Concours canadien de journalisme

Page 1

National Newspaper Awards

Kathy English & Nick Russell

EDITED by / Édité par Michael Simpson

PUBLISHER / Éditeur Jim Poling Sr.

EDITORIAL CONSULTANT / **PRINT MANAGEMENT** / Conseiller à la rédaction / Gestion de l'impression Dawn Martin

NNA 50th ANNIVERSARY CO-ORDINATOR / Coordonnateur du 50e anniversaire du CCJ Bryan Cantley

DESIGN CONSULTANT / Conseiller à la conception graphique Len Fortune

Page 1
Concours canadien de journalisme

ISBN 0-9684864-0-1

Page 1
National Newspaper Awards

ISBN 0-9684864-0-1

Association canadienne des journaux
890 rue Yonge, bureau 200
Toronto, Ontario

Achevé d'imprimer par Bryant Press,
Scarborough, Canada

Canadian Newspaper Association
890 Yonge St., Suite 200
Toronto, Ontario

Printed and bound in Canada
by Bryant Press, Scarborough

Black & white imaging /
Graphisme monochrome:
Ron Hartwell

Translation / traduction:
Johanne Norchet

CONTENTS

TABLES DES MATIÈRES

INTRODUCTION
Kathy English & Nick Russell
Page viii

● **CHAPTER / CHAPITRE 1** ●
News as a Reflection of Canadian Society
Page 1

● **CHAPTER / CHAPITRE 2** ●
The Opinion Shapers
Page 83

Acknowledgments

THE IDEA FOR THIS ANTHOLOGY CAME FROM TWO CANADIAN JOURNALISM TEACHERS WHO HAD never met one another. Though they live in different regions of Canada and are separated by 20 years in age, Nick Russell and Kathy English unknowingly shared a passion for newspaper journalism and its history and a belief that Canada's best newspaper writing should be celebrated and collected for future generations. Both regarded the 50th anniversary of the National Newspaper Awards as the ideal opportunity to do that.

Russell and English would like to thank the Board of Governors of the National Newspaper Awards for supporting and funding this project. We must especially acknowledge Wayne Parrish for convincing the board to take the risk such a project as this entails. Thanks also to board members Jim Poling — this work's publisher — and Angela Ferrante, for her guidance in helping us reflect the bilingual reality of the National Newspaper Awards.

On that note, special thanks to Alain Dubuc of *La Presse* in Montreal, who wrote the essay that accompanies the *Voix* chapter of French winners, and Johanne Norchet of the *Montreal Gazette,* who translated all the appropriate portions of the book.

We are also grateful for the judicious, careful editing of Mike Simpson. He is a writer's editor who tampered little with substance, but perfected style.

We would also like to acknowledge designer Dawn Martin for making words on a computer screen live on these pages and Len Fortune for his inspired cover design.

Special thanks to Bryan Cantley, vice-president of Member Services for the Canadian Newspaper Association and Secretary of the National Newspaper Awards. His contribution in all aspects of this book cannot be overstated.

The newspaper librarians across Canada who assisted in collecting these stories also deserve thanks, especially Sonja Noble of the *Toronto Star,* Celia Donnelly of the *Globe and Mail* and Donna MacHutchin of the *Montreal Gazette.* Thanks, too, to Adele Ritchie and Nancy Kutas of the Canadian Newspaper Association, who proofread the French text.

Kathy English also acknowledges Ryerson Polytechnic University's Scholarly, Research and Creative (SRC) committee for a project grant to assist with initial research costs.

On a personal note, Nick Russell would like to thank his wife Sharon for putting up with piles of papers, clippings, envelopes and correspondence on the dining table and the study floor for three years. Kathy English would like to thank her husband Gregg Serles and their children, Samantha and Geoff, for understanding those times when research and writing come first.

REMERCIEMENTS

L'IDÉE DE CETTE ANTHOLOGIE FUT PRÉSENTÉE PAR DEUX PROFESSEURS DE JOURNALISME CANADIEN qui ne s'étaient jamais rencontrés. Malgré la distance et l'âge qui les séparaient, Nick Russell et Kathy English partageaient la même passion pour le journalisme écrit et son histoire, et la même croyance qu'il était temps de reconnaître le journalisme écrit canadien et de le rassembler pour en faire profiter les générations futures. Tous deux étaient d'avis que le cinquantième anniversaire du Concours canadien de journalisme était l'occasion rêvée de ce faire.

Les auteurs aimeraient remercier le Conseil d'administration du Concours canadien de journalisme pour son appui et son aide monétaire envers le livre, et tout particulièrement Wayne Parrish qui a réussi à convaincre le Conseil de prendre le risque d'un tel projet, de même que Jim Poling, l'éditeur du livre, et Angela Ferrante pour son aide à refléter la réalité bilingue du Concours canadien de journalisme.

À ce chapitre, ils remercient particulièrement Alain Dubuc de *La Presse*, Montréal, qui a rédigé le texte qui accompagne le chapitre *Voix* où l'on retrouve les gagnants de langue française, et Johanne Norchet de *The Gazette* (Montréal), qui a traduit les diverses sections appropriées de cet ouvrage.

Nous sommes aussi reconnaissants envers la révision judicieuse effectuée par Mike Simpson qui a peu touché à la substance du matériel mais en a perfectionné le style; et envers Dawn Martin qui a fait vivre ces mots par sa présentation typographique et Len Fortune pour la couverture vibrante qu'arbore notre livre.

Des remerciements particuliers vont à Bryan Cantley, vice-président des services aux membres de l'Association canadienne des journaux et secrétaire du Concours canadien de journalisme: nous ne saurions trop souligner son apport.

Nous ne voulons pas, non plus, oublier les documentalistes d'un bout à l'autre du Canada qui nous ont aidés à recueillir les textes, particulièrement Sonja Noble du *Toronto Star*, Celia Donnelly du *Globe and Mail* et Donna MacHutchin de *The Gazette* (Montréal). Merci à Adèle Ritchie et Nancy Kutas de l'Association canadienne des journaux qui ont relu le texte français.

Kathy English remercie aussi le comité de la recherche et de la création de l'université polytechnique Ryerson pour sa subvention couvrant les frais initiaux de recherche.

Sur une note toute personnelle, Nick Russell tient à remercier Sharon, sa femme, pour avoir vécu pendant trois ans avec des piles de journaux, de coupures, d'enveloppes et de correspondance sur la table à dîner et le plancher du bureau; et Kathy English remercie son mari, Gregg Serles, et leurs deux enfants, Samantha et Geoff, pour leur compréhension de ces heures où la recherche et l'écriture devaient passer en premier.

INTRODUCTION

*Since 1949, the National Newspapers Awards have
recognized the finest in Canadian journalism.
This book salutes those journalists, their craft ...
and newspaper readers everywhere.*

By Kathy English and Nick Russell

IN FEBRUARY 1947, SOME NEWSMEN AT THE TORONTO MEN'S PRESS CLUB OFFICIALLY DECIDED TO look into the idea of establishing national newspaper awards in Canada similar to the American Pulitzer Prize for outstanding journalism that dated back to 1917.

It was an idea that had been talked about for some time around the bar of the press club at 99 Yonge St. (where, records indicate, members were limited to 24 pints of beer a month), but never really acted upon. This time though, directors of the club set up a committee to investigate and make recommendations for such awards. According to a memo written in 1950 by the late Charles Bruce, the former general superintendent of CP and inaugural NNA committee chairman, the committee decided, "that by getting something of this sort going, the club would have made a contribution to stimulating excellence in newspaper work in Canada."

The committee was adamant that the newspaper industry, not some outside commercial interest, must fund the awards. For some 20 months after approving the proposal to establish the Canadian National Newspaper Awards, the press club directors searched for ways and means to raise money to sustain such awards. Funds were not easily forthcoming and as Bruce's memo says, "It seemed for a while as if the whole scheme might die of malnutrition or something."

Toronto newspaper publishers were of course approached. Gwyn (Jocko) Thomas, then a club director and young reporter for the *Toronto Star*, well remembers that quest for funds. What the now 85-year-old retired reporter has never forgotten is the fact that his own publisher, Joseph E. Atkinson, owner of Canada's largest newspaper, refused to help out. "Joe Atkinson gave that same old answer when he never wanted to say no but didn't want to give: 'The time is not opportune,'" recalls Thomas.

The awards would come to be despite the parsimonious Atkinson (who died in May 1948). In November 1948, Bruce received a telephone call from George McCullough, the publisher and owner of the *Globe and Mail* who had also purchased the *Telegram* that same month for $3,610,000. McCullough agreed to give $3,000 a year for five years to get national newspaper awards started in Canada. (Incidentally, McCullough and Atkinson were long-time bitter enemies and, as Jocko Thomas recalls, "McCullough always hated the *Star*" — we can only wonder now whether McCullough agreed to fund the awards because the *Star* refused.)

The purpose of the National Newspaper Awards as expressed in a statement drafted by the directors of the press club was — and still is — "to reward achievement and encourage excellence in the newspaper work of this country." The first national newspaper awards were given for work done in 1949 in six categories: Spot News Reporting, Feature Writing, Editorial Writing, Staff Corresponding, News Photography and Cartooning.

While the names of all the winners of all the NNAs of the past 50 years appear in *For the Record* in this book, history demands the first award winners be recorded here. They were Edmond Chassé of Montreal *Le Canada* (spot news); Dorothy Howarth, *Toronto Telegram* (feature writing); Edgar Collard, *Montreal Gazette* (editorial writing); Stuart Underhill, *Canadian Press* (staff corresponding); Jack DeLorme, *Calgary Herald* (news photography), and Jack Boothe, *Globe and Mail* (cartooning). The award winners received $400 each, a large sum considering that the unofficial minimum wage for editorial employees at the *Toronto Star* in 1948 was $55 a week.

The first National Newspaper Awards were presented on June 10, 1950 at Toronto's Royal York Hotel. The *Toronto Telegram*'s coverage of the event reported that its "girl writer" Howarth received, "an extra round of applause as the only woman 'newspaperman' to write her way into Canada's 1949 hall of newspaper fame."

Howarth, who went on to become one of the *Telegram*'s best known reporters in the 1950s, fondly remembers her NNA win — especially the cash it entailed. With her $400 in hand, she bought herself a mahogany writing desk. Though Howarth does little writing these days, the desk still sits in the book-filled study of her midtown Toronto home.

Guest speaker on that first awards night was Alan Pitt Robbins, news editor of the *London Times*, who told his audience that newspapers cannot live solely off the splash of sensational beats and that routine newsgathering was just as important both to a newspaper and its public. Robbins praised the Toronto Men's Press Club for initiating the awards and said that yearly newspaper awards would surely go a long way toward improving newspaper reporting and editing standards. He said the successful "newspaperman" must combine three characteristics — individuality, enthusiasm and character.

As history has proven, the National Newspaper Awards survived and thrived, adding new categories such as sports reporting, feature photography and, in later years, column, critical and business writing. When McCullough's initial five-year guarantee of funds ran out, a number of major Canadian newspapers and newspaper chains — including the *Toronto Star*, Southam Newspapers and Thomson Newspapers — contributed to a trust to provide long-term funding for the awards which would be administered by a board of trustees.

This anthology of award-winning Canadian newspaper writing celebrates the 50th anniversary of the National Newspaper Awards. As such, it is intended as a "best of the best." (Winners in all the Photography categories are celebrated in our sister publication, *From See to See*.) Of course, just as "news" is difficult to define and many news judgments are based on instinct and experience, so defining "great journalism" is abstract and intangible. "History on the run" does not lend itself to fine writing. So what sets the material in this book apart?

All the 500-odd winners of NNA awards met certain criteria in their own time, but those criteria do not necessarily work today. For instance, one of the considerations which judges of the annual awards have not had to wrestle with is timeliness: Eligible entries in the awards each year had to have been written in that calendar year, and many, particularly Spot News and Spot Photography, had to be timely: It's the very nature of daily journalism that it be written on the fly, sometimes under the worst conditions of weather or communications or equipment, or even war.

But for an anthology such as this, the opposite is true: The material either has to have a timeless quality, or has to reflect the times — to hold up a mirror to contemporary history, society or culture. If it remains as riveting now as when it was written, it passes one test. If, on the other hand, it casts light on contemporary life and times, it passes another.

Of course, writing is paramount. But what was regarded as good writing half a century ago may not appeal to us in the same way at the cusp of the millennium. So, what is "great" writing? It is writing that sings, writing that is not accidental, not hurried, not flawed by errors of grammar or spelling or flow. It is writing that flows seamlessly. It is writing we want to read.

Part of this involves great leads (or "ledes" as old timers used to say, to make it clear they were not talking about "lead," the hot metal used for casting newspaper type). A fine lead must reach out and grab the reader by the lapels: It must shout "Read Me! — because I am exciting, important, moving or otherwise irresistible." Fine leads — indeed, all fine writing — should look effortless, yet may in fact be the result of hours of careful crafting, writing and re-writing until the author is sure she says what she wants in the most effective way she can. (And sometimes, fine leads write themselves in the cab on the way back to the newsroom.)

But there are other components to fine writing, components that verge on literature. Some of the best journalism uses literary techniques that we expect to find in Dickens or even Shakespeare. Good writers will illustrate complex ideas with effective imagery, they will draw graphic word pictures so the reader can visualize the scene, and they will be sensitive to sound, pace and tone. Such techniques are not the private preserve of "literature" in the sense of fine poetry and books, but are also — sometimes — useful tools for the journalist. And they are rarely accidents: Even if the writer is not saying to himself, "I should use parallel structure here," his inner ear is suggesting to him that having two phrases chime together sounds better than not. Indeed, many skilled writers will test out a piece of writing by speaking it out loud (or at least mouthing it at their computer screens), to see if it has the cadence that they seek.

In addition to all of this, there are "news" criteria: Good journalism is about finding stories, conducting revealing interviews, selecting the right material (and omitting the dross), organizing it well and writing it economically — all of it on some sort of deadline. (The deadline for the feature writer may be very different than for the editorial writer or the spot news writer.)

This book honours Canadian journalists and Canadian newspapers. It is a tribute both to those whose writing is included, and those who — unfortunately — we could not include because they didn't comfortably fit our somewhat arbitrary structure. Wags have transmuted the *New York Times* motto ("All the news that's fit to print") into "All the news that fits in print": This anthology, like every newspaper, is finite, and in the final analysis, it must all fit. We were forced to winnow some 320 winners in the writing categories down to 120. There were some tough calls to make. We hope you will see the reasons for our selections, but you can be sure we have had to reluctantly omit many other, excellent pieces.

In choosing stories for this anthology we have tried for some balance of geography, individual newspapers, time-frame and language. We also decided that multiple NNA winners (more than two awards) deserved automatic inclusion in this book. Undoubtedly they would have made the cut in any event.

The pieces included here are published in their original language, so you will find that many chapters contain both French and English selections. Chapter 7, *Voix*, is made up entirely of French NNA winners. A note on style: For the sake of consistency in this book, all stories have been edited to a uniform style, rather than retain the variety of formats used by different publications over the years.

Special tribute should be paid here to those many multiple winners of National Newspaper Awards in writing during the half century of existence. Some 50 writers have won twice or more (though Paul Watson may be the only one to win twice in one year!). Three-time winners include Peter Calamai, Gérard Filion, Joan Fraser, John Gray, Bob Hanley, Bruce Hutchison, David Prosser, Bob Reguly, Jay Scott, John Stackhouse, Gwyn Thomas, Michael Valpy, Paul Watson and Tony Westell. Deserving special mention are the two journalists who have won four NNAs: Edgar Collard and Peter Worthington. (Collard's spanned 20 years, Worthington's a decade.)

You will also find winning editorial cartoons throughout this book. Again, we had to limit our selections, but tried to include representation based on content, geography and recognizing multiple winners. A special salute goes to Roy Peterson of the *Vancouver Sun*, seven NNAs, and Duncan Macpherson of the *Toronto Star*, a six-time winner.

But perhaps we should also pause to recognize that — somehow — a few highly respected Canadian journalists slipped through the net, and never won a National Newspaper Award — people such as June Callwood, Nathan Cohen, J.V. Defresne, Michel Roy, Walter Stewart, Ray

Timson and Réjean Tremblay. In the name of excellence, we salute them as well as the thousands of other Canadian newspaper journalists who care passionately about responsible reporting and compelling writing.

PRÉAMBULE

Depuis 1949, le Concours canadien de journalisme souligne l'apport des journalistes canadiens et de leur métier.

C'EST EN FÉVRIER 1947 QUE DES JOURNALISTES DU TORONTO MEN'S PRESS CLUB DÉCIDAIENT officiellement d'étudier l'idée de mettre en place un concours canadien de journalisme semblable au prix Pulitzer décerné aux États-Unis depuis 1917 pour reconnaître l'excellence en journalisme.

L'idée faisait son chemin depuis quelque temps autour du bar du cercle des journalistes du 99 Yonge, mais rien de concret n'avait jamais été entrepris. Cette fois-ci cependant, les directeurs de ce cercle où, selon les dossiers de l'époque, les membres n'avaient droit qu'à 24 pintes de bière par mois, décidaient de créer un comité pour étudier la question et présenter des recommandations à cette fin. Selon une note de service rédigée en 1950 par le regretté Charles Bruce, ancien directeur général de l'agence CP et premier président du comité du Concours canadien de journalisme, le comité était d'avis que le cercle contribuerait ainsi à stimuler l'excellence en journalisme au Canada.

Les membres du comité tenaient à ce que ce soit l'industrie des journaux qui subventionne les prix et non des intérêts commerciaux externes. Pendant vingt mois après l'approbation de la proposition visant à établir les prix, les dirigeants du cercle des journalistes avaient tenté d'accumuler les fonds nécessaires pour soutenir le projet. Mais l'argent n'entrait pas rapidement et, comme le mentionnait Charles Bruce dans une autre note, il semblait bien que le projet était condamné à une mort prématurée. On avait approché les éditeurs torontois, et Gwyn (Jocko) Thomas, alors un des dirigeants du cercle et jeune reporter au *Toronto Star*, se rappelle bien cette tentative de levée de fonds. Il a aujourd'hui 85 ans mais il n'a jamais oublié que son propre éditeur, Joseph E. Atkinson, alors propriétaire du plus grand quotidien canadien, avait refusé d'y contribuer : « Le moment n'est pas opportun » avait déclaré Joe Atkinson. « C'était la réponse qu'il donnait chaque fois qu'il ne voulait pas donner un « non » catégorique », d'ajouter Gwyn Thomas.

Mais les prix verraient le jour malgré Joe Atkinson qui mourut en mai 1948. Ainsi, en novembre 1948, Charles Bruce reçut un appel de George McCullough, éditeur et président du *Globe and Mail* qui avait, la même année, acheté le *Telegram* pour une somme de 3 610 000 $. Il consentait à verser 3 000$ par an pendant cinq ans pour permettre au projet de voir le jour. En fait, Joe Atkinson et George McCullough étaient des ennemis de longue date, déclare M. Thomas : « McCullough avait toujours détesté le *Star* ». On peut se demander aujourd'hui si George McCullough a consenti à subventionner le concours parce que le *Star* avait refusé de le faire.

L'objectif principal du Concours canadien de journalisme, tel qu'exprimé à l'époque dans un énoncé de mission préparé par les dirigeants du cercle des journalistes, était et est toujours de reconnaître l'excellence et d'encourager le dépassement en matière de journalisme au sein de notre pays. Les premiers prix furent décernés en 1949 dans six catégories: nouvelle d'actualité; reportages; éditoriaux; correspondants; photographie d'actualité et caricature. Bien que les noms des gagnants de tous les prix décernés dans les cinquante dernières années soient publiés plus loin dans le présent ouvrage, l'histoire exige que les premiers gagnants aient leur nom mentionné ici. Les voici donc : Edmond Chassé (*Le Canada*, Montréal) — nouvelle d'actualité; Dorothy Howarth (*Toronto Telegram*) — reportage; Edgar Collard (*The Gazette*, Montréal) — éditoriaux; Stuart Underhill (Canadian Press) — correspondants; Jack De Lorme (*The Herald*, Calgary) — photographie d'actualité; Jack Boothe (*The Globe and Mail*, Toronto) — caricature. Les gagnants reçurent 400 $ chacun, une bonne somme d'argent à l'époque puisque le salaire minimum non officiel pour les employés de la salle de rédaction du *Toronto Star* était de 55 $ par semaine en 1948.

Les premiers prix furent présentés le 10 juin 1950 à l'hôtel Royal York de Toronto. Dans sa couverture de l'événement le *Telegram*, de Toronto, déclarait que Dorothy Howarth, leur « fille journaliste » avait été rondement applaudie puisqu'elle était la seule femme journaliste à avoir atteint ce temple de la renommée du journalisme canadien.

Maintenant âgée de 87 ans, Mme Howarth, qui devint éventuellement un des reporters les plus connus du *Telegram*, se rappelle ce prix avec émotion, et le fait que les 400 $ lui avaient permis d'acheter un pupitre d'acajou qui, bien qu'elle écrive moins de nos jours, conserve toujours une place d'honneur dans la bibliothèque bien remplie de sa demeure torontoise.

Ce soir-là, le conférencier invité était Alan Pitt Robbins, du *Times*, de Londres. M. Robbins avait alors déclaré à son auditoire que les journaux ne pouvaient pas vivre que de sensationnalisme et que la cueillette des nouvelles était tout aussi importante, tant pour le journal que pour ses lecteurs. Il avait aussi félicité le Toronto Men's Press Club d'avoir mis le projet en branle, soulignant qu'un tel concours ferait beaucoup pour améliorer la qualité du journalisme, tant du côté cueillette de la nouvelle que du côté qualité des textes. Le journaliste, avait-il conclu, en utilisant le masculin, devait avoir trois grandes qualités: de l'individualité, de l'enthousiasme et du caractère.

Comme l'histoire l'a prouvé, le Concours canadien de journalisme a survécu et a grandi. Il s'y est greffé de nouvelles catégories telles: le sport, la photographie de reportage et, plus récemment, la chronique, la critique et l'économie. Lorsqu'au bout de cinq ans, la garantie de subvention de George McCullough prit fin, bon nombre de grands quotidiens canadiens et de chaînes de journaux (y compris le *Toronto Star*, la chaîne Southam et les quotidiens Thomson) décidèrent de prendre la relève pour donner au concours des bases financières solides qui seraient administrées par un conseil de fiduciaires.

Cette anthologie de textes primés publiés dans des quotidiens canadiens célèbre le cinquantième anniversaire du Concours canadien de journalisme. Elle doit être considérée comme un recueil de ce qui s'est fait de mieux en matière de journalisme au pays. Les gagnants des diverses catégories de la division photographie sont répertoriés dans le second volume intitulé *D'une vision à l'autre*. Mais, tout comme la nouvelle est difficile à définir (et comme les jugements en ce domaine relèvent parfois davantage de l'instinct et de l'expérience), il en va de même pour ce qu'est le journalisme de qualité : c'est une notion abstraite et intangible. L'histoire à la seconde près ne se prête pas à une prose fleurie. Comment donc le matériel choisi ici a-t-il pu se démarquer?

Le matériel des près de 500 gagnants répondait aux critères de leur époque, critères qui ne sont peut-être plus les mêmes aujourd'hui. Ainsi, un critère dont les juges d'aujourd'hui n'ont plus à se soucier est la temporalité; à l'époque, il fallait que l'article ait été écrit dans la même année civile et, dans certaines catégories, particulièrement la nouvelle ou la photographie d'actualité, le texte devait être opportun. La nature-même du journalisme quotidien est qu'il doit être rédigé rapidement et souvent dans des conditions des plus difficiles: mauvais temps, problèmes de communications, bris d'équipement ou même bombardements.

Mais pour une anthologie, il en va tout autrement: le matériel doit être intemporel ou refléter la réalité de l'époque, de la société ou de la culture. S'il est aussi captivant aujourd'hui que lorsqu'il a été écrit, il atteint son objectif. S'il illumine une période de la vie contemporaine, il réussit encore. Mais la qualité de l'écriture doit primer avant tout. Il faut aussi se demander si une écriture de qualité signifie-t-elle la même chose à l'aube du nouveau millénaire qu'il y a cinquante ans? Qu'est-ce donc qu'un grand texte? C'est un texte qui vit, qui chante, qui n'est ni accidentel ni pressé, qui ne contient ni erreurs de grammaire, d'épellation ou de style. C'est un texte qui « coule » bien, un texte que l'on a envie de lire.

Il lui faut donc une bonne entrée en matière — quelque chose qui accroche le lecteur, qui l'invite à s'y attarder pour s'informer, s'émouvoir ou se divertir. Il faut aussi que le texte semble s'être échappé d'un trait de la plume de l'auteur même s'il lui a fallu des heures pour y arriver ou si elle a rédigé le tout à la hâte dans un taxi entre deux rencontres.

Mais un bon texte doit aussi beaucoup à la littérature. Le journalisme de qualité se sert souvent des techniques littéraires qu'utilisaient Balzac, Flaubert ou même Molière en parvenant à rendre des idées complexes au moyen d'images efficaces, à faire naître tout un univers au moyen de quelques mots, de leur sonorité, de leur rythme ou de leur tonalité. Ces techniques ne doivent pas être l'apanage exclusif de la littérature que l'on lit dans les recueils de prose ou de poésie — ce sont aussi et souvent des outils pour les journalistes. Ces méthodes ne surgissent pas par accident car, même si l'on ne se dit pas, « Si j'utilisais ici une sonorité sibilante, ce serait efficace », l'oreille suggéra les mots qu'il faudra pour arriver à l'effet désiré. En fait, nombre de rédacteurs relisent souvent leurs textes à haute voix pour en juger l'effet.

Il faut ensuite ajouter toute la dimension de l'actualité. Le bon journalisme, c'est aussi trouver les sujets, faire les entrevues, séparer le grain de l'ivraie, réorganiser les idées et rédiger le texte en gardant en mémoire les considérations d'espace et d'heures de tombée qui varient beaucoup que l'on soit éditorialiste, chroniqueur ou reporter.

Ce livre souligne le travail des journalistes et des journaux de notre pays. C'est un vibrant témoignage envers ceux et celles dont les textes sont publiés ici et envers les autres dont les textes n'ont pas été retenus parce qu'ils ne cadraient pas avec notre structure somme toute assez arbitraire. Nous avons dû, nous aussi, nous plier à des considérations d'espace, par exemple, en réduisant à 120 les textes des 320 gagnants de la catégorie reportages. Ce furent des décisions difficiles à prendre et nous espérons que vous comprendrez ce dilemme qui, par moment, nous a forcés à faire des choix déchirants en omettant certains excellents textes.

En choisissant les articles pour le présent ouvrage, nous avons recherché un équilibre en matière de géographie, de quotidien, de temps et de langue. Nous avons décidé d'emblée que quiconque avait gagné à deux reprises devait être présent. Les textes sont publiés dans leur langue originale. Vous remarquerez donc que certains chapitres contiennent des textes en français et en anglais. De plus, le chapitre *Voix* ne regroupe que des textes de langue française. A noter qu'en matière de style typographique et pour obtenir une meilleure constance tout au long du livre, les articles ont été revus pour leur appliquer les mêmes caractéristiques plutôt que de conserver les différents styles en vigueur dans les diverses publications au cours des ans.

Il faut particulièrement reconnaître l'apport de ces journalistes au moment où le concours fête ses cinquante ans d'existence. Près de cinquante d'entre eux ont gagné deux prix ou plus (Paul Watson est probablement le seul à avoir gagné deux prix dans la même année). D'autres en ont gagné trois dans leur carrière, y compris Peter Calamai, Gérard Filion, Joan Fraser, John Gray, Bob Hanley, Bruce Hutchison, David Prosser, Robert Reguly, Jay Scott, John Stackhouse, Gwyn Thomas, Michael Valpy, Paul Watson et Tony Westell. Une mention d'honneur va à Edgar Collard et à Peter Worthington dont la carrière a duré respectivement vingt et dix ans, et qui ont chacun quatre prix à leur tableau.

Le livre contient aussi des caricatures primées. Nous avons, ici aussi, dû limiter nos choix tout en gardant un oeil sur le contenu et en conservant une certaine représentation géographique. Les gagnants de prix multiples ont aussi une place de choix, y compris Roy Peterson du *Vancouver Sun*, gagnant de sept prix, et Duncan Macpherson du *Toronto Star*, gagnant de six prix.

Prenons aussi le temps de reconnaître quelques journalistes canadiens renommés qui n'ont jamais remporté de prix du Concours canadien de journalisme — des journalistes comme June Callwood, Nathan Cohen, J.-V. Dufresne, Michel Roy, Walter Stewart, Ray Timson et Réjean Tremblay. Au nom de l'excellence, nous les saluons de même que les milliers d'autres journalistes canadiens qui ont à coeur un journalisme responsable doublé de textes de grande qualité.

James G. Reidford

Montreal Star

It's a theme that still echoes today … the contrasting worlds of poverty and wealth. James Reidford of the *Montreal Star* took home the NNA for his 1950 editorial cartoon, his first of three national awards. He won back to back in 1956 and 1957 with the *Globe and Mail*.

Un thème encore présent de nos jours — le contraste entre la pauvreté et la richesse. James Reidford du *Montreal Star* a reçu un prix du CCJ pour cette caricature publiée en 1950. Il en recevrait deux autres, en 1956 et en 1957, durant sa carrière au *Globe and Mail*.

CHAPTER 1

News as a Reflection of Canadian Society

While this chapter primarily encompasses the Spot News segment of the National Newspaper Awards, there are also representatives from Features, Enterprise Reporting (continuous since 1972), and Staff Corresponding (a short-lived category from 1949–1971).

By Kathy English

ON MARCH 31, 1949, THE DAY NEWFOUNDLAND BECAME CANADA'S 10TH PROVINCE, THUS UNITING THIS nation from sea to sea, Dorothy Howarth, the *Telegram*'s "girl reporter" rushed to the telegraph office atop Signal Hill, high above the windswept Atlantic coast, flush with the heady discomposure of deadline. Disconnected words and images swirled through her mind as she struggled for a lead, knowing her editors in Toronto were waiting for her story. She gazed out across the vast sea; envisioning unseen, faraway land, and her thoughts fixed on the war that had so-recently torn Europe asunder. An idea, and the words to express it, began to form. Howarth began to write:

Today a country dies. Not as they die in Europe by enemy fire and sword or by aggressive annexation, but by its own hand, the democratic choice of its people. By a majority vote of only 6,401 of its citizens, Newfoundland today gave up its life as an individual nation in the British Commonwealth to become, instead, the tenth province of the largest Dominion in the Commonwealth, Canada.

Howarth's story reported on the despair and hope in the hearts of the people of Newfoundland. "We hate Canada, we hate Canadians. Come in here with your baby bonus and take us over," one man told her. "Of course we're glad to join with Canada," said a woman with a baby in her arms. "Look what it will mean to us. I've five children and my husband's work is uncertain."

With her deadline hovering, Howarth ended her story as eloquently as she began:

So it goes — half sadness, some downright anger, some anxiety and some downright gladness. No one quite sure about the future. Almost everyone realizing they've reached the end of an era and everyone waiting — waiting to see what Canada and Confederation will bring.

Howarth, now 87 and living in midtown Toronto, was awarded the first National Newspaper Award in feature writing for that story, part of a series on Newfoundland's decision to join Canada. Though 50 years have past, she vividly recalls travelling the island's outposts to discover how real folks felt about Confederation. Howarth was motivated both by the reporter's need to know and the reporter's need to beat the competition to the best story. In this instance, that meant going up against the *Toronto Star*'s man on the scene, a promising young reporter named "Bee" (Beland) Honderich, who went on to become the *Star*'s legendary publisher.

The uncertainty of this entity called Canada reflected in Howarth's 1949 stories resonates through this chapter and indeed through this entire anthology of 50 years of great Canadian newspaper reporting. Though the post-war years have brought Canada great wealth, worldwide recognition of possessing Earth's best living conditions and progress beyond the wildest dreams of anyone who existed in 1949, collectively we are somehow still waiting. Still waiting to see what Canada and Confederation will be. To determine where we are going as a new millennium dawns, we must, of course, understand from where we have come. The newspaper stories in this chapter provide the portal through which we can seek to understand Canadian society throughout the last half of this century that Sir Wilfrid Laurier once so boldly declared belonged to Canada. From Howarth's 1949 story, which opens this chapter, through to the 1981 NNA winning stories reporting on the patriation of a Canadian Constitution, we see the history of a country struggling to find and fulfill its destiny.

While the notion that news is the first rough draft of history is a cliché of journalism, it has become so because it is so apt an idea. Both the journalist and the historian seek answers to the question 'why,' with the journalist probing the present and the historian the past. If history is an enormous jigsaw with many missing pieces, journalism is the initial attempt to construct those pieces. When we look back to those pieces in such an anthology as this, we examine both journalism and history.

Consider, for example, Alexander Ross's 1963 *Vancouver Sun* story on Quebec's early separatist movement (page 13). Both the innocence and prescience of the piece ring with poignancy in light of the future we know was to follow. In his lead, Ross declares the future of Confederation "relatively secure" and the separatist Rassemblement pour l'Independance Nationale, led by Marcel Chaput, weak and divided:

Separatism as a means of achieving self-determination for French Canada isn't yet accepted as desirable or necessary. Most French Canadians still believe the Confederation marriage can be saved through concessions from English Canada.

Ross concludes his piece with an excerpt from an article written by the editor of an influential quarterly called *Cité Libre*, a man named Pierre Elliott Trudeau. In explaining why he was not a separatist, Trudeau wrote:

All the time and all the energy that we use to proclaim the rights of our nationality, to invoke our sacred mission, to trumpet our virtues, to weep about our misadventures, to denounce our enemies and to declare our independence have never made one of our workers more adroit, one civil servant more competent, one financier richer, one doctor more advanced, one bishop more learned or one of our politicians less ignorant.

Five years after Ross's piece was published, after Prime Ministers Lester Pearson and John Diefenbaker had their opportunity to build and unite Canada, Trudeaumania swept the nation. Canadians — both English and French — looked to the pragmatic Trudeau for renewal and reconciliation of an officially "bi and bi" country that had by then witnessed mailbox bombings in Montreal's Westmount by a new separatist group known as the Front de Liberation du Quebec.

By October 1970, though, we knew there were no saviours and no simple solutions when the FLQ kidnapped British diplomat James Cross and Quebec Labour Minister Pierre Laporte, and eventually strangled Laporte to death with the chain around his neck that held a medal of his Catholic faith. Trudeau invoked the War Measures Act, giving police unprecedented powers of search and arrest.

Still, as Tom Hazlitt's 1970 NNA story details (page 26), Montreal police bungled their search for Laporte's killers, spending 22 hours searching a Montreal house while the killers hid in a closet with a false wall.

Despite the affront on civil liberties brought by the War Measures Act, a vast majority of Canadians supported Trudeau's actions. His Liberal government lived on until 1979, scraping by with a minority in the 1972 election and a majority in 1974. But, as Richard Gwyn's 1980 story records (page 33), that wasn't the end of Prime Minister Trudeau. He rose again, rescinding his decision to resign from the Liberal leadership in time to lead his party to a resounding majority in the February 1980 election.

The pieces of the puzzle that is Canadian postwar history continued to be constructed with Trudeau's 1980 victory, setting the stage for what is probably the most significant event of the 50 years covered by this collection — the patriation of a Canadian Constitution. The winning NNA story by Canadian Press's Ottawa bureau (page 36) reported the Constitutional agreement in a straightforward manner, which historians of the future will look back on as a turning point in our development as a nation:

Prime Minister Trudeau and the premiers of all the provinces except Quebec called a truce Thursday, agreeing to patriate the constitution with a new amendment formula and a charter of rights. So ended 54 years of squabbling over bringing the British North America Act of 1867 to Canada so Britain will never again be asked to amend the constitution.

The CP story and Mary Janigan's *Montreal Gazette* piece (page 37) on the day-to-day implications of the new Canadian Charter of Rights and Freedoms signal the end to the politically-oriented stories in this chapter on news as a reflection of Canadian society. Many of the remaining stories reflect a much more disturbing Canadian society, the Canada that somehow bred our most notorious and vicious murderers. Their very names tell whole stories — Clifford Olson, Mark Lepine, Valery Fabrikant, Paul Bernardo — monsters who slaughtered our innocents and shattered our collective innocence.

Why do such stories belong in this anthology? Why did they win National Newspaper Awards? Indeed, as those who don't live inside the world of journalism may well ask, why do newspapers even cover these horrible stories? Any reporter who has struggled with knocking on the door to request a "pickup" picture from the parents of a fresh-faced young woman just found murdered, has undoubtedly struggled with these questions.

The answers lie in the very fact that as horrible as these stories are, they are *true*. We cannot hide from horror. It lurks as a possibility every day of our lives and it has long been a role of the daily newspaper to show us the ugliness, lest we sink into our comforts. Kirk Makin's 1995 NNA (page 76) for his coverage of the Bernardo trial struggled to make sense of why he sat in a downtown Toronto courthouse for three months to report the crimes of Paul Bernardo and Karla Homolka:

I would defend what I was doing on the ground that there are valid reasons to report the proceedings, if only to allow society to bear witness to this breakdown in humanity.

To bear witness to society is the journalist's calling. Whatever the story, be it the Constitution or crime, the newspaper reporter watches and writes. The story unfolds day by day and Canadians wait to see what tomorrow will bring. This is our future. To borrow the words written by reporter Dorothy Howarth, some 50 years ago, as a nation we will be waiting … "waiting to see what Canada and Confederation will bring."

• **1949** Feature Writing •

New province tomorrow: Hope, sorrow blend on Confederation eve

Dorothy Howarth

Toronto Telegram

ST. JOHN'S, Nfld. — Today a country dies. Not as they die in Europe by enemy fire and sword, or by aggressive annexation, but by its own hand, the democratic choice of its people. By a majority vote of only 6,401 of its citizens, Newfoundland today gives up its life as an individual nation in the British Commonwealth to become, instead, the tenth province of the largest Dominion in the Commonwealth, Canada.

There is no celebrating in St. John's today. People move quietly about their everyday business, through the steep up-and-down roads. Two-wheeled carts, filled with coal and produce, clatter in the cobbled streets. Fur-hatted policemen patrol their beats and long-shoremen wait on Water Street, leaning idly over the railing, above the docks where the tall ships come in.

"Ah, well, Miss, I think there are many of us feeling badly today, even though we be confederates," said the doorman at the British Commission office.

"How would you feel in Canada if the United States were taking you over today? It's like a country dying," said the librarian. "It doesn't matter how you voted, confederate or responsible government, today still means that we are no longer a separate country. We're only part of a larger one now."

Above the hall of an Irish Benevolent Association rises in defiance what claims to be Newfoundland's flag — pink, green and white. But far out the narrows from the top of Cabot Tower, whipped out in fierce wind, flies its real flag — the Union Jack. "That'll not change, thank God," said a policeman.

In the hearts of many responsible government people there is real despair. "We hate Canada; we hate Canadians," said a well-known St. John's professional man. "Come in here with your baby bonus and take us over and you'll name us a premier and cabinet that are like leopards that can change their spots. Now Tory, now Liberal. Well — once I was a Liberal but not anymore. I'll not be associated with that confederate outfit, I can tell you.

"Look at my office — it's the same at my house ..." Every blind in the place was pulled down to the sill — as if death lay inside.

There is a rumour that before the day is out a number of anti-confederates will take a funeral cortege through the town to bury high on the hill above the city the body of what is supposed to be Newfoundland. But their procession, if it is carried out, will wind right by the same frame houses, lining the hill, from which nightoil is still collected and from which issue nine and 10 children.

"Of course we're glad to join with Canada," said one woman, a baby in her arms. "Look what it will mean to us. I've five children and my husband's work is uncertain. Those Water Street millionaires have bled us long enough," she added, looking down into the town where the names of a number of merchants could mainly be read on the sides of their stores.

Store windows are the only evidence that Confederation has really come. Price tags on goods, with black lines drawn through the old prices, show the cuts. Nylons from $2.25 to $1.98, linoleum at $1 a yard down to 50 cents. Drugs and cosmetics in particular show a tremendous difference.

"It'll take me from three to six months to recover from the change," said one druggist. "I'll lose 20 per cent on most of my stock."

But his clerk, a girl, saw the other side of the story. "Now I'll only pay $1.25 for creams, I paid $2 for before — and cologne is $1.98 now instead of $2.50.

"I saw a cotton summer dress in a store window today for $8.95 — last summer I paid $15 for the same dress. Confederation will certainly make things easier for me, but I am sorry to feel that I must sign my passport Canadian."

There was an air of waiting over the whole city, waiting for what is going to happen, what Confederation is to bring in small things and in large.

"I was going to buy curtains for my living room, but I decided to wait and see," said a woman, window-shopping. Another window-shopper was interested in the drop of the price of linoleum. "I wanted new covering for my kitchen floor for Christmas, but we decided to wait. Now I see that I was wise to."

Waiting in government offices, figuratively biting their nails, are civil servants who have not yet been notified if their department is even going to exist after today. Several slated to take trips to Canada on official business, find that financial provision has not been made for their journey.

Up at Government House, where tomorrow the official naming and swearing in of the new premier is to take place, faces are a little red. It isn't too propitious that new government should be born on April Fool's Day — a day kept here in the rowdy English fashion. It is said that is the reason the ceremony will not take place until 1:15 p.m., the traditional minute for April Fool's Day to end.

The whole ceremony is being carried out as swiftly, as simply as possible with all the hush-hush trimmings of a military secret. There will be no fanfare: It was not even announced where or at what time the ceremony was to take place.

In schools there will be no special observance of the last day of Newfoundland's nationhood. One school-master said he thought he would probably address morning assembly for a few moments on the significance of the day, but other schools were ignoring it.

"We'll be singing our national anthem, 'Ode to Newfoundland,' in the morning and 'God Save the King' when we leave at night," another teacher said.

Biggest event of the day will be when the first sealer comes in, its decks slippery with blubber and blood from the raw seal skins piled on it. The *Terra Nova*, possession of the Eric Bowring stores, a Water St. merchant, was due today but because of high wind and its loaded decks, rolling in a heavy sea, it is still on its way.

"Oh you don't have to worry about where it comes in," said a clerk in the store. "Just tell the taxi driver; he knows where to take you. There'll be lots other people there."

Baked seal flippers and seal flipper pie will be on all menus when the first ship finally does arrive. "Tastes just like beef, with a bit of a fishy tinge," said a longshoreman. "You'll like it. Real Newfoundland dish. Can't make it Canadian whatever you do."

"I don't know if we'll have any here," said the waitress in the restaurant. "Sometimes we do," then giving out the change, she noticed the silver. "There — there's our 20-cent piece for you, and our little bitty nickel. Suppose they'll go out of circulation. But I kind of like them. I'll miss them. It'll be all Canadian money instead of our own."

She swabbed the table with her cloth for a moment. "I've a sister in Toronto. She makes more than I do at the same work. But I don't know, whatever happens, I still want to be a Newfoundlander."

So it goes all through the city: Half sadness, some downright anger, some anxiety and some downright gladness. No one quite sure about the future. Almost everyone realizing they've reached the end of an era and everyone waiting — waiting to see what Canada and Confederation will bring.

• **1951** Spot News Reporting •

Stanley Buckowski confesses

Gwyn "Jocko" Thomas

Toronto Star

San Quentin Penitentiary, Calif. — Stanley Buckowski, 26, who is awaiting execution in the lethal chamber here, told me today he killed Gloria and Bob McKay.

He said he shot the young Toronto couple in their own car on Civic Holiday, 1949, as Bob McKay drove wildly along Eglinton Ave. in an effort to attract police. Then Buckowski took over the wheel, dumped McKay's body in a North York ravine, and left the car with Mrs. McKay's body in a parking lot at Christie Street hospital.

Not long before he granted the interview in which he made the sensational confession, he had been told by Warden Clinton T. Duffy that the Supreme Court of the U.S. had granted him a stay of execution to review his case. Buckowski said he knew this was routine and held no hope.

The death sentence here was imposed for the murder of a 78-year-old woman during a house burglary.

The McKays, a happy young couple planning their dream home, might have never been killed, Buckowski said, if the work of a Toronto police artist who drew a picture of the suspected murderer of Alfred Layng hadn't been so accurate in his portrait.

At Wasaga Beach, where he spent the weekend after shooting Layng to death in the Loblaw robbery, he bought a newspaper. He saw the picture which Det. Maurice Inglis had drawn.

"I figured right then and there they knew I killed Layng," said Buckowski, between puffs of his cigarette. "I was desperate. If they knew I killed Layng, they wouldn't have any trouble knowing I had a car. I had to get out of there fast. I left my car beside the cabin I had rented and started out for Toronto.

"I got as far as Elmvale," he continued. "Everybody seemed to be looking at me. I knew the cops were out in full force. I tried a couple of cars but no one would give me a lift.

"At the side of the road, I saw a parked car. A young couple were in the front seat. She was asleep on his shoulder.

"I got in the back seat. I woke them. I told them I wanted to be driven to Toronto. I pulled out my gun and told him to get going.

"He didn't give me any argument at first. I was in the backseat and I held the gun at his neck at first and I told him not to try any funny stuff. He drove fast and I had to slow him down because he was trying to get the cops to come after him. When we got to Toronto, I told him to turn off at certain streets. He wouldn't do what I told him even though I warned him he could get shot if he didn't.

"Once he said, 'Go ahead, punk, kill me.'

"He seemed to get mad. He drove against red lights and was going 60 miles an hour. I couldn't make him slow down. He went against four or five more lights. He turned along Eglinton Ave., which wasn't where I wanted to go.

"I hadn't told him what I had done. What I wanted was for him to go along a side street. Then I would take the car. But when he started to drive all over the street on Eglinton Ave., near Bathurst St., I pulled the trigger. I kept pulling the trigger.

"She started to scream. I pulled the trigger on her."

Buckowski couldn't remember the time, but he said it was late the holiday Monday night (Civic Holiday).

There was heavy traffic both ways on the street but no one seemed to realize, he said, that the man and woman slumped over the dashboard had just been killed.

"I squeezed my way into the front seat and drove a few streets until I found a lonely spot where I intended to leave them both. I mustn't forget to mention the dog. He was a little sandy-haired spaniel. He'd been very quiet until after his master was dead and then he started howling.

"I pulled the man's body out of the car. I knew he was dead because I got him many times. She was still groaning. Just after I got his body out and dragged it to a place where I figured it wouldn't be found, the dog started barking some more. There was commotion. Someone was coming and I had to get out of there quick. She was still groaning.

"I dragged her over to the seat into the back and put a rug over her. Then I drove to Christie St. hospital parking lot which I knew because I spent 14 months there for treatment when I was in the air force.

"When I got there I knew she was dead. I went to a home of a friend where I spent the night. But I remembered the dog and the fuss he would make. Then I thought of the fingerprints I had left on the car. I went back, let the dog out, tied him to the bumper and then wiped out all the fingerprints."

"Next day I read the papers. I was in pretty deep ... Three people I had murdered. It was then I found out they had no idea who the murderer of Layng was. I'll tell you I felt sick. What a nightmare when I realized that what I saw of myself was not a police picture but a drawing."

Buckowski sits in a row of death cells with 21 other prisoners in an institution world-renowned for its rehabilitation of criminals. He entertains them with sweet clarinet music. But he won't talk about that, almost anything else.

Warden Duffy told me that efforts to draw him out of his shell of reticence had not been successful. According to penitentiary rules no prisoner had to see anyone he didn't want to see, police or anyone else.

But within five minutes of the formal request for an interview, which is done by typewritten form, Buckowski had signed the order that allowed me and Douglas Cronk, a *Star* photographer, to see him.

Yesterday, Buckowski was in a different frame of mind. "You'd better take shorthand because when I talk I talk fast and it's hard to get me to stop," he said.

Reaching periodically for a cigarette, he told me of his boyhood days at Essex St. public school. Miss Washington was a kindly teacher. It was the only name he could remember of his teachers.

"I got my entrance and then I started to hang around street corners," he said. "I was what you might call a good juvenile delinquent. I was interested in chemistry. I broke into places to steal things that I needed, electrical gadgets and those things.

"My first hold-up was done with a cap pistol. I went out to High Park and held up a motorist and took his car. That was in 1939. I was caught and I came before the juvenile court because I was only 15.

"Judge Mott decided against sending me to reform school. He sent for my father who was working at Galt and told him he was to give me a sound thrashing. I got a sound thrashing.

"Next I held up a filling station. I was working with another fellow. I had a real gun by this time, but I had no bullets. I decided to hold up a clothing store on Bloor St. Don't forget I was still 15 years old.

"The old guy that owned the store just laughed at me when I stuck the gun out. I was just a punk and I looked like it. We had a box fight. I hit him on the head with the gun. He fought me right out of the store. They grabbed me on the street. I got two and a half years.

"I thought I was a big shot. All I thought about was going out with the gang. I was hanging around Bathurst and Bloor Sts. I thought it was a sucker's life to work."

He burglarized and stole in Toronto until he signed up as an aircrew in the R.C.A.F. "I figured that would help me," he said.

He described a "reckless change" that came in his life. While stationed in a western Canadian city with the R.C.A.F., he persuaded a nurse in a hospital to introduce him to narcotics. "I even stole a lot from the dispensary because I knew I could make money."

Now Buckowski said he had found another source of easy money. "She had given me a shot. But she didn't know that when she wasn't looking I had stolen a lot from the dispensary," he said.

"I came back to Toronto when I was still in the air force. I got married. But I couldn't keep away from Bathurst and Bloor when I hung around with a gang.

"My wife, Jeannie, and I got an apartment in Rosedale. One night when she was at work as a waitress I got good and tight and burglarized a lot of homes. I don't know why I did it because Jeannie was making good money.

"One night I was walking down Yonge St. when the police grabbed me. I was going to meet Jeannie. They shook me down. I was mad. They said: 'How would you like to go to headquarters and be shook down?' and I went there. I had been breaking into houses before then. When they found out from my wife where I lived they went to the house and found diamonds, rings and a lot of other stuff I had stolen. I got 18 months in Burwash.

"I didn't get along very well there. Out in the woods you had cold dinners in 20 degrees below zero. The warden was a tough guy. All he knew was the strap.

"I had trouble with my hip and I needed medical attention. I couldn't get it there. My wife kept going to the parole board and I got out on the understanding I was going to the Christie St. hospital.

"I seemed to have turned paranoic at Burwash. Jeannie was working all the time and with my air force pay and allowances we had quite a lot of money saved up. Jeannie was working at a hotel as a switchboard operator.

"The operations I had to graft skin on my hip which I burned as a boy didn't do me any good. If anything, my paranoic condition became worse. I couldn't seem to make friends with anyone.

"When I got out of the hospital I had resolved to stay away from the corner and the boys, but the first I knew I was back with them. I was in burglary on a wholesale scale again in no time.

"Then I got it into my head to make a lot of money and retire," he continued. "I had in my burglaries obtained a couple of pistols. I sat home night after night because Jeannie was after me to stay there. She knew I was a chronic thief and she didn't want me out without her.

"I drank a lot and when I got nasty I used to beat up my dog, which was a spaniel just like the one the McKays had. So one night I went to the Alhambra Theatre and held up the manager.

"That was easy. More and more I thought that only suckers work for a living. Not long afterward I was at home waiting for the time when I should go and pick up Jeannie at the restaurant. I had a lot of drinks.

"It suddenly came to my head that the Downtown theatre, which had just opened, might really be easy. They had a lot of new staff and it should be a nice score worth $4,000 or $5,000.

"So I got to a spot outside the manager's office and I told him I was waiting for someone. I put on glasses and had a fedora hat. I waited until the manager came in, rapped on the door and held him up. That was easy too. All I did to get away fast was to hail a cab."

Buckowski said he had several thousand dollars in the bank and didn't need any more at the time he decided on the Loblaw robbery. Now he lived on Wellesley St. Saturday afternoon crowds convinced him a robbery would be worth $4,000.

"Now," he said, "I kept my guns in my locker at the College St. Y.M.C.A. I drove over there and got them. There were crowds in the store. I walked back to the manager's office and told him to fill the paper bag. He did. Just before I left I warned him not to make any scream for help.

"He seemed like a good guy that way but as soon as I got to the bottom he was safe so he started to yell. He shouted, 'Stop that man. I've been robbed.' He was safe.

"At first I didn't run because that would attract attention. Then the clerk (Leonard Leftly) grabbed me. I had my gun in my hand and I shot him in the leg. By this time there were lots of guys chasing me.

"Next thing I knew there was a fellow coming down the street with a woman and a baby carriage. Everybody was yelling for someone to do something. This fellow was putting his nose into something that wasn't his business.

"He grabbed me. I said, 'Let me go.' He didn't and I shot him in the leg. He still hung on. I shot again and he dropped. I guess the bullet went through his heart. He didn't mind his own business, but he was a good citizen.

"By all the odds on the dice, I should have been caught. The police say it is a puzzle to them how I got away. It's a bigger mystery to me. First, I ran up a blind lane with a 15-foot fence at the top. Behind me was a fellow. I could hear the howling mob behind him. He just about had me.

"I needed a run to get over the fence. He was so close to me I couldn't step back to get the run. I turned around with my gun and told him to get back or die. He did with his hands over his head. A run at the fence and I was over. Just then the mob came.

"I wasn't away even then. There were a bunch running around the other street. I got into an old car and tried to start it. It wouldn't go. By then someone was near me. I pulled the gun and they ran back. I dashed through a yard on to Sherbourne St. and then up to the St. Regis hotel.

"By this time, I had thrown my coat under a veranda. I told the girl at the desk to call a cab. I went to a washroom and cleaned up, going out when the cab came. I was just in the cab when the police car came up to search the hotel. The policeman was about to come to the car to ask me questions, but I guess because I had no coat he didn't. That night I went out and got drunk."

Buckowski had a new car he bought with earlier hold-up proceeds. "I thought the best place would be Wasaga Beach. I drove there from my apartment on Wellesley St. I don't know whether my wife knew about my being involved in the holdup or not. She was at work. But she knew me as a burglar and a thief," he said.

Then he narrated the story of how terror gripped him at the belief police knew he murdered Layng.

"All I thought of was that I was a marked man," he added. "I had to get away. Lord, help me, I didn't know they were a couple of sweet kids. My life is a nightmare that is soon to come to an end."

Buckowski has been the subject of an intensive sociological and psychological examination, as are all condemned prisoners in this prison which has 4,700 inmates.

Experts have gone into his boyhood life. This goes back to a remote section of Saskatchewan. There he was born of Polish-Canadian parents. F. L Ornellas, state prison sociologist, who has written thousands of words about him, ends up his report of Buckowski's father's death: "He died of a broken heart. He couldn't believe his boy was a killer."

● **1957** Spot News Reporting ●

Jeers, boos, catcalls tear
rally to pieces

Ted Byfield

Winnipeg Free Press

Surplus-suffering Manitoba farmers Saturday night pounced on the man who is responsible for selling Canada's grain crop, turning a carefully planned Liberal rally into a pandemonium of shouts, jeers and raucous booing.

The place was the crowded auditorium of the Morris High School and the man was Canada's minister of trade and commerce, minister of defense production and deputy prime minister, Right Honorable Clarence Decatur Howe.

The trade minister's presence set the farmers into a turmoil of hoots and hollers like those that came from the little man half way down the hall who kept jumping up to say, "I've been a Liberal all my life, Mr. Howe!"

But when it was over, he was shouting, "I've been a Liberal up to now, Mr. Howe!"

Local Liberals said that Mr. Howe had defied their advice and determined to sally forth into the teeth of farm unrest in the grain country.

But before he had left the Morris auditorium, the teeth had clamped down hard upon him and he had to battle his way off the platform, shouting over choruses of catcalls and jeers that he was wanted back in Ottawa.

And back to Ottawa he flew Sunday morning, behind him the rowdiest Manitoba meeting of the election campaign and some of its worst fiascos.

There was, for instance, the man who elbowed his way to the front of the hall at the height of the uproar and asked the chairman if he might not speak from the platform.

Mr. Howe didn't wait for the chairman's reply. He did the replying himself. No, the intruder could not have the platform. "When your party organizes a meeting, you'll have the platform then and we'll ask the questions," said the minister of trade and commerce.

"Well," observed the man from the floor, his arms folded jauntily across his chest. "I *AM* the president of the Liberal association for the constituency of Morris."

"But why," began the trade minister over the howls of the crowd, "but why aren't you up here?"

"I don't know," retorted Bruce MacKenzie, who *IS* the president of the Morris provincial Liberal association.

There was considerable shuffling and clearing of throats on the platform as Mr. MacKenzie was welcomed to it, patted affectionately on the shoulder by the minister of trade and commerce and escorted triumphantly to the microphone.

But the worst was yet to come. No sooner did Mr. MacKenzie receive the instrument into his hand than he used it to launch into an aggressive attack on:

(A) The federal government
(B) Its handling of the wheat problem
(C) Mr. C. D. Howe

In fact, he began with a little joke, the main point of which was that Mr. Howe had once sat between two provincial premiers as meat between the bread of a sandwich and that somebody had said it must have been a "baloney" sandwich.

It was at this moment that Mr. Howe discovered the hour was getting late and he had pressing business back in Ottawa.

A hurried conference was called behind Mr. MacKenzie's back on the platform in an apparent attempt to deal with the problem of getting Mr. MacKenzie away from the microphone and back into the crowd.

As the conference huddled, they cast anxious glances over their shoulders to hear what Mr. MacKenzie was doing to their meeting in language vigorous and bold.

The farmers had been told if they gave the government control of wheat sales, they'd have "an orderly market and social security ."

"We haven't got them!"

(Loud applause)

Mr. Howe had been "sliding around the main issue."

(Cheers)

Where but on a western farm did a man "have to go and borrow after an honest season's work?"

(Applause, jeers, hisses and whistles)

Rene Jutras, seeking re-election as MP for Provencher, came forward and suggested to Mr. MacKenzie that he might sit down. But Mr. MacKenzie was just warming to his subject.

How was the farmer to meet his obligations? "He hasn't got the stability and social security that the Liberal party promised ..."

The government was "not assuming its responsibility ... That was not "a good thing ..." That was not "a Liberal thing ..."

Mr. Jutras having failed to dissuade the illustrious MacKenzie, the deputy prime minister had a try. Mr. Howe shook hands with Senator Arthur Beaubien (who had been shifting from one position on his seat to another) and said he really ought to be going.

Mr. Howe came forward and put his arm affectionately on the speaker's shoulder and interrupted his speech. He said that he hadn't known there was going to be another speaker at the meeting. "So if you'll excuse me, I've made my speech and I'll be on my way," said Mr. Howe.

But it wasn't quite that simple. He retreated to the wings of the stage, but nobody else came with him. This put him in a dilemma. He could either push his way out through the crowd and risk being booed out of the meeting, or make an anti-climactic return to the stage, or stay in the wings indefinitely.

Meanwhile, events had been developing on the floor that made the decision for him. A man had some questions for the trade minister (currently hidden from view). Was he going to answer them?

Mr. Jutras was energetically waving to Mr. Howe to come out of the wings and get back on the platform.

"Who prepared the questions?" demanded Mr. Howe, reassuming the microphone.

The man said he had.

Mr. Howe said he wasn't going to get into a debate. The man would have to ask all his questions at once.

The man said he wanted to know "what is Ottawa's attitude toward the farmers in the West?"

Mr. Howe said he had to be in Ottawa first thing in the morning. He simply had to be on his way.

And was the farmer as well off as other Canadians and if the government thought he was, "how do they explain it?"

Mr. Howe broke in again to stress the importance of the Ottawa engagement and Mr. Jutras fully agreed. A lot of people had come out from the city for this meeting, said Mr. Jutras taking over the microphone from Mr. Howe, and they had asked that the meeting end "in good time so that they wouldn't be inconvenienced."

Since people were definitely being inconvenienced it was clearly time to end the meeting.

"Everyone recognizes that there is a problem," said Mr. Jutras.

"But Mr. Howe is not the minister of agriculture. He came here to deal with figures on the movement of grain … (jeers from the crowd) … We've done the best we can with the policies we have … We don't claim that we are infallible. We haven't solved all the problems … But with your help and suggestions, we try to work our way out of it.

"In any case, it is now 11:25 city time …

(Shouts and jeers)

"… and the meeting should be brought to a close …"

Senator Beaubien then arose to thank Mr. Howe. "I don't say everybody's prosperous," he said — to a chorus of catcalls and shouts — "but Canada is prosperous."

The chairman called for somebody to play *God Save the Queen.* When nobody would, he led the singing himself. And Mr. Howe hurried to the Fort Garry Hotel in Winnipeg where he spent the night before keeping the Ottawa engagement.

The crescendo in which his day ended was in crashing contrast to its gentle beginning at Carman, Man., where he addressed a meeting of about 170 in mid-afternoon in support of Dr. W. A. Pommer, seeking re-election in Lisgar constituency.

The trade minister appeared heavily fatigued and three times his head nodded and his eyes closed as the doctor was speaking.

But when he took the floor, it was with characteristic energy. "I look forward to election campaigns," he said. "It's the most enjoyable part of the four years of service."

It was "unfortunate" that there were not more Liberals elected from the West, he said, because eastern Liberals had to be called in to serve on the House agricultural committee.

In any case, Canada was enjoying a period of unprecedented prosperity. Her birth rate topped even India's and Japan's. It was true that there was "a problem" in wheat marketing, but "it's not a very serious problem and it's a problem that can be cleared up very quickly by the end of the year," he said.

Wheat exports in the last five years were greater than in any previous five-year period. Western wheat production was reaching figures "never remotely approached in the whole history of the West." Never in history had producers marketed and been paid for as much wheat as in the past five years, said Mr. Howe.

Such marketing problems as there were had begun last July with a "tremendous upsurge" of "unfair competition" from the U.S. give-away program on wheat.

Next the Suez crisis had increased shipping rates so high that grain couldn't be moved out of the Atlantic ports. To make things worse, the Lakehead opening was three weeks late and this slowed the annual crop movement.

But the government had been working hard to market the crops and was particularly gratified by developments like the Japanese trade agreement which might make Japan second top buyer. And now that the season was under way, "the crop is moving freely both east and west," he said.

"We still have a surplus problem. Perhaps it's no worse than last year. It's certainly no better. I refuse to get worried about these problems. It's the best possible protection against future damage to the crop in, say, a dry year or with damage of one type or another."

He paused to rap briefly Progressive Conservative Leader John Diefenbaker for supporting Ontario Premier Leslie Frost's bid to revise the tax-rental agreements.

Ontario wanted $100,000,000 more, he said, and if the deal went through Manitoba would be the "chief contributor."

The applause was restrained and polite at the Carman meeting, but immediately after it there occurred an incident which was a forewarning of what was to come.

A bronzed farmer rushed into the Carman Memorial Hall as Mr. Howe was leaving and thrust a piece of paper into his hand which purported to show that it cost 76 cents a bushel to grow oats. "Why'd you cut the price from 60 to 55 cents?" demanded the farmer.

Mr. Howe asked him where he got the figure.

The farmer said that it was from "statistics."

"You look pretty well fed," said the trade minister, patting the farmer on the stomach with the back of his hand.

The argument lasted for about another two minutes and the farmer departed. He said outside he wasn't a member of any political organization. He just wanted to know. He didn't like the answers, "but what can you do about it?"

Mr. Howe had dinner at Morris and the 580 people who filled the school auditorium began arriving long before he came.

It was "very gratifying to have people turn out in such large numbers to these gatherings," said Mr. Jutras in opening the meeting. Possibly he had been "carried away," he said, in his work for the constituency in Ottawa in the past four years. In the next four years he would try to do more at home.

In any case, he was working on some major projects like a proposal to carry Winnipeg water south to the border and to develop a new dam in the area to help diversify agriculture and bring more cash crops to the area.

Mr. Howe repeated his Carman speech with little variation, and a small gathering in the front row led sporadic applause when he pointed for it.

But half way through, the crowd began to show some initiative of its own. When the trade minister came to the part about the grain moving freely east and west, there were unsolicited chuckles and cackles in the crowd.

Three-quarters of the way through, new trouble arrived. A farmer sat down in a rear seat and began to make a little speech of his own in parody of the trade minister's. It could be heard only in the rear, but it started the rear of the crowd laughing in the wrong places.

Mr. Howe: "They say we're a government of old men …"

The farmer: "Yeah! Why doncha retire on pension ?"

Mr. Howe: "… and we've dealt with the butter and the cheese problems …"

The farmer: "Yeah, that's for the east. What about the west?"

Mr. Howe: "… I'll just sit down, then and let you ask some questions…"

The farmer: "Ah come on, don't sit down …"

When the trade minister concluded, the applause from the front was clearly mingling with boos from scattered parts of the hall.

The chairman called for questions. Instantly one man arose and he "agreed entirely" with what Mr. Howe had said about prosperity in Canada.

"That's fine and if there are no more questions," said the chairman, but that was as far as he got. There was definitely more questions.

A farmer wanted to know about the quotas this year.

"Where are you from?" asked Mr. Howe.

The man was from Brunkild.

"Well," said the trade minister, confidently hauling out of his pocket a lengthy sheet of paper, "let's be specific. We'll just see exactly what happened there … Brunkild, you say, eh … Brunkild …"

It became apparent that the minister was in difficulty with his paper. Mr. Jutras sped to his side and they hunted the list together.

Finally Mr. Howe said: "We don't seem to have Brunkild on here." There was unkind laughter in the crowd.

Mr. Howe said there would be at least a seven-bushel quota in the area at most points.

"I differ with that," said a man on the wings.

And a seven-bushel quota wouldn't leave much grain in the area.

"I differ with that," the man said again.

Another questioner read a newspaper clipping which said Mr. Howe blamed the surplus at Weyburn on the boxcar shortage and a letter from the wheat board saying the boxcar situation wasn't to blame. Who was the farmer to listen to, he asked, and the crowd cheered.

Who would take a five-cent loss on oats if they weren't delivered this year, another farmer demanded. "You will," roared somebody in the crowd and there were more cheers.

Somebody else wanted to know how the country could afford to give away war planes and not wheat. Millions of people were starving.

Mr. Howe said he would ask the questioner to be more specific. He had sought through the UN for places in dire need of wheat and had found none. Starving countries were rice-eaters. And the only planes given away were obsolete ones to re-arm our allies.

"Do you think it's all right to give obsolete planes to our allies?" asked another questioner.

Mr. Howe said the government was guided in these things by the external affairs department. "I don't decide who gets planes. I just make them."

As he was talking, the Liberal association president was moving toward the front of the hall and an already obstreperous meeting was on the way to becoming bedlam.

And all the questions weren't over when the meeting ended. As Mr. Howe made his way to the door, one of his questioners approached him. "I still want an answer to my question," he said.

"Look here, my good man," said Mr. Howe. "When the election comes why don't you just go away and vote for the party you support."

"In fact," said Canada's deputy prime minister, "why don't you just go away?"

• **1963** Staff Corresponding •

Quebec separatists split by rivalries

Alexander Ross

Vancouver Sun

MONTREAL — As long as Quebec's separatist movement is in the hands of men like Dr. Raymond Barbeau and Dr. Marcel Chaput, the future of Confederation is relatively secure.

But if their movement is ever commandeered by the responsible politicians who are running Quebec today, get ready to have your passport stamped in Hull.

For separatism — as a means of achieving self-determination for French Canada — isn't yet accepted as desirable or necessary. Most French-Canadians still believe the Confederation marriage can be saved through concessions from English Canada.

But if those concessions aren't forthcoming, and soon, leaders of both major Quebec parties say the only alternative is an amicable divorce and an independent republic of Quebec.

In that case, it would probably be men like Premier Jean Lesage and his colleagues who would lead Quebec out of Confederation and into nationhood. Not because they wanted to — but because English Canada, by indifference and stupidity, forced them to it.

Is this likely to happen? Not very. For one thing, Quebec is in a stronger position than ever before to use its concept of biculturalism on the federal government, and on the provinces where French-Canadians live in large minorities.

For another, the separatist movement at present is numerically weak and divided by petty rivalries.

Its leaders, charming and articulate though they may be, are not the sort of men to common continuing public support.

Take, for instance, Dr. Raymond Barbeau. At 32, he is the elder statesman of the separatist movement — its brightest, most thoughtful advocate and the founder of Quebec's oldest separatist organization, L'Alliance Laurentienne.

Dr. Barbeau collects knowledge the way some men collect postage stamps. He has more degrees, diplomas and certificates than he can remember, and he is on the lookout for more.

"Knowledge is everything to me," he says. "Right now, I'm studying medicine on my own. You can't know too much." To prove his point, he hauled a stack of medical textbooks from his briefcase and laid them on the table for my inspection.

He is a great believer in proving things. It was a careful reading of all the English and all the French philosophers, he says, which proved to him that separatism is the answer for Quebec.

That was seven years ago.

Ever since, by writing three books, editing a separatist magazine and making speeches, he has been busy trying to prove it to everybody else, too.

He has all the answers, and he is not overburdened with false modesty.

"I'm the elder statesman of separatism," he assured me in his barely furnished office in Montreal's Ecole des Hautes Etudes Commerciale. "It's fair to say that the whole separatist movement started under my impulsion."

That is not exactly true. Separatism has occurred at fairly regular intervals throughout French Canada's turbulent history (some people think it is caused by sun spots), and today there are several other separatist leaders who speak with as much authority, if not the cocksureness of Dr. Barbeau.

It is almost an article of faith with Dr. Barbeau that Confederation not only hasn't worked, but that it can't be made to work to Quebec's advantage.

"The cards are stacked against us," he says. "We're only 30 per cent of the Canadian population now, and because we can't control immigration, we're only going to get more outnumbered as time goes on.

"If Quebec can't win concessions from English Canada with 30 per cent of the population, how are we going to win them with 20 or 15?"

Dr. Barbeau not only believes that Confederation is hopeless. He is sure that most French-Canadians agree with him already. And so, at the age of 32, separatism's old statesman is breezily confident that he will living in an independent republic of Quebec long before he is 40.

He makes it sound almost easy.

The only separatist party functioning so far, the Quebec Republican Party, headed by Dr. Marcel Chaput, plans to run candidates in all 95 ridings at the next provincial election. This should be held in three or four years.

"And we will win," says Dr. Barbeau. "Everyone in Quebec is a separatist, even if he doesn't know it yet. We'll form the next provincial government, and then we'll go to Ottawa and start negotiations for independence."

Suppose Ottawa, despite this mandate, says no?

"Then we would have to fight," Dr. Barbeau answers. "But it will never come to that. Canada can't vote for self-determination at the United Nations and refuse it at home."

In preparation for that moment of truth, Dr. Barbeau has disbanded his Alliance Laurentienne, and, as he puts it, thrown its resources behind Dr. Chaput's Republican Party.

Dr. Barbeau is busy forming a sort of separatist academy of about 75 invited members, who will be required to undertake studies on the practical problems of Quebec independence.

Should Quebec join NATO? Should Quebec form a common market with the rest of Canada?

While Dr. Barbeau works out such details, Dr. Chaput, from his tatty walk-up office in an old stadium in East Montreal, is doing his best to transform the independence ideal into political reality.

Interviewing Dr. Chaput is a little like interviewing the Pope.

Dr. Chaput, acting on the principle that a reporter from *Le Monde* or *La Presse* wouldn't expect to interview President Kennedy in French, will not speak English inside Quebec.

If he makes a speech in New Brunswick or Ontario, however, he will speak in English.

And so, through an interpreter, I addressed my questions in the third person: "Would Dr. Chaput care to comment on …"

Sometimes he would nod involuntarily at my questions, which he understood perfectly, but wait for the French translation. Then he would give his answer in French, and I would wait for the English version.

After an hour of this elaborate and time-consuming game, I think we were both having trouble keeping straight faces. But for anyone who insists, as Dr. Chaput does, that Quebec is a separate country, it's an excellent ploy.

What he said was remarkable. I had read his book, *Why I Am A Separatist* (a best seller in Quebec) and could quote chapter and verse of the separatist theology before I asked for the interview. And so, whenever I fed in a question, the answer would come back as predictably as popcorn from a vending machine.

He strongly reminded me of Dr. Norman Alcock, the founder and head of the Canadian Peace Research Institute.

Both are ex-organization men who got an idea, turned it over in their minds until they had anticipated all possible objections, wrote a book about it, and then founded an organization to put their idea into practice.

Dr. Chaput doesn't concern himself with the practical problems of independence, any more than Castro worried about export quotas while he was fighting Batista.

"That's not important now," he would say when I would ask him whether the republic of Quebec would join NATO, internationalize the St. Lawrence Seaway or accept nuclear weapons. "What's important now is self-determination for Quebec."

Why is he so sure this cannot be achieved within a revised Confederation?

"The English Canadians," Chaput answers, "stand to lose too much. After being used to ruling and dominating, they would suddenly find themselves reduced to the status of equality."

By contrast, he says, an independent, unilingual, Christian Quebec, enjoying normal trade and external relations with North America, would be a better bargain for both Confederation partners.

This can be an attractive idea, even to English Canadians.

But for most Quebecers, Dr. Chaput hasn't yet proved his case. They still believe that French Canada can best solve its differences with English Canada by repairing its own house.

Pierre Elliott Trudeau, editor of an influential quarterly called *Cité Libre*, summed it up in a recent article explaining why he is not a separatist:

"All the time and all the energy that we use to proclaim the rights of our nationality, to invoke our sacred mission, to trumpet our virtues, to weep about our misadventures, to denounce our enemies and to declare our independence have never made one of our workers more adroit, one civil servant more competent, one financier richer, one doctor more advanced, one bishop more learned or one of our politicians less ignorant."

• **1964** Feature Writing •
Canada's momentous 5 days in April

Peter Newman

Toronto Star

OTTAWA — For sheer drama, impact and audacity, no political event of the Pearson Years can match the process by which the federal government managed to obtain Quebec's endorsement for its third and final version of the Canada Pension Plan, tabled this week in the House of Commons.

Those five momentous days last April, when the Quebec-Ottawa pension agreement was negotiated, already have become clearly identifiable as a major turning point in Canadian history. The talks, reconstructed here in detail for the first time, achieved much more than a pension formula.

The accord came at a moment when Confederation seemed in real danger of breaking up. Jean Lesage had cornered himself into a position of having to impose double taxation in his province, a move that would inevitably have led to an open break with Ottawa. Lester Pearson seemed about to lose the sole claim to statesmanship which had survived his disaster-filled first

12 months in office. That he was the only federal politician who would hold this nation together.

The success of the dramatic April 7-11 negotiations suddenly made everything seem possible again. Lesage obtained the funds he so desperately needed without being forced into a position that might have driven even the moderates in his province towards separatism. Pearson was granted another chance to get a renewed grip on the country's problems. All the people of Canada were able to look forward to the benefits of a new dimension in social insurance. The nation had won a reprieve.

This was made possible by the fortuitous coming together of five very different men. Each brought to the negotiations a highly specialized talent — together they possessed exactly the qualities required to ensure success.

Lester Pearson contributed a superb sense of timing, honed during a lifetime in diplomacy which had taught him that large problems can be solved only by allowing them to ripen to precisely that point when decisive action becomes acceptable.

Jean Lesage took the occasion to prove that he was a Canadian first and a Quebecer second, and that in his own person was embodied the best, perhaps the only, solution to the English-French rift threatening the fabric of Confederation.

Tom Kent, Pearson's policy advisor, used his cool, priceless ability to reduce large questions to manageable proportions, to work out the details of the complicated formula which eventually satisfied both Ottawa and Quebec.

Maurice Sauve, the federal minister of forestry, brought to the confrontation tough-minded independence and integrity, providing the key link between the sources of real (as opposed to titular) power in both camps.

Claude Morin, Quebec's deputy minister of federal-provincial affairs, contributed a sure instinct for the possible gained during graduate work in social security problems at Columbia University, to tie up the Quebec side of the bargain.

The events which brought these five men together began to take shape at the federal-provincial conference, held in Quebec City from March 31 to April 2.

The conference had turned into a disaster of stunning proportions. It had been called in the hope of reaching some kind of compromise, among other things, on a federal pension plan. The pension scheme had first been introduced by Judy LaMarsh on June 18, 1964 as part of the instant legislation of Pearson's first "Sixty Days." The original plan had been scuttled by Quebec's objections to its pay-as-you-go philosophy and a new scheme was tabled on March 17, 1964. This one had taken Quebec's abstinence for granted and was supposed to be more in line with the Ontario pension approach. But that province made it clear that if Quebec could have a plan of its own, so could Ontario.

At the Quebec City conference, Ottawa's emissaries sat stiff with embarrassment while Quebec civil servants outlined their provincial plan to the premiers. It was indisputably a better piece of social legislation than the Ottawa version. Following the presentation, Pearson turned to a colleague and quipped: "Maybe we should contract into the Quebec plan." Robarts of Ontario and Roblin of Manitoba said as much publicly.

The unhappiest participant in the conference was Lesage of Quebec. His concern was not pensions. He knew he had the best plan. He had come anxious to negotiate for extra tax revenues and found to his dismay that no one was prepared to discuss his problems.

(Quebec had been granted $42 million of an $87 million increase in equalization payments at the previous federal-provincial conference in November, and as far as Finance Minister Walter Gordon was concerned, the federal treasury could afford no more.)

The Ottawa delegation had come to Quebec willing to offer its "contracting out" formula for shared-cost programs. That and nothing more. At the end of the conference, a frustrated and angry Lesage warned that the next provincial budget would impose double taxes which he'd blame on Ottawa's intransigence.

The experiment in "co-operative federalism" on which Lester Pearson had bet his political life, suddenly was coming apart at the seam. At the same time, his pension plan, meant to be the main plank of the Liberal platform in the next election campaign, had been scuttled.

The full gravity of the situation didn't hit most of the federal participants until several days later. But even while the conference was still meeting, Claude Morin, Lesage's chief advisor on federal-provincial relations, had telephoned his former colleague Maurice Sauve in Ottawa to warn him just how badly things were going. They had become fast friends during the 1960 provincial campaign when Morin had helped Sauve draft the articles for the election platform which later swept Lesage into power. Now, Morin was appealing to the only Ottawa minister in whom he felt total confidence, to help stave off what he feared might be a national disaster. He confirmed that the Quebec budget, due in only 15 days, would angrily blame Ottawa for provincial tax increases.

As the precious days dropped away, the Pearson ministry remained inert. Maurice Lamontagne had stayed in Quebec City to begin a round of desultory negotiations with Bona Arsenault, the only provincial minister who'd talk to him. Neither man spoke with the accent of power.

During the five days after the conference, Maurice Sauve met several times with Tom Kent, who is not only highly influential with the PM, but, alone of the people in that category, sympathizes with Lesage's problems.

On the morning of April 7, Kent gave Pearson a long memoranda, outlining a daring formula which would allow Ottawa's requirements and Quebec's requests to be met in one package deal.

Pearson decided to call a meeting of senior ministers at his home the following evening to discuss the proposals. But Sauve, fearful of the time element — Lesage's double taxation budget was now only a week away — and impatient to get Quebec re-involved in negotiations, had already telephoned Morin to find out whether he would receive an informal delegation from Ottawa the following day. Morin readily agreed.

Late that afternoon when Kent and Sauve walked, grim-faced, into Pearson's office to ask permission for the journey, the prime minister greeted them bitingly with, "So what's the new disaster?" He heard them out, and made his decision: "I don't want it said I didn't do everything possible to save Confederation. Go ahead, but keep the trip secret."

It was 6:40 p.m by the time Kent and Sauve left the PM. With only 30 minutes to pack, the two men caught the 8:10 T.C.A. flight to Quebec City. Sauve's secretary had made reservations for them at the Chateau Frontenac Hotel, but in order to preserve the secrecy of their mission, she booked Kent's room in the name of Claude Frenette, Sauve's executive assistant.

When Kent and Sauve switched aircraft in Montreal, they found themselves near Jules Lesage, the premier's son, who was full of probing questions. "Just a routine visit," Sauve smiled weakly.

Morin came to Sauve's hotel room at 9:30 the following morning, bringing word that Lesage would receive them at 3 o'clock that afternoon.

By the time Morin left at 11:30, he had been briefed on Kent's compromise and reacted favourably to its terms. That afternoon, the Ottawa emissaries slipped through a side entrance into Lesage's office. Rene Levesque and Paul Gerin-Lajoie joined the talks. After Kent and Morin had outlined the formula, Lesage sprang out of his seat and on the spot postponed the date of his provincial budget presentation to allow more time for a settlement. Gerin-Lajoie and Levesque supported Lesage's enthusiasm. Although many issues remained unsettled at 4:20 when the meeting broke up and Lesage shook hands with his visitors, tears of pure happiness were in his eyes.

A provincial government plane brought Kent and Sauve back to Ottawa by 7:30 p.m. They rushed to the prime minister's home, where five senior ministers (Sharp, Gordon, Favreau, Martin and Lamontagne) heard the report of their odyssey. General shock at the magnitude of what was being proposed persisted until the meeting broke up.

The next day (Thursday, April 9), Kent and Sauve continued to work out the final details of the federal plan which Morin (and the Quebec government's pension expert, Claude Castonguay) would take up at a secret Ottawa conference, planned for that Saturday morning. On Friday, Judy LaMarsh, the minister nominally in charge of the pension legislation, was informed of the talks. But she pooh-poohed their importance and went off to Niagara Falls for the weekend.

Saturday morning the final and most important confrontation took place in an office adjoining the East Privy Council chamber. Kent, Sauve, Dr. Joseph Willard, deputy minister of welfare and

D.S. Thorson, an assistant deputy minister of justice, represented the federal side, with Morin and Castonguay at Quebec's end of the table.

The bargaining began to meet obstacles, particularly in the attempt to mold the two pension plans. After a discouraging lunch at an Eastview hotel, the two sides grew even further apart. By 4 p.m., when a messenger knocked on the door and informed the Quebec delegation that a D.O.T. plane would be available to fly them home, they resignedly began to push their chairs away from the negotiating table.

At this point, Kent decided to go to the washroom. Sauve followed him out. The two men quickly went over the list of outstanding differences between the pension plans. Sauve suggested what he thought Quebec might be prepared to accept, and they reopened the negotiations. In the next three hours, both sides made major concessions and the Canada Pension Plan, as it now exists, came into being.

The over-all agreement turned out to be a costly settlement, worth $200 million out of the federal treasury over the next two years.

The pension plan compromise was only part of the package. Its principal terms were these:

1. Quebec agreed to a constitutional amendment permitting federal pension benefits for widows under 65, orphans and disabled contributors.

2. Quebec agreed to modify its pension plan, bringing it more into line with Ottawa's mainly in cutting the transition period from 20 to 10 years, but including other significant alterations, among them the contribution rate.

3. Quebec agreed to take part in the federal-provincial tax structure committee.

4. Ottawa agreed to revise parts of its pension plan, mainly the investment of reserves which was surrendered to provincial control.

5. Ottawa agreed to grant Quebec an additional three per cent of income taxes in lieu of the federal students' loan and extended family allowance plans.

6. Ottawa agreed to double the rate of its withdrawal from the personal income tax field, giving the provinces 21 per cent in 1965 and 24 per cent in 1966. (This change brought the tax-sharing formula to 27-21-75, remarkably close to Lesage's target of 25-25-100.)

The following Monday morning, Kent telephoned Morin to double-check the details of their agreement. At 5 p.m. the same day, Pearson finally revealed the proposed agreement to his full cabinet. It was one of the most impressive performances of his career. Each of the objecting ministers — at one point the majority of the cabinet — found himself the target of a rare display of impassioned persuasion by the prime minister. Two days later the Pearson and Lesage cabinets approved the deal and on Thursday, April 16, the other provincial premiers were advised of the changes. On April 20, the terms of the package were made public.

In the Commons, Tommy Douglas hailed the agreement as "a real victory for national unity." Bob Thompson praised Pearson for avoiding a serious crisis in national unity and even John Diefenbaker called it "a step forward."

But it was Paul Gerin-Lajoie, speaking in the Quebec legislature, who provided the most moving eulogy of the great pension entente.

"In the story of Canada," he said, "April 20, 1964, will become an outstanding date and the men who have taken part in these events will see their names in the pages of history."

• **1966** Spot News Reporting •

Star man finds Gerda Munsinger
Robert Reguly, with Robert MacKenzie

Toronto Star

M UNICH — The girl Canada calls Olga Munsinger is alive and well.
Her real name is Gerda Munsinger. She is tall, blonde and shapely.

I found her in a chintzy flat in an affluent district of Munich, wearing a gold September birthstone ring that was a gift of a former Canadian cabinet minister.

I had a 15-minute chat with her last evening and have just returned from a longer discussion over lunch today.

I did not tell her of Justice Minister Lucien Cardin's statement yesterday that the girl at the centre of the 1961 sex-and-security case alleged to involve Conservative cabinet ministers died of leukemia four years ago.

But I did say that her name had been mentioned in the House of Commons.

Immediately, she said: "Perhaps it's about Sevigny?"

Pierre Sevigny was Associate Minister of National Defense in the Diefenbaker government.

Gerda said she had been his frequent companion in the years 1958, 1959 and 1960. That birthstone ring was a keepsake he bought for her in Mexico.

She'd traveled in a twin-engine government plane with him to Boston "for the races."

She'd visited his Beacon Arms Hotel suite in Ottawa. He'd visited her apartment in Montreal.

Once, "I attended an election banquet at the Windsor Hotel in Montreal. Diefenbaker was there and so were most of the cabinet."

Gerda said she also knew a second Conservative cabinet minister — "very well".

One of her minister friends was once called in by "somebody in Ottawa" for a warning to "go easy" on their relationship in public "because an election was coming on."

I told Mrs. Munsinger, now a coffee shop manageress, that her name was at the centre of Canada's biggest political storm in years as a result of Cardin's statements.

She took the news calmly and said: "If the justice minister wants any information, why doesn't he call me?

"You know where I live. If you can find me, surely he could."

She volunteered to come back to Canada to tell all she knew "if they keep pushing my name around in Canada."

Then, she seemed to have second thoughts.

She said she wanted physical protection if she returned to Canada to testify at any inquiry, expressing fears for her life from a Montreal businessman-racketeer.

At today's lunch, she apologized for having been slightly reticent at our first brief meeting last night.

She had been afraid, she said, that I might be an emissary from the racketeer in Montreal who she said "had good reason to keep me quiet."

Later, I asked her what she had to say about the charge that she had been a Communist spy. Without batting her long eyelashes, she answered: "If I were a spy, would I be working for a living?"

Then she turned to what she obviously found a more pleasant topic. She walked across the comfortable living room and came back with a copy of the Social Register of Canada.

"I know and I can call many people in here. I tried to phone Sevigny last night in Montreal but he wasn't home." She said she was once known as "Ricky" as well as Gerda by her Montreal friends.

She categorically denied that she had left Canada under pressure.

"No Mounties visited me before I left. I had been homesick for years for Munich and after I came back, intending a visit, I decided to stay."

She recalled her marriage to Mike Munsinger, an American GI who took his discharge in Germany. They were divorced in the 1950s.

Gerda remembered the date of her arrival in Canada as Aug. 7, 1955.

She came aboard the *Arosa Star*, a ship which later became famous as the *Yarmouth Castle* when it burned in the Bahamas last August with heavy loss of life.

In Montreal she said she worked as a waitress and as a secretary.

Before returning to Germany she made a brief trip to Cali, Colombia, in 1960. She intended to marry a newspaper heir but thought better of it and returned to Montreal.

She was born Gerda Hessler of Koenigberg, East Prussia, where her mother still lives. Gerda fled East Germany "as a refugee" in 1948 — at the age of 19.

Friendly and uninhibited as she was in our first talk, Gerda Munsinger was waiting for her wealthy businessman boyfriend, "Mr. Wagner."

Her still shapely figure dressed smartly in black-dotted gray wool, her centre-parted hair curling long at the sides, she sat and eyed the clock; an attractive woman, though past the first bloom.

The Avenue Road-style one bedroom apartment would cost around $175 a month in Toronto.

The furniture is attractive but rather heavy with fringe drapings.

A few months ago she was working as a waitress at a popular restaurant.

It was through the restaurant that I found her. And Gerda, storm centre that she is, was remarkably easy to find.

I was at the door of her apartment within three hours of my landing at Munich Airport.

I went straight to the coffee bar where, I had learned, she had been a waitress in mid-1965. The proprietor scratched his head. Yes, he remembered the street, but the number … no, he couldn't be sure.

He gave me the two numbers he thought most likely. At the first I tried, a smart, four-storey apartment building, it was there on the wall of the foyer — G. MUNSINGER, in capital letters on a neat nameplate. But no one answered the buzzer.

I stood on the sidewalk, watching the blondes go in. One … two … three … any one of them could be the mystery girl.

At 6:45 (12:45 Toronto time) I pressed the buzzer again. A girl's voice called, "herein bitte."

I went on up, saw her in her doorway and said "Gerda Munsinger?" She said "yes." I identified myself and asked if I could talk to her.

She agreed — but even then she was apologizing for having so little time.

She answered the questions she wanted to answer and left me to guess the rest.

And the rest was plenty.

● **1967** Spot News Reporting ●

Drop 2-nation plan or I step down, Diefenbaker says

Anthony Westell

Globe and Mail

Conservative leader John Diefenbaker appealed to his party last night to repudiate the two-nation theory of Confederation.

Speaking with deep emotion, he warned the party and Canadians from coast to coast that

Confederation was heading toward crisis and breakup and he said solemnly and slowly: "I cannot be interested in the leadership of this party under a policy that is borrowed from Liberalism."

The Chief, who will be 72 on Sept. 18, left slightly open the question of whether he will be a candidate to succeed himself in the leadership contest tomorrow.

He has until 10 a.m. today to file his nomination papers and enter the race against the nine declared candidates.

When he sat down at the end of his dramatic 45-minute speech to 8,000 persons in Maple Leaf Gardens, the old grey fox of politics still left them guessing.

Conservative national president Dalton Camp — the cool, calm man who led the party into challenging the leader's authority at this convention — listened carefully to the speech last night, and commented: "I cannot see anything which indicates to me that he will be a candidate or that he won't be."

Marcel Faribault, the Montreal businessman who was the architect of the two-nation statement that the party's policy planners have accepted, said he found Mr. Diefenbaker's speech: "Infinitely sincere, infinitely touching, infinitely sad." But he thought it meant that the leader was bowing out.

To many observers, Mr. Diefenbaker's speech sounded more like a tragic farewell than a challenge to battle.

He seemed to set impossible terms for entry into the leadership race. Declaring that he could never accept the two-nation theory and alluding to his position in the leadership race, he said to the delegates: "You make the decision for me when you decide the policy."

But the decision has been made. The Conservative thinkers' conference at Montmorency Falls last month adopted the two-nation, or two-founding-peoples, concept of Confederation. It was approved by a study group at this convention on Tuesday, with hardly a dissenting voice. And it went through the national policy committee with no difficulty on Wednesday.

There is no provision now for the convention to review the decision. The policy committee will report to the full convention tomorrow, but the agenda allows no debate or vote.

Mr. Diefenbaker admitted last night he was appealing to the party to reverse its stand. He was not threatening, but asking it to break out of its agenda and repudiate its policy decisions. There is no way the party could do that by the time nominations close this morning, even if it wanted to.

But Mr. Diefenbaker could still enter the race and allow his candidacy, in effect, to be a party referendum on the two-nation policy. His aides were encouraging that view last night. They warned that the speech should not be interpreted as a withdrawal from the leadership.

Mr. Diefenbaker was saying nothing. Back at the Royal York Hotel he was beaming and full of zest and willing to chat with reporters about everything except his intentions.

Mr. Diefenbaker is a fighter. In 50 years of political life, he has never backed away from a scrap, never — as he said last night — refused his duty. It would not be surprising if he decided today to fight. But last night he spoke as an old man looking back over his life and ready — or almost ready — to retire.

He said that in the normal course of events he would be retiring in two or three years in any event — but offered to race anyone in the Gardens a mile. He turned to his wife, Olive, and said softly that she, too, had carried her burdens.

And speaking directly to Young Canada, he encouraged them to follow him into public life and to be able to say at the end: "I tried, I did what I could in my day and generation."

Mr. Diefenbaker came to the Gardens last night to face one of the great political occasions of his life behind a 12-man pipe and drum band, marching with head up and gazing fondly at Olive in her mauve dress and mauve and pink hat.

There had been grave fears that Mr. Diefenbaker would be bitter, would attack his enemies within the party, would even lead a walkout.

Uncertain what he would do, the delegates and the thousands of observers gave him a reception as he entered that was warm, but polite rather than enthusiastic.

When he rose to speak, there was a fair round of applause but none of the hysterical excitement the Chief used to generate in mass audiences.

Instead of being bitter, he was mellow. Instead of threatening, he pleaded. There were no attacks on his opponents but plenty of flashes of good humour as he told his familiar jokes about Sir John A. Macdonald.

Then, in the second half of his speech, Mr. Diefenbaker turned to the serious question of the two nations and made clear his great and deeply felt concern.

All his life, he said, he had fought for the equality of all Canadians, regardless of their origin. He knew it would have been easier for him if he had borne his mother's Scottish name rather than his father's German name.

Now, the two-nation theory would place six million Canadians who were of neither English nor French origin in a secondary position.

"My message to you tonight is this," Mr. Diefenbaker said. "The Liberal Partry has placed these people in a secondary position by the two-nation policy. We ought not to follow."

He gave his assurance to French Canadians that he had always respected their rights and that they were safe within Confederation. "Recognition of the two cultures was, and must remain, the vary basis of Confederation," he cried and applause rose from the floor.

But he went on to say that the rights of Canadians, whether of the founding races or others, must not be put on the auction block for political gain, must not be put up for grabs.

Every French-Canadian statesman since Confederation had rejected the idea of two nations. "The theory that Canada is two nations can only lead to division and deconfederation."

In deeply emotional tones, Mr. Diefenbaker said he had spoken of one nation 50 years ago and he was not going to change now. When Prime Minister Lester Pearson enunciated the two-nation theory, he had stood against it.

Twice, Mr. Diefenbaker drew parallels between the position of West Berlin and the position Quebec would have if it was a separate nation within Canada. "I am not going to agree, whether it's popular or not, to build a Berlin Wall around Quebec."

And again he said, "We don't want any Checkpoint Charlies in this nation" — apparently suggesting there would be a controlled border around Quebec.

It was an interpretation of the two-nation concept that few, if any, Conservative policy thinkers would share. Mr. Camp remarked later that he could never accept the two-nation theory as Mr. Diefenbaker understood it; it was an interpretation he had never thought of.

But Mr. Diefenbaker had no doubts, in his speech, that the theory would lead straight to crisis and to the end of Canada. He dug from his deep knowledge of Canadian history to support his view that Sir George Etienne Cartier and Sir Wilfrid Laurier, even Quebec nationalist Henri Bourassa, had seen Canada as one nation, not two.

He argued that Confederation had been designed to join two nations in one and said the Tories were marching backward to the days before 1867, were undoing the great work of the Fathers of Confederation.

He had marched with the party for 50 years, had supported policies he did not always agree with, had been loyal to leader after leader. But he could not and would not turn his back on the beliefs of a lifetime to accept two nations.

"I plead with you," he said dramatically to the hushed crowd. "I plead with you, and I know how far you have gone along this road."

Several times, he raised his eyes from the audience to look directly into the television cameras and speak to Canadians from coast to coast. "I am looking into the hearts of Canadians everywhere," he intoned.

And he said he was making a direct challenge to conscience — to the conscience of the party and of the country. With his customary, wandering style of oratory, Mr. Diefenbaker was speaking at one moment to French Canadians, then to the delegates, next to the nation, specifically to youth.

He recalled his childhood in East York, he remembered what he had said in 1917.

He went even further back to talk of Canada in 1841, and he told French-Canadians: "Your freedom in our country came because there was a British monarchy — that has to be underlined."

He spoke of the rewards of public life — not monetary, but in satisfaction. He was warmed by the knowledge of the hundreds of letters and telegrams he has received this week, including many from Quebec asking him to stop the two-nation heresy.

People had said he was too concerned with an average Canadian. "I can't help that, ladies and gentlemen, I am one of them."

John Diefenbaker last night was not an average Canadian. Convention Chairman Edwin Goodman put it into words when, after leading rousing cheers, he said: "I know I speak for every Conservative when I say no Canadian has served his party and his nation with more distinction and more dedication."

• **1968** Feature Writing •

The immigrants' dilemma in Canada

Sheila Arnopoulos

Montreal Star

(Part of a series)

Ever since the great migrations of the 1890s when thousands of immigrants from all over Europe began to fill the empty farmlands of the Prairies, Canadians have pointed with pride to the creation of the "great Canadian mosaic."

For most English Canadians, the concept of the "Canadian mosaic" as opposed to the "American melting pot" has become a romantic idea, suggesting a tapestry of images suitable for treatment by the Feux Follets.

Through misty lens, Canadians, whose heritage goes back to Britain and France, see a jolly panorama of garlic-munching Italian mama mias, Ukrainian girls in yellow braids and red boots, Greek women in black shawls listening to bouzouki music, and "mad" Hungarians with hidden gypsy souls. The average Canadian is, of course, not that naive. The mosaic is not simply folklore. It is also the notable contributions of people such as architect Dimitri Dimakopoulos, contractor Johnny De Toro, agricultural scientist T.K. Pavlychenko, medical researcher Dr. Hans Selye and theatre director John Hirsch. This is a country of opportunity, of freedom, of class mobility, he will say. And the remarkable success of these immigrants proves it.

But beneath these half-truths lies a forgotten "third solitude" containing thousands of people who even after 10 or 15 years in this country know very little beyond the visible ghetto wall which separates their particular ethnic group from the rest of the Canadian mosaic.

One mile from the heart of Montreal are Greeks who have never learned to speak either English or French; Portuguese who work for $30 a week in dim St. Lawrence street factories, afraid to form unions because no one has told them it is not illegal to do so; and Italians who have no idea that the Department of Manpower will subsidize them while they learn the language and skills suitable for the labour market.

Last year Montreal received approximately 45,000 immigrants. About 60 per cent of these people had to meet special qualifications based on education, training, knowledge of English and French, and demand for their particular professions or skills.

Six thousand of these particular immigrants were trained in engineering, physical sciences, teaching, medicine, architecture and accountancy. Another 6,000 were skilled workers in the manufacturing and mechanical trades.

These highly trained people fill tremendous gaps in top levels of the labour force. To illustrate how much our economy needs these types of workers, the Department of Manpower and Immigration released figures showing that one architect in three, one engineer in four, and one doctor in five is a post-war immigrant.

Many of these immigrants were from Great Britain, the United States and France, and will relatively quickly become part of the English or French communities. Other groups — from Egypt, Israel, Germany and Switzerland, for example — will have a harder time integrating. But the task will not be insurmountable.

It is the other 40 per cent — the so-called sponsored immigrants — who have the greatest problems finding jobs, making ends meet and becoming part of the new society.

In Montreal these people are largely Greek, Portuguese and Italian. They are the ones who swell ghetto communities which stretch from Park Ave. to St. Denis and Pine to Jean Talon.

A large proportion of these people come from villages, have little education and no skills. Urban living, let alone North American society, is a totally foreign experience. They are here because they have been sponsored by some relative already in Canada. They are theoretically eligible for such things as language lessons and occupational training by the Manpower Department. But because their welfare has been entrusted to relatives who may not know English or French, they are ignorant of even the most basic services at their disposal and hence do not take advantage of them.

These are the people who become the city's "slave" labour force. These are the people who go out to work at twilight to clean the toilets of the chromium-plated buildings of Dorchester canyon, who mop hospital floors, who dishwash in restaurants, who work long hours in the garment factories of Park and the Main. These are the people of the inner city whose weekly wage, shown to be less than 65 dollars, officially categorizes them as "poor" or "deprived."

Although we like to feel we have enlightened immigration policies — and indeed much was done during the past two years under Jean Marchand — the unskilled labourers of 1968 are part of a tradition which goes as far back as the 1830s.

In those days it was the Irish who were at the bottom of the social and economic scale. Pushed out of Ireland by the potato famines, they were the ones who came to work on projects such as the Rideau Canal System where they were reported to have "worked like horses," and "died like flies."

Later on during the 1880s, it was the Italians and Chinese who provided labour for the building of the railways. Today, it is largely Greeks, Portuguese and Italians who do the unskilled work in the expanding Canadian cities such as Montreal.

There have always been groups who have had to put up with the worst jobs and the lowest social status. With time, they have moved up. But in Canada the situation was aggravated by immigration policies based on primitive 19th century theories of racial superiority.

As sociologist John Porter has noted in his well-known book, *The Vertical Mosaic*, racial theories of the present century by no means began with the Nazi period in Germany. Decades earlier, Canadian and American politicians and writers, including humourist and economist Stephen Leacock, were denouncing immigration policies which encouraged "poor" stock from Latin and Slavic Europe and thus "diluted" the "superior" Anglo-Saxon and Nordic breeds.

Class and ethnicity became inextricably bound — and a "vertical mosaic" based on occupation and national origins was created with the British at the top and the southern and eastern Europeans at the bottom.

Reputed biological qualities were used for and against the immigration of specific national groups, for it was these qualities which suited them for particular tasks.

Porter claims that "these ideas of race and inherited biological qualities, so important in the building up of a class system and in the social process of assigning newcomers in the economic system, did not die easily."

Up until 1962, for example, there were still preferred and not-preferred sources of immigrants built into Canadian immigration policy.

Only last year were discriminatory clauses completely removed to allow immigrants from anywhere in the world to compete with one another on equal grounds.

The Department of Manpower and Immigration admits that Canada cannot develop its resources without newcomers. Last year over 30,000 professional and technical people were admitted. The department estimates it would have cost the Canadian economy more than $130,000,000 to provide this training.

At the moment, one-sixth of the population is foreign born. Since World War II, 3,000,000 immigrants were admitted to Canada. DBS figures show that 60 per cent of Toronto, 50 per cent of Winnipeg, and 20 per cent of Montreal are of ethnic origin other than English or French.

With the falling birth rate of French-Canadians the Quebec government is looking with less suspicion on immigration and is trying to develop policies which will woo the immigrants into the French rather than the English culture.

The illustrate the extent of the French-Canadian population explosion in the past, University of Montreal demographer Jacques Henripin points out in an article that "during the last two centuries, world population multiplied by three, European population by four, and French-Canadian population by 80."

Since 1947, the French-Canadian birth rate has fallen by half, and since 1963 by nearly one-fifth. Yves Gabias, the new Quebec minister of immigration, says that "if present trends in birth rate and immigrant option for English culture continue, Montreal in 15 years will be an English-speaking city."

Nothing has more pointedly illustrated the possibility of the fading-out of French-Canadian culture than the events of the past few months with the St. Leonard crisis, the implication by Jean-Guy Cardinal the English language rights for "neo-Canadian" will be progressively reduced, and the creation of a provincial immigration department, which according to reliable sources, will encourage only those immigrants who will join the French-Canadian community.

Immigration, which is such a vital factor in Canada's economic prosperity, is a complicated arena of activity where deep-rooted social, political, as well as economic, interests vie with one another to fit the immigrant into traditional slots. There is, in fact, no one facet of our community which has not had some part to play in the shaping of the future for today's immigrant.

A microscopic view of the "Canadian mosaic" reveals a psychotic array of pieces which are extremely difficult to place in perspective.

One thing is certain: Many immigrants are disillusioned by the reality of the "mosaic." Antonio Spada, a former Italian newspaper publisher who has been here for 25 years, describes it as a convenient way for the "French and English charter groups" to keep ethnic groups second-class citizens.

Even the smallest scratches on the surface reveal symptoms of the problems. For example:

• A Czech dentist finds that to practice dentistry he must not only pass an entrance exam but also go back to dental school for two years.

• An Italian living in St. Leonard refuses to send his child to a French school. "I've come to America, "he says. "Not Quebec. I already have one minority language. Why should I acquire another?"

• A Portuguese, already fluent in French, can't understand why the federal immigration authorities in Lisbon didn't explain to him that without English employment opportunities in Montreal are limited.

• A French-speaking Jew from Morocco finds he cannot find a job in the French-speaking community.

• Social workers in the inner city area find they are the only ones concerned at a grass-roots level with the problems of the ghetto-bound immigrant.

• A 15-year-old Spanish girl living around Park Avenue is told by her father that it shows scandalous immodesty to be seen in a bathing suit.

• A wealthy Greek restaurateur, who started on St. Dominique St. and now lives in the Town of Mount Royal, turns his back on his "lower class" compatriots for whom he could lobby and help.

• A Montreal manpower official is "stunned" to learn that a woman on Jeanne Mance St. has been here for 10 years and speaks neither English or French. "She must be an exception," he says. "But there are thousands like her," he is informed. And he stares in disbelief.

• **1970** Spot News Reporting •

FLQ trio hid 3 hours in closet as police searched just inches away

Tom Hazlitt

Toronto Star

MONTREAL — The main suspects in the murder of Quebec Labour Minister Pierre Laporte hid in a Montreal apartment occupied by police for 22 hours last weekend, reliable sources report. The suspects then escaped by means of a closet with a false wall, the sources said.

The almost incredible story came to light in bits and pieces late yesterday. It was still being denied by the Montreal police early today.

But other agencies sadly and almost regretfully provided a wealth of detail and documentation.

Sources said Paul Rose, 27, his brother Jacques, 23, and Francis Simard, 23, escaped capture precisely a week ago when police arrested Bernard Lortie, another of the wanted men, at a west-end Montreal apartment.

As police pounded at the door last Friday night, the trio climbed into a carefully contrived hiding place 40 inches wide by 14 inches deep. They stayed there for 22 hours while squads of police searched the apartment and took scientific tests.

When the police left, they flipped open the back door and escaped. There are no clues to their whereabouts.

A Montreal police spokesman denied the whole thing emphatically.

He said: "The guys searched everywhere in that building. They must have discovered that hole at the time. They're pretty thorough people. They wouldn't have missed a thing like that."

However, it was learned that senior officers of the RCMP and the Quebec Provincial Police were invited to an extraordinary meeting last Tuesday morning at which the escape was revealed and explained.

Since then, an Ottawa source revealed, an official RCMP bulletin has explained the escape to senior officers under the caption "top secret."

Detailed photographs are now being circulated within the Montreal force.

At that time Rose disappeared into a building and "never came out." When police were next able to pick up the trail, Laporte was dead.

Here — from a number of sources close to the investigation — is a blow-by-blow description of what happened a week ago yesterday in a respectable apartment at 3720 Queen Mary Rd., almost in the shadow of the University of Montreal.

At 7:30 p.m. police surrounded the middle-class apartment and asked caretaker Michel Champagne to supply them with keys to all the apartments.

The police had with them a telephone number found on a piece of paper in the St. Hubert house where Laporte was killed 19 days earlier. Just why it took them 19 days to connect the telephone number with the address at 3720 Queen Mary Rd. has never been explained.

At the door of third-storey apartment No. 12 the police knocked three times and said in French: "Open up, it's the police."

Eventually, a girl answered the door. The police swept in with machine-guns at the ready. For them it was one of hundreds of raids, most of which yielded nothing.

They swept through the living room, kitchen and two bedrooms. In the clothes closet of the first bedroom, they saw a pair of male shoes peeking through items of female attire. They reached through more female clothes to the rear of the closet — and found Bernard Lortie, 19.

Warrants have been issued charging Lortie and the others with conspiracy to kidnap Laporte.

Lortie, two girls and a juvenile, the brother of one of the girls, were quickly shipped off to the

Provincial Police prison on Rue Parthenais for questioning — and 14 hours later Lortie was to give sensational testimony at the opening of the inquest into the death of Laporte.

The police immediately seized all available documents, ripped open suitcases, pulled mirrors from the walls and cut open the chesterfield.

Their search yielded enough tips to result in 80 raids in downtown Montreal.

But they failed to notice that the walk-in clothes closet where they seized Lortie had been skillfully doctored, evidently by a master craftsman.

A floor plan of the building reveals that in the two adjacent bedrooms the clothes closets are located back to back, and in the larger of the two the rear wall had been recessed approximately 14 inches.

A low bench had been installed which would permit three people concealing themselves. New joists were erected and the panel — precisely precut to the right size — was put firmly into place by means of small, square-headed screws.

The conjecture is that one of the group was always on guard on the apartment's balcony, overlooking Montreal's wax museum near the corner of Queen Mary Rd. and much-traveled Côte des Neiges.

At the first glimpse of a police car, the Rose brothers and Simard climbed into the false closet.

Someone — presumably Lortie — quickly sealed them in by inserting and tightening the screws. Then Lortie hid himself as best he could.

Police assume that not all the men were supposed to be in the same place at the same time, and Lortie remained in the clothes closet simply because no more than three people could get into the hiding place.

But all this was unknown to the police when they arrived. Having captured Lortie, they set about conducting a frantic search, knowing that minutes were precious if they were to capture the other suspected murderers.

All through Montreal telephones were ringing, and about 1,000 policemen were brought together to stage 80 raids on the basis of information turned up in the Lortie suite in the first few hours.

The assemblage of policemen was briefed on what had occurred at 3 a.m. and at 4 a.m. they struck simultaneously throughout the city. These raids turned up nothing.

Meanwhile, more specialized searches were taking place in the apartment as fingerprint and scientific analysts moved in.

An investigation is under way as to what the squads of police may have said during the 22-hour period they ransacked the apartment, while their quarry crouched and squirmed a few feet away.

But no one tapped the wall of the make-believe clothes closet and if they had, police experts said, the wall would have sounded as true an any of the other walls in the 45-year-old building.

Instead the police pursued their search for 22 hours. They unlocked the padlock, walked into the apartment — and found the back door wide open.

A frantic search revealed a slight difference in measurements between the widths of the two adjoining closets.

A crowbar confirmed the worst fears of the police, and the hiding place was discovered.

Fingerprint experts provided the grim details. The thumbprint and fingerprint of Paul Rose were found on the bolt which unlocked the back door leading to the fire escape and freedom.

Fingerprints of all three men were found everywhere in the apartment and in the secret hiding place.

Some police sources have suggested that the three might have been in the apartment at some time but not while the police were conducting their search.

But a communication filed between the QPP and the RCMP director in Ottawa on Tuesday rules out this possibility. It notes that the Montreal police swear they locked the back door when they left and it was open when they returned.

There is further evidence of a biological nature that humans inhabited the hiding place for a long period.

And it is only logical to assume that if the hiding place had been empty when the police arrived,

Lortie would have used it.

Down at provincial police headquarters on Rue Parthenais, Lortie met his captors in an atmosphere of grim defiance. He refused to say where his co-conspirators might be.

And he added: "I came with you because you caught me unarmed. But the others have guns, and they have decided not to be taken alive."

At this time Lortie knew that his comrades were locked up in the false cupboard, but he had no way of telling whether they would be discovered or not.

Police sources believe it is quite likely that the three fugitives in the cupboard were heavily armed as they writhed in their tiny prison, and were prepared to blast their way out at the first sign of discovery.

During the inquest last Saturday, Lortie testified that he left the Armstrong St. house in St. Hubert, where Laporte was held from Oct. 16, the day before the labour minister was murdered.

• **1975** Grande enquête •
Le drame de l'enseignement
du français au Québec

Lysiane Gagnon

La Presse

Au niveau collégial, l'incohérence s'accroît dans ce qu'on appelle encore « les cours de français » (terme qui, comme au secondaire, recouvre n'importe quoi) … mais on arrive ici dans un milieu d'enseignants beaucoup plus sophistiqué, partagé entre des exercices intellectuels de très haute voltige, d'interminables querelles idéologiques et le cynisme le plus caractérisé :

• Dans un cégep montréalais, la majorité des professeurs du département de français a décidé, par un vote en bonne et due forme, qu'il ne fallait plus pénaliser les étudiants pour les fautes qu'ils commettent dans leurs travaux écrits, parce que toute correction « relève d'une idéologie bourgeoise » ; et aussi parce que l'écriture est « l'apanage de la classe dominante ».

• Dans un cégep de Montréal, les professeurs de français ont mis dans un chapeau des notes de 70 à 90 (sur 100) et les ont attribuées au sort aux examens de fin de semestre de leurs étudiants respectifs. C'était, semble-t-il, pour contester le principe d'évaluation des étudiants, procédé qui lui aussi relève « de l'idéologie bourgeoise ».

• Dans un cégep de la région de Québec, les professeurs du département de français ont demandé, plutôt que des sessions d'ordre pédagogique, des stages de psychothérapie collective, histoire d'apprendre à travailler ensemble et à surmonter les dissensions idéologiques et philosophiques qui, semble-t-il, les empêchent de mettre leurs expériences pédagogiques en commun.

D'une manière générale, il y a chez les professeurs de français au collégial un grand courant qui se manifeste à divers degrés et qui se résume ainsi : pour peu qu'un professeur ose maintenir dans son enseignement un certain niveau d'exigence, il se trouve classé par ses collègues comme étant « de droite » (« Couler un étudiant, dit l'un d'eux, c'est passer pour un beau salaud, et c'est mal vu, en outre, par l'administration, qui ne veut pas voir les classes engorgées par des doubleurs. »)

La prédominance d'une idéologie qui se veut « de gauche » a des effets encore plus profonds : beaucoup de jeunes professeurs de français, frais émoulus de l'université, et influencés par la linguistique, le structuralisme et la sémiotique, contestent l'objet même de leur enseignement, c'est-à-dire qu'ils ne croient ni au français (sous l'aspect qualitatif), ni à l'écriture, ni à la littérature.

De plus en plus, en effet, les milieux de l'enseignement collégial sont atteints par des idéologies qui sont bien loin des épouvantails qu'agitent les pouvoirs en place : non, les professeurs ne font pas de propagande en faveur du PQ, ils trouvent au contraire que le PQ n'est pas assez à gauche ; non, ils ne font pas lire aux étudiants des livres marxistes, ils ne font pas lire du tout parce que les œuvres écrites, à travers les âges, ont été produites par les classes bourgeoises ; non, ils ne militent pas contre la loi 22, ils estiment que la langue n'est pas une valeur en soi, que les normes linguistiques n'existent pas, que l'essentiel est de pouvoir « se faire comprendre », et que « la langue du peuple » c'est « le québécois » et non pas le français.

Les plus sophistiqués de ces enseignants estiment enfin, à la lumière de leurs propres lectures, que c'est par le langage que la bourgeoisie maintient son pouvoir (bien parler, bien écrire, c'est appartenir à la classe dominante), et prônent l'éclatement des structures linguistiques, ce qui est une manière plus confortable que d'autres de faire la révolution. Il faut tenir compte ici de l'influence qu'ont eu sur le milieu enseignant des revues comme « Stratégies », « Tel Quel », des auteurs comme Roland Barthes, Althusser et les diverses écoles de la linguistique moderne.

C'est résumer bien grossièrement une argumentation ultra-savante (et d'ailleurs assez hermétique pour un reporter ordinaire, et sans doute aussi pour les étudiants des cégeps). Mais le fait est que, dans une très large mesure, le français au collégial est enseigné par des professeurs plus « idéologisés » que jamais à des étudiants moins politisés que jamais, et qu'une partie de l'enseignement se déroule sous le signe de la lutte des classes — qu'on apprête à toutes les sauces — phénomène ironique quand on sait que les étudiants ont de plus en plus tendance à décrocher de la politique et des idéologies ! Dans beaucoup de cégeps (et surtout dans les régions de Montréal et Québec), les idéologiques, et les professeurs divisés selon des lignes idéologiques, et les professeurs qui s'en tiennent à une philosophie humaniste, littéraire et libérale (dans le sens large du terme) sont souvent considérés comme des êtres à part.

« On finit par avoir peur de faire tout ce qui pourrait être interprété comme une contrainte à l'endroit des étudiants. On a peur d'être jugé réactionnaire. Je me rends compte que je diminue mes standards et mes exigences d'un semestre à l'autre … »

Car l'argumentation ultra-savante des professeurs qui ont en trois ans d'université découvert la vérité se traduit dans la pratique par le laissez-faire, la facilité et la démagogie envers des étudiants qui (tous les professeurs le confirment) demanderaient plutôt, quant à eux, des cours plus structurés.

Au collégial, les programmes comportent pour chaque étudiant quatre cours obligatoires de français, ce qui représente environ trois heures par semaine (sur un total de 20 à 35 heures, selon qu'on est au général ou au professionnel, dans telle ou telle concentration.

Passons rapidement sur les concentrations « lettres », où la majorité des étudiants se retrouvent quand ils n'ont pas été acceptés en sciences ou en sciences humaines, mais signalons que les professeurs de français s'entendent sur le fait que leurs meilleurs étudiants sont ceux qui sont en concentration « sciences » … pour la simple raison que ceux-là ont franchi des critères d'admission plus élevés, et qu'ils ont davantage l'habitude du travail, de l'effort et de la rigueur.

Les quatre cours obligatoires de français se répartissent en général ainsi : roman, essai, théâtre ou poésie, et l'un des cours est consacré à la linguistique. Non seulement les programmes diffèrent-ils considérablement d'un cégep à l'autre (dans un cégep de la banlieue Montréalaise, on a aboli ces cours au profit d'une approche strictement audio-visuelle, et les étudiants apprennent à manipuler des appareils et à faire des scénarios), mais il n'y a aucune continuité par rapport au secondaire. La majorité des professeurs des cégeps que nous avons interviewés ignoraient ce qu'est le programme-cadre de français au secondaire, mais constataient que leurs étudiants avaient tous été formés de façon différente, et que la plupart auraient besoin de cours de « rattrapage » de niveau presque élémentaire.

Comme au secondaire, on tente au collégial d'axer les cours sur la communication plutôt que sur la littérature proprement dite, et, comme à l'élémentaire et au secondaire, de favoriser le développement de la créativité, du sens de l'initiative et du travail d'équipe. Comme aux autres niveaux, on met l'accent sur l'audio-visuel (dans un cégep de banlieue, les étudiants montent des diaporamas et ne font à peu près jamais de textes écrits), et sur la rentabilité immédiate : si possible, que tel scénario soit diffusé, que telle pièce de théâtre soit montée, que tel écrit soit imprimé etc. La dissertation n'existe pas plus au collégial qu'au secondaire, et les quelques exercices écrits qu'on donne aux étudiants (analyses de textes, commentaires à partir d'une question, etc.), n'excèdent pas cinq pages et doivent généralement être encadrés d'un questionnaire précis pour guider l'étudiant.

« Les étudiants sont incapables d'élaborer d'eux — mêmes un raisonnement logique, admettent tous les professeurs que nous avons rencontrés — et qui représentaient eux tous une dizaine de cégeps — et ils n'ont aucun esprit de synthèse. Ils sont incapables de faire la différence entre la langue écrite et la langue parlée, et écriront, parlant d'un écrivain : « Il était ben pogné » ou « Il était bien down », ou résumeront ainsi un passage de roman : « Alors, le gars a sauté sur la fille … ».

Les cours de français sont par contre beaucoup plus ouverts sur l'actualité : on invitera souvent un écrivain, ou un poète, à rencontrer les étudiants ; les périodes consacrées au français seront souvent à mi-chemin entre la littérature, la science politique ou la sociologie, et les étudiants s'y exprimeront, verbalement, bien plus librement qu'auparavant … Mais le développement de la spontanéité, n'était-ce pas l'un des objectifs du cours élémentaire ?

Dans les cours qui portent sur les genres littéraires, les professeurs déterminent seuls — selon leur idéologie et leurs préférences personnelles — ce qui sera étudié : cela peut aller des bandes dessinées québécoises à des auteurs hermétiques comme Alain Robbe-Grillet, en passant par la projection d'œuvres d'art.

Histoire de voir ce que se fait concrètement dans les salles de cours, nous avons regroupé en « table ronde » une dizaine de professeurs de français qui travaillent dans sept cégeps différents de la région montréalaise.

Au fil de la conversation, alors que chacun expliquait ce qu'il fait en classe, et à mesure que l'on constatait l'incroyable diversité de leurs contenus de cours respectifs, les professeurs se sont mis à discuter entre eux — à un point tel qu'ils ont signalé au reporter que cette « table ronde » représentait exactement ce qui se passe dans une assemblée départementale, où s'affrontent des thèses opposées sans que l'on puisse se convaincre mutuellement. Au bout de trois heures, nous apprenions que ceux qui avaient des enfants (à l'élémentaire et au secondaire) les avaient envoyés dans des institutions privées. Le plus jeune et le plus « révolutionnaire » du groupe affirmait lui aussi que s'il avait un enfant, il irait à l'école privée.

Mais voici, à titre d'exemple, ce qu'ils enseignent.

Les cours qui portent sur l'essai peuvent être axés sur la sociologie, le journalisme (!) ou l'esthétique. (L'esthétique est la réflexion sur l'art, et c'est une discipline généralement réservée à l'université.)

Un professeur a choisi d'étudier avec ses élèves la littérature fantastique (Edgar Allan Poe, etc.), et les a fait travailler notamment sur un numéro spécial de la revue « Maintenant » (sur les femmes).

Un autre donne des cours « d'esthétique, et travaille sur les arts. « C'est ce qui me déprime le moins, dit-il, je ne vais quand même pas leur parler de Blaise Pascal ! »

— Et pourquoi pas ? Lance un autre prof, moi, je leur ai donné déjà un cours sur Descartes et ça ne leur a pas déplu !

Le précédent a tour à tour parlé, dans son cours, de Mondrian et de l'escouade de la « muralité » à Montréal, il projette sur écran des pointures et aussi des bandes dessinées. Il estime qu'on ne peut refaire au cégep la démarche qui aurait dû être faite au secondaire : « Les étudiants ne lisent pas. Il faut en tenir compte et s'adapter. »

Un autre professeur tente au contraire, dans son cours sur l'essai, de « donner des racines à des étudiants déracinés, » et leur fait étudier des essayistes québécois, du Refus global à Vadeboncoeur, en passant par les grandes revues (*Cité Libre, Parti-Pris*, etc.), qui donnent un aperçu de l'évolution des idées au Québec.

Environ 90 p. cent de la matière étudiée provient d'auteurs contemporains, dont beaucoup sont considérés comme d'avant-garde, » et dont la plupart sont québécois.

A côté d'auteurs plus faciles d'accès qui reviennent souvent (Steinbeck, Soljenitsyne, André Langevin, etc.), on trouve du Hubert Aquin, auteur plus hermétique. Et puis, le nouveau roman français (Sarraute, Robbe-Grillet), de jeunes auteurs québécois comme Nicole Brossard, et puis, ô surprise, Diderot … « Parce que j'aime Diderot », explique un professeur.

L'étude des biographies d'auteurs est complètement abandonnée : « Beaucoup d'étudiants ne sauront jamais qui est Hugo, Proust … » De même, car cela se tient, que l'étude de la littérature dans son contexte historique. Auparavant, en effet, on procédait en fonction des grandes périodes (la littérature du moyen-âge, la période classique, le romantisme, etc.). Aujourd'hui, l'étudiant pige, selon ce que le professeur lui propose, et plus ou moins au hasard, dans un éventail hétéroclite d'où est absente toute l'histoire de l'humanité avant le 20e siècle. L'étudiant lit, quand il lit, à la pièce, sans faire de liens entre divers ouvrages, et ceux qui, parmi les professeurs, veulent lui faire connaître au moins certains classiques de la littérature québécoise (Anne Hébert, St-Denys Garneau) sont jugés, par leurs confrères, plus ou moins d'arrière-garde.

Il va de soi que les grandes œuvres de la littérature française apparaissent rarement au programme (Villon, Racine, Chateaubriand, c'est « impensable »). Dans les meilleurs des cas, la littérature française commence avec Maupassant ou Zola, et l'on débouche sur autre chose que du québécois avec des auteurs américains comme Steinbeck, ou russes comme Tchékov.

D'une façon générale, on a tendance à proposer aux étudiants des articles de journaux et de revues (c'est moins long à lire). Exemple : au lieu d'un livre de Vadebonceoeur, un article de Vadeboncoeur fera l'affaire.

■ ■ ■

Il y a dans un même cégep un prof qui travaille sur la bande dessinée Beaujoual à l'heure où un autre étudie Albert Memmi avec ses élèves, et où un autre veut leur donner ce qu'il appelle « un choc culturel » avec Nicole Brossard et des modes d'écriture inspirés du structuralisme.

● **1979** Spot News Reporting ●

Quarter of a million flee Mississauga

Canadian Press

Toronto Bureau

MISSISSAUGA, Ont. — The threat of deadly chemical gases being wafted by winds from the site of a burning derailed train has forced an estimated 223,000 persons out of a 130-square kilometre area in the largest evacuation in North American history.

No serious injuries have been reported although about 220,000 residents in this city of 250,000 were urged by police to leave their homes on Sunday.

The evacuation involves more than twice the population of Prince Edward Island or four times as many who fled the Three Mile Island nuclear accident in Pennsylvania earlier this year.

Most persons who were advised to leave appeared to have done so, but the blaze left an aftermath of snarled traffic this morning on the Queen Elizabeth Way which cuts through the city as commuters headed to work in Toronto.

An additional 3,000 residents of Oakville, a city just west of Mississauga, were advised to leave Sunday night when easterly winds pushed chemical-laden smoke from burning and leaking tank cars containing propane, chlorine, caustic soda, butane and toluene toward that city.

Prime Minister Joe Clark told Ontario Premier William Davis at a first ministers' conference on energy in Ottawa today that the federal government was prepared to help in any way and armed forces personnel were standing by if needed.

At first, the chemical gases in the air caused only minor eye and throat irritations. However, police feared that an overturned tank car containing 90 tons of chlorine which was precariously close to flaming wreckage could blow up.

If it did, deadly gases would escape.

Staff Inspector Barry King of Peel Region Police said he had been advised by a member of a chemical emergency team sent from Dow Chemical Ltd., Sarnia — which owns the tank car — that the fire could burn for another two days.

The team was considering ways of sealing what was described as a minor chlorine leak as firemen poured thousands of gallons of water and special coolant on the blaze.

Gordon Bentley, chief of the Mississauga fire department, said the situation was stable this morning and officials were slightly more optimistic because the fire was contained and the tanks next to the chlorine container were coated with ice from sub-freezing temperatures overnight.

"It's a very, very lazy dormant flame," Bentley said. "We are completely happy with the situation as we see it at the present time."

Staff Inspector Ewen MacDonald Of Peel police shared Bentley's optimism.

He said the cold weather makes smoke and fumes disperse in the atmosphere more quickly than would happen on a warm day.

Maris Lusis, an Ontario environment ministry official, said this morning the amount of chlorine leaking from the overturned tank was slightly higher than readings taken overnight.

Lusis said, however, the concentration would have to be up to 10 times higher to present a serious danger to health. He said the amount of chlorine in the air diminishes quickly as ministry air monitors take readings away from the fire site.

Huge towers of flame and earthshaking explosions hit the largely affluent, residential area of Mississauga just before midnight Saturday night when 25 cars of a 106-car Canadian Pacific freight train derailed after an axle broke on a car.

A lack of lubricant in a wheel bearing caused it to burn out, said John Magee, chairman of the Canadian transport commission's safety advisory committee.

The glow from the fire reminded one teenager in the area of "a space ship from another galaxy." For an older resident, the initial mushroom-shaped cloud raised images of an atomic disaster.

In what Mississauga Mayor Hazel McCallion called "an act of God," the train derailed one kilometre away from the most densely-populated area of the city.

Saturday night when the accident occurred, two of the derailed cars exploded immediately and the resulting fire caused a third major explosion. By late Sunday night, three more had blown up.

Another car, filled with thousands of gallons of propane, "had become unstable and may explode," Russ Cooper, Peel Regional Police commissioner, said late Sunday night.

The burning tank car was adjacent to the one containing 90 tons of chlorine. If chlorine is mixed with water, it forms hydrochloric acid, which is fatal if inhaled. If subjected to extreme heat, it forms phosgene, the deadly gas used in the First World War.

No serious injuries were reported.

Police went from door-to-door, used loud hailers, radio and television to inform residents that they should leave the area. The evacuations were conducted without any suggestion of panic.

One man who traveled through the city early today said the only sign of anything unusual was the heavy pall in the air and the flames.

"Had I not known that 220,000 people had been evacuated I would never have guessed that anything unusual had happened."

Police believed that most residents told to leave had done so.

The usually-busy city streets were eerily empty Sunday night, but the disaster site was hidden from view in a hilly, wooded area.

Police cars sat at every intersection and 400 police officers patrolled the evacuated areas to discourage looters. There were no looting incidents reported.

Some officers had been on duty for almost 24 hours despite an influx of 250 Canadian Forces personnel and help from the RCMP.

In Mississauga, almost 700 patients in two hospitals were either sent to private homes or taken to hospitals in Metropolitan Toronto and Oakville in a fleet of 57 ambulances from as far away as St. Catharines, about 80 kilometres away.

Later, patients in Oakville, a town of 69,000, were transferred to Burlington and Hamilton hospitals.

Helicopters carried critically-ill persons to intensive-care units.

About 300 residents of several old-age and convalescent homes were taken to homes outside the city or transfered to other institutions.

The Canadian Red Cross was coordinating operation of the evacuation centres with the assistance of various police forces, Canadian Forces, St. John Ambulance and volunteers.

Families and their pets slept on makeshift mattresses strewn on the floors of the centres. Food and blankets were provided by various departments of the federal and Ontario governments and other contacts available under the Red Cross disaster relief plan.

Evacuated citizens were housed in a Burlington high school. However, the number of pets brought along caused a bit of a problem and they were taken to the local animal shelter.

At the derailment site, about 200 men, in addition to Red Cross support staff, were trying to bring the flames under control.

• **1980** Feature Writing •

The resurrection of Pierre Trudeau

Richard Gwyn

Toronto Star

OTTAWA — Through the morning and afternoon of Thursday, Dec. 13, the day the government fell, former Liberal cabinet minister Robert Andras phoned time and again to Pierre Trudeau to urge him not to defeat the government on its budget.

Each time Andras called, Trudeau was unavailable. None of the calls was returned.

Late that afternoon, a senior Trudeau aide promised Andras that Trudeau would see him at 9 p.m., three-quarters of an hour before the vote.

Andras came for his appointment. And waited … and waited. And finally left.

At 9:30 p.m., a quarter-hour before the Commons' division bells began to ring, Trudeau was driven in his maroon Pontiac from Stornoway residence to the Commons. He went straight into the chamber. At 10:23 p.m., Trudeau smiled as Commons Clerk Bev Koester read the result: "Yeas, 139. Nays, 133." The government was defeated; the election was on.

No one knows precisely Trudeau's moment of truth — that is, the moment when he made up his own mind to remain leader, as distinct from the moment when he told others of his decision. Probably Trudeau experienced no moment of truth, but a dawning realization of his possibilities.

Trudeau may have missed Andras by accident. Certainly his chief aide, Jim Coutts, and Party Deputy Leader Allan MacEachen did all they could to keep him away from anyone who might have put up a strong argument for not defeating the government or, later, for Trudeau not returning as leader.

As the days passed, however, Trudeau became actively involved in his own role as a passive victim of events. Trudeau delayed until the last possible moment talking to the one person who could have convinced him not to return as party leader.

That person was Donald Macdonald, a former minister of finance and Trudeau's certain successor as a Liberal leader.

Late in the afternoon of Monday, Dec. 17, a few hours before he announced his decision to his aides, Trudeau called Macdonald. Trudeau asked him one key question: If he did not again assume the leadership, would Macdonald do so?

Yes, he would be a candidate at the leadership convention, then scheduled for Jan. 18, Macdonald told Trudeau. Trudeau thanked him. The next day Trudeau announced that because "duty" called, he would stay on as leader.

Here's what really happened.

Early November: Jim Coutts, Trudeau's chief aide, and his close friend Senator Keith Davey, strategist in the last election, detect signs that Trudeau plans to step down as Opposition Leader. To dissuade him, they commission Liberal party pollster Martin Goldfarb to survey voter opinion in four Ontario ridings. Goldfarb calculates that his results, if extended across the country, would give the Liberals a huge lead of 15 percentage points.

Coutts and Davey take the poll to Trudeau. He disputes its validity.

Then he tells them: "What you don't understand is that even if you are right and I could win, I don't want to be Prime Minister again."

Nov. 19: Two federal by-elections are held. The Liberals win Burin-St. George's; the New Democrats win Prince Albert.

Trudeau is in Toronto, at the annual meeting of the Ontario Liberal Federation. He meets privately with Macdonald, tells him he intends to resign, and urges him to run for the leadership.

Nov. 21: Reporters jam the National Press Building theatre for an early-morning press conference. They listen, stunned, as Trudeau tells them: "After spending nearly 12 years as leader of the Liberal party, I am stepping down."

Dec. 10: Former finance minister John Turner declares he will not contest the Liberal leadership. Macdonald, now the certain winner, says he will announce his decision shortly.

Tuesday, Dec. 11: At 8 p.m. in the Commons, Finance Minister John Crosbie begins to read the first Conservative budget speech in 17 years. He takes as his text, "short-term pain for long-term gain." To reduce the budget deficit, taxes will go up by $3.7 billion.

The contents of Crosbie's budget have been filtering out to reporters weeks in advance. The only surprise is a casual comment by Trudeau to reporters late in the evening: "We are going to have to vote against this budget."

Wednesday, Dec. 12: The key figure now is Allan MacEachen, former deputy prime minister and his party's top parliamentary strategist. As a small 'l' liberal, he's genuinely outraged by the heavier taxes on low- and middle-income earners. More important, he is a fiercely competitive Liberal partisan.

The other key person is Jim Coutts, Trudeau's chief aide for four years. Coutts wants revenge for the defeat in the last election — revenge on Clark, whom he's held in contempt since the days when both were at the University of Alberta and whom he later nicknamed "the Wimp;" and revenge on behalf of Trudeau, whom he idolizes, and whose portrait in oils he keeps above his fireplace.

At the weekly caucus this morning, Trudeau urges MPs to vote against the budget. He warns, though, that should the government go down, he would not lead the party. This warning persuades MPs who back one or another of the leadership aspirants that they can risk an election without Trudeau remaining as leader.

MacEachen's is the decisive voice. He damns the budget as socially regressive. He warns that unless Liberal MPs oppose the budget, their credibility will be demolished on the eve of the election he's certain Clark will call soon. The MPs applaud MacEachen and vote to oppose the budget.

Few Liberals yet take this decision very seriously. One who does is Coutts. On his own initiative, Coutts commissions Goldfarb to survey hastily selected Ontario and western ridings. Goldfarb is to test voter policy preferences in a possible election. Much more important, he is to test voter preferences for Liberal leader.

Thursday, Dec. 13: At 9 a.m., Clark's staff assembles for their daily meeting. Conversation stops when legislative assistant Nancy Jamieson tells the group, "I don't think we've got the numbers."

The numbers could have been there. For a government to go down, it has not only to be pushed but to go down itself, by accident or intent.

Some Conservatives want to go down. They count on the public being outraged, and the Liberals being leaderless.

Most want to stay up. The Cabinet is beginning to be pleased with itself, but is tired, hanging on for the Christmas recess.

In the end, the government goes down neither by intent nor by accident but by incompetence.

At full strength, the Conservatives muster 136. With the five Creditiste MPs, this makes 141, compared to the Liberal-NDP tally of 140. (The Liberals will support the NDP motion of non-confidence.)

Three Conservatives are away: Lloyd Crouse, on holiday in Australia; Alvin Hamilton in hospital, but unbreakably paired with Liberal Serge Joyal; External Affairs Minister Flora MacDonald in Europe.

MacDonald is the key. Present, she would bring the Conservatives to 134. The five Creditiste votes could increase the tally to 139. The opposition, down from its maximum because of Joyal, would number 139 too. If the vote is tied, Speaker Jim Jerome has made up his mind to support the government.

To survive, the government needs Flora MacDonald.

By Thursday, MacDonald has moved from Paris to Brussels. There, at 10 a.m. local time, 4 a.m. in Ottawa, a Telex from Clark's office informs her about the vote. The budget will be tested tonight, the Telex explains. It adds: "We have no/rpt no/intention of asking FM (Foreign Minister) to return stop Despite bold talk we believe diplomatic flu will hit Liberal benches."

MacDonald continues to her next appointment.

By now, Andras knows no Liberals will suffer from flu.

None of the tension touches government House Leader Walter Baker. He spends the morning planning the Commons business for next week.

Baker has one last chance to save the government. He can postpone the budget debate — by changing the Commons order of business — and give MacDonald time to get back. But Baker is unruffled, genuinely. He recites legislation planned for the next week; the budget debate will continue.

Afterwards, reporters corner Baker. They tell him that the Liberals are at full strength and that Creditiste Leader Fabien Roy now has declared he will abstain. Baker's face goes ashen.

It is too late to halt the budget debate.

The government's defeat is now certain. By telephone, MacDonald is ordered to return. She checks, and reports that the last trans-Atlantic flight left half an hour earlier.

Clerk Koester reads the results: "Yeas, 139; Nays, 133."

Friday, Dec. 14: Most press comment is critical of the Liberals for defeating a government elected so recently and for bringing on a election, now set for Feb. 18, while leaderless. Even in private, Liberal MPs sound either uncertain or confused.

At 10:30 a.m., Liberal MPs and senators assemble for a special caucus. It's their job to decide whether to ask Trudeau to return, and risk him rejecting them, or not to do so and risk wasting one half of the campaign picking a new leader. Eleven hours later they decide to place their bets on Trudeau.

Sunday, Dec. 16: In the evening, Trudeau returns to Stornoway. Representatives of the caucus and the executive go out in a snowstorm to report officially that he's wanted back.

The group, however, has something far more important to tell Trudeau. Goldfarb's survey is done. He has detected wide and deep anti-Clark feeling. The Liberals are far in the lead; Trudeau, as leader, would put them even further ahead.

As important to Trudeau's decision is something that the group deliberately does not tell him. Through the weekend, stories leaked to the press speculate that Trudeau will have to stay because a mid-campaign leadership contest cannot be organized.

On the contrary, Liberal insiders already have planned a brilliant scheme. Regional conventions would be held from Halifax to Vancouver. Candidates would fly from city to city in the campaign plane and make their speeches, after which delegates would cast their votes in sealed ballots. These would be opened, and the new leader picked, at a convention in Ottawa Jan. 18.

MacEachen and Coutts argue that the scheme is unsound and uncertain. The group agrees not to mention it to Trudeau and he, usually so inquisitive, doesn't ask.

Monday, Dec. 17: Trudeau spends the day asking MPs, party officials, friends and aides, in person and by phone, what he should do. He talks to Gerard Pelletier, ambassador to France. He talks to Michael Pitfield, former clerk of the Privy Council.

Not until late Monday afternoon does Trudeau make the most important call of all. Six and a half days have gone by without Trudeau talking to Macdonald, the person most affected by what has happened and by the decision Trudeau must make.

Their conversation isn't long. Trudeau asks Macdonald the key question: If he does not run himself, will Macdonald commit himself to run, and thus guarantee the party a leader who could win the election?

Later, in an exclusive interview with the *Star*, Macdonald recounts his reply: "I said that if a vacancy existed in the leadership, I would be a candidate."

Trudeau has his answer, and his replacement.

That evening, from Stornoway, Trudeau tells a few insiders such as Coutts of his decision. (Trudeau's office staff isn't told, and so prepare two alternative statements for him.)

Tuesday, Dec. 18: Just before Trudeau enters the National Press Building at noon, a woman stops him on the sidewalk. In broken, Italian-accented English, she asks, "Mr. Trudeau. Please tell me you will run." As he ducks into the building, Trudeau turns and says, "Si, Signora."

Inside, Trudeau tells reporters: "It is my duty to accept the draft of the party." A week later, Macdonald announces he will not be a Liberal candidate. So, another week later, does Andras.

• **1981** Spot News Reporting •

An agreement after 54 years of strife

Canadian Press

Ottawa Bureau

OTTAWA — Prime Minister Trudeau and the premiers of all provinces except Quebec called a truce Thursday, agreeing to patriate the constitution with a new amendment formula and a charter of rights.

So ended 54 years of squabbling over bringing the British North American Act of 1867 to Canada so Britain will never again be asked to amend the constitution.

"After 114 years, Canada will become, in a technical and a legal sense, an independent country for once and for all, "remarked a surprisingly restrained Trudeau at the end of a four-day first ministers' conference.

At the insistence of the provinces, the charter of rights Trudeau demanded be included was weakened so provinces could pass temporary laws conflicting with such basic rights as freedom of religion and equality among the sexes.

The compromise, largely the work of officials from six provinces negotiating until dawn in the hotel room of Saskatchewan Premier Allan Blakeney, does not mean an end to constitutional turmoil.

Quebec Premiere René Levesque refused to sign because of provisions guaranteeing minority language education rights, the lack of fiscal compensation for provinces opting out of national programs and rights guaranteeing individuals to move freely between provinces and work.

The package must be ratified by the British and Canadian Parliaments. The agreement will likely facilitate passage in London but the reaction of parliamentarians in Canada to Quebec's opposition, the loss of a Senate veto over constitutional amendments and a weakened charter is uncertain.

At the government Conference Centre, where Trudeau and the premiers appeared on national television to announce their agreement, it was all handshakes and congratulation except for Quebec.

"What we are celebrating here makes me very excited," gushed New Brunswick Premier Richard Hatfield.

"To say this is something of an emotional moment for all of us … is something of an understatement," exclaimed Ontario Premier William Davis.

"It's an honourable bargain for Canada," said Blakeney.

A smiling Davis turned to Alberta Premier Peter Lougheed at Thursday's closing session and declared: "He (Lougheed) may not want to acknowledge it, but he has moved."

For Trudeau, signing meant giving up his favoured amending formula and paring down his rights charter. For the provinces, accepting any kind of a charter represented considerable movement.

The charter contains such basic rights as freedom of religion, speech and thought; checks on police powers; prohibitions against discrimination based on sex, age, race and disability.

However, Parliament and the provinces can pass laws conflicting with specific clauses which would be reviewed after five years.

Trudeau insisted a section be included guaranteeing the right of individuals to move between provinces and work. The provinces weakened this by demanding provinces with employment rates below the national average could implement programs to favour the hiring of residents.

The nine English-speaking provinces agreed with Trudeau to guarantee schools for French-speaking minorities where numbers warrant. Levesque refused to provide the same for Quebec's English-speaking minority.

Provincial ownership of natural resources and the principle of rich provinces helping poorer ones through equalization payments would be enshrined.

Trudeau abandoned his amending formula proposal in favour of one supported by the provinces — the Vancouver formula.

Parliament and seven provinces representing 50 per cent of the country's population would have to ratify changes under the formula. Up to three provinces could opt out of agreements signed by the other.

Trudeau's proposals for vetos by Ontario, Quebec and the Senate were scrapped.

The federal and provincial governments have been discussing patriation intermittently and almost reached agreement 10 years ago at a conference in Victoria.

In 1971 Trudeau was working under the assumption he needed unanimous consent of the provinces to patriate and when Quebec balked, a potential agreement dissipated.

The difference now is that the Supreme Court ruled unanimous support is unnecessary. It recommended substantial support, but more than just two provinces.

• **1981** Enterprise Reporting •

Constitution will touch us all

Mary Janigan

Montreal Gazette

OTTAWA — It will touch every Canadian, somehow and somewhere. It protects the citizen from governments and bureaucrats. It will trigger an initial flood of litigation and put awesome power in the hands of the courts.

The 33-clause Canadian Charter of Rights and Freedoms will be, quite simply, the cornerstone of the Canadian way of life. It spells out fundamental freedoms, democratic rights, mobility rights, legal rights, equality rights and language rights, including minority-language education rights.

And then it sets all of these rights beyond the long and intrusive grasp of governments and bureaucracies.

Many Canadians believe that they now have rights which they do not in fact have. They have, for example, little protection against unreasonable police searches.

More importantly, many Canadian "rights" — including the basic freedoms in former prime minister John Diefenbaker's Bill of Rights — can now be changed by a simple majority vote in Parliament. A passing fancy could wipe out a Canadian "basic right."

The charter would change that, because it is "entrenched" — cemented into the constitution, the country's basic law which will always be difficult to change.

This means that the charter — once it becomes law — would overrule any conflicting federal or provincial law. It would take the agreement of almost every provincial government and of the federal government to invoke the amending formula and tamper with the right.

Critics of the charter argue that it will put dangerous power in the hands of the courts. A charter can only spell out rights — it cannot say how these rights will apply in every case. That means a lot of Canadians are probably going to be headed for court when the charter is passed and that the courts are going to be entrusted with some awesome decisions.

Charter defenders counter that the charter has been sifted through one of the most conscientious parliamentary committees in history. For 267 hours last winter, Liberals, Conservatives and New Democrats pored over the wording to make doubly and often triply sure that the Supreme Court would do what Parliament intended.

The charter only governs the relationship between people and their governments. Individual disputes continue to be governed by provincial human rights legislation.

The onus is clearly on governments — not citizens — to defend their actions. If the government cannot support its actions, the citizens' rights triumph.

Across Canada, federal and provincial governments are examining their legislation and regulations to make sure that they conform to the charter. Provincial governments, for example, will probably have to ensure that laws controlling the age for drinking and voting are the same.

The *Gazette* has consulted senior justice department officials to determine what each charter clause may mean.

But by consulting these judgments and current Canadian practices, the experts have determined that the charter is likely to have some of the following effects:

"The Canadian Charter of Rights and Freedoms guarantees the rights and freedoms set out in it subject only to such reasonable limits prescribed by law as can be demonstrably justified in a free and democratic society."

This is the commonsense rule that puts limits on all other charter rights. Freedom of the press, for example, is curtailed by libel laws. The freedom to leave Canada does not allow prisoners to stroll out of the prison gates and across the border.

The limitation does, however, give enormous power to the courts. Since the yardstick for extension of a right is "reasonable limits," judges will have to determine what this phrase means in case after case.

"Everyone has the following fundamental freedoms:
Freedom of conscience and religion."

The conscience clause will probably mean that doctors and nurses who object to abortions will be freed from any obligations to perform them.

If Canada resurrects the military draft, this clause could be invoked to escape active combat (even though some form of service could be required).

The first casualty of freedom of religion will probably be the Lord's Day Act, a federal law which prohibits business activities on Sunday, with certain exceptions.

"Freedom of thought, belief, opinion and expression, including freedom of the press and other media of communication."

If this clause had been around in the 1950s, former Quebec premier Maurice Duplessis would never have been able to ban and persecute the Jehovah's Witnesses; the Alberta Social Credit government of the late 1930s could not have passed a short-lived law demanding that newspapers print only pro-government news.

"Freedom of association."

This probably means that Canadian courts will rule that governments cannot stop certain groups of people from joining a union. And this means that staid government lawyers and all senior management will have the right to hatch unions.

This freedom also means the government will no longer have the right to ban such political parties as the Communist party of Canada, which was declared illegal three times between 1918 and 1945.

"Everyone has the right to be secure against unreasonable search or seizure."

This is a new right and it is going to have some powerful effects.

Writs of assistance — Federal Court orders which grant open-ended search and seizure authority to the Mounties — probably will be branded as unreasonable and banned. Individual searches under search warrants issued by a justice of the peace will also be open to scrutiny.

The new act would also prevent police from entering any public place without a warrant where they suspect there is a narcotic and to search everyone, even internally.

Recent raids in a Toronto homosexual bath-house could be deemed "unreasonable" because of the force employed. Ontario rules which allow police to stop cars at random to check licences — a method of detecting drunken drivers — could be thrown out as unreasonable searches.

"Every individual is equal before and under the law and has the right to equal protection and equal benefit of the law without discrimination and, in particular, without discrimination based on race, national or ethnic origin, colour, religion, sex, age or mental or physical disability."

This section is dynamite. It has upset the dissenting provinces who feel that social policy now is in the hands of the courts. And it has thrown the federal government into a tizzy since no one knows what some of these rights — especially protection for the mentally and physically disabled — mean.

It adds three new categories to the traditional Bill of Rights prohibitions: Age, ethnic origin and physical disability. And even though categories such as sexual orientation are not mentioned, the courts are free to rule that these are included.

"Equal benefit" could mean that hospitals in remote areas without abortion committees will be forced to set up these committees.

The age provision will probably end mandatory retirement at 65.

The prohibition against racial discrimination will end the law which lets Indian men marry white women and keep their status — "status Indians" qualify for numerous benefits and rights not available to other Canadians — while Indian women who marry white men forever lose their status.

The greatest challenge comes from inclusion of the "mental and physical disability" category since no one knows what this means. Any public building — constructed with taxpayer funds — now must include ramps for wheelchairs and other provisions for the disabled. And transportation systems may have to accommodate the handicapped — at massive cost.

The CBC — and perhaps all Canadian television stations — could be forced to close-caption all programs for the deaf.

The list is endless. The costs are mind boggling.

• **1982** Enterprise Reporting •

From bully to butcher

Vancouver Sun Team

Patrick Nagle, Moira Farrow, Nicholas Read, Paul Mugrove,
Miguel Moya, Wendy Long, Ros Oberlyn, Gillian Shaw,
Rick Ouston, Gerry Bellett, Jes Odam, Phil Needham

H e was a braggart and a bully, a liar and a thief. He was a violent man with a hair-trigger temper. But he could also be charming and smooth-tongued when trying to impress people.

Clifford Robert Olson had a Jekyll and Hyde personality. He posed as a happy family man and a devout church goer. But in reality he was a monster.

In his 42 years, Olson compiled a long list of crimes which kept him behind bars for nearly 25 years. And he capped this shocking record with the ugliest string of murders in Canadian history.

Looking over his life, the mind is shaken: Why was he let out of jail so often for good behaviour only to go straight back to crime? Why was his potential for murder and sex crimes not spotted during the many times he was interviewed by social workers, medical officials and prison staff?

He started life as a schoolyard bully and a petty thief. The only constant in his life seemed to be erratic behaviour. That was obvious right up to the opening of his murder trial when, after lawyers had spent months of work preparing his case, he suddenly changed his plea.

An early acquaintance who was at school with Olson describes him as a "habitual criminal from the age of 10."

Dave, who did not want his full name used, said one of his most vivid memories is of a teenage Olson being chased through a schoolyard by a Mountie after holding up a grocery store with a knife.

When police finally ran down Olson for 11 murders last year, he was drunk in a rented car with two hitchhikers.

In between there are burglaries, break-ins, armed robberies, forgeries, and at least five escapes from custody.

Then, Olson became older, the crimes became uglier and sexual. There were rapes, indecent assaults and buggery. The victims were of both sexes and then were as young as seven years old.

And finally, the murders. Eleven murders of youngsters aged between nine and 18. Three boys and eight girls.

They were slain by a man who was the complete opposite of a quiet, introspective loner, often the personality type involved in mass killings.

Olson was a compulsive talker. Everyone who met him remembered him. And it was usually because of his constant talking which he used most effectively to get his own way.

"I can well understand why those kids got into a car with him," said RCMP Const. Jim Hunter of Squamish. "He really had the gift of gab."

Olson was born Jan. 1, 1940, in Vancouver to Clifford and Leona Olson. He was their first child but soon had two brothers, Richard and Dennis, and a sister, Sharon.

The family had moved to Richmond by the time he went to elementary school. His father bought a small one-storey box of a house in a community built by the government for ex-service-men after the Second World War.

Olson quickly earned a reputation as a bully and a little bit of a con artist. Neighbours remember him sneaking into their backyards to pick raspberries and then knocking on the front door to sell the stolen fruit.

Some people, however, liked the good-looking youngster who was always polite to adults.

"He was sort of a laughable little cuss," recalled one neighbour who did not want his name used. "And he was cute as a bug's ear."

For 11 years Olson was at school in Richmond. According to the school board, he left Cambie Junior High in 1957 and was away from school for about six months in 1956 because he was "working." But Dennis Terry, a former schoolmate, recalled that Olson spent some time in a juvenile detention home.

"The police were always knocking on the door of his house or dragging him home from somewhere," said Terry. "They always looked for Clifford when there was any trouble."

Until he reached junior high, Olson was big enough to dominate the other kids but in his teens his growth tapered off. He's still only 5-foot-7.

"Though Clifford thought he was tough, he wasn't really," said Terry. "You could always back him down."

Olson's father talked to the press about his son's childhood in 1965 when the young man, serving time at B.C. penitentiary for breaking and entering, escaped from custody during a visit to hospital for treatment.

"He was always getting into fights at school and getting beaten up," said Olson Sr.

"One day he said to me: 'Dad, I'm going to learn to be a boxer.' As soon as he did, he began to make the rounds of the boys who had beaten him up and evening the score. Maybe that's his trouble — that chip on his shoulder."

The only success Olson had in his early years was in boxing. He won a runner-up trophy in a local Bronze Gloves tournament in 1954. Four years later he participated in a Golden Gloves tournament and won a trophy as "the most sportsmanlike boxer." But that's not how some of his former boxing associates remember him.

"In amateur boxing, his thing was to try to learn all the dirty tricks right away," recalled Terry.

The two youths met again after leaving school when they both worked at the racetrack in Vancouver.

"He was around the track for one or two years grooming horses as a summer job," said Terry. "He was thrown off the track when he stole some cheques."

Eddie Ciminelli was the trainer who employed Olson.

"Clifford seemed to like the job and he did all right at it," he said. "But then he stole a cheque off my window ledge. He wrote it out for $400, forged my name on it and cashed it.

"When I found I had no money in my account the bank showed me the cheque. They described who cashed it and I knew right away it was Clifford. He didn't deny it. I was very disappointed in him.

"I didn't press charges because his mother said she would pay me back a little at a time but I never heard from her. Clifford left the track then and I never saw him again."

Olson was 17 when he got his first jail term, nine months for breaking and entering with intent. He worked briefly as a millworker but was never out of jail long enough to develop a long-term job.

In jail, Olson often behaved well enough to win early release. But there were frequent escape attempts which added more time to his sentences. And he earned an unsavory reputation among his fellow inmates by informing on them.

Several prison staff, looking back on Olson in those years, had no hesitation in labelling him a psychopath.

Dr. Guy Richmond recalled that Olson escaped from the New Haven Correctional Centre in Burnaby and stole a power boat. He was then sent to the Haney Correctional Centre and later to the B.C. penitentiary and Oakalla (now known as the Lower Mainland Correctional Centre.)

Richmond, a doctor at Oakalla for 17 years, remembered how a doctor colleague inadvertently became involved in an escape attempt from the B.C. pen.

This doctor heard something bumping under his car while on the way to the institution. He discovered that a gun had been strapped under his car and had come loose.

The gun was strapped back under the car, the doctor held sick parade as usual and his parked car was closely watched by guards.

"After the parade two inmates detached themselves from the group and went to the car to get the gun — one of them was Olson."

Both men were apprehended.

Robert Green, now with the provincial correctional branch on Vancouver Island, was working at Haney when he met Olson in 1958.

"I remember him as a brash young kid," said Green. "He was very manipulative and he liked to put on a big show in front of other people. but when you got him into a corner, he backed right down.

"He was aggressive with the other inmates, nothing violent but he was kind of mean and miserable."

Herb Reynett, last director of the B.C. penitentiary which closed in 1980, said Olson had to be kept apart from the other inmates.

"The others had no respect for him because he didn't abide by their code of ethics," said Reynett, now warden of Collins Bay prison in Kingston, Ont.

"He was always telling stories on other inmates. He was an informer.

"Olson was always looking for a deal to better himself, so the inmates didn't trust him at all. To tell the truth, I'm surprised he wasn't killed — even when he got outside. He built up so many enemies."

Reynett said Olson liked to brag about his crimes.

"No prisoners formed a friendship with him. Any friends he developed he would start using and then they'd become enemies."

Michael Garcia said in an interview at Oakalla that he spent time in the B.C. pen with Olson in 1974 and described him as an "arrogant kind of guy."

Garcia, being held on a drug trafficking charge, recalled running into Olson once when he started bragging about how easy it is to rape a woman.

"He said things like, 'you just bop them over the head and rape them because they don't put up much of a fight.' Once I heard that I just walked away. The worst thing you can do is start talking to a rape-o."

Garcia said Olson was always demanding special privileges to make things hard for the authorities.

"He was the righteous type of inmate who was always demanding his rights," said Rev. Ross Manthorpe, prison chaplain at Oakalla. "He wouldn't ask you for something, he'd tell you and then say that if you didn't agree, he'd go to someone higher up."

He said Olson is what is known as a "progressive skinner" — he went from voyeurism to indecent assaults to rape, and, finally, to murder.

Olson paid an apparently sentimental visit to the B.C. pen in 1980 when it was open to the public for a last look before closing down. The last look cost him his freedom.

He trooped into the 102-year-old building with thousands of sightseers, unaware that there was a Canada-wide warrant for his arrest, and was arrested when one of his former guards recognized him.

Olson had last been there serving four years and nine months for a variety of offences including theft, forgery and false pretences, when he was released in June, 1978, on mandatory supervision but subsequently served time in Saskatchewan. The nostalgic return cost him another month in prison before the original term expired.

Olson then rented an apartment in Surrey, only seven blocks from where one of his victims, 12-year-old Christine Weller, was living with her parents.

Gwen Meister, manager of the building, said he was then living with the woman he later married — Joan Hale, sometimes known by her previous married name of Joan Berryman.

Meister said Olson stayed there for four months. He gave no notice when he suddenly vacated the suite and she later heard he was in jail.

At about this time, Olson apparently tried to establish himself in the construction business. He did do some construction work but he liked to pose as a much bigger operator than he really was.

He handed out shiny red and green business cards for companies such as Hale and Olson Construction Ltd. and Olson and Olson Enterprises Ltd., naming himself as either president or vice-president.

Olson married Joan at the People's Full Gospel Church in Surrey on May 15 shortly after their son Clifford was born.

After leaving Surrey, the couple moved into a two-storey apartment building in Coquitlam where Olson's parents lived. Olson Sr. is maintenance man for this building and two others, which have some form of joint ownership. Mrs. Olson Sr. is building manager.

But the apartment was for adults only, so when the baby was born the Olsons moved around the corner to another building which was part of the same ownership group.

He told neighbours he was in the construction business and that he and his father owned most of the apartment buildings in the area.

"He was always bragging about something," said Debbie Campbell, 26, who lived with her two youngsters, aged 4 and 2, in the apartment underneath the Olsons.

Darlene Baines was the only neighbour with good words for Olson.

"He was a nice friendly person," she said. "He wanted me and my husband and kids to go on camping trips with him."

Shortly after Olson was arrested, Joan vacated this apartment and moved with her baby to her parents' home in Kitsilano.

"We knew that he had served time," said Olson's mother-in-law, Kay Hale. "But we were awfully shocked, of course, when we heard about this."

The end of Olson's murderous summer came Aug. 12 when he was arrested while driving a rented car near Port Alberni on Vancouver Island. Initially he was held for alleged driving offences but police took him back to the mainland and on Aug. 14 he appeared in Burnaby provincial court on two counts of breaking and entering.

Police then started an intense interrogation which culminated in the first murder charge being laid against Olson on Aug. 20. He was ordered to the forensic institution in Coquitlam for a 30-day psychiatric assessment.

While a huge search continued for the missing children, the Crown began requesting stays of proceedings on a string of other charges such as breaking and entering, impaired driving, possession of a dangerous weapon, rape, buggery, indecent assault.

During the last week of August came the grisly discovery of the bodies of five missing youngsters — all found within a 72-hour period from Richmond to Whistler.

On Sept. 1, Olson was charged with eight more counts of first-degree murder. On Sept. 15, the special prosecutor announced that the psychiatric assessment had found Olson fit to stand trial.

Back in Oakalla, Olson complained of being harassed by inmates and guards and got himself removed to the Burnaby RCMP cells for a brief time.

On Sept. 21, the 10th and last murder charge was laid against him. On Sept. 24, he telephoned *Vancouver Sun* reporter Rick Ouston from jail with a string of complaints about his treatment. But even in the midst of his outrage Olson could not resist talking about the murders and even described the location of one of the bodies.

Two days later, Olson was moved to Burnaby again while the B.C. ombudsman, Karl Friedman, investigated his complaints. Friedman suggested some minor changes to ease Olson's conditions but said he found no evidence of "systematic harassment."

The trial opened in Vancouver last Tuesday. Sitting in the prisoner's dock in the starkly modern courtroom, Olson's behaviour was in character: He was restless, opening and closing his briefcase, taking notes, dropping his pencil and constantly turning to peer at the crowded public seats.

And on Wednesday, he dropped the bombshell that had been anticipated by at least one of the lawyers involved in the case. He changed his plea.

• **1984** Spot News Reporting •
Colin Thatcher trial

Peter Calamai
Southam News

J oAnn Wilson could not run from death that January night in her Regina garage.

An assailant clamped the screaming woman by the neck, like a terrier would a rat, while dozens of flesh-slashing, bone-breaking blows thunked onto her body. The 43-year-old ex-wife of prominent Saskatchewan politician Colin Thatcher raised her hands against the relentless onslaught of a vicious curved blade, something like a grass scythe.

The blade descended again and again, breaking and separating two bones in the right hand, fracturing her left wrist, slicing through all but the skin of the little finger on the right hand.

With Wilson's hands broken, bloody and useless, the blade rained 20 times on her unprotected head, slicing deep because of its curve and weight. On the top of her skull, an eight-cm (three-inch) gash was criss-crossed by three other cuts in a herringbone pattern.

Perhaps these blows alone would have killed Wilson, already the victim of one murder attempt. But they didn't. She died from an uncommon bullet that tore through her skull from just above the right ear, shattering into at least 14 fragments in her brain.

At some point, she was dragged across the rough floor of her garage, only a block from the Saskatchewan legislature. When she fell dead, her face bashed into the concrete.

That gut-churning picture was painted here Thursday by pathologist Dr. John Vetters, testifying in the fourth day of Thatcher's first-degree murder trial.

At least two members of the jury seemed on the verge of nausea as Dr. Vetters pointed out the location of each of Wilson's injuries on his own head and hands, speaking in the matter-of-fact tones of a professional pathologist who performed the autopsy on the Wilson body.

"I don't know if we need to go into all that detail," interrupted Crown Attorney Serge Kujawa when Vetters started describing the 14th group of head wounds.

"Because it is certainly getting to me."

It was a day of three expert witnesses like Dr. Vetters and of courtroom dramatics.

The dramatics came mostly from Gerry Allbright, Thatcher's peppery defence lawyer, who tried to shake an RCMP firearm expert's opinion about the probable murder bullet and the gun most likely used.

After more than an hour's cross-examination, Staff Sgt. James Somers still insisted the "most logical" murder bullet, judging from the recovered fragments, was a .38 caliber, silver-jacketed dum-dum usually restricted to police use in Canada.

The most likely gun, he insisted, was a Ruger make, either .38-special or .357 Magnum.

Minutes later, former gun dealer Ronald Williams testified he sold Thatcher two boxes of such bullets in Palm Springs, Calif., on Feb. 28, 1982, along with a Sturm Ruger Security-Six .357 Magnum handgun that would fire them.

"It is designed to stop people," Williams replied when asked why he recommended that particular ammunition.

Williams also said a gun holster recovered from a Saskatchewan government car used by Thatcher is similar to one he sold the former cabinet minister along with the gun and ammunition. No handgun has been introduced into evidence and police have testified they found none during searches of Thatcher's Moose Jaw home and his condominium in Palm Springs.

Thatcher's former mistress testified Wednesday that she watched him place a handgun inside a toy box when packing a suitcase to return to Canada from California. She said a toy box found by police in Thatcher's Moose Jaw home looked like the same one.

As the evidence fell into place, defence lawyer Allbright attacked the RCMP firearms expert for not recording how much the bullet fragments weighed, for not trying to reconstruct the murder bullet from the 14 flattened and shattered fragments and for not knowing whether similar ammunition could be legally bought in Canada.

In one of the first moments of the trial that seemed lifted from a television script, Allbright pulled out three concealed boxes of ammunition and smacked each down on the rail of the witness box in front of the expressionless Somers.

"I'm going to show you the stuff you can't get in Saskatchewan," said Allbright curtly.

Replied Somers: "You were obviously more successful in purchasing it than I was."

The RCMP expert later engaged in his own dramatics. The pieces of the bullet clattered into the pan of a portable scale at the front of an expectant courtroom.

As a judge, jury, lawyers and spectators watched, the wavering pointer of the scale settled on a number.

"83 point 6 grains," announced Somers. (A grain is a specialized ballistic measurement of weight; 700 grains equal one pound.)

That fragment weight, said Somers, fitted with his most logical choice for the murder bullet, which was a 95-grain bullet. Some small particles were not recovered from Wilson's brain but had been seen on X-rays.

Allbright also argued the murder bullet proposed by the RCMP officer would have caused more damage.

"I find it highly unlikely that it would exit the skull," said Williams, whose knowledge of firearms seemed as broad as his mammoth chest.

The trial continues today.

• **1988** Spot News Reporting •

No reason for police to shoot, family of dead teenager says

Dale Brazao, Kevin Donovan

Toronto Star

The family and friends of a Mississauga teenager shot and killed by police while driving a stolen car say there was no reason for opening fire.

They are demanding an independent probe into the death of Wade Lawson, 17, who was hit in the back of the head with a single bullet.

"There was no need for gunfire, nobody in the car had a weapon," said Dale Ewers, 16, who left the car seconds before police opened fire among the prestigious homes on Ewers' street.

But police say the officers fired "in defence of their lives" when the stolen car Lawson was driving raced toward them. Only the back window of the car Lawson was driving was shot out. The others were undamaged.

A second youth who was a passenger in the car, Dwight Hilton, was slouched down in the seat and was not hit by the gunfire.

After the shooting, the officers worked frantically to save Lawson and they handcuffed Hilton to a tree to prevent him from running off.

The shooting took place on Willowbank Trail, in the wealthy suburban Cawthra-Burnamthorpe Rds. area, at about 7:45 p.m. Thursday.

Peel Region Police Chief William Teggart said last night the Peel homicide squad will conduct the initial investigation, which will take until early next week.

After that, he will ask the Ontario Police Commission to set up an independent investigation, using investigators from the Ontario Provincial Police.

A coroner's inquest has also been called and will probably begin in January.

Shortly before the shooting, Lawson, his cousin Dale Ewers and friend Dwight Hilton had been driving around in a car police say was stolen.

Ewers, 16, told the *Star* he had just been dropped off in the driveway across from his home when a blue car "came out of nowhere."

Ewers said he did not know who the occupants of the car were and suspected they were a group of "Outlaws," a gang from Toronto that he and his friends feared.

"I was walking towards my house. When I got to the middle of the street, that's when the unmarked car came out fast, so I just ran," Ewers told the *Star*.

"I was running through the backyard and that's when I heard three gun shots," Ewers said.

Ewers fled the scene and eventually called his mother later from a mall, saying he had heard gunshots while on the street and asking if anyone was hurt.

Later he went to a Peel police station when he was told his mother and sister were there being questioned. He was released early yesterday and no charges were laid.

Joyce Ewers, Dale's mother, said she was unaware of the shooting for about an hour. She said police came to her door several times saying they had picked up two of her son's friends and that he had been a passenger in a stolen car.

Eventually, Joyce Ewers was told what had happened and she was taken to a Peel police station for questioning. She said she spent three harrowing hours in the station and wasn't allowed to use a telephone or the bathroom.

"I begged, I pleaded, I bawled, and they kept me in that room until after midnight," she said.

Lawson was listed as brain dead soon after he was taken to Mississauga Hospital. He stayed alive on a respirator for about 15 hours after the shooting.

As family stood around his hospital bed yesterday morning, they watched doctors disconnect his life support system at their request. Lawson died 15 minutes later at 10:59 a.m.

Police have said little about the shooting.

"We really can't get into any details of this right now. There's going to be an inquest and a full investigation that will be making public its own findings," said Inspector Rod Piukkala, who is heading an internal probe into the shooting.

Police issued a terse statement yesterday morning setting out a few details of the shooting.

In that statement, senior officers said Peel police say the two plainclothes officers each fired "several shots" at the car when it drove directly at them.

The two detectives had the Ewers' home under surveillance because they suspected Dale Ewers had taken part in the theft of a car from a Mississauga dealership the night before.

Senior officers claim the detectives saw the black Nissan Maxima, bearing stolen New York licence plates, drive up to Ewers' home at about 7:45 p.m. Police say the officers identified themselves and ordered Lawson to stop the car.

"They approached the vehicle and identified themselves to the male occupants, who failed to comply with the request to stop," the police statement said.

"The stolen high-powered vehicle then accelerated at a high rate of speed directly at both officers, who were forced to take evasive action, thereby avoiding death or serious injury.

"In defence of their lives, both officers discharged several shots from their firearms at the suspect vehicle, resulting in the driver being struck."

The stolen car came to rest on the sidewalk west of the shooting scene, against a fence.

The shooting has stoked the anger that many blacks already harbour for police, civil rights lawyer Charles Roach said yesterday.

"From our perspective, it seems that black people are more likely to get shot by police than white people in any situation," he said, citing the police shootings of Albert Johnson in 1979 and Lester Donaldson this summer.

Roach said it's difficult to imagine a scenario where police officers would have to shoot Lawson to avoid being killed themselves.

He plans to meet with Evelyn and Winston Lawson this weekend to determine the facts of the case and plot a course of action.

The black community, he said, will push for an independent civilian body to investigate the Lawson case and all cases where police have allegedly used excessive force.

Lawson's father, Winston, was devastated when he heard his eldest son was slain Thursday night and said he did not trust Peel to conduct the investigation.

"I don't see how you can shoot a kid for being in a stolen car," Lawson said, cradling a wallet-sized picture of Wade in the living room of his apartment at Jane St. and Sheppard Ave.

"This kid had never done anything like this before," said Winston, echoing remarks by other family members who said the dead youth did not have a criminal record.

"Justice seems to be different when it comes to a black person in this area," Lawson said. "I think the police are more willing to shoot a black youth than a white one."

With files from Andrew Duffy and John Duncanson

• **1992** Spot News Reporting •

Murder in the mine

David Staples, Greg Owens

Edmonton Journal

On the day that Yellowknife lost its innocence, the nine doomed miners began with a normal security routine, then descended into the dark forever.

In the Giant mine's main change and shower room, the C-Dry, dozens of blue plastic tags hang from a large board, one tag for each of the mine's 240 miners.

Before entering the mine, each miner is to take the tag with his or her name on it to the shift boss. The shift boss then hangs the tag on a smaller board in his office.

At the end of the eight-hour shift, the shift boss returns the tag to each miner. This way, if something goes wrong, rescue workers can figure out how many miners remain underground by counting the tags on each shift boss's board.

At 8 a.m., the nine doomed men handed their tags to shift boss Don Moroz.

Nine men, nine miners, nine murder victims.

Eight of the nine men were married. In all, they had 19 children.

Six men were residents of Yellowknife and members of the striking union who had decided to cross the picket line and return to work. Three came from out of the territory, strike-breakers hired in the South, flown into Yellowknife, then bused in to work and live at the massive mine site 10 kilometres out of town.

Nine men, nine miners, nine pawns in a four-month strike marked by hatred, then violence, culminating in the explosion at 8:45 a.m. at Giant mine on Sept. 18.

That morning, the nine men joined a routine safety meeting, which lasted a half hour. Long-time Giant mine handyman George Samardija remembers looking across the meeting room to see Josef Pandev, the best friend he had ever had.

Pandev, 55, had only recently crossed the picket line. He was afraid of losing his pension if he stayed out. He looked forward to retiring soon to spend time with his grandchildren. "Joe Pandev wouldn't hurt a fly," Samardija says. "He would just smile and do his job."

Some of the men at the meeting had crossed the picket line because they wanted to make house or car payments, some hadn't worked in a few years and couldn't provide for their families, some bitterly disagreed with the tactics of the union, the Canadian Association of Smelter and Allied Workers Local 4.

After the meeting, the men headed down to work on the cage elevators in the mine's main shaft, C-Shaft. At about 8:30 a.m., 14 men got off the cage at the 750 level, meaning it was 750 feet below ground level.

Samardija was already there, working in the electrical house. He waved to Pandev.

"Hi, Joe. How are you?"

"Good morning. I'm OK."

Eight men loaded into a steel and wood man-car, a cart used to transport workers along the rail line to their work site. Another man climbed on to a loki, an electrical locomotive, which is used to push in the man-cars and haul out rail cars full of muck, the mine's gold-rich ore deposits.

The nine men headed off down the three metre by three metre corridor, or drift, as miners call all horizontal tunnels in the mine.

"They went to work," Samardija says. "Everything was like usual."

A few minutes later, Samardija heard an explosion. He could not tell where the blast came from. The sound of a blast always rumbles and ricochets around the shafts and drifts in a mine.

Samardija was not startled because such explosions are common in a mine, but nevertheless decided to call his shift boss. The blast had sounded a little louder than usual, he says.

Samardija asked the shift boss if anyone was blasting. The shift boss said he'd check and immediately called around.

At the same time, Samardija's partners, Henry and Serge, took a loki down the 750 drift, heading off to gather muck.

The shift boss called back Samardija to say no crews had been blasting.

A few minutes later, Henry and Serge returned with strange news. They told Samardija that the doors to the mine's main air vent, the B-Shaft, had been damaged and the 750 drift was blocked by an unmoving loki. Above the loki, the water and air pipes running along the drift's ceiling had ruptured. Pressurized air and water blew everywhere.

"We can't get through," Henry told Samardija. "The way is blocked. We're not sure what's going on down there."

A call was made to shut off the air and water pipes. With Serge and Henry, Samardija travelled down 750 drift on a loki to investigate.

When they came upon the loki blocking the way 2,080 feet from the C-shaft elevator, Samardija saw it was largely undamaged. But past the loki, he saw a man-car had been hurled from the track and obliterated, as had most of the men inside.

"Everything was blasted," Samardija says. "Everything was in pieces. It was hard to see the bodies. I got sick to my stomach."

At once, Serge took off running. Samardija also turned back.

"I was mumbling to myself as I walked along. I was saying, 'Oh my God.' I was crying. I was full of tears, my eyes were full, and you feel like you don't feel anything any more. In all my life I have never seen anything like that.

"Since then, my wife and I, every day and night we cry. We sit on our chesterfield and we cry."

Next on the scene were mine maintenance worker Jim O'Neil and shift boss Keith Murray, who had come to the 750 drift to check out the report about B-Shaft's damaged doors. O'Neil, 32, was one of 40 men who had defied his union to return to work.

"I went back to work on principle," he says. "We didn't believe in the strike. Many other people were working. Why the heck should we stay out?"

O'Neil says the union had been hijacked by a group of radicals, who only wanted to destroy the mine's owner, Royal Oak Mines Inc.

In late May, when O'Neil initially broke with the union, he received death threats just as he was to appear on Yellowknife's CBC Radio to speak his mind.

"From there life was chaotic," he says. "I went home that night and we loaded the rifles and we waited."

On the advice of the RCMP, O'Neil left town for northern Alberta for a few days. He later worked another job for a month. In early August, he and his best friend Chris Neill decided to cross the picket line.

That night, someone painted "Scab" on the garage door of O'Neil's new $265,000 home. Since then, O'Neil has set up floodlights and a video camera in his yard to protect himself, his wife and their baby girl. O'Neil believes he is high on a union hit list.

"I hate to say it but I guess we were prepared to die for the cause," he says.

O'Neil struggles to comprehend the violence.

"I think people got caught up in the whole thing. I don't know what happens to people, do they lose their minds or what? I don't really understand that sort of behaviour … I mean, this isn't a war, it's simply a strike where these guys thought they had something to gain."

On the morning of the catastrophe, as he and Keith Murray made their way along 750 drift to B-Shaft, O'Neil saw the light on Serge's helmet approaching fast.

"They're all dead," Serge said.

"He looked shaken," O'Neil recalls. "He just kept on running. Obviously there was something traumatic going on."

At once, Murray turned to O'Neil.

"You better prepare yourself," Murray said. "This could be our friends that we find killed back there."

The men, both of whom are trained mine rescue workers, made their way, moving only by the lights on their headgear.

"If you cover your light you can't see your finger in front of your face," O'Neil says.

At the B-Shaft vent, the big steel doors were bent and twisted, blown inwards. The long steel bolts holding the door frame into place had been peeled out of the wall.

As they continued on, the scent of an explosion hit them. They saw the loki, Henry and Samardija, his head down.

"I have never seen a man look so torn apart," O'Neil says. "He was just distraught. Just sickened."

As soon as O'Neil saw the blast site for himself he says he knew it was murder, "pre-meditated murder with a bomb."

Like about 100 other of the union mine workers, O'Neil has his blasting ticket. He says explosives just don't go off in a mine after falling from a truck or tram. They must be detonated.

To rig an explosion the miners use 22-kilogram bags of Amex (a mix of diesel fuel and fertilizer) and water-gel stick powder, which is set off by a blasting cap and B-line, an orange-coloured, shoelace-thick detonating cord.

"We don't have dynamite underground," O'Neil says. "We don't have the kind of explosives that just explode. It takes an explosion to make an explosion.

"It was so evident and so obvious it was murder from the first second I saw it."

Only the bottom of the man-car's steel frame was intact. Along with the bodies, it was blown to the ride side of the tracks.

"I looked for signs of life," O'Neil says. "I went from one man to the other looking for a pulse, looking for any signs of life and all the men were dead.

"It was a massive explosion in such close proximity. There was no chance of surviving."

The body check over, O'Neil and Murray went to either end of the blast site.

"We wanted to make sure that no one else would come through and see the catastrophe," O'Neil says.

A moment later, the shift boss, Don Moroz, arrived. He told O'Neil and Murray the names of the men who were on the man-car. Among them was Chris Neill, O'Neil's best friend.

"It was terrible," O'Neil says. "I asked myself, 'Why? Why did they do it?'"

More than 45 police officers from Yellowknife, Edmonton and Ottawa continue to investigate the catastrophe, trying not only to answer O'Neil's question of why, but also find out exactly who "they" are.

The only thing anyone can say for sure is that if the volatile labour dispute between the mine's owner Royal Oak and the union had been settled earlier, the nine men would still be alive.

The union's distaste for Royal Oak is a direct result of the good times the union had under the mine's previous owners in the '80s.

Both Falconbridge of Canada and Pamour of Australia were excellent employers, says striking miner Max Dillman, who has worked 13 years at Giant.

"The men were treated like men," Dillman says. "It just seemed like if you showed up for work and kept a clean record you were never hassled."

The average salary at Giant is near $80,000, with some men making more than $100,000. While the money was always great, it was the small touches that seemed to endear the two corporations to the miners: The company Christmas party for the children, the silver tray a worker received after 10 years service, or the fishing reel awarded after three months without a safety violation.

"It shows you're appreciated," says Rick Cassidy, the union's vice-president. "It makes way for better relations."

In all his years at the mine, Dillman says he didn't grieve one thing through the union because he thought he was treated well.

Says another striking miner, Conrad Lisoway: "When people in town asked you where you worked, you said, 'Giant,' and you said it with pride."

The mine generates $15 million to $17 million in spinoff revenue every year in Yellowknife, a city of 15,000 perched atop the rocky shore of Great Slave Lake.

The mine makes up almost 20 per cent of the local economy.

There had been a strike in 1980 under Falconbridge, but no replacement workers were brought in. When the miners stood up to the RCMP, escorting in oil trucks to Giant, a settlement was soon reached, with wages sky-rocketing.

The miners say they worked hard for the two companies, taking out 15,000 ounces of gold in August 1990, a record.

The workers were also close, a family, the union miners say, pulled together by the ever-present danger of working underground.

From the day Giant opened in 1948 to the start of the strike, 16 people had died in accidents.

In 1990, Pamour went broke. The bank took over in August. In November, a new group, Peggy Witte's Royal Oak Mining Inc., bought Giant for $33 million, a pittance compared to the $200 million Pamour had paid Falconbridge for the mine in 1987.

Witte, 38, the president and chief executive officer, is one of two women in Canada to run a major mining company. She was born on a farm in Nevada and began studying music before training as a metallurgical engineer at the MacKay School of Mines in Nevada.

She worked in the United States Bureau of Mines, where she developed gold and silver heap-leaching technology. She has several patents in the field.

The union miners at Giant saw her as an ambitious woman in a macho man's world.

The union's Cassidy believes Witte set out from the start to break the union, a strategy that led to the use of replacement workers this summer.

"What we need out of this is an anti-scab law," he says. "The use of scabs tears up friendships and communities … It just rips the town apart.

"No company should ever have the right to do this to a place."

Striking miner Dillman sees the strike as a test case for Canada.

"If they break this union, every union across Canada will go down."

The hard feelings began a few months after the November, 1990 takeover when Royal Oak introduced the STEP system, a program in which a worker takes "steps" towards getting fired by violating safety rules, showing up late, being insubordinate or not performing on the job. If a miner takes seven steps, he is let go.

"Everybody hated it," Cassidy says, claiming that if a man was late three minutes he took a step, even if he hadn't been late in years.

Under Falconbridge and Pamour very few men were fired, Cassidy says. Under Royal Oak, 13 men were let go in a year.

Other changes came as well, Conrad Lisoway says, all of them with the bottom line in mind.

"Their attitude was money. Production. We weren't people. We were production numbers."

While many mine workers had trouble with Royal Oak, a number of union members understood the new way of doing business. O'Neil says Royal Oak's approach was to cut down on accidents and costs.

"An employee could miss two days a week and it wasn't a problem with Falconbridge," he says. "Nobody used to get fired from Giant."

Since laziness went largely unpunished, O'Neil says, some miners stopped performing or worse. O'Neil says he has seen a man pull the wiring out of his mine vehicle's engine so he could slack off while the mechanic repaired the motor. "They would do anything to avoid work, one way or another."

A group of about 25 malcontents formed over the years, he says.

"I would never go and have a beer with these guys. They are people with deviant behaviour patterns."

At union meetings during contract negotiations, O'Neil says, workers who disagreed with the union were shouted down by the malcontents.

Samardija says he tried to speak out against a strike but nobody listened.

"As a matter of fact the union executive told me, 'Are you trying to split the union?' I said, 'No, you're doing a good enough job'."

In the summer edition of the union newsletter, *Fool's Gold*, union leader Bill Schram said the workers went on strike May 23 to maintain their hard-earned benefits and fight for improved safety conditions and job protection.

Of the six major gold mines in the territories, Giant mine has the worst safety record, says John Quirke, deputy minister of safety and public services.

Those are the kind of facts that Lisoway cites when he says, "The people who crossed the picket line lost their dignity."

But O'Neil says Royal Oak's offer, which would have seen the miners take wage and benefit cuts, was good for the times — gold prices were down, labour was plentiful.

When he met the replacement workers his belief that the union was out of touch was confirmed.

"Most of these guys have been out of work for two years. You hear the same story from each one of the guys. They're all from Quebec, Ontario and New Brunswick."

"Whoever thinks the strike was right is an idiot," Samardija says. "He didn't think with his brain. In this economic situation the contract was not bad. There was a few cuts, but you would not notice it."

Two weeks before the strike began, John Werner, the mine's general manager, received a bomb threat at home. Violence began and escalated after the union walked off the job.

First came threats and obscenities, next came rock-throwing. A police officer was knocked with a baseball bat. Power poles were knocked down, shutting off the lights both at the mine and in Yellowknife.

"Those pesky damned night ravens screwed up the power again last night," read a union bulletin in June. "It's tough to run a mine without power so these mysterious birdies are actually our allies in this fight ... curiously enough, it (the bird) only drinks Molson's 'Canadian' or Labatt's 'Blue.' Funny kind of bird, ain't it?"

On June 14, the RCMP riot squad used tear gas and batons on 200 strike supporters in a battle at the gate. Pinkerton's security guards were brought in.

Ralph Sinke, Pinkerton's security chief, called the mine site "Fort Apache."

A striking miner called it "Royal Oaka."

Forty-two miners were fired for their activities on the line and insubordination. Deputy fire chief Mike Lowing says there have been 60 calls for fire trucks and ambulances at the mine since the strike started. Normally, there would have been about two a month. A dozen fires have been lit, with buildings, wild land and the mine dump all set ablaze at different times.

In July, as federal Minister of Labour Marcel Danis refused a request from the territorial government to introduce back-to-work legislation, the explosions started. First a satellite dish near the mine was damaged, then an air shaft in the mine. And then came last week's explosion at 750 level.

Yellowknife Mayor Pat McMahon says most of the town's political leaders had appealed to Danis through the summer for help to end the strike. Danis at last met Royal Oak and the union on Thursday, six days after the catastrophe.

"I think that if there had been more determination on the part of the minister of labour we may have been able to get this settled before it came to this very big tragedy," McMahon says. "He let us down."

Northwest Territories Government Leader Nellie Cournoyea had no jurisdiction over the strike. She says the people who did in Ottawa ignored her repeated calls for help.

"You get treated as though it's only what you can take out of the North, rather than what you can give," Cournoyea says.

By Friday at noon all the plastic tags had been counted at Giant, but the bodies of the miners were so mangled that rescue workers could not be sure how many of the nine missing men were actually dead at the crash site. It was hoped that two men might still be wandering around the mine, dazed from the explosion.

The mine started to evacuate at 10:15 a.m. when stench gas was released. The rotten egg smell alerts miners to go to their safety stations to await instructions. Around Yellowknife, emergency plans were set in gear. Two ambulances were dispatched.

At the city's Stanton Hospital, Dr. Ross Wheeler volunteered to head to the mine after a request for help came from Royal Oak at 10:20 a.m.

Wheeler arrived at the top of C-Shaft to see RCMP Sgt. Wylie Grimm organizing operations.

"They seemed fairly certain in their own minds that no one was alive," Wheeler says.

It would be Wheeler's task to pronounce the men dead so the investigation could proceed, Grimm said. Shortly after 11 a.m., Wheeler was led down C-Shaft on to the 750 drift along with Grimm, Royal Oak vice-president John Smrke, a nurse, mine captain Noel O'Sullivan and several mine safety men.

"It was the first time I had ever been down in the mine," Wheeler says. "Quite frankly, I was scared. I have some fairly basic fears about being buried alive."

The journey along the drift was dreamlike, with the mine walls looking phoney, as if they were made in Disneyland, Wheeler says. The helmet lights danced.

"Wherever you look, that is where the light is. It kind of reminds you of a disco light show where the lights are flashing all over. It was very unreal."

Along the way, the group passed B-Shaft's blown doors. A tremendous wind blew into the tunnel, Wheeler says.

It seemed to Wheeler they had walked for a long time when at last they arrived.

"We got there and we all stared in stunned silence," he says.

Jim O'Neil and three other Royal Oak miners awaited them at the site.

"I remember looking into Jim's eyes," Wheeler says. "It was scary. He just looked like he was in total shock."

Wheeler set to work checking the bodies.

"I think one of the things I've always been able to do as a physician is when you get into this kind of situation you get into an emotionally shut-down state and you do the work that has to be done."

With the bodies and the man-car wreck smashed together, Wheeler could not make a sure count. "A couple I could examine closely. Others, it was impossible to get close to them."

He was told there were seven men in the wreck and he says he accepted that.

Sgt. Grimm approached him. "Doc, what do you think? You think they're all dead?"

"Yeah, I think they're all dead."

"OK," Grimm said. "You guys can leave now."

Wheeler returned to the surface. The disorienting impact of what he saw didn't really hit him until Tuesday. Sometimes in the middle of a conversation, he'll forget what he's talking about or even where he is.

"My short-term memory is not terrific," he says.

Often he feels like a stranger in a city he's lived in for 22 years.

"I was in an operating room this morning and it was really good," he says. "It felt like it was one area that hadn't changed in this town. I was safe in there. I was competent in there. My friends were there and we were doing good work and we knew what we were doing. Everywhere else I've been around town this week has seemed unreal."

Everyone has something to say about the murders, Wheeler says.

"One of themes of what people are saying is that Yellowknife has lost its innocence." People came to this city because it was safe, because people were friendly, because it was a good place to raise children, Wheeler says.

Now people are realizing someone capable of mass murder may live here. But the realization hasn't daunted people, Wheeler says. It is pulling many together, making neighbours realize the absolute need to stay in touch and on good terms.

"We'll never get back to that stage of innocence," Wheeler says. "But what we may do is that we're going to grow with this. As horrible as it is, we may end up being a more mature community and a better community."

Conrad Lisoway, one of the men fired by Royal Oak during the strike, isn't so optimistic.

"There's going to be hard feelings for years and years. Yellowknife will never be the town I moved into.

"I'm worried about my family more than myself. I have a two-and-a-half-year-old son … What if they decide to retaliate? How am I supposed to protect my kid?"

With the men pronounced dead by Wheeler, not only the police investigation began in earnest, so did the speculation, paranoia, persecution and retaliation.

On Friday night a bottle was thrown through the union office's window. A non-union worker burst into the office, yelled "Murderers!" and a fight broke out. Other fights went on around town. The bars were shut down at 9 p.m. Nine people were arrested, three for breaking windows.

"CASAW murderers," was spray-painted on one store and outside the union office.

The wife of one of the dead miners, Judit Pandev, went down to the sporting goods store owned by her neighbour Dale Johnson, a CASAW union leader.

Judit asked to buy a gun from Johnson so she could shoot him and other union members.

"I told him to watch his back. I told him to watch his kids," she says.

On Sunday, the RCMP shocked the city by announcing that the blast had been deliberately set. The nine deaths were murder, the police said.

Strikers angrily denounced the police for stirring up hatred by pointing fingers before their investigation was complete.

Peggy Witte called the explosion an act of terrorism. She had heard the news while she was vacationing in Hawaii, then chartered an aircraft to Yellowknife.

"This is the worst thing that can happen to the CEO of any company," she said.

Witte pledged the mine would reopen.

"Nine men have lost their lives to keep the Giant mine open. Royal Oak will make sure their lives have not been lost in vain."

From the start, the union desperately put forward the case that the blast was an accident, that it was Royal Oak's responsibility, that it was caused by a safety violation, an issue in the contract negotiations.

Union president Harry Seeton claimed the day of the blast that a worker in the mine told him the nine men were being transported with explosives, which is against mine regulations.

Through the week, union members held firm to this belief. In the rush to earn their bonus, Conrad Lisoway says, miners will take the chance and ride with explosives.

"I've sat on powder and I've had powder under my feet," Lisoway says. "It saves a trip."

Man-cars in the mine derail often, Lisoway says. The track is bad. The cars usually move as fast as a person walks, but sometimes they move fast enough that they slam into the wall when they derail.

If the man-car was really moving, if it carried Amex and also volatile B-line detonating cord, the union men insist an explosion could have been the result.

"I still think it was an accident," Lisoway says. "The fact is, I couldn't see myself doing something like that and I can't really see another human being doing something like that."

But at Royal Oak's daily 5 p.m. press conferences at the mine head office, vice-president John Smrke continually rebuffed the union's accident theory. No explosives were transported with the workers, he said.

Backing Smrke are his workers, including Samardija, who saw the man-car head off.

"There was no powder," Samardija says. "That is baloney. I don't like to even talk about it. It makes me sick."

Mine worker Milan Kunderlik worked with the men on 750 until two days before the blast, when he was transferred. He says the powder was hauled to the men by front-end loader scoop trucks, which take a large winding ramp road down into the mine. The scoops then put the powder into deep storage holes called powder magazines.

"If the union is saying they were taking powder on the man-car, it was impossible," Kunderlik says.

Despite the improbability of the union's theory, especially considering the RCMP's verdict, Dr. Wheeler says there is nothing wrong with the reaction of the striking miners.

"They have to believe that," he says. "The alternative is too horrible to believe, that the murderer is one of their own."

There are no automated cars at Giant. No matter what, the explosion would have killed someone, the first unlucky tram driver down the 750 drift. The blast was not just intended to blow up a mine corridor. It was not manslaughter.

The culprits likely entered the mine after the night shift went home at 4 a.m., says a mine worker, who rode the 750 line just before coming out.

Few people are in the mine in the hours before the day shift starts.

The culprits could have got into the mine any number of ways and used any number of tunnels.

"There are a million ways to get in there," Samardija says. "If you want to do something you can do whatever you want to do."

The mine site is a massive area, with no fence around some of it, O'Neil says. "Giant mine is on the edge of the wilderness."

As much as 160 km of corridors run through the mine. There are 13 main access airways, and numerous other smaller ones.

Air shafts and entrances to the mine are kept locked, but there were breaches in the past. Anti-Royal Oak graffiti was found underground on a mine vehicle earlier in the strike.

"There are old shafts all over," says a mine worker. "I would believe they would go in through some old shaft. That way they would not meet anybody."

O'Neil says he has heard the blast was caused by 45 kg of explosives.

"A blast like that would be humungous," Kunderlik says. "It would knock you down 300 metres away. With two bags of Amex you could easily blow up a concrete bridge."

O'Neil says the vehicles used by the saboteurs to get around underground have been discovered: A scoop truck and a battery locomotive, which was left plugged in, against company policy.

"Obviously whoever left that motor left in a hell of a hurry and didn't bother unplugging it."

The scoop truck was taken from its storage shed and dropped off at the 575 level, O'Neil says. The culprits likely walked out the rest of the way.

Among those who most desperately want an answer to the mystery of the murder are the strikers themselves.

"Let's get the questions answered before any blame is laid," Lisoway says. "We're just a bunch of blue-collar workers. We're not a bunch of terrorists."

The pain of the past week is cut into their faces. Dillman and Cassidy are both unshaven and look like they haven't slept since the bomb went off.

A few of the dead men were their good friends. Dillman wanted to call one dead man's family to offer his sympathy, but he was told not to. Another union man had tried and was called a murderer.

"If this isn't an accident then it's the work of an individual or of several people," Cassidy says. "It is no way the work of the union."

"It would have to be some sick individual to do something like that," Dillman says.

The good hearts of some of the union men were proven the morning of the catastrophe. At the union hall, strikers were monitoring their radio scanner, as usual, when they heard a call for two ambulances to go to Giant.

Word of injuries and death crackled on the airwaves soon after. In tears, striker Allan Shearing said, "We got to get down there."

Cassidy and Dillman set to work contacting the union's mine rescue team. Both Royal Oak and the territorial government were informed the union was ready to help.

Ten members of the rescue team rushed out to the mine, only to be stopped at the gate. They were told there would be no rescue. Everyone was dead.

Nine men, nine miners, nine names on the nine tags left unclaimed that Friday on the shift boss's board:

Josef Pandev. Verne Fullowka. Shane Riggs. Malcolm Sawler. David Vodnoski. Norman Hourie. Robert Rowsell. Arnold Russell. Chris Neill.

• 1993 Enterprise Reporting •
Who is Valery Fabrikant?
William Marsden, Andrew McIntosh, Carolyn Adolph

Montreal Gazette

(Excerpted from a 10-page special report)

On the afternoon of Aug. 24, 1992, Professor Valery Fabrikant walked into Concordia University's Henry F. Hall Building carrying three handguns. When he was taken out by police 90 minutes later, two of his colleagues — Matthew Douglass and Michael Hogben — were dead and two — Jaan Saber and Phoivos Ziogas — were mortally wounded.

Those four killings weren't the first sign that Fabrikant was a troubled and violent man. They were the culmination of a long history of aggression and manipulation that dated back to Fabrikant's early days in the Soviet Union. And they occurred in spite of the fact that many at Concordia loathed and feared the wiry mechanical engineering professor because of his threats and abusive behaviour.

How did Valery Fabrikant end up at Concordia? And in spite of all the warning signs, how did he come to take the lives of four of his colleagues?

This is the story of Valery Fabrikant: fake, liar, murderer.

AUG. 24, 1992, 3:05 P.M.

Dressed in a sport shirt and windbreaker, Professor Michael Hogben, 52, smiled nervously at a secretary as he headed down the narrow corridor toward Valery Fabrikant's cramped ninth-floor office in Concordia University's mechanical engineering department. As faculty association president, Hogben had an intimate knowledge of Fabrikant's grievances. He knew what Fabrikant could be like and he didn't relish confronting the abusive professor about his behaviour. Hogben basically believed Fabrikant was crazy. What's more, he had heard disturbing rumours that Fabrikant had made death threats and purchased guns. He worried about Fabrikant. Yet somebody had to lay down the law.

Hogben stepped into Fabrikant's office and sat down. He produced a carefully worded letter of reprimand from his briefcase. Fabrikant produced a .38 calibre pistol from his. Three gun shots rang out. One bullet crashed through Hogben's head. A second went through his chest, lacerating his heart. As he fell, a third shot was fired through his lower back. Hogben collapsed and bled to death on the floor clutching the letter in his right fist.

Electronic-mail transmission
From: Adam Steele, Concordia University.
Date: Aug. 24, 1992. 20:37:26 GMT.
Subject: Fraud and extortion at Concordia University.
"There is an unconfirmed report that Fabrikant is involved in a hostage-taking at Concordia right now ..."

Electronic-mail transmission
From: Amy L. Rovelstad, College of Engineering, University of Maryland.
Date: Aug. 24, 1992. 21:56:51 GMT.
Subject: Fraud and extortion at Concordia University (Canada).
"Yup. I just heard on (radio) that an unnamed engineering prof at Concordia had taken hostages. Sounds like he went off. I am now curious to find out how it ends. Let us know, someone at Concordia."

Electronic-mail transmission
From: Matthias Pohl, University of Oregon.
Date: Aug. 24, 1992. 21:56 GMT.
Subject: CNN — JUST IN.
"CNN reported that a gunman has killed two people at Concordia University. The gunman was described as a disgruntled professor of mechanical engineering ..."

For more than six months leading up to the Aug. 24 killing spree, Valery Isaacovitch Fabrikant, 53, had been trying to persuade the international scientific community that he was a genius scientist and a victim of jealous colleagues conspiring to throw him out of Concordia University.

Using the scientific community's electronic-mail system, he transmitted reams of documents that he claimed proved his colleagues were driving him out because he knew too much about fraud and extortion at the university.

He represented himself as the victim of ambitious, bogus scientists — scum or parasites, as he liked to call his colleagues — who, recognizing his superior genius, forced him to put their names on his scientific papers.

While many scientists ignored him, others, both at Concordia and elsewhere, readily believed his accusations.

Some concluded he was a genius, the "Einstein of engineering." These scholars, otherwise trained to be skeptical, eagerly jumped on his bandwagon. Many held to their views even after his murderous spree and his lengthy trial.

While almost five months of trial brought out the facts of the murders, they revealed little about the murderer and why Concordia University for years endured his psychotic behaviour — what three psychiatrists have called his severe narcissism and acute paranoia.

Who is Valery Fabrikant? And why did so many academics believe in him? That he was a dangerous psychotic there's little doubt. Adept at exploiting weaknesses and prejudices of others, he knew how to wield the modern tools of communication to create the image of a wronged genius that he thought would justify the murders he committed in such methodical, passionless intent. But he was also a scientist, a mathematician and a father with a wife and two children.

An investigation of Fabrikant's past reveals that he was above all a fake with a long history of violent and abusive behaviour dating back to his early days in Russia.

In this special report, the *Gazette* will recount Fabrikant's clouded history, both in the former Soviet Union and in Canada.

Our investigation shows that Fabrikant reluctantly left the Soviet Union after being fired from at least three jobs because he abused his fellow workers, threatened them and frequently flew into violent rages. He came to Canada not because he was a dissident or a refusenik, as he claimed, but because he couldn't get a job. Given a long leash in one scientific institute after another, he had run out of rope. The investigation also reveals that once he arrived in Canada:

• He falsified his curriculum vitae by altering the field of his PhD degree and other titles to try to get hired full time at Concordia.

• He fraudulently bumped up his students' marks at Concordia and also marked test answers correct that were wrong.

• He lied about being offered jobs and publicly berated professors who refused to hire him. He also tried to evade his teaching responsibilities.

• His books, which he claimed were classics, still languish in the publisher's warehouse unsold.

• He had no evidence for the accusations of fraud and extortion he made against fellow professors.

After a preliminary talk with the *Gazette,* Fabrikant refused to answer questions about his past. He later agreed to be interviewed on condition that this newspaper print a lengthy statement. The *Gazette* refused.

The *Gazette* investigation also raises serious questions about the Concordia administration's conduct in the handling of Fabrikant throughout his 12 years at the university. How could a person who was as abusive, rude and threatening as Valery Fabrikant find a home at Concordia for so many years? Was the university so tied up in rules and regulations that it was unable to take action against him? Fabrikant was on the faculty of mechanical engineering. But he knew almost nothing about mechanical engineering. He was a mathematician with degrees in mechanics and electrical engineering. Why did Concordia hire Fabrikant in a faculty where he had little or no expertise?

Furthermore, why did the university never bother to check his background in Russia before hiring him full time in 1991?

"In all my life, even when a small boy, I never got involved in a fist fight with anyone and if such a peaceful person like myself takes gun (sic) and starts shooting, something very terrible must have been done to that person."
— Valery Fabrikant in *Laurentian* magazine, November 1992.

It was a warm July day in 1979, and Valery Fabrikant stood on the railway platform in Brest, waiting to board a train that would take him across Poland, through Czechoslovakia and on to Vienna.

He was tired. It had been a long and cramped train ride from Moscow. His bags bulged with engineering books and his father's heavy woollen army uniform, which he thought might come in handy during cold Canadian winters.

Unlike most of the others on the railway platform, he was a reluctant emigrant. Until he was fired from his job, he had never thought of leaving Russia.

Now he had set his hopes on Canada. He later would tell friends that he chose Canada because Israel and the U.S. were too violent.

"He wanted a safe country for himself," said Efim Vaks, a Russian emigre who now lives in California and knew Fabrikant in Russia.

Standing next to Fabrikant on the concrete platform in Brest was his ex-wife, Galina. No one else came to see him off. Soviet Russia was glad to be rid of Valery Fabrikant.

Acquaintances remember Galina as a small, soft-spoken, slightly overweight but pretty woman who once appeared at a workers' dance with a large paper butterfly on her back.

About 15 years younger than Fabrikant, Galina had been his student. She had idolized him. She had championed his causes, supporting him in his numerous battles with Soviet academia. She stuck with him from job to job. And he had encouraged her worship, always insisting that his colleagues plotted against him because they feared his genius.

But when he decided to emigrate, Fabrikant discarded her. He divorced her because she couldn't have children and he wanted to start a new family in Canada.

Still, Galina promised to take care of his aging mother and alcoholic brother and she loyally came to say farewell.

Born in the Belorussian capital, Minsk, on Jan. 28, 1940, Fabrikant came from a military family. His father, a committed communist, was Lt.-Col. Isaac Fabrikant. His mother, Pesya Yudelevna, was a housewife.

When the Nazis invaded Russia during World War II, the family was sent 3,700 km southeast to Kok Yangak, near the Chinese border.

After the war, the Fabrikants moved to Ivanovo, a dreary textile city 233 km northeast of Moscow.

Fabrikant's school records show he excelled in all courses in primary, secondary and university studies, graduating with honours. He also was a star chess player and gymnast. Colleagues remember that he practiced one-handed handstands in his room.

At the Ivanovo Power Institute he wrote three research papers. On the strength of these papers, the Moscow Power Institute accepted him into its graduate school without the requirement of entrance exams. He studied under one of Russia's foremost engineers, V. V. Bolotin, a name he would later use to help him get a job at Concordia.

He graduated in 1966 with honours. It was then that the trouble began.

Twenty-six years old and unable to find a job in Moscow, Fabrikant was forced to seek employment in the boondocks of Russian academia.

Electronic-mail transmission
From: V.I. Fabrikant.
Date: Feb. 9, 1992. 17:46 GMT.
"… I was voted best teacher back in the U.S.S.R., and you may be assured that the quality of my teaching performance will never deteriorate."

Fabrikant travelled 200 km north to Rybinsk, where he took a minor teaching position at the Institute of Aircraft Technology. Two years later he experienced his second setback. For unknown reasons, he was demoted to the position of programming analyst at the nearby Aviation Engine Manufacturing plant.

That lasted only a year. He left under a cloud in 1970 to take a job as an instructor in theoretical mechanics at the Polytechnic Institute in Lenin's birthplace, Ulyanovsk. It was here that he met Galina.

According to his records, he was considered a "gifted scientist."

Two years later, in 1972, he was promoted to an assistant professor. But that didn't last long. Suddenly, in 1973, he quit.

His records show that he "left of his own volition." But as subsequent events would prove, this was a euphemism for being fired.

After Ulyanovsk, his career nose-dived. In what was considered a death blow to the career of a Soviet scientist, he moved from academia to light industry.

Returning to his home town of Ivanovo, he got a job as a research scientist at the Automatic Control Systems Institute, which employed about 1,500 people to conduct research for the textile industry.

Fabrikant's first boss, Efim Scheinberg, a tall, tough, heavy-set man, quickly became his arch enemy.

At one point, Fabrikant accused Scheinberg of stealing his scientific ideas. He threatened Scheinberg. A long-term quarrel ensued and was finally settled in Scheinberg's favour in the institute's comrades' court, a sort of in-house procedure for settling workers' disputes.

According to institute records and to witnesses, the proceedings became legendary because at one point Fabrikant attacked Scheinberg and tried to club him with a chair.

After the incident, Fabrikant was transferred to a division run by Vadim Livadonov, who now works for a state computer company.

Electronic-mail transmission
From: Alexander Anger, Hewlett-Packard, Santa Rosa, California.
Date: Sept. 1, 1992.
"… Although interesting in their own right as intellectual tomes, the description of the problems (in Fabrikant's scientific papers) leaves one wondering if any mechanical engineer who ever built a real structure could make use of them."

Livadonov, interviewed for this article in his spartan office in Ivanovo, said he remembered Fabrikant as a quarrelsome, belligerent person who picked fights with everybody.

"It was difficult to discuss things with Fabrikant because he quickly lost his temper and would hurl things like books," said Livadonov, choosing his words carefully. "It was constant tension and conflict. That was the routine. Every day something happened."

He called Fabrikant a "fraud" and said he was not a good scientist.

"He worked as a programmer, but his programs never worked in spite of the fact that they looked good on paper. His knowledge sometimes appeared to be sketchy rather than erudite," Livadonov said.

"He didn't finish his work. He would have an idea but he would not carry it out. Still, in some ways he was better than some of the others."

Igor Liakishev, who headed Fabrikant's division at the Ivanovo Institute, characterized Fabrikant as an "unreliable person" and dismissed him as "dishonourable."

Liakishev, who is now retired, offered two reporters who visited him vodka and tomatoes. As he lounged in his warm-up pants, Liakishev recalled that Fabrikant could never admit to a mistake.

"I once told him that he didn't understand what he was doing and that he wasn't fulfilling the assigned task. After that, he would write down everything I told him into a special notebook so he could catch me in a lie or something. Sort of throw my words back at me.

"He constantly claimed that envious colleagues were trying to keep him down," Liakishev said.

Electronic-mail transmission
From: V.I. Fabrikant.
Date: June 28, 1992.
Dear Colleague:
"Since I was a dissident back in the U.S.S.R., I have no doubt that there is a file named "FABRIKANT, CONFIDENTIAL" somewhere in the KGB vaults."

Institute records show that Fabrikant complained to the KGB and the regional and central committees about colleagues conspiring against him.

His colleagues said Fabrikant often cited speeches by Brezhnev or Lenin to prove that they were anti-communist and threatened to denounce them to authorities.

Fabrikant even antagonized the medical staff at a local clinic.

He was determined to have children. When repeated attempts failed, he went to a clinic to have his sperm tested.

Galina Osokina, an Ivanovo doctor, complained to Fabrikant's colleagues that he became belligerent after receiving the results of his sperm test.

"The results of the test didn't satisfy him and he started writing complaints to the health-care department about the 'improper work of Dr. Osokina.' He also began to make regular visits to the polyclinic, bringing a medical reference book, and he would try to teach the staff how to run a sperm test. He was a pain in the ass," Liakishev said.

By 1978, Fabrikant's job came up for renewal. The hearings are normally a routine procedure in which a board of about 11 colleagues votes to renew a scientist's contract. Fabrikant's hearings inspired a sort of cabal against him.

His bosses all told the *Gazette* that the leading scientists at the Ivanovo Institute colluded to vote him out because of his threatening behaviour.

"He didn't deserve it as a scientist," Liakishev said. "He was neither very good nor very poor, and there were people who passed the proceedings who were much worse."

Fabrikant's former colleagues agreed that it was almost unheard of to vote out a colleague.

The institute offered him a lesser position as a senior engineer at the same salary. But Fabrikant refused and launched a lawsuit.

He charged that he was being persecuted as a Jew, that the institute had insulted his honour and that his firing was illegal.

The civil trial took place in December, 1978 in the court of the Leninsky region of Ivanovo under Judge Kovaleva.

What eventually sank Fabrikant was the evidence of his previous job performances, which showed, according to the record, an uninterrupted pattern of abusive and belligerent behaviour. It proved that he was forced to leave his teaching job at the Ulyanovsk Polytechnic Institute under similar circumstances.

Fabrikant lost his case and was fired from the Ivanovo Institute.

With his disastrous work history, he was unable to find a job. So for the first time he began to think of emigrating to the West.

Soviet law required that he first obtain an invitation from a relative in the West.

He turned for help to a Moscow scientist he knew through his work at the textile institute. His name was Efim Vaks, and he was a refusenik who had contacts within the dissident community.

Efim Vaks had been waiting for more than six months for permission to leave the Soviet Union but had run up against a brick wall. As a result of his request for an exit visa, he had lost his job as a researcher in the textile industries.

Invitations had arrived for Vaks from Israel. But Soviet authorities repeatedly rejected them for petty reasons such as the invitations failed to mention one of his sons or a name had been misspelled — anything to make his life difficult.

Vaks's requests for exit visas were constantly held up or rejected. It was the usual KGB practice to harass refuseniks.

But Fabrikant was different. He knew Vaks vaguely from a past joint project with the Ivanovo Institute. One day, Fabrikant approached him to find someone in Israel who would send him an invitation.

"I asked some people who were leaving the country and gave them his name and said that he would like to have an invitation," Vaks recalled from his home in California.

About four invitations for Fabrikant arrived in the spring of 1979 at the Ivanovo post office. So eager were the Soviets to get rid of Fabrikant that the KGB took the unusual step of sending a courier to Fabrikant's home and demanding that he sign a form proving he had received the invitations.

Fabrikant, however, refused. He told the KGB he had changed his mind and wanted to stay. He went to the regional party secretary to protest the KGB action. The secretary, who knew all about Fabrikant from his constant complaints and court actions, told him he had to leave because without a job, life would be too difficult in the Soviet Union.

Fabrikant took the hint, signed the forms and made plans to leave the country.

Fabrikant and his ex-wife, Galina, stayed at Vaks's Moscow apartment the night before leaving for Brest. Vaks saw them off at the Moscow train station. He would wait another year before he was allowed to leave.

Six months after Fabrikant left Russia, Galina came to the Ivanovo Institute to visit his former bosses. She told them she had received a letter from Fabrikant. She said he was working as a professor in a Canadian university and was making $10,000 a month.

In reality, he was earning $7,000 a year as a research assistant.

"She wanted to prove to us that we had driven out a genius," Liakishev said.

It was a cool, damp day in early December, 1979 when Valery Fabrikant arrived at Concordia University and declared: "I'm a scientist escaped from the Soviet Union."

Through his black, horn-rimmed glasses, Professor T.S. Sankar studied this peculiar figure with sullen eyes, dressed in his rough-textured, ill-fitting Russian suit and big fur hat.

Fabrikant wanted a job. He had been ushered into Sankar's cramped office by his secretary, Elizabeth Horwood.

An immigrant himself who had become chairman of the mechanical engineering department, Sankar sympathized with Fabrikant and wanted to help. But there was nothing he could offer Fabrikant.

What little money Sankar had was for hiring graduate students for research projects.

Still, Fabrikant was persistent. He said, almost blurting it out, that he had been a student of V.V. Bolotin, a well-known Russian scientist. Sankar was impressed. He knew and respected Bolotin. So he offered Fabrikant a few thousand dollars to help with research projects.

He expected Fabrikant to turn it down. After all, Fabrikant was overqualified and could earn more washing dishes.

But Fabrikant grabbed the offer. Sankar was more than pleased. He told himself it would only be temporary. But for at least a few months, he could rely on an experienced researcher at a bargain price. As for Fabrikant, he had what he wanted: A foot in the door.

Electronic-mail transmission
From V.I. Fabrikant.
Date: March 1, 1992. 18:37 EST.
"Make no mistake, I am dead serious in what I am doing. I cannot fight all the crooks in the world, but I shall not rest until the bogus scientists in this university are exposed and Justice is served."

Fabrikant had arrived in Montreal with four precise goals: Find a permanent job, find a wife, have two children (boy first, girl second), and gain recognition as the Isaac Newton-James Maxwell of modern mathematics.

"He was full of hope. He was certain of the work he wanted to do and that it would be completely different from what he had left behind," said Inessa Golod, a friend who had arrived in Montreal from Minsk a month before Fabrikant.

To Golod and her husband, Anatoly, Fabrikant seemed friendly and at times even funny. They noticed he was strong and fit and regularly swam and did yoga.

But Fabrikant would pick up in Montreal exactly where he left off in the Soviet Union.

He would threaten and fight with his colleagues at Concordia and elsewhere, making enemies wherever he went. It didn't take long before Sankar discovered the real Valery Fabrikant.

Sankar assigned Fabrikant work on problems related to the stochastic process — the random behaviour of input forces over time — and handed him some scientific papers to read up on the subject.

But Fabrikant wasn't interested. Sankar recalled that he dismissed the papers, claiming they were riddled with unspecified errors.

Fabrikant said he preferred to work on contact problems instead — problems that examine what happens when two moving pieces of material contact each other. He bristled at outside interference in his work. So gradually Sankar let him be.

"He had definite preferences in terms of what he wanted to do, whether you liked it or not," Sankar recalled. Although Fabrikant was often intractable and did not always want to do what he was asked to do, Sankar continued to work with him because of his ability to generate research efforts in collabouration with Sankar and others.

What Sankar didn't realize at the time was that Fabrikant had convinced himself that he had discovered a new scientific method that would catapult him into the highest ranks of science.

"He once told me that after his death his work would be put on the same level as James Maxwell," said Leonid Roytman, an emigre Russian scientist who met Fabrikant at Concordia and who is now an engineering professor at City University in New York.

Physicists place Maxwell, the 19th-century British scientist, on the same level as Isaac Newton because he developed standard equations applicable in electromagnetism and many other areas of physics.

Fabrikant thought he had developed the use of tables of integrals to obtain precise solutions to mathematical problems. He intended to apply his methods, which were common in Russia, to contact problems in engineering, Roytman said.

Meanwhile, he also was busy solving a series of contact problems of a different kind.

Before Fabrikant left the U.S.S.R., his father died, leaving him a modest amount of money. Officials refused to allow Fabrikant to take it out of the country. Once in Canada, he wrote the External Affairs Department, demanding that Canada suspend grain shipments to the U.S.S.R. until he received his money.

Eventually, he received about $12,000 and used it to buy himself a Dodge K-car.

He also started looking for a new wife. "He wanted to be married so much," Inessa Golod remembered.

"In the summer, he would go to social dances at Beaver Lake and hope to meet beautiful young girls. I would tease him about his desire for a young wife and about his dressing, which was very conservative and unfashionable. In the winter, he would wear a big black hat and he looked like Nikita Khrushchev," she said.

Fabrikant struck out with Soviet Jewish women in Montreal, said one woman who asked not to be named. "He was trying to date a number of women, but not many liked him," she said.

He ran personal ads in Russian newspapers in New York, claiming he was 35 when he was actually 40. The ads didn't work.

Fabrikant became almost desperate. At one point, he complained to Roytman that he might have to bring over his ex-wife, Galina.

Finally, Fabrikant begged acquaintances in the U.S. for help. He called Efim Vaks, who had helped Fabrikant obtain exit papers in the U.S.S.R. and who had since immigrated to the U.S.

"He was obsessed with having children," said Vaks, who arrived in New York in 1980 and now works in California.

Vaks's wife, Larisa, eventually found Maya Tyker, then a 21-year-old Russian woman living in Brooklyn.

When Larisa phoned Fabrikant with the news, he hopped into his K-car and drove straight to Brooklyn. That same day, the Vakses introduced him to Maya.

Then, as Vaks recalled, things went a bit strange. It was late spring 1982 and still not warm enough to swim. But Fabrikant insisted that they all go to nearby Brighton Beach. So Maya, the Vakses and Fabrikant climbed into the K-car.

On the beach, Fabrikant stripped down to his bathing suit. He insisted that Maya remove her clothes, too.

"I want to see your skin to see if you have clean skin," he told her, according to the Vakses.

At first, Maya refused, saying she didn't have her bathing suit.

But Fabrikant ignored her and started unbuttoning her blouse and removing her clothes. Maya didn't resist.

When he had removed most of her clothes, Fabrikant looked her over and then told her to dress. In an interview, Maya Tyker denied the incident occurred.

Soon after the meeting, Fabrikant and Maya drove to Florida. Maya became pregnant. They married and returned to Montreal. Nine months later, Maya gave birth to a boy. A year after that, she gave birth to a girl.

Two of Fabrikant's four goals had been achieved. There remained the quest for a permanent job and worldwide recognition.

Pathological tendencies began to show in Fabrikant's character, and it wasn't long before Concordia heard disturbing things about its self-proclaimed Soviet refusenik.

At first his actions appeared simply annoying and could be attributed to the eccentricities of a slightly obsessive professor.

For example, after signing up for French classes in 1981, Fabrikant denounced the teacher because she smoked in class. He wrote to the university administration, demanding that she be fired.

But the French teacher incident was only one of many.

"He fought with everybody for the smallest, littlest things," Sankar recalled.

Soon his reputation for unrelenting fury at people he believed had wronged him spread to other universities. He was clearly fixated.

When University of Calgary professor Peter Glockner ran up against him in 1981, he came away convinced Fabrikant had mental and behavioural problems.

Fabrikant had applied for a job at the University of Calgary and didn't even make the short list. His rejection letter came from Glockner.

"He apparently took this very personally, because shortly thereafter I met him at a conference in Moncton," Glockner recalled. Fabrikant had been sent to the conference by Concordia.

"He buttonholed me and told me, 'What a rude and impersonal way of communicating a negative decision.' He demanded to know why he was not on the short list.

"The area in which he was active was not the area in which we were making an appointment. He would not accept that. He was furious. He felt he was the best candidate for the job," Glockner said.

What happened next is legend in Canadian mechanical engineering circles.

Fabrikant attended a Glockner lecture. Before it began, Fabrikant grew agitated, pacing around the room, making loud, rude remarks and badgering officials to begin the session.

"He was pumped up because he was ready for a fight. No sooner had I presented my paper when he started attacking everything that I said," Glockner said.

The moderator cut Fabrikant short, but Glockner asked that Fabrikant be allowed to finish. "He was simply interested in trying to embarrass me," he said.

Fabrikant called Glockner a disgrace and urged him to resign.

"He was shouting, being very abusive," Glockner recalled.

When the moderator cut off Fabrikant a second time, Glockner was relieved. But Fabrikant refused to let the matter rest.

At a later social function, Fabrikant again buttonholed Glockner and resumed his attack, shouting at him as people talked and sipped drinks.

"I just turned around and left. He was an absolutely unreasonable kind of a fellow," Glockner said. "I was not surprised to read that Dr. Fabrikant had finally blown his lid because he was ready to blow his lid 10 years ago."

Back in Montreal, Fabrikant bragged to his colleague and fellow emigre Roytman that he had "shown that (Glockner's) paper was a fraud."

Roytman was puzzled. "If you're trying to get a job, you don't act like this," he told Fabrikant.

Electronic-mail transmission
From: V.I. Fabrikant.
Date: March 1, 1992.
"My only crime is honesty."

In the early 1980s, Fabrikant was collaborating with Roytman, Sankar and M.N.S. Swamy, dean of Concordia's engineering department.

The collaboration was largely at Fabrikant's request, Roytman said.

"He wanted to collaborate with Swamy because it would give some lustre to his list of publications. Swamy was a very well-recognized person," Roytman said.

They worked on two papers. After the second paper, Swamy refused to work with Fabrikant because at the last minute he secretly instructed the publisher to remove Roytman's name.

"I was furious and I wanted Fabrikant to apologize and republish it," Swamy said.

Roytman told Swamy to forget about it.

"I kind of felt that even at that time he (Fabrikant) was an unstable kind of fellow," Roytman said.

Fabrikant never revealed at the time why he pulled Roytman's name.

Roytman recalled, however, that Fabrikant had once accused him of secretly publishing a paper on which he had done some computer calculations for Roytman. In fact, the paper was never published.

"It was of no importance, but Fabrikant thought it should be published," Roytman recalled. "I said no. Later Fabrikant accused me of publishing the work without him. I think that's why he took my name off."

Electronic-mail transmission
From: Joseph Merola, Virginia Tech.
Date: Sept. 1, 1992.
Re: Fabrikant
"As a matter of fact, single-author papers in an experimental area sometimes evoke the comment: 'Can't the person get along with anybody?'"

From 1982 to 1989, Fabrikant published 56 papers. In 37 papers, he was the only author. This low level of collaboration is unusual in engineering, where a collaboration of varied expertise is needed and expected, all engineering experts contacted by the *Gazette* said.

Prior to publication, reviewers edit the papers for possible errors and omissions. Their names are kept confidential. In Fabrikant's case, reviewers sometimes found his efforts obscure and questioned why the papers were being published. Some of these papers were collaborative efforts with T.S. Sankar, on which Fabrikant was the primary author and Sankar the consultant.

One reviewer criticized Fabrikant for claiming that a mathematical technique was original when in fact it had been employed in 1881. Another criticized him for including scientific references that were "hopelessly out of date." The problem Fabrikant was claiming to have solved was solved by another researcher in 1961, the reviewer added.

These criticisms infuriated Fabrikant and he demanded to know the reviewers' identities. When editors refused to release them, Fabrikant flew into rages.

Sankar repeatedly fielded calls from angry, offended editors who complained about Fabrikant's rude, abusive behaviour. "He told one editor that he should resign," Sankar said.

Fabrikant later published two monograph books, which were compilations of his own previously published work. Between 400 and 600 copies of each book were printed after Fabrikant himself submitted camera-ready, laser-printed manuscripts to Kluwer Academic Publishing in the Netherlands.

Fabrikant often boasted that his first book, published in 1989, would be a classic. Ditto for his second book, published in 1991.

"His first book didn't disgrace itself," Kluwer Academic president David Larner said from the Netherlands. "The second one has sold less well. We've still got plenty in our warehouse." Larner rejected Fabrikant's proposal for a third book in 1992 after his scientific advisers considered the work would not be very useful to the research community and would not sell.

Ironically, interest in Fabrikant's books grew only after the Concordia murders. The McGill science library's copies have disappeared. "I should have got him to sign a couple of hundred," Larner said, facetiously.

Electronic-mail transmission.
From: V.I. Fabrikant.
Date: June 28, 1992.
"An honest person, who has nothing to hide, would not be afraid to work near me."

Fabrikant approached several Concordia engineering professors and suggested joint research projects. But when Fabrikant became belligerent and abusive, each of them ended the relationship. His conduct annoyed, angered or shocked one colleague after another.

"He was a know-it-all. I didn't like his attitude," said Professor Sam Osman, who refused from the start to collaborate with Fabrikant.

In 1982 or 1983, Fabrikant offered to put mechanical engineering professor Richard Cheng's name on two of his scientific papers, even though Cheng made no contribution whatsoever.

"My response was: 'Look, I made no contribution to these papers. I can't consent to being a co-author. That's wrong.' After that, he stopped coming to my lab," said Cheng, a top robotics expert.

"Perhaps he really did want to expand into my area and genuinely collaborate with me. Perhaps one of the ways he knew was to offer me something in exchange for something in return," he said.

As Fabrikant became a professional outcast, he shunned mechanical engineering department social activities and kept a low profile in Montreal's Soviet Jewish community.

The Soviet engineer seemed a friendless loner; the Golods said Fabrikant's life was his work and his family.

"As long as he had a chair, his two computers and a work table in the bedroom, he was happy," Inessa Golod said.

The Golods recalled the time they invited Fabrikant to a vernissage organized by Anatoly to celebrate an exhibition of his new paintings.

Fabrikant telephoned Anatoly and declined the invitation, saying:

"I can't come. I don't understand your paintings. Don't invite me any more."

Anatoly was amused. "His idea of a good painting was one in which there was no dirt, no broken objects. Everything had to be perfect and clean. He didn't realize that there could be beauty in a broken red fence in the middle of a field."

Electronic-mail transmission.
From: V.I. Fabrikant.
Date: July 19, 1992.
To: Scientific community.
"I needed a regular tenured faculty position, and it was clear that T.S. Sankar (who was chairman of the department at that time) would never offer me one, since this would be the end of his ability to profit from my work ..."

Electronic-mail transmission.
From: V.I. Fabrikant.
Date: Aug. 18, 1992.
To: Scientific community.
"The shear (sic) number of well-founded grievances is an indication that the griever is being harassed."

Fabrikant's personnel file at Concordia was ballooning. From 1979 to 1988, the file had 28 documents, most of them routine.

Conspicuously absent was proof of his academic credentials.

But from 1988 to 1992, another 610 documents were filed. Most of these dealt with complaints and grievances launched by or against Fabrikant.

Indeed, he was applying the Fabrikant treatment with a broad brush. He abused secretaries, technicians and faculty alike. He called them scum, shams, frauds. In January, 1990, he told Catherine MacKenzie, who by then was associate vice-rector in charge of security, that "now I know that the way to get things done is to get a gun and shoot a lot of people." This statement came several weeks after Marc Lepine murdered 14 women at the Universite de Montreal.

When secretaries or technicians didn't jump at his every request, Fabrikant would say: "Excuse me, excuse me, I am putting on tape recorder. You are dishonest and lazy. You have probably been bought."

He went after Concordia's purchasing manager, Mike Stefano, when Stefano demanded Fabrikant pay for an $8,401 laser printer he ordered.

"I believe you are aware of the Pentagon scandal brewing in Washington," Fabrikant told him. "I am not interested in starting a similar scandal in our university, but if the harassment does not stop, I shall have no choice but to go public."

The printer dispute lasted seven months, during which the supplier cut off credit to the university and refused to service its other printers. At one point, a defeated Stefano wrote to Fabrikant's boss, Sam Osman: "I'm afraid I've had more than enough. When the (supplier) agreed to install the unit at no charge, (Fabrikant) countered with a demand for a one-year warranty. He told me he would pay the bill if you told him to. He then told you he'd pay the bill if the rector told him to. It appears that he will continue to escalate his demands at every opportunity."

Fabrikant eventually paid the bill, but only after the university agreed to finance an extended warranty.

Fabrikant also began secretly taping conversations with his colleagues, hoping to entrap them into making embarrassing statements about their peers.

Despite his threats and abusive behaviour, the engineering department promoted Fabrikant on June 1, 1990, to research professor. It was one step removed from a full-time faculty position.

Fabrikant had been teaching the odd class on and off since 1984. In their evaluations, students, the department personnel and faculty committees cited his high-quality research, his book publication, his good teaching performance and the fact that he had already been a professor at the Polytechnic Institute in Ulyanovsk, U.S.S.R.

What faculty members didn't know was that Fabrikant lied on his resume.

He claimed that from 1970 to 1973 he was a professor at the institute in Ulyanovsk. In fact, institute records show he was only an instructor from 1970 to 1972. He was then promoted to assistant professor. And in 1973 he was fired for abusive behaviour.

He also lied when he said in his resume that his doctorate degree was in mechanical engineering, which deals with machines and the production of power. His Russian scholastic records show it was in mechanics, a different field that is the basis of physics and astronomy.

■ ■ ■

The mechanical engineering personnel committee logged more than 30 hours of meetings in late October.

Fearful that Fabrikant would eavesdrop, as he often did, Osman ordered that his office doors be soundproofed. (At one point, committee members discovered Fabrikant loitering outside Osman's office at 11:30 at night. They called security to have him ushered out of the building. But he escaped through the basement. He would later claim he was assaulted.)

Eventually, the department committee voted not to renew Fabrikant's contract, citing his chronic abusive behaviour, his repeated attempts to evade teaching duties and his failure to supervise more graduate students.

"Many persons inside and outside the university have been subjected to harassment, threats, blackmail and allegations by Dr. Fabrikant," the committee wrote in its decision.

> *Electronic-mail transmission.*
> *From: V.I. Fabrikant.*
> *Date: March 1, 1992.*
> *To: Scientific community.*
> *"I am a world class scientist ... The more lawless the action the greater the probability that I lose my temper and do something outrageous."*

In the fall of 1991, Fabrikant took a course in handguns at a basement club in Ville St. Pierre. He passed the course on Nov. 22, the day after the mechanical engineering department sent its recommendation to fire Fabrikant up to the engineering department's faculty personnel committee.

After three meetings, the faculty personnel committee overturned the decision. The faculty committee claimed the mechanical engineering committee concentrated too heavily on his behaviour and failed to properly evaluate his research and teaching record.

Nevertheless, the committee criticized Fabrikant for not working within the department's research goals, for not supervising more graduate students, for not contributing to curricula development and for not teaching any advanced courses in mechanical engineering.

Instead of renewing his two-year contract, the faculty committee voted to put him on probation for one year, during which Fabrikant was to demonstrate he could satisfy all of the committee's concerns.

Without realizing it, the committee had Fabrikant trapped. He was in danger of being uncovered as a fraud.

He was not a mechanical engineer as he had claimed. He couldn't teach advanced courses in the subject in which he fraudulently claimed he had a PhD.

Fabrikant had already tried to obtain a transfer to the department of mathematics but was rebuffed. Nobody else wanted him. And admitting that he had lied on his resume would get him fired.

So, early in the new year, Fabrikant began what would become an international campaign to discredit the university and paint himself as a victim of "fraud and corruption" on the part of his colleagues.

■ ■ ■

Vice-rector, services, Charles Bertrand wrote his memo quickly. He glanced up at the clock. Almost 5 p.m. It was getting late. The rector's office was about to close for the June 24, 1992, holiday weekend and Bertrand needed an answer right away.

That morning, Valery Fabrikant had approached engineering faculty secretary Elizabeth Horwood to demand that she sign his application to carry a gun. Fabrikant needed five signatures.

The thought of Fabrikant with a gun terrified Horwood and made Bertrand shudder.

And it angered and scared vice-rector, academic, Rose Sheinin. She was aware of Fabrikant's threats against staff and faculty and she had always opposed his hiring because she believed he was disruptive and didn't fit in. But the university had opposed her.

This time, she and Bertrand agreed, the university had to act.

Bertrand hurriedly typed out the memo:

"It is our recommendation that he be immediately suspended with pay from the university. In our opinion, Dr. Fabrikant presents an immediate and continuing threat to the members of the university community as set forth in Article 29.07 of the collective agreement.

"As a condition for reinstatement in the university, Dr. Fabrikant must be required to produce a statement from a psychiatrist chosen by the university, attesting to his mental stability."

Bertrand read the memo to Sheinin over the phone. "Sign my name," she told him. Bertrand dashed out the door and headed up de Maisonneuve Blvd. to Bishop Court, where rector Patrick Kenniff was waiting. Bertrand was sure that Kenniff would agree to bar Fabrikant from the school.

Electronic-mail transmission.
From: Stephen Jonke, NASA Goddard Space Flight Centre, Texas.
Date: Aug. 25, 1992.
Subject: University rampage.
"What we have here is publicly available copies of notes from a madman before (his) killing spree."

The first six months of 1992 hadn't been good to Valery Fabrikant. His second book had been a disaster, his proposal for a third was rejected, and he was facing possible dismissal from his job.

The engineering department had put him on one-year probation during which he had to prove that he could teach advanced mechanical engineering courses.

It was becoming increasingly clear to his colleagues, however, that Fabrikant couldn't teach these courses.

At first, Fabrikant tried to get out of teaching altogether. When department chairman Sam Osman sent a memo to all department professors in November 1991 asking for their teaching preferences for the academic year 1992–93, Fabrikant wrote back: "No teaching. I'll be on sabbatical next year."

Osman thought it was just another attempt to shirk his teaching responsibilities. Fabrikant had no permission to take a sabbatical. Nor did he have a right to one. Osman told Fabrikant that unless he indicated his teaching preferences, he would assume that he had none.

Fabrikant felt cornered. His only refuge seemed to be the passive, sterile, international electronic-mail system called Internet. Created by the U.S. Defence Department in 1981 to promote communications between the military and industry, Internet has since become one of the most useful and widely used tools of communication for scientists worldwide.

Fabrikant worshipped its power. It gave him access, free of charge, to about 15 million subscribers around the world with about one million more linking up every month. He spent long hours, often on Sundays, pounding his frustration into what became his own private international broadcast network.

Early in 1992 his emissions started to reach a frenzied pitch. For six months, reams of memos, letters and reports with lengthy explanations and allegations of corruption came out of Fabrikant's computer and flowed into those of fellow scientists at Concordia and around the world.

Staring into his unquestioning computer screen, Fabrikant recreated himself as Mr. Excellence. His papers and books became classics. And his colleagues were bogus scientists and shams, corrupt and fraudulent.

A push of a computer button transmitted his delusive self-representations to the scientific world in lengthy transmissions that at one point were so voluminous they caused a huge backup in McGill's electronic-mail system.

McGill computer services pleaded with Fabrikant to stop repeating a programming error that often sent 45 copies of the same letter to the same place. But Fabrikant couldn't believe he'd made a mistake, and announced that McGill, too, was part of a conspiracy to make him look crazy, which he described as an "old communist trick."

While some scientists dismissed his postings as idiot rantings, others were more encouraging. Disgruntled students and some professors jumped on his bandwagon.

One of his biggest supporters was Professor Klaus Herrmann of Concordia's political science department.

Herrmann decided Fabrikant was the "Albert Einstein of mechanical engineering" and the victim of jealous colleagues. (He later admitted to the *Gazette* that he knew nothing about engineering and had never read any of Fabrikant's publications, but said he felt there were too many Asians and foreigners in the engineering department.)

Unknown to Concordia, Fabrikant also redoubled his efforts, begun in 1990, to purchase a handgun.

In February, he secured a gun permit for target shooting. Then on March 11, clad in his large fur hat and Red Army great coat, he went to a small gun shop in Pierrefonds called W.S. Avenue International and bought his first handgun — a palm-sized $69 pistol called an MEB 6.35, described as too small and inaccurate for target shooting. "It's a lady's gun," shop owner Bill Sinka said with a shrug.

Concordia's winter semester ended in April. Fabrikant spent part of May marking his share of exams for a first-year dynamics course that had been taught by him and three other professors.

Each professor is allotted a number of questions to mark. After the marking, each student's exam book is returned to his teacher, who adds up the score.

When Fabrikant added up his students' marks and the registrar posted the results, the trouble started.

The final marks were issued in late May. And it wasn't long before students started complaining. But they weren't the usual type of complaints. Students didn't complain about their own marks; they complained about other students' marks. And those marks had been given by Fabrikant.

"Students talk after an exam and compare answers," Osman said. "So they have a pretty good idea who gave what answers."

They began to complain that fellow students who hadn't answered the questions correctly received better marks than they did.

After receiving about 20 complaints, Osman grew concerned.

So he collected all the exam books from the professors and gave them to an outside consultant to analyze. Fabrikant grew concerned.

Several times he tried to find out from Osman's secretary, Elizabeth Horwood, why the exam books were recalled. She said she didn't know.

The consultant, who is a mechanical engineer and whose identity the university has kept secret, filed his report in July, 1992. His computer analysis of the marking revealed some startling facts:

Fabrikant had marked wrong answers correct for his students. When Fabrikant added up his students' scores, he fraudulently bumped up the marks 12 to 20 per cent.

Osman didn't receive the consultant's report until late July. His superior, Dean Swamy, was out of town, so Osman couldn't discuss it with him. Several days after Swamy returned, the shootings took place. So Fabrikant has never been confronted about the report.

Fabrikant knew that Osman intended to have the papers marked again. He must have worried that he would be found out.

In June 1992, Fabrikant also received his teaching assignments for the 1992-93 academic year. It wasn't good news. He was assigned four courses, two of which were computer design courses, one at the graduate level.

"He went into a panic," Osman recalled.

Fabrikant knew nothing about computer design or creating software.

Fabrikant once told Osman he thought it involved teaching students simply how to use software for drafting and design purposes.

Fabrikant begged to be reassigned. But Osman stood firm.

"Every mechanical engineering professor must know how to teach this course," he said.

In August, a week before his killing spree, Fabrikant went to court seeking an injunction against the university. He wanted the court to order Concordia to cancel his teaching assignments and grant him an immediate sabbatical. In his motion, he claimed he was a "world-class scientist on the verge of an important scientific discovery." And he admitted that the two design courses were "outside my field of expertise."

Electronic-mail transmission.
From: V.I. Fabrikant.
Date: Wednesday, Aug. 19, 1992.
To: Scientific community.
"A Russian proverb says: 'Any administrator is a scum by definition.' So, nothing what Concordia or McGill administrators would do may ever surprise me."

When Bertrand headed down the street to Kenniff's Bishop St. office during the late afternoon of June 23, Fabrikant was in a highly agitated, even panicky state. He feared he could be unmasked for fraudulent exam marking and his inability to teach more advanced mechanical engineering courses.

Bertrand wanted to send Fabrikant a strong message: "I wanted to say, 'We're fed up with your intimidation and your harassment, and we're not going to put up with it any more.' "

But his meeting with Kenniff didn't go well. Kenniff categorically refused to suspend Fabrikant. Kenniff has declined to be interviewed by the *Gazette*. Bertrand recounted what Kenniff said:

"Legally, he didn't feel he could suspend Dr. Fabrikant. He didn't have enough proof that he was a threat. He's the rector of this university; he's the only one who can suspend. It was his call and he didn't feel there was enough there."

Bertrand was stunned as he went back to his office. Of all the things he'd imagined doing about Fabrikant, doing nothing had never entered his mind.

Over the last year, he had heard professors and secretaries complain that Fabrikant had threatened them with violence; the faculty union offices had purchased video surveillance cameras because they feared Fabrikant might get violent during his frequent unannounced visits; the vice-rector, academic, had ordered guards stationed outside her door whenever Fabrikant was around; Concordia had hired armed security to protect the rector and several others; one university administrator installed a panic button in his office; and the dean of engineering had posted a guard at his door, fearing that Fabrikant might attack or kill him. Still, Kenniff didn't believe he had enough solid proof to take action against Fabrikant. So he ordered his executive assistant, Maureen Habib, to send a letter via internal mail to Grendon Haines, the in-house consultant who in 1989 had tried to help Fabrikant. The letter asked Haines whether he had any information that could support a letter to police requesting that Fabrikant not be given a gun permit.

Because of a foul-up in the mail, the letter didn't arrive on Haines's desk until July 25, one month later. Haines sent his reply five days later. In it, he recounted the bare facts of his meetings with Fabrikant and mentioned the death threats. But his reply, which might have lent considerable weight to the rector's letter, was too late. The rector had already sent his letter to the police.

Meanwhile, Bertrand left for his Maine vacation disappointed. But he consoled himself with the belief that Fabrikant wouldn't be able to buy a gun.

But nobody had bothered to check what kind of application Fabrikant wanted Horwood to sign. It was an application to transport a gun. In other words, Fabrikant already owned a gun.

Unable to persuade anybody in the engineering faculty to sign his application, on July 14, 1992, Fabrikant sent one to Kenniff. The rector's reply: a huge bold-faced 'NO' printed over one letter-sized page.

A week later, Fabrikant's wife, Maya, filed a request with the police for a permit to purchase a Smith & Wesson .38 special and a Bersa 84 7.65 for target practice. She told the *Gazette* she picked them out of a catalogue sent to her by Century International Arms Ltd., a Montreal gun wholesaler, because they were small and light.

Then on Aug. 6, the same day Fabrikant had been forcefully rebuked by faculty association union president Michael Hogben for his constant intimidation of staff members at the union office, she ordered the guns from Century's Henri Bourassa store. With money drawn from a bank account she shared with her husband, she paid for the weapons three days before the killings and carried them home. Fabrikant hid them in a suitcase to keep them away from the children. (In an interview, Maya at first claimed she never told her husband she intended to buy the guns. Later, however, she admitted they had discussed and agreed to the purchases.)

It was during these weeks that Fabrikant's neighbours in the apartment building at 5525 Trent in Cote St. Luc became worried about the engineering professor. When he wanted to unwind, Fabrikant was apparently fond of playing a second-hand piano he had bought.

Neighbours enjoyed his selections so much that when he stopped playing regularly, they started to call to ask whether he was OK. Maya assured callers he was fine, but the truth was she was concerned about his health and mental state.

On Aug. 23, the day before the shootings, several neighbours saw a solitary Fabrikant pacing round and round the nearby outdoor pool, hour after hour, immersed in thought and mumbling to himself.

Maya would later tell friends that Fabrikant paced up and down the apartment that night with a blank, fixed gaze, mumbling: "My life is finished, my life is finished."

■ ■ ■

Concordia's downtown campus is anchored by an enormous square concrete building with modular-shaped windows that don't open. It's dedicated to Henry F. Hall, a former natural-science professor and school principal remembered by students as warm and caring.

On Aug. 24, Fabrikant entered this starkly institutional structure wearing a dark blue suit and clip-on sunglasses that he didn't remove. As he rode the escalators up to the ninth floor, he carried a brown leather bag.

Professor Douglas Hamblin, associate dean of engineering, spotted him at about 2:35 p.m. coming off the escalator. Hamblin greeted him but Fabrikant barely nodded.

He walked past Hamblin and into the dean's office, where Cecilia Benavente, 26, a part-time secretary and receptionist, had just returned from lunch.

Benavente had been working in the dean's office for only a few months. She had heard rumours about trouble between Dean Swamy and a professor who, she understood, had even threatened to kill him. Indeed, Dean Swamy had asked her to be careful about who she let into the office. She did not know Fabrikant and did not know what he looked like. She didn't even know that he was the infamous menacing professor.

So, though she noted the presence of this odd little man with a big briefcase and sunglasses, she didn't pay much attention as he walked past several students and quietly checked to see whether Swamy was in. When he discovered Swamy was out, he left by another exit.

Fabrikant headed to the other side of the building to Osman's office. Osman was not in either.

So Fabrikant returned to Swamy's office. This time, when Benavente saw Fabrikant lurking around the office, she confronted him.

"Excuse me! Who are you and where are you going?" Benavente stopped him.

"Don't you know me?" an annoyed Fabrikant asked in his thick Russian accent. "I'm Dr. Fabrikant, a professor in mechanical engineering."

Fabrikant again checked out Swamy's office and, finding that he was still out, left.

He headed across the building to his office, where he had arranged to meet union president Hogben at about 3 p.m. The two men met by chance in the hallway. With Fabrikant leading the way, they walked through the narrow corridor to his office. As Hogben passed secretary Elizabeth Horwood he smiled at her. As Osman's secretary, Horwood had had 12 years of experience with dealing with Fabrikant.

Fabrikant's cramped office was barely 60 square feet, just enough for a desk and computer table. Fabrikant and Hogben sat face to face, almost touching each other.

What transpired exactly is unknown. But at one point Hogben pulled out a letter he had written to Fabrikant informing Fabrikant that owing to his "harassing" of union employees, he was not to speak to anyone else in the union office except Hogben and then only by appointment.

About five or 10 minutes went by and then three shots rang out.

They were heard by Professor Jaan Saber, who was across the hall in his office talking to his wife on the phone. With him was graduate student Peter Lawn, 26.

Saber went into the hallway to investigate. He peeked around the corner into the reception area to ask the secretaries about the noises. They thought they came from construction workers on the 10th floor using a staple gun.

Annoyed at the intrusion, he returned to his office. He didn't shut the door. Instead, he picked up the phone to resume his conversation with his wife and started writing out a complaint to the building supervisor about the noise.

Inside Fabrikant's office, Hogben lay dying, clutching his union letter in one hand. Fabrikant pushed Hogben's body aside so he could open the door and stepped into the corridor. The smell of gunpowder filled the air.

Saber had considered taking one of his two children to the office that day, but had changed his mind at the last minute. He was still on the phone to his wife when Fabrikant came through the open door with a gun in each hand.

"Don't point those at me, I'm not joking," Saber said angrily.

Fabrikant said nothing. He shot Saber once in the head and once in the stomach.

Saber screamed and fell to the floor. Fabrikant then turned and left.

"It's OK, you can get up now," Lawn said to Saber. He hadn't realized that Saber was hit, that the guns and the bullets were real, until he saw the blood soaking through Saber's shirt.

Hearing the shots and commotion, Saber's wife became frantic. She immediately hung up and phoned 911. One name stuck in her mind: Fabrikant. She had warned her husband not to get involved in his disputes. Stay away from him, she had said. He's dangerous. Now her worst fears were coming true. She grabbed her car keys and headed downtown to the Hall building.

As Fabrikant slowly walked down the corridor he saw Elizabeth Horwood, the 66-year-old department chairman's secretary, coming toward him. He shot at her. She screamed and pressed her body against the wall. More shots rang out. She lunged toward her office door. As she crossed the threshold, blood sprayed out from the front of her right thigh. "I've been hit," she thought. She slammed the door behind her. She knew it would lock automatically.

Fabrikant then left the mechanical engineering department and headed through a maze of corridors toward the department of electrical and computer engineering. Students and professors who saw him dashed into offices to call security.

Professors Otto Schwelb and Phoivos Ziogas had been chatting in Ziogas's office for more than a hour when Valery Fabrikant came through the open door.

The two colleagues were exchanging news about their children. Fabrikant walked over to Ziogas, who was sitting behind his desk, raised a pistol in his right hand and, with his arm extended straight as an arrow, shot Ziogas point-blank.

"Otto!" Ziogas said, rising out of his chair.

Otto Schwelb stood spellbound. Ziogas took one step toward Fabrikant, falling on his shoulders, grabbing him, desperately holding on to his assailant. Schwelb thought: "This is a joke." Then he noticed the small stain of blood building on Ziogas's forehead. Fabrikant's first shot had grazed his skull.

As Ziogas held on to Fabrikant, one more shot rang out. The bullet ricocheted inside Ziogas's abdomen, severely damaging his liver, pancreas, spleen and intestines.

As Ziogas slowly sank into unconsciousness, he slid down to the floor, still clutching Fabrikant's thin wiry body. As Fabrikant went down with him, Schwelb raced round the table, grabbed Fabrikant by his jacket and pulled him out of Ziogas's office into the corridor. In the scuffle, one of Fabrikant's guns and his glasses fell to the floor.

Outside Ziogas's office, Fabrikant wrestled free and the two men squared off, Fabrikant staring at Schwelb with "crazy eyes."

Schwelb screamed at him: "What have you done? What have you done?"

Fabrikant responded by punching Schwelb in the face.

"I really don't know if I punched him back," Schwelb said three weeks later, still bewildered at what had happened. "Somehow I didn't feel anything, pain or fright or anger. Nothing. I was like a robot and that's bad."

Fabrikant's punch was Schwelb's wakeup call. A medium-sized man with lean, muscular arms, he grabbed Fabrikant and started pushing and kicking and shoving him down the length of a 25-metre long hallway.

When he ran out of corridor, he pushed Fabrikant onto the floor of the end office and tried to shut the door. But Fabrikant's leg stuck out across the doorjamb.

Schwelb didn't care. His priority was Ziogas and so he rushed back to help him. He thought Fabrikant was disarmed. He didn't know that he had two palm-sized pistols in his pockets.

As soon as Schwelb left, Fabrikant picked himself off the floor and went toward Dean Swamy's office.

Swamy, his friend Professor Matthew Douglass and Professor Terry Fancott were having coffee in a kitchenette when secretary Susan Altimas came running in and warned them that Fabrikant had a gun and had shot Horwood.

Swamy immediately went into his office to call security and 911. He ordered Altimas to stay put. But Altimas ignored him and headed back to help Horwood. Fancott and Douglass went out to the reception area to warn students to clear out of the building. Fancott left the dean's offices.

Fabrikant suddenly came into the dean's reception area and pointed a gun at Cecilia Benavente. She thought it was a toy and told him to "get that thing out of my face."

He walked right past her. At that moment, Douglass came out of a conference room, raised his hands and said, "Hold on! Let's talk about this." Fabrikant shot Douglass three times from close range through the hands and into the right side of his head. Douglass collapsed.

Benavente and several others still in the office fled. Fabrikant started marching down a small corridor toward the office where Swamy was on the phone to vice-rector Charles Bertrand. But halfway there, he suddenly stopped, walked back to Douglass, whom he didn't even know, and shot him through the head.

He then left the dean's offices and headed back to Osman's office in the mechanical engineering department.

Inside Osman's locked office, Horwood and Altimas felt secure. They were on the phone to 911 when suddenly security guard Daniel Martin opened the door with a key. He came into the office with Professor George Abdou. Martin took the phone from Horwood and began speaking to 911. Horwood was about to sit down when she saw Fabrikant coming through the open door. He pointed a gun at her and fired. Horwood screamed. Altimas leaped toward a side door, yelling "Here!" As Horwood rushed through the open door, she felt the heat of a bullet across her upper arm. But Fabrikant had missed.

He then locked the doors and took Abdou and Martin hostage. He took the phone from Martin and told 911 that he had just committed several murders and wanted to talk to a television reporter to explain his killing spree to the public.

Fabrikant hung on for about an hour until he put a gun down to adjust the phone. Abdou kicked it out of Fabrikant's reach and Martin jumped him. The killing was over.

But once again the electronic mail circuits came alive as the scientific world gabbed about Fabrikant:

Electronic-mail transmission
From: John Manuel, University of Alberta.
Date: Aug. 25, 1992.
"I think there's (sic) enough facts here to give Fabrikant the benefit of the doubt instead of dismissing him as a madman with a gun."

Electronic-mail transmission
From: Benjamin Dehner, Iowa State University.
Date: Aug. 25, 1992.
"I'd say that what he did with his gun clearly makes him some sort of madman: what kind of 'doubt' could possibly justify his actions?"

Electronic-mail transmission
From: Brad Wallet, U.S. Naval Surface Warfare Centre.
Date: Aug. 27, 1992.
Subject: Fabrikant, mad or bad?
"Incidentally, anyone want to guess how many slime balls analyzed the situation and decided that what all this means is that Concordia now has several open billets for tenure-track faculty?"

Electronic-mail transmission.
From: William Reiken, Ryukoku University, Japan.
Date: Aug. 28, 1992.
"Perhaps the ones he missed will have a few things to reflect upon."

Electronic-mail transmission.
From: Michael Assels, Concordia University.
Date: Aug. 31, 1992.
"I can't believe what I'm reading here, day after day. A man murders three people (a fourth died later) *and he develops a fan club! Hello? Is anybody out there?"*

• **1993** Spot News Reporting •

Davis Inlet:
Suicide common thought in town

Michael Johansen, Beth Gorham

Canadian Press

Michael Johansen

DAVIS INLET, Nfld. — Six children were found high on gas fumes and nearly comatose in an unheated shack Tuesday night in this Innu village on Labrador's north coast.

Const. Simeon Jacobish found the five girls and one boy, aged between 12 and 14, shortly before 8 p.m. Temperatures had dropped to -40 Celsius and two of the children were unconscious.

"I went in and found the six kids huddled together in the freezing cold," said addictions counsellor Bill Partridge who was called to the scene by the native police. "They were down by the government wharf in a small shack with no heat.

"It was a surreal scene," Partridge said. He and others had difficulty moving the children to a heated location. He said the kids fought their attempts to save them.

"All six kids were expressing suicide last night," said Partridge. "They didn't want to leave. We had to force them."

When the children were finally brought to a heated building, they had to be kept there by force, he said. Eight adults kept watch on them for several hours to prevent them from escaping back into the cold.

"We had to plywood up the windows because they were trying to break the windows to get out," he said. "We took their coats and boots to prevent them from running. They were literally climbing the walls."

A chartered airplane took them to the Goose Bay area shortly after midnight. They are being looked after in a group home at Sheshatshiu, an Innu settlement.

Partridge said there is a report four other kids were also sniffing gas. They were still unaccounted for this morning and the residents of Davis Inlet were searching for them.

Partridge, however, said the existence of the four was not confirmed.

The apparent suicide attempts come almost a year after a fire took the lives of six children left home alone in Davis Inlet. Gregory and Mary Rich, parents of five of the six, face abandonment charges and are to reappear in court in March.

That tragedy served to underline the desperation faced by many residents of the tiny island community, considered by some to be the poorest in the country.

The Labrador Innu were relocated to Davis Inlet in 1967 with a government promise of improved living conditions. But the better housing, running water and sewage treatment never materialized.

Many homes today are no more than wooden shacks and few have facilities other Canadians take for granted.

The community has repeatedly called for government to move them back to the mainland and to help them fight problems such as alcoholism, violence and suicide.

Statistics from the health unit in the community show that 25 per cent of the adult population attempted suicide last year.

Beth Gorham

DAVIS INLET, Nfld. — Innu teenager Antonia Benuen stopped sniffing gasoline fumes last year, about the same time her parents quit drinking.

"When they drank, my parents beat me," the shy, pregnant 19-year-old said Friday. "I started to sniff when I was 15. I quit school."

Still, she's one of the lucky ones. Having survived a suicide attempt, she now tells her friends to stop the deadly gasoline habit. They don't listen.

On Tuesday, six Innu youths, high on gas fumes, attempted a mass suicide in this remote Labrador community.

The six, between the ages of 12 and 14, were recovering at a group home near Goose Bay, Nfld., on Friday.

"They seem OK," said Peter Penashue, a spokesman for the Innu Nation in Sheshatshiu. "Of course, it is very difficult to have any sense of what's really happening in their minds.

"They're all sleeping together in one bed, huddling — they're scared."

Penashue said provincial social services officials are considering paying to send the children, their parents and Innu interpreters to Pound Makers, a native treatment centre near Edmonton.

Benuen remembers many trips to group homes over the years.

She talks of the horrible pervasive chill of her crumbling wood house, warmed slightly by a woodstove.

But she doesn't talk about her suicide attempt last August.

Native policeman Simeon Jacobish remembers; he was called to the scene when she blew a hole in her chest with a shotgun.

"Suicide is the major problem I deal with — teenagers or adults," says Jacobish, huddled in a tiny, cold office belonging to the band council.

"There's no hope here. I don't see any future. A treatment centre would help. Services would help."

The six youths who attempted a mass suicide this week had run out of hope too. They were found in an unheated shack — nearly comatose.

Rescuers discovered they didn't want to leave — or live.

Their desperate attempt was shocking — even in a village accustomed to four suicide attempts a month.

"We are faced constantly with death," said Chief Katie Rich.

"But we have never seen that happen."

Alcohol counsellor Bill Partridge estimates that half this island community of more than 500 people are contemplating suicide at any given time.

"Most every child coming from a dysfunctional home has suicidal thoughts and tendencies," he says, adding many keep their thoughts to themselves.

This tragic village can be just as deceiving. It seems peaceful, especially at night, blanketed in snow with wood smoke curling in the air.

But many houses aren't insulated and they're falling apart. There are no roads, no running water, no sewer system.

Human waste is thrown outdoors in buckets. Dogs eat it. Children play in it.

Clothes are thin and ragged. There are scars and sores on kids' faces.

"We don't have those things that other people take for granted," says Rich, fighting tears. "I get really frustrated when I repeat myself to every (government official) who comes.

"It seems like both levels of government are playing games with us — with our childrens' lives."

Both the federal and provincial governments are responsible for the Innu. But Rich says they spend most of their time pointing fingers.

The community was relocated to its current site in 1967. Better services were promised but never materialized.

For years, the Innu have wanted to be moved back to the mainland where the expanding population would have room to grow and they would feel less isolated.

They've also repeatedly asked for a treatment centre in Labrador to fight addictions, violence and suicide.

If the Innu don't soon receive help to move, Rich says they'll do it themselves.

George Rich, vice-president of the Innu Nation, says it had better be soon.

"We're living on a time bomb here. It's going to go off any minute."

• 1995 Feature Writing •
The Bernardo trial:
The world of Courtroom 6-1

Kirk Makin

Globe and Mail

Having once spent a saucer-eyed evening at an S & M club in New York City (it was research for my school newspaper), I enjoyed a slight edge on my media colleagues when it came to figuring out Karla Homolka. The parallel between Karla and the clientele of the Chateau 19 Club came to me while my colleagues and I in Courtroom 6-1 were viewing a set of grainy 1988 snapshots depicting Karla nude, bound and gagged. She had the same glassy stare I'd seen on the patrons of the club as they were being whipped, stomped, nailed to the wall or stretched on the rack.

There was never any doubt that Karla Homolka was the star of the strange show that played out its three-month run at Toronto's downtown courthouse this week. Those of us covering the Bernardo trial were every bit as fascinated by her as was that portion of the public that didn't spend the summer shielding its eyes from the media coverage. Figuring out what created and sustained Ms Homolka was infinitely more challenging than scrutinizing that seething mass of uncontrolled testosterone, Paul Bernardo.

From our outpost in the mass of scaffolding and television trailers known as Camp Bernardo, we tried to make sense of this inscrutable individual who was largely responsible for transforming an unusually ugly tale of cruelty and murder into an international story. As I made the visual connection between Chateau 19 and the Karla snaps, I realized we had been wrong to make our judgments about her based on stereotypes. She may have been reared in a semi-rural area of St. Catharines, Ont., but her psyche was pure 19th Street and SoHo in Manhattan. It was those amateur bondage photos that helped convince me that the Karla Homolka who teamed up with Paul Bernardo in 1987 was simply answering her own particular sexual call of the wild. Arriving at a firm conclusion during the Bernardo trial — or indeed any conclusions — was welcome. Life for all of us in Camp Bernardo — the sixth floor of the courthouse on University Avenue and immediately outside the building — was filled with as many unanswerable questions as it was with small, piercing insights. And those of us who spent so many hours together in Courtroom 6-1 during the summer of this year tended to spend as much time disagreeing as we did agreeing.

There were 45 regular reporters, plus another 20 to 30 who dropped by occasionally. Most had been living with the case since 1993 when Mr. Bernardo was arrested, some even earlier. Ours was a hyperactive little community, consumed by conflicting deadlines and a strong sense that we were collectively involved in something big. Broadcast producers circled the courthouse with cellphones glued to their ears. Camera crews dutifully filmed familiar daily cycles: The victims' families and lawyers arriving in the morning; witnesses and shell-shocked spectators leaving in the afternoon.

The French-Canadian reporters probably had the toughest job. Not only did they have to make notes in a second language, but the most common words in the Bernardo lexicon — for instance, oral sex and analingus — often didn't translate well.

But the Americans were the funniest. A researcher for *The Jerry Springer Show* arrived one day blithely convinced she could arrange for Paul and Karla to appear on the program together before a live studio audience. Then there were the cosmetic kings and queens from Buffalo television stations. Some of them were fond of braying about how spineless we Canadian reporters were. Imagine not violating a court-ordered publication ban? Imagine not pestering the families of victims as they enter and leave the courtroom?

Those of us who were together for the entire three months shared the camaraderie of trial veterans, if only because the things we knew were often too searing to convey to friends and family. Particularly in the beginning, the mind was unwilling, the tongue unable.

This is not to suggest I arrived in Camp Bernardo a complete novice at dealing with the unembroidered cruelties that are played out daily in criminal courts. I've sat through dozens of murder trials, including a total of 15 months as the Guy Paul Morin saga crept toward his unjust conviction. I became accustomed to the demands of high-profile, emotional procedures such as the 1985 Ernst Zundel trial and Dr. Henry Morgentaler's abortion trial in Ontario in 1984. You can get used to anything, even Paul Bernardo.

And we all found our own ways of living through a summer exposed to so much misery. Still, many of the images will forever remain engraved in my mind: The ebullient power-saw expert, exuberantly explaining how metal cuts through flesh; prosecutor Ray Houlahan (or Ray Halothane, as we called him), who spoke in a clipped, almost academic manner, about Mr. Bernardo dropping Leslie Mahaffy's severed head on the basement floor; the sad-eyed Karel Homolka on videotape jokingly telling his daughter's future husband, "Okay, Mr. Bernardo, look after my kids"; the unearthly panting, whispering and rustling of clothes as Tammy Homolka was raped in her parents' basement on Christmas Eve, 1990, and of the equally unforgettable image of Tammy's mother Dorothy and sister Lori trying to block their ears as the tape was played in the courtroom; Leslie, her final minutes captured on videotape, being handed Karla's teddy bear Bunky to hug while the life was snuffed out of her.

Then there was Paul Bernardo describing how he worked under a tarp in goggles and hat while he sawed Leslie up, and using animated hand motions to describe how he moved a cement block containing her torso across his kitchen floor; ham-handed prosecutor Greg Barnett, grinning at his cleverness after unthinkingly starting up a circular saw in the courtroom and ripping another piece from Debbie Mahaffy's shattered soul; Kristen sobbing "I love you" 26 times as she tried to appease Mr. Bernardo — a scene I find myself unable to recall without being shaken to the marrow.

During the early days, before we had quite struggled into our journalistic suits of armour, there was much talk of lasting effects. The *Toronto Star* hired a psychologist to tend to its Bernardo Battalion, the swarm of reporters, columnists, editors and photographers assigned to the trial. You somehow knew they were going to be all right when they arrived back from their session, good-naturedly bitching about having wasted lunch with a shrink.

Yes, we had nightmares. Some of my colleagues have hinted that sex has pretty much become a thing of the past. Most of us will forever flinch when we hear the rock or rap music that droned eerily in the background of the tapes.

Even overhearing lovers exchange pet names summons unsavoury memories of a couple whose depraved relationship teemed with such endearments. Wiggle worm. Furry little creature. Little slut.

Ugh.

I well remember sitting on my porch until near dawn after Karla Homolka's first day of testimony, thinking furiously about this woman who had loved animals so much she couldn't bear to dissect a worm. Reconciling the pert blond figure on the witness stand with the treacherous creep in the videos was an impossible task. I couldn't comprehend her willingness to participate in the torture of children — girls like her, who dreamed of careers and marriage and children; who whimpered and cried out for their families; who looked to her as a fellow female who might deliver them from the cruelty of Paul Bernardo. And, to compound the already unimaginable pain, Ms Homolka and her beau would pluck their victims on special weekends: Father's Day will always carry a special torture for the Mahaffys; Christmas for the Homolkas; Easter for the very religious French family.

In short order, I found the constant expressions of sympathy that came the media's way almost embarrassing. I have yet to encounter a colleague who felt he or she wouldn't be able to deal with the Bernardo-trial experience — especially compared to the victims who are still living, a seemingless endless procession of psychological refugees: Raped, stalked, abused or dead women. At the head of the line, of course, are the families of Leslie, Tammy and Kristen.

Never in my experience have victims so dominated a trial. It seemed appallingly insensitive to oppose their attempts to block the playing of the videotapes. I sometimes felt guilty just being there. This sense was not alleviated by the slew of messages I and my colleagues received early in the trial from readers or viewers who likened us to various vermin and excretory products. I would tell myself these people didn't realize that interest in the trial was a simple extension of the human impulse to stop and gawk at an automobile accident. I would defend what I was doing on the ground that there are valid reasons to report the proceedings, if only to allow society to bear witness to this breakdown in humanity. But what an imposition.

In the early days, we would all catch our breath whenever the French and Mahaffy contingent stood up in the courtroom to make one of their stately but dramatic exits. During adjournments, they would leave through a side door and run into the rest of us near the escalators. Like mourners at a never-ending funeral, the families, flanked by their ever-present police attendants, would stare fixedly ahead as their procession parted the flow of spectators and press. We would fall silent until the door of the victims' chamber closed.

I developed a crick in my neck turning to see the reaction of the Mahaffys, Frenches and Homolkas to the latest indignity visited upon their dead children. A muscle would invariably twitch in Doug French's cheek whenever his daughter, Kristen, was mentioned. Debbie Mahaffy, her face looking like a death mask, was stoic (though we knew she resented the fact that Leslie was not accorded the same outpouring of public horror that accompanied Kristen's abduction). Alone among the parents, she remained to hear the videotaped cries of her child fill the courtroom.

How did these people remain silent through lawyers' in-jokes, Ms Homolka's whiny rationalizations, Mr. Bernardo's bumptious insensitivity? How did they bear John Rosen's unfortunate objection to the trial judge about the families' "carrying on" in front of the jury? We got used to the routine. The ordinary citizen who came to watch the proceedings for just one day would lean forward at 9:59 as the pasty-faced Mr. Bernardo swaggered in with his armed escorts, his tongue self-consciously testing the air with a lizard-like flick. The press, meanwhile, would chatter on, oblivious.

We were especially chummy with the irreverent and utterly unpretentious defence team. Tony Bryant and John Rosen were so accessible that many a chat with the press was conducted while they stood in their underwear, preparing to don their lawyer's gowns in their work room. We would kibitz with the baseball-obsessed Bryant. We were concerned when Mr. Rosen, a consummate defence lawyer, steadily lost weight in the final stages of the trial.

The prosecutors were polite but more distant. When their entourage swept through the hallway in a self-contained bubble during recesses, I fancied they looked at little wistfully at the laughing knot of people surrounding the defence. It was doubtless as hard for them to see the press side against the star witness, Karla Homolka, as it was for the their professional and emotional stake in the case.

We even had a relationship of sorts with Judge Patrick LeSage, a remarkable man who balanced the tremendous competing interests within the case as adeptly as anyone could. When issues relating to what could or couldn't be published grew confusing — and they often did — we would send him notes asking him for clarification. He always responded, sometimes with a glint of humour.

One small cluster in the Bernardo galaxy had little time to engage in anything beyond research and paranoia: the book authors. There were two sets of co-authors — one from the *Toronto Sun,* the other from the *Toronto Star* — and a freelancer, Stephen Williams, usually accompanied by his researcher and partner, Marsha Boulton. (Two other Bernardo books had been published even before the trial began.)

The book authors often set up camp in the hallway outside the courtroom, alternately schmoozing police officers or warily watching their opponents do the same. All the authors knew that only one or two of the five books will do well. Considering the stakes, it struck me as heroic that they could maintain the stiff formality they reserved for one another. The Bernardo teams from the *Star* and *Sun,* in particular, had been at journalistic war since the time of the Kristen French murder. The pressure to produce and break stories, greatly complicated by the publication bans that littered the legal proceedings, was immense.

There were only occasional signs of the pressure under which they lived. One was the day a witness mentioned having been paid several thousand dollars by the *Sun* in 1994 for some schlocky photographs and letters Ms Homolka had written from prison. Chequebook journalism! The *Star*'s genteel Nick Pron, who had never quite lived down missing that particular scoop, never had a happier day. I thought the poor fellow would hand out cigars.

Without a doubt, the most surreal experience for the Bernardo pack occurred during the first playing of the videotapes. The audio was often incomprehensible, so during each adjournment we would press together in an anteroom. Bibi, an angel-faced court registrar, would read the transcript of those repulsive taped scenes, line by line, profanity by profanity, scream by scream. Reporters would occasionally break through her soft recital to bark something like: "Hold it, Bibi. Was that 'Lick my ass' or 'Lick it, ass'?"

Another moment of unreality: Sixty reporters crowded at the front of the courtroom during a recess one day to look at a sheaf of autopsy photographs showing one of the victims.

"Why, exactly, do we need this?" I wondered aloud to a colleague.

"I don't know," she replied. "I guess after all this time, you just need to see." Unlike the pensioners and slightly wonky "court rats" who make up the audience in most Canadian courtrooms, the Bernardo trial attracted a heavy component of fluorescent green hair and nose rings. The case prompted one offbeat artist to hang bride-and-groom effigies in courthouse trees. Another doused animal blood on a sculpture in front of the building. We even had a character decked out in Lycra who, as he was hauled out of court for praying aloud on his knees, began shouting, "Internet! Internet!"

The trial accented the arresting visual, the quick clip, and moved at a faster pace than any I've covered. The brain was yanked from one image to the next. If you left the courtroom, you inevitably missed something powerful — flashes of emotional, important factoids from witnesses or video by the Handycam Twins themselves.

Many of these clips are unforgettable: Mr. Bernardo suggesting he might need some professional help. Or Ms Homolka performing a very creditable, screechy imitation of Edith Bunker singing the theme from *All in the Family.* My favourite was the sound of her voice on the video soundtrack as her groom pans across the Pacific from their hotel balcony during their honeymoon: "How far inland do you think the sharks come?" she asks innocently.

One video that sticks with me was screened twice but never reported in the papers, being just another blip during a trial day: A bright and bouncy Paul Bernardo trains his videocamera through the couple's shiny, new home while a song by Freddie Mercury and David Bowie blasts in the background. He excitedly points out kitchen nooks, the jacuzzi and his tools (including grandpa's circular saw) in the basement. Karly Kurls and the Big Bad Businessman, first-time homeowners, warble a verse from *Our House,* by Crosby, Stills, Nash and Young.

It would be impossible to produce a more ominous rock video. Neither actually said, "Here's the walk-in closet where Kristen will sleep, pray and vomit. And here's the jacuzzi where Paul will squat, grunting like a fevered pig, over Kristen's face." But each of us in the audience, sitting in stupefied silence, certainly must have had such thoughts. I remember my foot tapping guiltily on the courtroom floor, stopping abruptly, stubbornly starting again.

Central to the trial, of course, was the plaguing question of domestic abuse. Was Karla Homolka a victim? This question ultimately transformed the proceeding into the trial she never had.

After watching every second of testimony, it seemed evident to me that she was beaten at various times in her marriage, though not to the extent she claimed. In her looking-glass world,

Ms Homolka would have us believe a battered, terrified woman was involuntarily sending those pathetic mash notes asking her assailant to abuse her more. Sorry, can't buy it. In fact, about the only part of her testimony I found easy to accept was her account of how her husband killed Leslie and Kristen.

Even then, the point was surely not whether she fully enjoyed it, half enjoyed it or derived only minimal kicks. What mattered was that she could have saved the lives of three girls, but didn't. I strongly suspect the police, prosecutors or victims didn't buy the victim scenario, either. Their mistake, albeit an understandable one, was feeling they had to justify her deal by helping her don the mantle of victim. Still, the feelings of disappointment in the police and prosecution ranks were almost palpable when it became clear the media were not impressed with Karla. Nor was it the sort of disapproval the press traditionally conveys during a trial. This was the Bernardo trial, where so many conventions ceased to have meaning. Newspaper columnists drained their thesauruses denouncing Ms Homolka and her snide aggressiveness. Television legal analysts (an O.J. Simpson innovation) spoke freely about the difficulty of believing this strange woman.

The female journalists were onto Ms Homolka first, almost as though they instinctively smelled on her the telltale odour of fraudulent teen angel from their own youths. Women covering the trial were at first perplexed, then impatient, with the male journalists who for a time gave Ms Homolka the benefit of the doubt. The high point of the trial was not Paul Bernardo's testimony. He was easy to figure out. A classic Ted Bundy formula: An emotionally barren childhood; a superficial charm; an utter lack of conscience. To observe his almost childlike absorption in the prisoner's box while his torture tapes were played, you'd think they had turned on Game Seven of the World Series. A psychiatrist noted in a report that it was a miracle of self-control that Mr. Bernardo didn't drop his pants and start masturbating during the videos.

Watching the accused man, I often thought of Mr. Bundy, the best-known North American serial killer, who once said something like, "Why all the fuss about a dead girl? There are billions of other people out there."

No, as much as it would chafe Mr. Bernardo's ego, the biggest moment of the trial came when the self-possessed Karla Homolka flounced almost insolently to the witness stand.

From the opening moment, when Mr. Rosen thrust photographs of the three decomposing victims in front of Ms Homolka's face, it was clear we would see a cross-examination probably never to be equalled.

We got to know her inside out — from her splayed genitalia to her constricted soul. It is the essence of Homolka's illness that she cannot accept how thoroughly we know her. Even now, she is assuredly convinced that her inner reality was twisted out of shape in that courtroom; that no more than a glimmer of her true self showed through.

But as adept as she was at burying the truth, as coolly as she engineered her plea bargain, as cleverly as she spun her courtroom anecdotes about her life of hell with her former husband, she made a critical mistake. She forgot he was a compulsive saver. Among the boxcars of carefully inscribed movie stubs and Canadian Tire receipts were more than enough exotic love letters to blow her story of victimization into the next galaxy. And yet after gutting her for almost two weeks, Mr. Rosen slumped in a chair outside the courtroom after their final skirmish and said he had somehow failed.

A few moments from a trial can often capture the essence of an issue. When it came to the conundrum of who Karla Homolka truly was, I had several such moments on my personal list: Her letter to a friend denouncing her father's "selfishness" for continuing to mourn the death of Tammy; telling the police that the deaths of Kristen and Leslie were hurtful to her, "Because you get emotionally involved with these people. I felt I was friends with both of them"; her decision that since Kristen was going to die, they ought to do it on Easter Sunday, when they would have dinner with the Homolkas, thus furnishing them with an alibi; and, finally, a heartfelt soliloquy by Ms Homolka on her Hawaiian honeymoon while, thousands of kilometres away, the Mahaffys were wondering whether the body parts being fished out of Lake Gibson belonged to their daughter. "I just want to tell you the beauty of this beach and everything here doesn't even come close to equalling the love I feel for you," Homolka breathed into the videocamera mike.

■ ■ ■

Just as it would be hard to describe the zen of skiing while whizzing down a mogul run, the psychic meaning of the Bernardo-Homolka union tended to elude journalists reeling through their 13th rerun of *Karla and Paul on Their Hawaiian Honeymoon* and *Leslie Begs for Her Life*. I find myself looking forward to the discussions that are bound to sweep the nation in the weeks ahead. Maybe something useful will actually come out of this national romp in the sewer.

In the meantime, I fear we are all in some way casualties of this wretched case. As rare and random as a Paul Bernardo may be in a country of 30 million people, how much more paranoid is every parent of a daughter as a result of him? How many teen-age girls are less confident to travel the streets?

One of the few individuals unlikely to care is Mr. Bernardo, the viler of the two, yet the one who received far less scrutiny at his own trial.

Unless some guard accidentally leaves his cell door open some night, he will almost certainly die in prison of old age. As psychiatrist Angus McDonald summed up in a report for the Crown: "If he is ever released into the community, it is entirely predictable that he would resume his previous lifestyle — although probably never again with a willing female accomplice."

Earlier detection would have put a halt to Mr. Bernardo's path of destruction. Had he been convicted of the rapes he is suspected of committing in Scarborough, for example, he would have spent several years on ice. The authorities would have been aware of him when he got out. Tammy, Kristen and Leslie would be alive today, probably embarking on careers, marriage and motherhood. And the Bernardo-Homolka team would have had no chance to wrap their tentacles around children in a death embrace. In other words, Tammy, Kristen and Leslie would today be young women, probably embarking on careers, marriage and motherhood.

And Karla Homolka?

What is so inconceivable is not that an impressionable adolescent, regardless of how headstrong she is, could become ensnared in the web of a master manipulator. What matters is that she made an adult decision on Dec. 24, 1990, when she served up her sister to her boyfriend. And when she dragged Leslie Mahaffy down to the root cellar and began making Father's Day dinner, she crossed a territorial line. When she held a mallet over Kristen's ravaged body while the girl cried out at the sight of her father on television imploring her to stay strong and escape, Ms Homolka moved onto a different continent. And when Karla — washer, wiper and vacuumer of evidence extraordinaire — douched Kristen's insides to remove traces of her co-conspirator, and then helped toss the naked corpse into the brush, she voluntarily removed herself from the planet.

Karla didn't take responsibility. She still hasn't. Insulated by therapists and encircled by friends and family who probably cannot be blamed for grasping at any tolerable explanation for what she has done, Ms Homolka still doesn't get it. In this respect, she and Paul Bernardo are still psychically joined, both of them unrepentant murderers.

The psychiatrists seem to feel Karla is unlikely to ever repeat her crimes, if only because she will probably never meet another male like Mr. Bernardo. It is a comforting but altogether too hopeful conclusion. Once she is given her freedom, wackos ranging from garden variety on up to potential Paul Bernardos will gravitate to her like flies to garbage. Perhaps, having learned her extraordinarily costly lesson, she will reject them.

However, knowing Karla as we do, it is easy to extrapolate that her future mental health will depend greatly on whether her excuses have been accepted. Most people won't accept them. Outside her tiny coterie, her life will probably be spent among disbelievers. If she remains in Canada — and what other country would have her — she may be obliged to skip from one community to another as her identity becomes known. Her innate insecurity and paranoia will bloat and perhaps overwhelm her.

That, I suspect, will be Karla Homolka's real sentence.

Robert Chambers

Halifax Chronicle-Herald

Robert Chambers claimed his second NNA for his take on the Gerda Munsinger sex and security scandal that rocked the Progressive Conservative party. Chambers started working for the *Chronicle-Herald* in 1933 and claimed his first NNA in 1953.

Robert Chambers est allé chercher son deuxième prix du CCJ avec cette caricature sur le scandale de ce qui deviendrait connu sous le vocable de l'affaire Munsinger qui avait touché le Parti conservateur. Il avait débuté sa carrière au *Chronicle-Herald* en 1933 et reçut son premier prix du CCJ en 1953.

CHAPTER 2

The Opinion Shapers

*A selection of the winners from NNA categories
for Editorials (continuous since the awards began in 1949)
and Columns, a category begun in 1980.*

By Nick Russell

THE BRITISH CALL EDITORIALS "LEADERS" WITH GOOD REASON: EDITORIALS SHOULD PROVIDE leadership in the community, helping readers to identify important issues and look at them in new ways.

The press recognizes that their responsibility goes beyond simply reporting events: They have an obligation to help the audience understand and evaluate events; as respected TV journalist Helen Hutchinson once said, to "put the beads on the string." Or in the words of George Bain, writing in *Maclean's*:

A well-argued and well-written editorial may occasionally cause a reader to say, 'That's it, that's what I was thinking.' In other words, the editorial may precipitate a previously unarticulated thought.

Reporting is the easy part; explaining can be an even bigger responsibility. Newspapers with no editorials (or only ones borrowed from elsewhere) are announcing loudly to the world that they have no opinions and they have no stake in their community.

Editorials also provide a couple of useful roles within the newspaper itself, providing an outlet for journalists to air their views and to write creatively. Here's an opportunity for people who are intimately familiar with the community to write about it. Often the editorial writers have lived for some years in the area, have written about and studied local politics, and bring a maturity and breadth of vision which few others could provide — city managers have axes to grind (protecting their turf) and elected officials are often only modestly equipped for their task. And here the journalist can write with clarity, precision and literary skill. Some editorials will have to be written on deadline, but others can be mused over, at least for a day or two.

In English-language papers, there is a tradition of anonymity with editorials: They are written to represent the views of all those persons named on the masthead, rather than of an individual writer. And yet the pieces included in this collection represent the work of some of Canada's best-known editorialists, for, despite the anonymity, some editorial writers become highly influential in the community and even the nation. Bruce Hutchison, despite a long lifetime based in Victoria, B.C., was the confidante of prime ministers, and the Dafoe family had decades of influence far beyond their Winnipeg newspaper.

How much influence do editorials have? That's difficult to measure, but more people read them than may be suspected (various surveys suggest that between 55 and 80 per cent of regular newspaper readers read editorials), and they tend to be an older, more affluent and more educated segment of the population: The decision-makers, the movers and shakers. These readers recognize that editorial writers do not operate in a vacuum. They often represent the views of large numbers of voters, or may influence the decisions of voters.

Because editorials represent the collegial views of the newspaper management, editorial writers are not just spouting their own opinions (though conversely they would be ill-advised to try to write editorials for a management with whom they disagree). Neophyte editorial writers could also usefully remember three Don'ts:

- Editorials don't have to be long.
- Editorials don't have to be deadly serious.
- Editorials don't have to be negative.

Sometimes one paragraph is all that is necessary to make a point, just as a touch of humour may leaven an uncomfortable message, and it's often useful to congratulate, and not simply criticize: Joan Fraser, once interviewed about her role writing editorials for the *Montreal Gazette,* said, "If you never write anything but angry editorials, people will tune you out after about three days." Ralph Hancox, for instance, whose winning 1966 piece for the *Peterborough Examiner* is included here (page 88), responds to criticism of Canadian journalists in a fair and open manner, rather than the knee-jerk repudiation that some might be tempted to write. And Andrew Cohen, in his 1996 winning editorial on Dominion Day for the *Globe and Mail* (page 103), explains persuasively that Canadians have a lot to celebrate, rather than complaining about the bad news. There's no reason to equivocate, and there's no reason to be abstruse: A complex idea does not need $10 words to explain it. Bruce Hutchison's winning entry, for instance, deals with a long-standing and complex furor over kickbacks for tree-cutting licences, but is succinct and elegant. It contributed to the first prosecution ever of a Commonwealth minister of the crown.

What should editorials be about? A good editorial may draw attention to something that has gone unnoticed (Edgar Collard, for instance, wrote his piece in 1959 about the post-war housing boom [page 87], putting trends in perspective); it may put topics on the public agenda (John Dafoe draws attention to Prime Minister Mulroney's indecisiveness [page 95]); it may encourage the community to participate in good causes or consider important issues.

But at the same time editorial writers know they are not solving all the problems of the world: It may be much easier — and a cop-out — to inveigh against drug-dealing in the Golden Triangle than it is to explain the new local cat-licensing bylaw. The editorial that simply concludes "This deserves serious study" has achieved little. But the writer on a small, local daily need not shy away from the bigger issues: Jacke Wolfe was only 25 and newly arrived from the U.S. when she wrote clearly and effectively about Ottawa's implementation of the War Measures Act for the *New Westminster Columbian* (page 90).

A range of editorial viewpoints and of columnists has become increasingly necessary in recent years with the disappearance of competing newspapers in many communities. This puts an extra burden on editors to provide a range of opinions (and a large hole for Letters). But the danger, of course, is that the editorial page will therefore become wishy-washy and lacklustre — "on the one hand this but on the other hand that"— to avoid alienating a segment of the audience. Fence-sitting solves nothing. Many of the editorials reproduced here express strong opinions, despite their appearing in one-paper towns.

What credentials do editorial writers need? They must have a passion for current affairs, must read voraciously and must have an encyclopedic knowledge, ranging from the arrival date of the first robin to the history of the Crimean War. They must keep their doors — and ears — open to community leaders. But they also need to ride buses and talk to ordinary folk in beer parlors and at ball games.

Columns, on the other hand, also provide a safety-valve for staff opinions, and their role in the community may be similar: Some columns are designed to inform, some to persuade, and some to entertain. But columnists, more than editorial writers, have an opportunity to develop a tangible writing style. Readers may look forward to a particular columnist not just for what she says but for the way she says it.

Editorial columnists can also be fiercely partisan, even expressing views opposite to their editorial page colleagues. For them, there is no need to be "balanced" and give both sides of an argument: Their role is to provoke debate and get people thinking. Thus Carol Goar's 1986 column about Prime Minister Mulroney's strengths (page 99) may have riled some readers, but it's fair and it's provocative. And Harvey Schachter, summarizing his views on the forthcoming Ontario election for the *Kingston Whig-Standard* in 1985 (page 96), is outrageous, sardonic and cutting — all designed to make the reader think once, twice, a hundred times before voting Conservative.

The editorials and columns included in this chapter demonstrate a wide range of topics and of styles, but they show that editorial writers have to grapple with some of the most important issues in society, and they can do so with colour and flair.

• **1957** Editorial Writing •
Premier Bennett's duty

Bruce Hutchison

Victoria Times

The Supreme Court of British Columbia has rightly dismissed the libel and slander case which Mr. Robert Sommers used to delay and confuse the course of justice for two years. The court could not do otherwise when Mr. Sommers — after announcing that he had resigned from the government to spend all his time vindicating his honour — refused to appear and face his accuser, Mr. Sturdy.

But the decision handed down by Mr. Justice Clyne, though thoroughly sound both in law and justice, leaves all the important and disturbing questions of public policy unanswered.

First, what of Mr. Sommers himself?

It is no defense for him to plead, from his secret hiding place, that he is too ill to testify when the court offered him the opportunity to be examined by a competent physician and he refused to appear even for that purpose.

The simplest fact is that he has faced charges of wholesale bribery for two years and has not disproved or seriously sought to disprove them. And Mr. Sturdy has never withdrawn an iota of his original indictment; on the contrary, he has expanded it by introducing various new charges.

■ ■ ■

It is to be assumed, of course, that Mr. Sommers will immediately resign from the Legislature. After his performance he can do no less. If he refuses to resign, the Legislature no doubt will unseat him, as it is bound to do in these circumstances.

His disappearance from public life, however, will not touch the second question: What of Mr. Bonner's extraordinary record as first law officer of the Crown, charged with the enforcement of equal justice among friends and opponents alike?

That record is not only unworthy of Mr. Bonner but almost unbelievable.

At first he brushed off Mr. Sturdy's charges as absurd, and not worth the Attorney-General's consideration. Later, when the Legislature realized the gravity of the charges and the Opposition demanded an investigation, Mr. Bonner refused to act.

He said he could not act because Mr. Sommers had sued Mr. Sturdy and that the case was sub judice. It would be wrong, said Mr. Bonner, for him to do anything which might prejudice the impending trial. And so the prolonged farce of Mr. Sommers' suit went on.

Meanwhile, Mr. Bonner instructed the Royal Canadian Mounted Police to investigate secretly the charges that, only a few months earlier, he had considered unworthy of his attention.

The report of the police has never been revealed and, says Mr. Bonner, will never be revealed. All the information the Legislature has received about the report is the statement of Mr. George Gregory, a lawyer of good standing, that it makes serious accusations against Mr. Sommers.

■ ■ ■

As a result of the collapse of Mr. Sommers' suit against Mr. Sturdy, Mr. Bonner has two clear duties to perform — duties that he should have performed 22 months ago.

He must consider whether the charges against Mr. Sommers, which have never been refuted, merit direct action by the Attorney-General's Department, like any other charges of a criminal nature; whether Mr. Sommers and those accused of bribing him should be prosecuted and thus given the opportunity to clear themselves.

Apart altogether from the position of Mr. Sommers and certain timber interests, Mr. Bonner must get to the root of this whole ugly business and find out whether in fact the administration of our forests has been corrupted.

So long as Mr. Sommers' suit against Mr. Sturdy was in the courts Mr. Bonner could make a colourable, though not a convincing, excuse for doing nothing. That excuse has now disappeared. There is no case in the courts. No matter is sub judice today. No trial can possibly be prejudiced by Mr. Bonner's action since there is to be no trial.

Was Mr. Sommers bribed, as alleged by Mr. Sturdy — and alleged not in general, but in specific detail with names, dates and figures?

If bribes were paid, who paid them and for what purpose?

What was the consequence of these transactions, if they occurred, to the distribution of forest management licenses?

If forest management licenses were granted as a result of bribes, should they be cancelled?

In short, if there was corruption how far did it go, whom did it include and, above all, how did it affect the public interest?

■ ■ ■

All these questions involve criminal offenses, punishable under the Criminal Code. Moreover, they raise suspicion against many honest holders of forest management licenses who have had no opportunity to defend themselves.

It is therefore Mr. Bonner's simple and unavoidable duty to make sure that all these questions are fully investigated and fully answered.

He can perform that duty quickly and decisively by setting up, at long last, a Royal Commission of inquiry.

Or, perhaps more conveniently, he can request Chief Justice Sloan (who previously refused to consider these matters) to reopen his forest inquiry and ascertain whether any of the forest management licenses discussed in his report were affected by bribery. For clearly the Legislature will be in no position to consider the Chief Justice's latest recommendations on future forest policy until it knows whether that policy has been administered honestly in the past.

If Mr. Bonner is not prepared to institute such an investigation, if he is determined to smother the Sommers case now, as he smothered it in the beginning, then Mr. Bonner should resign forthwith.

■ ■ ■

There is a third question left unanswered by the collapse of the suit against Mr. Sturdy: What of Mr. Bennett?

While Mr. Bonner is Attorney-General and thus vested with vast and peculiar powers, Mr. Bennett is still leader of the government. The final responsibility for all its acts is his. And Mr. Bennett knows very well that not some trifling peccadillo by a former cabinet colleague but the integrity of the whole government, the honesty of public business and his own honour are at stake in this case.

If Mr. Bonner (now unfortunately absent in Europe at an important moment which he could have foreseen) is not inclined to do his duty as Attorney-General then Mr. Bennett, as premier, should compel him to do it or dismiss him.

The primary duty here — the duty of getting all the facts and punishing the guilty, if anyone is guilty, of placing the public business beyond any breath of suspicion — rests with Mr. Bennett. If Mr. Bennett is an honest man, as we believe him to be, he will not rest until his obvious duty has been done.

• **1959** Editorial Writing •
The new grass roots

Edgar Collard
Montreal Gazette

Suburbia has been coming in for a good deal of harsh criticism these days. Many an expert has been saying that these communities outside the big cities have become traps for the unwary.

These suburbs, according to these critics, always are "sprawling." They have sameness and dreariness. Those who live in them dwell with spiritual desolation on their little pads of earth. They build picture-windows only to look out on the street, or into a neighbour's picture-window.

Life is unreal, dull, conventional. In its own way, it is crowded and intrusive. There is no true privacy, no independence of spirit, no freedom. Suburbia is filled with those who wished to escape from the city's crush. But now they dwell in inert disillusion, though the bravest of the brave are shaking the dust of suburbia from off their shoes, and are heading back home to the big city.

But those who live in these new suburbs do not feel nearly so sorry for themselves as the critics pretend to feel for them. Most of them are extremely well content, and have good reason for the way they feel. In their suburban homes they have gained much of what they wished. And they have no intention whatever of fleeing back to the big city, as to a sanctuary.

Most people who live in suburbia have, often for the first time in their lives, the very real satisfaction of owning their own homes. They have a sense of belonging to their homes and having their homes belong to them. They have a bit of garden (rare in town, where the garage has taken sway). Even when suburbia is not quite the rural life it might sometimes supposed to be, it is at least a good deal nearer to the sense of earth and sky.

The dweller in suburbia is far more likely to feel that he has a part in the government of his community, and to realize the problems of government. He is more likely to know his alderman, even his mayor, as neighbours.

If the snow is not removed as he thinks it ought to be, he knows whom to phone, and has a considerably better chance of having his grievances re-dressed. The old cityman's cynical saying, that "you can't fight City Hall," is far less likely to be accepted by the suburbanite, and far less likely to be true.

He may also have a far closer and more responsible feeling towards the other institutions of his community. He has seen the school built. He knows where his school taxes go. He knows his children's teachers and the principal. The Home and School Association is probably a very practical and lively organization.

The suburb is likely to have its planned shopping centre, with space for parking. Zoning, which in the city is a vague and wobbling thing, is very real in the suburbs. Most of the suburbs about Montreal have done a rather good job in keeping the different areas for different purposes and in preventing overlapping and intruding.

No doubt those who live in suburbia would all prefer to have ranch houses built in estates, with picture-windows looking upon lakes or mountains, and with a curving motor road from the gates to the main entrance. But such things do not come to many anywhere.

What the suburban dweller has found is a place of his own, where the air is less poisoned with exhaust, smoke and soot, where there is a bit of grass and garden, where springtime and autumn mean something, where summer is not one long wail about the humidity, and where, in winter, the snow, strange to say, is white.

There the suburban dweller, enjoying many advantages and carrying out many responsibilities, has put down his roots as a property-owner. His roots are strongly attached to the place where they grow. Whatever the critic may like to say, his roots nourish him and he has no desire to be uprooted.

Perhaps, and not least, it is only after living in suburbia that many people have learned what it is really like to be a citizen. And for the country, as well as for the person, it is a wonderfully worthwhile discovery.

• **1966** Editorial Writing •
Canadian papers faulted

Ralph Hancox

Peterborough Examiner

In his talk at the Canadian National Exhibition on Friday, Richard O'Hagan, who is Prime Minister Pearson's press secretary, said that newspaper coverage of Ottawa "did not add up to the most edifying picture of a journalistic community meeting its primary responsibilities as well as it might." There was not enough self-criticism in the press of this country, he said, and he criticized the training of newspaper journalists.

These criticisms are common enough, though infrequently voiced on public platforms. Their validity, like that of all criticism, depends very largely on the vantage point of the critic. Mr. O'Hagan has access to much information in his position as press secretary to the Prime Minister. He also has, or should have, an intimate working knowledge of government and its institutions of an order that few journalists can have. Thus it is easy for Mr. O'Hagan to see discrepancies between what he knows and what a working journalist reports in the course of his work.

In some ways, Ottawa is well-served by a coterie of correspondents who cover national affairs. In others, national coverage of Parliament, Government and the Departments, seems to result from a very jaundiced and bellicose attitude towards the nation's business. This is unquestionably one of the sources of Mr. O'Hagan's discontent.

But there is a much larger difficulty that arises out of the geography of the country and the sparsely-spread population outside metropolitan areas. These same difficulties have led to a growing concentration of ownership into fewer hands, and to the pooling of services among newspapers. This last technique is one which is approached with some caution. Pooled service means less diversity. At the same time, wide diversity of coverage means the kind of expense that only large newspapers can afford.

As for self-criticism, newspapers universally appear to be very sensitive. When they are criticized there is a knee-jerk response that results in a lusty kick of protest. Despite the earnest self-examination that is carried on, perhaps largely unknown to Mr. O'Hagan, the effect is not necessarily invigorating to the press as a whole. It results in a stolid front, the main purpose of which is to keep the institution of daily newspapers intact and to approach all innovations with caution.

Generally speaking, Canadian newspapers contain more information from more sources than their counterparts in the United States. They also give better international coverage of events than the popular press of Great Britain. In Quebec, there are two or three French-language journals of vigour and enterprise that enjoy deserved reputations for astute commentary and criticism. In the English-language press in Canada, several daily newspapers enjoy an international reputation for their coverage and poise.

On the other hand, there is considerable room for improvement, both in coverage and comment, and in criticism and commentary. This will largely come about through the insistence of informed and articulate readers — who are, in the end, the true watchdogs of the press. As for the training of newspaper journalists, this is a problem that must soon be tackled by newspapers which have traditionally depended on the attractions that newspaper work offered. Today, there is such a variety of interesting and satisfying careers available, that this reliance is not enough to produce sufficient suitable recruits and unless some concerted attempts are made to attract a variety of people into journalism, newspapers must look forward to some anxious moments in the discharge of "primary responsibilities."

• **1969** Editorial Writing •

There is no honour in a gentle death

Martin Dewey

Toronto Star

Man should not die gently, wrote Dylan Thomas. He should rage, rage against the dying of the light.

Countries can die too, gently or with rage. Canada is taking the quiet route.

A finance minister is drummed out of Ottawa for advocating fiscal policies that are just a little too Canadian. A monumental reappraisal of our tax structure gathers dust in Ottawa because we can't afford to be too Canadian in that area either. A task force blueprint for gaining some small measure of additional control over our economy is filed away because — well, just because.

We elect a Prime Minister who sets his lance against the dragon of Quebec nationalism while shrugging off the larger, hungrier dragon that whips its tail to the south of us. One dragon threatens to lose us a province; the other, a nation.

The death rattle grows louder. We lay plans to extricate ourselves from military entanglements in Europe. For what purpose? Not to carve out a distinctive Canadian role in world affairs, as so many had hoped. The troops are being brought home, it appears, to man the northern outposts of Fortress America; to scan the skies for missiles that might be heading for Chicago or Cleveland.

The late U.S. secretary of state, John Foster Dulles, inadvertently warned us of our fate several years ago when he said nations are no longer conquered by armies but by dollars. George Ball, the former U.S. ambassador to the UN, proposed our epitaph when he predicted that simple economics would inevitably dictate the ultimate corporate merger — between Canada and the United States.

But must we die so gently? Or should we begin to rage, rage against the dying of the light? And, in raging, is it possible we might ignite some last spark of will that could grow into a flame of self-preservation?

Some of the economic remedies are gathering dust in filing cabinets in Ottawa. We must maintain and strengthen our system of cultural antibodies — our press, our magazines, our television, our theatre. We must also identify the grasping filaments that reach northward to turn our labour unions, our social clubs and our board rooms into vehicles for the aspirations and ideologies of others.

We must reserve some of our rage for those who are willing to let Canada die for private gain — businessmen who don't recognize the word sovereignty because there is no provision for it on the balance sheet; politicians who equate heavy inflows of foreign money with "good times" and who are willing to let future generations pick up the pieces.

Rage can be legitimate and healthy. It could also be the salvation of a worthwhile country. We have been dying too gently.

● **1970** Editorial Writing ●

PM's desperation act against FLQ is stern test of our democracy

Jacke Wolfe

New Westminster Columbian

We realize that desperate measures are sometimes necessary in desperate situations. And certainly everyone must agree that the situation involving the kidnappings and the FLQ in Quebec is extremely serious.

But we still have very grave reservations about the implementation of the War Measures Act. Perhaps it would be simplest to list the issues that now concern us:

• The War Measures Act has far wider powers than is necessary to control the current situation. Parliament could have been asked to make amendments to the Criminal Code expanding police powers of questioning in connection with conspiracies against the government. The death penalty could have been imposed for kidnapping of innocent political hostages.

• It is always extremely dangerous in any democracy for a government to assume unlimited powers for any length of time. The prime minister has asked for the Act to be in force up until April 30, 1971. This is entirely too long. Presumably, the act is being implemented to deal with this one specific situation and, if it is, the maximum time should be extremely short — even more than two weeks would be excessive.

• Many actions have now been labelled "crimes" in the hysteria of the moment. Anyone "in possession of posters, stickers or pamphlets of a political nature" is now liable to arrest and detention without recourse. The news could be censored, and controls could be placed over the use of any private property. Police have blanket authority to arrest, detain and deport those suspected of insurrection without legal recourse. Private property can be confiscated and disposed of by the government.

• In implementing the Act, the government is not specifically limited to dealing with the FLQ situation. With wide police powers, the RCMP could also arrest, detain and deport persons suspect of any crime or conspiracy. And we suspect that the temptation to use these powers would be very strong.

• Finally, and more seriously yet, Trudeau has promised to try to write a new statute which would be less sweeping than the War Measures Act and which could be used in circumstances similar to the present ones.

The reservations we have about implementation of the Act are insignificant beside our fears of what such a new act could bring. At least when the War Measures Act is involved, everyone must be convinced that this is really a national crisis for which temporary measures are required. A lesser act, with the connotations of not being related to very critical situations, would be far more dangerous.

The government could give itself controls over political activity that might be put into effect for comparatively trivial reasons.

Surely, if we truly believe in democracy, we must have more faith in our governmental system than this. For centuries we have given lip service to the idea that evil roots itself out in a democratic society. Those with evil motives and evil methods are exposed for what they are, and voted out by the populace. Or they simply lose their popular appeal in the face of the advantages of a democratic, orderly system.

We implore the Commons to give the parliamentary and democratic system a chance. Surely the government must be closely watched in its administration of this Act, and the period of its implementation must be severely limited. The proper and orderly administration of justice, suitably legislated by Parliament, can handle the current crisis.

The means must not justify the ends. Democracy can never be maintained by dictatorial methods.

• **1978** Editorial Writing •

Trudeau and the fatal flaw

John Grace

Ottawa Journal

It is, of course, Victoria revisited. Canadians have been through all this before with Prime Minister Trudeau, and they will go through it again after the next election. The constitution bill which Mr. Trudeau has produced will not pass this Parliament nor the next. Nor should it.

Mr. Trudeau is seeking to achieve by cleverness what he could not achieve by consensus. He is trying to build a monument by himself (and to himself) which he could not convince others to build with him. The bill introduced to the Commons this week is a testament to his failure. It is the product of constitutional experts and legislative draftsmen, not of national will.

This is the fatal flaw of what Mr. Trudeau is attempting. The specific proposals are capable of revision and amendment. They are, indeed, presented as a starting point for discussion in the months ahead. But unless there is a national consensus and will that there should be these changes, Mr. Trudeau is building his constitutional castles on sand.

Lester Pearson, a far more able negotiator than Mr. Trudeau, also attempted the two-phase approval method of constitutional reform. It didn't work for him and it certainly will not work for Mr. Trudeau.

If constitutional reform is to have any chance, it must be initiated by a federal government enjoying a fresh, powerful mandate and immense goodwill across the country. The present Trudeau government is at the tag-end of its existence. It is a lame-duck government, tired, dispirited and on the political defensive. Its weakest area of support is among English-speaking Canadians, precisely where a government trying to carry out basic and valid constitutional changes should be strong.

The disabilities of the Trudeau government alone are enough to make the proposed constitutional timetable utterly unrealistic. The whole process has the smell of an elaborate pre-election production staged for the good of the Liberals rather than in any reasonable hope of accomplishment. But the proposals are turning out to be unacceptable in themselves. The House of the Federation, disguised as reform of the Senate, is a dog's breakfast. The concept is undemocratic in addition to being unworkable. The Conservatives' House of the Provinces is no better. Unfortunately, the Liberals' transparent plagiarism of the House of the Provinces idea seems to have led Joe Clark into a totally premature commitment to abet Mr. Trudeau's constitutional proposals.

The so-called reform of the Supreme Court is also highly suspect. Put aside the question of whether Quebec should have one or two more Supreme Court judges, or whether the court should be enlarged. That is not the crucial matter. The danger is of turning the Supreme Court into some kind of national arbitration board by having judges appointed to represent various regional interests. The Supreme Court is the ultimate court of law in the country. Justices are there to interpret law. They should represent themselves, not sides or regions of Canada.

The changes Mr. Trudeau is putting forth may be legally within the federal jurisdiction's right to make. In practice, those which are not merely cosmetic go right to the heart and nature of the federal system. Their implementation without provincial concurrence would be a violation of the spirit of federalism. It would make agreement possible in the crucial areas where provincial agreement for constitutional changes is essential. Mr. Trudeau has already had Claude Ryan's cold response ("unilateraly unacceptable") to the federal strategy.

There is a temptation to say, get on with constitutional changes. The country is weary with the decades of talk, and there are changes which should be made. But Mr. Trudeau's bill will not placate Quebec's nationalists and save Confederation. It will make the governing of an already fragmented country more difficult. Federalism is not strengthened by diluting federal institutions or by making them unwieldy.

• **1982** Editorial Writing •

Teetering on the brink of an historic tragedy

Joan Fraser

Montreal Gazette

Beyond the summer lull, the thunder-clouds are building over Claude Ryan's head. If the provincial Liberal leader manages to retain his job despite the widespread animosity to him in his own party it will be, on current form, something of a miracle.

That is, of course, properly a matter for the party itself to decide. Certainly there are glaringly serious flaws in Mr. Ryan's leadership. What is distressing, however, is that so much of the current discussion seems to be blaming him for the wrong things. It does no service to Quebec or to the Liberal party, let alone to this man of great dignity and worth, to have the debate so badly distorted.

It is not true, for example, that Mr. Ryan is a traitor to the French, or to the English, or to federalism, or to Quebec. Quite the contrary. He has never wavered from the admirable dedication to personal freedoms, to French Quebec's blossoming, to minority rights and to a strong Quebec within a united Canada that was the basis of his campaign for the Liberal leadership four years ago.

Mr. Ryan is blamed by some French Quebecers for being a sort of hostage of the English. That is ludicrous. His position on English rights is, in all essentials, unchanged from the one on which he was elected leader; a far greater recognition of English rights in education and elsewhere than the Parti Québécois would offer, but continued vigilance and protection for the French fact.

Many anglophones resent him for not going further, and in particular for his speech last fall pointing out the obvious: That unless the Liberals can appeal more to francophones they have no hope of getting elected. Agreed, Mr. Ryan stated this simple truth clumsily. But that awkwardness did not merit such wholesale bitterness.

Many Liberals also resent, to the point of suspicion about his federalist credentials, his position during the constitutional debate. This newspaper was among his strongest critics when he voted for the Parti Québécois resolution condemning the accord reached by the federal and other provincial governments. That position, however, was entirely consistent with the kind of principled federalism, based on consent of all major partners, that Mr. Ryan has long upheld. It detracted in no way from his commitment to Canada.

Indeed, his conduct then despite such vociferous opposition demonstrated once more Mr. Ryan's great political courage. He simply is unwilling to let short-term politics influence a position he believes to be right; another recent example is his proposal to give up Quebec's claim to Labrador.

Perhaps the biggest single accusation against Mr. Ryan is that he lost last year's election. Here, the critics are getting closer to the real problems of his leadership.

It may be that no Liberal leader could have won that election against a living myth of the stature of Rene Lévesque, and Mr. Ryan did manage to bring the Liberals' popular vote within a whisker of the PQ's. It is also true, however, that he made an astounding error in political judgment when he decided not to make independence an election issue, thus allowing the PQ to shelve almost all discussion of the first and most important article in its program.

That lack of a basic political instinct is crucial. It is perhaps inherently linked to Mr. Ryan's determination — enunciated in his leadership campaign and since then — to make the Liberals a party distinguished by its "unalterable respect for intelligence" one that would never stoop to "methods used to sell soap or beauty products."

Mr. Ryan's dedication to rational ideas and discussion has given the Liberals some of the most coherent and constructive positions in politics today. But his unwillingness to recognize that politics is and must be a series of civilized compromises, and that the most admirable platform in the world is no help if the people do not understand it, is a major political flaw. He has said more than once, in effect, that he would rather be right than be premier — a most risky position for a political leader.

He too often ignores the fact that a decision made for principled reasons may have an effect exactly opposite to what was intended — as did his constitutional vote in the National Assembly, which the PQ used to bolster its case for independence.

The Liberal leader has done badly in another key task, keeping his party united and motivated. It is no use to castigate the party membership for this; a leader's job is to inspire others to work with, and for him.

It seems more than likely that if Mr. Ryan could get elected he would be one of the greatest of Quebec premiers. Whether he can get elected is a different if crucial question, one that will properly concern party members now considering their duty.

But if they decide he should go, they should be very clear in their minds and to the public about why they are doing so. If they reject Claude Ryan it will be a personal tragedy for Mr. Ryan, who is one of the finest of Quebec's citizens. But if out of ill-considered spite they also reject the best of what he represents, that will be a tragedy of historic proportions for all of Quebec.

● **1983** Column Writing ●

What has Trudeau done in 15 years?

Allan Fotheringham

Southam News

The night in the Ottawa ice rink in 1968 when the Liberals were about to choose their new leader, America was busy burning down their cities.

As the eight candidates made their crucial speeches before voting next day, Martin Luther King was assassinated and the blacks of the world's most advanced democracy set out to avenge their saint.

Those of us in the press seats kept sprinting between the Lincolnesque words of Joe Greene to the press room and the television sets recording first Detroit, then Baltimore, Chicago and Pittsburgh erupting in flames.

This week, with the attention on a Tory leadership convention, is the 15th anniversary of that April day when Pierre Trudeau (as he was then known) became the prime minister.

In 15 years, he has gone from being the best-liked to the most disliked politician in Canada.

He is the longest-reigning leader in the western democracies.

The U.S., so rich at the base, so unstable at the top, has gone through five presidents since Trudeau was chosen and then confirmed by the Canadian people: Lyndon Johnson, Richard Nixon, Gerald Ford, Jimmy Carter and now Ronnie Reagan.

Britain is now on her fifth prime minister in the same period: Harold Wilson, Edward Heath, Wilson again, James Callaghan and now Maggie Thatcher.

Chancellor Kiesinger was running West Germany when Trudeau came to power, followed by Willy Brandt, Helmut Schmidt and now Helmut Kohl.

France has gone through Couve de Murville to Giscard d'Estaing to Mitterrand. And we won't even mention Italy.

Trudeau has now been in power longer than all the Progressive Conservative leaders since the First World War. He has been more successful, in terms of longevity, than Meighen, Bennett, Manion, Bracken, Drew, Diefenbaker, Stanfield and Clark put together.

If he wishes to beat the record of French-Canadian prime ministers, he could in April of 1984 surpass the term of Sir Wilfrid Laurier.

What else has he done in 15 years?

We could spend a week. When he came to power, he inherited from Lester Pearson four provinces with Liberal governments. Two more were elected later.

Today, as we know, there is not a single provincial Liberal government in the land.

There is not a single Liberal in the provincial legislatures of the growing end of the country — the western provinces where the resources reside and where the population, is flowing.

He turned Ottawa into a nominally bilingual town, thereby saving — or at least delaying — Quebec from leaving the country.

He has probably assured that there will never again be a unilingual prime minister, as the unilingual Lester Pearson accurately predicted.

Thanks to his stylish profile, and the reputation of his estranged wife, he now attracts more attention and respect abroad in the world than he does at home.

Of the eight good candidates who originally lined up against him in 1968 (there are only three, possibly four, who can be taken seriously in this race) this is the result:

Robert Winters, the runner-up, is dead of a broken heart.

Joe Greene is dead of a broken body.

Paul Martin is writing his unending memoirs.

Paul Hellyer, the most confusing and confused man in modern politics, is in journalism — a suitable fate.

Eric Kierans is in intellectual opposition.

Mitchell Sharp depends on government largesse.

Allan MacEachern is the only man left in government, a discredited force.

John Turner waits on his Elba at the corner table in Winston's, ready for the call.

There is not a single respected leader around the Trudeau cabinet table who can speak with assurance for the three-quarters of Canada that is non-francophone.

His relations with the press (while somewhat irrelevant) are, to be polite, poisonous.

This is our progress report, after 15 years.

• **1985** Editorial Writing •

Making decisions in government

John Dafoe

Winnipeg Free Press

As Parliament broke for its summer recess, Prime Minister Brian Mulroney summed up his thoughts on one of the great issues of the day, free trade with the United States:

"I think that — uh — trade enhancement — uh, a trade enhancement program — uh, uh — of any kind in Canada — uh, uh — would probably meet with an overwhelming degree of — uh — ambivalence.

"… Put out an idea like that and you can count on the country to come down squarely on both sides of the issue — to say nothing of the government."

Mr. Mulroney could have given the same response to virtually any question, on any subject at any time during his first 10 months as prime minister of Canada. Canadians have discovered that, when they gave the Progressive Conservatives their immense majority last September, they did not elect a prime minister, they elected a weather vane which cannot even make up its mind which way the wind is blowing.

The hallmark of Mr. Mulroney's government to date has been, as the prime minister so aptly puts it, "an overwhelming degree of ambivalence." Most of that ambivalence has been supplied by the prime minister himself. More often than not, when a minister tried to set out a clear and decisive position, he found himself undercut by Mr. Mulroney. External Affairs Minister Joe Clark, Finance Minister Michael Wilson and International Trade Minister James Kelleher have all found themselves in that position over the past few months.

Government decisions have been rare since Mr. Mulroney took office and most of them have tended to be negative — dismantling the National Energy Program, cutting down the Foreign Investment Review Agency, giving up the federal government's demand to be the dominant partner in the development of oil off the coast of Newfoundland.

Dismantling some of the work of the previous administration is part of the job of every new government and the Mulroney government's actions in those areas are likely to have a good effect on the Canadian economy. But most new governments do have some positive ideas of their own and do try to put them into effect during their first parliamentary session. If 60 days of decision can be foolhardy, 300 days of indecision are positively idiotic.

The question now is whether Mr. Mulroney will go on for the next four years of his mandate searching constantly for his elusive consensus, maintaining his overwhelming degree of ambivalence until he is certain that absolutely everybody, everywhere in the country, is on his side. If he does, his term of office is unlikely to be useful either to the country he serves or to the party he leads. Ten months of ambivalence have already weakened the party's popularity. A few more could wash it away entirely.

Pierre Mendes-France is not the sort of fellow Brian Mulroney would select as a role model. After all, he did not survive as prime minister of France even as long as Joe Clark did as prime minister of Canada. Yet, Mr. Mendes-France did attach his name to an aphorism which defines the challenge which faces Mr. Mulroney and all of those who aspire to political leadership:

"To govern is to choose."

• **1985** Column Writing •

100 reasons not to vote Tory

Harvey Schachter

Kingston Whig-Standard

To summarize my series of provincial election columns, let's look at 100 reasons to not vote Tory on Thursday:
- After 41 years, it's time for a change.
- Ontario has had a deficit for 10 consecutive years.
- At a family income of $15,000, Ontario levies the highest taxes of any provincial government in Canada.
- We have a premier who refuses to debate his opponents in an election campaign.
- The Ministry of the Environment's budget has been cut back by 25 per cent the last three years.
- Ontario universities receive the lowest funding from their provincial government, on a per student basis, than any other provincial university system in Canada.
- The Ontario government has been stalling for years on freedom of information legislation.
- Provincial support of education has been declining drastically.
- We have an environment minister who believes only rats are hurt by PCBs.
- Tories favour the rich: At a family income of $100,000, taxes are the third lowest in Canada.
- Ontario ranks last among all other provinces in funding of the arts.
- The Ontario Tory government is the only one of three in Canada that continues with regressive health-care premiums — highest in the country.
- The Ontario Tory government makes Brian Mulroney look like a piker when it comes to patronage.
- The Tories' handling of the trust company fiasco was inept.
- The Tories have failed to enact new legislation to prevent another trust company fiasco.
- The minimum wage in Ontario has been lowered from 47 per cent to 40 per cent of the average industrial wage, hurting the working poor, who lack bargaining power.
- The Tory government has protected, rather than controlled, Ontario Hydro.
- The Tory Ontario government has failed to enforce its (inadequate) rules and standards for occupational health.
- The Tory government has failed to take action to curtail the acid rain emissions of Inco and Ontario Hydro.
- Ontario is the only province with no long-term program of loan assistance for existing farmers.
- The Tory government has done little to increase the supply of housing.
- The 1983 tax surcharge on Ontarians, unlike the custom in other provinces, was levied on everybody earning over $12,000 a year, rather than simply on the rich.
- The decision to fully fund the separate school system was unwise.
- The government has no moral standards. It gets its direction from polls.
- The Tory government has been slow to fund day care.
- The Ontario Tory government has reduced the level of support of tile drainage loans from 75 to 60 per cent.
- The government's decision to eliminate Grade 13 without really ending it was cowardly camouflage.
- Our last environment minister told us the pollution of Toronto's beaches was caused by seagulls.
- The handling of separate school funding — phasing in the program within one year, before adequate preparation — is senseless.
- The government has failed to proclaim the hazardous spills bill passed by the legislature six

years ago.
- Seventy-six per cent of hospitals will have to reduce services this year because of provincial underfunding.
- The Tories have been promising us denticare since 1943 without delivering.
- The Tories allowed the potent anti-pornography film, *Not A Love Story*, to be restricted to filmings before small groups.
- Eighty Ontario beaches have been closed because of pollution in the past two years.
- The Ontario Tory government doesn't provide wheelchairs for the handicapped over age 19.
- The government spends more per capita on advertising than the federal government or any other province.
- The Ontario Tory government has refused to address the problems of the natives on the English-Wabigoon river system.
- Ontario has 26 per cent of the nation's farms, but accounts for between a third and more than a half of each year's farm bankruptcies.
- Youth unemployment is unconscionably high in Ontario.
- The site the Tories originally chose for Ontario's major waste disposal site was porous and leaky — just like the government.
- The Tories refuse to ban extra billing.
- Frank Miller refused to debate women's issues at the recent PC leadership convention.
- In the 10 years since the Tories promised to close the wage gap for women, it has narrowed by only 5.2 per cent, a rate that would require 50 more years of Tory power to complete the task.
- The premier has failed to stand up for Ontario consumers on oil prices.
- The Ontario government is suppressing information on Great Lakes polluters.
- Eastern Ontario lost 3,914 acres of improved farmland every year during the last decade.
- The premier admits rural abortion facilities are inadequate but refuses to improve them.
- Ontario's share of the Canadian Gross Domestic Product has declined by 10 per cent over the last 15 years.
- The Tories' Minaki Lodge wasted $45 million of our money.
- Assistance to farmers facing soil erosion is pitiful.
- Average wages and salaries in Ontario have fallen in real terms in six of the past seven years.
- While pledging restraint, the government services department hiked spending on consultants five-fold from 1978-84.
- Government advertising increased 17 per cent last year.
- The government showed contempt for us in its tossing out of election goodies.
- The government never established the assistance fund it promised for Eastern Ontario and Northern Ontario farmers during the last election.
- The Ontario government refuses to tell us how much it spends on consultants.
- The Tories blocked a private member's bill that would have established an electronic video Hansard similar to parliamentary coverage.
- Farmland is disappearing at the rate of 15 acres an hour.
- The budget for sewage waste filtration projects was cut by $76 million over the last four years.
- The Ontario government refuses to fund groups arguing against the Hydro lines that will cut through eastern Ontario.
- Justice Secretary Gordon Walker gave out $413,000 in speechwriting and consulting contracts to close associates, without tenders.
- The government refused to fund environmental groups fighting for Ontario citizens in the Love Canal court case.
- Frank Miller was given a zero rating by environmental groups.
- The Ontario Tories took 14 years to solidify their block-Spadina pledge.
- Frank Miller says tampons are non-essential items.
- The Tory government promised a tritium recovery process at the Pickering nuclear site and

then reversed itself.

• Frank Miller promised lean government and then gave us the largest Ontario cabinet in Ontario history.

• The government subsidizes tobacco farmers to change crops.

• The Ontario government has exempted 67 Ontario Hydro projects from Environmental Protection Act hearings.

• The government has failed to fund legal aid properly.

• At least one-third of the major companies polluting the Great Lakes from the Ontario side are violating Ontario's pollution standards.

• The Tory government has cut back on alternative energy.

• The Tories gave $3 million to an American tomato paste producer while giving short shrift to a competent Canadian firm.

• The minister of agriculture refuses to talk about the Hay Bay Farms issue.

• Midwifery is illegal in Ontario.

• Our past premier thought nothing of taking a government jet when he wanted to watch a baseball game with his pals one evening in Detroit.

• The government repeatedly offers contracts without tenders.

• Fines for pollution in Ontario are minimal, providing an incentive to pollute.

• The former justice secretary removed a hotel wall — at our expense — for a photo opportunity.

• The elected cabinet is second in power to the premier's breakfast clubs.

• Frank Miller thought there was no conflict in having a Crown company employee run his leadership campaign.

• It's hard to tell the elected politicians and civil servants apart at Queen's Park.

• The Tories showed extreme bad faith by eliminating the select committee on Hydro as soon as we gave them a majority in 1981.

• Keith Norton and Bob Runciman both skipped all-candidates' meetings this election.

• The government has not kept its pledge to regenerate one acre of forest for every acre cut.

• The government stopped tax assessment of homes during the election because of partisan political considerations.

• As minister of industry and trade, Frank Miller had the second worst record in the government in promoting women.

• The government refuses to change its method of planting trees even though other jurisdictions found the system ineffective.

• Ontario was the last province to agree to the child-rearing dropout provisions of the Canada Pension plan.

• The Tories forfeit $1 million a week by refusing to ban extra billing.

• The government pays $246 million a year to nursing home operators without properly regulating those homes.

• The government is quietly stock-piling chemicals for spraying forests after the election even though non-toxic methods would be more effective.

• Since 1978, there has been an 18.2 per cent reduction in provincial funding for roads, and, as a result, 28 per cent of all municipal roads in the province are considered inadequate.

• Our waybill system for toxic wastes — which depends on an honour system — is ineffective.

• The deputy-premier, Bette Stephenson, misused her position in supporting a development that will financially benefit herself and her family.

• The government has taken years to not decide on aluminum pop cans.

• The Tories have been nonchalant about foreign ownership of land.

• The gap between Frank Miller's ideology and his election statements is too large for comfort; we can't be sure what we'll get after the election.

• The government approved the $12 billion Darlington project despite projections — which proved correct — showing that it wasn't needed.

• Anything on which J. Lorne McDougall and Harvey Schachter agree — in this case, that it's time to turf out the Tories — must be correct.

• **1986** Column Writing •

Some nice things to say about Mulroney

Carol Goar

Toronto Star

OTTAWA — One of the quickest ways to bring a conversation to a dead halt is to say casually: "I can think of some good things about Brian Mulroney."

Eyes widen; sentences stop in mid-syllable; people don't know whether to smile politely or turn away in embarrassment.

As it happens, I'm being perfectly serious. I propose to mark the second anniversary of the Mulroney government — when everybody else is cataloguing its faults and failures — by pointing out a few of the things that the Prime Minister has done right.

Anyone who watches Mulroney closely has to be impressed with his dedication. He works as hard or harder than any of his aides or cabinet ministers. He spends an average of 16 hours a day on the job, has a working knowledge of most areas of government policy and never takes a real, don't-open-a-newspaper holiday.

He can't be doing it for the money, or the perqs. His $132,000 salary is less than half of what he earned previously as president of the Iron Ore Co. of Canada, and the prime ministerial residence at 24 Sussex Drive is no match for the home he once occupied in upper Westmount, along with the rest of Montreal's corporate elite.

Nor is his lifestyle one that most Canadians would envy. He doesn't smoke, doesn't drink and spends most evenings at home with his briefing books. Even his trips abroad aren't as glamorous as they are made out to be. A prime minister's schedule doesn't allow much time for sightseeing or candlelight dinners.

This is not to say Mulroney lives like a monk. He has limousines and jets to whisk him around, aides to do his legwork, a summer home in the Gatineau Hills, and the use of a luxurious condominium in Florida every winter.

Still, no one who is familiar with Mulroney's daily agenda could accuse him of cheating Canadians taxpayers of either his time or his devotion.

Another of the Prime Minister's unsung virtues is his awareness of the concerns of the ordinary Canadians. Unlike some of his predecessors, he has not allowed Ottawa to become a privileged ivory tower. He knows how much it costs to feed a family of six. He knows the unemployment rate of Newfoundland. He knows how the Blue Jays are doing.

And he cares about these things. He listens when his backbenchers report back from their constituencies. He plunges into crowds. He reads the papers, listens to the radio and watches television, and grills his friends and advisers about the mood of the land.

The Prime Minister's humble-boy-from-Baie-Comeau protestations can be irritating at times. But no one can fault him for forgetting who elected him.

Mulroney's sensitivity to criticism is no secret. He unabashedly devours his own reviews, then has staff alert journalists whose stories he considers unfair or inaccurate. What is less widely known is that the Prime Minister's aides also call journalists from time to time to say: "We didn't like what you wrote, but we've got to admit that it's true."

It takes a certain strength of character to admit that a reproof is merited, then to step back and think about it.

One of the more curious misconceptions about the Prime Minister is that he is indecisive. Most of the evidence points the other way.

In the summer of 1985, when it was clear the government had made a serious mistake in trying to de-index old age pensions, it was Mulroney who — over vociferous objections from his caucus — insisted the Tories back down. Last fall, when an all-party parliamentary committee could not make up his mind whether Canada should seek a free trade deal with the United States, Mulroney took charge, committing the government to one of the riskiest initiatives of its mandate. And last spring, when the right-wingers in the Tory caucus were on the verge of revolt over a government decision to extend equality rights to homosexuals, the Prime Minister laid down the law, warning the malcontents to go along with the measure or face his wrath.

There have been times when Mulroney has been slow to cut loose errant cabinet ministers or cut short developing scandals. But these delays have often stemmed from a lack of solid information or a determination to give his ministers the benefit of the doubt — not indecisiveness.

Finally, the Prime Minister is good at taking the sting out of confrontations. He exhibited this talent twice during his recent trip to the East Coast. The first instance was in Fredericton, where he faced a mob of angry rail workers who pelted his car with hard hats. By the time he left, an hour or so later, he was joking with their leader — "the guy with the good lungs" — about buying a membership in the Progressive Conservative party.

Three days later in St. John's, Nfld., he encountered a small band of peace demonstrators on his way into a cabinet meeting. Mulroney stopped for 10 minutes, politely listened to their concerns, explained his government's defence policy, and said he'd be happy to read their brief.

In neither case did he solve the problem. But he did show how far a little courtesy can go in defusing a crisis.

Does all this add up to good government? Obviously not.

Hard work is no substitute for vision. Recognizing a mistake is not the same as correcting it. Being decisive is quite different from being right. And knowing how to calm a crowd is a far cry from knowing how to satisfy it.

But, for once, that is all I intend to say about the shortcomings of the Mulroney administration. Read any public opinion poll and you'll find out how Mulroney has fallen from favour. Go to any cocktail party and you'll find out how he has fallen out of fashion. The government's mid-term reviews are uniformly bad.

At times like this, people like me feel an impish desire to loosen one of the wheels of the bandwagon.

• **1989** Column Writing •
Accord and discord

Jeffrey Simpson

Globe and Mail

(Part of a series)

One of Canada's leading experts on public opinion was conducting a focus group interview in Saskatchewan on other subjects when he decided to ask about the Meech Lake constitutional accord .

Every respondent, in a province whose government had negotiated and ratified the accord, denounced Meech Lake.

The respondents could offer no specific reasons for disliking Meech Lake, or even express reasons for general unease, because not one of them knew what the accord was all about. They articulate only a vague sense that Meech Lake represented something for Quebec, and therefore should be rejected.

From the beginning, Meech Lake has been an issue for the elites. It was prepared in secret, negotiated in private, and ratified with surprising speed by eight of the 10 provinces and the federal Parliament. Now it is stuck for lack of approval by Manitoba and New Brunswick.

The vast majority of Canadians reckon they have better things to do than to ponder Meech Lake. They have their own personal struggles and joys, and the constitution seems remote from both.

And yet Meech Lake is a dagger pointed at the nation's heart, not because of its intricacies, about which the vast majority is and will remain unaware, but because it has the unique capacity in our current climate of insidious and subtle discontent to remind English and French-Canadians of their growing lack of interest in, and mutual irritation with, each other.

As such, Meech Lake bids fair to become a clarion call for demons of the heart. Without knowing or caring much about its component parts, Canadians on both sides of the divide can read into Meech Lake their accumulated grievances.

In Quebec, Meech Lake will be seen as the irreducible minimum for further accommodation; in English Canada, or at least in large parts of it, Meech Lake has already become a maximal and therefore unacceptable demand.

The more Meech Lake is pressed upon English Canadians as something indispensable to Quebec, the greater the resistance is likely to become because there is a fatigue — where there is not hostility — with accommodating a part of Canada that manifests so little interest and conviction in the aspirations of the rest of the country. Conversely, the greater the hostility to Meech Lake, the greater the sense in Quebec that the rest of Canada remains implacably unwilling to accommodate the distinctiveness of Quebec within the federal system. Meech Lake, then, is loaded down with two different sets of emotional baggage whose weight will grow as the deadline for ratification draws nearer (with apologies to Gordon Robertson, who argues June 23, 1990 is not a deadline). That weight grows with each declaration of the dire consequences for rejecting Meech Lake.

Each time a leading politician puts the argument in terms of Meech Lake or disaster, Quebecers are reminded that Meech Lake will be the one and only litmus test of English-Canadian accommodation, and English-Canadians recall that Meech Lake is the latest in a series of what many of them consider endless and profoundly fatiguing demands for accommodation coming from the same place.

Meech Lake might yet be saved, for better or worse, if English Canadians believed its acceptance would truly mean that Quebec would become psychologically a more committed part of Canada, instead of believing that the accord will consecrate constitutionally the already widespread indifference in Quebec to the rest of Canada.

Meech Lake cannot be wished away. It is the receptacle for conflicting national visions and gnawing mutual irritations. These visions and irritations, lying just beneath the surface of public discourse, carry the seeds of abrasive discord.

● **1994** Editorial Writing ●

We should not be in the Persian Gulf war; pacifism isn't passive

Linda Goyette

Edmonton Journal

I 've been thinking all week about one man who stood alone in Canada against war.
He, too, had to listen to people who found polite ways to call him naive or ignorant or cowardly for opposing Canada's descent into the black abyss of warfare. He, too, knew the frustration of a doomed argument.

Yet in September, 1939, he stood in the House of Commons to argue that Canada should declare its neutrality because war breeds only war. He tried to make Canadians understand a critical point: His pacifism was not passive. He did not accommodate the evils of fascism, but argued for the protection of "real liberty" through the rejection of all violence.

"I believe the only way to do it is by an appeal to the moral forces which are still evident among our people, and not by another resort to brute force," he said. He was the only MP to vote against Canada's entry into the Second World War.

I envy J.S. Woodsworth, a half-century later, for the courage and intellect he could summon to the cause of human dignity. There were no rewards for him. He scraped into Parliament in 1940 with a greatly reduced majority and died in the bloody spring of 1942 without any public confirmation of his views. "The conscience of Canada," he was called in the eulogies, but it was a conscience people could ignore when it suited them.

I wish my generation had Woodsworth's strength of spirit. Few of us do. His position requires free thought and self-discipline; we have an abundant supply of the former but little of the latter.

Canada should not be in this war. Yet, according to a poll released recently, the majority of Canadians are for war in the Persian Gulf as long as somebody else does the killing and suffers the casualties.

What timidity, what spinelessness. When the conflagration ends, if it ever does, Canadians want to be able to say: We supported the United Nations; we did as the Americans told us to do; we didn't get any blood on our hands, and we're still a peaceful nation. This is impossible. It's as cowardly as the Mulroney government's assertion that we are locked into the war by the commitments we should never have made. Perhaps it's more cowardly.

War is wrong. Armies that use devastating weapons against children, women and men will never guarantee the collective security of the human race, not even if they fight with the permission of the UN and all the world's governments.

Collective security will come only when the great mass of humanity can harness the elites that condemn young people to war with such cruel regularity. Collective security will only endure when we learn to ignore our worst impulses, when we deny violence its breeding ground.

"Don't be ridiculous," reply the Voices for a Just War. "In the power politics of the real world, unleashed evil must be checked. Saddam Hussein doesn't listen to reason. You want to appease him and ignore his oppression."

No. Again, pacifism is not passive, it is not appeasement.

Mohandas Gandhi taught the world that lesson. Men and women who renounce violence are obliged to be fighters of a different kind, he said. They must combat evil with the untried weapons of love, truth and sane argument.

"I shall not bear ill will towards anyone," wrote Gandhi. "I shall not submit to injustice from anyone." He saw no contradiction in these two statements. There need not be a contradiction.

Those who argue against war do not tolerate the transgressions of the Iraqi dictator. There are punishing alternatives to war that the world could have used against Saddam and did not.

Canada had a peace option and a war option at every wretched step of the parade toward war. It chose the most belligerent alternative.

Like all nations, Canada could have restricted the manufacture and export of war's machinery. It did not.

Canada could have used its position on the UN Security Council to temper the war rhetoric. Canada could have argued — publicly — that the UN take precedence over the United States in the response to Iraq, that the Arab nations of the Middle East be given full opportunity to deal with the regional problem on their own, that international economic sanctions be solidified and given enough time to work.

Canada could have urged the U.S. — publicly — not to increase the number of troops in the Persian Gulf to the degree that war became inevitable. It could have lobbied forcefully in the corridors of the UN against the over-hasty ultimatum of Jan. 15. It could have refused to condone that ultimatum.

Even now, Canada has choices. It could refuse to take part in the direct military action against Iraq. It could explore diplomatic options for a ceasefire. It could demonstrate its true commitment to the UN — and to peace — by financing and operating refugee camps, field hospitals, civilian relief and regional reconstruction with all the money it would have spent on war. Canada could do this — but it will not.

The people who defend this war — always at a comfortable distance from the bombs and blood — use three arguments to support Canada's involvement. First, they say that a military challenge to Iraq could prevent a potential apocalypse in the future because the coalition will destroy Saddam's nuclear, chemical and biological weapons. Second, they argue that this collective war will give the UN a new credibility to protect peace. Finally, they say that the modern technology of computer warfare will spare civilians and limit the fighting to weeks rather than years.

Who are they to suggest that the apocalypse is not already upon us? Who are they to say the UN will have any credibility in the Arab world, or in the Third World, when it has been so manipulated by the U.S., the only superpower?

Who are they to tell the screaming children of the Baghdad bomb shelters that they are not suffering because they are not dead yet?

The Iraqi people, the Arab people, the Muslims of the world — they are not Canada's enemy. Yet the world will wage war against them with a brutal fury that may never touch Saddam and his coterie. Where is the sense of it?

Our troubled planet can't afford another war. The U.S. is spending an estimated $500 million a day in the gulf; the allies are spending between $125 million to $140 million per day; and who knows what Iraq is spending.

Yet the world's richest countries refuse to declare war on poverty, hunger and disease. The UN estimated last year it would cost about $2.5 billion per year to prevent 100 million children from dying from preventable illness and malnutrition in the 1990s. The U.S. spends that amount every five days in this war; $2.5 billion is the approximate cost of five Stealth bombers. Humanity has lost nature's gift of reason.

The people who support the use of military force to accomplish political ends — those who say, "just this little war and then we'll stop" — are the truly naive. They marginalize, and ridicule, the advocates of peace. But it is their arguments, and selective analogies about Neville Chamberlain, that are simplistic, not ours. They ignore the true history of human suffering.

War is wrong. Stand alone.

• 1996 Editorial Writing •

Canada, the unfinished country

Andrew Cohen

Globe and Mail

Dominion Day, 1996 — Across the breadth of the country, the veil of anxiety is lifting. After the titanic clash of last autumn, the forces of division are in repose, if not retreat — if not forever, at least for now. On this anniversary, the threat of disintegration is less pressing than it has been for a half-dozen years. While the silence is not reprieve, we welcome it as an ailing soul welcomes the morning.

If there is a peace over the land today, it isn't because our demons have taken flight. They have not. The inconclusiveness of the referendum was a kind of perverse Canadian compromise. Without the intervention of good sense, Quebec will put the question, again, and Canada will put its case, again. Until then, our future will remain under house arrest.

Uncertainty is our birthright, and we are learning to live with it. The endless conversation over the distribution of rights and powers has become the glue of our nationhood. Its properties are too often narcissism, jealousy and myopia. After 129 years of accommodation, we recognize that it is quintessentially us. It is our fate, this navel-gazing. As fates go, though, it isn't so bad.

Look around. As all great nations have a projet de société— a dream or vision which inspires their peoples to excellence — they also have a *bete noire*, an obsession or weakness frustrates their progress. For the United States, it is race. For Great Britain, it is class. For Italy, it is corruption. For Germany, it is history. For China, it is ideology. For Russia, well, it is all of the above.

For Canada, it is the Constitution, the lightning rod of our discontent. This isn't just a matter of the secessionists in Quebec. True, they are the only ones seeking to dismantle the federation, but they do not represent the only danger. They make tacit common cause with the cries of interest groups, the demands of victims and the carping of the regions, all bubbling happily in our cauldron of complaint.

If youth is wasted on the young, is Canada wasted on Canadians? Perhaps. For all our space and security, for all our bountiful riches, we have become inexorably a nation of sumkeepers and accountants of envy — bearing grudge, keeping score, taking offence, lacking memory. Behold Canada, writ small.

And yet. The principal reason that Canada has endured since 1867 is that its promise has always been bigger than its people. Having built so well, we succeed in spite of our ourselves. Our resentments collapse under the weight of our history. Our envy fades in the face of our geography. Our parochialism recedes amid our diversity.

Compared to the problems of other peoples, the Canadian Malaise is trifling. Ours is the self-indulgence of a country which, by any honest measure, is a solution in search of a problem. To nations riven with war, poverty, crime, terrorism, disease and illiteracy — which is most of humanity — our unrelenting introspection is an extravagance. The wonder is that for all that we quarrel about who gets what, we have still managed to create the most blessed nation on Earth, an assertion probably never more true than today.

Indeed, on this first of July, the land is strong. The country has been through enormous change in the last decade, and the good news is that we are still here. Free trade, constitutional debate, the recession, the restructuring, the referendum. However agonizing, we have survived — a little tougher and a little more wary, but still moderate, generous and tolerant.

We have secured our markets and found our way in a competitive world. We have eliminated the deficit in most provinces, and can think of addressing the accumulated debt. We have restructured industry, reduced the size of government and recast social programs, usually to preserve them. We have continued to absorb immigrants and welcome refugees and fulfill our international obligations, if less broadly, on aid and peacekeeping when it would have been easy to renege on them.

No, this isn't the New Jerusalem. Bad things happen in Canada (although we'd like to think they happen less often). The underclass riots in our streets and the homeless sleep in them. Women fill shelters and the hungry crowd food banks. Children are killing children, and too many of them are killing themselves. The military is in disrepute and the police are under suspicion.

Because our political class forget the past, they fumble the future. Lacking a vision beyond the consommé of cliches served up by untutored speechwriters, they have failed to touch the soul of this unfinished country, as Bruce Hutchison aptly called it. Their challenge is to challenge Canadians to become, at home and abroad, something greater than a chorus of laments. And so, as F. Scott Fitzgerald wrote, we beat on, boats against the current.

When Lucien Bouchard suggested that Canada wasn't a real country, we flew to the ramparts; if we do not know what we are, we know that we are. Yet Mr. Bouchard, who subsequently recanted, touched the ambiguity in our soul. Curiously, the doubt about ourselves is entirely our own. The world knows who we are and bids us to be less hard on ourselves. We should listen more carefully.

Canada is real to the Hungarians, Ugandans and Vietnamese who came here fleeing oppression. It is real to the Bosnians who are separated by our peacekeepers and real to the Dutch who were liberated by our soldiers.

It is real to the Jews of the concentration camps for whom "Canada" meant cornucopia, and real to the children of the Third World who have been fed our grain, taught by our teachers and treated by our doctors.

It is real to the South Africans, Israelis and Czechs, who study our Charter of Rights and Freedoms. It is real to Americans who hail Shania Twain, Peter Jennings and Carol Shields. It is real, oh, so tragically real, to that Somali youth who died at the hands of Canadians with "Canada"on his lips.

Dominion Day, 1996. Canada retreats from the abyss, binds up its wounds and draws its breath. Forever phlegmatic, forever unsentimental, it remains the country that dares not speak its name. For Canadians, we suspect, remaining whole in a fragmenting world is expression enough.

Duncan Macpherson

Toronto Star

Duncan Macpherson claimed his sixth NNA for this cartoon illustrating the tenuous political situation after the 1972 election left Pierre Trudeau's Liberals with a shaky minority government. Macpherson's legendary career at the *Star* began in 1958.

Duncan Macpherson est venu chercher son sixième prix du CCJ pour cette caricature illustrant la situation politique tendue après les élections de 1972 qui avaient donné aux Libéraux de Pierre E. Trudeau un gouvernement minoritaire. Il avait débuté sa carrière au *Star* en 1958.

CHAPTER 3

Journalism as Literature

Many of these items in this chapter are selected from the Features category — continuous since the NNAs began in 1949 — but two of these selections actually won for Spot News Reporting and one for Enterprise Reporting.

By Nick Russell

THERE ARE NO LITERATURE POLICE. NOBODY HAS DRAWN A LINE IN THE SAND, ON THE ONE SIDE Journalism and on the other Literature. The best that can be said is that much journalism is not literature, but some is; much literature is not journalism, but some is. Many newspaper stories, while not being sustained pieces conceived by the writers as literary works, nonetheless use literary techniques from place to place. Most of the works in the current chapter fit this category.

Someone once said journalism is literature in a hurry, history on the run. Much journalism is committed on deadline, with little time to refine the language or polish the way the story is told, which we would expect of literature. Yet journalism often involves telling stories, developing a narrative with flow and structure beyond what is imposed by the content. It may not be Margaret Atwood, but it can still be a darn good read. The journalist has to decide what is suitable to the story she is telling, what she is capable of, and whether she has the time and desk support for something more polished or sustained. Literary journalism goes beyond the obvious, the dry recital of facts: It is value-added, data told in an enjoyable way.

To make such a distinction is not to be critical of the average news writer: Readers seek facts on which they can act, information to live full and rich lives. The wordsmith working in the fiery furnace of daily journalism cannot spend hours shaping and reshaping his work. Hence many reporters rely heavily on formulas, bolting together the various basic elements like building a Lego house.

Sometimes, however, the writer has the luxury of a little more time, perhaps writing a feature that can wait for Saturday's paper. Clearly not all journalists are able — or want — to write in a literary way. The reporter who simply has a tin ear and cannot "hear" the cadence and rhythm of his writing, will not write with much style or flair, though he may still report accurately and effectively.

Likewise, the reporter who has read good writing critically, with an ear tuned to how literature works, is more likely to be able to use some of these techniques himself when he needs them. And there's one more vital element: The intelligent and sensitive editor. Without the support of editors who provide the time and the creative editing, the writer's aspirations may die before the writing even starts. The works in this collection represent a collaboration between inspired writers and sympathetic editors.

I'm not using "literary journalism" here in the sense of a genre of writing. (Some use it to describe the writings of people as varied as Daniel Dafoe and Tom Wolfe —a synonym for "new journalism." For discussion, see Norman Sims' book *Literary Journalism*.) Rather, I use it to describe creative literary techniques employed by journalistic writers. The simplest news story may benefit from the use of repetition or parallel sentence structure somewhere, but that's a far cry from a George Plimpton or Tom McPhee. Such devices as alliteration, metaphor, repetition and parallelism may be seen as the realm of poets: But why not the journalist, too?

Let's examine a few such techniques:

Dialogue: Reporters quote sources constantly. But they rarely quote the to-and-fro of a discussion, more usually relying on the words of a public speaker or the answers of an interviewee. Yet genuine dialogue adds great depth and interplay to a story. Dick Beddoes, in his amusing piece about the baseball player's wife (page 245), describes the banter between her and reporters at a news conference:

"The players need their wives badly, she said. "Pitchers can't sleep a wink after a game. Do you know what Don does after a game?"

"No. What?"

"He replays the whole nine innings ..."

This allows Beddoes to introduce a new anecdote. Less stylish writers would have simply used reported speech ("She added that many players were tense after a game and would replay the whole nine innings.")

Euphony: Some words have a pleasing sound. Others sound harsh and provoke negative feelings. Poets and creative writers recognize that even individual letters of the alphabet have dark or bright overtones: The long 'e' and 'o' sounds of Ebenezer Scrooge and the short 'i' of The Grinch sound evil and are deliberately selected.

Foreshadowing: The inverted pyramid news format starts with the ending, so hinting at the outcome or some future development doesn't work . But it may well work in more discursive, featurish pieces. Nigel Gibson's wonderful study of motorcycle accidents (page 136), for instance, starts (second paragraph) with a prediction:

"When that boy is good, he'll be very good," the doctor who delivered him couldn't help remarking. "But when he's bad, he'll be twice as bad and twice as strong."

And of course the story hinges on the boy being "bad."

Similarly, when Tim Padmore and Chris Gainor set out to tell Terry Fox's story (page 145), they recognized that readers knew how the story must end. Nonetheless, they created a sense of tension and suspense, starting with another very telling quote from Fox's basketball coach:

"Just making the team was a tremendous feat. I've never seen a kid with more desire."

Thus the coach hints at Fox's astonishing motivation and determination, in the face of overwhelming odds, and even failure.

Irony: This is a dangerous weapon, best omitted from mainstream journalism. Genuine irony involves a value-judgment, with the writer expressing approval in such a way as to clearly condemn. It's also risky, of course, because readers cannot hear a tone of voice or see a facial expression which would hint that the writer actually means the opposite of what she's saying.

Metaphor: A metaphor involves substituting one thing for another, so would seem to be the very opposite of journalism. A sustained example is Nigel Gibson's description of motorcycles, where he quotes an Indian legend of killer horses, then, after the opening anecdote (12 paragraphs describing Barry Catel's fate), he moves from the specific to the general with:

Once again, in sheds and basements across Quebec, the two-wheeled chrome monsters are stirring from their winter sleep. Their canvas shrouds off, their bodies stripped down, greased and gleaming they lie in wait for spring: Waiting for the right moment to burst into life and hit the open road with their young masters.

At a much simpler level, Ray Guy (page 119) describes the train he is boarding as "panting to be off," Brenda Zosky (page 139) mentions "mountains of evidence" at an inquest, and Dick Beddoes says of his stripper, "Two dimples made small whirlpools in her cheeks."

Pace: Writers can vary the pace of a story by manipulating sentence length, choice of words (ponderous polysyllables will slow down a story), use of transitions, and other techniques.

Parallel structure: Patterned repetition gives structure and punch. Journalists use it often. The *Vancouver Sun*'s wonderful profile of Clifford Olson (page 40) begins:

He was a braggart and a bully, a liar and a thief.
Any other variation of that would be significantly less effective.

Punctuation: Every writer needs to know some basic rules. But journalism has developed its own conventions, rarely, for instance, using semi-colons, colons, dashes, ellipses or parentheses. Yet these are sometimes useful tools. Brian Stewart, for one, makes bold and effective use of many of these (page 127).

Repetition: Stewart uses the phrase "presumed innocent" with clanging effect at least four times in his study of a man who has clearly been presumed guilty by the legal system. Stewart also uses a single word with neat effect:

In short, Simpson is in jail because he is a poor man.

Then he begins a series of paragraphs with "Because ..." Within one of these, he again uses repetitive structure:

Because Simpson is in jail, he cannot earn enough money for adequate legal counsel, but instead must rely on a heavily overburdened legal aid system ...; nor can he properly instruct counsel; nor can he look after his family; nor can he buy proper clothes for his trial. (Note, too, the use of semi-colons.)

Pierre Foglia shows a wonderful sensitivity to this technique in his column *Virus* (page 325) in the chapter titled *Voix*. The first, long, paragraph begins, "C'était ..., " followed by the staccato "C'était tout le contraire." And he continues with another, long paragraph beginning "C'était ..."

And Claire Dutrisac (in her cool description of heart surgery, page 125) uses the thumping rhythm of the heart-beat to build to the climatic moment where the heart is jump-started: Everyone, she says, holds their breath for a moment, as if their own hearts have stopped in sympathy:

Un instant qui paraît une éternité, un instant qui sépare la vie, la vraie vie de la mort... Battra ... ne battra pas ... battra ... IL BAT!

Rhythm denotes some recurring pattern of emphasis. It is obvious in classical poetry but much rarer and less useful in journalistic prose. Nonetheless, occasional patches of rhythm may help. Again, examine, "He was a braggart and a bully, a liar and a thief." The two parallel phrases have a matching cadence which is no accident. Just see how the sentence deflates if written as "He was a boastful liar, a thief and a bully." Gibson's motorcycle piece has rhythm, and the final couple of paragraphs have a rich, poetic cadence.

Sentence length: Long sentences will tend to slow a story down, and short ones will speed it up. Too many of either will be boring. So, a variety of lengths is usually best, until the writer needs to change gears or create a specific atmosphere, such as the excitement of a chase. Pierre Foglia, for instance, is a master of this, using long, thoughtful paragraphs that build to a coup de grâce of just four or five words.

Andy MacFarlane begins his *Reporter's Longest Walk* (page 193) with a nine-word sentence, and the tension grows as his next 17 sentences average 14 words each. In the process, there are some sentences of 26 or 27 words, but others of just two. The *Vancouver Sun* piece about Clifford Olson uses a similar pace: The lead (the first five paragraphs) is composed of six sentences, averaging just 10 words. And even the words themselves are dramatically short. Greg Weston and Jack Aubry also use sentence length with great effect as they reconstruct the murderous rampage of Marc Lepine (page 169).

Similes: These often help the reader to understand or visualize complex or abstract ideas. Some writers use them for emphasis: Ian Brown, writing about life in a local high school (page 150), notes how intimidating it is to be summoned to the school office by a loudspeaker in the classroom:

It's like being yanked down to purgatory by some electronic monster.

Heather Mallick says attending a school reunion "is like volunteering for surgery without anesthetic" (page 178).

Tenses: Logic suggests that much reporting is about what has happened, and therefore the past tense will dominate. However, journalists often use the present tense to add drama to their story, and it's particularly effective in features. Good writers select that first verb with particular care, because it's probably the most important single word in the entire piece. Look at these samples:

He hoists the rifle to his shoulder, presses his right cheek to the hardwood stock and slowly squeezes the trigger ... (Weston and Aubry on Marc Lepine)

Puffs of smoke rise from the surgical opening in the head of a patient ... (Marilyn Dunlop witnessing brain surgery)

Even the colourless verb "to be" can draw the reader into the action:

It is 6 a.m. Kristine Taylor reaches out of bed and hits the radio; she needs concentrated AM funk to get moving ... (Ian Brown on high schools.)

Tone of voice: A story, or part of a story, can be grim or happy, or impart to the reader some other emotion. But while the tale itself will influence this, the writer can deliberately manipulate this by using a combination of the techniques described here.

For contrast, look at the opening of Pierre Berton's *The story behind those 'Let Me Be Your Friend' ads* (page 279) which is dryly dispassionate: He chooses a clean summary of events, to establish his fairness and neutrality, so that when his anger eventual spills over, it is all the more powerful. Similarly, Jean Pelletier (page 212) and Claire Dutrisac both brilliantly understate the entire piece, letting their exciting tales tell themselves, without any verbal pyrotechnics.

Transitions are — largely — the little words that sweep the reader from one thought to the next: "But ... And ... Nonetheless ..." Journalists use them constantly. But transitional phrases and thoughts are useful, too. (See Dick Beddoes' use of dialogue, described above.)

Viewpoint: Viewpoint is not the same as point-of-view. The writer's opinion (point-of-view) is generally irrelevant in news and features. But every writer constructs every story from a particular viewpoint: In news, the writer is usually the neutral observer, so the viewpoint is outside the story, looking in. But sometimes the story may involve the writer, so he or she writes as a participant. Catherine Dunphy writes as one of "the Carmelita Team" who looked after a dying cancer victim (page 164), but mostly uses "we" and rarely intrudes her own feelings beyond admitting her initial doubts and fears. Laurie McKechnie writes very personally about his battle with alcoholism without attempting to universalize the piece. And when Val Sears summarizes his love-hate relationship with John Diefenbaker (page 143), part of the appeal of his feature is his outspoken criticism, summarized in the middle:

I didn't like him, if like is not too watery a word for such a man. I thought he was a bully and that he twisted the truth. But I rejoiced in him ...

Vocabulary: Obviously journalists must always strive for the "right" word. But there's much more to it: The careful writer must gauge the intellectual level of her readers or listeners, which may vary not only from newsroom to newsroom (the *National Inquirer* versus the *Peterborough Examiner*), but within the paper (Editorial Page versus other pages?) and even between one article and another. Vocabulary may also be selected for specific effect, and of course loaded words can be used to tweak the readers' emotions. For instance, Josh Freed sets a grim scene for his piece about Moonies (page 141) with the first sentence:

The seemingly endless gravel road halted abruptly at a high barbed-wire fence and a wooden sentry post.

The phrase "seemingly endless" hints at mystery and fear, "halted" and "sentry post" have militaristic overtones, while even "abruptly" is dramatic and unsettling. He could have written, "The long road to the Moonies Ranch led to a gate ..." with far less effect.

These are just a few of the techniques occasionally employed in good journalism. In addition, a cluster of literary "rules" impact news writers. The best writers are intimately familiar with the rules of writing, but are not imprisoned by them. For instance, the *Vancouver Sun* team, writing about Clifford Olson, effectively break the rules about "and":

Then Olson became older, the crimes became uglier and sexual. There were rapes, indecent assaults, and buggery. The victims were of both sexes and they were as young as seven years old.

And finally, the murders.

The first sentence is made grimmer by the deliberate omission of "and." Yet the second paragraph begins with "And," which the textbooks tell us we are not supposed to do.

Val Sears says everyone will remember Diefenbaker, "And have a story about him." Those stories may be contradictory, he adds, "Still, that's the way Dief will be remembered. In stories." This two-word sentence has no verb, which helps to summarize and punctuate the point Sears is making. So there goes another rule: Every sentence must have a verb.

Bill McGuire breaks that rule and then some, with dramatic effect. He begins his memoir about catching polio as a youth (page 148) with two longish paragraphs of description. After a preliminary, dry establishing shot, he writes 10 staccato sentences averaging 10 words each; several of these have verbs with no subjects and even no verbs or subjects. The "I" is clearly implied, but the narrative is far more dramatic for their omission.

More complex is the structure itself: The Who, What, When, Where, Why of daily reporting are necessary components, but good writers will add a thread of narrative to a story. Many features, for instance, instead of being in "inverted pyramid" form, will be circular, with a beginning, a middle, and an ending circling back to where they began. Nigel Gibson, for instance, ends by returning to his early the image of the demonic monsters. Others simply let the chronology of the events carry the story along: Lepine's life, or Ray Guy's railway saga.

And sometimes the writer is more subtle; G.E. Mortimore seems to be writing about a traveling clinic (page 118), and Stewart seems to be writing about Alfred Simpson, but these are vehicles for much more complex studies of tuberculosis and of justice.

All of this suggests that the good journalist does far more than reach for the nearest cliché, clicking together the Lego blocks of language. (Subject, Verb, Object. Quote quote quote, he said.) He writes for the eye and the ear (in those rare moments when he has time to think and to polish). To achieve that, he reads voraciously, not to imitate but to enjoy, and to expand his own possibilities.

Yet having said all this, we must note that the National Newspaper Awards has never had a section labeled "Literary Journalism." This category is titled "Features," and some pieces use literary devices from time to time, while others use little or none. Their claim to a place here is that they display clear, bright writing, often are longer pieces, and are usually the result of significant research, rather than the more hurried work of, say, the Spot News category. There is some outstanding writing here, writing that deserves to be honoured not just as fine journalism, but as fine Canadian Literature.

• 1950 Feature Writing •

Goodbye, demon rye

Laurie M. McKechnie

Toronto Telegram

(Part of a series)

It was a giant, economy-size hangover — the granddaddy of all that 20 years of bibing and guzzling had produced.

It was a "doozer" but it was distinguished by more than its size. It had been deliberately induced as a therapeutic measure. And it was achieved with only a two-ounce libation of a moderately good brand of rye.

With that hooker and its disproportionately devastating reaction, I embarked upon what, after several weeks of expanding well-being, gives every promise of being the happiest, most productive, most satisfying period of my life.

I am still an "alcoholic" in the sense that the word describes an illness or an allergy for which there is no known "cure." Nothing now known to medical science can so amend my metabolism — my body chemistry — that I can become again a "social drinker."

Never can I safely take "just one."

But I am no longer an addict. I'm no longer a drunk. Alcohol is no longer of the slightest importance to me except as a hospitable cup to be offered a guest in my house. I can enjoy many uproarious memories involving a party, a bar or, at least, a drink. But I know that, for me, those beautifully rosy pasts could never have developed into a happy present.

Maybe I'm no longer "the life of the party." But at least I can remember next day all that happened the night before.

Perhaps I'm a little bit virtuous — maybe even disgustingly triumphant right now. But mostly I'm just plain happy …

I haven't found a new world. But I like the old one a whole lot better. There is a new kind of exhilaration that sharpens the senses into appreciation of small things. And the calendar of my daily life is no longer darkened by ominous figures of deep remorse and black despond, shadowy anxieties and gloomy forebodings spawned by that other traitorous kind of exhilaration.

This new sense of wellbeing dates from that last huge hangover I mentioned. It results from a complete independence of alcohol. True, that independence is maintained and continued to some extent by fear of the awful consequences of even a two-ounce drink. But fear daily becomes less and less important as a deterrent while the physical and psychic self return to normal health which requires no deceptive boost from the imposter, alcohol.

There is not the slightest doubt in my mind that this initial period of abstention, supported by a little white pill daily, will grow into total abstinence for the remainder of a lifetime. Some time hence the "crutch" which supports my resolve may be tossed aside, but it matters little whether it is months or years because the daily ingestion of antabuse is no more bother than swallowing an aspirin tablet.

My own experience, therefore, gives me every reason to believe that the age-long hope for a reasonably sure cure for chronic alcoholism has been realized. Antabuse, the accidental discovery of a Danish researcher, may not be a miracle drug; it may not be what the medical profession regards as a "specific"; but it is certainly an adjunct with which a little determination can win permanent sobriety.

Antabuse is the Danish trade name for a drug with the tongue-defying title of tetraethylthiuarum disulphide. Mixed with alcohol in the human system it produces a violent reaction comparable to some results when gasoline tangles with alcohol on the highway.

It is definitely not a nostrum nor is it something to be taken casually like a vitamin pill by someone who has a "morning after" feeling that they'd like to quit drinking. It is, most certainly, not something that a well-meaning wife can surreptitiously introduce into the breakfast coffee of her errant spouse.

A tablet or two of antabuse taken by one whose system has not been thoroughly cleansed of alcohol can have disastrous, even fatal, consequences. It can be obtained, legally, only on prescription and it should be administered, in the first instance at least, only on the advice and guidance of a physician who has had experience with its effects.

Oh! Those effects! How vividly they remain in my memory. I was a patient in Shadow Brook Health Foundation Hospital, formerly the posh country home, a few miles north of Toronto, of a Toronto stock broker. The circumstances which led up to my admission and the treatment which I followed, I shall deal with in subsequent instalments of this story.

I propose now to jump ahead to the day of that big hangover; about "T-Day" or the day of my "TEST." I had been warned the night before that I would get nothing for breakfast more than a cup of clear tea. (And by that time I had developed a terrific appetite.) I had had a thorough medical check-up.

In pyjamas and dressing gown I went from my own room to the bedroom that was to be the scene of my ordeal. Added to the sumptuous furnishings of the room were a cylinder of oxygen with its appended tubes and mask and a white enameled stand from which I knew there could be suspended the apparatus for intravenous feeding. Ominous portents!

The doctor and the nurse were there to receive me, she to pop a thermometer into my mouth and he to strap the tourniquet on my arm so he could read my blood pressure. The gadget containing the indicator was in a metal case and he seemed to enjoy plumping its icy weight on my bare chest.

With these little attentions completed, the pert little number in white appeared with a tray. I recognized a brand of rye to which I had been rather attached.

"How about a drink?" a staff doctor invited heartily.

To be absolutely truthful, I didn't really want it. The jitters were two weeks gone. I had no real need of a drink and I was a little frightened about what I had heard from others would happen. But I knew what was expected of me. I poured a good two ounces, filled it up with water (I always drank water with my whisky. Ginger ale or soda were bad for the stomach, I always thought). The first taste brought that familiar shudder. But the next was pleasant enough. And as I sipped I began to panic. "My God," I thought, "nothing's different. This antabuse stuff hasn't worked … My wife will be furious … The boss will fire me when I go back at it again."

The panic mounted. Somehow I didn't want to finish the drink. My heart was thundering in my ears. I was gasping for air. An iron band seemed to be tightening around my chest.

The nurse giggled. She held up a mirror.

Good Lord. Was that me? My eyes were staring out of the reddest face I had ever seen. I looked down. My chest glowed as if I had fallen asleep in the sun. My head pounded.

"Walk about a bit. You'll feel better," the doctor suggested — deadpan.

I edged off the bed, reeled a few paces, fell flat and crawled back to the refuge of the pillow. There was no pain I could put my finger on. I just felt awful. I was nauseated but I couldn't throw up, not even when that nauseating doctor (with firm fingers on my pulse) suggested that I might enjoy "a nice slice of fat pork or a Laura Secord."

I don't know whether they used the oxygen mask. I seem to remember that I slipped off into a terrible dream, then roused again several times. I know they didn't use the "intravenous."

It had been mid-morning when I took the drink. At some point about noon, I dropped off to sleep completely. It was about four hours later that I awoke — with a splitting headache. My first stirring brought that white form in the chair to her feet.

The cup of clear tea she brought was pure nectar. And it wasn't long before that ache that pierced from the forehead to the nape of the neck began to recede.

That evening I went down to dinner. And enjoyed it … but tomato juice was the only cocktail I needed.

• **1951** Feature Writing •

Private Tony Edmond grows up

Bill Boss

Canadian Press

TOKYO — It was the end of a campaign, a bitter heartbreaking defeat …
It has been a desperate rearguard action, a one-man show, all the way back from a beleaguered Korean mountain-top north of Kapyong.

It had been waged in a lonely slit trench in the heat of battle, in the regimental aid post, in the field surgical hospital to which he had been evacuated by helicopter, through long weeks in the convalescent hospital in Kure, Japan, and here in Tokyo where in an army medical centre he awaited the plane home to Canada.

For he didn't want to go.

He didn't want to go. He was determined to stay, to get well again, to go back and fight as he had never fought before.

But there he was, airborne. Over suburban Haneda airport the silver CPA North Star sparkled in the late afternoon sun and wheeled sharply eastward, scattering his hopes in its slipstream. Like a glassblower in the forge of that setting orb, the aircraft drew finer and ever finer the tie between him and his battalion until, somewhere over the Pacific, it imperceptibly gave. And a new life, for a different man, drew ever closer ahead.

He was 24, had been around before. He'd sailed in ships, had known the adventurous tang of merchant navy life. He'd been strong, too, had gloried in hard work, in exercising the rich pile of muscle down his back and chest and the great sinews of his arms.

But that was all "before." Wrap into one packet all the things he'd done, the places seen, the persons known in the six months ago since he'd come away a boy.

It was a man who was going home.

He'd undergone the fighting soldier's change, the incommunicable experience that only the man who has faced it understands.

In the agony of the climb, winded, dead tired and weary from the 75-pound load on his back, he'd forced himself to "get there." He never grumbled or complained. Once on the top he'd nerved himself to the suspense of waiting. In the heat of battle he'd steeled himself to "take it." At grips with the enemy he'd marvelled in the very combat how body and soul slough all fatigue and thrill at his command of every reflex and reaction, how automatically it went, how every new and desperate peril summoned up new resources from within his being to sustain him.

He'd lived with death and walked beside himself. He'd come up bloody, mangled, murmuring, "Thanks, God, I can take it." The depths and heights hold no new terrors for the man who's found himself.

His crucible was the moment when a Chinese grenade came into the trench from which he, as leader, was directing his section's battle. It shredded his arm. It gouged his bowels. It cost him blood and pain.

Improvising his tunic into a bandage, he carried on the battle.

He couldn't shoot. But still he had grenades.

He locked them between his knees, the lever firm against his flesh lest they explode inside the trench when he drew the pin with his good left hand.

It was a slow, painful method for the pace set by the oncoming Chinese masses. He doesn't know how many he threw, just that he kept them going over until one Chinese, closer than the rest, poked a carbine into the trench and fired at point-blank range. His guts again.

That did it. He crumpled over and for a while his position was ignored.

But still that will to live drove on. "I can't die now," he thought. "I won't die."

Thinking back over it later, he said:

"After all that happened I just couldn't, wouldn't give in.

"It was like when we were climbing the hills. I always just said to myself that I just had to get there. I had to now."

As the battle allowed he crawled out of his trench, dragged himself slowly with one hand, unable to make much use of his legs because of the torture to his stomach, and inch by inch got down a few feet below the mountain crest. Hanging grimly onto brush and grass and thorn — whatever came first within his grasp — he followed the line of the ridge over to his platoon commander's dugout, briefed him on the situation forward and then allowed his wounds to be dressed.

He couldn't be evacuated that night.

That was the night during which finally the Chinese overran the Canadian position and for three hours United Nations artillery poured concentration after concentration down upon it in murderous lacings which ultimately drove them back.

Morning was well advanced before stretcher-bearers were able to get him down to the regimental aid post, 2,000 feet below and 1$\frac{1}{2}$ miles away. A helicopter got him back to the field surgical hospital.

Already his rearguard action was under way. He was determined to return to the unit. That something inside him that had changed told him it was where he belonged — a man with men, whose common language ran deeper than the words they used or the thoughts they uttered. There are things the soldier never talks about.

It was in Kure that they told him his days of soldiering were over — he had lost a kidney, he would have to take it easy for a long while, he would have to go home and find some job not too demanding on his mutilated body and his sapped strength.

He wouldn't believe it, that what he now most wanted — to be back with "the boys" — had eluded his grasp, that now that his whole approach to soldiering had changed, the whole avenue had been placed "out of bounds." He was being shorn of part of himself.

He had himself paraded before the medical officer. He wanted a reboard, a chance to stay. It was no go. The answer was final: "Home for you."

In Tokyo he tried again. Another parade. The same request. The same answer. It was hell when he met some of the old gang on their Tokyo leave. Their accounts of events since his departure, their gossip, the flavour of the old comradeship stirred up again an almost-laid-to-rest nostalgia.

He tried again, and still no go.

And so he left.

His name? It hardly matters.

What happened to deepen the look in his eye, to sober the note of his voice, and endow his personality with the stamp of the man who's really found himself through the reality of the battlefield, goes on daily over here.

He's just one of the many who, according to their sensitivity, to their receptivity, "grow up" overnight in war.

Nothing happens in the army that won't, in another way, perhaps, happen to a man on Civvie Street — it just speeds up the process.

His name? Pte. Tony Edmond. He may be sitting alongside you in a Toronto streetcar, or at the opposite table in a Glace Bay, N.S., restaurant. They're the places he calls "home."

• **1955** Feature Writing •

Gigantic U.S. bombers straddle entire globe

Frank Lowe

Montreal Star

WITH THE U.S. STRATEGIC AIR COMMAND — In the turbulent days of the 18th century, it was the all-powerful Royal Navy which enforced an uneasy peace on most of the world. Today, 200 years later, the United States Strategic Air Command, a force made up of elite fliers, incredible aircraft capable of carrying nuclear bombs and bases scattered throughout the Western world, has taken over this role.

Only today things are a little different. A globe, the only one of its kind in the world, stands in SAC Headquarters at Omaha, Neb., to highlight that point.

The globe, waist-high, is a solid white ball. On it are depicted no continents, no oceans, no place names. Instead, there are blue stars and blue circles. Connecting the stars and circles are red lines.

The significance: The stars are SAC bases where, 24 hours a day, every day in the year, aircraft capable of carrying nuclear bombs stand ready to roll at a moment's notice. The circles are predetermined Russian targets, already picked out on a master plan, which would be annihilated if Russia ever made a threatening move.

The red lines are the routes SAC bombers — bombers which can fly more than 45,000 feet up in the weird, deep blue world of the stratosphere and at speeds close to those of sound — would take.

For a Canadian, this somewhat gaudy globe is an eye-catcher. It shows clearly that the majority of the stars and the majority of the circles face each other across a white expanse which, while not named, is obviously Canada. Across this expanse, like strange red rivers flowing against nature upwards over the top of the world, are the three main routes SAC bombers would follow in order to knock Russia out of any war it might instigate.

It could almost be said, because of this, that SAC is also a Canadian force. Its bombers would be our main protection against aggression across the Pole.

Canada's main defence effort, in fact, is geared to mesh with SAC activities. Our three radar lines would flash the word if aggression took shape from the north. Our fighter aircraft would fling themselves high into northern skies to try and knock down these invaders — all so SAC bombers could begin to roll and unleash on Russia the horrors of nuclear massive retaliation.

Sir Winston Churchill, a few years ago, credited the ability of SAC to do just this with postponing World War III. SAC officers, a dedicated group of men who for 10 years have lived with the terrible concept of nuclear warfare, privately consider their force as the only military outfit in history "to win a war which was never fought."

But while the presence of SAC has probably been a deterrent to armed aggression, its work is far from finished. Russia also has its "SAC," and the U.S. force is engaged in a strenuous race to make sure it always stays a jump ahead.

This is how SAC works, as I saw it during a tour in Omaha; Westover, Mass.; Loring, Me., and Lockbourne, Oh., and by riding in its high-flying bombers as they "bombed" Montreal and effortlessly streaked over more than half the length of a continent in a matter of hours:

SAC is made up of three air forces — the 8th Air Force in the eastern United States (a new base is going up at Plattsburg), the 2nd Air Force in central United States and the 15th on the west coast. In this force in the near future will be 54 wings, each wing comprising anything from 75 fighters to 45 bombers. Its manpower is estimated as close to 200,000. Already it has cost the U.S. taxpayer $8,500,000,000.

In addition to the three air forces, SAC also has the 3rd Air Division at Guam, the 2nd Air Division in England and the 5th in North Africa. It is an open secret that in addition to these bases, SAC has others it can use.

SAC's main armament, the planes which keep the peace the way Britain's sail-driven battleships did two centuries ago, is a double-barrelled affair. First are the B-36s, powered by six reciprocating and four jet engines. They can fly from the United States, Guam, Britain or North Africa to Russia with a thermo-nuclear weapon and return. There are several hundred of these mammoth aerial dreadnoughts.

Then there are the B-47s. These are powered by six jet engines and fly at more than 600 miles an hour, or better than 50 per cent faster than the B-36s. But they can get to Russia and back, too, with their dreadful burdens because they can be refuelled in mid-air. There are about a thousand of these fleet and deadly monsters on duty today.

Of course, bombers can't operate alone, nor can fighters. Each SAC air force, and division, is completely self-sufficient. Each one can pick up on a moment's notice to travel any place in the world — and be capable of performing its combat job as soon as it touches down at its new field or base.

Units of SAC practice this business of setting up new homes constantly. From Loring a wing will move to Britain, then to North Africa, then to Thule and way across the world to Guam. And when it moves, and when it arrives, it doesn't need any help.

First the bombers leave. As they move out to the runways, the planes pause over sealed "mobility bins." The hoists which are built to lift bombs into the bay of the plane come down and pick up the bins. In these boxes, by direct order of the commanding officer never opened no matter what the local emergency, are sufficient spare parts to keep that plane operating for 30 days.

(SAC officers are firmly convinced that if World War III does break out despite their best efforts, it can't possibly last more than two weeks because of the terrible destructive power which can be unleashed.)

Next the huge flying tankers, carrying fuel for the thirsty jet bombers, take off. Into C-124

Globemasters are loaded complete hospitals, key personnel, security police, heavy tools needed for repairs. Each SAC unit is self-sustaining.

After a decade of practice — SAC will be 10 years old next March — all this is completely automatic. No special orders are needed. Those are worked out and standardized by this time. The commanding officer says "go," and even if the unit commander is on leave, or sick, the entire complex machinery begins to function.

Should war break out tomorrow, the same would be true. A master plan is already in being. One word sent over the complex communication network would set the bombers rolling. There would be no additional paper work, no last-minute decisions to make, no red tape.

Each individual aircraft crew, so detailed is this plan, already knows what its individual target would be in the event of war. The crew has, time without number, studied mock-ups and photos of this target, until the enemy site is more familiar than a hometown. And, again times without number, this crew has made simulated bombing runs on cities in Canada and the United States which resemble, in one way or another, the target which would be its wartime objective.

Over the years, by watching each practice mission, SAC planners have come to know what percentage of aircraft will fail to get off the ground because of various troubles. They know the percentage which "abort," or fail to reach a designated target, because of failure in one or more of the complex electrical gadgets which guide these bombers in the pathless wastes of the stratosphere.

The plan even has a percentage set aside for "attrition" — the planes which will be intercepted and shot down before the target is reached. All these tangibles and intangibles — the routes, weather, mechanical failures, enemy awareness — have been calculated and allowed for.

And despite these factors, SAC staff officers still insist that should Russia ever gamble on all-out war, every one of her major production centres, her war-making potentials, would be "howling wastes" within a matter of hours.

While all this sounds comforting to a resident of the Western world, it is not making SAC officers complacent. Well aware that the Russian "SAC" is forever growing and groping for new methods of attack, the U.S. SAC on the eve of its first 10 years of existence is constantly looking to the day when it will be an even better deterrent against aggression.

SAC is already "a weapon of decision." Now the problem is to find out how many minutes, or even hours, can be trimmed off the time needed to bring this weapon smashing down on an aggressor. Naturally, the first step is to build faster and yet faster aircraft capable of carrying the bomb load and fuel necessary to allow a plane to wing from one continent to another and then return. With the B-52, an eight-jet bomber "as fast as any fighter," expected to be in operation by next year, this problem is well in hand.

But even the B-52, or any advance on that plane, is not the ultimate answer if world tensions last indefinitely. The "ultimate answer," if the Russians keep intent on world domination, is to have SAC bases lined with thermo-nuclear guided missiles, permanently in place and each one "zeroed in" on a prime Russian target. Then, should war come, a press of a single button would send these deadly, unmanned tubes of destruction hurtling through the skies and around the world at incredible speeds to wipe out Russia's war-making potential.

That is the lethal SAC of the future. But it must be admitted that the SAC of the present is not exactly a harmless toy.

• **1958** Feature Writing •

Science in station wagon
fights disease, squalour

G.E. Mortimore

Victoria Colonist

Two muddy station wagons bumped and squelched their way across the grasslands of the Chilcotin plateau and halted near a small house with imitation-brick siding.

If an observer had wiped the grime off each car, he would have exposed the gold-lettered legend: "Canada, Department of National Health and Welfare, Indian Health Services."

The coating of dirt was evidence of the miles that Jack Bogart, X-ray technician, and Mrs. Frances Owens, Indian health nurse, had traveled to reach scattered villages.

The house with the imitation-brick siding was that of John William Baptiste, chief councillor of the Toosey band in Williams Lake agency, and his wife Yellicy. The curious name of the latter was a corruption of "Elsie" which, through usage, had gained a place in the official register.

The chief had agreed to lend his home for the clinic. Jack Bogart unloaded the pieces of his portable X-ray unit from the back of his station wagon, and assembled the unit in the bare room that served as the Baptistes' combined kitchen and living room.

Meanwhile, Mrs. Owens was in a small adjoining room, setting up her documents, vaccine and hypodermic needles, each needle in its own sterile tin where she had labouriously packed it the night before.

There was no electric light here. Jack and a young Indian in a grey mackinaw heaved a portable power plant from the car, hooked it up, and started the engine. The putt-putt of the generator was the signal to the village that the clinic was ready to accept customers.

Most of Toosey's 100-odd persons lived on the other side of the creek, in slanting log cabins with weeds sprouting thickly from the sod roofs, or in boxlike new frame houses with wash-tubs and saddles hanging on the walls. At least one house was under construction.

Now the people made their way across the plank bridge to the chief's house, cowboys with Stetsons and bandanas, mothers in loose-fitting cotton dresses carrying babies in narrow baskets, toddlers with grubby faces and solemn brown eyes, wrinkled old men, stout old women with scarves around their hair and legs encased in several pairs of coarse grubby stockings.

They lined up placidly. A faint smell of earth, horse and sweat pervaded the house. As a volunteer clerk, I helped check off the names on the list of band members and type X-ray cards for each: Names like Charleyboy and Eagle Lake Johnny; English or French descriptive names like Grambush (Grande Bouche — Big Mouth) betraying the humourous contempt with which the grandparents and great-grandparents of these Indians had been regarded by traders and homesteaders.

Useful only as fur-hunters, mistresses and primitive souls to be salvaged, those earlier Indians had been named as casually as puppies or kittens. They died in such numbers from tuberculosis, smallpox, measles, influenza and other white man's diseases that it didn't seem to matter what labels they had. They would soon be gone, and their names with them.

But the surviving Indians began to develop some resistance to the new diseases. The white man felt twinges of conscience, and for the first time made earnest, widespread efforts to save Indian lives. The population began to grow again.

And so the travelling clinic of the Indian Health Service happened to be here, photographing the chests of Eagle Lake Johnny and the Charleyboys and the Grambushes and their numerous children, to guard them against the tuberculosis which — only a dozen years ago — had been eating up their race.

Beside some of the names in the register of the band were the letters TBS in red ink, to signify that previous TB surveys had shown that person or members of his family to have the disease. Twelve years ago nearly every Indian family had someone dead or ill from TB. Now the red entries were becoming sparse.

Looking up the members of the Toosey band in the list was not easy. Some children had been brought up by aunts or maternal grandmothers, and there was confusion about their parentage. Some had two or three different names. Other people had drifted in from other reserves, and were listed elsewhere. Others, long absent from the reserve or married to whites, had white status on the health service records. These could be X-rayed, but were not strictly entitled to any other health service.

But the paperwork barriers were overcome, and a parade of Indians moved up and placed their shoulders on Jack Bogart's lead screen.

Frances Owens, an attractive tousle-haired widow with the face of a hard-boiled saint, was busy injecting children against smallpox, polio, tuberculosis, whooping cough, tetanus and other diseases; comforting hurt and scared children; examining prospective mothers, and tactfully hinting to some women that they should clean up their homes and their persons to reduce the risk of infection.

On the side, she undertook such tricky jobs as trying to induce a young man to marry the girl who was going to bear his child; and urging another man to hike into the mountain meadows and fetch his brother, a former TB patient, who had run away from the X-ray clinic because he was afraid of being sent back for another term in Colqualeetza Indian Hospital at Sardis. If the brother could reach him in time, this man might catch up with his X-ray at another village.

People do not often run away from the clinic nowadays. They know it is there to help them.

• **1967** Feature Writing •

Long, tedious trip overland by rail in Newfoundland

Ray Guy

St. John's Telegram

"What? By train!" asked the surprised CN ticket agent when I phoned for reservations.

"Right," said I. "St. John's to Port aux Basques. And return the next day. No, I'm not travelling on a pass."

No shame to the poor man. Well he might marvel. The CN still gets some passengers undertaking the 547-mile trek but one asking for a double dose with no time off for a rest cure between must be a rarity.

Even the Royal Commission on Transportation has declined an invitation by the railway unions to try it just ONE way. The *Telegram* rushed me in where royal commissions fear to tread.

And, as I said to myself frequently between Gravol ("for the prevention of nausea and vomiting") tablets and complimentary CN meals during the course of the 1,094-mile experience: "What a hell of a way to make a living."

The railway wants to do away with the 86-year-old train passenger service and speed travellers back and forth by bus. Strenuously opposed are the railway unions and the St. John's city council which fear loss of jobs and business, and Joseph O'Keefe, MP for St. John's East.

Railway employees are circulating "save the train" petitions. Opposition Leader Gerry Ottenheimer says no changes should be made until the public has been polled.

Here is my straw vote on it for Gerry and this advice to the venerable members of the Royal Commission: Stick to your guns, chaps, and don't risk the trip.

Come on with the buses. Train travel in Newfoundland is a tedious, gruelling, outmoded, slow and painful way to get about. Planes, cars, buses, motorcycles, or roller skates must be better. Crawling across on your hands and knees can't be too much worse.

The island's railway had "second class" built into it from the start. A bill passed by the government in 1881 stated that "the railway intended to be constructed shall not be what is deemed in England or the United States, a first-class railway."

Donald Gordon, former president of the CNR, implied shortly before his resignation that Newfoundland still could not afford better than second class.

It would take at least $150,000,000, he said, to straighten out our crooked little railway and move the rails one foot, two and a half inches further apart.

Newfoundland's rails are now a substandard three feet, six inches wide — the only narrow-gauge line of its length left in North America.

Our rail cars and diesel engines have to be especially made and are the same size as those in use in some of the small banana-belt countries of South America.

Still, says Mr. Gordon, the narrow-gauge is not to be sneezed at. With the $179 million in improvements made since Confederation there is now no reason to convert to standard gauge and "wisecracks about the Newfie Bullet are no longer warranted."

On the other hand, railway union leader Esau Thoms says CN has become sloppy about its passenger service. More people would go "the way of the worry-free" if the cars and service were spruced up.

Whatever the cause, CN's train passenger service is going downgrade with the throttle open. For the first six months of this year CN carried 43,585 people; in 1965, for the same period, they had 83,744.

Gordon D. McMillan, CN's area manager, said recently: "The *public* is abandoning the rail passenger service — not us."

Perhaps the public shouldn't be faulted too much on this account.

So away we go. If forced, or for some weird reason you want to travel across the island by train, you must present yourself at the old stone terminal Water Street West not later than 11:30 p.m. on Mondays, Wednesdays or Fridays.

The first thing that may strike you (apart from porters burdened down with baggage) is that the inside of the station has been redone in CN modern.

Light panelling, fluorescent lights, new drink machines, pay lockers for parcels and electric blue jackets for the lads behind the counters.

Once outside on the train platform, however, you will soon find that the railway is still attached to its traditional colours — Nazi green and chopped liver.

And there, panting to be off, stands your conveyance. Identical in size to those chugging through the Honduras jungle, it consists of a 1,200-h.p. narrow-gauge diesel towing a couple of mail cars, four "day coaches," a diner and five "sleepers."

At the outset, let me admit that I cheated. I had a sleeper … $23, meals included. I chickened out of the supreme test — jogging across the island in a "day coach."

People do. Those who can't afford a sleeper or who are travelling by train for the first time and aren't aware of the terrors involved.

A stroll through a "day coach" at 2 a.m. is an unforgettable sight. The Black Death has struck. Twisted bodies sprawled in fantastic shapes. Mouths agape. Hideous snores and groans.

Bottles rolling from side to side as on a derelict vessel. Frightened children crying. Limp arms and legs flopping in the aisles as the train jiggles and jolts through the night.

A degrading experience for those forced to travel on Newfoundland's second-class transportation system designed for second-class citizens.

There are two things which prove impossible in a CN "day coach" — sleeping and raising a window.

Only twice in my life have I succeeded in wrenching open a CN window and in one of these cases it later crunched down on my elbow.

Sleeping more than 10 minutes at a stretch in the day coach is the equivalent of swimming

Cabot Strait in a suit of armor. The seats are so cunningly designed that writhe and twist as you will, some part of your frame will come in contact with bare metal or wood or glass.

The Bullet averages at least one "killer lurch" every 10 minutes. You either stay alert or risk getting your face smashed against the windowsill.

Could the solution be a sleeper? Since the westbound leaves near midnight, CN beds you down as soon as you step aboard.

Sleepers and day coaches alike, however, have the same type of ventilation system. Sleeper windows will rise a few inches — to reveal another sooty pane containing a small strip of dirt-clogged screen.

More air could pass through a mosquito's nostril. No. The CN method is to pump all cars full of fumes, smoke and grime in downtown St. John's and hermetically seal them.

The characteristic smell on the CN is of coal smoke and stale urine. The coal smoke is, as has been explained, pumped aboard and locked in at St. John's.

The latter fragrance is emitted mainly by the washrooms. So incredible was the stench in the Bishop's Falls (sleepers are named after prominent stops along the railway) water closet I was led to investigate others. They were all alike. The men's, anyway.

Situated over the pertinent fixture in the men's convenience is a card quoting the Canada Criminal Code on spitting and gambling in public places.

I would lay a two-to-one bet that no one can take a deep breath in a CN train washroom and still remain standing. You take a deep breath outside, hold it as long as possible and when that gives out risk pinching little breaths and shallow gasps.

From time to time a porter circulated through Bishop's Falls sleeping car dispensing a few quick squirts of Florient air deodorant then bashfully hiding the can under his jacket.

He was like the fly spitting in the ocean.

And so to bed. All is quiet in Bishop's Falls sleeper, the tranquility broken only by the rhythm of the wheels — whackety whack, whackety whack, smash, bang, lurch — and the rending screech of rusty metal rubbing together where the cars are coupled.

Soon the air is rent by an internal commotion which revolves around a flurry of enthusiastic oaths delivered with a Scottish accent.

Heads pop out, top and bottom, from behind the chopped liver curtains. The grand old Scottish curses are redoubled.

Eventually, the racket dies down, mystified faces withdraw behind the curtained walls. Peace reigns once more. Whackety whack, whackety whack, smash, bang, lurch.

Then at 2:30 a.m., "up she goes" again. This time the Scotsman far surpasses his previous efforts. The lights are turned on. The porter is summoned. The fragrant air turns blue. There are threats and curses and angry words which take at least 20 minutes to subside.

Only next morning are the details revealed. In every CN car there is at least one drunk.

Those who would deplore this custom have obviously never travelled across the island by train cold sober. Just as the invention of ether relieved untold suffering in the operating room so does alcohol have its place on the CN.

Our drunk had taken a case of beer into his top bunk and supped away as the Bullet jogged merrily through the night.

In the berth below lay one half of a Scottish couple, now resident in Toronto, and returning from a holiday in quaint, hospitable Newfoundland.

The first row started when the chap in the upper dozed off and spilled a bottle of beer on the tourist in the lower.

The second fracas, half hour later, occurred when the jolly traveller in No. 3 upper became nauseous, leaned out, and spewed all over the occupant of No. 3 lower.

In came the porter, wrested the remainder of the beer away from the bad boy and threatened to heave him off. At which he began to snore. He slept peacefully until dawn.

"Oh, it's not been a bad holiday," observed the Scottish tourist next day. "Just before leaving we went to a rrestaraunt forr a bite and a fight started. They locked the dooors and there we were in the midst."

"Aparrut from that and yon bluddy idjot lost night we had a verra nice time. Aye, we plon tae coom back next soomer. We lairned this time tae save a few dollarrrs along the way."

For all that, his wife looked a bit washy and made frequent trips to the brake for the only fresh air available.

"Odd," said he. "She generrruly hos a cast irron stomik when travelling. Moost ha been thot bit of business lost night."

Later, as we neared Port aux Basques, boozy Bill, still three parts, began pestering the porter for the return of his beer. Denied, he commenced tongue-banging and insulting the Scottish couple.

"Let's gang up and heave the bastard through the port-hole," suggested a Bell Islander, fed up by now with this treatment of visitors to our shores.

At that the culprit scuttled off and was not seen again in Bishop's Falls sleeper for the duration.

But one good thing about Newfoundland trains is that you need never be stuck for someone to talk to.

Black strangers come in and sit down and within five minutes have launched into the story of their lives from the cradle to the present — whether you want to hear it or not. Plus what you can gather by eavesdropping.

I soon learned that in Bishop's Falls car there were the Scottish couple and two other mainland tourists, two sick people coming from St. John's hospitals, three welfare cases, two relatives of railway workers travelling on passes and six youths and two girls going to the mainland for work.

Sitting opposite me were an extremely distraught looking pair, mother and daughter.

"Oh, my God, my God, my God," the younger one would sigh profoundly. The mother, leafing through a *True Story* journal, also gave signs of distress.

It was soon disclosed that they were "on welfare," that the younger had spent some time in the orthopedic hospital, was now discharged and her mother had journeyed in to take her back home.

During her stay, the daughter had cultivated a boyfriend in the great city. I presumed her disconsolation was due to the parting.

There was talk of marriage at Christmas.

"I was talkin' to 'en the other night," said the mother. "'E got grade eleven, 'aven't 'e? 'E can get a job on that. What do 'e want to go back to school for? Said 'e was afraid 'e wouldn't pass. Said 'e had a lot of worry."

"'E got a lot of worry!? snorted her offspring. "What the 'ell do 'e think I got! My God, my God, my God. My dear, you'll never see me going to the h'alter by Christmas."

They had a small "picture in a minute" camera with which they would photograph each other from time to time. This diversion seemed to raise them out of the dumps a little.

Then they settled back to make rather cold-blooded plans aimed at ensuring the proposed Yuletide nuptials would come off.

"As soon as we get back you'll write 'en a letter. Next week we'll send 'en a parcel with a cake into it."

The daughter had a four-pound bag of toffees which she generously passed round in the general area. After the fourth candy I declined and, by way of a pleasantry, said I must "watch my figure."

At this, my younger neighbour launched suddenly into a flurry of wails, groans and sobs. I was dumfounded at this outburst.

"Save your tears, my dear," said her mother over the top of *True Story*, "h'or you won't 'ave none left for later."

Upon closer scrutiny I discovered that the young one was definitely in what used to be called an "interesting condition."

They gradually calmed down and took a few more pictures, which seemed to do them a world of good. My faux pas was apparently forgiven. We finished the toffee.

As they detrained at their destination I wished them good luck.

"Same to you, sir. Sniff. Sniff," said the daughter.

"Come on. 'Urry up. My God. I'll never h'undertake another trip like this. Com on. Knock off snuffin'. I 'lows if your father 'aven't got nothin' left from supper I'll knock his 'ed off."

Conversation drifted back through the rattles and squeaks from other parts of the car.

Two girls who had lately worked in a St. John's tavern were on their way to Toronto seeking employment. They were got up in what they figured was the height of Toronto style.

One of the tourists, a woman who hailed from Toronto, was telling them about the wonders they might see in the big city. One of the young emigrants sat there bug-eyed while the other giggled nervously.

Toronto Tourist was obviously enjoying their reaction: "What? You've never ridden the subway? Oh, you'll LIEE-k it! They go like CRAAAY-zy!" Bug eyes. Giggles.

Then in came a young man, also bound for employment in Toronto. But he had been there before and in consequence assumed no slight swagger.

The two innocents abroad then heard another account of the golden metropolis and the Toronto Tourist had a little of the wind taken out of her sails. He promised to look out for them on the journey along. Bug Eyes relaxed a bit and Giggles wasn't quite so nervous.

The trip to Port aux Basques took about 20 hours. We left St. John's near midnight and jolted into the western terminal about 7:30 p.m. the next day. In 1898 it took 27 hours and 45 minutes.

As we staggered off the Bullet a friend of theirs, who had driven across in a car, greeted the Scottish couple brightly:

"Well, here you are at last. We slept at home in bed and still got there before you."

That was the kind of remark we could all do without. Those who took the train because they didn't know better didn't need to have it rubbed in.

Those who couldn't afford to come any other way didn't need to be reminded further that they were second class-citizens.

The return trip began at 10 a.m. next day. More whackety whack, whackety whack, smash, bang, lurch and the screech of rusted metal. And the porter with his ineffective little squirts of Florient.

And the joggling limbs and rolling bottles and frightened children crying in the day coaches. It will take a day and a night to reach St. John's.

Away from the dreary, rocky Port aux Basques, past the wide beaches and surf and rolling sand dunes of Cape Ray, up through the portals of the Long Range Mountains into Codroy Valley.

Who's aboard this trip? A small crowd. Two elderly and former Newfoundlanders returning for a visit. A lively and silver-haired woman who soon reveals that her father was a Spanish captain.

Six lads returning to the island from Toronto "for the winter" — unable to kick the inherited habit of summer work and winter rest begun centuries ago in the fishing boats.

A young mainlander who said he was a freelance photographer with a sudden impulse to come to Newfoundland and stay for a year.

Two sick people on welfare going to the hospital. Five people travelling on a railway pass. Seven girls going back to school. One woman, who was deaf, kept telling everyone how because of her affliction she missed her train in Montreal and had to wait two days for another.

But there is a mixup in tickets and most of the interesting passengers get moved to another car, including the daughter of a Spanish captain and the young freelance photographer.

Sitting opposite me is the deaf woman who took off her shoes, rolled down her nylons and put up her feet. She is the loudest chewer of gum I have ever heard. Even above the whackety whack, whackety whack, smash, bang, lurch you can hear her top plate clicking and scrunching.

She came from her daughter in Ohio? Poor soul, I thought. She figured her daughter would take her in and keep her. But they couldn't stand the way she chewed gum. So she was coming back to live out the rest of it alone.

Behind me are the elderly and former Newfoundlanders.

"Look mother, there they are. See them there. That's Newfoundland to me," says the man. Damned if his voice doesn't tremble a bit.

I think he is right. You don't see them just like that on the mainland, even in Cape Breton. Scrubby, scrawny, pitiful, miserable spruce bushes growing on the cliffs by the sea.

The train tows you past the untidy backsides of a string of small communities and larger towns.

Past lonely shacks scattered over the barrens with moose horns over the doors and children with no school out front.

It has been a good year for juniper, if nothing else. From one end of the island to the other they are green, fluffy, luxuriant — so vigorous they look like a strange, new species.

Up the Codroy Valley and Humber Valley where you get the feeling you are trespassing on the private domain of the paper companies. Their roads and signs and tractors and men are everywhere.

Through Corner Brook and Deer Lake which are Bowater's and Lundrigan's. Over the barren Gaff Topsails which nobody wants except the people in the shacks with the moose horns.

The CN in Newfoundland has not yet got around to installing the glass-roofed scenic dome cars they picture on the diner menus. A film of St. John's soot and grime dims our windows — and you can't get them up.

Whackety whack, whackety whack, smash, bang, lurch. The deaf woman in the top bunk is ringing for the porter. When nobody comes she tries to clamber down by herself, can't, and crawls back.

Next morning, she complains to everyone that she didn't sleep a wink because the porters were laughing and carrying on "until all hours" with the young girls in the lower berths. A lie.

Through the early morning fog we crawl into St. John's, along the greasy Waterford River, past the chopped liver freight cars in the railyards and the Nazi green day coaches waiting on the siding.

Out into the familiar St. John's air which the CN has provided its passengers in stoppered cars for the whole journey.

The victims of the day coaches stumble off, numb, red-eyed and bewildered into the arms of the aggressive men calling "taxi, taxi."

Come on with the buses. It won't be the easiest way in the world to travel but compared with the trains it will be fairly comfortable and mercifully quick.

Some things about trains I'll be sorry to see go. For one thing, the scenery isn't all barren and scrubby spruce — and you have lots of time to admire it.

At both ends of the railway at Cape Ray and Holyrood there are stretches where the train all but takes to the water travelling for miles along the beach. Seabirds and waves create an inspiring panorama.

No more impressive entry into the island could be imagined than the gap through Table Mountain into the splendid Codroy Valley.

I like the way the railway skirts closely the rivers and lakes — Georges Lake, the Humber River, Deer Lake, the Exploits. It's murder on timetables but as a scenic route it can't be beat.

And some second thoughts on shacks. When is a shack not a shack? When it's a summer shack.

Isolation and a certain crumbling at the edges are attractive features in a summer place. In these respects many of the buildings by the railway in remote places far surpass the summer subdivision colonies by the highways with their white paling fences.

It would be comforting to think that all the remote shacks along the railway were summer places. But what of the children playing out front in late September? Still, they might commute to a regional school every day by helicopter for all I know.

Then there are the railway personnel who still manage to do their job and be courteous about it even under trying circumstances.

Sure, the water looks dirty, but the way the waiters can balance three plates on each arm as the dining car all but turns end over end takes your mind off it.

The elderly ladies miss their table linen but they still feel elegant when the waiter asks, "Would Modom care for after dinner mints?"

And absolutely the best way to go home for Christmas is by train with the university crowd going cracked, the out-of-town shoppers burdened down, the holidaying workers opening their bottles a bit early, a guitar in every car and everyone exceedingly warm and merry and the snowy hills rollicking past.

The thing I'll miss most about trains is the way they encourage people to talk. I'll miss the people who do you the honour of telling you all their troubles and hopes starting within five minutes after they sit down.

But these people deserve better than second class.

● **1968** Nouvelle d'actualité ●

Claire Dutrisac témoin d'une
transplantation cardiaque

Claire Dutrisac

La Presse

Si l'habit faisait le moine, il est certain qu'hier matin, je me serais crue infirmière. Tout comme les infirmières qui assistent l'équipe chirurgicale, je portais le casque, le masque, la robe verte et les pantoufles.

À mon entrée, dans l'une des salles d'opération, le receveur était sous anesthésie et presque prêt à recevoir le greffon. Dans l'autre salle, on vérifiait si le coeur du donneur était en bonne condition. Le jeune homme ayant succombé à une hémorragie cérébrale massive, on voulait être sûr qu'aucun épanchement de sang n'avait pas endommagé le coeur; fort heureusement, il n'en était rien.

On commença donc le prélèvement du coeur. C'est une opération délicate qui exige environ une heure. Le coeur du donneur est sectionné le plus haut possible. C'est-à-dire qu'on en conserve autant qu'on peut. À l'inverse, celui du receveur est coupé le plus bas possible, pour la même raison. Car au moment de la suture du greffon, pour l'ajustement des deux coeurs, si l'on peut ainsi s'exprimer, on se laisse une marge au cas où il faudrait couper encore un peu de chacun.

Cette intervention sur une personne décédée n'a aucune analogie avec une dissection ou une autopsie. Elle s'accomplit avec le même souci d'asepsie et de précision qu'une opération sur une personne vivante.

Contrairement à ce qu'on imagine, il y a très peu de sang répandu dans une salle comme dans une autre. Une fois le coeur sectionné, on le place dans un bassin et il baigne dans du sérum physiologique. Comme les deux interventions sont syncronisées, le receveur, à quelques minutes près, recevra un « coeur neuf ». Les fonctions de la respiration et de la circulation du sang sont assumées par le « coeur-poumon artificiel », ce qu'on appelle communément la « pompe ».

Cette pompe recueille non seulement le sang qui circule normalement dans le système vasculaire (artères et veines) mais également celui que le patient peut perdre, dans le thorax, au cours de l'intervention. Elle permet également d'abaisser la température du coeur jusqu'à 20ºC (environ 65ºF). Ce refroidissement des deux organes facilite l'opération.

Elle assure un contrôle absolu sur la circulation et restitue graduellement au système du patient, selon les instructions du chirurgien, le sang veineux qu'elle a reçu, épuré, oxygéné, refroidi puis réchauffé. C'est également par la pompe que se fait l'anesthésie. Pendant que durera la suture du greffon, le malade ne respire pas, le pompe le faisant pour lui.

Dans chaque salle d'opération, des écrans reproduisent le graphique des électrocardiogrammes qui renseignent sur les réactions du malade.

Dire que le facteur « temps » dans une intervention chirurgicale est d'une importance majeure, surtout en cardiologie, est un truisme. Dès l'instant où le chirurgien commence à suturer les deux coeurs, le bord de l'un étant superposé à l'autre, c'est une lutte contre le temps. La dextérité du chirurgien entre en ligne de compte mais également la précision, la rapidité et la coordination des gestes de toute l'équipe, sans jamais oublier les anesthésistes et les techniciens pompistes.

Si cette opération, la partie la plus délicate de l'intervention, n'exigeait pas une extrême habileté, s'il ne s'agissait pas d'un humain, le profane pourrait assimiler cette suture à un travail de couture. La comparaison, un peu grossière, permettra peut-être au lecteur d'imaginer la scène.

Mais on sent très bien que chaque seconde compte. Au fur et à mesure que l'opération avance, une légère tension se fait sentir. Le chirurgien vérifie fréquemment certains détails, comme le degré de refroidissement, le débit de la pompe, etc. Avant de tenter de faire fonctionner le coeur greffé, le chirurgien laisse passer un peu de sang dans les cavités, afin de s'assurer que les sutures sont en nombre suffisant. Si la moindre goutte de sang perce, on procède à une suture supplémentaire. Il faut que le coeur soit parfaitement étanche.

On est prêt pour le grand moment : celui où le chirurgien, à l'aide de deux électrodes, stimulera le coeur d'un courant électrique afin qu'il commence à battre et assume ses fonctions normales. Tous les yeux sont tournés avec une anxiété visible vers l'écran où l'électrocardiogramme indiquera le résultat obtenu.

Sans même qu'on s'en rende compte, on suspend son souffle, on a l'impression que nos coeurs, à nous, cessent de battre pour un instant ... Un instant qui paraît une éternité, un instant qui sépare la vie, la vraie vie de la mort ... Battra ... ne battra pas ... battra ... IL BAT !

Et avec une force qui nous laisse béants d'admiration. Les mots me manquent pour décrire ce moment où chacun, de toutes ses forces, espère ce battement, attend ce battement, veut ce battement. Dans le cas de M. Paris, ce fut formidable. Les médecins qui m'entouraient exprimaient leur satisfaction. Moi, je gardais extérieurement un très grand calme mais, tout au fond, j'étais soulevée d'enthousiasme.

Si un pas immense vient d'être fait dans la voie du succès, la tâche du chirurgien n'est pas encore terminée. Si la tension est moindre, elle subsiste encore. Car l'équipe, dirigée par le Dr Grondin, devra équilibrer la pression artérielle et la pression veineuse. On surveille toujours avec attention le va-et-vient du graphique sur l'écran.

Tantôt la pression artérielle monte: 100, 160, 200, tantôt elle retombe jusqu'à 60. Le même phénomène se produit en ce qui a trait à la pression veineuse. Les chiffres indicateurs sont lancés d'une voie forte dans la salle d'opération et des substances médicamenteuses sont administrées pour rétablir un rythme normal dans le réseau vasculaire. Quand le Dr Grondin s'esquive, on sait que tout va bien. On respire mieux. Ses assistants termineront le travail, c'est-à-dire qu'ils refermeront le thorax et surveilleront l'état du patient. Il reste l'attente et un immense espoir.

Dès l'instant où le coeur du donneur a été prélevé, des chirurgiens de l'hôpital Royal Victoria sont venus prélever les reins. La famille Bastien avait accepté que les organes utilisables de leur fils servent à sauver des vies humaines. Un des reins seulement a servi à une transplantation.

La jeunesse et la force du donneur, la rapidité avec laquelle la famille a pris sa décision en ce qui concerne le don de ce coeur, la jeunesse relative de M. Paris, la grande compatibilité entre les deux coeurs, tout permet d'espérer le succès de cette greffe. Le fait que la vie artificielle des organes du donneur ait été plus courte que dans le cas de Mme Rondeau (on a gagné au moins une douzaine d'heures) est aussi d'un heureux augure.

L'Institut de Cardiologie de Montréal, sous l'impulsion du Dr David est en train de se tailler une réputation mondiale.

La famille Bastien a beaucoup mérité de la science et la science à son tour a beaucoup mérité de la société.

Le moment le plus pathétique d'une transplantation cardiaque, c'est sans contredit l'instant où, par un choc électrique, le chirurgien remet en marche le coeur greffé qui, dès lors, devra fonctionner par lui-même. Ce moment d'émotion, je l'ai vécu et j'ai ressenti l'allégresse générale.

On ne peut alors s'empêcher de penser, tant l'espoir et la confiance nous habitent: « Sauvé ! » Sans doute, est-il à cet instant précis trop tôt encore pour une telle prédiction. Mais au moins, le patient vit et le coeur greffé laisse croire qu'il pourra continuer à assumer les fonctions du coeur dans l'avenir.

Pour une profane, assister à une transplantation du coeur constitue une aventure exaltante où divers sentiments remuent en soi : admiration devant l'habileté et la dextérité des chirurgiens, devant le travail de toute une équipe pour sauver un homme condamné.

À cet enthousiasme devant la performance de la science médicale se mêle aussi un « certain sourire triste » si l'on pense que tout à côté un être jeune est mort.

Est-ce terrible à voir ? La réponse varie sûrement d'un individu à un autre. Moi, je dis carrément non. Tout s'agence avec tant d'harmonie, tous les membres de l'équipe, médecins, infirmières et techniciens-pompistes oeuvrent avec une telle coordination qu'on pourrait imaginer que ce travail est facile. Soulignons ici le rôle trop souvent ignoré, mais d'une importance capitale, de l'anesthésiste.

On m'a aussi demandé : quelle est l'atmosphère de la salle d'opération? Il y a des moments de sérieux extrême, des moments de grande tension, suivis souvent d'une détente nécessaire à l'accomplissement d'une tâche de cette envergure.

Pour le « receveur », la transplantation, c'est une porte fermée qui s'entrouvre …

Jeudi soir, la femme du receveur, M. Gaétan Paris, qui attendait à l'Institut sa chance de survie, décidait de lancer un appel à la collaboration du public. Elle craignait que son mari ne succombe avant que l'occasion d'une transplantation se présente.

Vers la même heure environ, la mort fauchait un jeune motocycliste de 23 ans, Yvon Bastien. Il fut transporté à l'hôpital Jean-Talon. Son état était très grave et ses chances de vie très minces. Les médecins de l'hôpital appelèrent des spécialistes de diverses disciplines en consultation, dont un neuro-chirurgien, un cardiologue et un spécialiste en chirurgie cardio-vasculaire.

Le cardiologue, le Dr Gaston Choquette, fut appelé vers 11h30 p.m. Il examina le jeune Bastien et en sortant de la salle, il se trouva en face de M. et Mme Bastien qu'il connaissait très bien et qui lui dirent: « C'est Yvon qui est là ! »

Le Dr Choquette avait examiné Yvon, il y a cinq ans, et avait constaté que son coeur était très bon. Mais, m'a-t-il dit, dans l'état où il était, je ne pouvais le reconnaître.

Quand tous les spécialistes eurent diagnostiqué la gravité du cas, hémorragie cérébrale massive, la famille d'Yvon décida de le faire transporter à l'Institut, d'abord pour qu'on tente encore de le sauver, ensuite, pour qu'on utilise son coeur et ses reins après le décès éventuel, s'ils pouvaient servir.

Quand il fut établi qu'il était impossible de sauver la vie du jeune homme, on procéda aux tests de compatibilité. Sur sept éléments, dont certains sont majeurs, d'autres mineurs, un seul élément moyen était incompatible. Quand le décès fut établi, un respirateur et certaines substances assurèrent la vie des organes en vue de la transplantation. M. Paris, avec l'aide de l'équipe médicale et technique de l'Institut, allait tenter sa chance.

• **1969** Feature Writing •

Case against the Crown, or how you can spend a year in jail before trial

Brian Stewart

Montreal Gazette

Last year a black youth we'll call Alfred Thomas Simpson reversed an underground railway that had shunted lost generations of his ancestors off to inconspicuous corners of the continent.

Like so many of his contemporaries, he chose his early 20s to escape the rural backlands of Nova Scotia, leaving behind impoverished family farms, depleted softball teams, back dirt roads and hopeless futures for the distant city lights of central Canada.

So far, a not uncommon story. Thousands before him growing up in Nova Scotia since the war had succumbed to frustration and those two historic magnets — grey sea-lanes out of old Halifax harbour, and CPR Specials roaring westward past the neck of the peninsula.

If it now seemed this neck was its own noose, the ship piers and rail terminal had become to a new generation what Cork harbour, Liverpool and Harper's Ferry had been to fleeing Irish, Scottish and Black forefathers.

And if many were trying simply to escape Atlantic isolation, and still more were leaving for profit, there were plenty enough like A. T. Simpson driven by more compelling reasons …

His father had died after a lifetime of futile struggle against the rocky land of his farm — a sad plot of no-where's-ville vaguely pinpointed as part of Nova Scotia's freakish black-belt. Certainly there was nothing left to bind him to the land, and his own education faded out by grade nine into fitful employment in the grimy mines of New Glasgow. His future appeared one of unrelieved bleakness.

Last June, however, he made his move and migrated to Montreal with his wife and two small children where, in rapid succession, he established a new home, landed a good job in a garage, and gained a reputation as a pleasant, quiet-spoken man and excellent employee.

A family, a home, a job, and a reputation, it must be said, all of which have been destroyed since the night of Sept. 23rd last. On that evening, a generally quiet one in Montreal, the police were alerted that a woman had been raped. The next morning they arrested and charged Alfred Thomas Simpson with the crime.

That was more than eight months ago, and Simpson is still locked in Bordeaux Jail awaiting his trial. He has pleaded 'Not Guilty' and stoutly protests his innocence. He is also "presumed innocent" by law.

And if he is very lucky he may get a chance to defend himself before he spends a full year-and-a-half behind bars.

The merits of the case to be made against Alfred Thomas Simpson cannot be discussed.

The merits of the administration of justice in the Simpson case, however, are open to question. Serious question.

During the past two weeks a host of top legal experts, practising lawyers, welfare officers, prison officials and court administrators have been asking questions — questions about the legal system.

For whatever the eventual result of the Simpson case, it cannot be said that Justice is being done, nor is it easy to believe that Justice will ever be done.

For a start, one needs only review the history of Simpson and his family since the arrest. It goes like this:

He made his first court appearance on Oct. 2 when he was remanded without bail for preliminary hearing set for November 4. At the crucial moment when bail was discussed he appears to have been unrepresented by legal counsel.

Taken back to Bordeaux, he was locked in one of the two trial wards that house roughly 300 men. He is still there eight months later.

On Nov. 4, the preliminary hearing was held and he was sent for trial on Jan. 7 — the next court Assizes. (All rape cases must be tried by jury in the Court of Queen's Bench, of which there are only two divisions in Montreal).

On Nov. 11, a prison chaplain told him his 11-month-old son had died in a hideous accident — scalding himself to death while playing with a bathtub tap.

Simpson, understandably distressed, applied for permission from the prison authorities to attend his son's funeral. His plea was refused, and on that rain-streaked November afternoon the chaplain and his wife buried the infant while he remained locked in his cell.

The judicial system which spends $5 a day to house and feed men who cannot raise bail, but will not spare a guard to let a man still "presumed innocent" attend his own son's funeral, appears cruel and preposterous.

A word, therefore, about the prison itself: While "C" and "B" wards are designed to detain men awaiting trial — trial wards — ex-prisoners and prison officials interviewed agree conditions there are actually much worse than in the regular prison wards.

Restrictions are as severe, the food as deplorable, the monotony twice as bad. Trial ward detainees have no work details to break the endless monotony.

Nor must it be forgotten that not only are these men "presumed innocent" but court statistics clearly suggest a great many may indeed be found not guilty.

Contrary to popular opinion, it is known that a fairly large percentage of men jailed before trial are later found not guilty, or have their cases withdrawn or dismissed.

Despite this, Simpson and the others remain subject to Bordeaux's restrictions, which include two telephone calls a week "with pull" and two half-hour visits with relatives a month — hardly enough to maintain the fabric of a family or even prepare for a trial.

While Simpson sat helpless in his cell awaiting the January Assizes, more tragedy over-whelmed his family.

His family was already reduced to public welfare, when scarcely a month after his son's death, Simpson's three-year-old daughter was diagnosed as suffering from cerebral palsy and was admitted to The Children's Hospital.

This proved the last straw for his wife, who collapsed under the strain and suffered a nervous breakdown.

Simpson, already having lost a son, a job and a reputation, now learned that his remaining child was headed for a temporary foster home and his wife confined to Douglas Hospital.

All this time the machinery of law chugged forward at much the same historic pace that had helped push the Prince of Denmark to the brink of suicidal despair.

On Jan. 7 he was handcuffed and led to court only to have his case postponed another two months until the next Assizes on March 3.

March 3, however, both divisions of Queen's Court were still wading through a backlog of cases and Simpson was again led back to Bordeaux to await another Assizes May 5. He had now spent five months behind bars.

At his last Assizes, however, a new factor entered the case of Alfred Thomas Simpson: Bail.

"For as long as money bail has been used to insure that defendants appear for trial, it has discriminated against poor defendants."
—U.S. President's Commission on Law Enforcement and Administration of Justice

"Failure to raise a certain sum of money should never be the reason for the accused remain-ing in custody ... financial security in advance must be eliminated from our release practices before trial."
— Martin Friedland: *Detention Before Trial*

It is widely accepted in legal circles that the present system of money bail practiced in Quebec destroys the concept of equality before the law.

And since the Provost Commission's recommendations, the pledge by Justice Minister Turner to review the status of bail, and trailblazing efforts to eliminate it in the U.S. and Ontario ... there is no doubt that it will soon be changed.

However, it is still very much alive in Montreal courts — and on the morning of March 3 Simp-son was offered his liberty for $2,000, by a judge who granted bail to express his disapproval of the Crown's excessive delay in bringing him to trial.

Simpson instead offered the court an equivalent property bond his mother was prepared to post on her Nova Scotia farm — quite plainly the only security he could have.

This was rejected by the court because the property lay outside Quebec. Simpson was hustled back to his Bordeaux cell.

At his last court appearance, on May 5, the court system which had held Simpson prisoner for seven months was still not in a position to proceed. Instead his case has been postponed until September — which will coincide nicely with his first anniversary in jail.

However, a court official scanning the growing backlog of cases last week told this reporter Simpson would be very lucky to come to trial before October and warned the whole affair could drag on much longer.

In fact there are now no less than 26 rape cases waiting to be filtered through the two courtrooms of the Queen's Bench. A third court has been promised for September, but it is doubt-ful this will make much impression. As several lawyers pointed out, some cases take up weeks of a court's time.

In any case one wonders — when it appears Montreal's court system is grinding to a halt — why justice officials are only now talking of a "third" court. The Queen's Bench can be divided into as many sections as there are judges available — why not, as many lawyers suggest, have four courts, or even eight courts.

Granted, the system would be put to some inconvenience rounding up extra court space, but the need would now seem great enough to demand action to protect individual rights.

As it is, Montreal has an unenviable reputation for delaying trials of men held in custody when it suits the Crown's purpose. When contacted, one official after another sighed and admitted: "But this case is not uncommon now ..."

For confirmation of that, one need only study the handling of suspected FLQ terrorists, many of whom ran the full gauntlet of legal procrastination.

Simpson's case has now attracted the attention of Prof. Brian Grosman, head of Criminal Law at McGill University and himself a former defence attorney as well as Crown Prosecutor. He terms Simpson's eight-month ordeal, "A perfect, and classic, example of the harshness of the money bail system that still prevails in Quebec.

"And what is really disturbing is that he is not unique ... that his case is not a cause célèbre when it should be," he adds.

Officials who know the trial wards at Bordeaux bear this out completely. Simpson is just one out of dozens imprisoned for excessively long periods before trial.

Prof. Grosman also points to another interesting factor in Simpson's case — there is no public prosecutor in charge of it, and no central administration that ensures men in prison are given priority in obtaining early trials. In Montreal, "No one knows about the case other than some paper in some court filing cabinet ..."

(A new system being introduced in some areas of the United States is designed to ensure men in custody are given the right to a trial within 30 days.)

Prof. Grosman has good reason to worry about the lack of pre-trial study of Simpson's case: He has twice defended men on rape charges who spent months in prison only to have all charges against them withdrawn after the trial prosecutor took his first look at the evidence.

In one, the defendant spent 13 weeks in jail, lost his job, his fiancé, and saw his family disown him. Then, exactly one hour before the trial opened, the prosecutor looked at his file and announced: "There is no case!"

Now, Canadian law insists, "the Crown must proceed with reasonable speed after the accused has been committed for trial."

Simpson, it will be remembered, was committed for trial last Nov.r 4. The Crown cannot seriously claim that throughout the subsequent three Assizes it has acted with "reasonable speed."

Considering the enormous number of cases before the courts such delays are understandable perhaps — but when they entail such deprivation of liberty they are patently unreasonable and unacceptable. The wise gentlemen who drew up the English Habeas Corpus Act of 1679, one of the great landmarks of our judicial system, appear to have had a very clear concept of what was unacceptable:

A section of that Act insists an accused must be liberated "if the Crown does not cause him to be indicted at the first term after his committal, *and to be tried at the second term.*"

Under this provision, Simpson should have been released from custody (though charges against him would remain) as far back as March 3. Montreal lawyer Morris Fish suggested this week the Simpson Affair could become a test case, "to see if Habeas Corpus is still applicable in Quebec in 1969."

Apart from the delay, there seems no justification for keeping Simpson, and many others also "presumed innocent," locked away in jail before trial. The "money bail" system that holds him prisoner is denounced everywhere as archaic and unjust, and for good reason:

• Simpson is not in jail because we know he's guilty (we know nothing of the kind). Nor is he in jail because the courts fear he will flee ... or because he is felt a threat to society. He is in jail only because he cannot raise $2,000 cash.

In short, Simpson is in jail because he is a poor man ...

Grosman: "The whole problem of bail and pretrial detention involves also the whole problem of equality before the law. And if a man's freedom depends on how much he has in his pocket, then there's something wrong with the system."

• Because he is in jail, his chances of a fair and equal trial may well be jeopardized. Canadian statistics in Friedland's famous *Detention Before Trial* and similar U.S. studies all show defendants in custody are convicted more often than similar, but richer, defendants out on bail for the same offences. Jailed defendants are also given heavier sentences ... and jailed defendants are sentenced to jail more often.

Precisely because it appears certain that "custody is prejudicial to the outcome of one's case," Quebec's Prevost Commission has recommended a complete overhaul of the province's bail system that would follow legal reforms in Britain, the U.S. and Ontario — including greater use of "own bail," or bail on one's "own recognisance." But in Simpson's case, the price tag for an equal trial still stands — $2,000.

Magna Carta, 1215: "To no man will we sell, to no man will we refuse, rights or justice."

• Because Simpson is in jail, he cannot earn enough money for adequate legal counsel, but instead must rely on a heavily overburdened legal aid system (now swamped under a 75 per cent increase in cases over the last year); nor can he properly instruct counsel; nor can he look after his family; nor can he even buy proper clothes for his trial.

• Because he cannot raise a mere $2,000, Simpson may serve out more than a year in jail for a crime he may never have committed. It can happen:

A cursory check with the *Quebec Year Book*, for example, shows that in 1965 fully 11 per cent of all people brought to trial for indictable offences were acquitted. That adds up to more than 1,000 persons ... and the figures do not show how many cases were dropped before trial, nor how many individuals served time in jail for crimes of which they were never convicted.

A pretty good idea can be gained, however, from Friedland's study, an exposé that rocked the Ontario court system and led to the introduction of a more liberal bail system.

He noted that fully 24 per cent of all persons brought to trial were not convicted and many more had charges dropped against them (more than 700, of whom more than 270 were jailed more than one week and 60 spent three weeks to two months in prison).

He concluded: "It is not strictly necessary to rely on the 'presumption of innocence' to form the conclusion that indiscriminate detention before trial is unsound ... when one knows that there is, in fact, a reasonable likelihood that the accused may be innocent."

• But the saddest aspect of all is that Simpson's guilt or innocence is now purely academic. His family has already been destroyed, his job and reputation are shot, a full year of his life has been wiped out ...

It is not hard to see what the courts should have done — correct procedures first adopted by the New York Vera Foundation and the Manhattan Bail Project are being widely advocated and adopted throughout the continent:

Either the man we call Simpson should be considered too great a risk to be freed — in which case he should have the option of immediate trial — or he should be freed on minimal bail or no bail at all. He could even be placed in limited detention: Allowed to work during the day, placed in custody overnight.

It is difficult to conceive of equality before the law when some men are liberated because they have $2,000, while others are stripped of their freedom because they don't.

And others, perhaps, must face the haunting thought that Simpson, or others like him, are innocent men destroyed by the system. If Simpson is eventually found "not guilty," society will do nothing to make amends; express no sorrow; offer no compensation; nor spend a dime to pay for a stolen year ...

At the end of a long talk about Simpson, Prof. Grosman mused over the possibility:

"And what if he's acquitted after all this? Do we give him any compensation for a destroyed family, his lost job, his lost reputation? We say 'you lucky man — you're free,'" he said, and then added:

"What do we do, we fine people ...?"

• **1974** Feature Writing •

Godzilla versus the kids

Carol Hogg

Calgary Herald

I t's a block-long line-up in front of the cinema.
   It's eating two boxes of popcorn, a bag of Smarties and an orange pop.
It's screaming during the monster fight.
It's hooting during the love scene.
It's getting away from your parents.
It's a phenomenon known as the kids' matinee.
And it's dying.
Like church, like the fox-trot and other institutions dear to the hearts of North Americans, the kids' matinee is struggling to stay alive.

The thing is, it no longer pays. And that's a fatal ailment.

Only six of Calgary's 24 theatres still show regular children's matinees. And it's not a paying proposition, even in these few theatres.

Pressed for a reason why they continue something that, at best, breaks even financially, cinema executives don't come up with any very convincing answers.

Jim Moore, city supervisor for Odeon Theatres, says, "We do it because we've always done it. It's a traditional part of running a theatre.

"I don't know how long it will be before somebody farther up in the corporation says, 'Hey, this isn't paying — why are we doing this?'"

During a recent school holiday for a teachers' convention, local theatres brought in special attractions that drew capacity audiences reminiscent of the hey-day of the matinee.

A visit to the matinee at such a time is like a trip back to childhood.

A line-up of waist-high patrons starts to coagulate at the theatre door at 12:05. The first feature is scheduled to begin at 1:30, when Godzilla, the monster with the heart of gold, will settle things once and for all with the (gulp) Smog Monster.

The queue lengthens, its members standing patiently, shifting from one foot to another. Conversation is fragmented.

"How much money you got?"

"I have to go to the bathroom."

"I'm going to buy two popcorns."

"I betcha Godzilla wins."

"We should kick these doors down."

The doors obligingly open and the theatre slurps up the string of kids, the cash register ringing them in, 75 cents at a time.

Inside the theatre is bedlam. It is an ant-hill in cross-section. Floors and seats are hidden beneath a sea of squirming bodies.

There is a protocol involved in attending a matinee. You do not simply take your seat and wait for the feature to begin.

You race to your seat, deposit your coat, jump on and off your seat three times in rapid succession to make sure the spring-up device functions satisfactorily. Then, trailing your muffler, you make a dash for the snack bar, struggling up the aisle against other incoming bodies, letting out the odd shriek. At the snack bar you buy a popcorn and a pop. Balancing one of these in each hand, you go to the bathroom …

All of this is well under way before the average adult can accomplish his blinking adjustment to the theatre gloom after the afternoon sunshine.

The roar cannot be described as dull. It has a distinctly piercing quality. When the theatre lights go out and the screen lights up, this roar does not subside, it intensifies — to a peak beyond measurement in mere decibels.

Phase Two of audience protocol: Deposit gum under seat; pelt Smarties at any adult foolhardy enough to enter the theatre.

Snippets of overhead conversation tell the rest of the story:

"These shows aren't really scary."

"You don't know me — I'm scared already."

"It's the music that scares me the most."

"Hey, there'th the Thmog Monthter."

"Holy shoot!"

"Hey, it's going to have babies."

"Look at the slime."

"Neat-o."

"C'mon Godzilla."

"Yeh, c'mon God baby."

"Way to go, God baby."

"I wish I had a cigarette."

"Yeh, me too. I forgot my cigarettes."

"Ugh, look at that slime."

"That's what you're going to have for supper."

"Yeh, French cuisine."

"Look, it's oozing all over."

"Who do you think will win?"

"Well, Godzilla's the hero, stupid."

"I know."

"Godzilla will win and then go away."

"Hey, he's bleeding."

"He's struck a leak."

"C'mon God baby."

"Lend me a quarter?"

"There's the mad scientist."

"Lend me a quarter?"

"That skeleton's still smoking."

"Yah, neat."

"Yeah, neat-o."

"The Thmog Monthterth getting up again."

"He's trying to shoot you, God baby."

"How much can this guy take?"

"Get him, Godzilla. Shoot him with your eye."

"All I want's a chocolate bar. That's all I want."

"Poke his eye out."

"I have to go to the bathroom"

"God never dies anyway."

"Where's he going now?"

"To another movie house."

At such a time, the matinee phenomenon looks as healthy as ever. But a number of special circumstances were at work. The teachers' convention made it a four-day weekend. That made it worthwhile for theatre management to bring in special attractions such as *Godzilla Versus the Smog Monster* and *The Wizard of Oz*, which are so good they draw full houses even at 75 cents a head.

The situation on an average Saturday is quite different.

The price of admission drops to 50 cents a head, and even then, theatres are less than half-full.

The economics are simple — if 200 seats are sold at 50 cents apiece, the gross is only $100. The price of the film alone is likely around $50, which doesn't leave much profit margin after paying staff, clean-up, lights and heat, and wear-and-tear.

"Quite frankly, when it comes to the financial side of kids' matinees, I don't like to look too closely," Mr. Moore says.

"As recently as two or three years ago, the matinee was still a paying proposition. Then audiences began to dwindle, and this year it's just no good at all."

Part of the problem is that movies suitable for matinee use are no longer being produced in any numbers.

"But it's phoney — the government wouldn't let it get that bad."

"Shut up, eh?"

"Yah, let's listen to the movie."

"Oh shut up."

"You shut up."

"No, you shut up."

"Shut up."

"Shut up."

Most of the films made today are violent and/or sexy and have a Restricted or Adult rating.

Prints are no longer available of old matinee stand-bys such as Roy Rogers, Gene Autrey, Abbott and Costello and The Three Stooges. And anyway, the tastes of the children of today lean away from westerns and slapstick. They like monsters and a few cartoons.

With suitable prints evaporating from both ends, the source of matinee movies is drying up, with the result that matinee fare becomes terribly repetitious.

"With the Adult classification in Alberta, there are very few films that kids can go to any more, except with their parents — and I don't know of a 13-year-old who wants to go anywhere, let alone to the movies, with his parents," Mr. Moore says.

"A mother phoned me the other day and complained that she had a 14-year-old boy, and the only movie in town he could get into was a Disney film."

What's left for matinee showing can be divided into three basic categories: Monster, cartoons and family films.

Three of the Canadian Theatres — the Plaza, Westbrook and Tivoli — generally show monster films and cartoons. A fourth Canadian Theatre, the Brentwood, offers a fare of cartoons and family type shows.

"And do you know, matinee attendance at the Brentwood is worse than at our other theatres," says Ron Tiboni, city supervisior for Canadian Theatres.

The Odeon Theatre has a policy of showing family films, such as the *Wizard of Oz*, *Island of the Blue Dolphins* and *Gypsy Colt*. And this type of film does no better than the monsters or cartoons, says Mr. Moore.

"Our policy of shying away from the monsters is really an attempt to appeal to parents to send their kids, rather than appealing directly to the kids. But our attendance figures show it doesn't work any better. My opposition sticks to showing horror — a very mild form of horror, Family-rated. But I figure if it doesn't make any difference to attendance figures, we might as well show the family films to avoid giving the industry a bad name. I suppose if horror paid off, we'd be showing it too, but it doesn't so we might as well show family movies." Mr. Moore says.

Although special features can withstand a 75-cents admission price, parents object to having to give their children more than 50 cents admission on an average Saturday. After all, the kids can stay home and watch TV for free.

■ ■ ■

But although television is an ever-present competition to movie matinees, theatre operators do not single it out as a major factor in the decline of matinees. Movie-houses continued to fill up with kids long after TV came on the scene.

After all, kids don't really go to matinees because of what's on the screen. Rather, they go because it is an exclusive club which welcomes only those under the age of 13 in possession of two quarters. In short, it is a place where a kid can be a kid.

Adults are not made welcome — either by the kids or by theatre management.

"We always warn an adult at the box-office that he likely won't enjoy the experience. If he insists on going in, we usually ask him to sit in the back row — to isolate him for his own sake, and also for the sake of the kids who like to get away from adults for awhile," says Mr. Moore.

An adult who stumbles into a children's matinee will feel like Gulliver in the land of the Lilliputians. In the course of the event he is likely to acquire a gob of chewing gum on the seat of his pants, ringing ears, and several small unidentified flying objects on the back of the head.

It is this "kids'-club" mystique which enabled the Saturday afternoon matinee to withstand the advent of TV.

What has really written The End to the phenomenon of kids' matinees is the shift of residential neighbourhoods. Many theatres are located in areas which no longer have many children living there.

"We don't hold any children's matinees in our downtown theatres at all any more," says Mr. Moore.

"It's hopeless, just hopeless to hold a kids' matinee in a theatre like the Uptown or the Grand anymore. The last time we tried, we attracted an audience of 25 kids per showing. Needless to say, it didn't pay.

"To sum it up — where the theatres are today there are no children. Where the children are, there are no theatres."

Mr. Tiboni points to the same factor in Canadian theatres. "Take the Tivoli. It's not that good for kids anymore because that area (Mission) is all going to apartment buildings. The Plaza (Kensington) is not too bad yet. Despite increasing numbers of apartment buildings, there are still kids living in this area. But the best of all is the Westbrook, which is surrounded by residential areas."

Parents may be willing to give their kids 50 cents, but it seems they are not willing to chauffeur their kids around to theatres on a Saturday. Very few cars pull up in front of the theatre to drop off kids or pick them up.

"If they don't live within walking distance of the theatre, they just don't get to the matinees too often," Mr. Tiboni says.

"While many existing theatres have lost their surrounding neighbourhoods, other residential areas have sprung up without a movie house."

Nevertheless, the matinees still offer one of the cheapest baby-sitting services in town. A rate of 50 cents for four hours is pretty hard to beat.

Mr. Tiboni estimates that a good half of the audience at any kids' matinee consists of preschoolers. Eight to nine-year-olds make up a large portion of the rest of the audience.

"We get very few kids in the 12- to 13-year-old bracket," he says.

While the matinees tend to be financial break-even propositions, they are very hard on staff and facilities.

One theatre manager describes the average mess left behind after a kids' matinee as "pretty heavy." Some of the theatres use "kids' brigades" to clean up the ankle-deep welter of popcorn boxes and other litter.

"And of course there is still the odd case of slashed upholstery. We just spent $400 fixing three seats that were slashed during a matinee last week," Mr. Tiboni says.

"Sometimes they don't mean to wreck a seat. They just find a little hole in the upholstery, get excited, and start picking at it until it turns into a big rip.

"We try a little to hold down the general ruckus — keep them from standing on the seats and things. But by and large, a matinee's a time for kids to be kids and we like to let them have fun," he says, getting back to the essence of the phenomenon.

Many adults today have fond memories about Saturday afternoon matinees when they were kids.

"It was wonderful," says one silver-haired man.

"Mom would give us each 11 cents to get in, plus five cents more for penny candy. I remember once there was this gripping scene where a car was rolling over. And then it said 'To Be Continued Next Week.' Well, the next week happened to be in Lent, and we were not allowed to go to the movie. I still wonder today what happened to that car."

A movie called *The Black Whip* inspires fond reminiscences from another adult.

"We saw it three times, and it was better each time. Great ending. The Whip, you see, turned out to be this frail little girl ..."

Mr. Moore, too, has a special warm spot in his heart for the kids' matinee as an institution. He was a manager of a city theatre in the heyday of the Saturday-afternoon children's matinee.

"We used to have a birthday cake every week. I was a great matinee manager. I used to get up every week and make a fool of myself, leading games and things.

"In those days, the theatre was a social centre, with kids' committees and things. It was always all local neighbourhood kids who came. We knew most of them by name.

"The manager was very important. You used to have a lot of kids telling you about what happened in school during the week. There were always kids who just had to speak to you, no matter where you were in the theatre or what you were doing. They just wanted to say, 'Hi, I'm here.'

"And there was always stuff coming down off the balcony, and someone would tattle, and the ushers would have to go up there and try to find out who did it," Mr. Moore says.

"I guess when you ask why we continue to have kids' matinees, if I were honest, I would say just for the love of it. Like a lot of other people, I'm terribly sentimental about it. Sentimentality is the only reason left for carrying on."

Mr. Tiboni emphasizes the financial problems with kids' matinees.

"By rights we should be charging one dollar a kid to get in. As it is, we don't even break even, not with the cost of the film. We plan to keep on showing kid's matinees — but we won't be making money at it," he says.

"We feel somehow we have an obligation to the neighbourhood. But guess the neighbourhood is telling us they really don't want this," says Mr. Moore.

"The way it's going, I suppose the kids' matinee is going to disappear. It looks like it's coming to an end, and I don't like it to come to an end. It should be a protected species. We've tried a lot of different things but nothing seems to work.

"There's no use asking where it's going — it's gone."

• **1975** Feature Writing •

Soon, the riders will return

Nigel Gibson

Montreal Gazette

"The moon was down over the mountains when the white horses, their nostrils filled with the stench of blood, swooped down into the valleys, seeking out the children.

"Dazzling the little savages with their speed and beauty, they lured them on to their backs, carried them laughing and screaming into the black hills and dashed them to pieces on the rocks below ..."

— From an Indian legend

David Barry Catel should have been a twin, but his twin stopped growing in the womb, and was dead at birth.

"When that boy is good, he'll be very good," the doctor who delivered him couldn't help remarking. "But when he's bad, he'll be twice as bad, and twice as strong."

Growing up in the weary streets and pool halls of Cartierville, the strapping hazel-eyed youth did his best to live up to the old doctor's prediction.

He fought his way up and down the block, cut up a few garden hoses in the neighbourhood "just to see what it was like," played a mean game of football, and rode his motorcycle as long and as hard as he could, from early spring, through the icy winds of late fall into winter.

His mother, Shirley, resigned to her maternal fate, used to tell him if he lived to be 21, she'd deserve a medal.

Barry was 21 last June. His parents and two brothers surprised him with a small party in their family bungalow, and he in turn surprised his mother with a gold medallion inscribed: "For making it this far Mum, 53-74."

He didn't make it much further.

Shortly before noon, on a sunny early October morning, as he roared along O'Brien Blvd. on his powerful 750 Norton, dressed in a white leather jacket and an old pair of jeans, he smacked into the side of a car pulling out of a shopping centre.

Barry's ribs splintered on impact, puncturing his lungs. His silver helmet flew off and his head hit the concrete, shattering his skull and sending bone fragments tearing through his brain.

The huge bike, its fibreglass gas tank ruptured, crashed down on him and burst into flames.

A passing post office employee doused the blaze with a portable extinguisher, and although badly burned, Barry was still breathing when St. Laurent police pulled his unconscious body out from under the smoldering wreckage.

He was dead on arrival at Sacred Heart Hospital. An autopsy was performed, and coroner Maurice Laniel returned his verdict: Death by violent means without criminal responsibility.

Once again, in sheds and basements across Quebec, the two-wheeled chrome monsters are stirring from their winter sleep. Their canvas shrouds off, their bodies stripped down, greased and gleaming they lie in wait for spring: Waiting for the right moment to burst into life and hit the open road with their young masters.

There are more than 140,000 registered motorbikes in Quebec — about 50 per cent of the Canadian total — and every year the grim toll mounts.

In 1971, 90 people were killed and 2,000 injured in bike accidents here.

In 1973, the casualty list soared to 5,446 injured and 178 killed — an increase of about 100 per cent in two years.

Although official statistics are not yet available, last season's toll, according to emergency medical personnel, was the worst on record and with winter sales of bikes booming, this summer promises to be the bloodiest of them all.

"They've got it coming to them," says one ambulance driver who spends much of his summer picking young victims off the roads and rushing them to the nearest hospital.

"These kids are crazy, sick and they think they own the streets," the driver says, shaking his head in disgust.

"If it was up to me, I'd leave them where they fall — as an example to others … How else are they going to learn …?

"Ever see a motorcycle accident? It's pathetic," the driver says. "They don't behave so high and mighty then. No sir they don't.

"Just lie there moaning and kicking their legs in the air like a rabbit that's taken a load of buckshot in the gut and doesn't know what happened." He laughs bitterly.

"That is if they still got all their grey stuff, and their necks aren't broken. The ones with the busted necks just lie there pissing their pants."

The driver laughs again.

Dr. Peter Cohen of the Royal Victoria Hospital's emergency department doesn't like motorbikes either.

"The accident rate is fantastically high," Dr. Cohen says. "There are almost as many people coming in for motorcycles during the summer as for cars, and there are many more cars on the road."

Most common injuries are to the head, neck, arms, chest and abdomen, but, Dr. Cohen says, "there are no injuries they are protected from.

"One fellow came in here last summer with the chain of his bike embedded in his leg and groin. The groin was torn apart, the leg had to come off, so we amputated …"

Head and neck injuries are the worst. Even if the victims survive the accident, they are often paralyzed for life, or linger on in deep comas beyond hope of recovery.

Many hospitals have their wards of shame, gloomy chambers filled with broken young bodies, hooked up to feeding tubes and urine bags, staring into space and drooling.

Their brains crushed beyond repair, they lie stiffly on their air mattresses, oblivious to the efforts of the medical staff struggling to keep them alive — pounding their emaciated chests, day after day, hour after hour, suctioning thick gobs of mucus from their lungs. Feeding them, washing them, dusting their raw bed sores, turning them, and suctioning them again until at last the battle is lost. Pneumonia sets in and the long agony ends.

"It doesn't matter what type of protective gear you wear, you can't protect the neck," Dr. Cohen says. "Neither can you pad the sidewalks, the trees and the concrete pavement."

There are no driving tests for motorcyclists in the province. Only an eye test and a written examination are required.

By contrast, the Ontario motorcyclist driver must pass a more detailed written examination as well as a practical road test involving an obstacle course and various braking and safety exercises.

In Quebec, it took an angry public campaign, spearheaded by the staff of the Montreal Neurological Hospital, for the province to make helmet use compulsory three years ago.

Even then, penalties for infractions were made ridiculously lenient: $5 or $10 fines or 48 hours in jail.

The cult, however, has its supporters.

Peter, a 24-year-old history student who lost both legs in a bike smash-up last fall and has been in hospital ever since, is one of them.

Peter's girlfriend Nancy, 23, who was riding with him when he crashed into the back of a car, didn't take long at all.

She was thrown 50 feet and killed instantly.

"That's the way she would have wanted it," Peter says dreamily. "She was quite a chick. She wanted a bike for herself.

"When I get out of here, I'm going to get one for her. Ride it for her too …"

Behind the euphoria, the hype and the rising death toll lies a multi-billion dollar industry — and another big Japanese success story.

In the beginning, there was the legend according to James Dean, Hell's Angels, Marlon Brando, Peter Fonda and the great Hollywood escape machine.

In the middle-60s, however, the Japanese bikes hit the shores of North America and the legend became big business.

Over the last decade, four Japanese companies — Honda, Suzuki, Yamaha and Kawasaki — have seized almost complete control of the $3 billion North American market.

U.S. companies such as Harley Davidson have fought back with their star-spangled version of the great American dream machine, but they have all but been drowned out in the hype of the big four.

Honda City started in 1965 with a small store on St. Catherine St. Now, they have five stores and are opening a sixth in Kingston, Ont.

The three stores in Montreal alone sold more than 1,000 bikes last year, and bad publicity isn't a problem.

Outside the store, a group of kids in jeans and sneakers gather to stare open-mouthed at the gleaming machines on display. Running their hands respectfully over the bright chrome fittings, and dreaming of possession.

It's not that easy for a kid in inflationary times. A medium-sized bike now costs about $1,500 — up several hundred dollars over the last few years.

But that doesn't stop them.

Barry Catel was also a believer.

"He never was much for cars," his younger brother recalls. "He wanted to be free and bikes were the way for him."

"He wanted to go to night school. His job was getting him down at times. But roaring down a country road, with the wind blowing in his face, he was free.

"He drove fast, had a few tumbles, but he was a good driver."

"It would never happen to him," his mother adds.

But it did, and when it was all over, long before it should have been, he was just a charred young corpse in a closed coffin.

"The mortician phoned us to say there was no way they could fix him up," his mother explains.

"I'm sure it was instantaneous, but I can still picture him lying there, all burnt and crying, 'mummy, mummy, please help me.'"

"It doesn't matter who you are. When you're in that coffin, you look dead," his father Derek adds. "It's the best way, even if nothing is wrong with you …"

"He couldn't stand ugliness," his mother says. "Ugliness he couldn't stand.

"Ugliness like a flower that was dead, or the wrinkles on an old person's face.

"He never wanted to be ugly. He never wanted me to get old. But if you told him he loved beauty, he would deny it, because only sissies did that. He didn't like anybody to see he was soft."

The Church of the Good Shepherd in Cartierville was packed with young people. The coffin buried under a mountain of flowers.

Outside on the lawn, a young piper in a kilt and white knee socks played for his dead friend.

"It was a fine haunting song, very sad," Shirley Catel recalls. "He looked so alone, and the song sounded like it was coming from above …"

At the Mount Royal cemetery under a clear blue sky, the young people filed by for the last time, showering the coffin with flowers.

It's all over now, the flowers lie wilted in the melting snow, and Barry Catel rests free and in peace forever.

Soon it will be summer, and in the hushed stillness of the night, the riders will return.

Roaring past the cemetery, down the winding mountain road in the shadow of the cross, reaching out for the bright city lights beyond …

• 1977 Feature Writing •

The system failed and killed a child

Brenda Zosky

Toronto Star

Somehow the system broke down and killed Vicky Ellis.
She died in a sea of trendy psychological theories, obscure legalities and the niceties of etiquette between child-help agencies.

Vicky's death was a majestic failure for Ontario's child care industry. Just about every facet was involved, and they blew it.

Four ministries touched the case: Health, Community and Social Services, the Attorney General's Department and the Solicitor General's Department.

About $2 million was spent on the family during the past seven years.

Thirteen social and health institutions were involved.

Nine different professions, including psychiatrists, police, judges, lawyers, social workers and others had a hand in it.

Still, Vicky is dead. In the end, nobody really protected her right to live.

How could it happen?

Mountains of evidence tabled during the five-week inquest into her death make it almost impossible to understand why, with all that expertise, the vulnerable newborn was left with her mother.

There are the appalling police photographs of her sisters, one after death, one near death; both bruised, dehydrated and dirty, with patches of raw, punctured flesh.

There are the written reports about the tragic physical and emotional neglect suffered by all Vicky's four brothers and sisters.

Neglect killed two. The others were taken by the Children's Aid Society (CAS), which feared for their lives.

In spite of this sordid history — and there are stacks of information about it on record in the coroner's court — Vicky was left virtually alone with her mother, a woman diagnosed as psychopathic.

The baby was dead 21 days after Judge Norris Weisman decided it was safe to send her home.

On Feb. 9, Ruth Parry, a social worker at the Family Court Clinic run by the Clarke Institute of Psychiatry, told Judge Weisman she would "stake everything I know" on her conviction that Vicky would be safe in the care of her mother.

When the judge announced his decision to take Parry's advice, he commented: "The evidence presented by Mrs. Ruth Parry was by far the best I've heard in my court" and called it "complete" and "perceptive."

But during the inquest, both Coroner Elie Cass and crown attorney Michael Morse suggested that Parry had been "carried away" by the personal challenge of treating the mother, Deborah Ellis, rather then protecting the child.

They said she had lost her objectivity.

Parry herself admitted at the inquest that she had done an "inadequate" job of gathering background information on which to base her outspoken support of the decision to let Mrs. Ellis care for her child.

But Vicky Ellis' life might still have been saved if Judge Weisman had decided to admit one piece of key evidence: A coroner's verdict on Vicky's sister Darlene, which cited "physical and emotional neglect" as a reason for death.

Weisman called it "collateral evidence" and ruled it inadmissable.

Parry says if she had seen the coroner's verdict, she would not have let Vicky go home — to her death.

But while it is easy to single out turning points in the case and individual decisions that contributed to the tragedy of Vicky Ellis, child care and legal professionals say that doing so only disguises the real problems.

The underlying issues the experts raise are: Poor communications between agencies; a system that forces family court judges to be too dependent on expert witnesses; the imprecise and unscientific nature of the social sciences which rely on constantly changing theories, and a giant child care industry geared more to preserving the family unit than protecting children.

Central to the debate about what went wrong is the incredible list of things that social worker Mrs. Parry didn't appear to be aware of when she convinced Weisman to let Deborah Ellis keep her daughter.

She didn't know that the mother had been taking sedatives (Valium and Noludar) for 10 years.

She didn't know that a psychiatrist at Toronto Western Hospital had written that "anyone attempting to relate to her (Deborah Ellis) in a therapeutic way is destined to defeat ..."

She didn't know that Mrs. Ellis, after being convicted of neglect in a criminal court, had disappeared, violating probation.

She didn't know that Darlene Ellis had died of neglect.

She had not seen the police photos of the battered children.

She didn't know circumstances surrounding the drowning of Parrish Ellis, who was left unattended in the bathtub.

She didn't know that Deborah Ellis had named a particular babysitter as being responsible for Darlene's death.

These are just some of the things that Mrs. Parry was not aware of, even though they were in either one or all of the CAS files, family court files, hospital files and police files.

Somehow the information never reached the woman charged with total responsibility for the Ellis family.

Why not?

Chief Judge Tedford Andrews of the provincial court family division said in an interview: "I have always had concern that agencies are so jealous and so self-righteous in their approach that there frequently is a lack of communication between them."

"Are we helpless?" asked crown attorney Mike Morse at one point during the hearing. "Will we have to attend yet another inquest into yet another Ellis death?"

• **1978** Feature Writing •
Danger: Moonies at work

Josh Freed

Montreal Gazette

The seemingly endless gravel road halted abruptly at a high barbed-wire fence and a wooden sentry post.

It was midnight and the end of a three-hour van ride from San Francisco when I got my first glimpse of Boonville Ideal City Ranch — training headquarters and alleged "brainwashing" centre for Rev. Sun Myung Moon's Unification Church.

I had come to learn what had happened to Benji Carroll, a close Montreal friend who had become involved with the Moonies. The little I knew of the ranch made me cautious, having been informed that hundreds of people had undergone rapid personality changes here in only a few days.

I was so nervous about my visit I had left a signed statement with friends, asking them to retrieve me if I would not leave on my own.

On leaving the van we were herded toward a shadowy tin structure and urged to bed down immediately. Inside, scraps of thin foam and a wooden floor awaited. Bodies were sprawled everywhere.

A morning drizzle was just waning when a live rendition of Raindrops Keep Falling on My Head roused me from a fitful sleep.

In seconds, bodies were leaping into their clothes and exuberant hands were hauling me into a circle of people gathering to sing wake-up songs.

"Good morning everyone!" boomed a clean-cut guitar player, wearing a V-neck sweater and a toothpaste smile. "How are you?"

"Ter-r-r-rific!", dozens of smiling faces replied thunderously, bursting into 30 minutes of cheery morning tunes. It was 7 a.m. on a wet Tuesday morning, and life at Boonville was rolling into gear.

Tucked into the gentle rolling forest of Mendocino County, 120 miles north of San Francisco, the 700-acre camp was a pleasant site with simple accommodations. Standing in the fresh country air, surrounded by wholesome faces and vibrant singing, my original paranoia seemed far away and unfounded.

Everything we did was punctuated by endless cheering and general noise — in particular the "family cheer," a seemingly innocent little chant called a "chooch" that required us to link arms and holler:

"Ch-ch-choo, ch-ch-choo, ch-ch-choo, Yea! Yea! POW!"

Even the dead hours of night were eventful at Boonville. All night long bodies shifted mysteriously about the Chicken Palace, as vehicles carried new people in and spirited others away.

By morning, about a third of the faces I had bedded down with the night before had changed. When the strains of Red Red Robin came filtering through a light veil of sleep, I had already decided that this second day would be my last in Boonville.

The previous night's activities had ended as they began with a barrage of singing, chanting and confessions. Food throughout was a tasty combination of starches, with hardly a grain of protein — a diet that a former camp cook later told me is budgeted at 50 cents a day per person.

Now, on the second day, I was assigned a shadow — a pleasant enough fellow who thudded along beside me wherever I went, even the bathroom, talking nonstop.

Fortunately, by this time, I had developed a number of small tricks to preserve my sanity — minute gestures that somehow helped me to keep my sense of self.

I found that I could avoid holding hands during singing if I grabbed one of the few songbooks and held it for my "brothers" and "sisters" to see — an unselfish gesture that kept one of my hands busy for a precious half hour.

The unsettling stare of the Moonies could be beaten back by relentlessly returning it until they looked away. Good eyes and alert reflexes helped me snatch salt, pepper and the like before a Moonie could do it for me.

I even gained a measure of satisfaction by chanting mindless ditties to myself at occasional moments.

It is astonishing how important these trivial tricks seemed when I felt every fibre of my person being sucked into this anonymous collectivity. The pull of the group was so strong that at times, inexplicably, I felt like giving in myself — despite what I knew.

Several bright and normal people who came up with me were clearly swayed by the group's indoctrination techniques, shedding their critical faculties quickly in the intense environment. While brain-washing may or may not be the correct term to describe the process, it is a terrifyingly effective means of influencing people.

By the end of my two-day stay, family members were putting enormous emotional pressure on me to stay "one more day." I did not, but ex-Moonies later explained to me the stages that would have followed. All had undergone the same experience.

The next step would have been a fantastic sales pitch to stay for the weekend session. Lying is routine, they say, as family members make use of information gathered during "sharing" periods.

Disillusioned teachers are told they can work in the project's alternative school (non-existent); single men see the promise of an interesting girl-friend (unfulfilled), and shy people find a flood of appreciative new friends (temporary).

The weekend session is a powerful and a moving experience, attended by hundreds of people. It is followed by intense efforts to convince your now fuzzy mind to attend a five-day "advanced" seminar at another Moonie site — where "3,000 years of history" are explained in 10 lectures.

The overwhelming intensity, spirit and seeming normality of the new life around you does the rest, as the project seems more and more to be a once-in-a-lifetime opportunity.

Reality somehow shifts a few degrees. Isolation, dwindling sleep, little protein and no time to re-evaluate what is happening cause you increasingly to lose perspective. You never really decide to stay — you simply defer indefinitely the decision to leave.

In the days and weeks that follow, the religious aspects of the camps seem increasingly convincing as well, ex-Moonies say. You feel special — in touch with some kind of force — and may even have religious dreams or experiences in early weeks, before dreaming stops altogether.

And when Moon's name begins to come up in lectures, two weeks later, it somehow doesn't seem to matter as much as it might have once.

Day by day he becomes more important, his ideas ever-present, until one day it seems only natural — a sudden revelation — to realize he is the Messiah responsible for your new life.

It is the final burst of enlightenment, and you dedicate your life to convincing others to come to Boonville and learn about Moon the way you did.

You have become a Moonie.

• **1979** Feature Writing •

Going quietly wasn't the Chief's way

Val Sears

Toronto Star

It was not like him to go quietly.

Alone, sure. He was always alone, all the good and bad times, except for three women, a mother and two wives, dead now.

But the John Diefenbaker I remember should have gone out banners unfurled, cursing his enemies, swearing to return, shouting defiance at all the petty men who would sever his mystic bond with Canada, with the prairie earth, with … the people.

Instead, he died alone in his study. Just quietly slumped over his paper and went gently into that dark night. Not like that furious old man at all.

I remember Dief. There's not a man or a woman or a child in the country who ever met him or even stood close to him who doesn't remember him. And have a story about him.

A lot of the stories will be the same. But they'll all be different. Because no two people saw Dief the same way, nor heard what he said and took the same meaning. His words crossed and looped and stopped, leaving an innuendo dangling so you had to finish the truth yourself. And if you got it wrong — or he said later it was wrong — then you were the fool, not he.

Still, that's the way Dief will be remembered. In stories. He wanted so much to be memorialized as a great prime minister, as a fighting civil rights lawyer — which he was — as a great Canadian, which he was as well.

But he left a small legacy of legislation, few great parliamentary deeds done, little changed. Instead, he governed by visions, by a mysterious linkage with "the people" that would guide him infallibly to do right as his hero, Sir John A. Macdonald, had done in building Canada.

I first met Dief in 1960 when I was assigned to Ottawa as bureau chief for the *Star*. He was at the height of his power. He bestrode the narrow world of Ottawa like a colossus.

He had humbled the upstart Lester Pearson. He had won the greatest parliamentary majority in Canadian history. The civil service hated him and feared him. They liked the Liberals.

Once, determined that it was Canada's role to help "free the captive nations," he ordered a speech written on that militant theme. His staff were too embarrassed at the naiveté and presumption to prepare anything but a watered-down series of platitudes.

Dief read it, threw it back at his aide, subsequently a distinguished ambassador, and thundered, "Take that back to your Liberal friends down the hall and have it written the way I ordered it."

The fact was that Dief loved his own language, loved to improvise, loved to play his audience and, even when necessity forced him to use writers, he would throw away whole sections — already made available to the press for publication — if the crowd was responding best to his anecdotes.

He was an inept governor. He didn't much like legislating, although he loved the swirl of rhetoric and power in the House of Commons. Dief came really alive during elections with "everyone against me but the people."

He did not like Quebec electioneering, of course. He spoke terrible French and drew small audiences. On many trips by train he would carry an "instant crowd" in a back coach which got out at stops to bunch around him for the photographers. Filled with Scotch, they would expand to impressive proportions of roaring applause.

At one platform, the mayor introduced him to his son — "mon fils." "How do you do, Mr. Monfeese," Dief said.

I didn't like him, if like is not too watery a word for such a man. I thought he was a bully and that he twisted the truth. But I rejoiced in him. We all did. He was splendid copy and when he spoke, although I had heard the speech on the campaign a hundred times, it was a joy to listen to the new intonation, the different timing, to repeat the climaxes until Dief heard us and scowled.

He called me "Smears" or "Sneers" and once devoted 20 minutes of a 40-minute speech to attacking me personally for something I had written. He was shaking with indignation and with … well, I don't know what.

Dief was furious. He had told a Montreal audience it was his attacks on the Soviet Union that had got Nikita Khruschov so mad he had taken off his shoe and banged it on the table at the United Nations.

I had pointed out that Diefenbaker had spoken more than two weeks before the incident, so it was unlikely the shoe-banging had to do with anything the prime minister had said.

It was the low point in our relationship.

He was convinced the entire press was against him and trying to destroy him, a feeling that was mortally encouraged by a smart-ass remark of mine while getting on a campaign plane — "Come, gentlemen, we have a government to overthrow."

It meant nothing, but he repeated it endlessly as evidence that we were villains, all of us. He said once the only person in the press gallery he really respected was Norman DePoe, the then-chief correspondent for the Canadian Broadcasting Corp. in Ottawa and the best they have ever had.

Dief, of course, was especially loved on the prairies by people who largely shared his feeling that the east was stuffed with barbarians after his blood.

In his speeches, he would always devote 15 minutes to "the same old bunch," the Liberal ministers who had ruled before and were now seeking to impose their vile wills again.

Once, in a small prairie town, I was sitting beside a local editor at the press table. When Dief got to the "same old bunch" section, I scribbled SOB on the pad and leaned back to enjoy the familiar refrain. The editor leaned over, saw my shorthand for "same old bunch" and ripped the pad to pieces, yelling: "You eastern bastards are all the same. You hate him, don't you? You hate him."

He once, and only once, gave a long rambling speech about attending the founding convention of the United Nations and discovering a cigarette box in a wastebasket on which was written the draft of the United Nations constitution.

This was a palpable lie — as Mike Pearson told me — because the draft ran to hundreds of words and was prepared far away from San Francisco. And American cellophane boxes couldn't be written on anyway.

When I pointed out the discrepancy, Dief threatened to sue me for calling the prime minister a liar.

He told me once, in a rare private interview, that his speaking style was intentionally convoluted.

"Sometimes, I start on a sentence," he said, "and realize that it is taking me where I don't want to go. So I switch direction in the middle and go somewhere else. That way they can't catch me."

He was hard to catch, damn hard. And yet you knew as you sat there, drowsy with his speech rhythms, waiting, hoping for some new fact, that there were discrepancies.

He was full of humbug about nuclear weapons, as well. It was a vital issue during his administration. Should Canada arm her Bomarc missiles with nuclear warheads or not? Dief wouldn't say yes and wouldn't say no. He simply stalled.

He didn't realize that his own ministers were becoming restless with the unresolved issue. The rot was setting in.

He didn't need advisers or economic experts or foreign policy analysts to govern. All he needed to do was to consult the people, plug into the reservoir and all would become clear. And anyone who didn't see that was crazy. And a traitor to boot.

Finally, of course, he was surrounded by traitors and unbelievers and addled drunks and mindless supporters and genuine critics who thought he was destroying the Progressive Conservative party, never mind the country.

He lost it all one day in Maple Leaf Gardens when he was defeated in a leadership fight he knew he couldn't win. After the first vote, when the end was clear, he looked at his wife, Olive, by his side and said it was time to go. Oh God, it was way past time. But he couldn't acknowledge it. He had to suffer humiliation. He would not give up. Not then. Not later.

I saw him only a few times in those last years. Two years ago, *Star* photographer Boris Spremo and I spent three days with Dief in Barbados. He was preparing the third volume of his memoirs.

He was little changed. His jowls wobbled, his lips twitched in that kind of half-laugh, half-sneer he used on people he distrusted, like me.

After one particularly long and revealing interview, he said to an aide: "I didn't tell him anything, did I? He didn't catch me on anything, did he? Well, I knew he wouldn't get me."

In the last campaign, I had thought to interview him in Prince Albert and asked his aide to make the arrangements.

"Sir," the aide told Dief, "Sears is coming to interview you. Now you must be tactful and not say anything nasty about Clark."

"You mean I can't even call him a sonovabitch?"

I think he meant Clark.

• **1980** Enterprise Reporting •

The start of Terry's long, long road

Tim Padmore, Chris Gainor

Vancouver Sun

*T*he kid was too small for the game and not exceptionally talented.
    "Just making the team was a tremendous feat. I've never seen a kid with more desire."
That's how Alex Devlin, basketball coach at Simon Fraser University, remembers a 19-year-old named Terry Fox who scratched his way to a substitute spot on the junior varsity team.

But Fox never got a chance to scratch higher.

Late in the season, his right knee began to hurt. "We were playing on a hard, rubberized floor and everyone had knee and ankle problems and that's what I thought I had," Fox said. He didn't bother telling his coach.

"After the season, when it got worse, it got to the point where I couldn't put any weight on the knee at all any more. I had to hop out of the house and down to the car so my dad could drive me to the doctor."

Dr. Robert Heffelfinger had been the Fox family physician since 1969 and knew Terry as a very healthy boy who needed little care beyond that required to repair the knocks of an athletic life — a fractured wrist at one time, a mild shoulder separation another.

He examined the knee. It was swollen and tender and Fox couldn't bend it properly. He suspected a significant problem — cancer a possibility, but a remote one — and referred his patient to an orthopedic surgeon, Dr. Michael Piper, for X-rays and diagnosis.

Fox kicks himself for not going to the doctor even earlier, but he had done the right thing: He had brought his trouble to the doctor when it was clear that it was persisting unreasonably.

The tentative diagnosis was osteosarcoma, a relatively rare bone cancer that tends to strike the young and the healthy.

In hospital, there were more X-rays and batteries of tests looking for substances secreted by tumor cells and searching for evidence of other tumors.

Each test with no word increased Fox's anxiety. "I thought it might be the cartilage or ligaments and later that it might even involve amputation, but I didn't put the word cancer to it.

"When the whole family came, I knew something was wrong. The doctor said I had a malignant tumor and I asked 'What's that?' — I didn't know, and he told me and said he was going to do an amputation in four days and that there might still be cancer cells in my blood and they were going to do chemotherapy treatments.

"It was a shock. I cried and cried."

Adjustment to the shock is complicated by the myths people entertain about cancer.

Often, the cancer is attributed to an injury. (Fox injured his right knee in a car accident the November before, but there is no scientific evidence suggesting there might be a link to the cancer.)

People may assume there is little or no chance for a cure.

They may imagine that cancer is contagious, and fear for their loved ones.

Most damaging are the horror stories — the grandmother who died in agony, the friend of a friend shattered by chemotherapy, films like *Love Story*. Those who are cured, those who find chemotherapy no more distressing than taking aspirin, and those whom the disease inspires to find meaning in their lives are seldom heard from.

No sign of other tumors had shown up in Fox's leg, or elsewhere. (His lungs, a common site for osteosarcoma to spread to, were examined particularly carefully.)

Osteosarcoma cells spread easily along "tissue planes," the divisions between bundles or layers of tissue. The object of surgery is to remove every viable tumor cell and the most conservative course would have been to take off Fox's leg at the hip, along with all the upper leg muscles that might harbor a stray sarcoma cell.

But the operation would have been much more crippling than a mid-thigh amputation and since there was no sign of spread, it was decided to go with the less drastic operation.

After the operation, Dr. Piper formed a stump by sewing muscle and skin around the end of the bone. Nineteen days later, a temporary leg was fitted to the still-swollen stump by Ben Speicher of Hodgson Orthotics, and the first permanent leg was fitted four months later. But Speicher's skills were not really tested until much later when Fox asked for a leg that would carry him at a trot for 5,000 miles.

The trick is learning to use the artificial knee. The complicated motion involves throwing the knee forward while weight is placed on the other leg.

The stump is held in the plastic socket of the prosthesis by suction. There are no belts. Air inside the socket escapes through a valve when the stump is inserted and an airtight seal is formed.

The most complicated part of such legs is the knee.

Like real knees, they must take a lot of punishment and provide solid support, yet be flexible when the user is sitting, walking or running. Artificial knees are expensive, and there are many types to meet varying needs.

Barely two weeks after the amputation, Fox was admitted to the B.C. Cancer Control Agency hospital to be evaluated for the drug treatments that he had been told about.

It is likely that even then the cells that would fell him three years later were lodged dormant in his lungs.

To qualify for adjuvant therapy a patient has to be considered at high risk for relapsing. This is certainly the case for osteosarcoma, Fox's disease, which recurs 80 per cent of the time if the only treatment is surgery.

In fact, it was publicity about drug therapy given another famous victim of bone cancer, young Teddy Kennedy, son of the senator, that spurred the widespread adoption of chemotherapy in the mid-1970s.

Fox was immediately considered for admission to an experimental protocol at the cancer agency. The experiment is to find out the better of two therapies, both of which use a pair of cancer-killing drugs called methotrexate and adriamycin.

Each drug is effective against osteosarcoma, but because it is a rare tumor, doctors have not yet worked out the best way of administering them.

It seems clear the results are better when both are given, catching the cancer in a sort of chemical crossfire. But should the treatment alternate the two drugs? Or is the best procedure a course of adriamycin followed by a course of methotrexate?

A random assignment — basically a coin toss — sent Fox to the alternating treatment branch of the trial.

But if the crossfire was killing cancer cells, it was also killing healthy ones.

Both drugs cause nausea and hair loss. Adriamycin occasionally causes significant heart damage, leading to a form of congestive heart failure.

"They made you sick, tired and fatigued. They wiped you out," remembered Fox. For him, the worse was adriamycin. When he was taking the other drug, he said, he would be ill overnight, but then feel somewhat better, although his appetite would not return for a couple of days.

And his hair fell out. That was the worse part. "I cried and got upset for a longer time when they told me I was going to lose my hair than when they told me I was going to lose my leg."

The matter of side effects from chemotherapy has created a great deal of confusion.

By their very nature, many of the agents are toxic to normal cells as well as to cancerous ones.

However, that doesn't mean that taking one of these drugs is going to make a patient throw up or their hair fall out. The most common thing that limits the dosage of a cancer drug is damage to the white cells and platelet-forming cells. Like cancer cells, these blood cells multiply rapidly and hence are sensitive to drugs that interfere with their reproduction.

But you don't feel a low white blood cell count. You will suffer only if the count goes low enough that there are not enough white cells to fight off infection. If your platelets get low enough, you may suffer internal bleeding.

It's the doctor's job to skirt these dangerous shoals, while keeping the drug dose high enough to kill the cancer.

Some chemotherapy drugs are virtually innocuous compared to the legend. An example is the drugs used for many kinds of leukemia, which are taken by mouth and usually have no unpleasant side effects.

Ironically, patients sometimes complain if there are no side effects. Dr. Mike Noble, a New Westminster cancer specialist: "Patients sometimes say, 'I didn't get sick, does that mean it's not working?'"

Fox's treatments were continued, every three weeks, for 14 months, with only rare exceptions when a treatment might be delayed or a dosage adjusted because of side effects.

In September, the adriamycin was stopped. Fox had reached a lifetime limit for the drug; if he had received more, he would have risked serious heart damage. The last methotrexate treatment was March 31, 1978, a date that Fox marked carefully. "At the end, they gave me a little party in the pool room at the agency. The nurses all came down and they gave me a little cake."

It was one of the pleasant moments of an episode that, for him, was often distressing.

"When I get sick, I want to be alone. I want to be shut away from everyone else, and I was always in a four-bed room," he said. But worse than the lack of privacy were the constant reminders of his own worst moments. The contrast with his dreams was almost too much to bear.

"Right after the amputation, I was on an orthopedic ward with a bunch of kids. That type of atmosphere for me was easy, I was recovering and getting stronger. I had always been the healthiest person I had known, and I was the healthiest person in the room (at the cancer clinic). Other than having one leg and a 50 to 70 per cent chance of living, I was healthy," he said, without irony. "But when I was sick and vomiting in a room with other people, hearing those things, that's what you shouldn't have to do."

When people come into the cancer clinic, said chaplain Colin Johnstone, they are often shaken by what they find.

"The hospital is a very, very primitive earthy place and people go through culture shock when they come to this place where people are sick and emotions are raw, but where there is also a lot of very deep caring."

For many, the four-bed rooms allow that caring to work. "You say, 'What the hell, he's seen me at my worst,' ... and the rooms can lead to tremendous strength and support.

"The trouble is, there are a lot of people who are very, very private, like Terry, and they like to be alone."

"Terry hated this place for what it symbolized. Others look at it as a safe haven."

One reason, he said, is that the staff are not afraid of cancer.

In fact, they like it there, something most people find hard to understand.

Nurse Sharon Burke: "If we tell anybody, nurses, friends, that where we work is a cancer clinic they say, 'Isn't that depressing.' … And these are intelligent people!

"I say, 'No, it can be really sad sometimes, but you see a lot of strength in human beings.' The strength people show, the strength Terry showed running across Canada, is equalled by a lot of patients, in the coping they do day to day."

• **1983** Feature Writing •

Almost-forgotten horror still remembered

Bill McGuire

London Free Press

It was a hot July 6 at Centennial Park on the banks of the Ottawa River that summer of 1951. We were playing baseball for the town championship, about midget age. Had my usual game. One hit, picked off first while showing off, misjudged a routine pop behind second and kicked it into centre field. No real damage. Think we won.

Next day, I didn't go to work in my dad's store. Had a headache. Never had one before. Bummed around all afternoon. Sneaked a cigarette and didn't want it. Went to bed about 6 p.m. with a fever, feeling rotten.

Two hours later, complained of a pain in my hips. "Polio," my mother said. In comes the family doctor (remember those days?). Around 10 p.m., I am walking into the Pembroke General Hospital feeling strange. I can't bend over to untie my shoes. What the hell is going on? I just put them on 20 minutes ago. Ask my brother to take off my shoes. He tells me what to do with them, Ottawa Valley style. Thanks, Roy.

My spine is tapped. I can still feel it. Woke up seven days later in an Ottawa isolation hospital. No pain. Family circled around the bed in hospital smocks. Mother refused to wear face mask. Good on you, Mom. She had been told I was dying and that it was only a matter of hours until the creeping paralysis reached the heart.

Remember a priest administering last rites. A waste of time, Father, I'm only 16. Can't move a muscle and am lying down. Mirrors are attached to bed so visitors can be seen. Beside the bed is an iron lung, a fearsome looking machine. The only time I had ever heard of an iron lung was from a midway barker urging a crowd to "come in and see the 'luvlee' lady who eats, sleeps and lives in a tube." Had visions of kids paying a dime to watch me huffing and puffing in a cylinder. I never went into the "lung" but technicians would rev it up every day and its eerie breathing still haunts me.

The reason I was face down, and would be so for the next three months, was that my buttocks had been burned to the bone by hot water bottles stuffed around and under me on the two-to three-hour, 160-kilometre ambulance trip from Pembroke to Ottawa. The driver, I was told, demanded $100 cash from my father before I was released to the hospital. Wonder what would have happened if he hadn't paid? Would I still be in the back of the ambulance?

Part of the burn treatment was a daily shot glass of peroxide poured into the cavities. I could hear it fizz, but couldn't feel anything for the first couple of months.

For some reason, the paralysis stopped below the heart, just touching one lung. No one knows why and I'm not pressing to find out. After three weeks in isolation — no visitors except family — I was transferred to the Ottawa Civic Hospital where they had a whole wing turned into a polio ward. Nurses hated that section with a passion. It was to be my world until mid-November. It was populated by men and women, boys and girls, Catholics and Protestants, rich and poor. Some died, some didn't. Polio had no respect.

Memories of that normal, four-bed green quadrangle — the love, the pain, the happiness, the loneliness, the shrieks of laughter in the daytime and the screams in the middle of the night — are indelibly etched. The room was later to become a disaster area, serviced only by the lowest of the student nurses or by those being punished.

Back home, the family was being ostracized. Neighbours and friends would talk to my parents only from the sidewalk. Pembroke, a town of about 12,000, was hit hard by the disease. The house was fumigated and scrubbed down. Everything washable was washed. Health officials probed and pricked for clues. Where had I been swimming, what had I been doing, what had I been eating, who was I hanging around with, what colour were my eyes? An older sister with children of her own was warned not to see me. She did. I remember her wiping the sweat from my forehead. I still owe you, pal.

The guys hated me. All beaches were closed for the summer, dance halls shut down, crowds of any type were discouraged, the movie houses were empty. My buddies felt that if I was going to get it, I should have got it earlier — then the schools would have had to be closed.

My Civic roommates were Tom McCool from my home town, a student one year behind me in my school; a Polish youngster about 12 from Barry's Bay (let's call him Dick) and Len, an adult from Renfrew. Len was only paralysed down one side of his face. His physiotherapy was whistling. And all he knew was Blue Moon. Day-in and day-out, he whistled that damned tune.

Staff said Dick was an irrepressible imp. I say he was a rat. He was mobile, had polio in his right arm and when he wasn't cradling it with his left hand, he would be stealing my dessert. Once he caught a baby mouse in the corridor, hid it in the room until an unsuspecting nurse with a tray of medicine and juice arrived routinely at 4 p.m. Her screams of terror when he produced his pet and the crashing of the medicine tray had alarm bells ringing and orderlies running.

On another occasion, he threw a bowl of corn flakes at me, missed and hit the wall above my bed. He just never did like corn flakes. At the time, I couldn't even move my thumb to press the buzzer for a nurse. It was a day before movie actor Gene Autry was to visit the polio ward with the attending press. Staff had worked for days getting the place spic and span. On his arrival, our door was closed and a scribbled "contagious" sign pinned up. I guess Gene rode off into the Ottawa sunset but it is only a guess.

The worst, bar none, the worst thing about polio for me was the tube to the bladder through the penis. The agony was relieved by the relief but you knew it was temporary.

For some reason, that part of the anatomy was not affected by the paralysis and led to many an embarrassing moment. A healthy 16-year-old penis, it is said, has no conscience.

The happiest moment of my life was the instant I wet the bed one afternoon in that long, hot summer. Everybody cheered. Even Jimmy, who had been moved into our room. It was good to hear Jimmy break his silence. I could never tell how old he was. He had been hit by polio a year earlier and his head had grown, but his body hadn't.

A lumberjack in his late 20s was admitted one Thursday, two days before he was to have been married in the village of Killaloe. I heard of him a couple of years ago. He was earning a living in a wheelchair weaving baskets. An Ottawa woman, the mother of three, was told the same day I was that she would never walk again. Her cries before she was sedated turned the wing into a horror chamber. A Pembroke man in his early 30s, father of two, had died of polio that day, before they could transfer him from his home to hospital.

My first introduction to physiotherapy occurred one morning just after breakfast when a bubbly little lady huddled over me, held a Kleenex in front of my face and told me to blow. My first reaction was that she was crazy. But I did and the tissue hardly moved. "Out of shape," I apologized. It was the beginning of a five-month daily program. A love-hate relationship. Loved her for what she was trying to do, hated her because she was doing it. Her vocabulary surely expanded as she stretched atrophying leg, arm, neck, back and torso muscles.

Part of the procedure for all polio patients at that time was known as the Sister Kenny treatment. It consisted of hot packs — pieces of insulated cloth — steamed in a pressure cooker and applied every hour in an eight-hour shift. We wore only G-strings and perspired so much that bed clothing had be changed nearly hourly. No wonder the probationary nurses hated that wing. We were plied with salt pills, but that little rat Dick kept stealing mine. He had a jar full and wouldn't use any. He said he was saving them for a pet calf back home.

Then there was Aldean. Forget her last name but she was the first true love. She controlled my mind 24 hours a day. Nothing else was important. She didn't visit but I could understand. The distance and the fear of polio, you know. She married some guy in late August.

The doctor in charge of the polio section was taking a tour of medical students around in early August when he stopped at my bed. He pulled off the hot packs and calmly announced, "This boy will never walk again." The students nodded and jotted notes. The tour moved on and a young nurse cursed softly, perhaps because she had to replace the hot packs.

His statement never sunk in. Who said youth was wasted on the young? He didn't know I was working on a football scholarship at De La Salle Oakland in Toronto and that I had to be there early in September. Never made the school appointment — but I was on my feet by the first of October.

One afternoon, a classmate dropped in, armed with a bottle of scotch. He had lied about his age and joined the Princess Patricia's Canadian Light Infantry. He was going to Korea and we decided to have a drink. I was taking mine through a straw, his was hidden in a tea cup. No one knew — until after he left and the regular 4 p.m. check, including temperature, was taken. Again the alarm bells ringing, and orderlies running. The fear of relapse gripped staff. They showed no sense of humour when it dawned on them that I was drunk.

On Oct. 3, 1951, Bobby Thomson hit a home run for the New York Giants — the shot heard around the world — to win the third and deciding game of the National League playoff series against the Brooklyn Dodgers. Two days earlier, I had taken my first step in a waist-high walker. How come Thomson got all the press?

Released from hospital during a November snowstorm. Had to wear a new pair of flight boots. Could hardly manage with light slippers. Flight boots were the "in" thing back in those days. Like the ones columnist Del Bell still wears. Let me assure you, my first trek across busy Carling Ave. to a parking lot was not exactly a sprint.

Looking back after 30 odd years, I sort of feel sorry for people without a limp. They have missed the good times of the polio experience. So where are you, Tom and Len and yes, you too Dick? Let's get together and toast Jonas Salk, whose vaccine can make polio almost a forgotten horror.

• **1984** Feature Writing •

Day in the life of
Bramalea Secondary School

Ian Brown

Globe and Mail

It is 6 a.m. Kristine Taylor reaches out of bed and hits the radio; she needs concentrated AM funk to get moving the way others need coffee. She has a mere three hours to get ready for school.

Mr. Wedlock, the principal at Bramalea Secondary School, where Kristine is enduring Grade 11, keeps telling school assemblies that "academic excellence" is what high school is all about.

Like any other kid, Kristine knows better. High school is music and fashion, otherwise known as recognition and acceptance. Because the music you like dictates the way you dress, Kristine has a good two hours of Michael Jackson funkomatic dressing to do before she steps out the front door.

She approaches it like an Olympic athlete in training. First she showers and curls and gels her highlighted shoulder-length blonde hair, to create the piled-string Michael Jackson look. That's the easy part. Next she does her face: Foundation, blush, those complex sunrises over the eyes, the full pink lips like two slices of papaya. That's another half-hour, not counting touch-ups through breakfast.

And what outfit? Kristine spends up to $300 a month on clothes. Maybe the black India cotton clam diggers, and the black satinized pumps ... the black and turquoise V-necked sweatshirt. And yes, definitely three-inch earrings.

Finally, at 8:30, Kristine steps out the door and begins her careful walk to school. She looks as if she stepped out of *Vogue* for a walk in Bramalea. She definitely does not look 16.

But she is 16, almost awkwardly shy, and wants for all the world only to be an "esthetician," which is guidance counsellor talk for hairdresser. The principals and the educators can talk about "back to basics" curricula, as they are these first few weeks of school in Ontario and elsewhere across the country. But inside, in class, girls like Kristine Taylor are what high school's all about these days.

8 a.m. Bramalea Secondary School is between subdivisions A, B and D in Bramalea, a "planned bedroom community" of 160,000 half an hour northwest of Toronto. It was originally designed for 40,000. It's a nice, endlessly average place: Two cars in every carport, lawn signs that say things like "The Five Tremaines."

The school resembles an enlarged clock radio, smaller but otherwise almost indistinguishable from the Simmons Beautyrest, Domtar and Ford factories lazing across the surrounding fields where many of the students' parents work. It's suburbia, Your City, Anyplace, Canada.

The blandness of this neighbourhood often strikes Ross Wood on his way to school, where he works as a guidance counsellor. "Having a job is a very, very high priority for these kids. To be employed, to be stable, to be independent. We often have to do some reality testing, and say — Look, Jack, what's your number one, your job or your school? And that's a reflection of the parents' attitudes."

In Bramalea, school is another part-time job. Homework is secondary to driving until 3 a.m. for Pizza Pizza or a job at Canadian Tire, so teachers don't assign much. If only a third of the Grade 9 population makes it to Grade 12, and if half those subsequently drop Grade 13, and if only 45 per cent of the remainder go to university — well, Bramalea's a practical sort of place. Never mind the technological revolution.

9 a.m. The electronic tone sounds over the loud speaker in Mr. Polisena's Grade 11 home room, and the class staggers to its feet for the national anthem. The anthem is followed by the disembodied voice of Mr. Lancaster, one of the vice-principals, reading the day's announcements. "From Mr. Byrne and Reach for the Top. The practise for today has been cancelled;" a prefects meeting; the J.W. Broiler factory needs part-time help ... the messages drone on. Often during a class, the speaker comes alive and Mr. Lancaster asks so-and-so to come to the office. It's like being yanked down to purgatory by some electronic monster, and the kids dread it. The disembodied voice is the only contact many have with the school's administration.

Mr. Polisena's home room is also his first class, Art for Beginners. Already, in the second week of school, a quarter of the class is missing, and another third haven't done their homework. The day is starting slowly.

9:03 a.m. Last chance to make out in the hallway. The couples lean against their lockers; the embracers linger forever. You would think the Queen Mary was tied up outside and they were separating for the duration of the war. No one pays them any attention. In high school, passion is as ordinary as breakfast.

9:10 a.m. Mrs. Stetic's Grade 11 English class is reading Sinclair Ross's *The Lamp at Noon* aloud. The Peel Board of Education's collective agreement specifies an average class of about 17, but Bramalea is growing; 29 kids are crowded into this aqua-coloured, cinder-block room.

Mrs. Stetic, who has a reputation as one of Bramalea's best teachers, is well aware that she's competing with Boy George and rock videos for 70 minutes of her students' attention, so she runs a 20-minute film strip on the Depression to prime the students for the story's Dust Bowl setting.

The only hitch is a punk rock/new wave blond who wants to be in the military police. She's a tad irritable this morning, and she's making a hell of a clatter with her three-ring binder, the noisemaker of choice at Bramalea Secondary. "Young lady," says Mrs. Stetic, "if you don't have time to settle down before you get here, maybe you should do it in the washroom, because we don't have time to put up with your temper tantrums." Silence.

Luckily, Ross's story works its spell. At two points in the reading, a churchy hush falls across the class. One comes when Mrs. Stetic mentions an acquaintance who lost $30,000 in the Depression. Money talks to these kids. The other, longer, more poignant hush, occurs when Ellen, the wife in the Ross story, longs for her husband, for his "great hunch of muscle-knotted shoulder."

10:20. Ms McGiverin's Media Arts class (Grades 11 through 13) is presenting the posters she asked them to create to introduce themselves.

If the posters actually reflect the characters of these teenagers, Canadian adolescence is an endless bath in consumerism. Only a few display any family members. In place of people, there are products: Guitars, food, telephones, beer, rock stars. From the younger ones, a few stuffed animals. Everyone "loves" money.

Monica, a pretty girl with a faintly dyed-blond forelock — a sign that she is a fan of the new wave group Duran Duran — stands up. She points out the components of her life stuck to paper. "I like the telephone. I like Coke. I like my soaps. I like money. I like hearts. I like Calvin Klein jeans." The litany of likes continues from student to student, personalized consumer creeds for a crowd that has nothing but wants everything.

Eventually, a 16-year-old heavy-metal fanatic gets up on his hind legs. He wears the standard uniform of the metalhead: Led Zeppelin T-shirt, jeans, shoulder-length hair. His poster is crammed with pictures of booze, guitars and one picture of a 747 airplane, "I'd like to get a 747 plane like Led Zeppelin has because I like Led Zeppelin and they're the greatest."

Ms McGiverin asks whether he has any plans for the future.

"I want to be a guitarist. Or a refrigeration dude because they rate $28 an hour."

The class laughs nervously without knowing why. What's so strange is the extreme contrast of this young man's goals. He leaps from the fantasy of being a rock guitarist to the dreamless reality of being a refrigerator repairman. He knows nothing in between.

If there is a lost generation these days, the high school generation may be it.

11:00. It's Picture Day in the gymnasium. The complete "colour package" is going for $13, and everybody has been warned not to wear white. Jeff Blimkie, one of the school's few punks, is therefore literally upholstered in black leather; leather studded jacket, black pants, black leather studded wrist band, even (unusual for Bramalea, where jogging shoes seem to come attached to the feet) shin-high black leather "bovver" boots. A bottle opener hangs from his belt.

Blimkie claims he's "just a person who stands up for what he believes in, a non-conformist." All he wants now is for his hair to grow out. When it's a foot long, he's going to get a mohawk cut, a single furrow of hair running from brow to nape. Punks normally use soap to make their mohawks stand on end. "The glue's the best, though, for the foot-long mohawk," Blimkie insists. "Elmer's glue. It washes out after four washings.

11:45 a.m. During gym class on the football field, a student refuses to slap his hands up into the crotch of another boy to receive a football hike. "But sir," he complains. "That has sexual overtones."

"Sexual overtones!" says the gym teacher. "That doesn't have sexual overtones. Where were you brought up, anyway?" Answer: Bramalea.

Noon. During the first lunch period, the strict social classes of high school society fall into place in the cafeteria. The divisions are regimental and based entirely on what music one likes and what clothes one wears. Once "in," a group member plays up the distinctions from other groups to increase the value of belonging.

At one end of the spectrum are the punks, the established radicals, fans of The Clash, UK Subs, The Exploited and other already mainstream punk groups. Dyed jet black hair is de rigueur; last term it was albino blond.

At the other end are the heavy-metal fans, the rockers who live and drink and pass out for Led Zeppelin, Judas Priest and Exciter. Metalheads are considered to have difficulty remembering their last names, but they enjoy radical outcast status.

In between are the preppies and the trendies, the funkers (Michael Jackson et al) and the New Wavers. "They'll listen to anything," a punk observes.

Underneath these formidable class distinctions lies the central social ache of the high school student: The desire, as one girl puts it, "to fit in." It's nothing new; but whereas 40 years ago it was books, today it's music. Never mind, as Andrey Kobilnyk, a Grade 13 student who left Bramalea for a free school last year, points out, "that most music today is just landscapes."

Those who fit in best develop an arcane chain of being of the clique's devising, or stand out by virtue of their clothes. It's not enough any more just to have big breasts: You have to have big breasts and six earrings and eye makeup that looks like an oil spill. As for jocks, they're going the way of the dodo at Bramalea. Not only must you know what kind of guitar the lead singer of AC/DC uses, you have to be knowledgeable enough to refer to him by his first name, Angus. The ultimate prize for such a command of detail is the Grail every student can identify instantly: "Recognition."

The game disturbs some people, but everyone has to play. "Theatre and fashion stuff is becoming the important thing," says Lisa, a quite sophisticated girl who tries to carve her own status by specializing in old movies. This is especially true as every new stylistic innovation is snapped up by a media-dominated trend machine. "People don't understand teenagers any more, because teenagers are becoming so weird," Lisa says. "Everybody wants to be so different." A few students still achieve distinction academically. But in middle-class Bramalea, where the economic future is as flat as the landscape, scholastics matter very little.

For all their devotion to this or that set, the students — particularly the girls — also hate the social structure with a passion. "The biggest problem in high school," says Debbie Powell, a black girl who may end up leading the cheerleading squad if Bramalea can afford the pompoms, "is a lack of sense. There's a lot of competition among women for clothes, for guys. But it doesn't depend on clothes. It depends on your personality."

But personality has no visual currency. "Guys like an easy lay," says Colleen, a diminutive Grade 11 student. Colleen strikes you somehow as a latter-day version of Holden Caulfield's old girlfriend who kept all her kings in the back row when she played checkers. "Guys go for that. Guys are so naive."

The fear is that if you don't put out, you don't belong. You become a "gumby." Of course, you can become a gumby the first day of school by wearing the wrong plaid stretch pants, too.

The entire steamy affair of sex begins in Grade 8, and reaches full throttle when the boys turn 16. "When guys turn 16, they've just got this big thing to become big swingers," says Lorraine. At that point the girls think of guys and school in somewhat the same way: Both are faintly pre-historic. So why depend on guys? "Oh," sighs Colleen. "Everybody wants a guy." The tough part, still, is having one and maintaining your integrity.

It seems ridiculous, of course — *adolescent* in the extreme. Adults know better. But as Ty, a Grade 11 student, points out, "school is a little world inside a big world."

3 p.m. Class ends. Debbie Powell and her four-girl "rhythm section funker session" sign up for cheerleading and make their way to the student common room where 13 black and white kids are shyly practising break dance routines for the upcoming school cabaret.

(Race is not a problem at Bramalea, unlike several schools in the area. The black population is small as yet, and the possibilities for racial clashes are few.)

The rehearsal goes on hold when a repairman comes to fix the Coke machine, which is constantly breaking down. He's on his hands and knees behind the machine when Debbie walks over to him. "Are you here to fix the refrigeration?" she asks.

"Yeah," says the repairman.

"You get $28 dollars an hour, right?"

3:15 p.m. Ms McGiverin, who teaches English and drama, is walking from school across the grounds of the church next to the school when she sees a Grade 9 freshman being taped to a tree. As Ms McGiverin elbows her way through the crowd of kids, Perry, a 16-year-old Bramalea student, tells her to "f - - - off." Three times, to be precise. Perry figures he's off school property, and safe. But the off-property argument is as faulty as it always was, and Perry lands a week's suspension from school.

3:45 p.m. In Seminar Room A, where principal Garth Wedlock is holding a meeting of department heads, the studded arm band has just been banned. Mr. Wedlock wants the names of students who wear them.

A balding teacher dressed in the standard teacher uniform best described as Bureaucrat Moderne, raises his arm. His concern is studs on any kind of clothing. "I don't want to break into the kid's fun," he says, "but is this dress always appropriate? Yonge Street is one thing, but Bramalea's another."

But the man is defeated. Studded belts and jackets are allowed. Armbands, however, "are a potential safety hazard."

4 p.m. In the smokers' quad a clutch of punkers and trendies make plans to crash a party later that night.

A bottle will be apprehended once everyone returns from their part-time jobs at 8 by trekking to Bramalea City Centre, a vast indoor shopping centre and psychological vacuum populated by "mall rats". For Bramalea students, it is Main Street, a commercial nirvana where they can be surrounded by what they know best: Products they don't have.

For a couple of bucks, one of the "Grampaw mall rats" — 25-year-old burnouts who loiter in the video arcades — will buy most anyone a bottle. For $5 more, he'll sell most anyone a gram of cocaine cut four or five times. "You can get anything you want, except maybe heroin," one of the kids claims.

Then the party starts. The problem is where. On a hill in a park? At the home of someone who lets his kids drink? Mostly they happen in the car.

The students drink a lot; even Mr. Wedlock admits it's a problem. They drink "for more or less energy," as one student puts it, to find something that might approach real emotion.

Of course, it will be better in the spring. By then, with any luck, the principal will have eased off on his first-term rigor. Then it will be possible to skip first class again, hit the beer store at 10, park out behind the Dramatic Arts building, haul out the lawn chairs — the lawn chairs, no less — and settle into a morning of heavenly drinking.

4 p.m. The halls are deserted now. Mike Holmes is getting ready to leave. Holmes will be 16 next month; next year, he intends to go to UCLA to study film. He has the marks; Mr. Young, who's no slouch, claims he is "one of the best students I've ever taught." Until then, Holmes is waiting; waiting to leave high school, to leave Bramalea. "Bramalea is stagnant," he says. "I'd either want to be really poor or really rich to experience something new. I'm sick of being middle class … that's the trouble with school. You can predict what is going to happen that day."

He too is beginning to feel the tightness of the punk's uniform he wears — and Holmes wears it looser than most. Still, he says, "I'd rather be called a punk. There's a lot of what I call trendy punk, but really, punks are anyone who wants to be different. The test is to see if they can be themselves."

• **1987** Feature Writing •

Saved by a scalpel of light

Marilyn Dunlop

Toronto Star

Puffs of smoke rise from a surgical opening in the head of a patient stretched out on the operating table.

Brain surgeon Charles Tator is directing a laser beam into the core of a tumor growing inside the woman's skull and pressing against her brain. With exquisite precision he focuses the beam to pulverize bits of tumor, charring it, or to cut out pieces.

Recently the pressure from the tumor had begun to give the 65-year-old woman seizures. "The tumor has probably been growing there for years," Tator says. "It's amazing how large a tumor can grow before it causes symptoms that suggest it is there." But eventually space inside the skull runs out. The skull can no longer accommodate more tumor growth.

A photographer and reporter from the *Star* were given permission to observe the operation by the surgeon and by the patient, who requested, however, that her name not be disclosed.

The woman had been wheeled into Operating Room 3, in the new neurosurgery unit at Toronto Western Hospital about 8 a.m. this day. Anesthetists put her to sleep and attached the monitors that would record all vital signs. They inserted into her throat the tube to a ventilator that would do her breathing in the hours to come.

Tator, assisted by Dr. Anita North, Toronto Western's chief neurosurgery resident, and another resident, Dr. Fred Kim, positions the patient's head to give them the best possible access to the tumor, fixing her head in a head-holder so there is no chance of movement. A halo-like metal frame — a $10,000 brain retractor — surrounds her head and will be essential later when the tumor is being separated from the brain.

This tumor is on the surface of the brain, not deep inside it. But it will turn out to have knobby edges that have pushed into the brain to a greater degree than Tator could see beforehand from imaging techniques.

Cat scans (computerized brain X-rays) and angiograms (pictures of blood flow) have shown him the tumor stretches over a fairly large surface and has many blood vessels. The images are displayed on a viewing board on the wall of the operating room. But they can't tell him whether the tumor is a cancer or is benign. He fervently hopes it's benign.

Soon after 9 a.m. the surgeons make the incision. The patient's hair has been shaved from the region of the tumor. The doctors cut through the scalp and the muscle below it to the bone underneath. The muscle is stripped away from the bone and folded back from the opening. The skull bone is about one quarter inch thick. Anita North uses a power drill to carefully cut "burr" holes and Tator manipulates a fine saw to cut along the line from burr hole to burr hole. "The bone is abnormal," Tator says. It's been affected by the tumor, causing an overgrowth of bone.

Standing on a stool beside the operating table, nurse Margaret Loh deftly hands Tator instruments as he calls for them, picking them off the high table arched over the blue draping covering the patient. In operating rooms, blue and green signify sterile areas. A warning to anyone who is not scrubbed in: Don't touch. The surgeons lift a piece of bone a bit smaller than a hockey puck. "Bone wax," says Tator and Loh gives him piece after piece of wax that he presses into the surrounding bone to stop the bleeding. He's also cauterizing blood vessels with a two-pronged electric device, called a bipolar, that shrinks and seals tissue. The pedal that operates the power is under Loh's right foot. "Bipolar on," says Tator. The device hums. An automated male voice gives him the power level.

"Irrigation," he says and an assistant squeezes sterile water into the wound, keeping it moist and washed. Suction wands clear away blood so the surgeon can see what he's doing. The blood they soak up runs through clear tubing into bottles hung on the walls.

"Okay," says Tator. "The bleeding is under control." He snips away a bit more bone. "Gives us a little more space so we can work," he says. The main piece of bone is removed completely and stored in salt water, to be wired back in place at the end of the operation.

It is 10:15 a.m. and head operating room nurse Colleen Pynn wheels in the laser machine. Its long, flexible arm is encased in sterile plastic. Warning signs are stuck on both doors of the operating theatre, alerting anyone wishing to enter that the laser is in use. While it is being used, everyone in the room must wear protective glasses in case the beam deflects from some surface and hits an eye. The laser (its name standing for light amplification by stimulated emission of radiation — a concept first dreamed of 75 years ago by Albert Einstein) has been called "a scalpel of light." The beam of the cutting tool is invisible but it is accompanied by a tiny red "aiming light" — a different kind of laser similar to the ones lecturers use as pointers. The twinkling red guide light tells the surgeon where he is aiming.

A nurse bustles in to speak urgently to Tator. An emergency operation is about to begin in the next operating room and North is needed to assist there. Can Tator spare her? He nods. North hurries out.

More blue draping is placed around the wound. All that shows is the opening, a gaping window through which the surgeons will search out and destroy the ugly threat to the patient's brain. The wound seems disembodied. Hard to realize one is looking inside the skull of a living person.

Three layers of membrane cover the brain. The tough outer layer is called the dura mater. Tator and Kim prepare to open the dura. "I can feel the tumor and it is very, very firm," Tator says. Indeed he will see later that it has become so calcified the core has turned to bone.

"The dura does not look normal," Tator says. "The tumor has infiltrated the dura. We may have to put in a graft." The surgeon cuts through the second layer. "That's the brain there," he says. "I don't see the tumor edge yet. We want to go around the periphery of the tumor."

Attaching flexible strips to the halo-like brain retractor, Tator gently sets them in place against the small area of brain that has been exposed. The retractor will gradually ease back under the skull the bit of brain that is exposed. "The retractor is a wonderful system. It gently retracts the brain," he says.

Gently is a word he uses often. It is the key to successful brain surgery. "If we don't traumatize the brain much, it will tolerate surgery and will be all right," he explains. But that is easier said than done with a tumor like this one, with its bumpy exterior adhered to brain tissue.

"Nubbins on the tumor have burrowed into the brain," the surgeon says. "We'll just gently tease them apart," he tells Kim. "Give me the microsscissors."

With infinite care, he works around the edge of the tumor. "It's like a mushroom," he says. "See that large vein. Be nice to preserve that. We'll just gently retract the brain from the tumor and the tumor from the brain, teasing them apart."

He's almost ready to use the laser. Tator screws an arm support into the metal halo frame. It will steady his hand while he uses the laser. "Everybody got goggles on?" Cloth strips placed all around the wound shelter the brain, now hiding back under the roof provided by the skull.

Tator begins to core the tumor, like coring an apple, the laser pulverizing the centre of the tumor and gradually shrinking it to get it to move away from the brain. His right foot operates the laser pedal. "When the aiming light is sharply focused, the laser vaporizes tissue. When you move it farther away, less focused, it chars more and cauterizes, stopping bleeding."

There are puffs of smoke and a slight smell of burning. Nurses bring in a smoke evacuation unit. From her perch looking down on the table, Loh tapes on the blue draping tubing that will suck up smoke. It helps, but smoke and vaporized tissue also get sucked by the tubes that take up blood, plugging them. Nurses change the suction tubing and containers, keeping them working. Suction is essential. This tumor is so vascular it spouts like a fountain at times. Tator works the cauterizing device almost constantly.

It is 11:50 a.m. and the surgeon wants to send a little piece of the tumor he is removing to the pathology laboratory for analysis. With biopsy forceps he cuts a sample and Loh drops it into a small container like a shot glass.

"The tumor is getting most of its blood supply from the base of the skull," Tator notes, "but some of the blood is right from the surrounding brain. It steals blood vessels from the brain and that's one reason she had seizures. Parts of the brain were deprived of good blood supply."

Tator is now using the laser like a scalpel. "I'm cutting out chunks of tumor as if the laser was a knife, rather than vaporizing it." Bits of tumor he hands to the nurse are accumulating in the shot glass. "We've uncovered another little bit of brain," Tator tells his assistant. "Cover it up. Put a cloth strip between the tumor and the brain."

The pathologist reports in over a loudspeaker phone. "Dr. Tator, the tumor is an angioma." An angioma is a tumor composed mostly of small blood vessels.

"Benign?" asks Tator. "Yes, it looks benign," the pathologist replies. "Terrific!" he says happily.

The good news helps make up for the discoveries that the tumor is bigger than he expected and has poked more extensively into the brain. "The brain looks a little squashed, not as healthy looking right here at the dome of the tumor," he says. "It has also imbedded itself into the skull at the spot where it originated."

Noon: Dr. Christina Benedict, an anesthetist, enters to relieve a colleague who has been the guardian of the unconscious patient for the first four hours. "Here comes the second shift," says Tator. "First class but second shift," he grins.

Benedict will be on duty in the hospital from noon today until 8 a.m. tomorrow morning. The anesthetic equipment and monitoring devices are behind a blue drape at the side of the operating table. Neuro-anesthesia calls for special knowledge, Benedict explains. "For one thing we hyperventilate the patients to shrink the brain a bit and we also drop the carbon dioxide level." It helps protect the brain from swelling and from damage. The patient is covered with a warming blanket that maintains a normal body temperature, and lies on a water blanket to avoid pressure sores. Nurses have put padded heel bootees on her feet to prevent sores that develop quickly when one lies still for hours. "Nobody lies this still in their sleep," says head nurse Pynn.

The surgery is taking longer than Tator had expected. "This tumor threw a couple of curves at us." He had anticipated being finished about 2 p.m. and had been scheduled to perform another operation later. The second case is postponed.

A fellow neurosurgeon, Dr. Mark Bernstein, pops in. "Dr. Bernstein specializes in removing tumors deep in the brain. He's conducting research into ways to improve such surgery. Compared with the surgery he does, this case is easy," Tator says.

"How's the laser doing?" Bernstein asks. "Beautiful," is the answer.

"This is one of the largest tumors we've used a laser on," Tator says. So far Toronto Western Hospital is the only one in Metro to have a neurosurgery laser. When the new brain surgery unit was opened last February, some of the five neurosurgeons at the hospital described the astounding progress in brain surgery technology that has taken place in the last 20 years. When they were in medical school such technology was undreamed of. The full recoveries seen after neurosurgery today were few and far between before 1970.

Among the technical advances is the operating microscope, a marvellous invention that enables the surgeon to see the tissue on which he is working magnified 25-fold.

The operating microscope in this theatre is mounted on the ceiling and can be moved into place at the touch of a button. Like the laser, it is wrapped in sterile plastic. The laser can be attached to the microscope if the surgeon so chooses but today Tator uses the hand-held laser and will use the microscope during conventional surgery.

It's 1:35 p.m. and Nurse Loh is about to step down from the high table to get some lunch. Pynn is scrubbing in to replace her. "Before you go, Margaret, would you give us the microscope," asks Tator.

When it's in place, Tator sits astride a saddle stool, peering into the microscope at the enemy that still remains within the skull of his patient. Kim looks through a second set of eyepieces on the microscope. The nurses can see the magnified view on a television screen.

"I want to scrape tumor right off the bone and it could bleed. Are you okay for blood?" the surgeon asks anesthetist Benedict. If bleeding is extensive the patient may need a transfusion. "Okay," she says from her perch behind the blue drape.

As she sees her job, it is to be advocate for the patient throughout the time he or she is so vulnerable and unable to fend for themselves. And, she says, that can at times mean standing up for the patient against the surgeon if it should seem that what is to be done might not be in the patient's best interest. Today she has little worry of disagreement with the surgeon. Benedict and Tator work together smoothly with obvious professional trust.

There's another guardian of the patient in the room. In one corner, a technician keeps watch on a monitor that would alert the doctors if anything was going wrong within the patient's brain. Researcher Dean Linden, with Tator, has developed a system that keeps check on nervous pathways. It can reveal any changes in the patient's sense, ability to see or hear and motor activity, despite the patient's state of unconsciousness and immobility. "It improves the accuracy and safety of the surgery," says Linden, who developed the system in animal models. It's now being used routinely in all neurosurgery cases.

Periodically, the technician can send a signal to the patient's nervous system and a computer screen displays the response. At 2 p.m. the technician reports: "No change, Dr. Tator. Everything is stable."

Steadily, with infinite patience, Tator eases the tumor away from the brain. "Safer than pulling the brain from the tumor," he remarks. "The tumor is more spread out over the base of the skull than I anticipated — instead of one centimetre at the base, it is actually five centimetres."

To stop the bleeding as he works, Tator sets in place tiny bits of white surgical gauze. They look like snowflakes. They're called surgi-cells. They turn black as blood soaks into them. "Set them in flat, one at a time," he tells Kim. The doctors also used tiny squares of cloth — "paddies" — to stop the bleeding. The paddies will be pulled out later by blue strings attached to them.

At 3:35 p.m., head nurse Pynn has finished her shift. "Thanks, Colleen," says Tator. "Anytime." she says. "Well, anytime between 7:30 and 3:30." She's a 20-year veteran of operating rooms.

3:55 p.m.: "I think we're nearly finished. We'll just check it over under the microscope to make sure there are not tumor cells at the base of the skull we're leaving behind."

4:25 p.m.: "I think we're finished as soon as we cauterize the base of the tumor. Now is the time to make sure there is no bleeding anywhere. Okay, now we'll coat the whole floor of the tumor with surgi-cells. Give me lots of irrigation while I'm taking off the paddies." Two nurses count the paddies, ensuring none is left behind, hidden by coatings of blood.

"When a tumor has been pressing against the brain for so long, the brain is always raw looking," the surgeon says. The brain is also soft and mushy, making more difficult its separation from tumor.

There is now a large empty space, large enough to hold an egg, in the patient's head. "That was all filled with tumor," Tator says. "This is the temporal lobe, this is the frontal lobe and you can see the ridge between them."

The next stage is to cover the brain again. Most times the dura can be put back in its place. But in this case, the dura was so infiltrated with tumor it cannot be used. Tator will use a membrane-sheathing muscle of the temple — the tissue that was partially detached from the skull at the start of the surgery.

"It's more important to cover the brain than to cover muscle," he explains, gently snipping the layer of thin tissue (fascia) from the muscle.

5:25 p.m.: Tator cuts from a piece of blue paper a pattern for the piece of covering he is creating, and holds it over the wound. He's satisfied the fascia he has snipped loose will be big enough.

Chief resident Anita North returns, the other operation completed. "You want to unscrub and get something to eat?" Tator asks Fred Kim. Kim doesn't have to be asked twice. He's been in the operating room since 8 a.m.

So, of course, has Tator.

With the power drill, North makes holes in the skull for the wires that will hold in place the piece of bone that was removed.

At 6:20 p.m., Tator positions the bone in place. It will be more than 10 hours after he took his place at the head of the operating table that Tator leaves that spot. He's worked without lunch, without even a cup of coffee or a trip to the washroom.

He's showed no signs of fatigue or irritation. One can't imagine him shouting, ever. His calmness pervades the operating room, making it a gentle place, where an injured brain, like a hurt, cringing fawn, can be given a healing touch.

"He's the only guy I know who can call you at 6 a.m. or 6 p.m. and you're glad to hear from him," says Dean Linden. No matter it will be a long day or a whole night of work ahead.

"I've worked with him for 17 years and I still don't know how he does it," says Tator's secretary. "He didn't finish his day until 10 p.m."

The day before, a Sunday, he spent on call at the hospital.

He was back in the operating room the next morning.

And the patient is doing well, her seizures almost certainly a thing of the past.

• 1988 Feature Writing •
Coming home to die

Kelly Toughill

Toronto Star

When Anne Hill dressed the corpse of her youngest and dearest brother, she expected to be angry, perhaps even to feel disgust. Instead, she felt a great honour, a lightness and release, a wash of love.

Her brother died on a cold January night four months after returning to the small town near London, Ont., where he was born. In the fresh daylight, black-suited funeral attendants came to take him away. They unfurled a dark rubber bag in the parlor of the old family home, then pulled on thin latex gloves. The explanation was mumbled quickly. They wouldn't embalm or dress the corpse of someone who had died of AIDS; they wouldn't even touch him with bare hands.

Hill's brother Richard had been a beautiful man, proud of his fit, lean body until it was devoured by the virus that eventually killed him. It fell to his sister and his best friend to tend the physical remains of the man they both had loved.

"We dressed him perfectly, even his socks and underwear," she recalls. "Richard never went out his front door unless he was immaculate. I just couldn't let him leave like that. I could not bear that."

All over Canada, people with AIDS — acquired immune deficiency syndrome — are going home to die. Some return out of necessity when no longer able to care for themselves, others come back earlier. All hope the return to their roots will stave off the terror of dying alone.

The exodus has sparked extraordinary feats of both cruelty and compassion as friends, neighbours and families grapple with a modern-day plague most thought only happened someplace else, to someone else's kin. Many have discovered that even where there is no hope, there can still be immense love.

Anne Hill isn't angry at the quiet men who refused to follow the standards of their trade and embalm her brother's corpse. She feels a sort of pity for them, that they failed to overcome their ignorance and chose instead to wallow in their fear.

In the end, she is glad she had the chance to dress her brother. It took an hour to coax the stiff, bloated body into a fine Italian suit, a white silk shirt, tie, belt and the silver cuff links that were a gift from his grandmother. It was hard work, and at one point, when the corpse flopped back, resisting their efforts, they began to laugh.

"I know that sounds odd, but it was funny, there was laughter in the room with us," she says. "It was a tremendous release to laugh that way. I felt very honoured to dress him. It was like a weight was lifted off of me."

Anne Hill's experience is just one example of how others are affected when people return home with AIDS. The trend is challenging entire communities, stripping bare the deepest emotions of family, friends and strangers, revealing untapped wells of love, and of fear.

Here are the stories of three very different homecomings: Of Bryan Hawley, whose hometown of Cloyne quickly rallied to his support; of the late Andy Armstrong, whose elderly parents cared for him night and day in their tiny London apartment, and of a man named Bill whose return has been both bitter and sweet.

■ ■ ■

"I hate it when people say I've come home to die," says Bill, 33. "I didn't come home to die, I came home to live."

Bill loves Owen Sound. He always planned to retire here one day, just not so soon.

He returned two years ago after more than a decade of working odd jobs and studying philosophy in Toronto and Waterloo. The ridges of his skull shine through the skin of his face in a gaunt pallor common to people with AIDS and his stride has been reduced to a slow hobble.

But Bill has not yet been diagnosed with full-blown AIDS. He is in an earlier stage of the disease and takes more than two dozens pills a day, including a heavy dose of morphine to control the pain.

It's easy to understand Bill's love for his hometown on the shores of Georgian Bay. It's a small city of large houses and solid churches hugging a deep blue bay. Wildflowers line the side of the road; nearby forests shelter gentle waterfalls.

Bill lives with his parents in the bottom of the gulch, near downtown. Sunflowers, bright pots of petunias and a spindly rose bush line the drive. The front steps are worn bare by the traffic of generations and the carpet covering the porch is a frazzled, matted gray. But the home is comfortable and warm.

During a recent interview with the *Star*, Bill's mother was making pickles in the kitchen, accompanied by the twang of country music on the radio. The house was filled with the sweet smell of fresh cucumbers and the cheerful, mindless chorus of Elvira.

"I never treat Bill with the 'oh-you-poor-fellow' approach," his mother says. "I always tell him things could be worse. You know you can't give people too much sympathy or they'll come down with the poor-little-me's. And the poor-little-me's never did anybody any good."

Bill talks a lot about the area's natural beauty, but little about the people who live here. When he does, it is to mention the handful who have offered support or, more precisely, who haven't turned him away: A former camp counsellor who talked with him on the street about his disease; girls in a coffee shop who called him brave for telling the truth.

The full story comes out slowly, with much pulling and probing: The teenagers who taunt him with the gruesome chant, "AIDS Kills;" the landlord who changed the locks while he was in the hospital; how his diagnosis haunts the family home like an unwelcome guest everyone is trying to ignore.

"Bill's had a really rough time; this town has treated him just awful," says a shopkeeper who is his friend. "He's had no help, no support at all."

It would be different if Bill had returned home with tuberculosis or incurable cancer, she says. Because AIDS first hit gay men in North America, it is inextricably identified with homosexuality. Those with the disease, their families and even casual acquaintances, are all coloured by the taboo.

The stigma is so great in Owen Sound that the shopkeeper asked that her name not be used in this article.

"I really feel bad about this. Bill's a great guy and we want to support him all we can, but you just don't know what Owen Sound is like."

Bill was very circumspect about his homosexuality as a teenager. It's one reason he left for Toronto 14 years ago, to "bury himself in the crowd."

Now he has returned; there is no going back in the closet, and no way to hide his illness — even if he wanted to.

"I'm obviously gay and I'm obviously ill, so I obviously have AIDS. There's just no getting around that," he says.

For most families who welcome home people with AIDS, that is the No. 1 issue: What to tell others.

Anne Hill remembers how her family was divided when her brother came home to die. Richard had struggled against the stigma of the disease for years and helped found the AIDS Committee of Toronto. But when he returned home, his mother told everyone her son had cancer.

Hill says few people were fooled: "In a small town, revealing the diagnosis is a matter of honesty, not privacy."

London physician Dr. Iain Mackie believes the hurt is greater when families lie.

Hiding the diagnosis can offend those who are ill, making them feel as if the family is ashamed of their disease. It also creates a wall of secrecy between those who are grieving and the people they would normally turn to for support.

One man, who told no one how his son died, agrees: "Until my son fell ill, I was the jerk in the office telling the AIDS jokes. Now there is nothing I can say when someone tells them back to me."

Bill's mom insists it is for his sake, not her own, that she wants to hide the truth about his illness. She cites the landlord who evicted him because of AIDS and says she doesn't want to see her son hurt like that again.

It is the biggest sore in their home, this disagreement over how much to reveal. Bill desperately wanted his full name used in this article. He thinks it is important to show people that he is not ashamed of his disease and to help educate others about its perils. But he fears his family would kick him out.

In the end he asked the *Star* to use only his first name and to photograph him in profile. He knows many people will recognize him anyway.

Most of Bill's day is spent reading and practising calligraphy in his small, bright bedroom. His daily regimen includes a walk through town, an ordeal that is planned in advance, with rest stops along the way.

"I miss having someone to talk to," he says, listing the drawbacks of life with AIDS in Owen Sound. "I need someone to talk to about the things I can no longer do."

Bill's homecoming has been hard on the whole family, says his mother.

"There's been a lot of stress. I've been spending a lot of time at the bingo."

Bill says his family hasn't faced the fact that he is dying. He worries that they never will. Many people who are dying — and those who love them — go through a time of denial.

Somewhere inside a lever is pulled that shuts off the truth, as if the brain could stave off an inevitable future by refusing to believe in it.

Bill's mother vows that next spring she and her husband will sell the big house Bill loves so much and move to an apartment. There will be no room for their first-born son.

"Bill knows it's imperative he get his own place," she says. "We want a smaller place, and some time to ourselves now the kids are all grown. That may sound cold, but Bill knows he can't stay here after we move."

■ ■ ■

Nothing makes Olive Armstrong angrier than the stories of parents who refuse to take home children with AIDS.

She bangs both fists on a card table and spits the words with pure fury: "How can they do that? It makes me so mad! Any mother who doesn't take her son home will regret that decision with every breath she takes for the rest of her life. She'll never be able to live with herself again."

The outburst is a surprise, disconcerting. One does not expect fierce passion from this carefully coiffed woman who wears her 76 years with such grace. It is similarly odd to listen to the Armstrongs chronicle their son's last three months of life. The words describe a time of horror and hardship but their faces are lit with joy, the painful recollections conjuring up a love that still thrives.

Andy Armstrong flew to Florida in January, 1987, to tell his parents he had AIDS. He showed them the purple splotch on his arm and introduced them to the medical terms that would consume their attention for the next eight months: Kaposi's sarcoma, human immunodeficiency virus and acquired immune deficiency syndrome.

The next time he visited their winter home, he was leaning on a cane. He died Sept. 11, 1987, at the age of 37.

Death is rarely a painless, peaceful process for people with AIDS. The AIDS virus destroys the immune system, leaving its host vulnerable to other infections. Many people with AIDS suffer through rashes, insomnia, diarrhea and dementia in addition to the skin cancer and pneumonia that most often kill them.

Most continue to work in the early stages of their illness, returning home only when no longer able to care for themselves. Families care for them during the final, most painful stage of the disease.

Olive tended her son for three weeks in his Toronto apartment before taking him home to London.

"I was barefoot up to my ankles in urine," she recalls of those weeks. "Nobody can tell me you can't care for AIDS patients with love and compassion, because I did it."

Andy's health deteriorated quickly in London. His legs were paralyzed, he became increasingly confused and was in almost constant pain.

"Andy regressed to the age of two in the space of just a few months," says his physician Mackie. "It was a very painful thing for the family."

A nurse came a few times but virtually all of the work of caring for Andy, who topped six feet and 180 pounds, fell to his elderly parents. They bathed him and changed his sheets at least twice a day. Nobody complained.

"My back hurt so much that I could only sleep on the sofa, because it was hard," his mother says. "If Andy rang for me at night, I'd roll onto my knees, get up into a crouch and get over to the table to pull myself up before going in his room. By this time, of course, he might have wet the bed, so I would change the sheets. But the important thing you see, was for him not to know I was hurt."

One morning Andy lay down on the sofa and couldn't get up. His parents couldn't move him, he was just too big. Mackie said Andy had to go to the hospital. Everyone knew he'd never be back.

"That's the only time in my life I've ever cried," says John Armstrong. "Andy looked up at me from the sofa and said, 'Poppa, did you cry during the war?' And I said, 'No, son, I didn't. I love you, son.'

"I have faced death so often in my life that I thought I could take Andy's death in stride, but I couldn't with the boy, I just couldn't. I thought I was hardened to all that, but I guess you're never hardened when it is someone who is so close to you."

An unusual thing happened while Andy was home; his parents became close with their son's gay friends.

John Armstrong describes himself as a "mid-Victorian" man who never knowingly met a homosexual until the day he found out his son was gay — the same day he learned his son was carrying the AIDS virus.

But he welcomed Andy's friends when they came to visit. Now, a year after Andy's death, a few still make the journey to visit with his parents.

"There are two fellows, I really feel deep down that they're trying to compensate us for Andy's death," says John Armstrong.

Andy was in the hospital a little more than a month before he died. His parents spent most of their time there. His mother baked him custard or cookies every day.

As Andy slid further into dementia, he took to asking his parents when he was going home. They tried to jolly him along, saying they couldn't get a cab or couldn't find his shoes.

One day, Andy got a mixed-up idea that his parents were moving from their small apartment to a large home.

"Will there be a garden there?" he asked his mother.

"Yes Andy," she answered.

They talked all afternoon about what they would plant in the imaginary garden come spring.

The hardest moment for Olive Armstrong was when another son told her she had to let Andy go.

"I prayed for weeks. One night I just leaned over and put my arms around Andy in his hospital bed. I said, 'Andy, God gave you to us for 37 years. I'll always be grateful for that. But now I have to give you up. I have to give you back to him.'"

He died less than two weeks later, late one night with his mother sitting beside him.

His father has one clear regret about that time: "I never talked to Andy about his death. I was always the cheerful one, kidding around and teasing him about the nurses and the food. Now that's sort of eating inside of me."

The Armstrongs say they have never for a moment regretted that their son came home.

Olive Armstrong is tormented by the stories she hears of families who reject their children with AIDS. "Which is the worse heartbreak: To have your son die alone somewhere or to have him die in his mother's arms? He's going to die anyway. How can they not understand?"

■ ■ ■

Bryan Hawley, 30, spent last summer drifting and fishing on the big lake near his childhood home, thinking he had just a few months to live.

That was more than a year ago and Hawley is still living in the small white home down the road from Marble Lake in Cloyne.

"If I really thought I was going to make it, I'd be in Calgary," Hawley says. "But I don't. I have come home to die."

Hawley, like Bill, loves his hometown, but unlike Bill's bitter homecoming, Hawley has been warmly welcomed back by the tiny resort community where he grew up. Family and friends cheerfully spend their day taking him to the hospital in Kingston, 110 kilometres away; one good friend helped start a group to educate people about AIDS; every week last winter, the minister at the Anglican church urged the congregation to pray for him.

"Cloyne is a good place," Hawley says. "It's not like Toronto, where you don't know your neighbour. I think people care about each other more in small towns. For me, coming home has been very positive."

Tiny Cloyne has one grocery store, a camp supply, three churches, a school, a museum, a white clapboard town hall and one motel. About 300 people live there, most earn a living off the tourists who come to hunt and fish in the wild, rugged bush of the Canadian Shield. In the early summer the black flies are so thick that people don old-fashioned hats with a green-mesh veil wrapped from collar to brim.

Hawley returned home the first week of July, 1987. He was in Calgary in May, hoping to work at the winter Olympics, when he fell ill. Doctors diagnosed pneumonia, and AIDS.

"I guess I've always run home when times got tough. I've always found the support I needed here."

His family told people Bryan had pneumonia, no more. One day an old friend called Bryan and asked if the rumours were true.

"Cathy said, 'I hear you have AIDS. Is it true?' And I said, 'Yes.'"

Bryan's mother June says she couldn't talk about AIDS at first; it was too scary. But she is glad the truth finally came out.

"I feel more relaxed with everybody now they know about it. People have been very good, very supportive. My friends just can't do enough for Bryan."

There is no more family secret about Bryan's AIDS, but there is still some strife.

One brother doesn't want Bryan to play with his young children, afraid that somehow the experts are wrong about how the disease is spread.

(The AIDS virus is found in body fluids such as blood and semen and is most often spread during sex, the sharing of dirty needles or from pregnant mother to child. It can't be spread through touching or hugging someone with the disease.)

The family doesn't discuss Bryan's illness. One time Bryan and his mother watched a soap opera in which a girl was dying of AIDS. His mother started to cry, but they still didn't talk about it.

Last fall Bryan and a friend, Cathy Ballar, started a local AIDS group. They raised money to buy pamphlets and bring in speakers for information sessions all over the Land O'Lakes Region. One night more than 60 people packed the town hall to learn about AIDS. They wanted to know how the disease is spread and if they were in danger. One teenager asked if it was still safe to swim in the lake near Bryan's home.

"People used to think AIDS can't happen here," Ballar says. "Now they can't say that, because it has. For many people here, nothing is real until it gets to Cloyne. Now AIDS is real."

Despite the information sessions, some people still can't overcome their fear. Ballor is one of them. She knows she can't catch the virus from touching her friend, but she still can't bring herself to hug him.

"I feel awful about it. I know there's no danger, but I just can't do it. Maybe some day I will."

One of the most difficult things about having AIDS in Cloyne is the long drive to Kingston for medical care, Hawley says. It's a complaint echoed by other people with AIDS in rural Ontario. The hospital in Owen Sound has twice referred Bill to Toronto and London for treatment, and Bill worries the local hospital won't have the expertise to cope when he becomes more ill.

Hawley says the best thing about living at home is just being around people he knows, people who care.

One night last winter he was taken by ambulance to the hospital in Kingston. They put him in a room where another man with AIDS had just died.

"I was so scared. I was terrified. But the ambulance attendants helped calm me down. They were people I knew, a woman I'd gone to school with, not anonymous strangers. That helped a lot."

Hawley doesn't think much about the future or dwell on his own death. He tries to live in the present and enjoy simple pleasures such as the splendid scenery from his window and the seasons rolling by.

A short distance from his home, a gray granite cliff looms over a still lake and a wild forest. A shred of a poem by Walt Whitman is carved deep in the rock, three lines suggesting we are all bound to the world for an eternal journey and that death is just one step along the way.

The words were etched seven decades ago, but are eerily appropriate today, echoing down through the years like an epitaph for the future, for people like Bill and Andy and Bryan, and for those they will leave behind:

My foothold is tenon'd and mortised in granite
I laugh at what you call dissolution
And I know the amplitude of time.

• **1989** Feature Writing •

The team that helped Carmelita die

Catherine Dunphy

Toronto Star

It was rotten weather the day of Carm's funeral — dark skies, cold, hard rain. The second day of November, a bleak and depressing month anyway. She would have hated it.

Except for the priest, quoting the Bible — she would have liked that. "In my father's house there are many mansions" — then slyly: "I can just see Carm up there doing a few deals now." Carm, nun turned nurse turned real estate agent with five phone lines running into her east-end home, would have laughed with us in that candle-lit church that day.

And had she been standing there with us at the graveside, shivering, wet, shoulder-to-shoulder for body heat as much as moral support, she would have appreciated Malcolm Savage arriving with her brown-and-white cocker spaniel, Hogan, dripping but still dapper.

Her reaction would have been discreet — a flicker not a double take — a sidelong glance, a slight curve of the closed mouth, eyebrow arched for a second, eyes lit up.

If you knew her, you knew what to look for. And we really knew her. We were the Carmelita Team, 50 of us, some her friends, some strangers, some health-care professionals, more amateurs. Some were gifted, gracious and comfortable with the reality that Carm was dying and we all die; others were stiff and afraid and damn good escape artists.

We counselled, listened, held her hand and guided her through her final journey. We gossiped, entertained, diverted. Some cleaned up her vomit, toward the end, changed her diapers; other — me included — bought her jelly beans. In the end it didn't matter what we did. What mattered is we were there, through the 16 months that Carmelita Lawlor fought like hell to beat cancer.

She got lucky when she got Dr. Linda Rapson. This is no ordinary doctor, but an acupuncture advocate who made house calls and whose practice is now devoted to pain control. Linda was central to another team for another dying woman, made famous in June Callwood's moving account of the death of Margaret Frazer in *Twelve Weeks In Spring*.

Many of Margaret Frazer's team were from Holy Trinity Church, so Rapson turned to a core group of them when she realized that here was another patient who was a single woman with family scattered across the country, whose independence streak cut a wide swath and who was determined to die at home.

Linda brought Callwood's book to Carm with an offer: Carm could have her own team. If she wanted.

"The key thing is whether she would take people she didn't know to be on the team," Linda recalled.

Yes, she would, and part of the team lore is that Linda collared everyone she knew, people she ran into in supermarkets, anyone.

"She called me one Sunday and asked if I wanted to be on a team, and I thought she meant baseball and said sure," recalled Carol MacKay, who drove Carmelita to many of her chemotherapy and blood treatments.

Carmelita had cancer of the lymph nodes, bone and liver, but its primary cause — the starting point as it were — was unknown. The same kind of cancer had killed her father. Her prognosis: Death, almost certainly within the year, probably in a month or two.

And so Carm's old friends, new friends, people she had sold homes to who became friends, neighbours, Linda's colleagues on the board for the AIDS hospice Casey House, all signed on for one shift a week. Meanwhile, Holy Trinity hired a co-ordinator for the growing hospice program, Mary Duncan, who quietly served as a behind-the-scenes resource for this — and other — teams.

But Linda knew from her experience that something very crucial was missing: The co-ordinator. She advised Carm to think carefully about who she wanted. Carm thought about it for two weeks and then phoned and left a message on Betty Gorman's answering machine.

"I hadn't seen her for maybe seven years and I came home to this message from Carmelita that she had cancer and that she wanted to talk," Betty said.

"Carm made the perfect choice," Linda stated.

"The team was very, very loyal," Betty said, deflecting the praise. "People wanted to be there. They didn't view it as a chore. There were times, though, when I thought I didn't want to make one more phone call. I don't like being on the phone much."

But she was, scheduling our shifts, noting when we couldn't make it, accommodating our absences, never — not once — complaining or even indicating it was an inconvenience.

"In the beginning, someone — either Carm or Betty — said people would never feel guilty if they cancelled. And we never did," said Liz Ferguson.

In the beginning it was a lot of fun. Carmelita, as Malcolm Savage noted, was a gracious hostess.

When my colleague here at the *Star*, Rebecca Bragg, very casually asked me if I wanted to fill in for her every so often I said 'Sure, why not?' This woman lives close to me, she sounds interesting — a nun then a nurse then into real estate — and besides, it's about time I did something for someone other than my immediate family.

Here's what I didn't say: She's dying and that scares me. I'm a fun person but I'm not so sure I'm a good person. What if she dies on my shift? (Carmelita later told Rebecca this was everyone's fear — Carm dying on their shift. She said it with that look on her face — amused, wicked. I used to tell her she was a brat.)

I will never forget the first time I saw Carm. For one thing, she was 6-foot-2. For another thing, she was bald. I don't remember a word she said, I just remember thinking, "She's so big. What if she gets really sick? How will I cope? I'm not a nurse."

As it turned out, none of use had to worry then. Carmelita thrived in the centre of the team's circle; she grew stronger, not weaker. Those phones rang incessantly; there was always someone in the house and another on the way.

Flowers? There weren't enough vases. In the living room plants grabbed all the sunlight. In the crisp blue and white kitchen, bottled water, bags and bags of carrots for the carrot juice she decreed she must have, health food store stock. And in the pantry, cases of Ensure, a nutritional liquid.

The dining room table, shoved against the wall, was piled high and deep with papers — only Carm knew what was where. Team lore has it somewhere there was the fabled Log Book — the book for keeping records of who gave Carm what, mood swings, things to do, musings. It was a central part of the Margaret Frazer team, only no one in the Carmelita team could ever find Carm's log. We figure she hid it; she'd do something like that.

Also in the dining room was the Codetron machine, Linda's miracle worker. Carmelita believed in it too. Some of us hated it. We had to untangle eight black cords, moisten sponge ends with water at a temperature that had to be just right, then tape the sponge ends one by one on the X's Linda had marked with black pen on Carm's body. They used the Codetron machine to electronically stimulate the body to produce pain-reducing endorphins.

There were also healing sessions, visualization courses, meditation tapes, potions — someone brought her crystals and a bottle of something called Willard Water, soon the subject of many team jokes.

What an adventure it was then for her. There was a team meeting disguised as a Christmas party to which Carm wore a wig, made a dramatic entrance with Hogan, and "looked like a million bucks," Linda said. There was the team's custom-made Christmas card featuring a glorious colour photo of Hogan taken by team member Cindy Green. It, too, went down into the team annals, as it was belatedly noticed that Hogan was, er, excited.

Carm spent last Christmas with her sister in Vancouver, then came back to organize with gusto a surprise birthday party for Linda. She went out to dinner with Rebecca, Betty Gorman and Margaret McBurney at Nekah, Toronto's hottest new restaurant, and "ate every morsel of six courses," Rebecca remembered.

But they lingered so long over dinner Carmelita had to cancel the team member who was to stay overnight. Rebecca remembered her panic.

"Obviously, she had a fear of being alone," Rebecca noted, then began to wonder: Shouldn't the team be helping her get over her fear instead of feeding it? What the heck were we as a team doing anyway? She didn't seem to really need us yet.

"I remember once being a few minutes early for my regular Sunday evening shift, standing on the porch and seeing Carm scurry down the street trying to get there before me. She'd been out visiting a neighbour; I wondered what I was doing there when she was so strong," said Rebecca.

At one of the regular team meetings, she suggested we cut back a bit on team visits, give Carmelita some time alone. But most disagreed: They knew what Carm wanted — constant care, they called it. Some of them knew she was scared to be alone, that she had spent the first weeks after her diagnosis walking the streets, all day, all night, terrified, frightened of going back alone to her home, the one she was born in.

But I didn't know that then and I too had some doubts. By this time I had been promoted to a regular Monday night shift and there were nights I had to force myself to go.

I didn't want to always talk trivia; but deep down I knew the real problem was I was getting much more than I was giving. (Carm, sensing my dilemma, began to save dirty dishes so I could wash them for her and fool myself into thinking I was useful.)

I met fascinating people in her living room — Sister Margaret Feeley, who took her vows with Carm; Sister Anne, a nun for 72 years, a wonder; Doug O'Neill and Jim Shea, who used to exchange wicked, witty Gothic tales of dubious veracity with Carm Friday nights; music therapist Mary Rykov; Malcolm Savage and his wife Stella; the paragons from Holy Trinity — Sheila File, Elaine Hall, Hilda Powicke — and people like Enid Richardson, fighting her own health problems.

For a while, I was never alone with Carm. There was always someone else in that living room. Others were more casual about it; Cindy Green shrugged and laughed: "Sure Carm manipulated us. She was good at it too."

Others saw it differently, more benignly: "Carm had her own kind of plan for us all. She fitted us in her own way," said Malcolm.

Many in the team were good people, extraordinary people wrapping Carm in their peace, their serenity. They helped her reclaim her faith, face death in little bits and pieces, work through regrets she might be having. They did real things for her — they sat through nights holding her hand if she was having a panic attack; they stayed with her through chemotherapy; they repaired garage doors.

I entertained. Carm had different roles for each of us — "She had us exactly where she wanted each of us," commented Margaret McBurney — and I was good at my part. But sometimes I had to dig deep to get the energy to do it. Maybe I, too, needed to talk about serious things, important things, inevitable things. Like death.

But slowly — oh, so slowly — I was beginning to understand that the rest of the team knew this. They knew I was one of her "good-time people" and they respected that. They valued everything everyone did because as Lonette Rieb said: "Carmelita got to round herself out with the team."

Carmelita Lawlor was tall, a tough businesswoman, but she was dying and she was scared at night and she didn't want to be alone. So she needed us, even if only to organize — and attend — another celebration, another party.

The good times didn't last, of course. In the spring, Carm started losing a lot of weight, her face becoming more the colour of chalk. She moved from the chair to the couch. The chemotherapy was eating up her calcium, causing her mind to wander. Her ankles were swollen, she always wanted warmer socks.

About the beginning of September there was one terrible night — she was so sick and so frightened Rebecca thought she would be dead by morning, and Malcolm sat in a straight back wooden chair in her room all night holding her hand.

Once again the team had a meeting; this time the word went out via the team's efficient phone tree. Be there, this was important, Carm is coming down to the crunch.

We sat in a circle in a Scarborough living room and listened to Linda's matter-of-fact discussion on what to do when Carm dies. I squirmed as she talked about staying calm — there is no rush after all, Carm is dead — and telephoning her at her home, office or cottage.

That thought came flooding back: "Please, not on my shift."

Carm began spending more time in the hospital. Once I took my daughter with me there and Carmelita, in pain and grieving privately because she could see her autonomy slipping away along with her health, rallied. With that grave courtesy children so warm to, she talked — not chatted — to my seven-year-old, ignoring me most of the two hours. My daughter had a wonderful time and always asked about her friend Carm.

But another time Betty Gorman had said Carm had been swamped with visitors all day and I didn't have to keep my regular shift. Truthfully, I had been counting on not going as I had my book club meeting, something near and dear to me. I said I would stay only an hour then leave for my meeting.

What an hour that was. Carmelita was distant and demanding — she wanted the bed up two centimetres, down four; pillows plumped, removed, plumped again; the dessert heated, cooled, and on it went until I was an hour and 20 minutes late for my book club. Seething, I announced I was leaving in what I hoped was a pleasant voice. Carm gave me her first smile of the evening. It was triumphant. "You missed your book club," she said.

She was fighting death. She had no intention of going gently into that good night. She didn't want to die. She wanted a miracle; she wanted to be healthy again; cured. But by fall she needed professional nursing (the team still came but the overnight shift was stopped when a night nurse was hired).

When a niece visited her, she tried to pass off the nurse as a friend.

She wouldn't finish Callwood's book about the serene death of Margaret Frazer because, "she didn't want to be like Margaret; she didn't want to die," Linda explained.

She bought a thick sweater for the winter; she made plans for Christmas and when Linda made one of her many house calls, she would have on fresh makeup and nightclothes. She worshipped Linda, who believed as she did, that hope can buy time.

She spent Thanksgiving weekend home, having a special dinner with Sister Margaret and Betty Gorman. She wore the turtleneck Enid had given her and a Peruvian sweater she had purchased to help out someone I knew. Her colouring was high and she sat tall and sipped white wine out of her crystal goblet.

It was her home-front finale. Betty booked the team until Nov. 25 and left on a long-awaited overseas trip. But not long after, Carm's health dipped and she was back in hospital. The team kept up its shifts and kept its covenant: Carm would not die alone.

On Saturday, Oct. 28 at 6 p.m. she died. She was only 56. Malcolm Savage was there, Mary Duncan was there, Sister Margaret and another friend, Sister Theresa, were there. They held her hands; they held each other's hands as she died peacefully.

Carmelita didn't get her miracle and she didn't die at home. Perhaps deep down she wasn't even totally at peace with her own mortality when she died. But she had a good death.

Linda believes the team gave Carm an extra year of living, in which Carm re-evaluated her priorities and opened up and laughed. She told some of the team she was astonished at all the people who gave her so much and wanted nothing in return.

Some of us learned something: We are at ease with illness, we can face dying now. Some of us don't know that.

We all got something — Carm spelled it out in her will — Enid the portable phone, Cindy the ghetto blaster, Elaine Hall the washing machine, luggage for Anne Winter, Betty Gorman the microwave. Mischievous gifts — Betty always refused to use the microwave and Enid remains baffled by the phone.

She left money in trust to Linda for palliative care, and also some money to throw a big party for the team.

So we'll get together in the New Year and tell Carm stories and reminisce about when we were a team. Were? We still are a team. Enid is knitting my daughter a sweater. Linda is a new friend, so are others.

Ties still bind. Betty says she and Carm decided at the beginning that no one on the team should feel "overwhelmed," but we all do feel that. Just look what we got from those 16 months.

Thanks Carm.

• **1990** Enterprise Reporting •

'Just small game'

He was going hunting —and the prey were 'feminists'

Greg Weston, Jack Aubry

Ottawa Citizen

(Excerpts from a two-part series)

MONTREAL — He hoists the rifle to his shoulder, presses his right cheek to the hardwood stock and slowly squeezes the trigger, just like his uncle the paratrooper had taught him as a little boy. The barrel sweeps to the left and stops, his eye now fixed just beyond the front sights.

"What are you going after?" the gun store clerk asks.

"Just small game," he says, lowering the rifle.

He probably noticed the big banner as he walked out of the Montreal gun shop that day: Good luck and good shooting.

Just small game.

Two months after Marc Lepine stalked his prey in the halls of a Montreal engineering school, the mourners' flowers have wilted but the impossible puzzle of a twisted young mind remains.

Lepine left behind only a few pieces of his macabre jigsaw, scratched on a handwritten suicide note stuffed in his coat pocket underneath a box of unspent rifle shells.

Much of it is a tirade against feminists who have "always ruined my life."

On another line he writes: "I have been unhappy for the past seven years."

Starting in the summer of 1982.

Marc Lepine had never been really happy — hellish years of child abuse at the hands of a violently chauvinist father; more years of loneliness after his parents split and his mother was out trying to support a family.

Only in his teenage years had he found any semblance of happiness, mainly through an intense friendship with a neighbourhood chum named Jean Belanger.

It was in the summer of 1982 that Monique Lepine sold their house in Pierrefonds and moved with Marc and his younger sister Nadia to another part of Montreal.

The rented apartment at 2675 Marlborough Ct. in St. Laurent was a modern two-storey rowhouse in a pleasant suburban neighbourhood.

And it was much closer to Marc's new junior college and her own nursing director's job at St. Jude's hospital.

But it was far enough away from Pierrefonds to break Marc's bonds of friendship with Belanger.

He had already been rejected by the army. Now he was spending the summer washing dishes in the kitchen of his mother's hospital.

Belanger visited Marlborough Court before they lost touch: "Marc didn't seem very happy there. We had been together for so long. I guess maybe he was lonely. He didn't have much to do."

Lepine began spending long periods locked in his small bedroom crammed with huge stacks of his beloved books, a wood table where he tinkered with electronics, and a computer — his obsession — donated by one of his mother's friends at the hospital.

Lepine enrolled in a two-year program in pure sciences at CEGEP St. Laurent junior college, continuing his high school path towards engineering school.

Perhaps it was his loneliness. Maybe the courses didn't come as easily as they had in high school. At the end of his first term at St. Laurent, he had flunked two subjects, his first academic failures ever.

Belanger remembers Lepine telling him he would get home from CEGEP in the evenings and

169

"just sit in front of his computer and start playing with it. That had become his hobby."

Shortly after Lepine turned 18 that fall, he filed the papers necessary to officially bury Gamil Rodrigue Gharbi, the name given him at birth by the father he loved to hate.

Lepine and his mother lived alone at Marlborough Court for most of the first two years after Nadia went off to boarding school. That was okay with Marc. He despised his sister's taunts.

The second term at CEGEP, in the winter of 1983, went much better than the first. His marks ranged from the 70s to the 90s, and he was well on his way to fulfilling a boyhood dream — to graduate in engineering from Montreal's Ecole Polytechnique.

Dec. 6, 1989. In the cluttered turquoise bedroom, he pulls the new Kodiaks over the cuffs of his blue jeans. He loops his belt through the sheath of the hunting knife and buckles it.

He reaches for the rifle. The curved 30-round magazine clip of high-powered bullets hangs from the stalk like a rectangular banana. He stuffs the gun into a garbage bag.

He folds the letter and puts it in his windbreaker pocket, then jams a box of 20 shells in with it. Another box of them is stuffed in the other pocket.

He tugs the "Tracteur Montreal" baseball cap down over his forehead, picks up the garbage and heads for the rented car.

It is just after 4 p.m.

In the fall of 1983, Lepine began what would become a long sequence of curious career moves.

At the end of his first of two years in pure sciences — the usual route to engineering school — he switched into electronics technology, a three-year vocational trades program.

Lepine excelled at his new vocation — 82 in industrial electronics; 87 in control systems and so on down the list.

Marcel Leroux, head of the CEGEP's professional electronics program, said most of the professors can't remember Lepine.

"He was not super-brilliant, but neither was he stupid. He really was low profile."

CEGEP director Claude Boily says Lepine was never seen by any of the institution's psychologists "and there were no reports in his file noting that he had any behavioral problems."

But he was also becoming increasingly hyperactive, always in a hurry. All nerves. And acne. Severe acne that embarrassed him.

Nadia's boarding school roommate, Isabelle Lahaie, used to visit the Marlborough Court apartment regularly: "Marc was a good guy. But he was closed. He had a strange look — his eyes were lit up, he had the same smile all the time … You could see he was unhappy."

For the next two years, Marc Lepine's world was CEGEP classrooms and his Marlborough Court bedroom.

As he headed home for the Christmas holidays that year, Lepine was only nine courses away from graduation — seven in the winter term, two in the summer.

But 15 days after the winter term began Jan. 31, Lepine simply stopped going to classes.

There were no discussions with anyone at the school. No explanations. No notice. Just gone. He was 21.

Nadia's former roommate Lahaie speculates: "That's when Nadia left … to return to live with her mother and get on his (Marc's) back fulltime.

"I can still hear Nadia telling me: 'If you really want to get him mad, call him Gamil — and tell him he is ugly and stupid.'"

The headlights moving along Bordeaux St. have slowed to a solemn procession in the freezing drizzle.

There are 15 wrought-iron stairs to the street. Normally, he takes them two at a time. This time he is calm.

He climbs in the small car he rented earlier in the day, turns the key and joins the procession down Bordeaux St.

Just before — or just after — he quit CEGEP in his final term, he applied for admission to engineering at the Ecole Polytechnique.

Not surprisingly, he was rejected.

Then he enrolled in two summer courses, but dropped them before he started.

Lepine was finished with school for a while.

For the next 16 months, the shy brainy kid was washing dishes, serving food and mopping floors at St. Jude's Hospital for the chronically ill.

On July 1, 1986, Lepine moved away from his mother — and his sister.

Lepine's apartment No. 401 was a modern one-bedroom with a small cement balcony on the top floor of a boxy 24-unit block 4185 St. Martin Blvd. in the northwest Montreal suburb of Laval.

The $10 an hour he was making at the hospital was plenty to cover his $300 rent. He didn't drink. He didn't smoke. No drugs. No girls.

The place was always clean, he never complained, never made trouble for his neighbours. And the rent was always paid on time.

Building superintendent Luc Riopel said: "He was a good guy. But he lived in isolation and did not appear very happy."

Lepine was always running, heavy-footed, crashing through doors at full speed. No one complained, except the day he hit the front door so hard he broke off the crash bar.

"He told me he didn't like working at the hospital. It was not what he wanted to do for a living. It was just a job for him. His real interest was in computers. And war books. He had a lot of war books ..."

The wipers are streaking the freezing rain across the windshield as he turns on to the long, steep drive that leads to the six-storey yellow engineering school at the top of the hill. The parking booth is 50 metres up the slope. He pays the attendant $5.

The car pulls to a stop in front of the student entrance. A tow-away zone. He doesn't much care. He won't be back for it anyway. The letter in his pocket says so ...

Dominique Leclair was 19 when she met Lepine that summer in the kitchen at St. Jude's. Her father runs the hospital and was good friends with Monique Lepine when she was his nursing director. He gave Marc his job.

But that's not why Dominique befriended Marc Lepine.

"I was kind to him because he was so hyperactive and nervous, nobody would talk to him at lunch or break time ... Everyone else tried to avoid him because he was a bit strange because of his shyness."

Lepine's hyperactivity and his job didn't mix either.

"He was always rushing things. He would never be calm."

He raced the food carts the same way he did everything else. Always in a hurry. Soup got spilled. Dishes got broken.

Every time he made a mess of something, his reaction was always the same: "Ah shit."

Finally, he was put on food-serving duty in the cafeteria where his pace would at least be tempered by the task. But the steamy kitchen atmosphere had festered his already unsightly acne problem.

Dominique recalls: "The employees would say they didn't want him to serve them their lunch because of his acne. They were mean."

Lepine was stuffed back in the kitchen where no one would have to look at his pimples.

He tried growing a beard to hide the acne, but it was scraggly and seemed to make the rest of his complexion worse. He would cut it off and grow it again like a suburban lawn.

No matter how hard he might have tried, Lepine just couldn't shed his shyness. Even with Dominique, he would stir his food and stare at the floor when he was speaking.

Dominique never had any inkling he might be interested in her romantically. "Maybe if I had asked him out, okay ... But I didn't sense he had any of that feeling. We were just friends."

Part of the problem was Marc Lepine figured he was just plain ugly. That's why he didn't have a girlfriend.

Dominique remembers him saying: "I've asked a lot of girls out, but they have all refused. I know so many girls, but they won't go out with me. I'm not good looking ..."

He is walking slowly, 48 paces along the cement path to the four sets of steel and glass doors, the ones beneath the huge sign Ecole Polytechnique de Montreal.

The gun in the garbage bag is hanging at his side as he steps into the crowded, noisy foyer.

Just another engineering student with another piece of equipment.

The college guards in the glass cubicle to the right pay him no heed. Nor do the other students. It is the last hour of the last day of classes before Christmas holidays.

In September, 1987, after Dominique had gone back to school, Lepine quit the hospital, probably not far ahead of being fired.

The next time Dominique heard the name Marc Lepine was the day her first cousin Maryse Leclair died. By sheer coincidence, she was Lepine's last victim.

Lepine turned 23 shortly after he quit the hospital, and enrolled that fall in three courses at the nearby CEGEP Montmorency.

His marks were all good: 81 in advanced algebra; 75 in a course called the ethics of politics; 84 in mass communications. As in the past, his 15 weeks at the CEGEP were thoroughly unremarkable.

After Christmas, he stayed on in his St. Martin apartment and spent most of his free time with a new Apple computer he had bought with his savings from the hospital.

On Feb. 29, 1988, two months after his course ended at CEGEP Montmorency, Lepine filled in an application for a computer programming course at the privately-run Control Data Institute in downtown Montreal.

He lied about his work at the hospital, and listed "David Caron, friend" as the person to contact in case of an emergency. The address he gave for Caron doesn't exist and the phone number was Lepine's own apartment.

Not surprisingly, computer whiz Lepine got 90 per cent on his admission test and began to take his courses on March 11. He was 23.

The $9,000 fee for the 15-month program was covered by a $5,940 student loan, and the balance by Lepine in $200 monthly instalments which he never missed.

Jean Cloutier, director of the institute, described Lepine in familiar terms: "He was an isolated hard worker. Very much above average ... His marks throughout were probably in the top 15 per cent."

Cloutier said about the only thing remotely notable about Lepine was the way he dressed. No blue jeans; they were banned. But he always looked sloppy. Always wore a baseball cap.

And the acne. Everyone noticed he had bad acne.

In June, 1988, Lepine moved downtown from his St. Martin Blvd. apartment in suburban Laval.

On moving day, his landlord Riopel recalls that he never mentioned anything about taking computer programming at Control Data — or anywhere else.

"He told me he was going off to join the Armed Forces ..."

He is moving up the beige stairwell from the ground floor to the second, new Kodiaks on terrazzo, the stainless steel railing sliding through his free hand. Thirteen steps to the landing. Another 13 to the top. Through the red steel fire doors.

Down one hallway, into another and another. The second floor is a maze of confusing corridors, lounges and student supply shops.

Room 230 is the only classroom on the floor, hidden at the end of a wide corridor lined with photocopiers, beyond a set of steel doors, the last room at the end of another narrow twisting hall.

He must have been there before.

Bordeaux St. is typical of blue-collar Montreal — a narrow one-way collage of overhead wires, parked cars and skinny, red-brick walkups.

The second-floor apartment at 2175 Bordeaux would be Marc Lepine's last home.

The neighbourhood wasn't far from Control Data, and Lepine's mother had moved into a new condo three blocks away. The rent was right — $285 a month — split with an old high school acquaintance, Erik Cossette.

He was Lepine's age, a little shorter, with curly blond hair. A theatre student, the landlord says. Their mothers had kept in touch.

Beyond the brown front door with the dirty glass window, the apartment was typical of student digs: A narrow hallway with worn-through linoleum. One sickly green bedroom. A smaller one in turquoise. A dilapidated bathroom in deep blue. A dirty beige sitting area. The yellow kitchen.

Marc got the small bedroom, about eight-by-ten. His mother helped him paint it turquoise.

The size of Lepine's room made it more chaotic than usual. A sofa bed along one wall; the Apple computer and a clutter of electronic parts on the desk in front of the window. The view is a blind alley and a spaghetti of telephone wires.

Everywhere there are piles of books, floor to ceiling, two deep. Even in the clothes closet.

There are two prints on the wall. One is a war scene. Nothing about women.

And there are video-cassettes, lots of them, mostly Pay-TV movies taped from the television and VCR in the sitting room.

Lots about war in those.

He is through the beige steel doors into a narrow concrete hall. The garbage bag falls off the rifle. Seven paces, then right, then left. He walks slowly through the doorless entrance at the front of the cavernous cement-block classroom.

He stops a metre from the two female students giving their fourth-year presentations. He appears calm.

He orders the women to move to one side of the room, the men to leave. There are titters. They think it's a prank. He fires a shot into the ceiling.

"I want the women," he says. "You're all a bunch of feminists."

"I hate feminists."

Gina Cousineau had never seen him look so dapper, so prosperous, as that evening he walked into the 1988 high school reunion for the class of '82. A black shirt done up to the neck. Black pants. A nicely tailored black sports coat.

Marc Lepine had been certain he would find his old pal Jean Belanger at the party, though they hadn't spoken in almost four years.

But Belanger was in hospital with a crushed leg after a garage door fell on him.

Lepine called him the next day and told him he was thinking of joining the army. It was the last time they ever spoke.

Lepine spent the entire reunion evening with Gina, Belanger's teenage sweetheart, the third member of the high school happy threesome.

Gina remembers the evening well, the last time she would ever see her old friend: "He looked like he always looked, that big smile. He always had that smile on his face, even if things weren't going so well."

Lepine never strayed far from Gina and her new fiancé the whole evening. He always ordered Coke at the bar.

Gina asked him if he had a girlfriend: "He told me, 'I had one, but she dumped me.'"

The reunion was in late August, 1988. He was almost half-way through Control Data.

He never mentioned Control Data.

"He told me he had just lost his job and was going back to university in the fall. He didn't mention which one."

Gina asked him how he lost his job at the hospital: "He said he had made one small mistake during his three-month probationary period and, bang, they told him to get lost.

"He told me he had been fired by a woman and that another woman had taken his place.

"He was really mad about that ..."

There is mayhem in the main corridor outside Room 230. The 50-odd men who left as ordered are screaming at people to run. Inside the classroom, six women are dead. The other three are wounded.

He is out in the main corridor again, down at the other end by the photocopiers. He keeps his back to the wall. Wheels. Fires. Wheeling and firing again.

The wounded are moaning for help. The woman selling posters dives behind her table. He is six paces past her. He stops, turns. The rifle recoils.

Sylvie Drouin thought he was a pretty "good-looking guy" that first night she walked into the chemistry class in February, 1989. Five-foot-nine, 160 pounds, curly brown hair. A beard. A baseball cap. Sure, he had bad acne. But she didn't care about stuff like that.

She asked him to be her lab partner. Drouin was 28, four years older than Lepine, and already had an arts degree from Laval University. Like him, she is shy.

Both of them were also taking the CEGEP chemistry course as a key prerequisite to engineering school.

Over the ensuing weeks, Lepine would continue his studies at Control Data in the afternoons from 1 p.m. until 6 p.m., then spend two nights a week at the nearby CEGEP de Vieux Montreal taking the chemistry course.

Sylvie Drouin would also become perhaps the closest Marc Lepine could come to a relationship with a woman.

It got off to a rocky start: "The first few weeks in the lab, he was very severe with me. I was never correct. He was being a fascist. The lab was never done well enough. He was always right ...

"And he was giving me these orders all the time. Wash those things. Don't do the calculation like that. Go and get something. Do this. Don't do that."

He called her "fraulein."

After two weeks of harassment, Drouin told him to either back off or find another lab partner. Lepine didn't say much in reply, just frowned and scowled. But he was at least more civil after that.

As usual, Lepine mastered the work easily and would get a final mark in the 90s.

But Drouin says Lepine was a bundle of nerves sitting next to her. "He was good at the theory, but at practical things he was no good. He was so nervous, he would make mistakes. His mind would wander. He would put too many drops in the solution, that kind of thing."

Every time Lepine would make a mistake, something that made him angry at himself, his reaction was always the same.

"Ah shit."

Drouin was taking another night course in computers and asked if he would help with her homework. She suggested maybe she could come to his place.

"He was really pleased to help. He needed to feel important to other people."

The next night, Drouin made the first of a dozen visits to Bordeaux S. over the ensuing three months.

"In the beginning, he was a lot of fun. I remember the first time I walked in and he told me to sit on the chair and he showed me all these things he could do with his computer — colours, three-dimensional stuff, that kind of thing."

But Lepine wasn't so much interested in helping as impressing. "He didn't want to do them (the problems) with me. He didn't teach me. He just wanted to solve the problems himself and hand them to me."

He didn't want to talk about his family. "He just said, 'Oh, I have a mother in Montreal.' That's all."

Every night Sylvie visited Bordeaux St., Lepine would always insist on walking her back to her bus. Very gentlemanly. But that was it.

She certainly wasn't pressing him into a romance: "I think in his mind, the girl has to worship everything he does, that everything he does is right. Like in those first few labs ...

"If you follow him and his ways, things are fine. If you don't, there is nothing. He gets very cold and withdrawn."

Drouin's initial attraction to Lepine had evaporated: "I like the different kind, not whackos, but different. But to be with a guy like that, you would have to give your whole life to him, just follow him."

Early in their relationship, Drouin made the mistake of casually asking Lepine if he had a girlfriend. "He was surprised I would even ask the question. He got mad. He said, 'What do you want to know that for?' So I shut up ..."

He turns through the student lounge. Left again, the rifle sweeping air. He moves along a now empty corridor. New Kodiaks on red tile floor. He is at the end. He starts to turn left. He stops. A door clicks shut behind him. A female employee of the finance department is just closing up for the night.

He spins. The gun cracks once. Then again. And again.

He wheels back into the stairwell. A student who has come to check out the commotion freezes. He is male. The gunman laughs and disappears down the stairs.

It was March 31, 1989. Lepine was two months and two relatively easy courses away from finishing his computer programming work at Control Data.

At 6 p.m. that day, he signed out on the attendance sheet and never came back.

Institute director Cloutier says everyone there was completely baffled: "With his background in electronics, plus his high standings in programming, he was well on his way to becoming a computer genius."

Lepine returned some books to the institute two weeks later and mentioned in passing he had decided to change careers. They never saw him again.

Lepine never mentioned it to Sylvie, pretending for the next two months that he was still enrolled. But she noticed his mood slowly started to change.

"He slowly got more difficult to communicate with. He became very withdrawn and closed."

In the chemistry class, lab assistant Andre Tremblay remembers Lepine's eyes were perpetually bloodshot, as though he weren't sleeping.

Drouin tried to include him in her social life, but to no avail.

"Once we had a party on a Thursday night in a bar downtown and I asked him if he wanted to come. He was alone and he seemed very down.

"He just said, 'No, I don't drink and I never go in that kind of place.' There was no discussion."

The only time he ever asked her to stay late during one of her visits was to watch one of the movies he had on VCR.

"They were pretty well all violent stuff, not just war films but science fiction, police movies. I told him I didn't like violence and went home."

One day, Lepine arrived in chemistry class with a full-page story from a Montreal tabloid about a policewoman named Angele who had just saved an old man from a burning house.

Lepine didn't think women should be on the police force. They weren't big enough or strong enough.

Lab instructor Tremblay remembers Lepine making the bizarre remark that there were only six women on the Montreal police force.

How did he know that? Tremblay asked, suggesting there must be far more.

"And he said, 'To date, I have only found the names of six of them in newspaper stories ...'"

The last time Sylvie Drouin saw Lepine at Bordeaux St. was one afternoon about a week after the last chemistry class.

"I had come away from there with a very strange feeling like I would never see him again, that I didn't want to see him again and I didn't. I told him I might call in the summer but I never did."

Lepine was "very strange, in a very hurried state, like someone with something very important on his mind. It was as though he had something to do that no one else could know about..."

Sylvie Drouin had been accepted into engineering at the University of Quebec in Trois Rivieres.

Marc Lepine told her he was going to the Ecole Polytechnique in the fall.

The stairwell from the second floor empties into the foyer near the main doors where he had entered the school minutes before. He is 15 steps away from them. The rented car is still there. He can see it. He could leave. But he doesn't.

He moves across the foyer to the huge cafeteria.

There are people everywhere. The gun recoils. And again. And again. Then pandemonium. Three more young women dead.

He is back in the foyer by the main doors. Again, he could leave. But he doesn't.

Erik Cossette never did notice anything particularly alarming about his roommate on Bordeaux St.

Lepine was "emotionally repressed," a dud with women, and while he often made sexist remarks, those were "no more disturbing than what one hears from many men."

Cossette describes a quiet intellectual, fascinated by technology, intrigued by history and world politics, and always happy to help a friend.

"Doing favours was his way of expressing his affection for people."

Cossette said Lepine had become an avid reader of gun magazines, but it just seemed to be "an interest like any other."

Sometime around the end of the summer, Cossette decided to go backpacking in South America and moved out of Bordeaux St.

On Aug. 29, Lepine walked into the Montreal headquarters of the Quebec Provincial Police to pick up an application form for a firearms acquisition certificate.

As he was leaving the building, he ran into his sister Nadia's old boarding school friend Isabelle Lahaie.

"He told me he was finding out how to get a gun. He said it was for hunting."

Lepine was back at the police station Sept. 4, Labour Day, with the completed application and his $10 fee.

As long as he was not a mental patient and had no record of violent crimes, Lepine would be licensed to buy as many guns as he could afford.

As it happened, his application got buried in the pre-hunting season rush and permit No. AA2092373 did not arrive at Bordeaux St. until mid-October.

It was about that time the clerks in the Checkmate Sports store on St. Hubert St. remember first seeing Lepine browsing among the gun racks, asking a lot of questions.

Since Cossette had left, Lepine's cousin, Michel Thiery, had moved in to Bordeaux St. He was a couple of years younger than Lepine, blond and clean-shaven.

The neighbours didn't notice anything unusual about Lepine in the fall. There were his calls for grocery deliveries. A bit odd. The store is right across the street.

And there was the late-night laughter. One voice. No other sound.

He is back in the stairwell. Up 13 stairs to the landing. Up another flight to the second floor. Up two more flights and through the red doors with the sloppy "3" magic markered over them. He turns right, past a wide corridor. Past the security office with the closed door and frosted glass.

He turns right, down the second corridor. It is 22 paces to Room 311, one of three classrooms on the left. He looks through the glass in the door. He is smiling when he enters the room at the front. Someone has just pulled the fire alarm. The bells are clanging in his ears.

It was around 1:30 p.m. on Nov. 21 and Lepine was making his last visit to Checkmate Sports on St. Hubert St.

Ninety minutes later, Lepine had chosen a Sturm Ruger Mini-14, the same kind a lot of police SWAT teams use. The weapon is a semi-automatic. Fires each time the trigger is pulled without reloading.

The gun comes with a five-shot magazine. Lepine asks for a banana clip that will spit 30 bullets, one after another, into the chamber. Just pull the trigger.

Lepine grabbed five of the powder blue boxes stamped "Remington 223" from the assortment of ammunition piled a metre high in the middle of the floor. Twenty shells in each. A hundred rounds.

It is a critical choice.

The bullets Lepine bought have solid slugs that go in one side of a target and clean out the other, not like hunting shells that expand on impact and blow the insides out of an animal.

Lepine bought them because they are the cheapest ammunition.

Store owner Gilbert Rosenberg would later say: "If Lepine had known what he was doing when he was buying the shells, the 13 people injured (at Ecole Polytechnique) would be dead today."

The clerk suggested Lepine buy a carrying case. The folks on the bus might take an open assault rifle the wrong way.

The total on the bill comes to $765.03, but Lepine doesn't have enough money. He is embarrassed.

"Ah shit," he said.

He leaves a $100 deposit, says he is going to his bank and is back with the cash in less than 30 minutes.

Shortly before 4 p.m., Marc Lepine carried the black rectangular plastic case out of the store.

They thought they had heard something that sounded like shots about two minutes before. The female student giving a presentation at the front of Room 311 had paused, then continued.

Suddenly, he bursts into the room and orders everyone out. Maybe just the men. No one can quite remember. No one moves. Another joke. He fires a shot. Everyone is diving under desks, cowering. Terrified.

There is another sudden burst of gunfire. Blood on the desks. More on the floor. Someone is moaning. Now he is walking across the desks.

Monique Lepine last saw her son on Sat. Dec. 2, four days before his rampage.

She would later tell friends she could recall no peculiar behaviour, no telling comment. No final hug. Nothing unusual.

The landlord also dropped by Bordeaux St. several times that weekend to collect the December rent. No one answered the door. No one answered his subsequent phone calls.

For the first time, the forever meticulous Lepine had not paid his rent on time.

On Monday evening, Dec. 4, the First Choice pay-TV channel in Montreal featured an extraordinarily violent Chuck Connors film, dubbed into French, called *Commando Terreur.*

The film is about two terrorists who take students hostage in their school. Some of them are shot. The terrorists are Arab.

Lepine watched a lot of violent films, and he was a subscriber to the pay-channel. It is not known if he tuned in the movie that night.

At some point in his final days, Lepine sat down and penned his now infamous three-page suicide note, essentially a eulogy to personal failures.

He bemoans that he was rejected by the army for what he calls "anti-social behaviour."

And most of all, "feminists have always ruined my life."

On the third page are listed the names of 15 prominent women, including six female police officers — the same ones he had discussed with his chemistry instructor eight months before.

The letter is not a blind rage. Some of it reflects an eerie sense of calm and rational thought.

He instructs that his old refrigerator be given to his landlord in lieu of the month's rent he hasn't paid.

The rest — his books, the computer, his bicycle — will go to his childhood pal Jean Belanger.

He is thinking about the end. Getting his house in order like anyone dying of a terminal disease.

The letter begins: "I will die on December 6, 1989."

It ends: "Marc."

He is at the front of the classroom, at the lectern where she had been giving her term-end presentation when he walked in and shot her. Three other women in the room are dead. She is moaning.

He pulls the knife from the sheaf on his belt. It is not like a trigger that causes detached targets to fall. Not like the trigger that is about to blow the top off his own head.

The moaning stops. There is blood on his hand. Blood on the blade. The knife clatters to the tile floor.

They hear his last two words.

"Ah shit."

• **1996** Feature Writing •

Northern exposure

Heather Mallick

Toronto Sun

There is a town in north Ontario
With dream comfort memory to spare.
And in my mind I still need a place to go.
All my changes were there

— Helpless, by Neil Young

High school reunions are a bad idea, as are all sentimental occasions. It is inadvisable to go back to anything. Old boyfriends should be erased. Funerals should be minimalist. If people don't send you Christmas cards for two years, strike them off the list. Be businesslike.

Going to your high school reunion is like volunteering for surgery without anesthetic. But I attended this one, my first, because all my relatives and school friends who weren't going (Kapuskasing is an acquired taste and not all of us had acquired it) plus all the people I know who have ever been north of Orillia, begged me to go.

In other words, go have what will probably be a bad experience so that you can write about it, and we can live it vicariously without having to put ourselves out. What follows is an entirely truthful assessment of my hometown, and I accept that I won't be invited back.

High school is a purely North American institution and its intensity can be glimpsed only by those who didn't experience it. My husband, for example, who is British and has standards, thinks that high school is where young Canadians are educated. He does not understand, as we do, that high school has nothing whatsoever to do with education. It has to do with the process of "socialization," with sex and drugs and yearning and clothes and girl gangs and what passes for entertainment and a mental stage where everything — and nothing — is interesting. Actual classroom time was incidental to the business of becoming a grownup, of spending time with your friends, of feeling your way underwater.

An hour after the harrowing flight from Timmins and a high-cholesterol breakfast at Belly Buster's, we head for the high school where they are holding a welcoming wine and cheese, sans cheese, in the sweltering gym. I will drink anything, especially now, but the reunion wine — a specially bottled chardonnay we'll name Chateau Kap after a beloved local bar — is corrosive. I wonder why it isn't chilled and realize suddenly what has been bothering me about the whole town.

The wine isn't chilled because this is not a place where you have to chill wine — it is cold here, always. This pretty town whose verdancy my husband is exclaiming over is behaving out of character. It looks like Niagara-on-the-Lake.

My Kapuskasing is a white, Siberian misery and if they were being strictly accurate, they would have held the reunion in January. I meet a classmate who tells me the reason he left Kap permanently was that in 1980, it snowed in every single month of the year and he could no longer tolerate it. The whole weekend, I am uncomfortably hot, because I never thought for a moment it wouldn't be freezing.

One thing hasn't changed — the bugs. I get mosquito bites so bad they leave scars. Visitors from Toronto are shocked to be told proudly by a Kap resident that no, the blackflies don't just appear in the evening, they hover all day. We reminisce about the caterpillar invasions — trees were leafless, cars skidded on the gooey road — and remember the year of the locust? Or were they just deerflies? What about those enormous beetles that we would occasionally find ponderously crossing the road in a procession? Where did they come from? Where were they going?

I begin to realize that there are so many things Kap people take for granted that southerners can't get over. We never salted the roads, instead leaving them to pack down to the consistency of hard soap, which provided sufficient resistance for snow tires. We used block heaters. When we got snow up our pants, we didn't mind because it wasn't going to melt till we got inside, maybe. We killed animals and ate them, but in a casual way so that you never saw antlers on anyone's wall because hunting wasn't a novelty. Everyone smoked, and still does, Player's Light, and people wore hockey T-shirts that said Puck It. The women all had small-town hair — terrible perms committed by hairdressers with criminal records.

My husband was desperate to go to Kap with me (to find out how you turned out this way, was how he put it, but he has always treated me the way a horticulturist would tend a genetically freakish plant) and, amazed by my consent, was on his best behaviour. He did have an unfortunate manner about him though, sort of like Prince Philip making stilted conversation with someone who has turned over a new leaf after getting out of prison. I overheard someone telling him about catching sturgeon and him responding, "Not a very attractive fish, is it?"

A man of insight, you'll agree, but I think as a subconscious punishment for his crime of being British, polite and well-dressed, I insisted he take me to the Model City Mall and hang out by the garbage cans outside the hot dog stand just the way all the guys did in high school. We sat there and watched women come out of the hair salon with the worst hair in existence, hair that literally looked as if it had been set by a Mixmaster, beehives with giant unblended curls, and the victims looking terrified, and I said, there, do you understand small towns now or do I have to take you back into Wal-Mart? Do you want me to gain weight and look 52 at 36, like that woman in the bright green sweatshirt that reads, "When Irish eyes are smiling, they're usually up to something"? Would you like to move to a small town and raise a passel of kids? Would you like to get up from supper every night and head off for your shift at the mill, picking those oft-used plugs out of the ashtray and shoving them in your ears? Go out to dinner on Saturday night and eat cream of carrot soup and hot pork with a side of order of toast? One word from you and we can do that! Stop saying my town is charming!

It was one moment of hysteria in an otherwise pleasant weekend.

It's actually useful to take an outsider to your hometown because you then see things through foreign, endlessly appreciative eyes. When I saw London, England, for the first time, I didn't see the grime and the stinginess but rather the beauty and the potential of it. Kap, like all northern towns, has a makeshift air about it, a certain raffishness.

One of the sweetest moments was revisiting the town library. Libraries are a safety valve for small towns, just as bars are, and as a teenager I brought home novels in bulk, not liking non-fiction at that age. The library seems to be as good as ever, one of the few places in town that has not deteriorated or been replaced by that attractive, but somehow samey, coloured, corrugated siding. (Why is everything built of synthetics in the middle of the world's biggest forest? Because it's cheap and practical.)

Change in this town was wrought by two things: The exodus caused by the mill downsizing, and Premier Bill Davis's last-moment decision to fund Catholic schools.

His move destroyed the French-English balance in the town, and sent many of the bilingual kids to the French high school, which is known as Cite des Jeunes, thus virtually wiping out my high school which was partially torn down and rebuilt as a combined junior and senior English school This pointless exercise means that my high school is now known as an "education centre." Kap, if it was worth five million precious dollars to you to reshuffle an age group that I recall proudly as being a bunch of happy, badly behaved illiterates, have it your way.

T.K. Jewell must have had a fit. He was the principal of my high school (and subsequently the town's mayor), a courteous and correct man whose icy English-accented precision had all the students terrified. We came in every day, listened to the anthem, recited the Lord's Prayer and waited for a speech from T.K. over the public address system (Mister Jewell to you, Miss Mallick) in which he enumerated our failings. He was a splendid principal, achieving discipline by strength of character, remoteness of manner and a sort of polite sarcasm.

He was the first person I encountered at the reunion and I realized as we conversed (alert questions on his part, frenzied babbling on mine) that he is black. That's the kind of town it is, where the mayor is the only black person in town and nobody notices that they don't notice.

In a TV documentary about Kap, T.K. Jewell described his small southern Ontario background. He said he was raised to believe that a black person had to maintain strict standards for himself in a town, that one had to behave better than others in order to thrive.

Is this true? It is certainly true that he always kept himself slightly apart from other people. I'm now wondering if there were Jews in Kap or Ukrainians, or indeed anyone whom we didn't take strictly at face value, just as they expected themselves to be taken. Everyone had a complete lack of "side" or snobbery. It was a profound shock to me in 1992 to hear for the first time — in Toronto — vicious anti-Semitic, anti-black and anti-gay remarks. I did not respond to them. My hometown had never prepared me for such a thing.

A small-town reunion gives you a feeling of familiarity and connection that is a shock to the system. Everyone knows you here, even if you think they don't, and it is an uncomfortable sensation. Big cities have a bad reputation, but as the travel writer Jonathan Raban once wrote, "Not knowing one's neighbours may be a privilege, not a dreadful fate. To be without a family is, for some, a luxurious and honourable escape from a state of repressive social bondage." Solitude is the prize, as well as the penalty, of city life. To live in a small town means to abandon privacy.

Or does it? Anonymity is a jewel. I greatly enjoy going to parties in Toronto where I know no one, as my chances of being surprised and entertained are so much greater. But then city people do pin you down. What do you do? they ask. What's your net worth? is what they might as well be asking. How many divorces have you had? Are those scars from plastic surgery?

The nicest thing about the whole reunion was that no one asked once in that grasping big city way about how I made my living. What are you doing now? they might say, referring to anything from marriage to children to where our last vacation was. Overwhelmingly, everyone in my class had children — never one, always two and sometimes four or five — but still seemed relaxed. I spent a week recently with a 15-month-old baby. I watched that child peel open a jelly doughnut, dump it in the pool, take it out and play badminton with it and then eat it. I am not even relaxed thinking of it. How do these women achieve such serenity?

Overwhelmingly, the women were open and generous and still attractive. Generally speaking, the men had aged badly and were just as boring as they had been in high school. In many cases, they were more so and communicated by grunting. Many were engaged in classic wife-avoidance tactics that afternoon, like golf, and fascinatingly, the wives expressed no regret at their absence. How did I ever yearn for the younger versions of these useless men?

I do not miss high school — no sane person does. After a few thimble-sized glasses of the Chateau Kap, I started to remember what I didn't like about it. They made us wear these tasteless navy blue nylon uniforms for gym class, with our names embroidered on the back — everyone detested them. (Or maybe they didn't; this is only my version of events.)

I hated gym. It always made me feel the way I assume homosexuals feel plunged into boot camp in Fort Dix.

Once when I was 13, the gym teacher asked me to demonstrate a somersault on the balance beam, which seemed to be to be several storeys off the ground. I looked at her in disbelief, but I did what I considered to be this silly, uncomfortable, graceless thing.

I silently swore that someday somehow I would not have to wear unattractive clothes and possibly injure myself following the absurd instructions of sweaty masculine women. I would not have to break wrist veins serving in volleyball. I would find someplace where I was valued for being a girl and would spend my adult life lounging around reading Henry James, eating delicious food and having affairs with clever older men who said clever things. I had this deep suspicion, from casual things that teachers had said to me, that there might be a percentage in being smart, in being the kind of person on whom nothing is lost.

All girls go through a phase where they realize that sex might be their ticket out. In small towns, sex is your ticket in. If you wear tight jeans and stilettos and hang out at the mall, you will have your future decided for you.

I considered this, but I think I was faking it even then. As Joni Mitchell said about trying to be Bohemian, "Even on the scuffle, the cleaner's press was in my jeans." About a third of us stayed;

the rest left never to return.

There were so many thousands of people crowded into the hockey arena for the Saturday night reunion party that we were forced outside. Like teenagers, we stood around drinking beer and talking about nothing much.

I said how sorry I would have been if the mill had died, taking the town with it. One of the nicest people I went to school with — there's one in every class, a Wayne Gretzky type, the kind of gentle, self-confident young man who always makes sure the retarded students aren't left out of things — reproved me for what he believed to be false sentimentality.

It would not have mattered if the town had been destroyed, he said firmly. Memories cannot be taken away. People go where the jobs are (a notion often expressed that weekend). They simply pick up and build new memories somewhere else.

He was saying that the quality of a place lives in the head, and I suspect he is right about this. Any genuine feeling I have for those days is generalized, and doesn't come directly from the town or the school or even individuals.

Places like Kap don't lend themselves to nostalgia. This may just be a conceit, but if there is anything in me that is sensible, hard-headed and ultra-Canadian, it comes from living in a northern town. It's an attitude thing. You southern people have your own softer memories; you wouldn't understand the harshness of mine.

Terry Mosher

Montreal Gazette

The style of Terry Mosher, aka Aislin, is unmistakable. This biting comment on Quebec Premier René Lévesque was Aislin's first of back-to-back NNAs. Aislin began his career with the *Montreal Star* and his work has appeared around the world.

Le style de Terry Mosher, dont le nom de plume est Aislin, est facilement reconnaissable. Ce commentaire grinçant sur le premier ministre du Québec, René Lévesque s'est avéré le premier de deux prix du CCJ en deux ans. Aislin commençait sa carrière au *Montreal Star* et ses oeuvres furent publiées de par le monde.

CHAPTER 4

How Canada Saw the World

*This category has changed its name over the years, from
Staff Corresponding (1949–1971) and Foreign Reporting
(1985–1989) to International Reporting (since 1990).
Selections are also included from
Spot News and Feature Writing.*

By Kathy English

"It was a reporter's golden fantasy come to life — at someone else's expense."
— Peter Worthington, 1984, *Looking for Trouble*

EVERY SEPTEMBER, ON THE FIRST DAY OF JOURNALISM SCHOOL, WHEN NEW STUDENTS ARE ASKED to tell their classmates what has brought them to j-school, invariably at least one student will state with great passion that he or she has ALWAYS dreamed of being a foreign correspondent.

While the cynic may well be inclined to inquire whether that student might consider first spending some time on the night police beat, the idealist will encourage that dream. After all, few among us can honestly admit that we never once shared a piece of that same dream.

The golden fantasy of the foreign assignment has fueled the early career of many a young reporter. Of course, to borrow a phrase from another book, many are called but few are chosen. And as the stories of the chosen few selected for this chapter illustrate, the reality of foreign reporting is more complex than the fantasy of travelling the world at a newspaper's expense. (Still, one can't overlook the words of *Globe and Mail* foreign correspondent John Gray as recounted in David Hayes' 1992 book *Power and Influence*: "Those fuckers are paying me to do this!")

For the record, it should be noted that Worthington, who won four National Newspaper Awards, two for foreign reporting, actually footed the bill and used his vacation time for his first overseas story, the 1956 Suez crisis. *Telegram* editor Doug MacFarlane was reluctant to send an "untried junior reporter" abroad, writes Worthington in his 1984 memoir.

It has been stated that there really isn't much difference between being a good cop reporter and a big-time foreign correspondent. Both demand curiosity, tenacity, integrity, accuracy, enthusiasm and the ability to recognize and tell a compelling story.

But the foreign correspondent is often driven by something more — a passion for adventure and world history. As former CTV news correspondent Ab Douglas explained in his 1993 book, *On Foreign Assignment: The Inside Story of Journalism's Elite Corps*, "The born foreign correspondent will never be content to cover the routine of city hall or a Legislature. He or she is driven by an unconfined curiosity about the world and a desire to give the public a ringside seat at the world stage."

The stories in this section show that throughout the past half-century, the reporters who have brought the world to Canadians have had ringside seats to history in the making. In the past 50 years, they've brought us the chill and thawing of the Cold War, the beginning and blessed end of apartheid and the rise and fall of the Berlin Wall. Their datelines have familiarized us with previously little known names on the map, among them Biafra, Bosnia, Uganda and Somalia.

Foreign writing at its best should take us to some faraway place and make it as understandable as our neighbourhood. The NNA winners here have successfully achieved that. In his 1955 dispatches from Moscow, I. Norman Smith (page 190) compares a Soviet department store to Eaton's in Toronto and its crowds to those walking out of the Forum in Montreal. Smith's stories, written in the early Cold War era, demystify the Soviet Union by showing Canadian readers that despite being Communists, the Soviet people are at heart simply human beings:

I guess what I am trying to say is that the people of Moscow do not LOOK cowed, or beaten or unhappy or pattern-formed. A closer look at their faces doesn't reveal a general or average countenance much different from what might be the general countenance in Ottawa, Toronto or Montreal.

Thirty-nine years later, following the dissolution of the Soviet Union, the *Globe*'s John Gray wrote of a much more wretched Russian populace cowed by decades of communism (page 233). Together Grey and Smith provide journalistic bookends to the Cold War.

Andy MacFarlane, who won a 1959 NNA in spot news reporting for his coverage of the Cuban revolution that brought Fidel Castro to power (page 193), also strives to help his readers identify with his foreign dateline. He tells his *Toronto Telegram* readers how a short walk through a raging, frenzied mob, "left me as cold as a zero morning walk up Bay St." MacFarlane crafted Hemingwayesque, simple sentences to convey the "nightmare of lawlessness" he witnessed on the streets of Havana:

As I write this, pistols and machine guns crack and chatter in the streets outside the Hotel Sevilla Biltmore. Blood smears the sidewalk and gutter ... A body lies where it fell outside the front door.

Fear and danger are part of the job description for foreign correspondents assigned to cover war and revolution. MacFarlane has said that in covering those stories, "all the cliches are true ... my mouth actually did get dry and my legs actually did turn to rubber." Jack Cahill, whose tale of harrowing escape from Saigon (page 206) when it surrendered to North Vietnamese forces in April 1975 remains as powerful today as when it was first published in the *Toronto Star*, discussed that fear in his 1987 book *Words of War*: "We were all scared. The correspondent who is not scared in such circumstances is stupid. But a feeling of fatalism sets in.

"There is nothing at all you can do about the events around you, except to follow the correspondents' edict and 'take care' not to do anything rash. And this feeling of fatalism is mixed with the exhilaration of being on the big story and the joy of the company of friends who are among the best professionals in our business."

Cahill's NNA citation for that story praised his initiative. Ironically, as he later wrote, "It was the story I tried hardest in my life not to get." Cahill's *Star* colleague Gerald Utting may well have agreed about the circumstances that led to his 1977 NNA for reporting from Uganda (page 209). Utting's award-winner recounts his imprisonment by Ugandan dictator Idi Amin.

For most of this century, Canadian newspapers have been criticized for a lack of initiative in covering the world. While the Canadian Press was originally established in 1910 to obtain a supply of foreign news for its member papers, most of its copy came from the Associated Press. Critics — especially those favouring a Canada closely aligned with Britain — decried the fact that Canadians received news from abroad gathered by American reporters.

The call for more Canadian foreign correspondents has been sounded repeatedly in the past five decades, but the cost prohibits all but the larger, big-city newspapers and wire services. Of the 36 awards given for staff corresponding, foreign reporting and international reporting (the various categories for foreign news since 1949), eight each have gone to the *Toronto Star* and the *Globe and Mail* and another nine to the wire services, mainly Southam News.

Those writers sent abroad by the *Star* and *Globe* and, until its demise, the *Telegram,* have undoubtedly produced the finest foreign writing of the past half century. Among the eminent journalists whose pieces are included in this chapter are Pierre Berton, Robert Reguly and Paul Watson of the *Star*, and Norman Webster, Jan Wong and John Stackhouse of the *Globe*.

Their stories reflect a tradition of foreign correspondence best expressed by a former foreign editor of the *New York Times* who instructed his corps of writers to, "Imagine you are being asked to write a letter home every week to describe a different aspect of life in the area you are assigned."

That demands reporting that seeks out the stories of real people whose experiences allow Canadian readers to bridge the gap between their own lives and the experiences of those touched by the most important events of history.

Thus Jan Wong explains the trafficking of Chinese women through the story of Ma Linmei, a Chinese woman sold to her husband for about $425 (page 225). Robert Reguly recounts the stark reality of race relations in America, circa 1968, by writing about two Detroit housewives, the "hefty Mrs. Helen Glowacki" and "grandmotherly Mrs. Mary Krosec," readying for a race war at target practice with their .22 revolvers (page 197).

Paul Watson, who has won two NNA's for foreign reporting and a Pulitzer Prize for his 1993 photo showing an American soldier being dragged through the street of Mogadishu by angry Somalians, juxtaposes mundane details of everyday life with the horror of wartime in his "letter" home (page 228). Watson takes his readers to the local cinema where war movies such as *Rambo* play daily and "when battles break out, theatre-goers simply take cover under the balcony and keep watching the film." But, he advises, "There is nothing normal about Mogadishu, unless you're among the damned who have to live there." Watson's underlying message suggests the "moral" of so many of these foreign stories — as Canadians, we live the good life.

• **1953** Staff Corresponding •

You're black, or you're white, in Africa

Jack Scott

Vancouver Sun

JOHANNESBURG, South Africa — You make your choice, such as it is, at three o'clock in the morning.

You've arrived in Johannesburg at that ungodly hour, eight hours late because of a defect in a tail-heater of your Pan-American Clipper away back there somewhere over the North Atlantic. Was it two days ago or two months ago?

The form that the weary immigration official hands to you gives you two choices. You are required to make a cross beside one of them.

You are either 'European' or you are 'non-European.' From now on it matters little if you are Canadian or American or Eskimo. You are either black or you are white. It is that simple and that tragic.

Having committed yourself to being a member of the master race, the formalities of inspection are brief and perfunctory. The customs official, unable to locate a number on your typewriter, grins and yawns and marks down the only numbers he can find — 6, 5, 4, 3, 2, which are there on all typewriters to adjust the pressure of the keys. You wonder what he would do if you did not have this privileged complexion.

You walk into the main lounge of the airport to await the bus that will take you into the city. It is a large lounge with cane chairs and low tables. A 'non-European' steward (for you have begun to think this way) brings you tea. Leading off the lounge is a small fly-specked room perhaps 10 feet square. There is a sign over the door: 'Nie Blanke Sitkamer.' That is the lounge for the non-European.

It is the first of the 10,000 signs you will see with those words, 'Nie Blanke.' Not-white.

From now on you will drink your tea and wash your hands and eat your food and use the toilets and drink the water and use the entrances that are there for you, the European.

You are in South Africa.

■ ■ ■

In the morning you are awakened in your hotel room at seven, and startled into springing erect by a motherly-looking woman who is pouring your tea. You will get to know this dear creature rather well, for when the colonial brings his tradition and his way of life to the far corners of the globe, he brings it with a vengeance.

The chambermaid will cart away your oxfords in the morning and return them honed to a gloss they never knew, bring you the newspaper (oblivious to the fact that you are sleeping in the raw), open the drapes across your window and draw them at night, find your pyjamas, which you thought were lost forever, in your bag, and lay them neatly on your bed with the covers impeccably folded back, bundle your dirty laundry and pop her head in every so often to see if there's anything she forgot.

In 12 hours you will wonder how you ever lived without her.

You go down to the dining room where the waiters are East Indian — that, of course, is 'Nie Blanke' — and while you ponder the menu you listen to the two people at the adjoining table. There is a woman and a man. The woman is the wreckage of all that a once-proud Empire held dear, complete with lorgnette. She does the talking. The little man beside her studies his nails from under the hoods of his eyelids.

"The mawster will have tomawto juice," she tells the East Indian who smiles and nods. "And let me see — ah, yes, the mawster would like kippers."

And you sip your tepid tomato juice, for here there is even a greater scorn of refrigeration than in England, and you catch the East Indian staring discreetly but contemplatively at the mawster and his good lady.

■ ■ ■

You have an air mail letter to be sent off and, having finished your cold toast, you walk out to the Enquiry desk.

The man behind the desk, as you can tell by his accent, is of Dutch descent. He would doubtless be more at home speaking Afrikaans, which is to the true Dutch tongue what French-Canadian is to pure French.

He wears an ornate, moss-coloured uniform with gold epaulets and gold chevrons on the sleeves. He is extraordinarily obsequious and so it surprises you when his manner changes and he turns to a black man, also in moss-green but without epaulets or chevrons.

"Weigh this, Jim," he says curtly.

"Yes, sir," says Jim. He puts the letter upon the small postage scales.

"Weighs less than half an ounce, sir," he says.

The white man wheels on him with such rage that it astonishes you. "Damn it, Jim," he says, "I've told you before there's no postage rate for anything under half an ounce. Why tell me its UNDER half an ounce, man? How many times must I tell you that?"

"I should have remembered that," the black man says, shaking his head.

The white man sighs extravagantly and turns to you with a smile you are intended to share. "They can't seem to learn anything," he says.

You look at him coldly, bewildered by the non sequitur of his diatribe and embarrassed for the coloured man.

"Traveller, are you, sir?" says the white man, all smiles and cordiality. "We certainly hope you will take to South Africa."

■ ■ ■

JABAVU, South Africa — One of the 10 million South Africans who will not go to the polls this Wednesday — but about whom this election is all about — is Leonard Mahlaba, a black-skinned native so humble that he hesitates in the presence of a white man to use the name of Jesus Christ, his one and only hope in this world or the next.

Late in the afternoon of the day I spent with Mahlaba and his family here on the segregated outskirts of Johannesburg I asked him if he had any heroes. Did he know of Abraham Lincoln?

"No," he said.

"Have you no one in whom you put your trust?"

Mahlaba thought a moment and then spoke in his native Zulu tongue for two or three minutes. When he had finished the young African interpreter I had hired for the day turned to me.

"He believes only in the promises of Jesus Christ," the interpreter said. "But he hesitates to tell you that for fear you will think him disrespectful. You see, he thinks of Christ as a European, a white."

Leonard Mahlaba is a man of perhaps 40. He himself does not know his age or where he was born. He is a short, wiry man whose black curly hair is closely shaved like a tight woolen skull cap. He affects long sideburns half-way down his cheeks and a tuft of a mustache. He smiles easily, revealing strong, wide-spaced teeth, but usually his face wears a look of solemn concentration.

Like tens of thousands of others, Mahlaba came to Johannesburg from the barren British protectorate of Swaziland in 1939 to find a wartime job in the city. He has worked for the past nine years as a handy-man in a Johannesburg furniture store called the Sun Furnishings Company.

Six mornings a week he rises at 5:30 a.m. and rides into the city in an ancient electric train in which hundreds of natives are crushed together like cattle. He is home, after standing in a queue for an hour or more, at 7.

He receives three-pounds-ten or about nine dollars a week and is envied by his neighbours whose average weekly wage is below seven dollars.

Mahlaba thinks of himself as a fortunate man, and in a comparative way he is.

Not more than a mile from his "location" (as the "apartheid" segregated native sections are called) are the worst of the Johannesburg slums where thousands live in wood and corrugated iron hutches facing into narrow mud alleys.

Before visiting Mahlaba I had wandered through one such "location." Naked, dirty children surrounded me begging for handouts. "Boss man got money, got smoke?" they pleaded.

I saw a typical one-room shanty where 20 adults and children sleep on the dirt floor, so crowded that their limbs overlap.

These are the breeding grounds of what the English language newspapers call "the native crime wave." "Flying squads" of husky white police in natty khaki and blue uniforms patrol their outskirts. No white man dares enter there at night.

Having seen this and with the stench still in my nostrils, I could understand Mahlaba's unreasonable pride in his own home when he showed me about on my arrival.

There are seven in the Mahlaba family. (He knows nothing of birth control and was embarrassed when I asked him about this; the only effective birth control is the pelvic weakness of the native wives who, through a combination of malnutrition and back-breaking work, often lose their babies during pregnancy).

Leonard's wife, Ann, is a thin and sickly little woman. When I arrived she was in the kitchen, barefoot, and in a faded cotton dress, holding her two-year-old son in the crook of one arm as she prepared the evening meal over a low coal stove.

The kitchen, like the rest of the rooms, was immaculately clean. On one shelf I noticed six heavy white cups, turned face down in their saucers, and lined up precisely as if by a ruler. There were yellow flowers arranged in a tin on the table.

I had brought along a box of Holland chocolates for Mahlaba's children. His wife could not seem to understand that this was a gift. The box was in the middle of the kitchen table, still wrapped, when I left.

Through the interpreter I asked Ann what she was preparing. She lifted the lids from two pots on the stove. The evening meal was to be spinach and porridge. I asked if the children had milk or orange juice. She said that when they could afford it they bought milk for their smallest child, but this was very rare. Mostly the children drank tea.

The Mahlaba home is numbered 1122B in the Jabavu "location" named for the first African professor at London University. Here are row upon row of small concrete duplex houses of three rooms apiece. The concrete partitions on the inside are built up just above head-level so that families in the adjoining compartments are on intimate terms.

Such quarters are rented under a municipal housing scheme for one pound 12 shillings and six pence (about $4.30 a month).

The "living room" of Mahlaba's house is perhaps 12 feet square. There is a table in the middle, and along one wall — the envy of every native visitor — a battered and sagging chesterfield which his employers had given him as a gift.

On the walls are sepia-tinted pictures of some of Mahlaba's relatives and two calendars, one showing Lena Horne in a moving picture scene, the other of "Miss South Africa of 1952," a white girl.

The kitchen is at the rear and off it is a small bedroom largely taken up by an iron double bed. Leonard and his wife sleep there with the baby between them. The other children sleep on the floors throughout the house.

There is no electric light (candles are used and figure prominently in Mahlaba's "budget"), but there is a water tap outside at the rear of the house. Here, too, are outside toilets, one for each dwelling, and Mahlaba and his neighbour had pooled their resources so that instead of each family using its own facilities one toilet was used by the women and girls and the other by the men and boys.

The names of the children reflect Mahlaba's intense religious feeling. The eldest boy is Elijah, aged 18, who works in a bakery in Johannesburg and earns two pounds, 12 shillings (about $7 a week).

Leonard explained sorrowfully that his oldest son would probably never earn a higher wage because his right arm had been mangled in a salt grinding machine and had been amputated at the elbow. When I asked if the boy had received compensation, Mahlaba did not understand and the interpreter explained that this was unknown.

The other children are Jacob, 11; Abel, eight; Josephine, five, and Petrus (or Peter) who is two. They are shy, appealing children. There is a strong family feeling and throughout most of the afternoon one or more of the children sat in Mahlaba's lap.

Unlike the European children, schooling is not compulsory for native children and while the sons and daughters of white families receive free primary education and texts the non-European pays for both.

Mahlaba explained that Jacob and Abel were attending a semi-religious missionary school. He hoped he would be able to keep them there, but with the growing strain on his income they would probably have to look for work before they are 12.

Leonard, conscious of his unaccustomed role as host, had sent Jacob to a nearby native store for a bottle of a carbonated orange drink called Krush. As we sat at the living room table sipping the sweet, syrupy drink I asked him questions directly and through the interpreter. Occasionally when he wanted to emphasize something to me, Mahlaba would use the small vocabulary of English he has picked up working with whites.

When I asked him if he had any views on Wednesday's election he shrugged and, through the interpreter, replied: "That's nothing to do with me."

"Don't you think there will be less chance of the African joining the human race if Dr. Malan is re-elected?"

"There is no equality between white and black. The white man is superior. God brought the whites to the country. They defeated the blacks. That is what we have to bear."

"Do you think the African will ever have equality with the whites?"

Mahlaba thought about this at length before replying.

"In health I am equal of any man," was the reply. "But the whites make the laws and the laws make the whites superior. We cannot share with the whites because we Africans are backward."

In an attempt to find his philosophy, I said, "I have a daughter just about the age of Josephine. Suppose we were to trade daughters and I were to bring up Josephine in my home. Would she still be the inferior?"

"No, no, no," Leonard protested, shaking his head vigorously. "Everything is education. That is what we most want. For our children to be educated like white children. But I know that we will never have it."

I asked the interpreter to question him as to how he felt about a feeling of security.

"This worries him most of all," the interpreter said after Mahlaba had given his answer. "He says, 'I will suffer much if I lose my job. If I am found to be without work I am liable to be sent away to the country as farm labour without my wife and children.' He says, 'I always fear that something will get lost or stolen in the furniture store for the African is always the one to be accused and punished.'"

Mahlaba had been listening intently to the interpreter's words and turned to me at this point to speak in English.

"We t'ank God we still have our job," he said earnestly.

"But how would the authorities know you were unemployed?" I asked.

Mahlaba answered by producing the frayed piece of white cardboard which is his pass and which he has carried since 1947. "If I am out of work I must go to them to have my pass renewed," he said through the interpreter. "If I do not go they will come for me."

He then produced another, smaller piece of paper which was my first knowledge that it is not merely the authorities, but the individual white man, who is the native's master. This was a pass that Mahlaba applies for at the end of each week from his employers so that he may travel across Johannesburg, if he so desires, to visit a friend on the other side of the city.

It was headed "Special Pass." Under the heading were the words: "Please pass native Leonard who has permission to proceed wherever he wishes on Sunday. Signed, Sun Furnishings Company."

Mahlaba neither drinks nor smokes. He would be entitled, he explained, to go in for a drink in one of the native "beer halls" in Johannesburg (a special beer is brewed for the native trade with an alcoholic content two per cent lower than that of the white man's beer), but he preferred to go directly to his home from work. In theory a native may apply for a permit to buy one bottle of brandy per month, but both Mahlaba and the interpreter explained that this privilege is usually limited to those natives who have "good white connections."

Mahlaba's main interest in life is his Sunday at home when he digs in a small flower garden and attends the services in the nearby African Gospel Church. When I asked the church's denomination, Leonard shrugged and grinned. "Very patriotic," he said.

In 1940, when Mahlaba's weekly wage was 30 shillings (or about $4.20) he and his wife, who was then also finding occasional work, saved enough to buy Leonard a black suit and Ann a "going out" dress. These they still wear on Sunday. Now, with the increase in their family they see no hope of buying more of the clothes they need.

When I asked if he could get by on his wages now, Mahlaba replied, "We get by with my son's help. If we have any left over we buy milk for the little one or meat. The meat is more expensive here out of the city. Often it is bad. It is she" — and he gestured to the kitchen where his wife worked — "who has the hard life." He shook his head sadly. "Very hard life for her."

What would he think was a livable wage?

Mahlaba spoke this time in English. "Would be not bad if four pound ($11.50)," he said, and returned to finish in Zulu. "I could then buy the blankets we need for winter. But I am paid now a high wage compared with others and I cannot expect more."

I had heard that there are "advisory boards" elected in such locations by the natives. While these boards are not able to go directly to the City Hall (it is out of bounds to non-Europeans) they are able, in theory, to make recommendations to the city's Department of Non-European Affairs.

When I asked Mahlaba if he was active in these elections he shook his head. "They can do little," he said. "Besides, what is true of white is true of black. The trouble with people in power is that they always want to run other people down."

It was now growing late and the living room, which had been flooded in sunlight through the open door most of the afternoon, was now in shadows. It suddenly seemed cold and desolate.

The interpreter and I, having said goodbye to Mrs. Mahlaba, arose to leave and as we stood in the door I asked one final question. "Would you ask him if he has any hope for the future."

Mahlaba listened to the question and both the interpreter and I were dismayed when his eyes filled with tears. He spoke quietly in his native language a moment and the interpreter turned again to me. "He says his hope is in death. Then, as he puts it, he will be finished in the ground where all men are the same."

• **1955** Staff Corresponding •

Plans change fast in Russian life

I. Norman Smith

Ottawa Journal

(Part of a series)

MOSCOW — A fellow feels no sleepier waking up in Moscow than anywhere else. The bed is good, the room is clean, the shoes are polished, the breakfast can be eggs preceded by a kind of lemon or raspberry pop, the coffee is foul, the tea is good.

I'm not suggesting this is the standard Russian breakfast or that any Russian who leaves his shoes outside the door picks them up clean in the morning. But this is the treatment the Canadians are getting and it is fine.

On this first full day in Moscow we encountered the usual difficulties a tourist encounters in a strange land that arise out of different tongue, different habits, and perhaps a national desire on both parts to make as much money as possible and spend as little.

In Russia it is a little more complicated because of mutual suspicion and sensitivity and also because they have struck an arbitrary rate of four rubles to our dollar which means we pay about four times as much for things as the Russian does, and also because a government bureau called "Intourist" is supposed to care for all our needs (provided we pay), but like many a bureaucracy it gets behind the play sometimes and our too-urgent minds are quick to smell a plot whereas it is just a nice Muscovite combination of inexperience and inefficiency.

This continuing problem of coping with the Russian facts of life is part of the fun of the trip, and is really only importantly a nuisance because it takes up much of our little time. Plans are made and unmade with startling alacrity, right hands aren't often acquainted with left hands and what's "laid on" here may be very much not acceptable there. Correspondents who have been here a long while assure us with a knowing smile we'll get used to it. I'll try to refer to it no more, but it's quite a rugged league just the same.

This morning amid the planning confusion I headed out on my own, across the Red Square to the large government department store. It is a massive place with goods of all kinds, restaurants, snack bars, statuary, fountains.

As noon hour approached, it was like walking out of the Forum at game end. Here were people of so many colours and types and sizes that one got a real idea of the scope of the 16 Russian Republics which make up the Soviet.

The buying was brisk and in terms of Russian income the goods seemed both desirable and reasonably priced — though prices varied according to the product with amazing spreads. That is, a chocolate bar or a refrigerator are beyond reason in cost; but clothes and meat and vegetables and books and implements seem at normal levels. Certainly people were buying and not just window shopping; and there were only a few queues. One line-up was for fur hats, the kind you'd want in below-zero weather. Possibly this was a new shipment in or a sale.

It was pleasant to note the friendliness and mutual curiosity of the shoppers. Each would look at the other's purchase and discuss it — complete strangers — and though the store is government run, as are all things, the clerks behind the counter seemed at least as courteous and friendly as any of our own in Canada.

The food is attractively presented and, barring oranges, I saw just about everything I could think of including nuts, luscious grapes, dates, really delicious cheese (I tried some), bread and rolls and cake and biscuits made with imagination that should shame those stereotype bakers of ours. Ice cream is good and a great favourite and is vended all over the streets.

I stress that this is a general department store jammed by the people in its broadest sense, and that folks who look to our eyes to be poor and ragged are buying at a gay clip.

Talking about food later to a foreign resident here, I was told there had been no famine in Russia since the war and that in the last few years especially, everyone had had plenty to eat. One could have stayed in that store (surely bigger than Eaton's in Toronto) a day with fascination, the people so variously dressed in farm clothes and city clothes, some in heavy coats and sweaters and heavy hats, others as though for summer, some in knee-high boots and others in "Western" brogues.

The women favour scarves as hats but otherwise are dressed as our women though without much "appeal"; the men run to a drabness in sober blue or black. This latter can mislead one into feeling it is a funereal or gloomy crowd, but a closer look at their faces doesn't reveal a general or average countenance much different from what might be the general countenance found in Ottawa, Toronto or Winnipeg.

Possibly you could say they take themselves more seriously than we do, but they are quick to laugh among themselves and even to clown. I guess what I am trying to say is that the people of Moscow do not LOOK cowed or beaten or unhappy or pattern-formed. They may be all of these things — I have been here but a day and am not talking politics or social welfare.

I am simply reporting that my eyes tell me that these people seem reasonably content and comfortable in their lot in life, and I say that after having walked entirely alone perhaps five miles on an ambling roundabout unconducted tour of the city, including some very slum-like areas where content and comfort would seem unlikely to dwell.

In the afternoon Mr. and Mrs. Pearson and the entire Canadian party marched through the centuries of Russian history that the apartments, chapels, council chambers and corridors of the Kremlin tell so vividly.

The Kremlin is really a fortress, which is what the word means, and within that fortress, growing larger with the centuries from the 11th onward, were huddled together sometimes in fear and sometimes in pomp and power all the dwelling and working establishments of Russia's rulers.

It was a fabulous visit. The wealth of the Crown Jewels in the Tower of London seems to pale before this collection of Czardom's crowns and adornments, before its golden coaches and jewelled saddles, before its malachite tables and ebony vases and assorted riches of perhaps untold value and uncounted variety.

We saw the St. George's Hall where have been celebrated Russia's victories, the little library where the Czars sought no doubt to get away from it all, the bedchambers, the gentle suites of the ladies, the sweeping formal staircases with imagined trap doors where treachery still seemed to be afoot, and bells that had rung for tragedy no less than victory.

And within these not-so-tall brick fortress walls of the Kremlin stand also churches and administrative buildings, the great plain dignified hall wherein meets the Council of the Supreme Soviet and lesser conference rooms, one of which was used by Mr. Pearson and Mr. Molotov in their talks.

I asked a guide where Premier Bulganin's office was. He took counsel with another guide and they mulled over the question with some care before pointing vaguely towards three large buildings each containing perhaps 200 offices. "In one of those offices over there, I don't know precisely which one," he said. I let it drop.

But if they don't care to reveal the location of the Premier's office they nevertheless have thrown open most of the Kremlin's storied halls and treasures, and open wide to the public. Even while our party with a Foreign Minister moved through the corridors we shouldered our way through crowds of sightseers who would attach themselves and listen to the guides and transla-tors with avid interest. Certainly we didn't object to their presence because it added liveliness to the panorama before our eyes, but the odd thing was that the Russian officials didn't object either. It seems that the Kremlin and its show places are now open to the public and if a Foreign Minis-ter wants to go too he must take his chance in the scramble.

One of our party who had been in Moscow a few years ago was amazed to see the public in the Kremlin. He had himself got in before but only with the greatest of persuasion and authority. Nowadays the lines form daily to gain entrance even as they do to visit the Lenin and Stalin tomb.

"The Kremlin belongs to the people now and they love to see it and possess it, so to speak." Thus spoke a Russian official and certainly his words were supported by the keen interest of the visitors who milled about the showcases elbowing their way good humoredly but firmly against all comers, including Canadians.

But even the diamond-studded horses' hooves can lose their appeal after a two-hour visit to such palaces and collections and his aides began to look anxiously to Mr. Pearson lest he too greatly spend energies which must stand with him on a long tour ahead. Finally he cried "uncle" and indicated he must go, but the principal guide or curator pleaded for "just a few more minutes because you must see …" And so he went on, and on.

Yet scarcely more than a short hour later Mr. Pearson and our outstandingly able ambassador John Watkins were hosts at the Canadian Embassy to Russian government chiefs, diplomats, the Canadian colony, some leaders in art and music and literature, and to some of the press.

It was a most extraordinary occasion. Molotov was there, and Malenkov the recent premier, and two other deputy premiers. When they arrived they made, shall we say, a brisk stroll through all of the crowded rooms, smiling roundly and pausing briefly.

Then in a small parlor near the bar the four deputy premiers and Pearson and Watkins and a gifted interpreter formed a circle, still standing, and proceeded amid much toasting and glass tin-kling, to talk of cabbages and kings, curtains, atoms and coexistence.

It chanced I was in the second circle, immediately at Malenkov's left — a gay sort of fellow he with a mischievous glint in his eye and a spritely spirit. A madder international conversation at "top level" I've never heard.

Mr. Pearson was at his very best, which is superb. He could discuss the brand of cocktails (maple syrup and vodka) that might lead to peace or he could answer head-on the rather sur-prising question with which Molotov opened fire. Molotov said: "It is said Canadian policy is in between British and American, is that true?" "We like to think we have the best of both," began Mr. Pearson with a smile, but he then played the rest of the answer straight and true for Molotov hadn't been fooling. It just seemed to be his idea of cocktail party small talk!

Each of the six had his shot at toasting co-operation and understanding alternately with little quips to help things along. Mr. Pearson said he and Molotov were members of the Foreign Min-isters trade union and should get on well; Molotov said they had replaced the iron curtain with aluminum and Mr. Pearson said he hoped they'd buy their aluminum from us.

When the Canadian minister feared he might be overwhelmed with kindness on his visit to Russia, it was Malenkov who quickly got the point and much as would Jack Pickersgill he chirped up: "It is not in vain, you see, that we are always toasting your health!"

The press provided a subject for some banter in which the Russians took a keen part. Mr. Pear-son told them they needn't worry about us being there because in Canada there was a free press and by that he meant we were free to publish anything he'd permit us to publish. The Russians weren't sure of the humour of this and the thing fiddled around among them for a while until Mr. Pearson gave them a cue to break up the group by saying he knew there was a ballerina present and much as he liked the deputy prime ministers he'd rather talk to her. But there was another exchange of serious toasts before the group did call it a night. I shook hands, incidentally, with Malenkov, thanks to an introduction by Mr. Watkins; so if we have a spy trial one of these years I suppose that should fry me properly over a slow fire.

But tell the inquisitor too, please, that I also met the ballerina of last night's Bolshoi perfor-mance, Blisetskay, and another who is to dance tomorrow night. This may not read like much sense but after seeing Blisetskay dance it is a most improbable thing to shake her hand for you had imagined she was elfin or fairy or perhaps a tiny particle chipped from the silvery moon.

But there she was, and talking excitedly about the enthusiasm of the young 12-year-old whom I had mentioned as being very talented; ah, she said, that little one you mention will be ahead of us all before long. But ballet, like anything else, comes only from work, and I was given an amazing and almost unbelievable story of the devotion of the student dancer who has given her life to the art. And during her story, bless her, she asked if she might please sit down on a nearby settee because her feet were tired each day after a performance. As mine had stamped through Russia from the 11th to the 20th century within the last 10 hours my sympathy came to her right from the soles of my feet.

Plee-sets-kaya (or Blisetskay) is the number two ballerina, second only to Ulanova; but there are some who feel the devotion to Ulanova is now at least partly due to her great career of the past (for she is no longer young) and that Plee-sets-kaya is Russia's greatest dancer. This is no discussion for an amateur to enter. I know only that she is charming and easy to talk to, that she is so frail and almost wan that you'd not believe her body could sustain her art.

But this day's diary entry is already over-long.

• 1959 Spot News Reporting •

Reporter's longest walk ...
slap through a revolution

Andrew MacFarlane

Toronto Telegram

HAVANA — I took the longest walk of my life yesterday.

It was only a couple of blocks along a sun-brilliant street, but it left me as cold as a zero morning walk up Bay St.

"Just walk; don't run. Anyone who runs is presumed to be doing so for a reason. It's the fastest way to get killed."

That was a U.S. correspondent, wise in the ways of revolutions, talking as we walked to a nearby apartment after we had been barred from our hotel.

Downtown Havana was in the grip of a raging, frenzied mob.

The rosy dawn of Cuba's "liberation" had turned into a black, blood-spattered nightmare of lawlessness and maniacal destruction.

As I write this, pistols and machine guns crack and chatter in the streets outside the Hotel Sevilla Biltmore.

Blood smears the sidewalks and the gutter.

The main floor of the hotel is a chaotic rubble of scattered glass, broken furniture, overturned roulette tables and smashed crockery. A body lies where it fell outside the front door.

From the street comes the howl of auto horns, braying since the morning when the word spread through the city that President Batista had fled.

There are shouts and crashes as the mob smashes everything that comes within reach of its clubs. Downtown Havana is a mess of shattered and burned wrecks of cafes, cars and offices.

At least 12 people are dead, shot in the battle between the police and the looters.

It all began quietly.

Batista and his aides and their families left the presidential palace about 4 a.m. yesterday. With them went carloads of tommy gunners, but they were not needed.

When the dawn turned Havana's cream-stuccoed buildings a rosy pink, there was not a sound. No one was stirring. The palace was empty, but no one knew yet. The guards were still on the roof with bazookas and machine guns.

The press made no announcement. The radio played music and news reports from elsewhere.

At about 10 a.m., we heard the first car horn. Soon there were hundreds of cars speeding around and around the main streets, blasting their horns. They flew Cuban flags and the flags of the rebel leader Fidel Castro's 26th of July movement.

There was jubilation. Everyone seemed to be happy. They sang out "Vive Cuba Libre" and waved at bystanders. At about noon I saw the violence begin.

A man ripped up a no-parking sign and smashed a parking meter off its base with it. Then he smashed another — and another. Soon there were three or four smashing meters a block at a time.

Then someone picked up a meter and hurled it through a shop window. Another followed it.

Within minutes a mob of hundreds in buses, trucks and on foot stormed through the street smashing windows with clubs, throwing furniture in the street, looting bars, smashing what bottles they could not drink.

They converged on my hotel, the Sevilla Biltmore. I watched while they stormed through a glass-fronted arcade of shops.

They burst into the hotel's casino and they ripped it apart. They threw potted plants through windows. Four more hotels got the same treatment.

Officials of the Castro 26th of July movement wearing red and black armbands tried to stop the looting. They pleaded with the mob, but it was too late.

Inside the hotel on the top floor was the wife of the hotel manager, locked in her apartment, afraid for her life. Her husband, a pillar of the regime, sought asylum in the embassy of Uruguay.

The hotel elevator operators took their cars to the top of the shafts and stayed there. The only way for those of us in the lobby to escape was to go into the street.

Two of us went to another hotel a block away where about 20 frightened people were milling around trying to decide where to go.

There was shooting in the street outside between the police and the looters. Then came a report that a three-foot long bomb had been dropped in the hotel garage.

That was when we started on the long walk-don't run to get to the apartment.

It was an unforgettable walk.

We saw a man running along the sidewalk pulling a friend out of the way of bullets that whined off the pavement. Then, as he tugged at his frightened friend, the "rescuer"crumpled.

He'd caught a bullet — right between the eyes.

In the midst of the street fighting a civilian stood in the open with a pistol.

He was shooting at everyone he could see — police, soldiers and other civilians. He hit no one.

We reached the apartment we had to go to, but on legs tensed for running, subdued for walking. In about half an hour there was a lull in the shooting and we made it back to the hotel.

Besieged guests were locked in their rooms. Many of them are U.S. tourists. The American embassy is trying to arrange transportation to get them back home, but last night there wasn't even a ship, and Cuba was in the grip of a general strike.

As the sun set over this troubled city, it glowed blood-red through a pall of smoke raised by the guns of rebellion.

• **1960** Staff Corresponding •

Tokyo sparkles 10 years later

Pierre Berton

Toronto Star

TOKYO — To return to Tokyo, after almost 10 years, is to return to a new city, so startlingly different that it is hard to remember the old one. When I was last in Tokyo, Japan was a beaten nation and looked it. MacArthur was Regent; the streets were alive with GI's, their pockets stuffed with Occupation script; there were great blank spaces in the town where the fire bombs had done their work. The Japanese were dazed, demoralized and subjugated; they could not even own a car that was less than 10 years old, since these were reserved for the victors. It was not a happy city.

Now all this has long ended and Tokyo stands on its own feet. Since I was last here something like three million additional souls have stormed her gates to make Tokyo the world's largest city — larger than London, larger than New York. It has also become the world's liveliest. From dawn until midnight it simply vibrates with life and passion.

In the old days the streets were almost empty save for carts, military vehicles and those queer, coal-burning taxis that chugged along so slowly. Now a farrago of vehicles — from bicycles to omnibuses — fight for a place on the narrow pavements. I have ridden in taxicabs in those homicidal cities of Paris, Rome and Cairo, but I never knew real terror until I took a taxi in Tokyo. The drivers all seem to be former kamikaze pilots clinging to old habits. They will hurtle cheerfully without slackening speed into a crowded laneway not much wider than their own vehicle. They will execute a fast U-turn on a crowded thoroughfare without warning. If the traffic is heavy they will simply head out into the wrong lane into the face of oncoming vehicles. In these taxi drivers one sees all the elan of the new Japan.

The police are lenient with them because the police are terrified of getting back their wartime reputation as bullies. They are so sensitive about this that students can riot easily in Tokyo, as they did last spring, and cars can be parked a good two feet from the curb. Thus, in small ways, and large ones, does the aftermath of war make itself felt in the world's largest hive.

There are no physical scars of war in Tokyo today and scarcely a vestige of the Occupation save for those tottering street signs that MacArthur's GI's erected so they would have a fighting chance of finding their way about the most baffling metropolis on the globe. But the signs are vanishing, and the Japanese show no inclination to renew them. It is as if the Japanese want to erase all memory of that seven years; humiliation, even at the expense of efficiency.

Thus, even for a long-time resident, a trip to the home of a chance acquaintance in Tokyo is like an excursion in the jungle. There are few street names or house numbers — and, remember, this is a city of nine and one-half million people, most of whom live in small houses and not apartment blocks.

Addresses are usually measured from certain well-known intersections. A man may describe his home as so many streets away from such and such a corner, halfway down the block and two doors from the saki house. Business establishments and private citizens print maps on cards showing how to reach them. Shops carry, in their advertising, instructions in Japanese characters to taxi drivers; without such help it would be hopeless for a foreigner to find them at all.

If they wanted to, I'm sure the Japanese could undertake the Herculean task of superimposing a modern street address system on Tokyo, for they seem capable of anything. (After all, they've built an Eiffel tower of their own, 50 feet higher than the Paris original, and perfected the Dick Tracy wristwatch radio). But they just don't seem to want to. They borrow what they like from foreign cultures while leaving their own intact. The geisha houses are equipped with air-conditioning and sometimes with Muzak, but they still operate. Scores of ancient temples knocked down during the war have been rebuilt at huge expense. They are just as they were before with one change: Most of them have pillars and roofs of ferro-concrete instead of wood, so that it will be harder to knock them down a second time.

And so I found Tokyo a city of almost frightening contrasts. I saw one temple which contained no fewer than 20,000 identical stone images of the same Buddhist deity; its goal, I was told, was to get no less than 84,000 images. I'm sure it will make its quota. On the other hand, I saw plenty of colour TV in Tokyo; Japan is one of only three countries which have it. And I also saw advertised a slide rule device (for one dollar) by which any woman interested in birth control can quickly compute her menstrual cycle.

One of the most revealing sights I saw in Tokyo was that of a labouring man squatting on his haunches in the time-honoured manner, dressed in loose white garments with a band around his head and a stubble of beard on his chin. Here was a figure straight out of a Hiroshige wood block print, but there was a difference. He was first of all eating a pink popsicle and, secondly, watching an outdoor TV set on whose screen was a young Japanese strumming the guitar and singing in English that Pat Boone hit about turning the juke box "way down low.'

I am told on impeccable authority that there are still rice paddies being cultivated within the city limits. This is hard to believe since the downtown area is now so crowded that real estate values are among the highest in the world. There is talk (still only talk, mind you) of persuading the Emperor himself to move out of the Imperial palace grounds, in the heart of the city, and turn those 500 moat-ringed acres over to office construction. Even more alarming, there is strong rumour that Frank Lloyd Wright's famous old Imperial Hotel will have to come down: It's only two stories high and it's hard to justify a two-storey building in downtown Tokyo.

Today it costs twice as much to rent office space in the Marinouchi district as in downtown Manhattan. Businessmen, moving away, have sold their telephones for as much as $500. "Key money," that Canadian postwar evil, is standard throughout town and the fact that there are plenty of people willing to pay it suggests how much Tokyo has changed since the Occupation.

"The Japanese are on a post-Occupation spree and the funny thing is there doesn't seem to be any sign the spree is ending," says Wallace Higgins, an ex-U.S. naval commander, who now lives in the Japanese style. A glimpse of Tokyo's sprightly night life, described in the adjoining column, is convincing evidence of this. It is this spree-like atmosphere, I think, that more than anything else marks the change in Tokyo and in all Japan. The period of the Great Loss of Face is over and almost forgotten. There is much more of a sense of fun in Tokyo today. There is also, happily, much more of a sense of dignity.

■ ■ ■

It is 9 o'clock on a Monday evening and my wife and I are strolling down the Ginza, which is Tokyo's Fifth Avenue and Broadway rolled into one. The sun has been down three hours, but it is brighter than any day, for Tokyo at night, all a-light, beggars description. Broadway, by comparison, is a pale moon, out-neoned by Tokyo's electric suns.

The signs are gargantuan and gaudy, multi-coloured and as ingenious as a Japanese mechanical toy. I watched one flashing toothpaste ad, several storeys high, go through 25 separate changes.

The main streets of Tokyo are always crowded, but the real crowds are in the side streets that feed the main drag like small creeks flowing into a mighty river. Off these side streets run narrower alleys, not much wider than a car, all lit like Christmas trees; and off these alleys run even narrower alleys, not much wider than a man, but also lit by signs that wink and beckon. 'Bar,' the signs say. Sukiyaki — Dance — Coffee — Jazz — Pretty English-speaking Hostesses.

■ ■ ■

This is the world's most cosmopolitan town; there is one of everything available. The best bouillabaisse I ever tasted was in Tokyo, and also the best smorgasbord and the best broiled steak. No wonder: The cows are kept in darkened barns, fed on beer and hand-massaged to distribute the fat evenly.

There is a coffee house called Tennessee where for a few yen you can linger all night over a single cup. My wife and I drop in and watch a group of seven Japanese youths to the snap of fingers and singing rock and roll with a genuine Southin' accent over which is superimposed a genuine Japanese accent. "Rove you!" one of them howls. "Rearry, rearry rove you."

We leave here and go to a tiny bar. "Sorry," says the bartender. "Japanese only!" It is an odd feeling to find oneself a member of a minority group, but we do not complain to the local Fair Accommodation Practices Commission. There must be 20,000 bars in Tokyo, and all of them seem to be on this alley. We simply move next door to a warm welcome.

■ ■ ■

"I love USA," says a cheerful but inebriated Japanese on the next stool who insists on sharing his drink with me, "Love USA! Not like Soviet!" It turns out that he is the owner of the bar, busily drinking up the profits.

"Americans our friend!" cries the capitalist, recklessly ordering more of his own stock. "You come from Boston, eh?" I tell him I come from Toronto, and he asks me for my phone number in Boston. He says he is going to visit Boston in 11 months, and he will certainly look me up. I give him my Boston phone number which is Empire 3-2211.

I feel a soft pressure on my hand and, turning, find that a beautiful girl in a kimono has taken the stool next to me. "Nice!" says the girl in the kimono, squeezing my hand tenderly once more. I introduce her to my wife and she doesn't bat an eye. "Beautiful!" she says, meaning my wife and the pressure on my hand subtly becomes a sisterly one.

She is one of the English-speaking hostesses advertised by every saloon in town. Many other cities have hostesses, but Tokyo has more than any other. One bar alone boasts no less than 1,200.

But it is past 11 and, lo, they are rolling up the Tokyo sidewalks. The establishments are closing, not by choice, but by law. If a bar has hostesses, the law says, then the bar must close at 11: Innocent young girls must not be out alone on the streets after midnight. And so the bars close dutifully, more or less on time, and the signs wink out one by one.

● **1968** Staff Corresponding ●

Detroit housewives are packing guns

Robert Reguly

Toronto Star

DETROIT — In the Scarborough-like suburb of Dearborn, about 12 miles from this city's fire-gapped riot scene, the 30 housewives were pinging away at the black silhouettes of human targets.

"No wonder the kids like it," hefty Mrs. Helen Glowacki trilled at her newly discovered skill. A quick learner, she was showing grandmotherly Mrs. Mary Krosec how to spin out the cylinder of her snub-nosed .22 revolver for fast reloading.

"I'm taking the course because of riots mostly," Mrs. Krosec explained. "This year is going to be worse than last year. Maybe it's just a lot of rumours, but I want to be prepared."

The weekly class, sponsored by Dearborn's city recreation department, has graduated 250 women — most of them in their late 20s — has a waiting list of 500 and will be expanded. The lecture-and-live-fire classes are held in the basement of police headquarters.

The city's 112,000 population contains one Negro family.

Prompted by Mayor Orville Hubbard, an avowed segregationist, the call to arms is sparked by the endemic fear of crazed Negroes invading from the Detroit ghetto, something like the Barbarians sacking cultured Rome.

"If it's going to be a long, hot summer, I'm going to make it hotter for them," said one budding markswoman who wouldn't give her name.

Mrs. Rochelle Bridge, 20, a buxom blonde, said her husband works the midnight shift at the car plant and she was alone with her baby at night. "I don't want to get raped," she said, displaying the revolver she carried to the class in a shoe box.

In the Detroit ghetto the black are arming too. The Frederick Douglass Shooting (not gun) Club is one of three markmanship training groups known to exist.

All but six of the 43 persons killed in last summer's riot were Negroes. The next time, militants are demanding the casualty odds be changed to two "honkeys" (whites) for each black.

The virulently racist *Inner City Press*, a weekly ghetto tabloid, carries such headlines as White Invasion Planned, gives advice on how to make Molotov cocktails and how to run guns from Ohio (stash the weapons, pick them up later, carefully avoiding the police-patrolled expressways).

Since last summer, the black-white arms race has reached Armageddon-like proportions. Smith and Weston produces 1,500 handguns a day and is almost a year behind in orders.

Surplus World War II M-1 carbines are in such short supply that a factory in Plainfield, N.J., has tooled up to produce new models. Detroit police have reportedly bought 1,500 of the semi-automatic weapons.

Detroit's Mayor Jerome Cavanagh pleaded on television recently for "return to sanity. This arms race must be stopped."

In Detroit, newspaperless for five months, city hall has a "rumour control centre." People are asked to phone in the rumour, a staffer checks it out and reports back to the caller. Among the rumours:

• Blacks plan to invade the suburb of Birmingham, kill a white boy and girl in hopes of provoking a white counterattack, to be met by a Viet Cong-style ambush.

• White extremists plan to invade the Negro ghetto, kill a black boy and girl and ambush the black counterattack.

• Black Power extremists had organized a disturbance that was to involve stealing autos and burning them on the major expressways.

The Detroit police department has registered 7,400 handguns in the seven months since the riot — double the number in the same period the previous year. Rifles and shotguns need not be registered.

Black militants are telling soul brothers not to register pistols. About 3,000 handguns were stolen during the riot and few have been recovered.

Detroit police have asked for $9,000,000 to gear up for this summer — armoured vests, 500,000 rounds of ammunition, machine guns, eight armored cars, infrared sniper scopes.

Police Commissioner Ray Girardin said: "This is a revolution. This is not just a mob or gang fight. It's a question of the survival of our cities."

Black Power "leaders" (a divided, self-labelling group) applaud the police acumen; both they and the police see the situation as it is. Most white people don't. "What do these people want?" is the commonly met cry of frustration from the whites insulated from the ghettos.

"Get off my back, that's what we want," says Joe Strickland, a Negro Detroit reporter who knows the ghetto best.

"You'll find smouldering hate among the black militant people," he said. "Both sides are so touchy that it would take just some silly little incident to create a riot."

Everywhere it is an article of black militant faith, at least in public utterances, that Whitey is preparing for black genocide. A rumour given wide credence in the ghettos is that the federal government has prepared six concentration camps for black extermination.

The big arms race issue in Detroit is the Stoner rifle. Detroit police wanted to order 100 awesomely destructive Stoners and a flock of armored cars but the Common Council vetoed the order, at least for now.

But the blacks don't believe it. They feel the police can quickly get their hands on the Stoners and "tanks" — and the Stoner can punch its way through a brick wall to get at the people ("snipers") behind.

At the Cadillac-Gage factory in suburban Warren, Mich., I test-fired the Stoner 63A and saw the "Commando" police armored car go through its paces.

The Stoner fires the standard .223-calibre bullet used in Vietnam in another rifle, the M-16. In fact, the two guns were designed by the same man, Eugene Stoner.

The bullet is designed to tumble and exit sideways, making a big hole. It can hit a man in the shoulder, tear down through his chest and punch out through his leg. It is a dum-dum bullet in its effects.

The bullet goes through three-eighths-inch armor plate — the punched armor is on display for prospective buyers.

The Stoner is really a weapons system. Add or subtract a few parts and, presto, it becomes a carbine, a fully automatic rifle, or various belt or drum-fed machine guns.

It can shoot anti-personnel or chemical 40 mm grenades.

The Stoner system has been sold to 25 suburban police departments, an official said.

The boss man at the Stoner division said only 300 were available for police — all weapons returned from a Marine Corps test in Vietnam.

"We told the Detroit police we don't want to sell it to you," the boss said. "We got a lot of bad publicity already."

Though the blacks have focused on the Stoner as the most heinous example of police repression, the ones I talked to seemed unaware that the AR-15 rifle fires the same bullet with the same effect.

The AR-15, the civilian model of the army M-16, is being purchased by many police departments. The suburban Wayne County sheriff's department has bought five AR-15s, along with polycarbonate shield and combat boots for 90 men.

Fifty police agencies want to buy the amphibious "Commando" armoured car, used in Vietnam.

Cadillac-Gage has taken off the turret, given it the euphemism of "rescue vehicle," offers it at $30,000 as a "forceful and psychological deterrent to civil disorder." That's what its sales brochure says, the one with the cover picture of a Commando rolling undaunted last summer through the flaming Detroit ghetto. Five Commandos then were loaned to Detroit police.

The Commando carries 12 policemen who can fire through 19 gunports, is claimed impervious to tear gas and "firebombs" and can run 50 miles on thick hard-walled tires even if they are shot out. Optional is a "shocker kit" that electrifies the hull "to deter mob contact with the vehicle."

The police market for armored cars is so inviting that eight firms are canvassing the field, offering such attractions as guns firing tear gas, big and little bullets, discombobulating street-wide foam, literally balls of fire, and some curdlers that can cause a rioter to lose his bowels or just make his head ache fiercely.

In Detroit, the black militants are split among the declining "Tom" integrationists (give Whitey one more chance), the growing urban black enclave theorists, and the separatists.

The separatists are led by the Henry brothers, Milton and Henry, Black Muslims who believe it's strategically absurd to think that the revolution can be fought from the northern city bases.

Milton Henry wants the blacks to be given the states of South Carolina, Georgia, Mississippi, Alabama, and either Florida or Louisiana as a black nation.

To white skeptics, Milton Henry argues that eventually Whitey will get so fed up with the riots that he will gladly accede.

Milton Henry is no fired-up fool. He is an intelligent graduate of Yale Law School who has the same force of conviction that Quebec separatists had a decade ago.

An advocate of grabbing political power in the northern city is Rev. Albert Cleage of Central United Church of Christ.

Cleage urges his parishioners to arm to strike a "balance of terror," and through the inevitable black majority take control of the city. Detroit is 42 per cent Negro.

He preaches black pride. For centuries the white model of beauty and behaviour has been the model for Negroes in America. But to hell with that now, he says.

As part of this process, he depicts Jesus Christ and his mother, Mary, as black, a secret that the white Christians have kept from the Negroes.

Cleage last Easter unveiled an 18-foot chancel mural of the Black Madonna, a treacly work by Detroit artist Glanton Dowell.

Blacks who had been uneasy about adopting the Muslim faith (Arabs supplied the slaves to the white traders) flocked to the Black Messiah concept. The church has become the centre of the black nationalist movement in Detroit and, Cleage claims, for the whole country.

Not so independent is the local chapter of the Congress of Racial Equality. I attended a CORE meeting at which, amid impassioned speeches that Negro children were being "educationally napalmed," a resolution was debated to restrict a project to Negroes.

But the treasurer jumped up to protest that only whites donate to CORE, not a cent came from blacks. He had expenses to meet — "We owe over $300 for windows broken in the rebellion" — and didn't care where the money came from. The racist motion was defeated.

After the meeting, CORE director Hayward Wilson recounted the mystery death of a nine-year-old Negro girl, shot in an alley. He suggested it was the work of perfidious white militants.

"Oh, but that case has been solved," interjected a white woman member. She said two Negro boys, ages 7 and 10, had stolen the rifle and accidentally discharged it.

But the two reporters present from the *Inner City Voice* snickered at this explanation. How could two boys aim and fire a high-powered rifle? This white-devil attitude is reflected in their publication — and feeds the vicious rumours.

And Detroit has been without regular newspapers for almost five months.

In the face of the new black militancy and chronic white racism, can white and Negroes live together? You can't prove it by Cecil Erbaugh, former president of the Fitzgerald Community Association.

Six years ago, the one-square-mile community, eight miles from downtown Detroit, was entirely white. Today it is 70 per cent Negro.

The association was formed to welcome Negroes and form an integrated community. But Erbaugh, a retired union leader, gently cited the old law: "Integration is the short period in a neighbourhood's history between the time the first Negro family moves in and the last white family moves out."

"We tried to prove," Erbaugh said, "that this needn't always happen. However, the proof has yet to be demonstrated."

The whites moved out to the suburbs, after experiencing a drastic increase in vandalism, muggings, burglaries and a deterioration of schools.

Erbaugh showed me a mimeographed, unsigned sheet a Negro high school principal had brought into the office.

The sheet, distributed at the school, was headed: "WHEN YOU FIRST HEAR THE THUNDER (news or bullets) — THE LIGHTNING HAS ALREADY STRUCK."

It suggested blacks stock four to six weeks' supply of food — instant grits, lots of beans, water purification tablets, candles, barbecue stove, fire extinguisher, first aid kit, "portable pot (slop jar)," and "guns and lots of ammunition. Please do not register your guns. Do not get your guns in Detroit or Toledo, Ohio, because the salesmen are turning names into the Detroit police department."

Similar lists for "survival kits" are being put out by Breakthrough, a militant white organization that holds gun classes, has broken up civil rights meetings and marches.

Its leaflet pronounces the need to prepare against "bands of armed terrorists who will murder the men and rape the women."

Those nice housewives in Dearborn are heeding the call.

• **1969** Staff Corresponding •

Biafra: One reporter's search for
the truth in complex civil war

Peter Worthington

Toronto Telegram

It is now almost two years since the word "Biafra" first burst upon the collective conscience of the world.

Biafra is now an emotional issue almost more than it is a piece of African geography or a political dream. It is also a humanitarian question and a pawn in great power politics. It is a civil war; it is starvation; it is suffering. Biafra is a lot of things — all of them complex and confused.

It was on May 31, 1967, that Lt. Col. Odumegwu Ojukwu, military governor of Eastern Nigeria, declared secession from the federation of Nigeria and proclaimed himself head of state of the Republic of Biafra.

Five weeks later the civil war was on.

Few countries — or peoples — have been subjected to the rigors and sufferings that the Ibo people have who live in what is now known as Biafra.

It is not the political dispute, the civil war, that has wrenched the conscience of civilized people everywhere. It is the civilian suffering. It is children dying of hunger, malnutrition, disease.

Truth tends to become clouded with emotion, passion, controversy. Questions that were raised a year ago still beg today.

Is there a policy of genocide being waged by the federal forces of Nigeria? Reputable people say yes, equally responsible people say no. Where does truth lie?

One fact that is known, is accepted, is that people are dying from hunger. But just how many are dying is subject for debate.

Estimates of deaths range up to 10,000 a day. More conservative estimates from church and relief workers on the spot claim up to 3,000 a day are dying.

Federal Nigerian authorities scoff at these estimates and claim that if the numbers were dying that Biafran propagandists claim, there'd be no one left now. This is exaggeration, for assuming that 10,000 were dying per day for the past six months, it would total 1,800,000 — in an area that contains anywhere from 8,000,000 to 10,000,000 people.

Does starvation constitute genocide? The detached viewpoint is that blockade has always been a legitimate means of warfare.

Britain tried to blockade Germany in two wars, while Germany tried to do the same to Britain as well as to starve and beat Russia into capitulation.

The Americans have tried to blockade Vietnam and the UN has tried economically to blockade Rhodesia. There is nothing new in the techniques of blockade — it's just that it is seldom so successful as it is against Biafra.

In fact it is only when blockade is effective, when its victims are starving, that the accusation of "genocide" arises. Does it matter whether or not there is genocide if the end result is the same, if a race is exterminated?

Does it make it acceptable to the conscience of the world if a people are made extinct from a legitimate blockade and not from a deliberate policy of genocide? It makes small difference to the already dead and the soon-to-die.

There is an associated question of a genocidal "policy" being practised by the federal government, that is, the slaughtering of prisoners; atrocities on civilians; burning and looting of homes; indiscriminate bombings of hospitals, refugee camps, market places.

The International Observer Team to Nigeria categorically says that it has found no evidence of genocide or military misconduct. But the observers have never been to the Biafran side, have never seen the evidence of genocide the Biafrans claim to have.

The observers even refused to acknowledge that there is a place called Biafra, that it is "Eastern Nigeria." What is more, they insist that there is no need for them to go there. In other words, their minds are made up after seeing half the evidence.

The suffering alone seems sufficient to prick the conscience of mankind. Nigerians too are affected by the suffering, but see the blame as lying with Ojukwu and the solution being in surrender.

This also seems to be the view of Mitchell Sharp, Minister for External Affairs, who is on record as saying that it would be as worthwhile to tell Biafra to surrender as it would be to ask Nigeria to stop bombing hospitals.

The same argument could have been applied to Britain's back-to-the-wall fight in 1940, or Russia's in 1941. Surrender is certainly a tidy solution to the problem — and conflict — but it isn't always a realistic one.

Stripped of emotionalism the basic issue at stake in Biafran secession is the right of self-determination. Does a people have the right of self-determination — a people of the same ethnic strain, living in an identifiable geographic locality; a people of the same culture and similar aspirations; a people who fear repression, persecution and feel politically stifled?

From its inception the United Nations seems to have recognized self-determination as a basic human right.

This was spelled out in 1950, and again in 1952 when the General Assembly reiterated that: "... The right of peoples and nations to self-determination is a prerequisite to the full enjoyment of all fundamental human rights and every member of the United Nations shall respect that right ..."

The UN Declaration provides: "All people have the right to self-determination; by virtue of that right they freely determine their political status and freely pursue their economic, social and cultural development."

This is exactly what the Biafrans — or Ibos — feel they deserve.

Prof. Richard Gregor of the department of political economy of the University of Toronto, feels the Ibo desire is valid "in view of the past treatment of Ibos in Nigeria."

He sees the problem of self-determination in "tribal Africa" where if all groups chose to take the path of independence "it would lead to anarchy on the continent." Yet to him the Ibos are a special case.

Prof. Gerald Helleiner, also of the political economy department and who has lived and worked in Africa, is particularly aware of the "tragedy" if the experiment of tribal unification should fail in Nigeria, where it had at least been partially successful.

He sees Iboland, as it exists now, as being economically unviable, and that if Biafra had independence it would be a landlocked republic surrounded by a hostile Nigeria.

The only way he sees Biafra becoming economically viable within its present boundaries is "if enough people die to reduce the population density, which at present is perhaps the highest in the world."

Anyone who has visited Biafra will testify to the fact that if a referendum were held, up to 95 per cent of the people would vote to opt out of the federation and choose independence. The mystique, or dream, of Biafra has truly caught the Ibo imagination.

The Ibo case for independence is made stronger by the fact that when Nigeria achieved independence from Britain in 1960, it was the Ibos who fought hardest for unity and one Nigeria. The north, and even the west, were more inclined toward separatism.

The fact that Ibos now feel that union is intolerable, reveals how far the situation has deteriorated; the one-time espousers of the one-nation concept and the supreme nationalists are now disillusioned, frightened, and feel their very survival hinges on being separated from the rest of Nigeria.

Unfortunately, clarity and truth in the Biafran crisis have been obscured because of emotionalism and one-sided vision.

It is only rarely that individuals manage to visit both sides and to assess the virtues and failings of both arguments. This is as understandable as it is regrettable. It is difficult to get from one side to the other — both regard such people as potential spies.

After visiting Biafra you have to fly north to Europe and then fly south to Lagos. It is awkward, time-consuming and expensive.

Another factor of Biafran reportage is that visitors usually spend only a few days there. They visit a refugee camp, a hospital, a feeding centre, talk to missionaries, interview a variety of officials and relief people, and have their minds made up. Most of their information is second-hand, filtered through the experiences and prejudices of individuals committed to Biafra.

Hence the findings that reach the western press often are coloured, unwittingly misleading, certainly suspect. This together with the fact that many visitors to Biafra are hand-chosen "guests" of the Biafrans or church groups, adds another dimension of complexity to the cause of truth.

I spent nearly two months in the Biafra-Nigeria area. I managed to see both sides reasonably thoroughly; I was at the front lines of both armies; I met relief workers on both sides; I was bombed, shot at, lived on impossible Biafran rations — then repeated the performance on the Nigerian side.

I saw evidence of Nigerian atrocities, and have photographs of them. But I also witnessed federal compassion to Ibo refugees, who are fed better in Nigerian camps than they are in Biafran homes. In Biafra it is strong medicine indeed to see a woman drop dead from hunger, or a child sucking its thumb on a doorstep suddenly topple over dead from starvation.

I saw and spoke to prisoners of war on both sides, and they seemed reasonably well treated. All said virtually the same thing: We don't want to fight; we don't understand the war; our forces are demoralized; we want peace; we want to go home.

Only the Biafran prisoners insisted that if they were free they would fight on. If they were being cruelly treated, they'd not dare say this to strangers.

I went on tour with the observer team, and I came to respect their integrity and dedication. Yet I was appalled at their narrow vision, their limited terms of reference, their sincere conviction that they need not see the other side to determine truth.

I slept in vermin-infested beds or, when lucky, on the naked earth with the army — both armies. I met the top field commanders of both sides, and mixed with the fighting troops. I was duly horrified at the low calibre of battle and the flawed mettle of Nigerian and Biafran soldiery.

I do not pose as an expert — yet I have reached certain conclusions based on what I've seen, heard and experienced which I think are impartial, unprejudiced, true.

I have concern for the plight of Biafrans — yet a sympathy for the goals of federal Nigeria.

I suspect some of my conclusions will offend interested parties in Nigeria and Biafra. I do not think Nigeria is as guilty of genocide as, say, Ojukwu is. Yet I feel Biafra should be allowed to secede.

I admire the relief work of the Christian church — yet I feel the church is at least partly responsible for the war dragging on, for perpetrating the myth of genocide, for becoming involved in local politics.

The Red Cross is trying to serve both sides and is succeeding in offending everyone by almost unbelievable clumsiness and insensitivity to the character of the people they seek to serve.

The international observers, though sincere, have hobbled their mission and let principles disintegrate into expediency.

To me Biafra has a right of self-determination — but only for the central eastern state, which is Iboland. Biafra has no right to include Rivers and eastern states which contain other minority tribes like the Rivers people, Ibibios, Ijaws, Efiks. These tribes harbour no special love for the Ibos and nurse little allegiance to the concept of an independent Biafra.

There is no simple answer to the Biafran problem — but there is an answer. The dispute is complex, but not insoluble.

Truth, ever elusive, is hard to pin down. But something approximating it is, or seems, possible. And truth at least seems a useful starting point for examining aspects of the civil war.

This is why I went to Biafra and Nigeria.

• **1971** Staff Corresponding •

In the world of attache cases, a T-shirt

Norman Webster

Globe and Mail

PEKING — If there's a diplomatic hall of fame somewhere, one exhibit it should place alongside the pinstriped suits and attache cases is a certain T-shirt.

White, with long sleeves, it sports the U.S. stars and stripes on front — except that in place of the stars there appears the peace symbol.

Underneath is the slogan, *Let It Be.*

The shirt was given to China's top table tennis player, Chuang Tse-tung, by U.S. pingponger Glenn Cowan during the recent world championships in Japan.

Although it is doubtful that Chuang will walk down the streets of Peking in the shirt, he accepted the gift in friendly fashion and returned a picture-imprinted Chinese handkerchief.

The exchange was the most interesting of several friendly gestures between the U.S. and Chinese table tennis delegations at the championships. That friendliness, and the good publicity it brought, was doubtless one of the many considerations that led to the invitation to U.S. players to visit and play in China.

The result has been an astonishing week here. Consider what your psychiatrist would have made of these fantasies a week and a half ago:

• Premier Chou En-lai meets athletes from five countries in Peking's Great Hall of the People. The event is covered by — good grief — NBC, the Associated Press, United Press International and *Life*, the CBC in both English and French and a number of other foreign news organizations;

• A U.S. teen-ager with hair falling to his shoulders asks Premier Chou what he thinks of hippies;

• Premier Chou says they should do their thing;

• On an outdoor basketball court in Peking, an American takes a jump shot. A Chinese goes up for the rebound;

• A British group tours Peking's Forbidden City, formerly the Imperial Palace of China. It has been closed to all but a favoured few since the Cultural Revolution;

• Two startlingly bourgeois paintings in old-fashioned frames suddenly replace a slogan by Chairman Mao Tse-tung on a restaurant wall. The slogan read: People of the World, Unite and Defeat the U.S. Aggressors and All Their Running Dogs.

• U.S., Canadian, Columbian, British and Nigerian table-tennis players practice in Peking's Capital Stadium as Chinese players instruct them and work on the weak points of their game;

• Chinese guides shift uncomfortably as they are grilled on sexual customs, dope and other subjects dear to the heart of North American youth. One Chinese cannot conceal his amazement when an American talks with a grin about "Happiness in a pipe";

• A U.S. reporter sits down for lunch with Chinese students, a professor and a People's Liberation Army soldier. He begins a story: "When I had lunch one day in Yenan with Chairman Mao …"

• U.S. tourists snap photographs at the Great Wall of China as if it's the most natural thing in the world;

• "These are Americans," I announce in Tien An Men Square to a crowd of Chinese. They smile. Two months previously hundreds of thousands filed through the square denouncing "U.S. imperialism";

• A U.S. expert on computers enters a classroom at Tsinghua University, looks at an equation on the blackboard, takes chalk and works on it;

• Foreigners visiting Peking change their money for Chinese yuan. U.S. dollars are accepted;

• Chou En-lai says that U.S. journalists will be coming to China in batches. He says a new page has been opened in relations between the Chinese and U.S. people.

It probably has. In the past week and a half, China has shown just how supple and clever it can be in its foreign relations. And it all came off a pingpong bat.

There is no doubt that it wasn't a last-minute affair. The Chinese pingpongers went to the world championships in Japan with explicit instructions to smile. Led by Chuang Tse-tung, an approachable, friendly Pekinger who once ruled world table tennis, they did just that — responding favourably even to overtures from U.S. players. The media reported this surprising development.

What was not suspected was that China was preparing to break, in dramatic fashion, more than two decades of ice in Sino-U.S. relations.

It did so by inviting the Americans to join a number of other national teams already signed up to visit China.

Observers in Peking feel there must have been a contingency plan drawn up some time ago for a U.S. visit. When the decision was finally made and the invitation issued and accepted, the plan swung into operation, with impressively smooth results.

U.S. newsmen and organizations were probably not planned for originally. It took a couple of days to expand the plan. Decisions of this importance probably go right to the top, to Chairman Mao himself.

Once it was made, the floodgates opened. U.S. and other news organizations poured in. They are still coming.

For all the visiting teams, the tour in China has been a strikingly friendly affair. (The Americans and Canadians leave today.)

The friendliness is not surprising. Once the invitations were issued, there could be no doubt that the Chinese would go out of their way to be perfect hosts.

They did. Baggage was not checked at Customs. There was none of the red tape often encountered by visitors to China. Anti-U.S. slogans were removed from some prominent positions (although a few remained — you can't win 'em all.)

Film was allowed out of China without first being checked frame by frame. The Chinese Dragon was wreathed in smiles.

Smiles can sometimes be mechanical, twisting the mouth but not reaching the eyes. This one seemed genuine.

Such things are hard to state as certainties, but there seemed to observers to be real friendliness on the part, say, of the students at Tsinghua University toward their foreign guests.

Friendliness and curiosity. They stared in fascination at the casual clothes and grooming of some of the tourists — especially of Cowan, with his long hair, floppy hat, *Let It Be* shirt and bellbottom trousers. They seemed impressed by the spontaneity of the Americans, and responded warmly.

This is encouraging. It seems to show that the differentiation China makes between the nasty U.S. government and the fine U.S. people really means something to the Chinese. Anti-U.S. campaigns have not erased the line.

This line must be kept in mind when assessing the past week's events. Chou En-lai did not mention any opening of a new page in relations between Peking and Washington. It was people-to-people relations that he and everyone else talked about.

But the compartments are not watertight. If U.S. groups continue to visit and the Chinese reciprocate, the whole climate of relations between the two countries, including their respective governments, should change. The White House has already admitted that President Richard Nixon's decision to relax trade and travel restrictions against China, announced on Wednesday, was influenced by Peking's pingpong diplomacy.

Important differences of principle remain between the two capitals, notably on the questions of Taiwan and Indochina. There will be no breakthrough in governmental relations until Washington alters its policies in these areas.

What might emerge is a situation comparable to that between China and Japan. Peking-Tokyo relations are in dreadful shape, but China is cultivating Japanese groups — from parliamentarians to athletes — that favour closer ties with China.

Currently, China's top pingpongers are touring Japan, and they may eventually go the United States. "The table tennis team is China's Bolshoi Ballet," one diplomat remarked yesterday.

• **1975** Spot News Reporting •

Six days of hell on the run from Saigon

Jack Cahill

Toronto Star

ON BOARD USS SGT. MILLER — It had seemed so good and so safe when the Jolly Green Giant helicopter had disgorged us onto the flight deck of the USS Denver last Tuesday after our harrowing escape from Saigon's shell-battered airport.

But now the lights from Jolly Green Giants and smaller helicopters, maybe 20 of them altogether, flickered in the dark sky as we were put off the aircraft carrier and floated out into a rough sea in a small barge.

Some bureaucrat in Washington, Manila, or perhaps on the Denver, had ruled that only Americans could stay on the carrier and be landed in the Philippines and that western third-country nationals, including newsmen, had to go another route.

So now Mike Sullivan of the BBC, an Englishman, a Spanish TV crew and I, a Canadian, suddenly found ourselves refugees just like the hundreds of thousands we had seen on the roads while covering the war, and about to be treated exactly the same as the few who finally made it to sea in the final dramatic evacuation.

The refugee ship they took us to — the USS Sgt. Andrew Miller, veteran of the exodus from Da Nang in which 43 of its 10,000 refugee passengers died in two days, painted gray, 7,000 tons, manned by a civilian crew and a company of U.S. marines — did not look too bad as we approached it in a rough sea.

But members of the crew and armed marines shook their heads at us as we climbed aboard and one marine asked: "Hell, what are you guys doing in a ship like this? We've got no food. We've got no water. We've got no toilets. All we've got is people, hell."

"We've also got no accommodation for people like you or anyone. This is a cargo ship, you know," the sailor shouted after us.

"But good luck anyway."

The ship had about 2,000 refugees on it then and we thought it was packed tight, but they crammed in another 5,000 people in the next 24 hours.

Saigon fell at noon that day and all day long barges, sampans, fishing boats and fair-sized ships packed with people hovered around the Sgt. Miller, but the marines kept most of them away by firing into the water nearby.

Still the ship, apparently under orders from Washington to pick up as many refugees as possible, moved closer to the coast near the refugee centre of Vung Tau, until it was well within Vietnamese territorial waters and the coast was clearly visible.

About 1 p.m. a marine shouted "We're under fire" and shells began to explode in the water a few hundred yards behind the ship. We could see the flashes from the shore batteries and the splashes near the ship but we must have been just out of range because they always fell about the same distance behind as we moved out to sea.

A destroyer escort and a helicopter carrier escorting us sped off to sea as soon as the firing began.

We moved slowly, loading people onto the ship from big barges with high wire fencing on the sides like tennis courts.

About 3 p.m. the marines had to open fire to scare away a fleet of more than 50 boats, but one man jumped overboard from his small craft and swam for us and made it.

An old woman slipped and fell between a boat and the loading barge and a sailor and marine jumped into the crunch between the two vessels to try to save her.

But she was squashed and they took her body out to sea in a tug and dumped it overboard.

Just after 4, a South Vietnamese helicopter with three men and two motorcycles on board started to circle the ship. The men signaled frantically for us to clear the foredeck, but it was too crowded. We couldn't move more than two feet in the crush of people.

After about five circuits, the pilot decided to put it down on one of the barges alongside the ship.

The few people on the barge scattered as he made an almost perfect landing. But his motor hit one of the high wire fences, breaking into small shrapnel-like pieces which peppered the decks of the ship. Miraculously, only a few of the refugees were slightly injured.

Marines pulled the three men, apparently not seriously injured, from the chopper, turned hoses on it, forced the pilot back into the cockpit to switch off the red-hot sparking motor, pushed the helicopter into the sea, and resumed landing refugees within 10 minutes.

By nightfall we had taken on about 4,000 more refugees and the work continued throughout the night.

May 1: Our main trouble was that we didn't plan to be refugees in the first place. So when we were told at Tan Son Nhut we could take only one small bag on the evacuation chopper Sullivan and I chose to take only our typewriters and cameras.

The other refugees, or at least some of them, were somewhat prepared with awnings, a few hammocks, groundsheets, water containers, toothbrushes and soap. But we had only the bush-jacket suits we had been wearing for two days already.

During the night, however, a small family of third-country "round-eyes," mostly in the same position as ourselves with no clothing changes or other possessions, gathered around us, and in the morning we held a survival meeting.

We decided we would form our own family because it seemed much more likely that a family unit would survive eight to 10 days on the Sgt. Miller. And we staked out a position on the fore-deck which we would defend as our home.

The position was a coiled piece of thick manila rope, the forward mooring line; which stretched beside the gunwhale for about 12 feet and into the deck for about five feet.

A very loud-mouthed American man, who never told us his name but was in Vietnam buying scrap metal, kept going around the ship shouting such things as "Women and children first," and "If you ARVN (South Vietnamese soldiers) had fought better we wouldn't be here."

Nobody knew why he was there and he was no help at all. After the first few days, he vanished from our "family."

The ship was still in glassy smooth water, with water snakes and flying fish, still picking up refugees this day from the hundreds of sampans surrounding it, but now we had caught up with the main American fleet of about 30 ships, half of them battleships, half refugee carriers and supply ships.

We were the last U.S. ship out of Vietnamese waters.

The sun hit down from above and reflected up again from the steel deck so that it would have been impossible to survive for more than a few hours in the pen.

When Sullivan and I tried to get near the crew and marine quarters to ask for blankets or sheets to make an awning, two big marines pointed their automatic rifles and yelled nervously: "Back, back, get back." So we got back.

We decided to send the women to infiltrate the crew quarters if possible, and they had remarkable success. Within an hour they were back with sheets and string, pillow cases to make covers for our heads and a plastic bag of water.

Two hours later they had jobs as assistants in the galley and that night we shared a plate of chicken legs and asparagus, stolen from the officers' mess.

There were jokes, of course, about going for a stroll around the deck and complaining to the chief steward about our table.

May 2. Very bad day. The women have been told there's no need for them any more in the galley.

The sun is worse and there is no water until noon when a marine comes around the ship with a plastic container and gives us two cups each.

The ship has no toilet facilities except for the crew, but the marines have built six little platforms out of 2-x-4s and hung them over the sides.

There is a line-up 20 yards long for each of them and they are a gymnastic and esthetic challenge.

The worst thing is that the women both began to have their periods and there are no sanitary napkins aboard. The doctor gave them a small piece of cotton wool each, but in the end we have to tear up our only sweaty singlets for them.

The ship is a stink, a crush, a rattling noise. Down the holds it is worse. The holds smell of urine and sweat. Families are crowded into them so they can hardly move.

But our little crowded house made of sheets stands up despite a bit of breeze made by the ship's movement.

We're all thirsty, but we can't eat all of the meal of rice mixed with sardines they dished out from garbage cans that night.

There are a few other Americans and Europeans on board but we have little contact with them because of the impossibility of walking through the crush of people sprawled on the decks.

Two French women, who owned one of Saigon's best restaurants, at first inveigled their way into the crew's quarters, but now under the policy of complete equality for all refugees of all races, they have been kicked out and are worse off than most because they had no time to find a space and build a tent.

An Irish nun and a Vietnamese nun with a British passport sit stoically out in the sun under their black veils, occasionally moving about doing good works.

Jim Sturgeon of Winnipeg, who had a business in Vietnam for eight years, is working 18 hours a day distributing water, so when he occasionally comes to us we get a little extra.

The Vietnamese lie on the hot decks or in the hotter holds, the babies mostly quiet now. There seem to be no cries left in them any more as they curl up around their exhausted mothers. There have been many cases of dehydration.

At night on the BBC the refugees have heard that Canada will take 3,000 of them. They pepper me with questions. Most of them don't know where they are going, just somewhere away from Saigon.

Most of them like the idea of Canada except for the cold. They are pathetic people caught in a vise of fear of communism behind them and the unknown ahead.

We don't see much of the marines except when they arrive at our part of the ship to bring a cup of water and the one meal of the day, which is distributed from garbage cans.

They are mostly tough men with bulging biceps but many of them are amazingly kind with the children.

Some of them, especially the blacks, are pleasant to us and apparently concerned about us. They bring us salt pills and sometimes some extra water.

"It's the slave ship syndrome, man," one big black told us. "Us Americans have never got over the slave-ship days."

Some are not so nice.

"You guys remember that you're all just refugees to us," one of them lectured for no apparent reason. "Everybody's the same on this ship. All refugees. All the same. No special privileges," he said.

Tonight for dinner we had a few baked beans and some tuna fish with our rice. It was good, but you don't get all that hungry in these circumstances. You get terribly thirsty, so that your hands shake like an alcoholic when you lift the water to your lips.

The Vietnamese are listless now, lying on the decks under their makeshift sun covers if they have one, mostly just staring at the sky. A few people are shuffling about the smelly holds looking after children, but mostly there is a sick stillness in the ship. Only one person has died so far but many are sick.

The ship pulls into Subic Bay. It smells like a wet diaper and still we don't know whether we can get off or have to go on it to Guam — another four days away.

Then the marines carry off the sick on stretchers and some Americans disembarked and we are told third-country nationals will be next.

Ashore on Grande Island in the bay, which is the biggest naval base in Asia, they gave us Cokes and food and a display of remarkable American efficiency and kindness.

"Hey, some VIPs here," an air force captain called out to his colleagues at one stage and it felt better than being a refugee.

Nice, fresh, American ladies kept pushing food and cigarettes on us. Kindness and goodwill and sympathy.

But at this end part what you remember most is marine Capt. Bill Darrow, the island's security officer who pulled out his Spanish guitar and played flamenco to entertain the Spanish TV crew while we waited in his office for a boat to the main base.

You remembered then that there are no Saigon girls any more and Saigon is Ho Chi Minh City. The Hondas are impounded and bustling Tu Do St. is now empty of almost everything but political idealism.

Saigon has seduced the French and almost ruined the Americans. It is a whore of a city that might some day even corrupt the Communists.

● **1977** Spot News Reporting ●

I was captured, then captivated, by Amin

Gerald Utting

Toronto Star

LONDON — The Conqueror of the British Empire, Uganda's Life President Field Marshal Al Hajji Dr. Idi Amin Dada, VC, DSO, MC, grabbed me by the hand and pumped it.

"I am very pleased to meet you, Mr. Gerald Utting," he said. "It was me who ordered you to be arrested and put in prison by the military police."

I had been sent by my office to try to interview Amin and spent more than a week in Nairobi, Kenya, cooling heels, waiting for an answer to my application for an entry visa into Uganda.

With no sign of reply, I finally boarded an Air France jet in Nairobi — and walked straight into captivity when I stepped off the plane at Entebbe.

The meeting with Amin was last Sunday. I was wined and dined, then late in the afternoon I met with the Ugandan president, who was sitting on what the British call a shooting stick, watching a group of girls in traditional costume dancing to the rhythm of drums.

He was wearing a flowing shirt with colourful designs commemorating the 100th year of Christian missionary work in Uganda, a pair of slacks with a revolver dangling in a holster on his right hip.

I shook hands and when he told me he had personally had me jailed and I was looking better for it, I tactfully agreed.

"I have lost about 20 pounds of fat, your excellency," I said.

"Your wife will thank me for it," he beamed.

"Well, the diet of your military police has succeeded where two years of complaining by my wife got nowhere," I replied. It is definitely not protocol to disagree with a dictator with a gun on his hip, who has been accused of responsibility for 100,000 killings and tribal genocide.

Idi Amin explained that he had nothing against me personally, but I must understand journalists can't just come calling on him in Uganda in the hopes of getting an interview, because "so many have been shown around our country and then gone outside and told lies about us."

I assured him I would never do anything like that.

He smiled — an Idi Amin Dada smile, with a big, broad beam — and said: "I love the Canadian people, but your prime minister says bad things about Uganda. But I do not mind that, because I know the Canadian people like me and my country.

"I have one big message for the Canadian people. I believe that 40 per cent of your country is owned by the Americans and you must try to end this. You must fight against more economic domination.

"The people of Uganda know what it is to be exploited by an alien people and will support Canadians in their fight against foreign economic domination."

Well, naturally, I agreed with him on that.

I explained to him that I had come to East Africa to try to see him so that he could explain in person what he had intended to say at the Commonwealth leaders' conference in London last month.

He said he had not gone to London because British Prime Minister James Callaghan had sent him a letter asking him not to come. He spoke sorrowfully of this blow to Uganda's feelings about the Commonwealth.

He introduced me to five of his young sons, solemn, sturdy kids, ranging up to about 10 years. His obvious favourite was his youngest, Mwanga, who was dressed in a miniature commando camouflage suit.

"How old is he?" I asked, "Five," said the president, who refers to himself as the Big Daddy of Uganda.

"What rank is he?" I asked.

"He is just a private," said the proud father.

Then he smiled that big smile again.

"I think I might award him an order that I created while you were in prison, so you probably have not heard of it. I might give him the CBE — Conqueror of the British Empire. (There is a British award, CBE, Commander of the British Empire.)

We sat down on some lounge chairs and I started questioning the president and taking notes. We talked for an hour. He told me:

• He'd love to visit Canada, but he couldn't come unless he was invited because that's the way heads of state operated.

• He'd put Uganda's athletic team into training for the Commonwealth Games in Edmonton. Whether they'd go depended on whether the Organization of African Unity accepted the compromise on the New Zealand — South African sports issue reached at the Commonwealth leaders conference.

• He plans to visit Cuba late this month or early next month to see Fidel Castro and hopes to visit some other Latin American countries. With a devilish grin, he said he intends to stop at London's Heathrow airport to refuel. Would he stop at Gander, Nfld., to refuel? "Perhaps," he said, obviously wondering where the heck Gander is.

• He thinks Canadian mining engineers are the best in the world and he would like them to come to Uganda to help develop the country.

• He supports the liberation war against South Africa and Rhodesia but thinks they will be no pushover. He has no desire, he said, to see the whites destroyed, or even to leave Africa because "they are welcome to live in Africa, we need their brains and their technique. What we insist is that they must not try to rule the majority, which is Africans, by force."

• He insisted he is not a Communist and never could be.

The interview seemed to be over, and we headed back into the building for the field marshal to have a massage.

I and my escort walked right through, while the president went into a little massage room.

The field marshal, surely the most informal head of state around these days, stripped off his clothes, right down to a pair of bright red bikini underpants. He heaved himself up on the massage couch.

Two little masseuses in white smocks came in and started pouring oil on the field marshal and pounding it into his brawny legs.

His bulky stomach ripples not with fat, but with muscle.

The naked field marshal Amin is indeed a tremendous sight. A kind of black Hercules.

Inside that room were The Conqueror of the British Empire, a military police major guarding me, two masseuses, a Scotsman who services motor boat engines and an extraordinary Englishman named Bob Astles.

Astles, the same age as Amin, has been reported to be the power behind the throne in Uganda, a sinister head of the secret police and several times reported killed by Amin as a British spy.

However, he was quite alive last weekend because I saw him, was taken out on a cruise on Lake

Victoria by him, had lunch with him, and appeared on a TV show with him on Monday. Yes, I became a TV star in Uganda without even trying.

While the girls pounded away at his Amin's black frame, while the pipes skirled, we talked about the world and President Amin.

"They say I am in fear of my life, guarded by Palestinians and Cubans," said Amin. "Tell me, do you see any Cubans or Palestinians here?"

I said I didn't, and indeed there was no sign of such people — or even of particularly heavy security near the president earlier when he sat amid a crowd of hundreds in front of the main building of the resort hotel.

He asked about the "divorce" of Prime Minister Pierre Trudeau and Margaret.

I said they had separated, not divorced, and that Mrs. Trudeau wanted to pursue a career as a news photographer.

"Is she a good photographer?" he asked.

I told him there were different views of her talent.

"I would like her to come here and take photographs of me," he said. "I would get one of those secret photographers from the Soviet KGB to come from Moscow and then I would give her a big kiss and then the Russians would take a picture of us and that would be great fun."

Nobody in Uganda, aside from a select few, ever see such things as foreign newspapers or foreign TV newscasts.

But Amin is very conscious of them. He told me he had wanted Walter Cronkite to come to Uganda but the CBS newsman had elected to go to Rhodesia instead.

"Why not Barbara Walters?"

Astles said he didn't like her. "She wanted to come but we turned her down."

It was time for Amin to go back into the sauna to get the oil out of his pores.

"Perhaps we will show you more of our country before you leave," he said.

"Good night, it was very nice to meet you."

"Goodbye, Mr. President," I said.

The major took me down to my cell and took back the clean clothes I had been wearing. I got back into the filthy clothes I had on when I arrived in Uganda.

I was awakened at 4:30 a.m. and taken to Entebbe airport. I was led into an office and handed a phone. It was 6:15 a.m. Idi Amin Dada was on the line. He sounded a bit sleepy.

"Goodbye, Mr. Gerald," he said. "I am sorry we had to put you in prison. But I don't think anyone did you any harm. I think you found it interesting here.

"Go back to Canada and tell everybody how peaceful you found Uganda and how the Uganda people want to be friendly with Europeans and Canadians. I am sorry your Mr. Trudeau has led the campaign of lies against me.

"But we like you and hope you will tell the truth, just what you heard and saw yourself.

"Perhaps you will be able to come back to visit Uganda again and see how beautiful our country is. See our High Commissioner in Canada and he may be able to arrange it.

"We used you as a warning to other journalists they must not come here without permission.

"But, anyway, goodbye and good luck, Mr. Utting."

I said I enjoyed meeting him and found Uganda very interesting. Even getting slimmer wasn't too bad for me.

"Well, goodbye," he said. "Enjoy the flight and tell the people of Canada I love them very much." Nine hours later I was in London.

• **1980** Nouvelle d'actualité •

Des Américains cachés à l'ambassade
canadienne sont sauvés

Jean Pelletier

La Presse

WASHINGTON — L'ambassade du Canada a fermé hier ses portes à Téhéran, évacuant tout son personnel diplomatique afin de permettre à un « groupe » de diplomates américains qui s'y cachait depuis le début de la prise des otages le 4 novembre dernier, de recouvrer la liberté.

En falsifiant avec l'aide des services secrets américains des visas diplomatiques iraniens inscrits dans des passeports diplomatiques canadiens, l'ambassade du Canada dirigée par M. Kenneth Taylor, a permis à des diplomates des États-Unis d'échapper aux recherches des militants de l'ayatollah Khomeiny qui, depuis l'invasion de l'ambassade des États-Unis, essayaient de découvrir où ils se terraient. Il a fallu plusieurs mois pour que le Canada et le gouvernement américain parviennent à mettre au point cette opération audacieuse.

Une autre stratégie envisagée consistait à les faire sortir à titre de simples hommes d'affaires américains.

La Presse était au courant de cette situation depuis le 10 décembre dernier mais a choisi de ne pas en parler à la suite d'explications fournies par le gouvernement canadien et les autorités américaines.

« C'est une question de vie ou de mort, » déclarèrent à *La Presse* en décembre dernier des hauts fonctionnaires canadiens. « Si vous en parlez maintenant, cela équivaudrait à divulguer l'adresse de familles juives qui tentaient d'échapper à la Gestapo en 1941. »

L'annonce hier par le gouvernement canadien de la fermeture de son ambassade à Téhéran en a surpris plusieurs dont les autorités iraniennes à Ottawa qui ne pouvaient s'expliquer les raisons justifiant pareille évacuation alors qu'à Téhéran la situation semble être revenue au calme avec l'élection à la présidence de la nouvelle République islamique d'un politicien modéré, M. Abdul Hassan Bani Sadr.

De sources fiables, *La Presse* a appris que le gouvernement canadien a décidé d'exécuter son plan d'évacuation (avec l'assentiment des autorités américaines) après en être venu à la conclusion qu'il n'y avait pas moment plus favourable.

« Comment diable aurions-nous pu expliquer aux autorités iraniennes qu'au lieu des 50 otages, il y en avait en réalité beaucoup plus, » de déclarer à *La Presse* l'un des rares fonctionnaires à connaître le détail de cette opération qui rivalise en péripéties bien des romans d'espionnage.

« En les évacuant maintenant, alors qu'un calme relatif règne en Iran et que d'aucuns croient que tous les otages sont encore détenus à l'ambassade des États-Unis nous avions une meilleure chance de nous en tirer que si nous avions attendu un règlement final et négocié de la crise. »

Il faudra attendre que le ministère des Affaires extérieures du Canada rende public le détail de cette affaire pour mieux comprendre comment des diplomates américains parvinrent à trouver refuge à l'ambassade canadienne à Téhéran et s'y cacher pendant plus de deux mois, alors que les militants khomeynistes (dont l'attaque sur l'ambassade des États-Unis était murie de longue date et minutieusement orchestrée) étaient au fait des noms, du domicile et des déplacements de tout le personnel diplomatique américain à Téhéran.

« Nous n'y croyons pas encore nous-mêmes, devait déclarer à *La Presse* un diplomate canadien. Chaque jour fut un cauchemar. »

Et pour cause. Lorsque les militants publièrent les listes de leurs détenus, plusieurs familles américaines ayant des parents à Téhéran mais ne les voyant pas revenir au pays, dûrent être tenues au secret absolu du sort réservé à leurs proches.

« Que personne n'ait vendu la mèche est renversant, » de noter la même source. « Mettez-vous à leur place. Comment explique-t-on à son voisin que son mari, bien que fonctionnaire à Téhéran, n'est ni dans la liste des otages que diffuse la presse américaine, ni de retour au pays? »

Mais comme toute histoire de ce genre comporte un héros, celle-ci n'en a nul autre que Kenneth Taylor. L'ambassadeur du Canada en Iran, avec un rare sang froid, donna refuge aux fugitifs américains, les intégrant lentement au personnel de son ambassade, créant ainsi un écran de fumée face aux autorités iraniennes. Redoutant que ses télex ne soient déchiffrés par les services secrets iraniens, il parvint au cours des semaines à faire comprendre à Washington et à Ottawa qu'une opération de rescapage devait être menée tôt ou tard avec bien sûr la plus grande prudence et surtout dans le secret le plus absolu.

Si bien sûr en théorie on pouvait émettre des passeports diplomatiques canadiens à des Américains pour leur permettre de quitter le pays, ce stratagème risquait d'être mis à jour dès l'instant qu'ils essaieraient de traverser la frontière. Car, non seulement fallait-il être muni du bon visa de sortie émis par le gouvernement iranien, mais il fallait surtout survivre à l'inspection des militants révolutionnaires qui contrôlent vraiment tous les points de sortie en Iran.

Deux stratégies furent donc envisagées au départ. La première consistait à faire fuir les Américains la nuit, par la route via la frontière turque, à quelques heures de voiture de Téhéran.

En profitant de la précarité des communications entre la capitale et les provinces et du fait que la population locale est plus ou moins hostile au gouvernement de l'Ayatollah dans cette région de l'Iran, on souhaitait faire passer les fugitifs américains en «zone libre» en toute impunité.

La seconde approche se résumait à affronter carrément les officiers de l'immigration à l'aéroport de Téhéran en souhaitant que ces derniers ne verraient que du feu à des passeports canadiens en apparence parfaitement légitimes, ou encore à des passeports américains de simples civils. On espérait en outre que les douaniers n'essaieraient pas de les faire correspondre aux listes des diplomates étrangers inscrits aux registres du ministère iranien des Affaires étrangères.

« Très vite on dut se rendre à l'évidence que ces deux approches recelaient (c'était au début de la crise) malgré leurs avantages respectifs, un danger grave celui que l'un des fuyards soit reconnu à la dernière minute par des militants révolutionnaires aux aguets). On se rappelle qu'un homme d'affaire américain soupçonné d'activités d'espionnage fut arrêté à sa chambre d'hôtel à Téhéran par les militants khomeynistes lorsque ces derniers découvrirent de par les listes consulaires qu'ils obtinrent à l'ambassade des États-Unis que ce « businessman » se trouvait encore à Téhéran. »

Ce jour-là, la liste des otages passa de 49 à 50.

Pareil risque était d'autant plus considérable que certains du groupe des Américains réfugiés à l'ambassade du Canada risquaient d'être plus recherchés que les autres.

Kenneth Taylor, malgré les risques que comportait une telle alternative, choisit d'attendre et de multiplier ses contacts auprès des autorités iraniennes.

Systématiquement, pendant plus de 80 jours, il visita les leaders révolutionnaires à Téhéran, entretenant avec chacun d'eux des rapports tellement exceptionnels que le Canada devint très vite l'ambassade la mieux au courant de ce qui se passait vraiment en Iran.

Au Département d'État, de révéler à *La Presse* un diplomate, les rapports de Taylor qui leur était transmis via Ottawa étaient considérés comme parmi les meilleurs compte-rendus en provenance de l'Iran.

L'ambassadeur Taylor, d'autre part, eut le flair de jouer les intermédiaires auprès du chargé d'Affaires américain, M. Bruce Laingen, toujours retenu au ministère iranien des Affaires étrangères. Taylor rencontra ce dernier regulièrement à toutes les semaines, lui apportant à l'occasion des chemises et d'autres objets utiles, devenant ainsi aux yeux des autorités iraniennes une sorte d'intermédiaire américain sinon sympathique du moins « ouvert » à la cause de la révolution Khomeiny.

En parallèle à cette stratégie d'ouverture, Kenneth Taylor « étudiait » le terrain, examinant de près les diverses procédures de sortie tant à l'aéroport de Téhéran qu'aux autres postes frontières de l'Iran.

Il comprit graduellement le système d'émission des visas d'entrée et de sortie, des cartes d'embarquement, des tours de garde des différentes factions d'officiers khomeinystes etc. Étant donné que les Canadiens avaient des allées et venues regulières dans le pays, il put graduellement inscrire (c'est ce que l'on soupçonne ici) les « fugitifs américains » au sein du personnel de son ambassade, ou dans d'autres cas changer leur identité les faisant passer pour de simples civils américains.

La Presse apprenait hier qu'on ne saura sans doute jamais les techniques consulaires utilisées tant par le Canada que par les États-Unis dans cette histoire.

Puis vint ces derniers jours l'ouverture que tous attendaient; les élection iraniennes et l'accalmie de la clameur antiaméricaine en Iran à la suite de l'invasion de l'Afghanistan par les troupes soviétiques.

En décrètant que le Canada fermait son ambassade à Téhéran, Kenneth Taylor put profiter de la précipitation que cause invariablement une telle décision pour évacuer tout son personnel d'un seul coup sans que personne ne s'inquiète de ce qu'il se soit élargi soudainement.

Le 28 janvier dernier, à North Bay, le premier ministre du Canada M. Clark annonçait la fermeture de l'ambassade canadienne à Téhéran. Cette décision causa bien sûr un profond émoi dans les milieux politiques. On comprend très vite à la lumière de ces faits qu'il ne pouvait y avoir d'autres alternatives.

Cet article, en conclusion, ne donne que les grandes lignes d'une opération unique dans les annales de l'histoire de la diplomatie canadienne. M. Kenneth Taylor, et sans doute quelques fonctionnaires du département d'État et de la CIA à Washington, pourraient ajouter des chapitres passionnants.

« Kenneth Taylor devrait être décoré », devait déclarer à *La Presse* un diplomate canadien. Ils sont en effet peu nombreux dans la fonction publique ceux qui auraient pu mener à bien une opération aussi périlleuse.

• **1981** Feature Writing •
They want bread but get statistics
Peter Calamai
Southam News

NAIROBI — Famine is thriving in Africa today. So is pervasive deprivation, a hunger more widespread and intractable than simple starvation.

Both persist despite stacks of international studies, global pledges of aid, and a succession of ballyhooed national self-sufficiency schemes. Only in Africa do the dire Malthusian predictions still hold true: Population increase is out-running food production.

"Today the average African has 10 per cent less food than 10 years ago," says Edouard Saouma, director-general of the United Nations Food and Agriculture Organization.

But why can't Africa feed itself? Why does the continent with the largest area of arable land — half not even under crops — permit one in five of its 500 million inhabitants to suffer starvation or debilitating malnutrition?

For the past two decades Africans and apologists elsewhere have put forward a litany of reasons: Colonial inheritance, tropical pests and diseases, natural and man-made disasters, global trade discrimination, poor soil and unreliable rains, and, finally, the alleged corruptive effect of food aid.

But recently there have been admissions that the overriding reason for Africa's hidden holocaust of hunger is poor political leadership. The Organization of African Unity conceded as much in a plan of action for economic development, adopted last year. So have African commentators, like a Nairobi newspaper, the *Sunday Nation*:

"The real problem is the Africans' failings," the newspaper editorialized, "and, to a certain extent, their misguided priorities that have turned countries on this continent into virtual beggars."

The begging is particularly noticeable this year, with half of Africa's 50 independent nations facing "abnormal food shortages," the FAO's euphemism for widespread starvation.

The FAO says those states need 2.4 million tonnes of food aid, about a quarter of the continent's projected total food imports for 1981.

Politics aside, that shortfall could be met within Africa. The Republic of South Africa has an estimated seven million tonnes of surplus maize this year. Most black African countries eschew imports from the apartheid regime or, like Kenya, conceal the unpalatable truth through falsified documents.

Imports would be politically acceptable from Zimbabwe, where efficient white farmers this year generated a million-tonne surplus of maize. But Prime Minister Robert Mugabe has elected to use scarce railway capacity to export more profitable tobacco to Europe rather than maize to his hungry black neighbours.

Those two instances merely emphasize what experts have argued: The world's food problem is distribution, not quantity.

In some countries the peasants have been exploited by black leaders more than they were under white colonialists. Senegalese farmers, for instance, were paid starvation prices for their peanut crop in the '70s, yet as much as 30 per cent of the hard currency earned from peanut exports was spent on imported flour to make crusty French bread for the elite in Dakar, Senegal's capital.

Progress in agriculture was further impeded because many countries pursued strategies which, in hindsight, were wrong-headed. The development orthodoxy from Western agencies such as the World Bank stressed export cash crops such as coffee, cocoa, tea, even flowers for Europe's winter markets.

Some African leaders believed the Western experts. Others appreciated the better opportunities for personal enrichment offered by cash crops over small-scale food production.

Honesty and corruption produced the same result: Dedication of the limited domestic competence in research and marketing to luxury crops for export.

But in the mid '70s the yo-yo of international commodity prices combined with soaring oil costs to doom that approach.

Now the new orthodoxy is food strategies tailor-made for each country. So far 20 African states have subscribed to this latest trend, often as the price of obtaining increased external assistance.

Missing from the lists is one factor often wrongly blamed for hunger in Africa — overpopulation. Some economists even maintain that parts of Africa are today underpopulated for efficient agricultural production and nearly everyone agrees the continent could support far more people, as it did before the depopulation caused by the slave trade and 20th century epidemics.

Some would add food aid as another impediment to self-reliance. In a report last year the UN World Food Council observed: "Only a third of food aid is specifically earmarked to feed the malnourished. The rest is sold commercially and its impact on the hungry is hard to trace."

Evidence strongly suggests that food aid not only keeps the disease but also the cure at bay. In country after country low-cost wheat and corn from overseas undercut local farmers, them into poverty.

Prime Minister Trudeau's advocacy of food self-sufficiency at the Commonwealth summit is a recent conversion. In the '70s the Liberal government's aid agency, CIDA, spent four times as much on dependency-producing food aid as on grants or loans to improve Third World agriculture and fisheries. Another shipload of surplus wheat was a convenient way both to meet aid pledges and keep Prairie farmers happy.

Africans, in particular, fear the political dependency wrapped up with food aid even with imports they pay for. Leaders here shuddered when U.S. Agricultural Secretary John Block spoke of America's "weapon" of farm exports. They positively blanched at the remarks of South Africa's agriculture minister Henrik Schoeman:

"Full grain silos will mean that we can talk and negotiate from a position of strength. With the rising populations all around us, more and more black states will depend to some extent on this country for basic foods," Schoeman told South African journalists.

The move toward food self-reliance in Africa is also an implicit admission from black leaders that they cannot bargain effectively for a better deal in international trade so long as the ever-present threat of famine forces desperate sales of their products to raise money for food imports.

But domestic self-sufficiency will at least place solely in African hands the most basic need of the continent, a matter too long tossed this way and that by the whims and fashions of international trade, aid, and charity.

As first director-general of the FAO, Lord John Boyd Orr, wrote 15 years ago in his memoirs: "The hungry people of the world wanted bread and they were given statistics."

• **1985** Foreign Reporting •

Death of 16-month-old in South Africa

Michael Valpy

Globe and Mail

Siphiwo Goodboy Willi made his odd little way into South African martyrdom on the weekend. He got there four days earlier than some people wanted.

Perhaps it was one of those judgment calls that Goodboy, by going into his grave on Saturday rather than on Wednesday, better served his people's cause. There were, on the one hand, 50,000 people and the international press to see him off. On the other hand, there now is no proof of what killed him.

Maybe it does not matter. There are so many black deaths, so many mass funerals and, as it is, everyone believes the troops murdered him. Maybe all that did matter was how the last of Goodboy Willi looked on television, which was fine: His little white coffin, half a metre long by 25 centimetres across, sitting in a puddle at the bottom of a full-sized grave, a cold wind gusting.

In East London's black township of Duncan Village, 16-month-old Goodboy Willi played his part in his country's tragic theatre. So did the 16 others buried with him.

So did the pathetic creature, a tire around his neck and his bared buttocks bloody with lash marks, who was dragged through the funeral crowd by youths waving sticks and knives while thousands chanted, "Burn him, burn him."

So did the black nationalist leader who told the crowd they must be prepared to die, who told them to go back into the township after the funeral and destroy everything that belonged to the government, "to shoot, to kick, to burn — to do everything to be free."

So did the youths who left the funeral and obediently burned houses and a school, and attacked and killed Pieter Gordier and Attie Stols, two white building contractors driving in a car near Duncan Village. So did the troops who beat a man's head with rifle butts, and whoever it was who threw pepper gas in the open graves before the victims of Duncan Village's violence could be placed in them.

Lastly, so did Joseph Menold, 33, the 18th victim of the security action against Duncan Village who was buried on Saturday. He was of mixed-race, a so-called coloured; the others were black. Under South Africa's Group Areas Act, he had to be taken to the separate coloured graveyard.

With all that drama on Saturday — 50,000 people attending a six-hour funeral service in eZiphunsana Stadium and the events that followed — Goodboy Willi could only claim a bit part.

"Oh, God, how did that body manage to get buried? I want to know how that baby got buried," said a distraught Janet Davies, hearing the news late Saturday night that Goodboy had been included in the day's mass interment.

Ms Davies, a community worker, had arranged for a private autopsy to be performed on him tomorrow. On Saturday afternoon, there was a man wearing a pink sweater, one of the funeral organizers, carrying a document in his pocket authorizing Goodboy's removal from the mortuary.

The rioting started in Duncan Village on the night of Sunday, at 11, and went on for 48 hours.

The unofficial death toll is about 30. On Monday, Aug. 12, Goodboy was asleep on his bed inside his own house in daytime when troops came down his street, firing tear gas canisters, his mother, Joyce, said.

The gas drifted through the doorway. Goodboy, according to Joyce, started to swell and perspire and could not breathe properly.

On Saturday, Aug. 17, she took him to hospital. On Monday, Aug. 19, the hospital told her he was dead.

The hospital gave her two causes of death: A form of malnutrition called kwashiorkor and/or double pneumonia. A paediatrician, hired to perform the private autopsy by the church clinic where Ms Davies works, had read Goodboy's hospital medical reports and said they were inconsistent with kwashiorkor.

The clinic at St. Francis Xavier Roman Catholic Church wanted to prove that the baby had died from tear gas. Mrs. Willi had come to the clinic on three separate days last week to work out the legal procedure with Ms Davies required for a private autopsy.

But Saturday came first — the day of the mass funeral organized by the anti-apartheid coalition, the United Democratic Front (its members wearing T-shirts with the slogan: *Duncan Village Massacre*) — and Goodboy's body turned up in the stadium.

"His mother was under a lot of pressure," Ms Davies said. She did not elaborate.

The coffins were carried into the stadium by UDF marshals in khaki uniforms and laid across benches. For about five minutes, no one seemed to know where to put Goodboy. His little coffin was passed from marshal to marshal until they found a place for it. At one point, a marshal was holding it under his arm like a box of roses.

Later, after everyone had marched to the cemetery, a marshal jumped down into the two-metre-deep hole and the little coffin was handed down to him. The photographers and TV cameramen almost fell in behind him, getting pictures.

Goodboy's mother and father, quiet little people, poorly dressed, stood by unnoticed. Their son belonged to something beyond them.

A priest took off the paper rosette in UDF colours — black, yellow, red — he had pinned to his cassock. He crumpled it, and threw it in Goodboy's grave.

That was Siphiwo Goodboy Willi.

The man with the tire around his neck, dragged earlier through the stadium crowd, was said to be a police informer.

As the throng chanted "Burn him, burn him," he was thrown onto the platform where the priests were sitting. He knelt before them and begged for mercy.

Several people, labelled as informers, have been burned to death in the past few weeks by having a tire put over their shoulders, being doused with gasoline and set alight.

He was later moved to the back of the platform, where he lay on the floor. It was too painful for him to sit. Someone pinned a UDF rosette on him and pulled up his pants. He later fell asleep with his head resting on a priest's shoe. It is not known what happened to him.

One man found drunk was made to drink liquid laundry soap. The crowd was warned by marshals that similar punishment would be meted out to anyone found with a bottle.

A report came from the graveyard, half a kilometre from the stadium, that someone had spread pepper gas, which causes sneezing and eye-watering, around the open graves.

Right Rev. Kenneth Oram, Bishop of the Anglican diocese of Grahamstown, led a group of priests and journalists off to investigate.

The bishop knelt down beside a mound of earth, sniffed, sneezed and confirmed it had been done. "It looks as if it's been deliberately scattered by somebody or their friends," he said.

From the second-floor balcony of a nearby school, police watched the group of clergy and reporters through binoculars.

There was no Bishop Desmond Tutu at the stadium service to tell people to go home peacefully when it was over.

Rather, there were speeches from firebrand union leaders, from members of the banned South African Communist Party and from the regional president of the UDF, Steve Tshwete — jailed for 15 years as a member of the banned African National Congress — who told the people to fight the police and troops.

Mr. Tshwete, a middle-aged man with thick glasses looking like a mild-mannered school-teacher, which is what he is, was brought by car to the stadium from a hiding place. The other members of the executive of the Eastern Cape UDF are in detention.

He told the crowd: "We do not want to die, but we are prepared to die for this country and our hour of preparedness is now. We will destroy everything here, and on the ashes of apartheid we will create a new South Africa."

Government buildings in Duncan Village had already been burned down, he said. "It is not going to be very long before the fires start burning in Oxford Street ('white' East London's main street)."

He was cheered.

After the burials came South Africa's set-piece theatre. First came the sound of rocks being thrown. Then a column of smoke rose from a black policeman's house within sight of the grave-yard. When it was alight, the crowd began stoning a second house nearby.

Four army armored vehicles moved against them. They stopped by the second house and the troops jumped out and a moment later came back with two men, one of them screaming, "Boss, I didn't do anything."

Nearby, a soldier was bringing his rifle butt down on the head of a prisoner.

It was a quiet night, none-the-less. Another man beaten by soldiers, a girl shot, two people reported — but the reports not confirmed — to have been hit by army trucks. An already-fire-bombed school set alight again.

Barely newsworthy.

• **1988** Foreign Reporting •
Today's footsteps in antiquity's war zone

Christopher Young

Southam News

BEIRUT — The first thing you noticed was the silence. When I entered Sabra refugee camp in the company of a Lebanese driver, nothing at first seemed to be stirring. Even our foot-steps in the sandy street sounded intrusive.

Two men lay on their backs beside a front door, their legs buckled under them. A few yards away another man was curled up on his side in the fetal position.

We turned down a narrow side street, lined with small, boxy houses made of concrete, with walled courtyards and bits of garden.

A woman of 60 or so rushed out of one of the houses as we passed. Sobbing and wailing, she shouted words of grief and rage that were not hard to understand without the language. Her hands kept making signs of short distance, a couple of feet or so, as a fisherman describes his catch.

She was saying, my Lebanese friend confirmed, that a small child was inside, shot by the "Christian" soldier who had come to Sabra camp a few hours earlier.

At the dead-end of the street was a pile of 11 male bodies, like football players frozen at the end of a play, some face down, others lying in strange positions looking up the street watching us come.

As we approached more closely, we could see the thousands of flies, crawling over the faces in the hot sun, swarming down the collars of open-necked shirts, clustered round the places in head or torso where the bullets had entered.

On top of the pile of older men was one who looked like a teenager, almost in a sitting position, his startled eyes open, looking as though he was about to get up to greet us.

There were no guns in evidence on or near any of the bodies we saw.

A CTV cameraman walking in another street saw a woman shot in the back. Other women were seen crumpled with dead children in their arms.

The Beirut French-language newspaper, *Le Jour*, reported Sunday that a witness who escaped had described how a mother had pleaded on her knees with the soldiers to spare her five-year-old son.

The officer commanding the group ordered the child killed with the reply: "Later he would grow up to become a terrorist."

In a courtyard I saw seven men sprawled between a side door and a battered old car, typical of the dented, rattling vehicles that roar and screech their way around Beirut from early morning till late at night, whatever the latest military force that claims to be restoring order in the city.

This is why the silence had seemed so striking. Beirut is a noisy place, and the refugee "camps" on its southern outskirts are only districts of the city. They are not camps in any sense that a Canadian would understand the word, although they originated with refugees from the Arab-Israeli war of 1948 who at first were housed in tents.

The atrocity of Sabra and Chatilla was carried out by soldiers of the Lebanese Forces, the army of the Christian Phalange party that controls the government.

It is also widely reported that the Christian Militia of Maj. Saad Haddad was involved. Haddad's men have controlled a large part of Southern Lebanon under Israeli direction since the civil war of 1976.

The atrocity was committed under the noses and guns of the Israeli army, which encircled the Palestinian refugee districts and could not possibly have been unaware of what was going on.

Looking down those streets next morning, where only the buzzing flies, the footsteps of reporters and cameramen, the sudden wail of the few women who had somehow missed the bullets, interrupted the unnatural silence, it was all too easy to imagine the noises that must have been heard during the massacre.

The men were mostly gunned down near their doorsteps or up against walls, presumably called out of their houses, rounded up and then shot.

The women and children were mostly killed in their houses, wherever they happened to find themselves in the gun-sight of a soldier.

The numbers killed in the massacres of Sabra and Chatilla may never be exactly known, but they are in the hundreds, perhaps over 1,000.

Correspondents have reported seeing corpses being driven away from the scene in trucks. Some bodies were scooped together with bulldozers and covered with rubble. Even if it had been possible to go into every street, courtyard and house to count the bodies, that would not be all.

The Israelis have confirmed officially that the move into the camps by the Phalange troops was jointly planned. Israeli tanks encircled the camps, covering the exit roads.

The story that the senior Israeli officer decided two hours later that things "might get out of control" and used loud-hailers in an attempt to call back the Phalange, suggests both an obtuseness and a delicacy of action that are not at all characteristic of the Israeli army.

For at least two months, Israel had held its forces back from taking the ominous step of moving into Moslem West Beirut. Last Monday, with the controlled evacuation of the PLO fighters completed, the last elements of the American-French-Italian supervisory force withdrew from Lebanon. The Lebanese army began to take control of the city.

Late Tuesday afternoon, Bashir Gemayel, leader of the Christian Phalange and president-elect of Lebanon, was assassinated in a car-bomb explosion. More than 20 other people were killed and some 60 wounded in the explosions, which wrecked the Phalange party headquarters in the Christian district of Achrafiyeh in east Beirut.

That night the Israeli army moved into the Moslem half of the city, which it had so scrupulously avoided while the PLO was there. The reason given was the need to prevent reprisals from the Christian side for what was undoubtedly a Moslem atrocity against the president-elect.

Yet when the reprisal came — horrible and indiscriminate — the Israeli forces made no effective attempt to stop it.

● **1989** Reportage à l'étranger ●
La liberté à « quel prix » ?

Gilles Blanchard

La Presse

BERLIN-EST — Après m'avoir fait visiter son appartement, Steffen a ouvert une bouteille et m'a demandé de lui redire l'émotion des téléspectateurs nord-américains devant ce Mur qui tombait et des deux Allemagnes qui s'embrassaient.

Croyant lui faire plaisir, j'ai répété ce que je lui avais raconté quelques heures plus tôt dans ce bar où nous nous étions rencontrés. Je lui ai dit comment nous avaient émus ces images historiques de la liberté retrouvée, d'Allemands dansant sur le Mur, de soldats de l'Est et de l'Ouest s'entraidant pour protéger la foule. Mille images toutes plus belles les unes que les autres. La terre avait vu l'Ouest offrir des gerbes de fleurs à l'Est. La terre s'était sentie grandie …

Sûr d'avoir bien compris, Steffen, découragé, a fermé les yeux et secoué doucement la tête.

« Dans les rues, la moitié de mes compatriotes chantent la réunification mais on n'entend pas les autres qui pleurent la disparition de leur pays », commence-t-il. Il ajoute, en pointant sa poitrine : « Le Mur est tombé mais il en reste un autre, beaucoup plus solide. »

« Le 10 décembre, moi aussi je suis allé à Berlin-Ouest. J'y suis même retourné une autre fois. On m'a serré, on m'a félicité, on m'a offert du vin et j'avoue que j'ai été surpris par l'accueil qu'on nous faisait.

« Mais j'ai aussi ressenti une humiliation profonde. Tiens, il faisait froid et j'avais le goût de ce café qu'un marchand nous offrait gratuitement. J'ai cependant refusé leur charité et j'en ai voulu à mes compatriotes de s'offrir ainsi en spectacle. Et j'ai eu tellement honte d'accepter leurs 100 marks que je les ai tout de suite dépensés.

« Nous ne sommes pas les parents pauvres de l'Allemagne. Pourquoi nous offrent-ils le passage gratuit dans leurs autobus ? »

Steffen a 27 ans. Marié, il habite un immeuble délabré de Berlin mais il a retapé son immense trois pièces avec goût. Des livres et des dictionnaires partout, en allemand, en russe, en anglais ; il est professeur de langues.

Ses études l'on conduit de son village natal à la ville voisine de Magdebourg, puis à Moscou — un an pour parfaire son russe — et à Berlin.

Enfant du système, il croyait fermement au socialisme. Il s'enorgueillissait des réussites de son Allemagne : « En URSS, j'ai visité les fermes collectives de l'arrière-pays … » Il avait lui-même profité du socialisme. Fils d'ouvriers, il avait beaucoup voyagé — dans le bloc de l'Est — et fréquenté les meilleures écoles ; il y aurait toujours un appartement et un emploi pour lui, des soirées culturelles à prix modique dans de superbes théâtres et, surtout, la satisfaction profonde de contribuer au bien-être des autres.

Et qu'importe s'il fallait rouler Trabant ou Lada usagées, porter des vêtements moins bien coupés ou continuer d'attendre que l'industrie finisse par produire suffisamment de réfrigérateurs !

Qu'importe même s'il ne pourrait jamais économiser suffisamment pour visiter l'Amérique !

Plus de 300 000 Allemands de l'Est – près de 400 000, m'a assuré un officiel — ont fui leur pays depuis l'ouverture des frontières. Par la suite, si la douzaine de brèches pratiquées dans le Mur ont rassuré, elles n'ont pas complètement stoppé l'exode. Samedi dernier, 800 autres « visiteurs » ne sont pas revenus chez eux.

La saignée est importante : les fugitifs, ceux qui se sentent la force de se battre à l'Ouest, comptent parmi les éléments les plus dynamiques de la société. Dans les hôpitaux, par exemple, on manque de médecins.

La tentation est grande. Elle a même effleuré Steffen.

Et la RDA compte des centaines de milliers de Steffen. Ils avaient pris la rue pour réclamer une plus grande liberté et manifester contre l'immobilisme des gouvernants. Au moment de crier victoire, quand « Die Mauer » est tombé, ils se sont aperçus qu'on les avait trahis. Ce n'était pas prévu.

Ces ouvriers qui dirigeaient leur pays, le modèle du socialisme, s'étaient moqués d'eux. Ils étaient profondément corrompus. Ils s'étaient construits un village de demeures princières à quelques milles de Berlin. Ils avaient transformé des territoires fauniques en terrains de chasse privés. Ils avaient détourné des sommes colossales, en précieuses devises étrangères, dans des comptes de banque en Suisse …

Ils ont volé mes rêves

« Ils étaient des ouvriers au moment où les ouvriers vivaient dans la misère, explique Steffen. Ils savaient ce qu'était la pauvreté et ils vivaient comme des riches. »

Document soumis aux dispositions du droit d'auteur. Tous droits réservés.

Fraudé par ses maîtres, trahi par ses compatriotes qui choisissent de fuir plutôt que de reprendre à zéro, incertain même du réalisme d'un système que l'URSS elle-même abandonne, Steffen sent bien que Berlin-Ouest gagnera sa campagne en faveur de la réunification.

Le capitalisme finira par triompher. Il est déchiré : s'est-il trompé toute sa vie ou la faillite du socialisme est-elle imputable à la perversité de ses leaders ?

« Je ne haïs pas l'Ouest, réfléchit-il tout haut, mais j'ai appris que Berlin-Ouest signifiait drogues, sida, criminalité et néo-nazisme. Et ici, maintenant, c'est la corruption !»

« A cause de ma maîtrise du russe et de l'anglais, je pourrais facilement gagner ma vie à l'Ouest. Je n'en ai pas vraiment ressenti le désir, mais j'ai aimé regarder ces vêtements et ces objets luxueux dans les vitrines de Berlin-Ouest … »

« Je ne sais pas ; je ne sais plus rien … »

« Ils m'ont tout enlevé, même mes rêves! »

• **1990** Feature Writing •
Conscious of the troubles in
Northern Ireland

John Gray

Globe and Mail

BELFAST — The strange, sad story of a beautiful land and the loyalties of its people is painted everywhere in large and defiant letters, in vivid images.

To the outsider they are incomprehensible tribal incantations. To those who live in Belfast, they reinforce 300 years of history, with all its loves and hates and desperate fears.

No Surrender. Ireland Unfree Shall Never be at Peace. 1690 God Save the Queen. Out of the Ashes Came the Provos. Hang All IRA Murderers. Welcome to the Loyalist Heartland of Ulster. Shankill Road No Surrender. IRA 1 RUC 0. Join the UDA. Tiocfaidh Ar La-Our Day Will Come. One Faith One Cross. Taig Scum. Belfast says No.

There are giant paintings that cover a building: King Billy's triumph for Protestantism at the battle of the Boyne in 1690, masked IRA gunmen preparing to murder for the sake of a republican dream, Union Jacks, young men who starved themselves to death in prison.

On the few occasions when there is even a shred of humor, it is grim. On a wall in the Falls Road there is a sign that says Semtex is Ozone Friendly. That is not really funny: Semtex is the gift of the now vanished Communist government of Czechoslovakia to the world of terrorism, a high-powered and almost undetectable explosive that has killed scores in car bombs throughout Northern Ireland.

These are the mean streets of Northern Ireland. These are the streets that shape the country, though most of the people of Northern Ireland are never there; they know what they know from newspapers and television.

A lucky visitor is hardly aware of the Troubles. Away from the newspapers and television, almost everywhere you go there is a deceptive normality about the place.

The green hills roll endlessly into each other. Hedgerows and stone walls and wandering country lanes divide the peaceful patchwork quilt. Nobody ever calls the North the Emerald Isle, because history has made it different. But it is the same island, and it has the same soft beauty.

As anywhere else on the island, the practiced tippler will find the easiest avenue into a conversation is through a pint of Guinness and into a debate on the nature of the rich stout that is forever Ireland. They will tell you how it has to be drawn from the cask with care, in stages, and that if the froth is right you can draw your initial with your finger on the froth and it will remain legible until the bottom of the glass.

It is not a great leap from the dark mysteries of Guinness to the beauty of the island and expressions of sympathy for a visitor who must make his home in London. It is all more welcome than the daily news.

The places that have put Belfast on the consciousness of the world — the Falls Road, the Crumlin Road, Ballymurphy, Andersonstown, Ardoyne, Shankill — are where the Protestant and Roman Catholic working classes live, each locked into its own ghetto, the ghettos divided by a 10-metre steel-and-concrete "Peace Line."

Elsewhere there are few slogans on the walls, little barbed wire, no carpet of broken glass on the streets. And the pubs and drinking clubs are not divided by religion. Waves of sectarian sympathy wash into the plushest corners of the land, but the war itself is working class.

One of the most-wanted men of the Irish Republican Army lived for months in the middle-class comfort and three-piece respectability of Belfast's Malone Road area because it never occurred to his neighbours that a terrorist might be living in their kind of neighbourhood.

As Aidan O'Reilly says: "Money transcends these stupid things." If not a lot of money, then a little money and some distance.

Out in the neat suburb of Carryduff, where Mr. O'Reilly, an ambulance driver, lives with his wife Heather and their 2-year-old son Christopher, Ballymurphy and Shankill are a world away. Life in Carryduff is, as he says, very normal.

It is a mixed Protestant and Catholic area, and when the neighbours get together everyone is careful not to mention politics or religion. There are enough reminders of Northern Ireland's problems in the newspapers and on television.

The O'Reillys are a mirror of the neighbourhood: He is Catholic, she is Protestant. Christopher will go to the integrated school that is just down the road and, with luck, his father says, "he won't have the experiences I had."

Even if he escapes those experiences, when Christopher finishes school his father will urge him to leave, as the Irish have done for generations. Mr. O'Reilly's older brother is in Calgary, a sister lives in Britain, and he thinks a younger brother and sister may leave soon.

"The whole idea is to get educated and leave."

Mr. O'Reilly would leave for Calgary tomorrow, but his wife, who grew up in middle-class comfort, is happy enough in Carryduff. She has no demons to flee.

He grew up in a predominantly Protestant neighbourhood in East Belfast, where they still talk about largely Catholic West Belfast as "the Irish side."

It was not too bad until he was in his teens, in the late 1960s, at the beginning of the Catholic-led civil rights movement. The Troubles began, and "suddenly we had to choose sides."

On Kimberly Street, as in every other mixed neighbourhood of Northern Ireland, there was a low-grade war. The kids were the worst — "I thought I was a punching bag until I was 16," Mr. O'Reilly says. Once he and several friends were shot at.

The adults were not much better. Led by a pipe band and a thundering lambeg drum whose sound still gives him the shivers, Protestant parades would detour to march menacingly up to the Catholic houses. The O'Reilly family finally moved out after Protestant vandals broke every window in the house. Elsewhere, the same kind of thing happened to Protestants, of course.

Everything is history in Northern Ireland, and everyone has a different starting point. Nationalist political leader John Hume says despairingly: "Our respect for the past paralyzes our attitude to the future."

Mr. Hume may be right. But respect for the past — sometimes it seems like wallowing in the past — is comforting. It makes the present understandable and even bearable.

For Aidan O'Reilly and thousands of his generation, history is places such as Kimberly Street and the start of the Troubles. For the Protestants in the Shankill, history is the paintings of King William of Orange astride his white horse at the Boyne. No surrender in 1690, no surrender in 1990.

There is a corner of Milltown cemetery in the heart of West Belfast that is a monument to Northern Ireland's Republican and Catholic history. There is the grave of Bobby Sands, the first of the 10 hunger strikers who died in prison in 1981, the grave of another who was hanged in 1798, the graves of three IRA gunmen who were killed by the British Army in Gibraltar in 1988, and a grave site reserved for Tom Williams, an IRA man who was hanged in 1942 and is still buried in Belfast jail.

It goes on for row after row. Murdered. Killed in Action. Shot dead by the British. Died on a prison ship. And there are lingering signs of paint bombs on a few of them, for one man's hero is another man's terrorist.

And high up in the Belfast sky there is the constant and unmistakable sound of the army helicopter that always hovers in search of trouble in the streets below. This is the newest of high technology in search of a peace that has eluded Ireland since the larger island to the east claimed a role here more than eight centuries ago.

An invading army from England first landed in Ireland in about the year 1170. Since then the struggle has never really stopped. They fought about power and land and religion with a ferocity that is frightening to recall.

Ireland's Celtic inhabitants were stubborn about their independence and about their religion. Britain became Protestant and Ireland remained Catholic. Even the terrors of Oliver Cromwell did not cure the Irish of that. Then Britain tried to overwhelm them by numbers. Boatloads of Scottish Protestants were sent to establish a plantation in the northeast corner of Ireland that is now Northern Ireland.

Catholic graffiti in Belfast occasionally describes Protestants as "planters" and "visitors," as though they arrived just last year for a temporary stay. In fact they began arriving in 1606, at about the time Samuel de Champlain was founding a shaky little settlement at what is now Quebec City.

For Britain, the solution of the Irish problem was finally partition of the island. The dividing line separated 26 largely Catholic counties in the south and north west from the six largely Protestant counties of the north east that remained a province of the United Kingdom.

But history was not so easily settled, for "largely" is not all. The Protestants who had been a minority in the whole island were at last a comfortable and unthreatened majority in the north.

But there remained a Catholic minority, about a third of Northern Ireland's 1.5 million people. The civil rights struggles of the late 1960s and early 1970s were about blatant discrimination in housing, in education, in employment, and before the law.

When those complaints were rejected by a majority that would not relinquish its advantages, the Troubles began. And once they began they could not be stopped, because on one side or the other there is always a death to avenge.

South of the village of Crossmaglen the road crosses into the Republic and then back again before you have any idea you are in another country. Only someone who knows the area can tell you where the border goes — from that fence, along the side of the barn and then the concrete wall to the middle of the road, down the road for half a kilometre and then left along that hedgerow.

But it is not what it seems. Crossmaglen is Bandit Country. The village square is dominated by a police station that looks like a fortress of barbed wire and concrete, a steel-plated lookout tower, aerials, television cameras.

On the highest of the surrounding hills are fortified lookouts from which British soldiers survey the countryside. The soldiers are usually flown in by helicopter because even armored vehicles are easy targets for bombs on these narrow roads. Local history is a sniper here, a car bomb there, and a mortar attack from behind that hill.

At the headquarters of the Royal Ulster Constabulary in Belfast, they assure you that the crime rate in Northern Ireland is lower than anywhere else in Britain. Homicides per 100,000 of population: Detroit 59, Washington 31, Northern Ireland 7. Anyway, less than 10 per cent of crime relates to terrorism.

Still, the toll is grim. Since the Troubles began, more than 2,800 police, soldiers, paramilitary activists and innocent civilians have died as a result of shooting or bombs. More than 33,000 have been wounded.

In the package of crime statistics distributed by the RUC, it is carefully noted that in the same period car accidents accounted for 5,500 deaths and 120,000 injuries.

But of course you don't think about car accidents the same way. They are, after all, accidents. You do not have patrols of men with dogs and automatic weapons sweeping through the commercial centre of Belfast to stop car accidents.

It pervades the society. A few days after two men had been shot on the Antrim Road within an hour of each other, several people in North Belfast were talking about adapting their lives to a society where there are deliberate assassinations and random sectarian killings.

You stick with your own kind. You drive the children rather than letting them walk or take the bus. You make sure you don't go drinking in pubs and clubs that you don't know; otherwise you might not get home again.

"You're always listening to the news," one elderly woman said. "And I for one don't go to bed at all without ringing the whole family to see that they're all in their own homes and safe. And I suppose there are thousands like me around here."

For the better part of two decades the British government has been trying to find some balance of power in Northern Ireland that would suit both the Protestant and Catholic communities. So far a solution has proved elusive.

In deference to Catholic complaints, the limited self-government enjoyed by Northern Ireland was suspended in 1972. Everything except municipal government now is run from London. Every attempt to give the Catholic community some share of power has been fought bitterly by the Protestant majority.

Perhaps the start of a solution came in 1985. To the consternation of the Protestants in the various "Unionist" parties, London and Dublin agreed that they should consult regularly about Northern Ireland affairs and they should co-operate on security along their unmanned and unmarked border.

The Catholic Nationalists were delighted; for the Protestants this was involving a foreign government in Northern Ireland's affairs. The result has been a stalemate.

In recent months the British cabinet minister responsible for Northern Ireland, Peter Brooke, has been talking patiently with every shade of political opinion except Sinn Fein, the political arm of the IRA. But the stalemate continues.

When Rhonda Paisley talks of Northern Ireland's troubles, there seems at first a tone of conciliation and change. She is 31, an artist, and a Unionist city councillor in Belfast. An exhibition of her paintings has just opened in Dublin.

She talks of the young people of Northern Ireland who do not care about the quarrels of the past and who just want to get on with their lives. There is no justification for killing on either side, she says. "Catholic tears are no different from Protestant tears."

It is important to understand Ms Paisley's background. For more than 20 years her father has been the single most powerful figure in Northern Ireland. Rev. Ian Paisley, head of the Democratic Unionist Party, head of his own Free Presbyterian Church, is the implacable enemy of republicanism, nationalism and Catholicism.

British leaders have assumed that Mr. Paisley himself will not be won over. But they have always hoped that a younger generation of Unionist would view the island differently.

Ms Paisley is clearly different. Her father has made a career of defiance and rage; he describes the Catholic Church as the whore of Babylon and the Pope as the anti-Christ.

By contrast Ms Paisley is quite moderate. But on the essentials of Northern Ireland politics, nothing has changed. North and South can be good neighbours, but there can be nothing beyond co-operation, she says. She shrugs off Catholic concerns about rule by the Protestant majority. She is contemptuous of the Anglo-Irish Agreement.

John Hume has been the tribune of moderate Catholic nationalism for almost as long as Ian Paisley has been leading Northern Ireland's Protestants. He was one of those who pushed hardest for the Anglo-Irish Agreement. By rights he should be dispirited, but he doesn't seem to be.

He thinks that somehow time is on his side. Northern Ireland's problem is out of date and the quarrel is out of date, he says. He returns again and again to Europe. If Greeks, Italians, French and Germans can forge new relationships, why not the two parts of Ireland?

"We need an agreement on how to share the island. Then the future will take care of the relationship, because, having extracted the poison, people will grow together at their own speed."

There is not so much optimism when Rev. Tom Toner talks about the future. In Belfast's Andersonstown he lives at the sharp end of the Northern Ireland problem. In St. Agnes parish the unemployment rate among young men is 35 or 40 per cent.

"If you scattered 100,000 jobs around, that would make a difference," Father Toner says. "The whole thing would be transformed."

At that, Andersonstown is comparatively lucky. In areas like Ballymurphy the unemployment rate is closer to 80 per cent. Some of them will never get jobs.

Belfast seems to be riding something of an economic boom these days, but that is not a promise of jobs for everyone. Some of the jobless, he says, are afraid to leave the comfort of their own neighbourhood because of the danger of sectarian attacks. Some, because of lack of education, do not qualify for work. And some have been defeated by the despair of an underachieving society.

Father Toner has seen it all. He has lived in the parish all of his life. It is the kind of place you leave if you can. Only one family remains from the time when he was growing up.

He has been outspoken in his condemnation of terrorism, which has won him no friends in the IRA. But he was the prison chaplain at Long Kesh when the 10 young hunger strikers died. He has had to conduct funeral services for young IRA men shot by British soldiers and he has had to comfort their grieving parents.

To the outsider it seems an unreasonable and intolerable burden. Father Toner smiles. "We are always conscious of the Troubles. But you can't afford to be obsessed with it." But his is a sad smile.

• **1992** International Reporting •

Wife trade takes off in China

Jan Wong

Globe and Mail

GUBEIKOU, China — Ma Linmei's wedding was only in November, but she can no longer remember the date.

No wonder. She did not know any of the 150 or so guests invited to the feast. She scarcely knew her husband. What is seared in her memory is the amount he paid for her: 2,000 yuan ($425) — about four times what he spent on his tape recorder.

Sitting in her stone cottage in the shadow of the Great Wall, she ducks her head so that her hair masks her eyes. She plays nervously with the zipper on her cheap, green windbreaker and whispers that she wants to escape.

"But if I tried, they would beat me. I can't anyway," Ms Ma, 21, adds in despair. "I have no money."

The breakdown of Communist controls in rural China has brought prosperity to the countryside. But as capitalist-style reforms are liberating the economy, women are finding themselves enslaved as they were in feudal times. Before 1949, women were routinely sold as wives and concubines. By tightening controls over the countryside, Beijing stopped the practice in the 1950s.

Now, for the first time since the Communists took power, the buying and selling of women is becoming epidemic. This month, the problem reached the capital. Operating on a tip, police arrested a gang who had abducted at least five women from Beijing in the past two months.

No national statistics are available for 1991. But more than 10,000 women were rescued in 1990, the official *Legal Daily* says. In some regions, as many as 17 per cent of families had bought wives, it said. A published Western report, citing confidential documents, said authorities investigated 18,692 cases of abducted women in 1990.

The actual number could be much bigger because many cases are never reported. An abducted woman who subsequently has a child is less likely to leave her new home. If she is rescued, the husband usually keeps any male children as the price of her freedom. Any woman who returns to her home village will probably be stigmatized as a "broken shoe," an epithet for a prostitute.

In an interview, the Chongqing Women's Federation said that "even if a woman is sold, if she puts up with it, then it is legal under the Marriage Law." In an actual case described in confidential documents, authorities accused an abducted woman of bigamy; it turned out she was already married but had resigned herself to living with her new "husband."

China's economic boom of the 1980s has made trafficking in women a big business. In contrast to the the old days, gangs operate far-flung networks, transporting victims to distant provinces where they cannot speak the local dialect. Equipped with walkie-talkies, portable telephones and cars, the traffickers easily out-manoeuvre local police. Even if the women are rescued, they rarely can tell police much about their abductors.

In this isolated mountain-gully village of 11 families, Ms Ma is surrounded by her husband's clan. If she wants to write a letter home, she must depend on him. (Like many rural women, she is illiterate; her father pulled her out of third grade to work in his moonshine business.)

She cannot communicate easily, because of the different dialects.

"When she first came, she didn't understand a word," says her husband's 19-year-old cousin, Wang Shuping, who is unsure of her own marital fate.

The only way out of the village is by foot or bicycle, and Ms Ma does not know how to ride. The general store is 15 kilometres away by a winding road that is cut off each summer when the river overflows.

"Even if she wanted to run away, she couldn't," her husband's 62-year-old aunt said with a satisfied chuckle. "Where would she run to?"

Trafficking in women has flourished because of classic supply and demand. For the middle man, there is low overhead, high profit and minimal risk. Women are sold for an average of 1.5 year's pay for a state worker. And until recently, penalties were less than five years, the same as for the theft of two cows. (Authorities toughened penalties in the fall so that minimum sentences are now five years.)

On the supply side, rural unemployment has forced hundreds of thousands of impoverished women to seek work in the cities. "They're uneducated, so they're gullible," said Xiao Yang, Communist Party Secretary of Chongqing, China's biggest metropolis.

On the demand side, female infanticide and selective sex-based abortions have led to a male-female imbalance in the countryside. That, coupled with the desperate desire of women in poor villages to marry up and out, has created "bachelor armies."

"Women in the mountains want to marry someone in the foothills. Those in the foothills want into the plains. And those in the plains want into the cities," said Qu Weijia, a Beijing filmmaker who has researched the topic of bride-selling.

In this mountainous region, where stunted corn struggles to grow in rock-strewn gullies, the men have trouble finding willing wives.

Ms Ma's purchaser, Wang Chengguo, had grown anxious after several local women rejected him. A slight man with a pinched face and bushy hair prematurely streaked with grey from malnutrition, he was considered a poor choice: A weakling in an agrarian society where prosperity depends on brawn.

"I tried for two years to find a wife around here. People said I was too thin," said Mr. Wang, 24, as he untied a sack of pig feed from the back of his bicycle.

So last fall, he and two friends went on a bride-buying expedition. Mr. Wang chose Yunnan province, 2,000 kilometres to the south, because southern women have a reputation for working hard.

Four women and their families had already rejected Mr. Wang when he began negotiating with Ms Ma's father. Ten days later, the three of them boarded a train. When they arrived here, her father was shocked by the poverty.

"'How can your home be like this?" Mr. Wang remembers her father exclaiming. "I said, 'We told you our mountains were bigger.'"

Unlike the lush rice fields of Yunnan, the mountains are so steep here that the villagers say there is no direct sunlight for 40 consecutive days in winter. But Ms Ma's father was not upset enough to renege on the deal. He duly saw his daughter wed, and he departed 20 days later, leaving her with two changes of clothing and 10 yuan, 0.5 per cent of her bride price.

Unlike Ms Ma, many victims are lured with phony job offers at railway stations and bus stops. Others are drugged and abducted. Some men are simply trying to economize; an abducted woman costs half as much as throwing a traditional wedding, with lavish presents to the bride's family and local officials. And because peasant men regard wives chiefly as a means to produce the next generation, retarded women are popular.

"They are honest, don't run away, can live in peace with their husbands and yet still give birth to babies," a report said last year in the official Chinese News Agency.

One ring in Sichuan recently abducted and sold 22 mentally-ill women, according to *Chinese Women's News*. Cheng Jianwen, the ringleader, got the idea when he spotted several disoriented women wandering outside hospitals while he was searching for his own mentally-ill wife, who had run away from home.

But even sophisticated urban women are not immune. In a celebrated case a few years ago, a postgraduate student from a university in Shanghai was sold to a peasant. The woman, a Communist Party member and a class leader, was rescued after 71 days.

One problem is a lack of public awareness. While the official press often prints stories about abductions, most victims are illiterate. The government has eschewed other mass media for fear of tarnishing China's public image. Mr. Qu, the filmmaker, said his feature film on abducted women was cancelled while he was still scouting locations because of sensitivity to exposing the "dark side" of society.

"We only like to do positive propaganda," said Wang Zijun, an official of the Chongqing Women's Federation. As an example, she said that a television announcer recently read out the text of the new abduction law.

Victims include women of all ages. Some, like Ms Ma, are sold by their male relatives. In about half the known cases involving professional traffickers, the women are raped before being sold. Those who try to fight off one husband may be resold to another. One married woman whose abductors didn't realize she had been sterilized was resold four times.

Wang Jinliang, Wang Chengguo's grandfather, was an underground Communist Party member when this village served as a base for guerrilla fighters. He said he didn't spend any money for his own wife.

"She came on her own," says Mr. Wang, who at 88 is the same age as Chinese leader Deng Xiaoping. Born in the twilight of the Qing dynasty, he sees nothing wrong with his grandson's recent acquisition. "I really have no thoughts on it," he says, stroking his wispy white goatee and scratching his bare leg.

But Zhang Wenjun, 26, a neighbour who married for love, pities Ms Ma. "It's very painful for these women. They sacrifice themselves so their families can get money. But they aren't compatible at all with their husbands," she says.

Although Wang Chengguo spent only 2,000 yuan on Ms Ma, he thinks she may not have been such a bargain. Pining for home, she has lost so much weight her cheeks are hollow. Now she complains of anemia and refuses to work in the fields. He is envious of the two friends with whom he went bride-buying.

"Their wives are fine. Their constitutions are better," he says.

In a rare moment of privacy, Ms Ma whispers to a visitor that she will not have sexual intercourse with her husband. "He sleeps here. I sleep there," she says, motioning to opposite ends of the clay kang, the heated sleeping platform in their room.

Some families lose patience with reluctant wives. According to the official *China Youth* newspaper, the entire family may hold the woman down while her husband rapes her.

"Many peasant families ignore the resistance and tears," it said. "They think that after a while, she'll get used to it, that she'll cry a little, but after she has a baby she'll be obedient."

That is what happened to She Rongxiu. Eight years ago, Ms She (pronounced sher) answered a personal ad in the newspaper from a man looking for a wife. She was 20 then, and he dangled before her the chance to live in Beijing.

"I wanted to come to the capital, the big city," she recalled bitterly.

He sent 70 yuan for a train ticket from her home in Guangxi, 2,000 kilometres to the south. On arrival, she discovered her new husband was a peasant and her home was a hillside village. He had not actually lied; technically, the village, 100 kilometres east of Beijing, is part of the capital.

"As soon as I arrived, I wanted to leave. I hated it. This place was worse than where I came from," Ms She said.

As a sign of her low status, her new in-laws did not even bother to have a wedding feast. Almost immediately, she became pregnant. When her daughter, Hai Yan, was 100 days old, Ms She went home to her mother. "I didn't want to come back," she said. After a year, and a visit from her husband, she reluctantly returned.

But the village still treats her like an outsider. It has not given her a residence permit so she has not been allotted any farm land. And because children follow their mother's residence permit, her two children are not allowed to attend the village school. Hai Yan, now eight, lives with Ms She's mother in Guangxi so she can go to school.

A neighbour, an older woman, tries to comfort Ms She, pointing out that 20 other women in the village arrived as bartered brides. "Really, no matter where you are, you'd have to work hard. Life is about the same."

Ms She's second child, four-year-old Hai Ping, shyly enters the room. The bitterness evaporates as a smile transforms Ms She's face. Asked if she ever thought of leaving, she shrugs.

"What would my children do," she says, "without a mother?"

• **1993** International Reporting •
Mogadishu Diary

Paul Watson
Toronto Star

MOGADISHU — It was the thing to do at the Sahafi Hotel, after a long, hot day watching the war, to get a cold beer or a cocktail and go to the roof to see the helicopters in the sunset.

But with the latest hostage threat and all, there weren't many of us left on the October evening when fewer than a dozen American choppers were circling silently in the distance.

The four of us on the hotel roof — two journalists, a Somali interpreter and a contract worker with the United Nations — were actually a little bored.

It didn't look like much at first. Maybe a training exercise, or another botched snatch attempt in the long and bloody hunt for warlord Mohamed Farah Aideed.

Then there was a small, bright yellow flash of a rocket-propelled grenade exploding just behind the tail rotor of a U.S. Black Hawk helicopter that disappeared behind a hill.

Within minutes, as dusk fell, a convoy of about 12 U.S. army trucks and Humvees with probably 100 soldiers in them inched through the traffic circle across from the hotel.

From the rooftop, we could see dozens of Somalis running down back alleys with rifles and grenade launchers to ambush the troops on a mission to rescue their comrades from a crashed helicopter across town.

When the Americans came under fire, they opened up on any building they could see. Our low-rise hotel was one of the first targets.

We hit the floor, and pressed as flat as we could, while tracer bullets burning a fiery orange hissed barely an inch above the metre-high parapet just beside us.

Then the parapet burst into hunks of concrete that showered over us as a grenade blasted through the thin wall, leaving a rectangular hole almost a metre across.

All I could think was that the next one was going to hurt and, please God, don't let it hit my head.

And then another grenade hit with an explosion that left a steady buzz in my ears and sprayed more chunks of concrete everywhere.

The metal fragments we picked out of the rubble the next day were from U.S.-made 40 mm grenades, the same kind fired from launchers on U.S. army Humvees.

The raging battle that changed the course of the peacemaking war on Oct. 3 had begun, but it would be suicidal to go out at night for a closer look.

So we crawled downstairs and sat in the hallway as eight more grenades hammered the hotel over the next hour while I pleaded on a walkie-talkie for someone to get the soldiers to stop shooting at us.

When they finally did, we went back to our rooms, wrote the little that we knew, and settled in to watch fuzzy live coverage on CNN of Russians fighting in the streets of Moscow.

Mogadishu would have to wait until the next morning when my 31-year-old armed guard, Mohomud Hersi Ali, arrived with his AK-47 and we headed out to see the damage from 16 hours of all-out war.

Ali wanted backup for a trip into Mogadishu's most ruthless neighbourhood, where gunmen walk freely with heavy machineguns and rocket-propelled grenade launchers.

So another armed guard, a middle-aged man I'd never seen before, got into the back seat with me and pointed the barrel of his battered M16 assault rifle out the window as a warning.

We soon passed Somalis carrying away their dead slung in torn grain sacks or stacked in the back of pick-up trucks like cords of wood.

And we stopped at the smoldering wreckage of a downed U.S. Black Hawk helicopter where jubilant Somalis pointed the way to the dead American soldier being dragged through the dusty streets.

I wanted proof of the grisly procession because the last time journalists reported that Somalis were parading American bodies the Pentagon flatly insisted it simply didn't happen.

That denied the very essence of what was going on in Mogadishu, the daily brutality of a war in which helicopters fired at women and children and captured soldiers were tortured and torn to pieces.

And there were no pictures, apart from those of people waving strips of scorched flesh from sticks, to show just how far humanity had fallen in Mogadishu.

After about 20 minutes of stopping at each block in what was still a war zone to ask passersby if they'd seen the American's body, we were almost ready to give up and go home.

Then my driver, 43-year-old Mohamed Mohomud Ahmed, spotted a mob moving slowly down a steep side street, and he made a U-turn.

Our white, air-conditioned Toyota Cressida pulled up behind the seething crowd of about 200

Somalis and my gunmen got out to get permission for me to look.

I followed, with a camera slung around my neck, and the mob parted to show the ravaged corpse that was naked except for his green, U.S. army underwear.

His arms, bound at the wrists by thick ropes, were pulled up over his head and the Somalis hauling the body around made it flip back and forth like some horrid puppet as the crowd cheered.

Someone spat on the bloody and mutilated corpse and then an old man pounded it as hard as he could with his wooden cane.

As the mob grew more frenzied, my gunmen pulled me away and into the car, afraid that the blood rage was about to turn on us.

It was when the swarming crowd closed round the corpse again and moved on with their prey that I realized I needed more pictures.

In the few that I had, the dead American's underwear were askew, and as horrifying as the photos were, I thought the sight of a penis, not a mutilated corpse, would make them unpublishable.

I told Mohamed to drive after the crowd as it turned a corner, still dragging the corpse, and pausing every few minutes to invite more people to desecrate it.

My gunmen argued and said it was too dangerous, so I jumped out of the car and they had little choice but to follow me into the mob.

I'd taken just a few more pictures when my guards pulled me away again and pushed me into the back seat because they'd heard threats in Somali that I didn't understand.

As we sped off, I noticed I was trembling.

The faces on the street were a blur and I wondered whether the soul, maybe the ghost of a man I could never know, had watched what I had done. I prayed he would forgive me.

And so began another day of life in Mogadishu.

■ ■ ■

It's amazing how mundane madness becomes when you're surrounded by it for far too long.

Suddenly it isn't unusual for mothers and their kids to stand on street corners laughing as men shoot at each other a few metres away and the bullets whistle overhead.

Thousands of buildings, most anything standing in fact, are pock-marked with bullet holes or the shrapnel spray from grenades and shells.

Yet after time, they're just houses, homes and shops that could use a little fixing up.

And you're not shocked anymore at the sight of a little girl lying on a hospital floor in her own blood without a tear in her eye.

And you expect surgeons to work 26-hour shifts to save Somalis wounded in the war, pausing only to donate their own blood because the supplies have run out.

There is nothing normal about Mogadishu, unless you're among the damned who have to live there.

Once a white pearl on the Indian Ocean, one of Africa's most beautiful cities is now a ruin shared among foreign soldiers, Somali gunmen and the innocents caught between them.

Most of the cars were looted long ago, or locked up somewhere until the dreamed of day when it's safe to drive them again.

Until then, most of Mogadishu's more than 1 million people have to walk or buy rides on minibus taxis that wouldn't get more than a stare of disbelief from a scrap dealer.

They sputter down the streets spewing oily black smoke, often with a dozen or more people clinging on to the sides and the rear end or sitting on the roof.

Being a passenger takes skill because many of the taxis run with a 45-degree list and look ready to tip over if someone leans a little too much.

The only thing holding some of the worst ones together is rust, rubber straps, twine and a lot of hope.

Few of the taxis or cars have any windows and those that do usually have a bullet hole with a spider web crack around it somewhere in the area off the driver's head.

Somali car looters rarely take the risk of ordering someone to stop and get out. It's a lot simpler to just kill them.

■ ■ ■

Despite the banditry and Aideed's war with the UN, there isn't severe hunger in Mogadishu anymore and the markets are full of fruits, vegetables and meat butchered with axes.

Several hotels have even reopened and one, named after mountains that were named after women's breasts, has an outdoor restaurant like a lush oasis where waiters in black tuxedos serve roasted lobster, espresso and liqueurs.

Trouble is it's right on the front line of recent clan battles and heavy gunfire is hardly good for business.

The United Nations Development Program has managed to keep water running in much of the city.

Yet it's still so precious that one clan's plan to tap a water main last month provoked a battle with guns and rocket-propelled grenades that lasted a day and a half and killed at least one Somali.

Those who can afford to, buy water from vendors, often small boys who go door-to-door with donkey carts dispensing water from dented drums.

A few hundred thousand refugees still live in camps in and around the capital and many depend on wells or pools of water that bubble up from broken pipes.

One of the watering holes is in a field of rubble beside the walled UN compound where peace-keepers blew up all the houses to stop snipers from hiding in them.

Somali kids used the sloping slabs of concrete from the pancaked buildings as skateboard ramps for a while. But then some men chased them off so they could hammer away and salvage rusting steel reinforcing rods.

About the only entertainment the children had left was pestering soldiers, or pelting them with rocks on the bad days, building roadblocks with their mothers or watching war.

■ ■ ■

You'd think the men who do the fighting had seen enough of the real thing to make seeing the movie version a waste of money. Not so, says Mogadishu's film theatre mogul, Ali Hassan Mohamed.

Mohamed, who has 10 brothers and sisters living in Canada, was in pre-med at Brandeis University in Massachusetts when his father died and he had to return to Somalia 11 years ago.

He's been in the movie business ever since as the owner of Cinema Ekwatore, an open-air t heatre on a busy corner that's been in the middle of some heavy firefights.

When battles break out, theatre-goers simply take cover under the balcony and keep watching the film, said Mohamed, 47.

"When the shooting starts, people keep quiet," he added. "It's usually just for 10 minutes, or half an hour at the most. We don't stop the movie unless the bullets come inside. But that's never happened."

To make sure there's no bloodletting inside the theatre, Mohamed's armed security guards frisk customers at the door and make them check anything lethal for pickup on the way out.

The picture signs above the front door make the policy plain: No assault rifles, no knives, no pistols and no walking sticks.

"Inside, there are a lot of young people who might quarrel and beat each other," Mohamed explained. "A cane is a weapon too."

His projector has been on the fritz lately because it needs a light bulb that can't be found anywhere in Somalia.

But when business is good, Mohamed packs in more than 200 people a night on corroded metal stacking chairs, several of which only have three legs.

"I have to fix them, but I'm waiting for complete peace," Mohamed said, sounding a touch embarrassed. "If I do it now, people will come in and loot. They like new things."

Mohamed's formula is simple: Play the soppy stuff first when the customers are still arriving in the darkness and then give them what they came for — war movies.

"Students and intellectuals, big people, come here," Mohamed said proudly. "They don't want to fight among themselves, but they want other people to kill one another."

The top two favourites in Mogadishu's main movie theatre are Sylvester Stallone's *Rambo* and Chuck Norris in *Delta Force Commando*.

Sure, Somali movie buffs know the ultra-secret Delta Force commandos were in town trying to arrest Aideed and probably took part in the shooting that killed scores of his supporters, Mohamed said.

Yet they still cheer Chuck Norris when he gets a good shot in.

"When you watch a movie, you want the good guy to win," Mohamed explained. "And in the movie, Delta Force are the good guys, so they want Chuck Norris to win."

■ ■ ■

A few kilometres away, at least 5,000 soldiers and civilians live and work inside the heavily defended walls of the UN compound in a sweeping stretch of land that used to be the U.S. embassy.

The property is so big that the Americans were putting in a nine-hole golf course before the dictator Washington had propped up, Mohamed Siad Barre, was overthrown by Aideed's guerrillas in January, 1991.

In the largest embassy evacuation since the fall of Saigon, U.S. marine helicopters airlifted the American embassy staff and other foreign diplomats who had taken refuge there.

But it didn't get much attention anywhere else because thousands more U.S. and foreign soldiers were staring down Iraqi troops in the desert, ready to do battle in the war to liberate Kuwait.

As the helicopters hovered and headed back to sea, Somali guerrillas spilled over the walls and went on a months-long looting spree.

They even drove off with one of the embassy's black Cadillac limousines with tinted windows which reappears from time to time on Mogadishu's streets.

When the UN moved in, and the war with Aideed began in June, the compound became Africa's largest trailer park to provide enough offices and bedrooms for everything from commanders to secretaries.

Sally Ager-Harris, 28, and Louise Gare, 24, both work for the UN's chief here, retired U.S. Adm. Jonathan Howe, and they've been stuck inside the compound's four walls for almost five months.

They knew they were coming to a war zone when they arrived from Geneva looking for something new in June, but no one told them it would end up this bad.

"We knew of someone who had been out here with Medicins sans Frontieres (Doctors without Borders) and she'd been shot up," Gare said.

"We thought there might be a bit of shooting, but nothing like this."

It's too dangerous for them on Mogadishu's streets, so the two English women had to get a lift from a helicopter to the airport just to spend an afternoon on the beach.

The helicopter shuttles were cancelled when Aideed's guerrillas threatened to blow military choppers out of the sky, a promise they carried out with devastating effect.

Aideed declared a ceasefire a month ago when U.S. President Bill Clinton ordered his troops to back off from the disastrous manhunt for the warlord, accused of masterminding the murder of 24 Pakistani peacekeepers in June.

But the almost daily mortar, rocket and grenade attacks on the UN compound are still frighteningly fresh in the minds of anyone who works or lives there.

Ager-Harris, Gare and the rest of the UN staff carry heavy flak jackets and combat helmets with them to work each morning and then lug them home again each night.

To kill time until the next day's work, they can watch videos or tune into the Armed Forces Radio and Television Service, known in the military as A-FARTS.

It broadcasts on two FM frequencies with country music, soft rock, hard rock, rap, news, talk shows and live sports.

The TV station shows *David Letterman, The Tonight Show with Jay Leno, The Simpsons, CNN, Good Morning America*, even the World Series in the dead of night.

A steady diet of Letterman prompted the UN workers to come up with their own Top 10 lists, including The Top 10 Reasons for Extending Your Stay in Somalia.

Number one was free malaria tablets.

The disc jockeys on armed forces radio called Mogadishu "The Mog" for the longest time until things started going wrong and then they switched to calling it "The Dish."

Some say it's because the soldiers suddenly felt like they were under a microscope as part of a scary experiment.

Ty Kendrick is a former Military Police officer who guarded nuclear missile sites in Europe for 12 years before jumping to civilian radio, where he got messed up on drugs and alcohol, then cleaned up and finally signed up for a tour with armed forces radio.

His mission is to boost the morale of a force that's feeling beaten and sold-out by the politicians who sent them to Somalia without a clearly defined mission.

"They want to know that somebody gives a shit about them," said Kendrick, 32, of Nashville, Tenn. "And I care about those guys because I've been where they're at."

• 1994 International Reporting •
Moscow farewell

John Gray

Globe and Mail

MOSCOW — When the changes began three years ago, Alexandra Yeremeyeva, red-haired and lightning-quick with her scissors, known to everyone as Sasha, charged eight rubles for a haircut in a dingy second-floor salon in the Hotel Ukraine. She gave a half shrug in half apology when she took the money. Inflation, she said.

Inflation or not, Sasha was convenient. The Hotel Ukraine, one of seven gigantic wedding-cake buildings bestowed on Moscow by Joseph Stalin, is just across Kutuzovsky Prospect from my office. Sasha cuts hair as well as almost anyone, and faster than anyone I've ever seen. And even with inflation, the price was not bad — eight rubles was 25 cents.

Since that summer of 1991, as the Soviet Union started to crumble and Russia began moving away from communism and toward a market economy, Sasha has been one of my barometers of economic change. Last week her half shrug suggested amazement only, because people like her have stopped apologizing for raising prices. My haircut, she said, would be 5,000 rubles.

For a Canadian visitor, 5,000 rubles is still a bargain. Where else can you get a good haircut for $3.50? Even for Russians, when costs are measured against incomes, the price is not much. But the sheer increase — a jump of more than 600-fold in three years —is disturbing.

Three years ago, a kilogram of chicken sold for less than six rubles; today it is more than 3,000. Boiled sausage was eight or nine rubles, and now is almost 10,000. Buckwheat, the staple porridge of most Russians, especially the poor, is almost 800 times more expensive. A cabbage that used to cost two rubles costs more than 3,000.

Is it any wonder that the faces on the streets of Moscow and every other Russian city are strained and a bit desperate? Is it any wonder that Sasha, even with a monthly salary of 250,000 rubles, looks back with fondness on the good old, stable days of three years ago, when she earned just 200?

This is a society shattered by change. For a few people, the new ways have been invigorating, liberating and wonderful. For the others — even for the majority whose lives have been measurably improved — the metamorphosis has been so profound and unsettling that change has become a dirty word.

Sasha's income is not a king's ransom but she earns more than her sister-in-law, a scientist, who makes 50,000 rubles a month. Sasha's husband and their 20-year-old son also work, and the family has a three-room apartment, which means they live much better than most of Sasha's friends. But she is not happy.

Life today, she thinks, is far worse than it was. Like most Russians she is oppressed by crime. Criminals and hooligans are everywhere. Look at the young thugs in their expensive Western cars on Moscow's streets. Where do they get their money? They must steal it from someone, somewhere.

"Everything is beyond the limit — inflation, crime, everything." She once had no concern about the thoroughfares of Moscow. She attended just about every play performed in the city; theatre was one of the riches of her life. Now she is afraid to go out at night; she stays in the safety of her home and watches television.

She has not suffered personally from crime, but the son of a friend was murdered not long ago. Nobody knows why. Most Moscovites seem to have friends who have been robbed or murdered. Their worst fears were confirmed last week by horrifying television pictures of a corpse sitting upright in the driver's seat of a car, its head blown off by a car bomb. Police believe the underworld was trying to settle a score with a prominent businessman but got his chauffeur instead.

Crime is not as bad as it is in New York or Washington. But not long ago Moscow and every other Russian city was safe and peaceful. The state was rigidly controlled; the police were everywhere and knew everything. Now the all-powerful state seems almost powerless, and the police are incompetent, corrupt and regarded with total contempt. Perhaps equally unsettling is that Russia — especially Moscow — looks different. The market economy has let in Western commercialism, the most visible evidence being a profusion of billboards, neon signs and illuminated window displays.

The sight is shocking to Russians. Until a few years ago, the only signs were giant red banners, strung across main streets or draped on public buildings, that exhorted the brave and loyal Soviet peoples to build communism, to salute the solidarity of working people everywhere and to strive for world peace (or for whatever the ideological flavour of the month was).

In a way, the old banners were welcome: They interrupted the seamless grey monotony of most Soviet cities. An English woman confessed she kept getting lost during the year she spent studying in a small provincial city. She could not tell one neighbourhood from another, one street from another, sometimes not one building from another.

In those days, shops were few and far between, and they were dark and unwelcoming. If you were lucky, the bread store had a faded and dirty sign that said Hleb (bread), the store that sold dairy produce said Moloko (milk), and the vegetable store said Produkty (products).

Then things started to change, and nothing was more dramatic than the arrival of sidewalk kiosks, with their glittering displays of cigarettes, liquor, beer, chocolate bars, women's underwear, electronic calculators, sex magazines, radios and video cassettes — most of it Western, all of it previously unavailable.

Some of the kiosks are being removed, but those that remain are the most vigorous evidence of a growing market economy and they are a startling addition to the bland streets. Citizens disturbed by the unsightly outriders of commercialism are not mollified by the knowledge that Russia's kiosk trade is controlled by underworld gangs.

Another aspect of commercialism is the sudden ubiquity of the Western alphabet. Moscow city government tried to enforce a law requiring advertisements to be in Russian, with the Cyrillic alphabet, but that battle seems to have been won by Western chic. Billboards proclaim the virtues of cigarettes called Dallas, West and Hollywood, and boast in English of "American blend and international quality."

The ultimate symbol is best seen from the upper floors of a massive structure that used to be the Soviet state-planning office. It is now the new home of the state Duma, the lower house of parliament. As Russian deputies look toward the north, they see a large neon sign with Western lettering that says Samsung. For people like Maria Mestikhovskaya, Western influence is distant and remote, like a Mercedes passing on the street. She is 79, once held a good job in a factory and now has a pension of 60,000 rubles a month. She doesn't mind the Western ways in the new Russia, but you can't buy much Western for 60,000 rubles. "I was once in a hard-currency store. When I looked at things I just opened my mouth like a crow. Clothing, cosmetics, everything. My son said 'Let's go,' but I said 'No, not yet, I haven't seen everything.'" Even she is riding change. In February she moved from a communal apartment in which she had lived for 40 years where she was, she says, like a prisoner chained to a trolley.

Communal apartments were one of the truly destructive aspects of Soviet life. Individuals, sometimes whole families, were crowded into a single room; other individuals, or families, were crammed into other rooms, and they all shared the kitchen and bathroom.

Small wonder that communal apartments have a special place in the history of Soviet wretchedness.

Ms Mestikhovskaya's new apartment is on the outskirts of Moscow, and she doesn't mind. Her main room is the same size as her old apartment, and she has a hallway, a kitchen and a bathroom all to herself, a total of 31 square metres. In Canadian terms it is pitifully small, but she is revelling in it. She has rearranged her furniture three times.

"For 40 years I lived in that damned apartment. I couldn't do it any more. This is not exactly what I wanted, but I'm happy." One drawback is cost. The rent is much higher, and to get a phone her son had to pay out $500 (U.S.) as a bribe to local officials.

Another drawback is the other apartment dweller — a large rat, with long black hair and blue eyes, that is so bold it occasionally walks right up to Ms Mestikhovskaya and rubs against her leg. Recently the rat had babies.

She is as depressed by her friends as she is terrified of the rat. When they get together, all of them oppressed by thoughts of how expensive everything is and how much life has changed, she has to leave because she can't stand it. "It seems they're going to talk about it to the end of their lives."

Valentina Plaskina, who thinks she is about 80, is not so lucky. She has been stuck in the one room of a communal apartment in central Moscow for 17 years and she cannot afford to leave. She likes the policeman and his family who have another room, but she is angry with a drunk named Konstantin who never does his share of cleaning up.

She carries another kind of burden of the Soviet past. She came to Moscow from the city of Chelyabinsk in the foothills of the Ural Mountains. Until two years ago Chelyabinsk was a closed city: No foreigners were permitted anywhere near it because it was one of the centres of the Soviet Union's defence industry. Ms Plaskina concedes that her Chelyabinsk factory made bullets and she is reluctant to say more because such things were state secrets.

"We were brought up like this," she explains gravely. "We were trained like this."

She is eager for visitors. It is mid-morning, but she has prepared buckwheat kasha, the traditional porridge on which she survives. Her luxury is butter, and she slices a large piece, invoking the old Russian saying that "you can't spoil kasha with butter." She watches closely to make sure that I, already over-fed, feed myself again.

She used to be cheerful about the new Russia but now, she confesses, she fears life is getting worse, what with crime and the price of funerals. These days, the costs being what they are, you need at least 300,000 rubles (about $200) for a decent funeral.

At the end of a long sigh, Ms Plaskina suddenly smiles. Mockingly, she quotes one of the old Leninist slogans that sustained the Communist Party for decades: "I would like people to be happy, to have a bright future." Then she looks quite sad. The whirlwind of changes touches everyone differently. For Lydia Dolnikova, it means her conversation is filled with words like fear, frightened and afraid. She began work as a hairdresser 30 years ago, at the age of 16, in the days when a job was a job for life.

Today, there are no jobs for life. As the economy struggles to adapt to a competitive world, unemployment — formerly a capitalist concept — has appeared. Even the government expects that by the end of the year, 12 million of a work force of 70 million will be without jobs.

Last year there was talk about changes at Ms Dolnikova's work place. She started feeling insecure, so she got a job at a different hairdressing salon. Now she is worried about the new place because one young woman was fired after she got into an argument with the director.

She's also worried about her husband. He already earns less than she does and he is working in a factory that has seen massive cutbacks. More are to come. "What can a man do? I'm afraid he will start drinking. That's frightening."

In the old days, nobody was supposed to do anything that smacked of private enterprise. For a lot of Russians it is still distasteful, but street trading has saved many of them from poverty. Natalya Volkova, who is 40 but looks much older, has been unable to work for 20 years because of a kidney disease. She once got a pension but now survives by selling bread outside the Kiev train and Metro station. She buys in bulk at a local bakery and sells the bread to travellers passing by.

These days the weather is cool but it is nothing compared with the horror of the winter. She has to watch out for the police because technically it's still illegal to sell without a licence, although they usually don't fine her. She gets more than 3,000 rubles a day, on which she feeds herself and seven children. She shakes her head grimly: "I wasn't put on Earth for this kind of life, just to stand here."

But on the other side of the street three men from the southern Russian republic of Dagestan are each packing two large cardboard boxes of American cigarettes into plastic travel bags. They are hurrying to catch the train south.

Each box contains 50 cartons, and they can make 1,000 rubles on each carton because cigarettes are hard to get in Dagestan. Each man should clear 100,000 rubles on every trip. "What else can we do? There's no way to get a job," one says. "To live, it's enough, to survive, but nothing more."

Nearby, on a table fashioned out of a plank and cardboard boxes, a young man is selling bananas. He trained as a sailor in the northern port of Archangelsk but wanted a different life. He does a brisk business with passers-by. He is saving to buy his own business some day. The man who brought most of these changes to Russia, President Boris Yeltsin, suggested the other day that people are suffering more from the phenomenon of change than from change itself. He is right, but for Mr. Yeltsin and his reformers this is no consolation.

The judgment of the country was offered last December when the reformers were thoroughly beaten in parliamentary elections. Almost instinctively people tell you the country is worse off, then after a few minutes of discussion they say, well, maybe, and they shrug.

Mr. Yeltsin might have acknowledged that people are suffering from the stress of choice. The first stages of the market economy have given them a range of choice they never had before, and not enough money to take advantage of it.

In the dying days of the Soviet Union, a trip to a food store was depressing and vaguely disgusting. On my first visit to Gastronom Number Four on Dorogomilovskaya Street, I found a vista of empty shelves, a few jars of pickled tomatoes, a few chickens that appeared to have died of starvation weeks before and large tubs of butter. There were no fruit or vegetables, no vodka or beer; cheese had not been seen for weeks, sugar for six months. The floors and walls were grimy, the pervading smell was of rotting food and the women behind the counter were slovenly, dirty and aggressively unhelpful.

Today, Gastronom Number Four is quite a different place. It is clean, brightly lit, the shelves are full of sausage and fresh beef, packaged meats, fruit and vegetables, eggs, milk, cheese and butter, and all kinds of liquor and beer. The staff is cheerful. It is not a Canadian supermarket, but it's a lot better than it was three years ago.

Like most other retail stores throughout the country, Gastronom Number Four was state-owned and is now run by employees, a fact that has produced a profound difference in attitudes. There is a vested interest in being agreeable.

Galina Pakidova, director of the store, says simply: "They are starting to understand that the more we sell the more we make. We lived under the old system for 75 years. It's difficult to change all at once."

Consumer choice is not limited to food stores. Formerly dreary state department stores — Universalnay magazeen, known as Univermag — have been spruced up and stocked with everything from French kitchen appliances to packages of German processed cheese called Slicettes.

For the first time in their lives Muscovites can buy Western clothes. They can purchase colour film for their cameras and have it developed in 24 hours. They can buy music cassettes, compact discs and pirated videotapes — and the machines on which to play them.

When I first visited Moscow eight years ago, a customs man at the airport scoured my luggage in search of rock-and-roll tapes, which the government regarded as subversive. Even three years ago, customs seized eight books in my luggage and returned them only after a formal protest.

All that is now history.

Not long ago the Soviet government jammed foreign short-wave radio broadcasts. Now the BBC and Voice of America are carried in English and Russian on local stations, and Russian television networks relied on CNN for their coverage of the armed uprising last October in the centre of Moscow.

Yet such freedoms are of small satisfaction to those who are struggling to survive, who are out-siders in the new Russia. Mr. Yeltsin acknowledged the other day that half of Russia is on the poverty line or below it. Even for those who are well above the line, the changes have been dis-turbing. Sasha is 45 and she seems to have no real desire to scramble through the intricacies of Western commercialism.

We are having coffee in an expensive Western hotel just half a kilometre from the Hotel Ukraine, where she works. She had never been inside the hotel and does not understand when the waiter suggests cappuccino.

As we leave, she hesitates, then asks if she can visit the hotel hairdresser. As we go inside, she looks around as though she has entered a different world — and she has. A haircut and shampoo at the Slavyanskaya costs $62.

Like many Russians, she thinks the new Russia is only for young people and foreigners, not for the old or even the middle-aged: "I want calmness. I want order. I want the law to be obeyed."

In the three years since the collapse of the Soviet Union, I have met only a handful of hardline cementheads who want to turn the clock back. But there is nostalgia and, for many, no joy.

• **1994** Feature Writing •

India's railway children

John Stackhouse

Globe and Mail

PUNE, India — The slum has been awake for an hour as Shankar wrestles himself out of a ratty blanket and nudges his three friends, huddled together for warmth. He barely notices the tear in his dirty white T-shirt, which was ripped in a fight last night. "We're late," he mutters to no one in particular.

This always happens when the boys stay up late watching Hindi dance films. Now they are in danger of missing the 8:45 train into the city. And that means they will miss breakfast at the hos-pital, where a nurse serves leftovers out the back door. Worst of all, they will miss the noon train to Bombay, with its handsome cargo of salesmen, middle-class families and college kids.

Soon the boys are up, enjoying the day's first cigarette. Shankar folds his blanket and observes his older companions. Rajesh, the money-spinner, sits on the floor checking the contents of his shoeshine kit, with which he earns 60 rupees ($2.40) a day. Aktar, the rabble-rouser, parks himself in a corner, sulking, as he does so often. Kishore, the smart one, paces about, hands in his pocket, taking in the scene. He joined the gang just two weeks ago. Their collective silence means they are all thinking about the same thing: the train.

From the moment they get up in the morning until the moment they huddle together under their blankets at night, India's railway kids dream of the train. Beaten by their parents, chased from their homes, dispossessed by society, all their hope is directed at the train and its singular promise that the next station will be better than the last.

No one knows how many Shankars, Rajeshes, Aktars and Kishores live on India's web of rail lines. Some say 10,000, others 100,000. It's like measuring a wave. Rising from metropolitan slums and remote villages, the railway children appear and recede, yet they are always there — not in one place for long, but always on the same journey.

The government prefers to deny their existence. Police ignore them or beat them, depending on an officer's mood. A few years ago, the United Nations Children's Fund (UNICEF) sponsored a program to provide them with basic education and health care, but when the Year of the Girl

Child rolled around, the boys were politely asked not to come back. The only reason the railway tolerates them is that they do the dirty work that salaried employees refuse to handle.

On the train, the railway kids are nobody's children. But the boys don't mind too much. They have their own dreams and journeys to follow.

Shankar's journey began last year on the other side of this patchwork of a subcontinent. He was 11, a frightened boy with an alcoholic father. "One night a friend said to me, 'Come, I know where we can get jobs.'" Shankar's big, brown eyes bulge with excitement as he tells his story.

"We snuck onto a train," he says, careful not to miss a detail. "We found a place on the floor to sleep. It was a good place to sleep. But when I woke up, my friend was gone. I looked everywhere on the train and could not find him. I didn't know where we were going."

Shankar got off at the next station. It was Pune, the last major stop before Bombay. A man on the platform greeted Shankar and promised him a restaurant job for 600 rupees a month. To a young boy 500 kilometres from his family, it sounded appealing, but after two months on the job he still hadn't been paid. When Shankar tried to leave the restaurant, the man beat him. One morning, he escaped and ran back to the Pune station.

Today, Shankar works the trains in his bare feet, wearing dirty shorts and T-shirt. He makes about 100 rupees ($4) a week shining shoes and doing whatever menial work he can find. "If I took a bath," he says, with the smile of experience, "no one would give me money."

Soon after Shankar and his friends make their way to the tracks, the morning's first southbound train sputters lethargically out of the station. It's a journey the boys make a few times every day, down the line for a couple of hours, then back to Pune, and then down again.

In the second-class section of the train, there is an unending procession of despair. Old women shuffle through the cars, begging bowls in hand, followed by the most macabre displays of deformity imaginable: Lepers with only stumps for arms, crippled men crawling along the floor, boys without legs walking on their hands.

Into this cruel sub-culture come the railway kids. Some gather discarded foil wrappers that they sell to scrap dealers. Others polish shoes, sell bottles of water or reserve seats. Anything for a rupee or two. Ashtar and Kishore, for example, sweep floors. Kishore is saving for a shoeshine kit.

No one makes rupees faster than Rajesh, who is 14. He moves deftly through the train from one pair of shoes to another, never looking up from the smelly, travel-worn feet that surround his work station. Rajesh grew up watching his father shine shoes in a Bombay station, and suffering the old man's nightly drunken fury at home. One day, Rajesh left. "My father has done this all his life," he says, his mouth exposing a jumble of crooked and stained teeth. "But I want to go a notch higher than my father. Maybe I'll become a handcart pusher. Or a porter."

As the train lumbers across western India's bucolic rice fields, Rajesh takes a break to count the 17 rupees he had just earned, enough, he announces, for a round of orange freezies. Little Omesh, barely eight, is thrilled. His shoeshine kit was stolen a couple of weeks ago, and he has not been able to buy a freezie since.

From the open train door, the boys stare at children toiling in the rice fields. The children in the fields wave. It is an odd sight. There is no money for them in the fields. No thanks. No education. No games. No joy rides. And no orange freezies.

When the break is over, the boys get set to move to the next car, but the door is sealed. There is only one route. Securing their shoeshine kits and whisks to their bodies, the boys step out the door and swing their small frames outside the speeding train, travelling at around 80 kilometres an hour, from one bar to the next, until they can step into the next car. They call it "coupling."

Little Babu was good at coupling, until one afternoon last summer when he slipped and was crushed by the train's rumbling wheels. When the boys heard about his death two days later, they didn't cry, nor did they stop coupling. They pooled their money, collected the body and paid for a proper funeral. They were all Babu had.

The government scarcely knows what to do about the thousands of children on the rail system. For years, it rounded up railway kids and street kids and put them in remand homes, hoping personal attention, health care and education would turn them around. But almost everyone knows remand homes are little more than prisons. Personal attention is a cane. Healthcare and education are minimal.

Subesh has been in and out of remand homes for six of his 14 years. They're always the same, he says: Regular beatings, lousy food, no fun. In the last remand home, in Delhi, Subesh volunteered as a cook's helper, borrowed the cook's keys and then locked the cook in the kitchen. A few minutes later, he and his friends climbed over the wall, pitched the keys and headed for the railway station.

On nearly every major railway platform, a social agency offers programs for the railway kids. But structured programs offer little appeal to children whose lives are defined by a railway schedule. Besides, how do you teach basic math to a kid who brings in over 50 rupees a day? How do you teach him geography when he knows every rail line in the country? How do you discuss social studies when he wrote the book?

At a recent seminar on street children in Bombay, social workers from around India listed education, nutrition, shelter, health and protection as the most important priorities. The 70 or so kids who live at Pune station have their own ideas — and education, health and nutrition are not on the list. They want protection from police, a place to lock up their shoeshine kits and English-language training. "I would make more money if I could talk to the foreigners," says Rajesh, always on the hunt for another way to make a rupee.

Gradually, adults are listening to their ideas. The Pune Municipal Corp. has given the boys nighttime access to a day-care centre in a nearby slum, a place where they can cook and sleep in safety. Railway officials have allowed a local group called the Association for the Rights of the Child to issue them photo identity cards to give them some security on the trains. And amazingly, the Indian government agreed this year to assume the costs of a couple of social workers who visit the boys to help them open bank accounts, deal with the police and obtain hospital-access cards.

"It's a real victory of sorts," says Girish Godbole, the India director of Save the Children-Canada, which started the program. "The government is finally recognizing these children exist."

Of course, there are some needs that social workers, police and governments cannot fulfill. By the time the railway kids are 10, most have turned to cigarettes and alcohol. By the time they are 14, it's drugs and substance abuse. By 16, they are paying prostitutes for comfort. They're a tough bunch, fighting on the platform, spending lazy afternoons in the local cinema, gambling through the night.

But in private, most of the boys show their vulnerability. They blame themselves for family rifts, and talk wistfully about winning back their parents' favour.

Away from the crowd, Rajesh's voice cracks when the conversation turns from his cruel father to his loving mother. Subesh talks softly about returning home with a peace offering of new clothes for his parents. Kishore, who ran away because his parents would not let him finish school, cries unashamedly as he talks about his younger sister. "She used to comfort me when my father beat me," he says. "I still see her face at night."

On the way back to the shelter in the evening, the older boys will buy food for dinner — tonight it's a rather good mutton curry — with money collected from the others. Subesh will stay a few steps behind, and quietly slip a five-rupee note to a crippled man who lives on the platform. And they will all talk about their dreams, even if no one is listening.

Kishore will describe his plans to finish school, to learn more about his warrior-hero Shivaji and to join the army. Rajesh will sit quietly repairing his shoeshine bag, keeping his dreams to himself. Aktar will talk about making it in the movies. "Don't you think I would make a good hero?" he asks. Little Omesh will tell of the trip he is planning to Bombay to see the ocean. "I have never seen one," he says earnestly. And Shankar will talk about going home. "Maybe when I have a good job," he says. "Maybe then, my parents will see me."

These are the dreams of children, dreams that fade with each passing station, dreams that awaken with each new journey.

Blaine

Hamilton Spectator

Pierre Trudeau's relationship with the provincial premiers was, on occasion anyway, stormy, and Blaine said it all with this cartoon. Blaine, who was a one-name artist long before it became fashionable, began his career in 1961 and has earned two NNAs, his first coming in 1974.

Les relations entre Pierre E. Trudeau et ses homonymes provinciaux étaient parfois houleuses — Blaine l'a bien fait voir dans cette caricature. N'utilisant qu'un seul nom bien avant que cela ne devienne la mode, Blaine commençait sa carrière en 1961. Il a deux prix du CCJ à son actif puisqu'il obtenait le premier en 1974.

CHAPTER 5

The Games of Our Lives

A selection of the winners from the NNA
categories for Sports Writing, which has been
continuous since 1957.

By Kathy English

"Ain't it bad enough to be a newspaperman without being a sports writer in addition?"
— Stanley Woodward, *Sports Page*, 1949

IT USED TO BE SO EASY TO MOCK THE SPORTS WRITER. AFTER ALL DIDN'T HE — AND IT WAS MOST certainly always a he — write about silly games played by grown men in silly clothes? Why, even sportswriters themselves referred to their corner of the newsroom as the toy department. Certainly Dick Beddoes' 1959 story on buxom stripper Patti Waggin ("it was something, friend, sitting there watching her breathe") is pure amusement (page 245). The toy department at its best. Today, sports coverage often commands more column inches of the daily newspaper than politics, the economy or any other single topic. Over the past 50 years, the boys in the toy department have matured and let the girls in. And together they've taught the rest of us newsroom types that sportswriting at its best means writing about the only game that really counts — the game of life.

Sports as a metaphor for life — why not? Sports has its winners and losers, heroes and bums and one can just as easily be one or another depending on how the game is played. Remember Ben Johnson?

Wayne Parrish's 1985 NNA-winning story about Johnson (page 259), written well before the sprinter won — and lost — Olympic gold, resonates with the irony only true life can create. Of course, Parrish could not have foreseen the events that saw Johnson stripped of his gold medal for testing positive for steroids at the 1988 Seoul Olympics. In retrospect though, Parrish's profile of a naïve kid from Jamaica seems to foreshadow his ultimate fall. As Johnson told Parrish,

"Sometimes nobody asked me anything, they just assumed I was not intelligent. In Jamaica you could do something about it and get away with it. Here there are laws."

Life as the great equalizer of the once mighty is played out in various other selections in this chapter. Gary Lautens' 1963 profile of boxer Jackie Callura (page 249), "a little guy who once was champ," reads like a script for the most archetypal of sports-as-life stories:

He was The Champ. People slapped him on the back and there were parades and a silver dish presented him by politicians who gave fancy speeches. But the bands don't play forever, not when you're an ex-champ and going to be 50 soon.

That theme is echoed in Red Fisher's poignant 1991 portrait of former Montreal Canadiens' coach Toe Blake (page 261), who spurred the Habs to eight Stanley Cups during his 13 seasons behind the bench. Fisher takes us to a small institution in west Montreal where Blake lives in a world of his own, defined by the vise of Alzheimer's. Fisher recalls the once fiery Blake for whom, "Winning wasn't merely a worthwhile target; it was everything. It was life itself." We live in an era that has appropriated the language of sport to express our most cherished goals. We strive to go the distance, keep our eye on the ball and hit one out of the park. Our biggest public gatherings occur in stadiums and arenas, venues where we freely express our deepest enthusiasms and emotions. Sports is our popular culture, providing daily entertainment and a lexicon of characters. How many young people know who Wayne Gretzky is long before they know the name of our prime minister?

George Vescey, the award-winning *New York Times* sports writer who began his journalism career as a religion reporter, believes sports has become nothing less than our modern-day religion. After all, "they both do it on weekends and they do it in big places and they celebrate and they got their fallen deities, their devils and their angels and their celebrations," Vescey states in the 1995 edition of *Best Newspaper Writing*, published by the Poynter Institute for Media Studies.

Can't buy sports as religion? No matter. Sports today is something Canadians revere even more than religion — it's BIG business. Indeed, the most striking development in sports during the past half century in which these National Newspaper Award stories were published was the evolution of sports as business, with big athletes earning big money for playing in big stadiums for big television audiences.

Television is, of course, the key to this development. No discussion of sports writing would be complete without acknowledging the critical role of televised sports coverage in the post-war era. The marriage of sports and television began in Canada on the evening of Oct. 11, 1952 when the Canadian Broadcasting Corporation televised its first sporting event — the third period of the Montreal Canadians-Detroit Red Wings hockey match from the Forum in Montreal. (For the record, the Habs defeated the Wings 2-1 with a late period goal on goalie Terry Sawchuk tipped in by Billy Reay off a pass from Maurice Richard.)

Within one year of that event, as sales of television sets skyrocketed across Canada, a full 10 per cent of the CBC's daily television schedule was occupied by coverage of the National Hockey League. In 1957, nearly five million Canadians tuned in to the CBC's first-ever, coast-to-coast coverage of the Grey Cup, pitting East against West. As Scott Young so succinctly stated in his 1958 NNA piece about what a Western boy must do on Grey Cup day — if he can: "That is, kick the whey out of the East."

Televised sports provided a challenge for the sports writer trained to report the score and crucial plays of the game. As former Toronto Maple Leafs' owner Harold Ballard wrote in his introduction to Allen Abel's 1983 book, *But I Loved it Pretty Well*, "Television was devastating to many sports writers. At the end of the game, before they could even unpack their typewriters, they were faced with the realization that their readers had already seen the game, probably in more detail than they had observed."

That challenge provided opportunity for the most talented of sportswriters — the storytellers — who broadened the definition of sports reporting to cover the personalities, and the politics, the money, the motives and the mannerisms, the anguish and the ethics of sports. On many newspapers in this country now, the best writing can be found on the sports page.

Great sports stories are nothing more and nothing less than great stories; the kind of good reads that resonate in our hearts and minds long after we've discarded our daily paper. The pieces in this chapter were selected for that reason, above all.

Consider Bob Pennington's 1965 *Telegram* story on the return of Eddie Shack to Maple Leaf Gardens following his exile from the big leagues to the Leafs' Rochester farm team (page 251). Elements of the classic short story shine through in this piece: The exiled hero offered an opportunity to redeem himself, the skate to redemption earned by backing down from a goading opponent (in this case Canadiens' bad boy George Ferguson) and, finally, a quiet escape into the night without even acknowledging his triumph.

Allen Abel's 1979 *Globe* award-winner exemplifies the ability of talented writers to make their readers see. In describing Moscow's fledgling gymnasts (page 256), Abel writes of a six-year-old girl strapped in a chair:

The chair begins to spin, slowly at first, then faster, faster, like a cybernetic electric beater, blending the little girl and her bright smile and her blonde pigtails into the secret recipe that has earned the Union of Soviet Socialist Republics a harvest of gold in the world athletic competitions of the past-quarter century.

Abel continues with this most vivid of images:

Across the hall, in a steam-heated little gymnasium, a dozen first graders in blue tights hang from the ceiling. Suspended by loops of rope at the ankles and wrists, they wriggle and squirm like emerging butterflies, which perhaps they are.

The days when sports reporters served as cheerleaders for the home team are long gone. The best sportswriters today are critics, not fans. Their experience and perspective gives their readers the less-heroic feats of sport, both on an off the field.

The talented Roy MacGregor's 1995 story on the bad boys of sports — among them Mike Tyson and O.J. Simpson — would unlikely have been published 50 years ago (page 263). MacGregor laments what he regards as "a quantum shift in the inherent values of sport.

"Cheaters now prosper (corked bats, hooking and holding in hockey, steroids in football and track)," he writes, noting that the crisis in modern sports is one of attitude. "There is something about the attitude of many professional athletes that causes them to feel they are not only above their fans, but above the law."

What MacGregor doesn't say, but we all certainly know, is this — in this game of life, bad boys never really win.

• **1958** Sports Writing •

A close look

Scott Young

Globe and Mail

VANCOUVER — Jim Trimble, a big, hard man, shut the press from his dressing room for 40 minutes after the game, but, even with that time to compose himself did not take the loss gracefully.

"Gentlemen, please, do you mind?" he said, until the gentlemen paid heed. "Talk to the players now. I'll be glad to talk to you later." Then he dressed and was gone. For that, many men will attempt to take the hide from him in print today, but he will survive.

Don't let anyone tell you that Hamilton lost this Grey Cup in the night clubs, either. While I am not an advocate of booze as a great body-builder, the Hamiltons are grown men and can take a drink or two and recover in less than two days.

The Winnipeg players had their night on the town too, but showed no signs of being afflicted with extreme lassitude or spots before the eyes. They were, by one touchdown, the better of two good teams. To prove it, they played a dedicated, battering kind of game that was very close to being a coach's dream.

In fact, as I was saying to the chaps in the press bus while we drove downtown after the game, that's the way WE WESTERNERS always hope that our teams will play in the Grey Cup.

What made them play it that way, this of all years?

I asked that of Norm Rauhaus. He is this year's dark horse hero, and has exactly the right background for it. In 16 years of growing up in Regina, and another six in Winnipeg, he has had built into his fibre the true-blue truth of what a Western boy must do on Grey Cup day, if he can. That is, kick the whey out of the East.

"Why?" he repeated. "Well, we've been out here for a week doing nothing but listen to that (short word deleted) that Trimble has been talking. We were all out there to show him how wrong he was."

Was Winnipeg shaken when Hamilton went into that quick two-touchdown lead? "There was a little silence on the ground, that was all. We knew we could still beat them." Indeed, while it would be difficult to find a coach who would agree that two early touchdowns might be a disadvantage, Hamilton seemed to coast after that — and a team that coasts, may get pushed around. Which happened.

It was impossible not to notice Rauhaus in that pushing around of the mighty Hamiltons. One of Bernie Faloney's passes sailed over his head to Ron Howell for Hamilton's third touchdown. Apart from that, he played, at his own estimate, his greatest game.

He intercepted one Faloney pass to stop a dangerous Hamilton march in the middle of the fourth quarter. He took a risky lateral from Ken Ploen after another march-stopping interception on the second-last play of the game. He also made what some persons think was the key play of a game that really had several — the blocked kick on the last play of the first half.

Just before that event, Bud Grant, Winnipeg's round-eyed mentor, had sent in word to put on a big rush (Grant said: "I was no genius on that one — it was the last play of the half and I thought we should go for the ball.") On receiving that message Rauhaus literally hid behind Winnipeg's left end, Herb Gray, as Cam Fraser lined up to kick. "I looked across the line at the guy who should block me, and he wasn't even looking," he said. "As the play began, I stepped out and drove in. I wasn't touched. I took the ball right here …" tapping his middle…"and was hardly even knocked off stride. Just kept right on going after the ball when it bounced into the end zone." He fell on it there. That was Winnipeg's first lead over Hamilton in a game and a half of Grey Cup play.

I asked Grant later what he would have his team do in the same position — in possession, near the goal line, with only seconds left on the first-half clock. "I'd be inclined to have my quarterback sit on it," he said.

Some hours later (boots, boots, boots), in a room off the Hamilton suite in the Hotel Vancouver, I asked Trimble if he regretted calling for the kick on that play.

"If I had to do it again 100 times, I'd do it the same way," he said. "I'd never surrender the ball in that territory even if the clock showed nothing."

Trimble had a few other things to say. For one, he had thought of not dressing Cam Fraser for this game because Fraser has not been kicking well, and Faloney has; but he left Fraser in, and Fraser had a terrible day. For another, "Some people say we got Winnipeg up for this game by needling them. If that's so, and they have to have that kind of stuff to get them up, they won't last long."

The third was about Ralph Goldston, thrown out of the game with 2:10 left in the first half, for punching Leo Lewis. The call was made by A. Taylor Paterson, third umpire, a Western official.

"I'm not contesting that official's call," Trimble said. "He was in a position to see. And I'm not trying to take anything away from Winnipeg, because the loss of Goldston can't hurt our club that much — although he's the core of our defensive secondary, and a real spark on offense.

"But all I see is Goldston on the bottom of the pile and before he's even up, this official's finger is pointing him out of the game. If he'd penalized us 25 yards or half the distance to the goal line, okay — but can that be good for football, to throw a player out of a game that is the culmination of a year's work? What would that official do in exactly the same kind of play, if he had to rule against Van Pelt, or Faloney? Do you think for a minute he'd throw out one of those players and ruin the game for 35,000 people?"

A good question. As he spoke, the city outside the open window was full of bursts of music, shouts, sirens of the harried gendarmes, auto horns, stray loud bars of wild Dixieland, and the tribal cries of football fans — none of it an answer, and none of it for him.

• 1959 Sports Writing •

The strip teaser

Dick Beddoes

Vancouver Sun

LOS ANGELES — You can do this here. You can sit in the New Follies burlesque theatre and watch a little cupcake pitch distracting curves.

The little cupcake wins, sex to nothing.

Later backstage, you can join the sporting press and meet the lady when she has a few more clothes on. Don't let anyone ever tell you the press isn't privileged.

Her name is Patti Waggin. She is a brunette strip-teaser, all slim and trim and superbly designed. In private life she is the wife of Don Rudolph, a left-handed pitcher with the Chicago White Sox.

Between them, the Rudolphs possess more exciting curves than the roller-coaster at Exhibition Park.

The scribes hammed and awed and snuffled, like they'd never been in a strip-teaser's undressing room before. Come to think of it, this hack never had. It was no more unsettling than being locked up with an Arizona gilamonster.

Finally a guy said, "Your husband, Miss Waggin … this Mr. Rudolph. Where did you meet him?"

Two dimples made small whirlpools in her cheeks. "We met in Colorado Springs," she said. "It was six years ago. I was dancing at a place and Don was pitching for the town team. One night he came in and saw my act."

"Was it love at first sight?"

Miss Waggin responded without a noticeable blush.

"Yes and no," she said. "Don stayed for three shows. I stripped three times, so he always said it was love at third sight."

Most of Miss Waggin is visible on the Los Angeles stage these nights, but her heart is with her husband. The big guy, up to now, has paused this side of pitching immortality.

"This year Don's going to make it big," she said confidently. "As soon as I finish this bumps 'n' grind schedule I'm going to join him."

"You're a player's wife," a reporter said. "You think all girls should travel with their husbands?"

"Oh, yes," she said quickly. It was something, friend, sitting there watching her breathe.

"The players need their wives badly," she said. "Pitchers can't sleep a wink after a game. Do you know what Don does after a game?"

"No. What?"

"He replays the whole nine innings. Every pitch. Sometimes he jumps out of bed, turns on the light, and pitches an inning like he did that afternoon. That's why he needs me."

"Yeah?" a man said. "How do you help?"

"Well, Don will be standing there in his pyjamas, pitching to Mickey Mantle, and he'll say: 'Then on the third pitch, Patti, I gave him a change-up, like this.' And I'll say: 'No, Donnie dear, it was a curve.'"

"So how do you know the difference between a change-up pitch and a curve?"

Miss Patti Waggin surveyed her newspaper guests with an arch eye. "Gentlemen," she said, "curves are my business."

The way it works, Miss Waggin explained, she keeps track of every pitch Mr. Rudolph makes.

"Before every game," she said, "I get out my score book and show my husband the hitters he curved last time. I also show him the hitters who hit him, and the kind of pitch they hit."

She wrinkled her pretty brow, looking perplexed. "Really, I don't see how bachelors ever win."

There was time, before Miss Waggin went out to play her G-string again, to ask a delicate question. "This is a, uh … a broad-minded age," a guy said. "Just the same, do your in-laws approve of a stripper as the wife for their son?"

"Oh, they do," Patti Waggin said gaily. "Donnie's daddy never saw me strip until one night last winter in his home town, Baltimore. His face got redder and redder. But afterward, I went right up to their table and just as I got there, Donnie's daddy was saying, 'You know what, son? We're staying for the second show.'"

● **1960** Sport ●

Le sport canadien a besoin d'un commissaire national

Jacques Revelin

L'Action Catholique, Québec

L'enquête relative à la future réorganisation du sport amateur au Canada suscite beaucoup d'intérêt dans la majorité des milieux sportifs de la vieille capitale mais, avant de communiquer les comptes-rendus de nos premiers entretiens avec les principaux dirigeants et moniteurs dont nous avons sollicité les avis éclairés, voici, brièvement exposés, les suggestions qui, selon nous, seraient susceptibles de revivifier l'attrait, le développement, et l'épanouissement des différentes activités athlétiques sur le plan national.

Même si le terme « centralisation » effraie certaines personnes, il est indéniable que les sports tout comme les arts devront être soumis à un organisme unique si l'on veut établir et réaliser un plan d'ensemble tout en simplifiant les relations et l'appui du gouvernement fédéral. Les efforts accomplis jusqu'à maintenant par les groupements disparates nous prouvent en effet qu'une centralisation est nécessaire car si telle ou telle association a obtenu par le passé des succès notables, ce fut toujours au prix d'incalculables dépenses d'énergie, d'un travail constant et acharné de dirigeants, dont l'abnégation se devait d'être parfois inconsciente pour se maintenir souvent sans entrevoir un seul espoir.

La création d'un conseil national des sports s'impose. C'est en se fiant à des gens compétents et responsables groupés ensemble que le gouvernement et les sportifs des dix provinces pourront entreprendre la grande rénovation désirée. Pour se faire, nous croyons qu'Ottawa devra nommer d'abord un commissaire, choisi ou non dans les rangs des fonctionnaires, mais en évitant surtout de tenir compte de sa couleur politique, si ce personnage se montrait digne de ses responsabilités, il devrait être préservé des renversements possibles du pouvoir.

De par son titre, le commissaire national des sports au Canada devrait posséder les mêmes prérogatives qu'un premier ministre, c'est-à-dire qu'il présiderait un conseil formé d'un nombre défini de personnages nommés à la tête des principaux mouvements sportifs canadiens par ceux qui en sont membres.

Cette suggestion n'est pas inédite car il existe effectivement au pays depuis longtemps l'Union Athlétique Amateur (A.A.U.) dont les activités ont permis au sport athlétique et strictement amateur de continuer à s'affirmer en dépit de l'indifférence des gouvernants. Cette association est cependant incomplète et par le fait même imparfaite puisque le hockey, sport majeur au Canada n'y est pas intégré, tout comme le ski, le tennis, etc … De plus, autre preuve de son insuffisance, l'A.A.U. n'a jamais pu obtenir malgré les demandes réitérées de ses dirigeants, l'appui financier indispensable pour l'aider à réaliser ses aspirations les plus humbles. Pour confirmer ces dires il suffit de se remémorer les restrictions qui surviennent chaque fois lorsqu'il est question de former une équipe canadienne en vue d'une compétition internationale.

En nommant un commissaire national des sports le gouvernement fédéral se dégagerait d'un fardeau, celui de recevoir sans cesse des demandes de subventions provenant de toute part et l'indisposant. Il lui suffirait, dès lors, de faire voter un budget annuel dont la répartition serait confiée au commissaire qui devrait être un sportif compétent et un administrateur averti.

Ce contrôle d'un seul homme, en apparence dictatorial, n'élèverait pas pour autant une barrière à l'autonomie des diverses associations sportives du pays. Chacune d'entre-elles conserverait ses principes, ses structures, ses propres règlements, et son champ d'actions particulier, mais devrait alors offrir certaines garanties pour bénéficier des privilèges offerts par le gouvernement.

Ce commissaire, en somme, n'aurait nullement besoin de s'ingérer dans les affaires internes des organismes sportifs d'envergure nationale mais serait avant tout l'intermédiaire, le porte-parole de tout le monde sportif au pays, tout en agissant comme arbitre ou conseiller advenant certains conflits nuisant à l'avancement d'un membre de la grande famille du sport.

Statué avec logique et réalisme, ce conseil national des sports serait la pierre angulaire de notre renouveau athlétique ; d'un renouveau qui pourrait être sans cesse florissant. Nous soumettons cette première suggestion aux sportifs québécois, et principalement à ceux que nous allons interroger durant les prochains jours. Ils nous diront s'ils partagent notre avis ou proposent un autre principe de base. Les experts ne sont pas toujours ceux que le grand public a consacré pompeusement c'est pourquoi les idées émises par les dirigeants sportifs qui se dévouent depuis des années dans l'ombre méritent beaucoup de respect et d'attention.

● **1961** Sports Writing ●

Sporting extras

Ted Reeve

Toronto Telegram

Suddenly it is awful quiet around the corner of Church and Carlton Street. C. Smythe is moving out to the sunny side of Shed Row. The men who are taking over at The Gardens are strong fellows who know their sport. So one of the outstanding big league operations in North America will continue aboard this beautiful battleship sort of a building.

Punch Imlach is a sturdy coach with great common sense in the best Hap Day tradition and with the Silver Savants solid on his side matters with the Maple Leafs will roll with all the old momentum. For which we are grateful. Yet, will you pardon an elder scribe a portion of time-out today to feel maybe a little bit sad or somewhat woeful (even if there is no reason for it, truly).

We happened to like the Little Pistol when he was a young, inquiring looking chappie from the First War pitching in with the famous Granites and the Varsity squads of those surging days of the Twenties. Driving one construction truck and using his engineering to be putting in sidewalks and side drives out in the west end with his own cement mixing shovel. Have admired him since though sometimes he made us so mad we felt like hitting him over the head with a fungo bat.

And now, with a couple of hundred other happy-go-luckies who knew the Maje maybe better than anybody else and who would go through that wall for him on any given notice, we think it would be the time to repeat a piece we wrote about his Building five seasons back; which went, from the heart:

Five and twenty years ago, come quarter day and the man with the dividends, the Maple Leaf Gardens commenced with a ceremonial display which in that year of 1931 A.D. (active depression) might well have been a wake.

One reporter we recall opined, amongst other matters, that from the grey seats one could hope to see Rochester on a clear night and then joined the rest of the populace in a one minute silence for the stockholders.

Have been wrong since about various events in the great glaciarium at Church and Carlton Sts., thereby being extremely fortunate to join in this anniversary of an amphitheatre that for athletics, and all round action, has actually been one of the busiest Arenas in the world. And the cleanest.

A quarter of a century of eventful seasons comes flooding back, of a necessity, on such a birthday. A sports saga, indeed, but of such an overwhelming part of, say, this sports observers' middle life time that the memories of the high excitement of fierce competition come even more so, now, of many, many side issues, sunny or sad ... of the men who made the action ... of the trips to other towns ... the setbacks and the celebrations ... the changes in the wide sphere of sport as well as the surrounding spin of the world events that fashion the attractions ... the very rooms and seating sections of the big house of hockey.

For when a scribe pauses here for a ponder it forcibly occurs to one that the Gardens, with its ever pressing program of events, becomes as much a part of a Toronto sports chronicler's life and daily journal as Mr. Crusoe's stockade was to the sturdy sailor with the steady habits. Or Mons. Cristo's air-conditioned tunnel, Master Thoreau's pond-side retreat at Walden or Tim Linkinwater's set of ledgers in the counting-house of Cheeryble Bros.

Like Charlie Silvera, the Yankees' bullpen catcher, we had a good quiet seat close to the uproar and with just enough company to keep it always interesting.

So we stroll again today through the great corridors into empty dressing rooms where we have seen so many famous hockey packs poised with the relaxed strength of the trained athletes, perspiration drenched shirts over padded thighs, hem-stitched eyebrows cocked alertly as they laced up skates again or reached for the taped warclubs as the rumble of the crowd rolls on above ... the last instructions for the next round of the fray. Witch hazel, wintergreen, oranges, steam, up and at 'em eagerness hanging in the air. Small wonder the old trainer in the verse can say, "I hope the heaven that I get will have some liniment and sweat ..."

Then that shambling sort of a quick-march of hockey players heading for ice, down the runway ... and instants later another Stanley Cup struggle is at issue ... Wide shouldered Bill Cook, Bun and Boucher are swinging about in passing patterns ... Schmidt, Dumart and Bauer are lifting the play with a surge into the beleaguered back-stops; Lach is wheeling over the blue lines as the Rocket spurts away down the right boards for the long, winging pass that sets him hurling almost on his left shoulder to the in-angle of the rear-guard for a back-hand blast.

Clapper has dropped a puck carrier with a solid bodycrash and Eddie Shore the Prairie Schooner pivots on his bent knees and brawny legs, lifts the puck ahead and is away ... straight down the centre leading a furious phalanx of burly Bruins to the charge.

It is late overtime again ... and again ... the rushers come reeling past the dour defenders, wet hair hanging in their eyes and the Arena one great cavern of sound ... and Broda turns aside another shot ... the rush rebounds with desperation speed on the other end. Bill Durnan spreads and a flashing glove deflects another air boring black biscuit ... the greatest of the last ditch struggles.

There is Apps seemingly going full speed on a break then giving it the extra stride ... faithful Nicholas Metz, swooping every-which-way in his amazing manner of almost sitting down while skating ... the Kid Line in full flight ... Barilko spinning an oncoming rusher high in the air like a ten-pin ... Kennedy digging in a corner, side-stepping a check, moving around another ... setting up a goal ... the methodical always dangerous Wings of Detroit ... led by some master of manoeuvres like Ebenezer Goodfellow or Gordie Howe and fired by a Lewis or a Lindsay ... Bill Cowley giving the puck to a defenseman, then pulling it back like a yo-yo, to lift it past again and ladle a perfect pass to some left winger. King Clancy ... as if coming off a spring board ... hitting the puck almost to centre ice ahead of him then bursting away in pursuit with an Irish whoop that would knock an echo off the topmost girder.

Clancy ... typical of how the memory of 25 seasons means the men there pictured ... No one would ever come out of a dressing room door quite like Clancy in his full Sandy Hill stride when he first came here from Ottawa and the Maple Leafs were on their way to the Stanley Cup that set the show upon the road. For Clance was there too, when the first machine began to sag ... when they almost knocked his head off in Detroit to take so much of the lift from out the club ... the start of the winters when the Big Line found combos who could check them and the rebuilding began ... as it always came, full circle.

Frank Selke taking the hard won experience of early Toronto campaigns to build the Forum into a twin pillar of hockey strength ... and C. Smythe, a fair working genius if ever one came along the sports beat, still full of zest ... But somehow walking by the towering red, blue and green and grey pews you think of the Maje and Frank high up there of a morning watching a workout as the cleaning crews were polishing away ... or Day coming off a train from Boston or Chicago with a score of details on his broad shoulders. Or of Henry Bolton up in the silent back offices looking at a seating plan that has filled in with opera crowds, with mass displays, with Memorial Cup fanatics, with the kids for the circus, with patrons of the ballet.

Or by the press room when it is quiet ... one does not think so much of stories typed on games now gone but rather of the great gatherings of grand sportsmen that we, in great good fortune, met therein between the sessions of the sport. The good Doctors who are the loyalest of the Leafs' supporters ... of dear old Rueben Bannister and Dr. Rush. Of our guide and friend, the late Horace Macintyre, MD of the sunny soul and all the good quiet fun we had on safaris in his company. Of Charley Querrie salting his comments of the passing fray with the lore of old lacrosse days, of even earlier chapters of Toronto headlines of the sports sheets. Of Bobby, Fergy and Baz and the older guard of the writers, who have been such staunch aids to us from the very start — to the younger lively lads of press and airways — Hesky, Steve all and all their henchmen and our old roomsie Josephus Perlove, the Jolson of the journalists, and the scouts around the circuit that we are planning once again. One more chorus, Joe, of Lazy ...

Another season ... number twenty-six — and a good dozen years flown since we sat one day upon the sands of Deal with the 'Old Man' on a pause in his inspection tour and looked across at the clock of Calais and talked of just such things which then seemed so far away.

So ... happy anniversary ... if you can wish a building such and this being a sturdy, solid structure in more ways than just girders and the bricks ... for it was built by that same sort of people, we toast old Twenty Five with a warm and grateful feeling for being with it.

That still goes.

• **1963** Sports Writing •

A little guy who once was champ

Gary Lautens

Toronto Star

He was just a little guy, maybe 135 pounds and armpit high, with thick glasses and a mushed-down nose, a forehead like a honey melon and a jaw the color of a cloudy sky. You might call him a squirt — until you saw the steelworker arms and the big, coarse hands with walnuts for knuckles.

This was at a dairy bar and he stood alone except for two dogs sniffing at his clothes. He patted them, went inside, came out with two sundaes which he put on the grass. He scooped out the ice cream with his fingers and let the dogs lick at the cold treat until they got the idea. Then Jackie Callura stood up again, alone.

Twenty years ago he wasn't alone. He was The Champ; people slapped him on the back and there were parades and a silver dish presented him by politicians who gave fancy speeches.

But the bands don't play forever, not when you're an ex-champ and going to be 50 soon.

As a kid Jackie helped his old man carry railway ties home for kindling, he sold papers in downtown Hamilton, and he fought on corners and in alleys when anyone made fun of his size or tried to take nickels out of his pocket.

Sometimes a guy named Rocco Perri came around to the house to stash stuff in the Callura basement. Nobody asked questions because Perri was a rough customer, the King of the Bootleggers; and, before he disappeared into Hamilton Bay with a cement suit (at least that's the theory), Perri was free with the dough among poor Italian immigrants hit by the depression.

When you're a boy you can remember the big spenders, good and bad.

To get a dollar, Jackie, ready to face life with a Grade 7 education and a left hook that whistled in transit, turned to boxing. For his first bout he wore someone else's oversized bathing suit with a safety pin holding up the crotch.

He had nearly 400 fights as an amateur. Crowds in Toronto and Hamilton and Buffalo — everywhere — loved him. He gave them blood. He was aggressive. And he was hungry for their money and attention. So he turned pro. A 125-pound slugger.

A boxer lives in crowds, savage, eager crowds that stand and cheer when a man is hurt and applaud the smack of leather on a chin and shout, "Finish him off!" when a fighter's knees buckle and his eyes turn to glass.

That was Jackie Callura's jungle.

He hit his peak in the late 30's when he fought out of Province and New Orleans and Toronto and Hamilton. Some paydays were worth $1,000 and towns argued to claim him as their own.

By the time Jackie met Jackie Wilson for the NBA featherweight title in January, 1943, he had been fighting about 15 years and was past his peak. However, he won the decision and the championship — but no money. He paid off his purse to get the bout.

He was the first Canadian since Jimmy McLarnin to win a world title, or a piece of one since New York state didn't recognize him.

Nine months later he lost the bauble to Phil Terranova, and the crowds started to thin out. They said he was washed up.

His brother, Angie, knew the feeling. He was a leading contender until a tough fighter named Allie Stoltz put a thumb in his eye and left him half blind and out of work.

They held a benefit for Angie to pay for eye operations — and somebody grabbed a big chunk of dough out of the pot. Boxing burns you at the stake and then offers a cigarette as a last request.

Jackie, the kid who carried railway ties home for his father, began dropping from sight — the odd bout in a tank town for a quick buck, an appearance where his hide could be used to fatten up the reputation of some local favourite.

Down is always faster than up.

But he had a home, a family, a restaurant.

Then, in 1951, the Callura name hit the papers again. His wife, Ena, had died mysteriously. A coroner's jury said it was infection from an abortion.

It was a sneak punch. Jackie didn't even know she was pregnant — and all of a sudden his world was shattered.

A "friend" of the family, held for (and later convicted of) perjury for evidence he gave at the inquest, said in court: "He's waiting outside with a gun right now."

That was in the March 30, 1951, papers. The "he" was Jackie Callura who, at one point in the trial, had to be removed from the public gallery when he stood up and shouted: "Tell the court how rotten this man is!" Every instinct, every feeling told him to lash out, to hit back, to trade hurt for hurt.

Jackie buried his wife, closed up the restaurant, watched the "friend" of the family get a light jail term. His children went to relatives and Jackie became a commuting recluse.

He works still in Buffalo in a steel plant. He visits Toronto and Hamilton sometimes. His children are grown up now and, to keep busy, he does roadwork or trains just as he did all those years ago. The dreams are packed away along with the silver dishes and the photographs of a young fighter who wanted to be champ.

And that is the story of the little guy with thick glasses who stood on this warm October afternoon feeding ice cream sundaes to stray dogs.

• **1965** Sports Writing •

Clear the track, Shack is back

Bob Pennington

Toronto Telegram

There was a touch of magic and mayhem and Kipling abroad in the smokeless air. Shack was back at the Gardens.

A new Eddie Shack. The old muscle and menace was there, but now it was allied to staggering maturity. The boy had become a man. The knock-about comic was playing Hamlet and the devil with those Canadiens.

Those who had written him off were proved wrong. Those who had laughed at him plunged into serious reconsideration. Perhaps there was even the odd official of the Maple Leafs club who mused last night —

Though I've beaten you and flayed you
By the living God who made you
You're a better man than I am
Eddie Shack.

And yet it all seemed so different last Saturday night when Shack walked into the office of Rochester manager Joe Crozier and said, "I'm quitting Rochester and hockey. If I can't play in the big league, I don't want to play any more. It's just not worth it financially."

At this time in hockey history, Shack's ultimatum was a grenade, not a bomb. He was a discard, a reject, a mere pawn in the complex hagglings that pass as trading procedure in the NHL.

Midnight came and Shack was still angry and determined and if there was a small cloud of self doubt in his hotel room he looked away from it. At one in the morning he was still sleepless when the telephone rang. Manager Crozier was on the line and Shack heard this invitation:

"Listen Eddie — forget what you were telling me. Punch wants you to fly to Chicago for tonight's game and I told him you would be there. You wanted a break. This is it."

When Shack arrived in Chicago, people noticed a subtle difference in his manner. He didn't want to make anyone laugh, which seemed strange. He was withdrawn and tense and the boys excused his silence by saying, "Even Eddie knows he can't fool around with this one tonight."

Shack didn't fool around. In fact, in the opinion of many shrewd judges, he was the best Leaf on the ice, justifying Imlach's desperate decision to give him a regular spot in a regular line.

The question was, however, would Shack lapse into his old ways of wildness with the roar of his own crowd echoing in the arena where he had once been a cause célèbre?

The answer, glory be, was NO. Perhaps it was all a grand illusion, but I don't think so and nor does Eddie Shack. He was hitting and checking with all his old power. Once three Montreal men converged on him to form a white wall, but still he got his shot away.

Above all he was an inspiration to his own men and spread alarm and confusion among the enemy. And on this night, at least, both his legs seemed to be skating in the same direction at the same time.

A game has many turning points, depending on the team you support and the players you are partial to. But if I was to suggest the turning point in last night's tie stemmed from Shack's refusal to fight John Ferguson I doubt if there would be many who would disagree.

The score was 3–1, early in the third period, when Ferguson, who had engaged in a running feud with Shack throughout, lost his temper, threw his gloves on the ice and started lashing out. Shack showed quite extraordinary restraint and no little courage in refusing to hit back. For this was K.O. Fergie who made the Forum ice run with Nesterenko's blood in the last Stanley Cup final.

After a clinch that would not have disgraced Ernie Terrell, Shack was pried apart and smiled with grim satisfaction as he heard Ferguson sentenced to a double minor penalty. The old Shack would have belted back like a poor man's Chuvalo and there would have been no subsequent power play in which Ron Ellis scored the critical second goal.

Edward Shack was not listed among the three stars of the game and I don't moan about that. He did not score a goal nor an assist and you don't often rate stardom by controlling your temper or refusing to don cap and bells.

What he did do was to set the fans roaring, the same fans who had treated his return with initial reserve and hesitation. He also enjoyed the supreme satisfaction of being honoured with a place in Leafs' power play by coach Imlach. Shack could be trusted … Shack had arrived.

We descended from the press eyrie expecting the reformed character to be holding court in the dressing room. Here, surely, was his chance to sip a little of the wine of retribution, to tell the world of hockey how it felt to emerge from the wilderness enriched by the experience.

Yet before many of his team-mates had even entered the shower, Shack had stolen away into the night. The only problem, as far as I could see, was that his reputation would linger on in the minds of those men with the whistle.

Imlach put it this way: "Eddie may pick up an extra penalty a night simply because he is Shack. On the road, the screams of a hostile crowd may even get him two. He's just a robust player — that's his style. But I thought he did a good job for us."

Imlach, you may feel, has done a great job for Shack by sending him to Rochester for a taste of stark reality. How else would this Don Quixote have turned the other cheek to Knuckles Ferguson?

• **1970** Sports Writing •

Clay-Quarry match meant much more than fisticuffs

Bob Hanley

Hamilton Spectator

ATLANTA, Ga. — It was a wild and peculiar combination of Negro pageantry, anti-war protest, fashion parade and duck shoot in a barrel.

In the old auditorium where Enrico Caruso once sang, it was stopped before it really began last night by a bloody, gaping, 14-stitch gash with the general ringside presumption that the real good alley fighter would have succumbed — ultimately and inevitably — to the fleet and scientific ring stylist.

Cassius Clay was better than ever. Jerry Quarry never reached him, and the fight was stopped from Quarry's own corner at the end of three.

Minutes later, the widow of Dr. Martin Luther King was presenting Clay with a medallion in her husband's name, glorifying America's most famous alleged draft dodger as "a man of dignity and peace."

At the other end of the auditorium, in a dressing room that was only 12 by 12, the enormous Quarry family retinue was in Irish tears, a four-year-old boy was crying, Quarry's wife was vomiting and Quarry's curses were muffled by a towel as a doctor stitched deftly around his slashed right eyebrow.

■■■

Quarry didn't quit — he forced his way past trainer Teddy Bentham and tried to continue, but Bentham had signalled Tony Perez, the referee, that his man had had enough.

Clay was fast as ever, had put more snap and sting into his left, and ripped open the cut with two left hooks and a hard right cross. Quarry took four tough rights in the late minutes of the third, weathered them well, but was never really in it.

On points, it was a shutout for Clay before a predominantly Negro audience in the little old opera house that was a symbol of white culture at the turn of the century.

But this indeed was a Negro night, one which celebrated Clay's permission to fight again after a three-year exile, even as his draft evasion appeals continued to wait upon court judgments.

It was the fight which no other city in the United States would take, and the racial impact and implications were apparent in the lineup of Negro dignitaries announced from the ring — Bill Cosby, Harry Belafonte, Sydney Poitier, Hank Aaron, Mrs. King, four former boxing title holders who were Negroes, Diana Ross and The Supremes.

Curtis Mayfield, in a psychaedelic costume, accompanied himself on the guitar for his own quavering interpretation of the national anthem. A stoutish coloured girl in a mini-skirt walked the numbered signs inside the ring between the rounds.

■■■

But that wasn't the half of it. The iridescent blaze of the wild costumes in the $100 seats was overwhelming. The up-close crowd was almost totally black and the weird styles, blinding colour choices in leather and fur, bespoke a kind of pageantry that would make Hallowe'en seem a night of mourning in comparison.

The ladies were in pant suits of lime, scarlet, silver and gold, with foot-high wigs in silver and orange, with inch-long eyelashes, or sometimes with deep-cut bra-less gowns of black and brown leather.

The gentlemen went to bizarre Bonnie and Clyde outfits with multi-coloured hats of exaggerated brims and there were such other male distinctions as a scarlet fur coat with a white shawl collar, all white evening dress with black shirt and white tie, a red derby, and a red-and-white striped opera cape.

It was a night of revolt — not only in fashion, but in support of Clay and the principles he protests. It was militant and anti-war and a kind of unified expression of the Negro elite that they stood behind Clay on this comeback night, in this old southern city that was the site of one of the last great battles in the war to end slavery.

■■■

In the dressing room afterwards, there were these quotes from the unmarked Clay who was suffering from a slight cold and the pressure of an afternoon in which he had rounded up tickets for two busloads of late-arriving friends …

"… I was not satisfied with my fight. I wanted it to go further. He didn't hit me in the head and struck only two body blows that I felt."

"… I think Quarry is a better boxer than Frazier because you don't have to worry about Frazier's jab — he hasn't got one. Quarry has good feet and he was moving, trying to sucker me into a left hook. That's why I kept reversing my dance — first clockwise and then counter-clockwise. I had to keep dancing — move in, stick him and get out quick."

"… I thought my left had a lot of snap but I don't remember which punches caused the cut."

"… I may have seemed fast in the first, but I was staying out of trouble. I was a little nervous and I was extra cautious."

"… A couple of days ago I made this drawing (he held it up) and it shows my prediction to myself that it would end in a TKO. I thought it might go 10 and I'd hoped for that much work. I need work."

"… I could go again in six weeks, but Frazier, make it an even two months — I'll be ready."

■ ■ ■

Accompanied by the Rev. Ralph Abernathy and by Senator Leroy Johnson, also a Negro, Mrs. King came to the large interview area which had been set aside for Clay, after he left his dressing room.

It was here that the presentation of the medallion was made with short speeches all around and Mr. Abernathy saying … "the recipient is a contributor to the cause of honour and dignity and is a living example of soul power."

It was not the old Cassius in any of his responses to sportswriters — before or after the fight. None of the old giddiness and silly poems. At least until after the courts delivered their judgments, Clay was a very symbol of courtesy, discretion and humility.

They mobbed him, cheered him as he came outside — some as a fist fighter, some as a prophet, some as a protester, some as a rights leader.

Such were the happenings last night in a city steeped in history and contrasts, of stunning architectural masterpieces in the new central core, of shabby shacks on the perimeter, of Peachtree Street, of Five Points, of well-marked battle scenes of the Civil War, and of the graves of Margaret Mitchell (*Gone With The Wind*) and the Rev. Martin Luther King.

It's a big sports town — the Braves, Falcons, Chiefs, Georgia Tech and Georgia State — but for all of its culture it has crammed in 200 murders since the first of this year.

It's a city with 50 topless dining and dancing spots on its great white way, but don't come around on Sunday. All the bars are shut on Sunday, and all the churches — countless red brick Baptist churches with tall white steeples — are open and crowded.

Burned to the ground in the war to end slavery, it has the race and social problems of a new century — same as they have in the north. It is big, and like all big cities it has a great deal of everything — good and bad.

Last night, everything was good for Cassius Clay, and everything was seemingly bad for Jerry Quarry.

"But it's not all that bad," said one of the writers who had fought his way to the door of Quarry's dressing room. "Lots of guys get cut worse than that just walking into doors. And they don't get paid between 300 and 500 thousand dollars."

Clay would do better — he could go close to a million gross — with the rich big Frazier prize still at the end of his come-back rainbow.

• **1975** Sports Writing •

Over to you, Roy

Trent Frayne

Toronto Sun

Have all the McMurtrys finally surfaced? Are there any more at home like John, Bill and good old Roy? What the hell got into that family, anyway, when they decided that anything tougher than Toller Cranston in one of his spiffy twirls was too violent for hockey?

First thing you know *Hockey Night in Canada* will be coming to you courtesy of Shipstad and Johnson, with Darryl Sittler and Karen Magnussen in the big production number. "Hide your eyes when they embrace at centre ice," the advertisements will cry. "Not recommended for children under 21 unless accompanied by a maiden aunt."

The third, and if luck is on our side the last, of the many many McMurtrys turned up yesterday on the front pages of all the papers with the latest denunciation of violence in the wonderful world of sports.

This one is big ol' rumpled Roy, who became Ontario's Attorney-General earlier this month, and as soon as he found a place for his hat in his new office he came out with an instruction to the coppers to "aggressively enforce the law," in a new crackdown on hockey. Come to think of it, he could have been a little more circumspect in using that word aggressively. Surely he's not suggesting the coppers haul out the billys and crack a few skulls.

Roy said he's worried that millions of television watchers are seeing "clear breaches of the Criminal Code" in hockey acts that set a terrible example for the tiny tots at home. I don't know what channels Roy gets on his set but there's no question they're not available on my tiny portable Sony.

The games I catch involve the Maple Leafs on Channels 6 and 9 and the Toros on Global. I find 'em more effective than Ovaltine. I find myself dozing off about a quarter to 10 most nights. Occasionally, to keep the old red corpuscles churning, I switch over to Judy LaMarsh on Channel 19 for a riveting discussion on Senate reform with some lively old dude from the Royal Ontario Museum. I'm glad Bill Dennison is no longer the mayor; I used to get so darned worked up when Bill came on with a fighting speech on sewage contracts that I'd have to go back to Leafs and the Washington Capitals to bring down the skyrocketing pulse rate.

The first of the many many McMurtrys to emerge was John. John is a guy who played some football with the Alouettes and the Stampeders and then threatened to make a career of attacking the violence of football, either in *Maclean's* or in the old *Tely* on those terrible days that assail all us hard-thinking columnists when there's nothing to write about and the paper's blank.

Next, along came Bill McMurtry, the one-man task force appointed by the government to investigate violence in hockey. This was in the wake of a hell of a fight in a Junior B playoff between Bramalea and Hamilton, and Bill wrote an outstanding report. He said high-sticking and spearing had to go, and he was absolutely right. Nobody wants stick-swinging and spearing, and the sooner they're gone from hockey the better.

But the point is, the point has been made. Okay, those despicable tactics have no place in the game but it's questionable if fighting fits the same cloth. It's been pretty clearly established that ice is a difficult surface upon which to find enough leverage to do much damage. And the NHL's own third-man-in rule has effectively curbed the dumb massed choruses.

I liked the way Roy McMurtry's predecessor, John Clement, looked at it: "It's a difficult thing … to decide when the natural enthusiasm of the participants really ends and wilful damage is inflicted," Clement said once. He thought there was "an implied consent that there is a certain amount of body contact."

Right on. In a high-keyed emotional contact game like hockey you've got an implied consent that you'd never find on the street where the Criminal Code protects citizens who don't want to be popped on the nose.

If McMurtry wants to make his edict stick, if he wants to apply all the protection to hockey players that's accorded Canadian citizens under the Criminal Code, then he's got to move on to all the contact sports. He can't stop at Tiger Williams, Danny Gare and Terry O'Malley, at Gordie Howe and Jim Dorey. He's got to have the coppers arrest very lineman who makes the bells ring inside the helmets of halfbacks in next Saturday's Argo-Hamilton game, too.

Before he does any of these things, though, maybe he'll take a look at yesterday's *Toronto Sun* where on Page 1 there's the stirring sight of a member of the Union of Injured Workers lying on the pavement in front of Queen's Park after a collision with McMurtry's cops.

First things first, Roy old boy.

• **1979** Sports Writing •

Turning tiny tots into Soviet champions

Allen Abel

The Globe and Mail

MOSCOW — In the basement of a palace in the east end of the capital of the largest country on Earth, they strap a six-year-old girl in a wooden chair and press a button.

The chair begins to spin, slowly at first, then faster, faster, like a cybernetic electric beater, blending the little girl and her bright smile and her blond pigtails into the secret recipe that has earned the Union of Soviet Socialist Republics a harvest of gold in the world athletic competitions of the past quarter-century.

Another button is pressed and the eggbeater stops. The little girl tumbles from the seat and is directed to a long, straight line of yellow footprints painted on the floor. Dizzy, confused, and alone — Mama is locked outside — she takes her first hesitant step.

A pair of physiologists from the All-Union Physical Culture Research Institute stand by, clip-boards poised …

Across the hall, in a steam-heated little gymnasium, a dozen first-graders in blue tights hang from the ceiling. Suspended by loops of rope at the ankles and wrists, they wriggle and squirm like emerging butterflies, which perhaps they are.

They are here, at noon on a sunny weekday, at the Palace of Sport of Moscow Central Automobile Factory, to practise the jumps and spins that some day may win them an Olympic medal in figure skating. If the little girl in pigtails succeeds in negotiating the yellow brick road, and if she passes the rest of her preliminary tests for balance, co-ordination and flexibility, she may be allowed to join them.

This is the U.S.S.R., where the Olympic Games will be held next year. It's a land where Olympic medals flow like liquid gold, the hockey team soars to new heights of perfection, the weightlifters smash records and the boxers smash each other.

Some seek a magic key to unlock the secret and because it does not exist, conjure up visions of clandestine laboratories where evil scientists transplant the muscles of gorillas into the arms and legs of little girls.

On another day in a downtown office, a university professor and national sport official will say that this — the swivel chair, the ropes, the young scientists with their clipboards — is the key to Soviet success.

"We do have a secret," Prof. A. Korobkov will say. "Our state system of medical support of sport is our secret, not secret methods or miracle machines or technical equipment. Our medical science studies all the people who practice sport, in every city, in every town, in every area. We have special medical and physical culture dispensaries, hundreds of them, and special methodological centres where reports are studied."

There are other keys. Sheer numbers, for one. For another, an attitude toward Olympic disciplines that reveres the gold medal as the highest possible attainment, rather than a stepping stone to cereal and underwear ads. In North America, the word "amateur" has taken on a derogatory connotation; "inexperienced, unskilled," the dictionary says. But not in the Olympic city. Not in the penultimate year of the XXII Olympics.

At the Palace of Sport, an instrumental version of Hank Williams' bouncy *Jambalaya* echoes from the loudspeakers as a young blond woman approaches, wearing, it turns out, a necklace that marks her as a Taurean. It is morning in Moscow, a city without gumbo, crawfish or, officially, astrology, a wintry morning despite the calendar that says April and here, in the arena, she shivers.

Her name is Natalia Golovanova. A long time ago, as time is measured in sports, Natalia was

256

awarded the title of Master of Sport of the U.S.S.R., having finished fourth in the 200-metre back-stroke in the national swimming championships. Since then, she has completed her studies at the Institute of Physical Culture and has been dispatched, as countless thousands of other former competitors have been dispatched, to the front lines of international athletic combat. She coaches first-graders. She is 23.

This particular palace is the home of one of Moscow's special sports schools, where Olympic champions germinate. Here, a talented novitiate first is indoctrinated into the Soviet sport system. Here, the first privileges arrive: Special meals, trips to summer camp, expert coaching.

It is called, not surprisingly, the Moskvich Sport School for Children and Youth, and there is nothing like it in Canada. Government documents claim that there are 5,900 such schools throughout the U.S.S.R., attended by two million young athletes, or about four per cent of the country's total school enrolment.

"I went to one myself," Natalia says. "But I did not start until I was 12. Here, a child can enter the school at the age of seven and remain for 10 years. But by the age of 14 to 16, the most talented usually have been put under the supervision of a national team.

"The whole thing begins with a team of sports researchers from the All-Union Physical Culture Research Institute. All children pass through this team. They are tested for physical condition and aptitude. On this basis, the researchers can say what sport is applicable to the child.

"We select the sport in which the child has the highest chance of succeeding. By the time he enters the sports school he should select one sport only at which he hopes to achieve world championship.

"Every summer, the children go away to camp for six weeks. There is a camp for each sport that is taught at our school.

"The children eat breakfast, lunch and dinner here. We make sure that they get vitamins and a good diet. It is possible that they may eat a light supper at home also.

"Of course, it may happen that the child does not like the sport for which he is selected. But usually, they want only to be a champion, and they go along with the sport in which they are told they have the best chance.

"If they do not, they still may take part in sport in the times reserved for the public."

She never mentions the word fun.

• **1980** Sports Writing •

The dream has become a reality

Archie McDonald

Vancouver Sun

Art Levesque awoke, as usual, at 4:15 without aid of an alarm clock and was at barn A at Exhibition Park by 5, exchanging good mornings with a smattering of people rubbing sleep from their eyes. Before opening the stall doors he greeted a ginger tom cat and various generations of that worthy's motley coloured offspring. He made a mental note to buy more cat food later in the day.

He checked the five stalls to see that the horses had passed the night in good health. Hustling Knight, a cheap claimer, got cursory attention but the filly in the next stall was sugar-talked as she snorted and voraciously pursued a tub of sweet feed — a mixture of oats, corn, and pellets — which Levesque carried into her stall. He called her "girl" a lot.

This was the start of an important day in the career of this particular girl, who would have her full name — Front Page Girl — in the program for the first time. Fourteen hours hence quinella players would see her as number five in the third race, a breathlessly short dash for two-year-old fillies who were all making their first starts.

"She eats everything up," noted Levesque. "Probably a better doer than her mother. She looks a lot like her mother, acts a lot like her, too, although she's probably got a little better temperament."

Maternal comparisons are inevitable. Front Page Girl's dam was a blur named Frannie. She was B.C. two-year-old champion 17 years ago, besting the great George Royal in two of three confrontations, but she had yet to produce a foal to emulate those performances.

"All I can say is they better have their running shoes on today," warned Levesque, now wielding a pitch fork. "The only thing that will beat her is if she stumbles out of the gate."

Levesque trains two horses on his own and baby-sits three others, including Front Page Girl, for trainer Jim Halket. Levesque worked for Halket when Frannie was numbered among a powerful stable bankrolled by Arthur Fouks. Runners such as Westbury Road, Black Pool, Jockey Cap and Hostiquette carried the red and white silks into virtually every Ex. Park stakes event. In those joyous days Halket was known as Diamond Jim.

He and his wife Fran now live comfortably on a farm in Langley and racing has become more hobby than livelihood. Racetrackers like Halket don't make their money from horses, but from the land. The ones who bought small farms on the outskirts of the city in the '40s and '50s cashed in their chips in the '70s. On this day he arrives at the track at 6:45. "Slow to get going on Monday mornings," he says.

Today Frannie's fourth foal is making her debut. Halket has gone to the post too many times and bet his money too often to get overly worked up over a first-time starter but he acknowledges he is long overdue for another quality horse.

"She's by Winning Shot — his last crop — and they are making good brood mares. I hope she turns out to be decent so we can carry on the breeding line. The only thing I don't want today is slop." He looks at the moiling sky and does not like his chances. "If you break just a little slowly, you get behind and that slop blinds you. But she's gifted with speed and Mena is a pretty good gate boy. But I'd like to hit a fast track."

Mena's first name is Joel, a solid journeyman jockey, who inherited the mount when Gary Demorest, who had galloped Front Page Girl and suffered the humility of being bucked off one morning, ended up, through the dealings of his agent, on Winning Minstrel.

Mena visits the barn and Halket calls him aside. Because a trainer has only a brief time to talk to a rider in the paddock before the race Halket wants to recommend to Mena that he not use the whip. "She has been shown the whip and tapped with it, but that's all. He might reach back and crack her and who knows how she'll react."

Front Page Girl returns from her gallop — two muddy laps around the three-furlong training track — and there is a suggestion that she is not exactly poetry in motion as she walks back to the barn. "Yeah she has a little hitch in her getalong," says Levesque. "She might be a little tender on one shin." Allan McKenzie, the exercise rider, notes that her troubles seem to disappear once she gets mobile.

"She's always gone that way," says Halket with a shrug. Again he looks at the sky. "I sure hope it doesn't come up slop."

Nature grants Halket his wish. Gradually clearing skies and a brisk breeze dry the surface from a mud pudding into small lumps of dirt which are rendered smaller and smaller by harrows. By the third race the track is rated as good, which is the next best thing to fast.

At 6:45 at night at the southeast end of Barn A the atmosphere has changed considerably from 6:45 in the morning. The people have swapped their work-clothes for downtown duds and they don't stand still for long. Race-trackers call it stall walking.

It is part of an anxious ritual. Front Page Girl had her water rations cut off three hours earlier, and was deprived of her evening meal. She knows something is up. Levesque and Fletcher wrap rundown bandages around her back ankles, a bit of padding covered by tape so that she doesn't scrape the seamoid joints on Ex. Park's sandy surface. She has not run down in training. The tape is only a precaution. Fletcher brushes her dark bay coat to a high shine and ointment is dabbed on her nostrils. "Ready as hands can make her," says Halket.

Fran Halket is apprehensive. "My stomach goes in a knot when they walk on the track," she says. Winning is not even a consideration. "I just want them to have a safe journey."

Frank Halket passes the time with June Anderson, whose husband is saddling Rifle Bird. June estimates Rifle Bird will need more experience and longer races to show her best. When her eyes light on Front Page Girl she exclaims, "My gosh, I can see Frannie like it was yesterday."

Jim Halket boosts Mena into the saddle, and reminds him again about the whip. "It's in the land of the gods now," he says.

The Halkets' box is in the clubhouse, almost on the finish line. All eyes rivet on Front Page Girl. Cripes, she's even money. Yes, she's acting fine. They're all in the gate. You've got binoculars, is anybody acting up? I don't think I'll look. She broke a little slowly. Where is she now? Second on the outside. Now she's in front. It's all over, Levesque predicts with an eighth of a mile to go.

Front Page Girl is by herself turning into the stretch, but Mongo's Kin is eating up ground. At the finish the winning margin is only a neck. Mena has not used the whip.

"She just went by that other filly on her own at the quarter pole," says the jockey, "and she was waiting for that other horse at the finish. She's a real nice filly but she's pretty sore. Maybe she bucked her shins."

"No, her shins are pretty good," Levesque assures the next day. "Maybe it's her shoulder. We gave her some bute after the race and she's walking pretty good today."

Halket would like to keep her in training, getting her up to a pair of five-furlong works. After that he would treat her shins and give her a rest on the farm. And then "if it looks like she's that kind of filly" aim at the rich races in the late summer.

Seventeen years ago Frannie was that kind of filly.

• **1985** Sports Writing •
Profile of sprinter Ben Johnson
Wayne Parrish
Toronto Star

One summer day eight years ago, a new kid shuffled on to the track at Lawrence Park Collegiate. Thin as a relay baton and wearing an old pair of high-top running shoes a size too big, he did one 200-yard tempo run, walked off the track and sat down in the stands.

When Charlie Francis, the presiding coach, went over and asked him what was wrong, the kid replied, "Leg weak, mon, gotta rest."

Francis shook his head and walked away. One 12-year-old sprinter more or less wasn't going to matter.

A lifetime later, Francis shakes his head again, this time at the memory. Even for him, it is hard sometimes to fathom just how far Ben Johnson has come.

At 23 — he was actually 15 that day at Lawrence Park, his under-nourished, 93-pound frame making Francis think otherwise — he's the finest Canadian male sprinter since Harry Jerome. It's not just the 100-metre bronze medal Johnson won at last summer's Olympic Games that says that but his consistently superior performances at major meets. While other sprinters like Tony Sharpe and Desai Williams have received more publicity, it's Johnson who has produced the big results.

And yet, he remains an enigma, largely if not wholly unknown by Canadians. Part of this is the fact he is a black from Jamaica. Of all the black sprinters, only Angella Taylor has managed to break through the barrier of public consciousness. At that, she does not begin to rank with a Brill or Joy or Konihowski.

In Johnson's case, there is something else. He's always been a shy individual. That, combined with his accent and a speech impediment, has often left the impression upon outsiders that he is less than intelligent.

That conclusion is not only incorrect — an hour's conversation proves him to be sensitive, thoughtful and, at times, eloquent — but sad. Yet, it is not atypical of the difficulties and prejudices encountered by many Caribbean youngsters who immigrate to Canada. To begin with, the culture shock is extreme. It runs the gamut from the weather — one recalls Williams' line when his plane from St. Kitts landed in Montreal and he saw everyone's breath in the frigid air: "Daddy does everyone in Canada smoke?" — to the lifestyle.

"Jamaica and here are two different worlds," Johnson said recently. "Back home, you would go out and get your fruit, go out and get fish. When you've lived like that, it's hard to get used to having to go to a grocery store."

Soon after his arrival, he and a couple of buddies were picked up for snaring and roasting a pigeon in a park. But how could one blame them? At home, that was their way of life.

The adjustment problems are underlined by the attitude of education officials. A recent controversy in North York, where 3,000 of 5,000 black students are from Jamaica, centres on the fact black kids who show the slightest difficulty with English or math or history are far more likely to be channeled into non-academic programs than white kids having the same problem. Officially, it's referred to as "streaming." Francis, who despairs of the effect it has had on many of his athletes, prefers to call it "dumping."

In Johnson's case, such treatment reinforced an image he'd had of himself since childhood. "When I was six years old, my mom sort of taught me I was dumb," he says. "I guess it was because I didn't talk too much around the house. I'd wake up in the morning, go out and come back at night. I played. We'd go get fruit to eat. We'd go swimming. None of my friends cared I didn't talk much."

He communicated best with his older brother Edward, who stuttered. When he was 12 or 13, Ben began teasing his brother by mimicking him. Before he knew it, the demon had taken hold of him too.

When he and five brothers and sisters followed his mother to Canada, Johnson, awed by the new world, retreated further into his shell. He took up sprinting only because Edward, who was much more outgoing, had done so and brought him along to workouts one day.

"He never hardly said anything," remembers Taylor of those early days. "He was so young then; on trips his brother wouldn't even let him order in a restaurant. Ben couldn't get a word in." As time went on, "he got more confidence. I got to know him better. I really like him. He's never rowdy or outgoing. He looks so shy to the public. I think that's why people stay away from him. But they don't understand him. He's great. It's his sense of humour, the things he says. He breaks me up all the time."

"It's a cultural thing," says Francis. "The whole sense of humour is different. It's like British humour. It's taken me a long time to pick it up. You know how it is, you have to be able to operate in everybody else's field to be appreciated."

When Edward Johnson left for college in 1978, "Ben began to really come out of his shell," says Francis. The previous winter, feasting on Kentucky Fried Chicken, his other shell had grown larger by 50 pounds. His stamina grew too and, while he still fought the perceptions of others — teammates often made him the butt of jokes — Johnson began to develop as a legitimate threat on the world scene. In the years since, it's he who has laughed last with better and better results. According to Francis, a large part of his success stems from the very quality that has led people to deride him — his retiring nature, which allows him to tune out the world before a race.

"At any meet, bad things are bound to happen," explains Francis. "People are always coming over and saying, 'How are we supposed to run with all this nonsense going down?' He doesn't see any of it. He can concentrate on what he's doing. He blocks all the rest out."

Echoes Taylor, "Ben has never had a beef. He knows what he wants to do and goes out and gets the job done."

Citing the Zurich race earlier this year in which Johnson led Carl Lewis for 95 metres, Francis says Johnson's absolute top speed is as good as anybody's, that only "a matter of mechanics" — his striding and body motion in the latter part of a race — stands between him and being No. 1 in the world.

Some say Johnson has changed since L.A., that he has come out of himself more, but he insists the transformation took place earlier than that.

"When I first came to this country, I didn't have the experience," he said. "That's why my brother did everything for me. It took time, but now I do everything on my own. I go to Europe to meets by myself."

He has heard the aspersions cast upon his intellect and felt their sting, but shows amazing equanimity about it.

"It is not fair when people do that," he said. "Sometimes nobody asked me anything, they just assumed I was not intelligent. I don't really take it to heart. In Jamaica, you could do something about it and get away with it. Here there are laws. So I have learned to be calm."

He has visited Jamaica, where his father still lives, just once in eight years. An older sister returned last year with a view to relocating permanently, but, finding the economic climate and mood on the island much changed, decided against it. Her experience reinforced Johnson's own feelings.

"It was a completely different life and sometimes I miss it," he says. "I miss all my friends, the warm weather, the sea. I lived on Montego Bay. But the economics is pretty bad there now."

He considers a moment, then adds, "I sometimes feel frustrated here in Canada, especially in the winter. But you adjust your feelings. There is where everything is good for me. I will die here."

● **1991** Sports Writing ●

What really counts: A visit with Toe Blake

Red Fisher

Montreal Gazette

It was cold, the man on the car radio was saying. Snow, he added, was on the way later in the day. Five to 10 centimetres, maybe, so bundle up warm.

The snow that had fallen in the area several days earlier had formed soft, white pillows on the short driveway leading to the building. On the second floor, a white, lined face peered out of the window, and then quickly disappeared. "Chateau sur le Lac, Blvd. 16289 Gouin Ouest" read the sign in front of the two-storey building.

Toe Blake sat in a hallway wheelchair, his head on his chest, eyes closed. The top of the exercise suit he wore was as gray as the weather outside. The only small splash of colour on it was the CH. The words "Montreal Canadiens," also in red, were below it. The exercise suit bottoms were blue. His hands were crossed on his chest.

"Hi, Toe," said Floyd Curry. "Look who's here, Toe."

His eyes remained closed.

"Don't wake him, Floyd. He needs his rest," a guy said.

"Toe," said Curry, "we've brought you some cookies. Wake up, Toe."

A slim black man named Andrew placed a hand on Blake's shoulder and shook him gently.

"Wake up, Toe," he said. "Let's get you up. You've got visitors, Toe."

Then he reached for the man who had been the very best of the National Hockey League's coaches for 13 uplifting seasons and shook him again. This time, Blake's eyes opened. An angry yell burst from his throat.

"That's it, Toe," said Andrew, his voice rising. "Let's get you out of this chair."

Almost two years have passed since Toe Blake was brought to this place. Only Andrew and the other warm souls who work there see him every day, talk to him, feed him and care for him, because they care. They smile a lot, talk a lot and, it's imagined, spread a lot of love around as only they can. They understand.

Andrew was on one side of Blake, holding and steering him into the bright, spacious dining room filled with empty tables. Curry, who once played on a Blake team, supported him carefully on the other side.

"There you go," said Andrew, easing Toe into a chair not far from the dining-room entrance. "There — isn't that good?

"Look what we have for you," he said, lifting a cookie toward Blake's mouth. "Eat, Toe, it's good."

Toe Blake, winner of eight Stanley Cups during his glorious seasons behind the Canadiens' bench, stared straight ahead, apparently hearing nothing, seeing less. It's what happens to people, Andrew whispered, when they're locked in the terrible vise that is Alzheimer's.

Or was he? Does anybody really know?

Once, everybody knew what Toe Blake stood for, how he felt, what he thought, liked, loved and hated. What he loved most was to win. Losing was what he hated.

He was rough, gruff, intimidating, wise, compassionate, unforgiving, scheming and hard-working — all of it dedicated to winning his eight Stanley Cups as a coach, including a National Hockey League record five in a row in the last half of the '50s. Winning wasn't merely a worthwhile target; it was everything. It was life itself.

Blake wore his strengths as a coach on his sleeve: The dedication, the humour and the violent temper. That, and more — all of it tied in with a remarkable hockey mind.

Frank Mahovlich was one of Blake's greatest admirers. He felt Blake took care of 50 per cent of what was needed to win.

"I've always felt that a good coach is the one who wins," Blake once said. "But 50 per cent? If that had been the case with me, my teams would have won a lot more games."

Goaltender Gump Worsley once was asked what made Blake special as a coach.

"There are 20 guys in that dressing room," replied Worsley, "and it's seldom you find even two of them alike. He knew each individual — the ones who worked from the needles, the ones who needed another approach.

"Between periods, he never blasted an individual," said Worsley. "He'd say some guys aren't pulling their weight. The guys who weren't knew who he was talking about and you'd see the heads drop. But he'd never embarrass anyone in front of everyone.

"His ability to handle players — I guess that's what you'd say made him great."

Was Toe thinking about Gump or Frank, sitting at the table yesterday, a plate of cookies in front of him? Once he was full of life and laughs and mischief and blessed with a thirst for winning. His eyes snapped and crackled with the joy of competition.

Now, at 79, his hair is white and his cheeks are sunken, but there was colour in them on this day.

"He looks good," said Curry quietly. "That's the best I've seen him lately. I was here a couple of weeks ago, and he really looked terrible. I couldn't believe that was Toe."

Blake sat at the table, staring. He didn't open his mouth until Andrew gently brought a cookie up to it.

"It's good, Toe," he said.

"Eat, Toe, it's good," said Curry, who has devoted the last few years to taking care of the man who took such good care of Curry the player.

"Why wouldn't I?" asked Curry. "He was such a good guy."

Toe reached for a second cookie, then a third and a fourth. On and on.

"He wants something to drink now," said Andrew. He lifted a small glass of cranberry juice to his mouth.

"Have a sip, Toe," he said. "Wash it down."

Toe drew on the juice.

"Merci," he said.

Andrew looked through his gold-rimmed glasses and smiled. So did Curry.

"His appetite is fantastic," said Andrew. "He don't refuse food. He'll finish all of this," he said, with a wave of his hand at the plate. "Most of the time, this is what he likes to do — eat. You haven't seen anything yet."

He placed an arm around Blake's shoulder.

"C'mon, eat — there you are, Toe," said Andrew.

"Does he watch hockey games on television?" Curry asked.

"Does he know what he's watching?" a guy asked.

"I would say yes, to a certain degree," said Andrew. "My belief is he knows. My own opinion is he knows."

Curry left to make a telephone call to his wife, June. Toe — who always wore a fedora during his years behind the Canadiens' bench — reached for the brown one Curry had left on the table. In his left hand, he held what was left of the plate of cookies. With the other, he pulled the fedora toward him. Then he ran his fingers over it — lovingly, almost. Then again and again.

"He seems to like your hat," Curry was told when he returned to the table. "It's almost as if he remembers what a fedora meant to him."

Curry blinked quickly. "It's a damned shame, isn't it?" he said. "Look at his hands. He still has hands like a bear. Geez, he was strong. Look — he's finished the cookies."

Blake stared at the empty plate. Then he lifted it with both hands, tilted it toward him and let the crumbs fall into his open mouth.

"Good, eh, Toe?" said Curry. "Very good. Remember me, Toe?" he asked.

It is that time of the year — a time for breathing in deeply and reflecting on what really counts. A time for remembering the good times.

Remember Toe.

• 1995 Sports Writing •

The bad boys of sport

Roy MacGregor

Ottawa Citizen

"Frank Merriwell would be appalled. We root for the bullies today. We glorify the scoffaws, admire arrogance, exalt egotism. No wonder the athletes think they can get away with any kind of antisocial behaviour. They're the new royalty. No wonder they act like Louis XIV."
— Legendary sports columnist Jim Murray

One week ago, when boxer Mike Tyson was released from jail after serving three years for rape, he stepped into a heated limousine stocked with Dom Perignon and pheasant and rode in a five-car convoy — four helicopters filming overhead — back to his 30,000-square-foot Ohio mansion where neighbours had tied yellow ribbons to their porches and his gates and where children stood cheering his return.

The convicted rapist returned from prison more famous than he had entered it, returned to an adoring world and talk of an immediate $140-million fight to determine the world's new heavyweight boxing champion.

Justice — the way it works in professional sports, anyway — had simply waited until he was back out to be served.

And how ironic that Tyson returned to his home with his new friend, former heavyweight champ Muhammed Ali. It is Ali, after all, who is widely credited with creating what is now known as attitude — as opposed, say, to "good attitude" — in professional sports. A generation earlier, Ali, too, had returned from prison a more famous person than he had entered. He served his time for draft evasion but had gained rather than lost his novel attitude: "I am the greatest!" And in a way he was easily the most famous celebrity in the world at the time.

The difference between Ali and Tyson is important. Both might be the best boxers of their times, but a generation ago there was something quite admirable about a man strong enough to go to prison for his beliefs. In 1995, how could there possibly be anything to admire in a man convicted of rape? What was there to recommend to the world in a man who, by age 19, had already been arrested more than two dozen times, a man who, prior to his conviction, had been accused of fondling, harassing, molesting or threatening to kill more than a dozen other women?

Perhaps we do not want to know the answer.

Today, the most famous celebrity in the world is O.J. Simpson, a former football star whose fame has skyrocketed since he was accused last June of all but severing the heads of his former wife, Nicole Brown, and her friend, Ronald Goldman.

Simpson, whose murder trial is being carried live around the world, is the author of a current best-seller on the incident and his autograph has become the most-sought-after in sports memorabilia circles, the value increasing dramatically if the signing took place after the killings. And Simpson, of course, has been happy to accommodate, using his ample free time to market his signature.

And it is not just a sleazy appetite fed by the supermarket tabloids and the television talk shows. The *Boston Globe* ran a fashion spread, "Justice on the chic," during the preliminary hearing, covering the proceedings as if they were taking place on a Paris runway rather than a Lost Angeles courtroom. It is happening at every conceivable level.

Perhaps it is a bit alarming to think that infamy can increase one's value in the sports world — that crime does indeed pay — but there is certainly enough disturbing evidence about to support an argument.

The sole rival to Tyson's release as the sports event of 1995 comes from the return of Michael Jordan to the National Basketball Association. Jordan, the highest paid athlete in the world — $42 million a year in salary and endorsements — quit basketball suddenly in 1990, claiming he was tired of the game after three consecutive NBA championships with the Chicago Bulls. He left, he said, to fulfil a lifelong dream of becoming a professional baseball player.

He may also have left, of course, because it was a better option than suspension. At the time, Jordan was under investigation for gambling, including a $1.75-million round of golf with a convicted cocaine dealer. His father had been murdered under mysterious circumstances. There is, one suspects, more to this than an unfulfilled dream.

As a baseball minor leaguer hitting .202 and riding a team bus, it was widely assumed Jordan's star would diminish. Yet it did not in the least.

In his year out of basketball, he made almost $50 million in endorsements. His advertising stock remained so high that, when rumours of his pending return to the Bulls hit the New York Stock Exchange, the stocks of companies connected to him rose a stunning $3.25 billion.

Jordan returned bigger than ever, slam dunking the dark cloud that had supposedly been gathering over his image.

But then, why should we be surprised? The world's best-known soccer player, Diego Maradona, greets reporters gathering outside his Buenos Aires home with an air rifle, injuring five with pellets. His fame quotient rises.

The most famous baseball player not in the Hall of Fame — Pete Rose — has discovered being banned from the game for gambling may be the best thing that ever happened to him. Rose has formed his own company to organize autograph galas, charging $65 for the effortless act of signing a bat.

Bob Probert, the best-known hockey player outside the National Hockey League, is on yet another comeback — despite being "banned for life" only five years ago. The Chicago Blackhawks signed the brawler to a four-year, $9.25-million contract a week after he lost control of his motorcycle and was found to have a blood-alcohol count nearly four times the Canadian legal limit. Out of the detox centre, he will soon be back in the penalty box.

"While ordinary mortals in public positions would likely be shamed into quitting, or at least be held up to public condemnation," the *Calgary Herald*'s Catherine Ford wrote about the Probert signing, "sports stars, as long as they are male, profit from the notion they are dangerous and out of control."

So it seems anyway.

■ ■ ■

The relationship between violence and sports is hardly new. It goes back to, and beyond, the throwing of the Christians to the lions, a sports spectacle that today would be rather politically incorrect but most assuredly a blockbuster television event if the rights were available.

There were once tournaments in which death was almost a certainty — in one early European competition held near Cologne in 1249, 60 knights died in a staged battle — and all the early crowd records were set at public hangings.

"We live in a freakish world," Muhammed Ali said in 1975, "a vicious world. People like to see blood."

They also, it would appear, liked to cheer bad guys. Long before the World Wrestling Federation made evil an art form, various sports deified certain bad boys. Baseball's Ty Cobb was as well known for his determination "to spike his grandmother" if necessary as for his lifetime .367 batting average. Hockey's Sprague Cleghorn was such a bad actor that in 1918, when he was sidelined with a broken leg, he was charged with assaulting his wife with his crutch.

"In the old days," the *L.A. Times* great sports columnist Jim Murray has written, "sports journalists pretty much restricted their coverage to runs, hits and errors. The coverage stayed pretty much between the foul lines. The writers had to know what kind of out-of-control human Cobb really was, but they spared the public. They let Cobb bask in a prism of his own accomplishments. Athletes were our new royalty. Cobb should have been in therapy. Or in prison. Instead, he was in the Hall of Fame. The first one there, in fact."

The classic example of the pampered, protected athlete has always been Babe Ruth, whose boozing and womanizing was ignored by sports writers who chose, instead, to portray him as a mythical figure who spent all his time visiting children's hospital wards when he wasn't pointing out where his home runs would land.

But Ruth was hardly alone. The truth was never even hinted at for the likes of Jim Thorpe, Hack Wilson, Grover Cleveland Alexander — or even sports' greatest icon, Notre Dame's George Gipp of Knute Rockne and "Win one for the Gipper" fame. Gipp, it turns out, was every bit the gambler Pete Rose was, even to the point of betting on his own games.

Along came the '60s, however, and everything began to change rapidly. Boxing's Muhammed Ali and football's Joe Namath more than others issued a challenge to the old and accepted ah-shucks humble approach of the Frank Merriwell books and begat bragging sports heroes who could back up their mouths with deeds. Ali was the heavyweight champion; Namath won the Super Bowl. Arrogance was chic.

By the time a generation had passed, ego insanity was ruling. "I consider myself different," said football and baseball and advertising star Bo Jackson. "I don't want to be put on a pedestal, but I see myself as a different being, not from this planet. It's as if I'm passing through here, a being that happened to choose this body, like I'm renting it while I'm here."

Athletes were different, and reporting was different. Watergate had an effect on all reportage, even on journalism's "toy department" — sportswriting. Whereas Dick Beddoes, the late *Globe and Mail* sports columnist, could tell a Senate committee in the spring of 1970 that "the profession is still burdened with hacks who make tin-can gods out of cast-iron jerks," more and more the cast-iron jerks were exposed.

They didn't much like it, and it caused severe problems at times between writers — rarely broadcasters — and those whose images were up for measure. A Cincinnati writer had the team meal dumped on him; a San Diego reporter had football quarterback Jim McMahon blow his nose over him; a Philadelphia hockey writer found himself being held down in a shower while members of the Flyers stripped him and assaulted him; a woman covering the New England Patriots was humiliated and sexually assaulted in the dressing room.

The number of "cast-iron jerks" grew. Even golf ended up with one: John Daly, whose 300-yard drives paled in comparison to his drinking and wife-battery and common assault problems.

And yet so often — and never so dramatic as in the case of Daly — these same jerks would capture the public attention in a manner in which not even Namath or Ali could have imagined. They were embraced, cheered. Their endorsement value began to soar.

When public interest began to plummet for professional tennis, it was widely said that the reasons had to do with the current stars; no one was bad enough. Pete Sampras, the current top male player, is just too nice. No tantrums, no thrown racquets, no obscene gestures, chewing out of officials, off-court scandals. The recent resurgence of Andre Agassi — Sampras' alter-ego in many ways — has been applauded with relief by those who make their money from tennis, particularly those who wish to sell products using bad-ass athletes.

"We applaud jerks," Joe Gilmartin recently wrote in the *Phoenix Gazette*, "and then wonder why our kids think it's cool to be a jerk. And the dissing of Sampras as dull serves as a sharp reminder that the jerks seem to get the most attention and adulation."

■ ■ ■

There can be little doubt in 1995 that there has been a quantum shift in the inherent values of sport. French philosopher Albert Camus may have once written that sports was "where I had my only lesson in ethics," but more and more Modern Sport is arguing counter to past beliefs.

Cheaters now prosper (corked bats, hooking and holding in hockey, steroids in football and track). No one needs an education to fall back on (not when rookie hockey players sign $12.25-million contracts). And, as Mike Tyson is proving this very week, crime does indeed pay.

When today's sociologists seek to understand what it is that caused the former image of sports — clean-cut and healthy — to shift to an in-your-face attitude, they end up, invariably, with one explanation that would have seemed incomprehensible to the world of Frank Merriwell.

Fashion. Sneakers and jackets and caps. The sneakers industry took off first, largely inspired by a fitness movement that created a booming market and then became a reality in which shoe manufacturers have somehow convinced poor, inner-city American kids that happiness is measured by a closet — if they are lucky enough to have a closet — filled with a minimum of 20 pairs of new sneakers.

Nike and Reebok began an advertising war that increasingly became a one-on-one attitude competition. Soon other companies had joined in and the connection between attitude and sports success was part of the collective value system.

When skater Tonya Harding began her fight to stay on the U.S. Olympic team in the face of charges that she was involved in the attack on rival Nancy Kerrigan, Nike sent $35,000 for her "defence fund." The company maintained it was just being civic-minded — innocent until proven guilty and all that — but think about it: Kerrigan was already sponsored by Reebok.

When British Knight began chasing the same market, they used promising young NBA rookies in television spots that showed them beating up on other players, blowing up opposing players, ripping down the backboards and urging youngsters to act exactly as they felt like acting.

In one of British Knight's most infamous ads, basketball star David Robinson asks viewers if they know how to say, "kick some butt." The company explained that "kick some butt" in this context really means "Let's go get 'em." Right.

In time, educators, police and social workers began sounding alarms. High-priced, high-tech sneakers had become part of the drug subculture: Kids selling drugs in order to pay for the necessary shoes, dealers enticing kids with expensive sneakers. *Sports Illustrated* soon ran a cover story entitled, "Your sneakers or your life." It was not a joke.

Jackets and caps also took off, with team logos becoming part of the U.S. gang culture. It soon became evident young men were being killed merely for wearing the wrong "colours" in the wrong neighbourhoods.

And what did the clothing manufacturers do in response? They began, more and more, to produce new merchandise featuring all team logos set on dark and black backgrounds — even if there was no black whatsoever in the original team colours.

Black, of course, was the colour preference of the street.

And the manufacturers, of course, were merely filling a need.

■ ■ ■

Boorish behaviour by a few tended to damage the whole. Baseball players — by far the most insufferable of professional athletes — are now held in such poor regard that even the advertisers who usually embrace jerks are staying away from them.

They are hard to love at any level. When Rickey Henderson set the all-time base-stealing record, he not only told the crowd that "I am the greatest ever," he let his teammates know that chipping in to buy him a Ferrari for his accomplishments was not what he expected — Rickey wanted a Lamborghini. Kirk Gibson attacked young autograph seekers. Mike Marshall went on strike, saying the Boston Red Sox should be paying for his wife's parking tickets.

Hockey players, on the other hand, remain — by widespread consensus of sports reporters — the least spoiled and least obnoxious, the image seemingly handed down by an endless string of polite, thoughtful, caring players: Howe, Beliveau, Orr, Gretzky. Players such as Pittsburg goaltender Tom Barasso — equally ignorant to sportswriters and children seeking autographs — remain an anomaly. It is even said that the Penguins' extraordinary success this season is directly linked to an injury that has kept Barasso out of the dressing room.

Being ignorant is not a crime. Even so, there is something about the attitude of many professional athletes that causes them to feel they are not only above their fans, but above the law.

"We feel as athletes — some of us — that we're special," NFL player Troy Vincent has said. "A person is making big money and he's on TV so he feels like he always has to be right. And a little woman, what she says doesn't mean anything. It's like: This is what I want! And you're going to give it to me! Or I'm going to take it!"

Canadian freelance writer Laura Robinson has spent considerable time researching sexual assault in Junior A hockey and, according to what she has found over the past few years: "There is an overwhelming evidence male athletes operate in a world where they feel untouched by laws."

Robinson argues: "Male athletes don't have a killer gene. Most male athletes don't sexually assault women and aren't violent, but recent studies show the chances of a male committing assault and sexual assault increase dramatically if he is on a team, and his sport stresses aggression and violence. This also is the kind of guy the sports media and the public adulate."

U.S. author Susan Brownmiller — *Against Our Will* — has even suggested that sports violence plays an integral role in maintaining male supremacy. All sports leagues vehemently deny any such connection, but it is noteworthy that, shortly after O.J. Simpson was arrested, the NFL dispatched counsellors around the league to discuss domestic violence in special sessions with the players.

The *Washington Post* also conducted an extensive survey that showed that, between Simpson's first run-in with the law concerning domestic violence in 1989 and his being charged in 1994, 141 U.S. college and professional football players were reported to police for violent behaviour toward women.

The *Post* found that victims and prosecutors invariably felt that the players had been given preferential treatment by police and judges — 61 of the cases were dropped — and that teams had little interest in disciplining players whose crimes did not affect the on-field performance.

Little wonder that a few years ago, *Sports Illustrated* could ask: "Have we entered an era in which bad apples are so prevalent in sports that you can't tell the players anymore without an arrest sheet? Are shame and fame becoming synonymous in big-time sport?"

■ ■ ■

In no sport has attitude had such profound effect on behaviour as basketball. The boorish conduct has now reached epic proportions — from former star Wilt Chamberlain's book boast that he bedded 12,000 women during his NBA career to red-yellow-and-green-haired Dennis Rodman's obnoxious behaviour throughout the 1994–95 season.

The fans, of course, love Rodman. He's fresh — in both senses of the word. Whereas the basketball highlight used to be the slam dunk, it is now trash talk.

"In the good old days," says NBA star Charles Barkley, "you just talked to have fun. Now there's a vindictiveness in your voice. I think it's in the players' mentality: They make so much money, they've got long-term guaranteed contracts, and they turn into jerks."

The arrogance is, at times, flabbergasting. When the Houston Rockets' Vernon Maxwell appeared in court for the third time in less than two years — this time for carrying an illegal weapon — his interpretation of events was that the arresting officer wanted to get on television.

Basketball's new angry side has had an alarming ripple effect as it comes down through the system. Some Toronto-area schools recently cancelled their basketball seasons because they could no longer deal with the violence or the cost of police surveillance at interschool games.

The best news about Jordan's return to the court may not be the remarkable 55 points he scored in an early game against the New York Knicks, but the fact that he — and others, such as former star Kareem Abdul-Jabbar — are finally beginning to speak out against attitude and the boors who have so embraced it.

The time has come, Jordan says, to grow up. It's time, he says, to "make people respect professional athletes as professionals — and not just jerks making a lot of money."

Unfortunately, the children cheering Mike Tyson's release may have already sounded the note that it is already too late in the game to change the players.

• **1996** Sports Writing •

Strong body, big heart

Erin Anderssen

New Brunswick Telegraph Journal & Saint John Times Globe

She curls her body over the cement block, nerves crackling, ears cocked for the snap of the starter's gun.

Driven by instinct, her muscles tighten and her feet spring away. Her head drops until her ears are squeezed between her elbows. She feels the shadows arching around her, and then she is alone with a wall of water and bubbles, and a long black line. For a few seconds, it is almost quiet. She shatters the surface. Her arms coil. Her legs slam down. And she swallows that first piece of air, tasting the flavour of the race.

If she is on, if the race belongs to her, she will skim along the surface as though the water is carrying her down the lane. Her strokes will look slow and languid even at record speed. The clock won't matter.

She will feel weightless, like she could swim forever.

It is cold and damp at 6 a.m., even in June. The Fredericton campus of the University of New Brunswick is deserted. Inside the Sir Max Aitken pool, 20 members of Fredericton's swim team have already started their morning practice. The distorted guitars of the Tragically Hip rumble through muffled speakers. No one is late. Coach Claude St-Jean is strict about tardiness. He expects all his swimmers — even Olympian Marianne Limpert — to be stretching on deck 15 minutes before practice starts.

In four weeks, Limpert will step onto the block in Atlanta, Ga., for the women's 200-metre individual medley (which includes the butterfly, backstroke, breaststroke and freestyle). She is expected to also swim two freestyle relays, but the medley is her race. She is ranked sixth in the world and the national record she set at Olympic trials in 1992 still stands today. Not even Limpert has touched it since. She will not say much about an Olympic medal, but the desire to break her own record consumes her. She wants it very badly. And she wants it to happen in Atlanta.

This morning, though, the Olympics seem far away. Limpert lines up in the fast lane with four other swimmers, dives into the water and starts a loping, front crawl, the first length of a long warm-up set that St-Jean has chalked on the board. 50-metre drill. She touches her finger to her back on every stroke, focusing on lifting her elbows. 50-metre pull. She swims with her arms only, a buoy held between her knees to keep her legs still. 50-metre kick. She streams down the lane holding a flutter board, churning white water. Again. 50-metre drill. 50-metre kick. 50-metre pull. And again.

Finally, St-Jean gives a new set of 25-metre sprints. "I'm giving you a five-second rest," he shouts over their grumbling. "I'm generous."

The swimmers slice through the water, counting their time on the clock after every length. Limpert averages 6,000 metres per practice. Almost 250 lengths of the pool in two hours. Ten times a week. She sometimes sings Christmas carols in her head to fight the boredom. She says, "You can go pretty insane after awhile, going up and down that black line."

Limpert bolts around a sluggish Ford in her red Volkswagen convertible and slips onto the bridge for Fredericton's north end. Practice ended in the weight room about 30 minutes ago and Limpert is late for her daily massage. Once on the bridge, she starts to relax. She jokes about how her driving scares her mother and grumbles about her unruly hair, sounding, for the first time, like a 23-year-old university student.

It is unusual for a swimmer to stay in the sport as long as she has — Atlanta will be her second Olympics. But Limpert has a strong, focused mind; she lives to swim. She has never had a serious boyfriend because, she says, "I've never met a guy I'm willing to give up swimming for." School has come second, a mix of physical education courses she no longer wants to pursue. When she studies languages at Montreal's McGill University this fall, she will practically have to start over. But she doesn't care. "This is my job," she says. "I can't imagine my life if I wasn't swimming."

Limpert's coaches say she is as intense as any athlete they have ever known. Among her friends, she is more likely to laugh at jokes than crack them, as though protecting some secret inner store of energy. On Canada's swim team, she is known for not getting rattled on race day. "She's never a basket case," says Shannon Shakespeare, a Winnipeg native who is slated to swim on the freestyle relay team with Limpert in Atlanta. "You don't have to worry about Marianne freaking out before a relay. She's always there to calm everyone down and get it together."

At the 1995 World Short Course Championships in Rio de Janeiro, head coach Dave Johnson needed a solid swimmer for the first leg of the women's 200-metre freestyle relay, someone who wouldn't crack under pressure. Limpert wasn't swimming well at the meet — she'd finished fifth in the individual medley, almost a second off her best time — but against the advice of other coaches, Johnson gave her the spot. "The lead changed hands five times," he remembers. "Some went out fast and died. Some went out slower and came back faster. And in the end, when all was said and done, Marianne touched the wall second, only five-tenths of a second out of first place. Because of that the relay team was still in the race and went on to win the gold medal. She came through big time."

It is obvious that this is the last place Limpert wants to be, sitting in sweats on the bleachers above the pool an hour before afternoon practice, struggling to answer impossible questions. She alternates between glancing at her watch and the clock high on the pool wall. She is polite and candid even as she fidgets, but her smile is strained. Her focus is on bigger things.

"I don't really know why I swim," she says after a pause. "Something is driving me to keep going. And I'm not going to stop until I've reached that level of success that makes me say, 'Okay, this is great, this is what I wanted to do.' Then I can move onto something else."

So Limpert is a mystery, even to herself. She cannot articulate what pushes her out of bed and into the pool at dawn to swim so many lengths. Her talent and drive are fed by an insatiable desire to win. She is miserable in defeat. "Her fuel is success," says Johnson, now the Olympic team coach.

In January, 1989, at the Montreal winter nationals, a 16-year-old unknown from Fredericton burst out of a 30th-place ranking in the 200-metre individual medley, shaved an incredible five seconds off her best time, and made the finals. Coaches started to whisper the Limpert name. But that night, she finished last, and when asked about her beginnings today, Limpert has to be reminded of Montreal. "I prefer to be on the podium," she says simply. "I want to win — that's the bottom line."

When she was nine years old, Limpert announced that she was going to the Olympics. "In the back of my mind, I always knew I would go." In the comfortable, brown bungalow across the road from the Fredericton airport where Heinz Limpert flew helicopters and his wife, Marianne, worked part-time as a secretary, that didn't seem so impossible. This was their only child; they were devoted parents. They had the money and the time to support her ambitions. Already, she had a good, strong kick and swam like a fish in the bathtub-shaped pool in their backyard. "It's not that we forced her," says Heinz. "It came by itself. Sometimes we even had to hold her back."

A tall, lean man with a hearty laugh and a gentle German accent, Heinz Limpert has his own Olympic ghosts. In 1963, he left Germany to study in Kitchener, Ont. The next year, he won the Canadian heavyweight boxing championship but was denied a berth on the Olympic team because he had not lived in Canada long enough to become a citizen. When asked about it, he waves his hand impatiently to stop the question and turns the subject back to his daughter, not wanting to steal her thunder.

Marianne Limpert was born a year after her parents married — on Oct. 10, 1972, in a tiny hospital in Matagami, Que., a northern logging town where engineers, surveyors and helicopter pilots dragged their families to work on the James Bay hydro project. In the winter, the temperature dropped to –35, and the summer air was thick with blackflies. To the German newlyweds, Matagami was the end of the world. It was not the ideal place to raise a child. They stayed only a few months.

Heinz eventually got a job at the Fredericton airport and the family settled in New Brunswick. When she was nine years old, Limpert joined the Oromocto Titans Swim Team at CFB Gagetown. It was a shaky beginning; she was disqualified from her first big race for not touching the wall during a turn.

"She would get very hard on herself," says Limpert's first coach, Susan Feitch. "But the potential was there that she would go great places."

Limpert looks scrawny in team photos, an impish grin creasing her heart-shaped face, frizzy curls drooping over her brow. She was splitting her time then between figure skating and swimming, but winning more often in the pool. She never repeated her mistake from that first race. In the pictures and newspaper clippings Feitch keeps in a shoe box, she is draped in medals.

When she was 14 years old, Limpert gave up figure skating for good. "I got tired," she says, "of landing on my butt." She quit the Oromocto club and started training in Fredericton to get more pool time.

Three years later, she surged into the finals at the Montreal nationals. At the Canada Games that summer, she won gold medals in the 200-metre individual medley and 100-metre breaststroke. By 1992, she was a national record holder, chasing world champions in the finals at the Barcelona Olympics.

Limpert's expression dims, remembering Barcelona. She stretches her legs over the bleacher and stares down at the chlorine-green water. "Here was my big chance but I took two or three strokes and I could just feel it. I didn't have that light energy. I was sluggish and heavy. This was the race of my life — there was no worse time for that to happen. I totally psyched myself out.

And you can't stop to think about anything."

Her watch suddenly beeps. It is 5:10 p.m. On the pool deck below, swimmers wander in, shaking St-Jean's hand in greeting. Practice starts in five minutes. "This is my alarm, so I remember to go down and get changed," she explains.

Limpert stands at 5-feet 11 inches, a sleek 140 pounds. She has an expressive face, sharp eyes and a strong jaw. Her stride eats up the pool deck. Her body is so long that, walking or swimming, she gives the impression of a movie in slow motion.

She arrives at practice smiling, shakes St-Jean's hand, and starts stretching. No one talks much. St-Jean doesn't waste time. He flicks the music on and gives the swimmers a quick warm-up set in the pool. Then he writes a 2,400-metre backstroke drill on the board. The backstroke is Limpert's weakest stroke.

"It's a fun one," he assures her.

"Oh, they all are," she scoffs back.

"She just read my mind," he grins, eyeing her shoulder roll down the lane. "And she doesn't like me very much. She knows what's coming next."

What's next is a 2,400-metre individual medley set, where the swimmers read their heart rate from a hand-held machine every few lengths, pushing to their maximum rate. Swimmers loathe the machine because there's no cheating it — swim a lazy lap and your heart rate will betray you. After Limpert's first four lengths, the machine reads 167 beats a minute. Her maximum is 196.

Limpert is backstroking down the pool when a male teammate kicking behind a flutter board suddenly snags her arm and pulls her up short. She is not hurt, but she is angry. The crash has ruined her focus. She starts down the lane again. Irritation shows in the tight line of her mouth and the way her arms slap the water.

"I'm getting out of here," St-Jean winces, and slides over to the next lane of swimmers. When Limpert touches the wall and turns for her next length, he doesn't look.

"It's just one of those nights," he says later. "The training is starting to get to her. You have to know when to stay away."

Limpert has gone through a number of coaches. Since leaving Fredericton in 1990 to train with Yeno Tihanyi, the Hungarian physiologist who coached Alex Baumann to two Olympic gold medals, she has moved around five times. She has a reputation for being demanding, but then, says Johnson, "Most of the compliant, do-what-you're-told-type athletes never amount to much anyway."

Limpert says, "There are some people who are difficult to coach because they're idiots. I think I'm difficult to coach because I'm too much of a perfectionist."

She stayed in Sudbury for eight months, boarding with her mother in the home of an old Polish woman, who could never understand why a pretty teen-ager was too tired to go to the movies on Friday night. Tihanyi was a stern taskmaster. He pushed his swimmers hard, and Limpert would come home at night too exhausted to carry on a conversation with her mother. When her race times started dropping, Limpert moved to the University of Toronto to train. Her mother went back to Fredericton.

"Marianne was not very patient," says Tihanyi. "She might have felt a little held back. I'm a no-compromise coach and I don't give swimmers too many choices. Marianne can't handle this type of approach. She likes to have her two cents worth."

Training went better in Toronto. In 1992, fighting tendinitis at the Olympic trials, Limpert set national records in the individual medley and the 100-metre freestyle. But in Barcelona, struggling almost from the start, she finished sixth. She had expected to win a medal. "I think she ran out of gas," says her former coach, Byron MacDonald. Eighteen months later, Limpert went home for Christmas and didn't return. "In her mind," MacDonald says, "she was getting stale. The honeymoon with Toronto was over."

Limpert trained in Fredericton for seven months before moving out to the new National Training Centre in Calgary, which boasted the latest high-tech equipment and sports medicine therapy. In August, 1995, she arrived at St-Jean's doorstep and asked to come home for good. "I respect all the coaches I've had," she says today. "I don't have any axes to grind. I was just looking for something different."

St-Jean, 41, is a compact man with a straightforward manner and a devotion to the technical precision of swimming. "If you were a gymnast on the beam," he is fond of telling his athletes when they make a sloppy turn, "you would be dead now." St-Jean has been coaching since he was 16 years old, mostly at low-profile Quebec clubs. In a sport with a strong western bias, he is a relative unknown. But Limpert obviously respects him. They have the easy camaraderie of good friends, as if always sharing some secret joke. "We laugh a lot," Limpert says. "For some coaches, once you're off the pool deck, that's where it ends. But not Claude. I need someone to hold my hand and give me that reassurance. Just being around Claude is calming for me."

St-Jean treats Limpert like the other swimmers on the team. During practice, she logs the same number of lengths as everyone else. St-Jean has made her spend the night in a sleeping bag on a classroom floor in Edmundston and, last weekend, she took a bus to a Quebec City meet when she had the money to fly. "Some coaches will do anything to keep their Olympic hopefuls happy," he says. "But I don't let her do anything she wants."

Tonight, at practice, he goes easy on her. She is tired, he knows, and impatient. "It's a long wait to the Olympics," he says.

Slowly, frustration melts into determination, and Limpert is digging into the water again. Her speed picks up, and on the machine, her heart rate jumps to 182 beats per minute. "You see," says St-Jean. "The whole mood is changed. She's back in the practice."

She finishes the 2,400-metre set swimming two lengths in 28.5 seconds, as fast as she starts some of her races. Her heart rate is 191, a few beats shy of her maximum. St-Jean is gleeful. "You see," he says again, grinning, "she can go faster."

The Olympics will not be easy. In a sport rife with steroids, all you can do is swim and pray the users test positive. Limpert learned this the hard way when she finished fourth in the individual medley at the 1994 world championships in Rome. A month later, the Chinese swimmer who won the race was caught using steroids. She was banned from competition for two years, including the Atlanta Olympics, but not stripped of her gold medal — a move that would have set Limpert on the podium.

To win an Olympic medal, Limpert will likely have to swim the individual medley in just over 2.13. She has never done it before. Even her national record of 2.15:15 is more than two seconds short of the current world champion, and she has not repeated it for four years. At Olympic trials in April, swimming what St-Jean calls a "safe race," she finished in 2.15.75.

That is not to say it can't be done.

In 1992 at Barcelona, when Mark Tewksbury stunned everyone by winning gold in the 100-metre backstroke, he shaved more than a second off his previous best time. Limpert had done it herself, only a few months earlier at the Olympic trials.

This time, Limpert will have the benefit of experience. She is in the best shape she's been in since Barcelona. Technically, her strokes are clean. Her dives and turns are faster and more precise than they were at trials this year. And in her mind, she is ready to race.

"If Marianne makes up her mind to do something," says MacDonald, "she's going to do it. She's going to go through a brick wall if she has to. I knew that when Marianne was in a race, tied with another athlete with 10 metres to go, it was going to be almost impossible to beat her."

Racing is Limpert's strength. She often wins in the last seconds, pushing her body mentally beyond what it can do physically. "She's able to reach a bit deeper," says Tihanyi, comparing her to Baumann, who set 14 world records. "Alex could race when everyone else was falling apart. And Marianne can do that."

This weekend, Limpert and St-Jean leave for a training camp in Gainesville, Fla., where they will cut back on her swimming and hone her strokes for July 25. St-Jean will not be there then — he is not one of the four national team coaches allowed on the pool deck in Atlanta, so he is staying home to watch the race on TV, connected to Limpert 24 hours a day by cell phone.

"Everything is there," he says. "She doesn't need me. In the ideal race, you just do it. 'Cause it will come out at the right time."

On race day, Limpert will stay away from the pool deck as long as she can, avoiding the tension of her competitors. She will concentrate on lifting her chin during the butterfly, on touching her hands and then her feet to the wall in one tight, clean motion, on saving her legs until that last 50 metres, on finishing the race as fast as she starts.

And then it comes down to two minutes alone with the water, and finding that one, rare spot where you're lighter and faster than ever before.

Brian Gable

Regina Leader-Post

Who decides how Canadians think? Brian Gable offers his answers in this 1986 NNA winner. The Saskatoon-born cartoonist has won two NNAs, his second in 1995 with the *Globe and Mail*.

Qui décide de la façon de penser des Canadiens? Brian Gable donnait sa réponse dans sa caricature de 1986 qui lui a permis de remporter un prix du CCJ. Ce caricaturiste né à Saskatoon devait en remporter un deuxième en 1995 alors qu'il travaillait pour le *Globe and Mail*.

CHAPTER 6

Money and Movers

*While Business has only had an NNA category of its own since 1987,
some of the entries in this chapter won earlier awards
for Enterprise Reporting, Spot News, Feature Writing
and Staff Corresponding.*

By Nick Russell

DURING THE SHORT LIFE OF THE NATIONAL NEWSPAPER AWARDS IN CANADA, BUSINESS WRITING has come of age.

The selections in this chapter are fascinating because they not only demonstrate the good writing of the time — as do all the sections of this anthology — but they reflect this maturing process. At the beginning of this period, there were few, good, reliable, fair business writers with any significant background in economics or business. Today, business writers are among some of the country's best and most influential journalists. Many are highly regarded as individuals, and the business sections for which they toil are respected across the country and closely monitored in the boardrooms of the nation.

What happened?

After the Second World War, Canadian journalism, like journalism elsewhere, was still recovering from its earlier reputation for "yellow journalism." As recently as the 1950s, a few newspapers were still party shills, striving on behalf of the Liberals or the Conservatives, and there were still vestiges of payoffs to a few reporters (the celebrated Christmas envelopes from politicians to friends in the Press Galleries). Today, such practices would appall any Canadian journalist.

At the same time, reporters in general were often poorly educated (Canada's first three journalism graduates emerged from Carleton University in 1946), and investigative journalism was largely unknown. Neither business nor journalism had thought much about ethics in general, and journalists were so poorly paid that having an outside job (say, writing a politician's speeches or doing press releases for a company) was accepted as a legitimate way of making a living wage. Few, if any, businesses had developed codes of conduct, and neither business nor journalism felt the need to be accountable to the public.

It seems incredible to read, today, parts of the Davey Commission Report (The Special Senate Committee on Mass Media), which 30 years ago reported that "in Canada the great majority of working newspapermen and women earn from their direct employers less than $9,000." (Vol.II, p.440). It continues, with a tone of approval or even envy, to note that this was padded out with such perks as "expense-paid trips to all manner of interesting places" provided by the travel industry and foreign governments:

"Distributed judiciously among the staff these trips can make for excellent employee-employer relations on one hand and confer upon the individual a substantial benefit. He makes trips to places he could never afford on his basic salary."

For most newsrooms, "freebies" such as a trip to the Volkswagen plant in Germany are long gone: Canada's daily newspapers, concerned to protect their credibility, insist on paying their way or not going at all.

The poor salaries also led to high turnover in the industry, and, as Davey noted in 1970, "Reporters have a discernible tendency to desert the business when they approach forty." Such a trend — typically senior writers moving to public relations — would particularly hit business departments, where journalists had earned good reputations and made good connections with industry, but had reached the top of the newsroom pay-scale (often just four figures), while they were seduced to PR by significantly better salaries and better working conditions.

Many writers, back then, could not resist the opportunity to escape dirty, smoky newsrooms, often working nights and weekends, in favour of the calm stability of writing press releases and CEOs' speeches. By contrast today, newsroom environments are eminently better, pay is better, and public relations may have lost some of its appeal.

Despite fears in the 1990s about the potential impact on newsrooms of advertisers and profit-driven proprietors, there was vastly more of this — at least from advertisers — back in the '30s and '40s. David Hayes, in his book about the *Globe and Mail* titled *Power And Influence*, described the early days:

Ever since the turn of the century, the Globe's *business pages had been devoted mainly to promoting the mining industry, and companies were willing to pay a premium for the uncritical coverage.*

The result was a too-cozy relationship between some reporters and some business people, and a lack of tough, critical journalism about industry.

Today, on the other hand, few newsrooms will tolerate writing stories about advertisers where there is no genuine news, nor will they consider showing stories to advertisers before they're published — both common practices half a century ago. And back then, reporters were, perhaps, more credulous: After all, they and their sources were all "gentlemen," so skeptical questioning and critical writing really wasn't "cricket."

By contrast, many of today's business reporters are women — people such as Kimberley Noble, who took both fine arts and journalism in college, and who has won two Business NNAs.

At the same time, business was becoming increasingly complex, with such developments as corporate takeovers, globalization and interlocking directorships, and there was a real need for interpretation and explanation. Christopher Waddell's 1987 analysis of the lumber dispute with the U.S. is a fine example (page 297). Another, early, example of this drawing the big picture is Arnie Myers' sweeping study of the British Columbia pulp industry (page 282): He carefully analyzes the environmental impact of the mills and makes insightful and informed predictions for the future, obviously the result of months of meticulous research.

All this, then, represents a period of steady growth and maturation. It's not that there was no business reporting earlier: Business departments had begun to appear and grow after World War I, but it took a while to earn their laurels. As Paul Rutherford says about both sports and business reporting in Canada between the wars, "They thrilled with a sense of the drama and excitement and significance of the little doings of these worlds, never troubling to criticize or question." (*The Making of the Canadian Media.*)

But it was only in this post-war period that daily business reporting truly began to emerge, helped along by the *Globe and Mail* introducing its Report on Business section in 1962. (The trend has continued with the founding of the *National Post* in 1998, with very strong emphasis on business reporting thanks to its acquisition of the *Financial Post*.) At the same time, hundreds of specialized business magazines were emerging, provoking the dailies to even better efforts.

To begin with, then, vigourous, critical writing such as Judith Robinson's revelations about kickbacks on federal highway contracts in 1953 (the first selection here) must have seemed a bombshell — and by a woman, no less! And Pierre Berton's campaigns on behalf of the little guy for the *Toronto Star* constantly caused a furour (page 279). After all, the term "consumer protection" had probably not yet been coined, and the apoplexy at such stories was as much surprise that the press would do this, as fury at the content of the stories. What the stories here represent, therefore, is a growing sense of responsibility in the business departments of the country's newsrooms, and the increasing importance of business as a beat. Many of these stories, for instance, won awards in the Enterprise Reporting category, not just in Business. Better-educated reporters were being hired, for better pay. The first had Arts degrees from university, but then some appeared in newsrooms with economics majors, to be followed by others with formal journalism education plus an economics background. (Canada still hasn't seen the influx of MBAs that U.S. newsrooms have undergone). These young turks were being given a chance to dig and to rock the boat, "and never mind the advertisers."

And what about the writing itself? Early business reporting tended to be pretty dry, heavy on statistics, financial reports, TSE movements and quarterly statements. As Carman Cumming and Catherine McKercher remarked in their textbook, *The Canadian Reporter*, "But much of the reputation for dullness is undeserved. Some of the best writing in the newspaper these days is in the business pages. Business and economics writers cover, arguably, some of the most significant news of the day."

Latterly, the writing has become positively vivacious: The tough analysis of David Crane's predictions regarding the northern gas pipeline (page 288), or Henry Aubin's fascinating insight into supermarket layout (page 291), are leavened by extremely accessible writing — clear, clean structure and simple vocabulary.

Notice, too, how Kimberley Noble makes her description of the Bronfman empire (page 298) more readable by opening with a homely anecdote about basketball. The no-holds-barred profile, too, made its debut, and swiftly began to humanize business pages from raw data to the people behind the data. So, Lawrence Surtees pulls no punches as he draws a picture of Paul Stern, the head of Northern Telecom (page 301).

Today's business writer will likely be an all-rounder: She may be writing one moment about a youngster starting up a novel Internet business, and the next moment about the impact of the Euro, about hockey pensions, or about the abstruse machinations of the World Bank. But she will be far more expert in her field than most of her predecessors just a generation or two ago.

• **1953** Spot News Reporting •

Awarded three contracts same year
seven cheques were issued by company

Judith Robinson

Toronto Telegram

REGINA — In 1950, the Harvey Lunam Construction Co. of Regina was awarded Dominion Government building contracts totaling almost $700,000.

During one week in November of that same year, Austin Edwin Dewar, Liberal member of parliament for Qu'Appelle, Sask., received from the Harvey Lunam Construction Co. seven cheques totaling $71,800.

I discovered these cheques while investigating the circumstances under which the Harvey

Lunam Construction Co. later defaulted on its Dominion Government contracts and left sub-contractors holding the bag for more than $230,000.

The cheques, cancelled because they were cashed, are in the storeroom of a Regina lawyer's office, along with hundreds of others, and books and records of the Harvey Lunam Construction Co. They were seized by this lawyer, a Lunam creditor.

Here are more facts:

The cheques are Harvey Lunam Construction Co. cheques on the Royal Bank of Canada in Regina.

All are:

• Signed "Harvey Lunam Construction co. per D. H. Lunam."
• Made out to Austin E. Dewar.
• Endorsed by Austin E. Dewar.

All were:

• Dated at Regina between Nov. 21 and Nov. 26, 1950.
• Presented at the Royal Bank in Indian Head, Sask. where Austin E. Dewar, M.P., lives, between Nov. 23 and Nov. 28, 1950.
• Accepted.

Two of the seven cheques, one for $15,000 and one for $11,000 and both dated Nov. 25, 1950, were endorsed "Deposit only credit of A. E. Dewar" over the signature Austin E. Dewar. The other five are endorsed only with the signature Austin E. Dewar or in one case, Austin Dewar.

At the time the Qu'Appelle member of parliament was given these cheques, D. Harvey Lunam had been awarded only one of the three contracts he finally received from the Dominion Government. These contracts, in the order of their letting, were:

• June, 1950 — Fort Qu'Appelle Indian Hospital, $333,264.79.
• Dec., 1950 — Regina Unemployment Insurance Building, $215,597.
• Dec. or Jan., 1950-51 — Fort Qu'Appelle Public Building, $132,787.23.

The second contract — the one on the Regina building — was awarded the Harvey Lunam Construction Co. by Order-in-Council P.C. 4660, on Dec. 29, 1950. This is little more than a month to the day from the date when two Harvey Lunam Construction Co. cheques, marked "deposit only," added $26,000 to the bank account of Austin E. Dewar in Indian Head.

The sequence of the cheques is as follows:

The first cheque of the seven is numbered 20346, dated at Regina Nov. 21 and is for $10,000. The second, number 20354, is dated Nov. 22 and is for $9,600. These two were accepted by the Royal Bank in Indian Head Nov. 23.

The third, numbered 20356, is dated Nov. 23 and is for $12,000. Endorsed, like the others, by Austin E. Dewar, it was presented at the bank in Indian Head on Nov. 24. All three were stamped "Paid" by the Royal Bank in Regina on Nov. 25.

The next four cheques all are dated Nov. 25 and have consecutive serial numbers from 20365 to 20368. The last in the sequence, for $9,200, was presented in Indian Head (Nov. 27) and paid in Regina (Nov. 28) a day ahead of its seniors. The three cheques, which came before it out of the Lunam Construction Company's cheque book on the same day, were not presented in Indian Head until Nov. 28 or paid from the Lunam company bank account in Regina until Nov. 29.

The amounts of these last three included the largest of the seven — for $15,000; the smallest — for $5,000, and one for $11,000. The cheques for $15,000 and for $11,000 were endorsed "deposit only" by Austin E. Dewar.

D. Harvey Lunam first came into the public eye in April of this year when John Diefenbaker, Progressive Conservative member from Lake Centre, Sask., charged in the House of Commons that Lunam had defrauded building material suppliers of over $150,000. Mr. Diefenbaker described the Lunam Construction Co. of Regina as a "fly-by-night" outfit which had received a number of government contracts to erect buildings in Saskatchewan, then defaulted before finishing them.

The sub-contractors, who claim their loss on these Dominion Government contracts is more like $230,000 than $150,000, have sought redress from the Dominion Minister of Public Works,

Hon. Alphonse Fournier. They have been refused.

The Honorable Mr. Fournier claims the government met its obligations in paying Lunam. If Lunam didn't pay the sub-contractors, that's their tough luck.

The sub-contractors — one received a cheque for 26 cents from the government for a job costing over $1,000 — say they trusted the government. They point to a clause in all public works contracts which provides that all wages, subcontracts and materials must be paid up to date before a general contractor employed by the government can claim progress payments from the government. This, the sub-contractors say, was ignored.

Qu'Appelle, the federal riding in which all this happened, abuts on and is to the east of Regina City. This is where an Indian Hospital costing over $300,000 and another public building, costing over $132,000, were to be built by Lunam.

Indian Head, where Austin E. Dewar, M.P., lives and where the seven cheques were cashed, is 42 miles east from Regina.

Mr. Dewar came to the House of Commons in 1949. He was new to federal politics then and thought to be a weak candidate — before the vote was counted in Qu'Appelle. Even the Liberals doubted his ability to defeat the sitting CCF member, Mrs. Gladys Strum, but in he went with the Liberal sweep.

The Parliamentary Guide says this about Mr. Dewar:

Born April 24, 1912, at Indian Head, Sask. S. of Mr. and Mrs. J. E. Dewar. Father's parents came to Canada about 1860. Mother's parents were U.E.L. descendants. Educated at Indian Head, Sask. Senior matriculation. M. June 29, 1940 to Mildred N., daughter of Helmi Bjorndahl, of Saskatoon, Sask. Two children: Gail Joanne and Garry John. Contractor. Member: "Rockets" Indian Head, Sask. Ex. Grain, Man., Ex-Hotel Owner; Ex-Farmer; Active in Can. Cancer Society; Red Cross; Board of Trade.

First elected to H. of C., at g.e. June 27, 1949. Party pol., Liberal. Rel., United Church. Address: Indian Head, Sask.

• **1960** Feature Writing •
The story behind those
"Let me be your friend" ads

Pierre Berton

Toronto Star

Oct. 8, 1959, I published a column entitled *A True Story About a Widow and a Mortgage*. It dealt with a series of loan companies controlled by two young Toronto lawyers, Arthur Lundy and Irving Solnik. The two chief firms at the time were Alleghany Finance and Quay Funding Corp. More recently the operative firms have been United Global Financial System and Valley National Financial Corporation.

You have probably seen their ads. Lately they have featured the slogan: "Let Me Be Your Friend."

In my original column I told how a widow from England, Mrs. Sophie Pratt, asked one of the Lundy-Solnik companies to be her friend. The results were disastrous. Mrs. Pratt thought she was borrowing money to pay off a third mortgage. It turned out that Mrs. Pratt was simply exchanging one third mortgage for another and that four years later she would still owe almost as much on her home as before.

Mr. Lundy and Mr. Solnik were very disturbed by this column. They said that there had been a terrible mistake in the case of Mrs. Pratt and offered to make amends. They said such a loan should never have been granted. More than that, as I reported in my column of Oct. 14, 1959, they offered to make some changes.

First, they said, they would change their advertising: The ads would be worded so prospective borrowers would realize that all these loans would be secured by first, second or third mortgages. They said they would publish a scale of rates showing the exact cost of each loan and the amount still owing when the loan terminates. They said they would modify extreme claims, such as the implication that all loans can be made in three hours.

Except in the *Star,* which has insisted on certain standards for mortgage advertising, these changes have not been made. The ads still say that the customer can get his money "in a matter of hours." They still don't show the cost of the loans or the interest rates or how much is owing at the end of the loan period. And (except in the *Star*) they don't mention mortgages.

Mr. Lundy and Mr. Solnik also offered to make some changes in their general method of operation.

First, they told me, they would now make certain that any prospective borrower, before he signed anything, would receive a statement showing exactly what the loan would cost him, what his monthly payments would be, and what he would still owe when the term was up.

Secondly, they said, they would do their best to stay away from the type of mortgage I wrote about — where monthly payments are set so low that the borrower owes almost as much at the end of the mortgage term as at the beginning.

Thirdly, they would try to arrange most loans so they would be fully paid off when the loan terminated.

Mr. Solnik told me that he was through with loans that carried 35 per cent interest rates. The risk was too great, anyway, he said. He added that it was his companies' intention to do away with bonuses, legal fees, disbursements, etc., and charge a straight interest rate so that the borrower would know exactly where he stood.

So much for good intentions. Let us now see how all this worked out in the case of a Dutch-Canadian from Oshawa named Gysbertus Huider.

Mr. Huider needed some cash to add a room on to his house. So last December he visited Quay Funding Corp. and asked them to be his friend.

I don't know if he asked to see Alexander Clarke, the kindly old gentleman who sometimes appears in these ads, or John McDonald, the genial man with the iron gray hair, or Robert Gray, the one with the cheery smile and the horn-rimmed spectacles.

I know that he did not see any of these men, however, because they do not exist. The names are invented; the photos come from model agencies.

Mr. Huider did not get his money in a matter of hours. It took some weeks and, in the end, all he got was $200.

When he entered Quay Funding's offices he had two mortgages on his home. One had a year to run. The other was not due for almost three years. The total amount he owed on both mortgages was $6,130.19.

When the Lundy-Solnik company was through with him, Mr. Huider had two brand new mortgages on his house. *And now he owed $8,795.*

In order to get $200 in cash, Mr. Huider allowed Quay Funding to negotiate two new mortgages to replace two old ones. The "finance charges" for this transaction totalled $2,300. In addition, "recording charges" totalled $190. In addition, Mr. Huider must pay interest at $7\frac{1}{2}$ per cent and 12 per cent, respectively, on the total value of the mortgages, plus all the added charges.

This works out to a real interest rate of 18.3 per cent on his new first mortgage and a real interest rate of 34 per cent on his new second mortgage.

And all Mr. Huider has to show for this is $200 in cash from the people he asked to be his friend. I'll repeat this for the benefit of those in the back who may not have thought they heard me distinctly:

Mr. Huider got exactly $200, plus the nebulous advantage of a slightly extended period in which to pay his debt. In January, he owed $2,665 more on his house than he owed in December. His monthly payments and his interest rates are now higher than they were before he applied for his loan.

I find this almost unbelievable, but I have the loan agreements and the reporting letter from Quay Funding before me, and I have had the mortgages checked. Mr. Huider is only dimly aware of what has happened. He still does not know what his real interest rates are.

There is something else, alas, that Mr. Huider is not aware of. His loan agreements call for him to make monthly payments of $90. This means that, in four years, when these new, expensive mortgages come due, Mr. Huider will have paid some $4,300 to the Lundy-Solnik firm.

Yet he will still owe more on his house then than he did when he first applied for a loan.

Last December he owed $6,130. Four Decembers from now, if he pays at this rate, he will owe about $7,300. He is paying more than 1,000 per cent interest per annum on his $200.

I have just been examining a recent ad for one of the Lundy-Solnik companies (Valley National) which shows the amiable features of the fictitious Messrs. Clarke, McDonald and Gray (but not the features of Arthur Lundy or Irving Solnik).

"It's a Shame For You to Be Short of Cash When These Men Have It For You," the ad reads. And then it goes on: *"Let's face facts. You've probably read our ads before. And perhaps they sound too wonderful to be true. Right? ..."*

Right, indeed. Oh, so sadly right.

● **1962** Staff Corresponding ●

Government must face fiscal troubles sooner or later

Michael Barkway

Southam News

The storm brewing over the head of the new government is piling up thick black clouds too ominous to be ignored.

The only question among serious financial and economic experts is whether it will break in a sudden deluge after the election, or whether — as hopeful children say at a picnic — it will "go away and come again another day."

While the Canadian dollar still scrapes along its floor, Finance Minister Fleming's June 1 announcement revealed that it has cost the Canadian government nearly $3,000,000 every business day since May 3 to prevent it breaking through the floor.

Even that may not represent the full cost because it is not known what "swap" deals in forward exchange may have been made to shift the losses forward into June.

Meanwhile, interest rates are rising — moderated but not stopped by the Bank of Canada — and the expansion of the money supply is being checked, though gently.

If the new government firmly declares a reversal of policy to tight money and higher interest rates, it should attract at least a modest inflow of foreign money which would support the Canadian dollar.

Yet there is some doubt in financial circles (both official and unofficial) whether even this will be enough to bring in the necessary amount of foreign capital.

Slide-rule calculations of the marginal profits to be made from higher interest rates in another country can move a lot of money in a climate of confidence.

If the confidence is lacking, the bait may be ignored.

That is why informed opinion is turning more and more to other ways of correcting Canada's balance of payments.

Devaluation has conspicuously failed to produce its traditional and theoretical effects.

Since the middle of 1961 imports have risen more sharply than exports. The newly-published figures for the first quarter of 1962 show that the import surplus continued to widen, even when the Canadian dollar was around 95 cents.

No serious economist now entertains the prophecy of a $400,000,000 surplus on 1962's merchandise trade which was made by Trade Minister Hees in a characteristic mood of exuberance. (It was not based on official forecasts from the Trade and Commerce experts.)

Most people now expect the unusual trade surplus of 1961 to be wiped out this year, and for Canada to return to a deficit on merchandise trade.

At the same time, the 1961 deficit of nearly $1,200,000,000 on "invisible" transactions is almost certain to be larger this year.

Nearly half of it consists of interest and dividend payments, which are growing each year anyway, and will now be increased by eight or nine per cent because of devaluation.

Freight and shipping charges also will be heavier.

The expected saving on tourist expenditures is most unlikely to compensate for these extra charges against us.

This means that the capital inflow of 1962 will have to be increased, not merely maintained, if we are to balance our accounts with other countries and hold the dollar.

Despite the rise of interest rates (for the fifth week running) and the Bank of Canada's gradually increasing restraint on the money supply, it remains open to question whether the capital inflow can be regained on a sufficient scale.

Moreover, even if it can, both Liberals and Conservatives have at last accepted the common sense view that we cannot indefinitely go on borrowing foreign capital to meet our current bills.

The only permanent and fool-proof solution is to start bringing our foreign spending into line with what we can earn abroad.

If devaluation will not achieve the result — and after nearly a year it shows no sign of doing so — some other means will have to be found.

• **1965** Feature Writing •

Prosperity: A deadly threat

Arnie Myers

Vancouver Sun

The greatest threat to British Columbia's inland waters in the years ahead will come from the dozen or more new pulp mills expected to be built in the interior.

Elaborate plans are now being made to safeguard the rivers. How effective these controls will be may not be known for five years or more.

The kraft pulp mill, prime symbol of B.C.'s prosperous forest industry, is a prodigious user of water. It takes as much as 50,000 gallons of water to produce a single ton of bleached kraft pulp.

The Port Alberni mill of MacMillan Bloedel and Powell River Co., for example, produces about 1,800 tons of pulp and paper every 24 hours.

To do this it must pipe in 42.5 million gallons of fresh water daily, and get rid of the same quantity of then-polluted water.

The Alberni mill's sewer lines pour out enough liquid waste to fill a 20-by-40-foot swimming pool five feet deep every minute.

Like all kraft mills, this one goes to considerable lengths to recover wood fibres and chemicals from its effluent before discharging it.

This is done as much for reasons of economy as in the interests of pollution control, because both fibres and chemicals can be re-used.

But reclaiming waste costs money and any mill eventually reaches a point where recovering the last fraction of waste costs more than it is worth, from a strict business view.

All existing B.C. pulp mills, therefore, pour huge quantities of chemical and fibrous pollutants into the receiving body of water.

According to present government policy, however, new mills in the Interior will be required to recover almost all their wastes.

The effluent is a complex mixture of dissolved chemicals used in making pulp, plus bits of bark, stray chips, tiny cellulose fibres and dissolved lignin, the glue that held the fibres together in the tree.

This coffee-coloured liquid can have a variety of effects on fish, shellfish and other aquatic life in the water into which it is dumped.

Many of the chemicals can be rapidly poisonous to fish if they escape in high concentration, through accident or inadequate recovery treatment.

Even in much lower concentrations, they can act as a chemical barrier to fish, deterring them from swimming through polluted areas.

The wood fibres and other solid materials affect fish in three ways.

They can blanket the bottom of a stream or bay, covering spawning grounds and destroying bottom-feeding life. The larger bits can harm fish directly, by irritating or clogging their gill membranes.

More important, as they decompose, the fibres use up a considerable portion of the oxygen which fish need.

This biochemical oxygen demand of the effluent from kraft mills, which are in the majority in B.C., is only about one-tenth of that of the outpourings of the older sulphite mills.

Whether or not a particular mill's effluent will harm fish and other water life depends largely on how quickly and efficiently the effluent is diluted and dispersed by the receiving body of water, and on how well the oxygen demand is met before the effluent is released.

The Columbia Cellulose Company's Celgar mill at Castlegar, as an example, dumps 12 tons of wood fibre into the Columbia River every day.

Fortunately, the river's flow is fast enough to sweep the fibre away and spread it over a long stretch of water. Thus, the effect of the biochemical oxygen demand is small.

W. R. Friesen, process engineer at Castlegar, said his company has had tests made by the B.C. Research Council three times a year since 1959, a year before the mill went into production.

These tests, he said — and the research council confirms him — have shown virtually no effect on the oxygen content of the river.

The Columbia at Castlegar contains about 10 parts of dissolved oxygen for every million parts of water. Celgar's effluent, Friesen said, has never reduced the oxygen supply by more than six-tenths of a part per million.

Similarly, the MacMillan-Bloedel mill near Nanaimo and the Crown-Zellerbach mill at Elk Falls on Vancouver Island have each been pumping about six tons of fibre into the water every day.

Both these mills are sited on fast-moving tide-swept channels. They have caused no serious pollution problems because their effluent is quickly swept to sea.

The Port Alberni mill is in a more difficult position, at the end of a narrow, 40-mile-long inlet which has only sluggish tides. (It takes three weeks or more for the tides to sweep debris out to open water).

The Port Alberni mill dumps its effluent into the mouth of the Somass River, which pours into the inlet, to take advantage of the faster flow of fresh water.

This effectively carries away most of the dissolved wood components and pulp-making chemicals. But wood fibres and other solids quickly settle to the bottom of the inlet.

The mill dumps 27 tons of solids into the inlet every day. Dr. Michael Waldichuck, of the federal Fisheries Research Board biological station at Departure Bay, estimates that only about one ton of the 27 is carried off; the other 26 tons sink to the bottom.

The bottom of the inlet near the mills is now covered with beds of sludge several feet thick. The mass of fibres slowly decomposes, releasing noxious gases harmful to fish and shellfish.

Occasionally this sludge must be dredged to clear a channel for deep sea ships. One dredging operation for a fish cannery site at Alberni resulted in a large fish-kill several years ago because the sludge and oxygen-starved water were stirred up.

Normally, however, according to Alberni mill officials, the escape of fibres has no effect on fishing. Good-sized tyee salmon are still taken regularly in the inlet.

The Crown-Zellerbach mill at Ocean Falls has caused a similar build-up of sludge on the bottom of Cousins Inlet. Crabs and other bottom fauna have long since been wiped out by the low oxygen concentration and the toxic hydrogen sulphide produced by the decomposing sludge.

The Columbia Cellulose mill at Prince Rupert is a sulphite mill, and its effluent has a much higher oxygen demand than that of the kraft mills. Waste from this one mill takes as much oxygen to purify it as the domestic sewage produced by the people of B.C.

Fishermen will still take herring in waters near the mills, although sometimes they find their nets full of dead fish. The once-prolific bottom life in the enclosed waters near the mill has been virtually extinguished.

There are other, less important kinds of pollution from the pulp mills.

The deep-brown colour of the effluent can itself be harmful, since by darkening the water it reduces the penetration of sunlight and thereby cuts down photosynthesis by aquatic plants.

Some mills also produce large quantities of foam, which results from the mixing of various acids and alkaline chemicals in their effluent.

This foam can carry high concentrations of chemical poisons.

"I'm sure it doesn't do any good if it gets washed up on oyster leases," said Dr. Waldichuck.

(The B.C. Forest Products Co. is currently being sued for alleged pollution of oyster beds near its Crofton mill.)

Waldichuck has devised a way to make foam disappear in a few minutes, instead of persisting for several hours, by mixing waste water from a mill in a specified manner.

Until now, all these kinds of pulp mill pollution have been confined, with the single exception of Celgar, to tidal waters in B.C.

Now, with planned development of new mills in the Interior, the province's major river systems face a new threat.

To keep this threat in check, the B.C. Pollution Control Board is working closely with the new mills and with various other government agencies to set strict standards for discharge of mill wastes.

Several of the new mills will be built on the Fraser or its tributaries, and the major concern is to protect the Fraser salmon runs.

The new mills will be required to monitor their effluent to measure its conductivity, its colour, its dissolved oxygen and its oxygen demand, and its alkalinity or acidity.

They will also have to measure the quantity of fibres and other solids they pour out, along with dissolved chemicals such as chlorine, nitrates and phosphates.

Strict limits will be set for each of these components, according to Charles Keenan, executive engineer of the Pollution Control Board.

All limits have not yet been established. However, the mill being built at Kamloops will be allowed to release only 10 parts of solids for each million parts of water.

For comparison, the Celgar mill discharges 100 parts of solids per million.

By this standard, the Kamloops mill will discharge only about 800 pounds of solids per day, compared to Celgar's 12½ tons.

According to Keenan, standards set for the Kamloops mill will apply, with some modification to suit local conditions, to all other Interior mills.

These high standards will require an elaborate array of pollution control devices, costing perhaps $1 million for each mill.

Besides the screens, clarifiers and other devices used by existing mills, the Kamloops plant will have two holding ponds where its effluent will be retained for 12 hours to allow solids to settle out.

Then the effluent will go to another lagoon where it will be held for a further five days to reduce its toxicity and oxygen demand. Only then can it be spilled into the river.

No chips, bark or undissolved bits of wood will be allowed to escape, Keenan said. Foam will have to be controlled. If the effluent changes the normal colour of the water, the colour will have to be extracted.

"These conditions are restrictive," Keenan said, "but not nearly restrictive enough for a small river.

"If we were to have a pulp mill built on a small stream, we would either have to write off that river — and this is an economic possibility if the stream has no other use — or we would have to impose such restrictive conditions that it might be impossible for the mill to operate competitively."

Restrictive though the new conditions may be, they are no guarantee of safety.

"Under all circumstances, there is a certain amount of risk involved," said Dr. Waldichuck. "We don't know what effect these mills will have on the migration and spawning of salmon. Research to establish the answers would take many years."

But Keenan is optimistic.

"There is no need for alarm," he said. "At this time, we have a tremendous factor of safety on our Interior waters.

"And the water permits of the new mills will be reviewed every five years to see whether we need to impose more restrictive conditions."

Dr. Waldichuck pointed out that even slight changes in the condition of Fraser River water could have subtle effects which might wipe out whole salmon runs, over a period of years, without ever killing a fish directly.

"For example," he said, "salmon that go up to the Stewart Lakes to spawn travel a matter of several hundred miles without eating.

"They have a certain amount of energy they have stored up to get them to their spawning grounds, but that amount is limited. There's some pretty precise timing involved.

"Any obstacle in their way will delay their migration and reduce their chances of getting there. If an effluent deters the fish, they might never reach the spawning grounds."

Despite such reservations, fisheries are confident about the Fraser's future and pleased with the enlightened and co-operative attitude shown by the companies building the new mills.

Lloyd Royal, director of the International Pacific Salmon Fisheries Commission, said recently pollution controls planned for B.C.'s new mills will be "far more efficient than any existing in the northwestern states."

"We're breaking through the barriers," echoes Robert McMynn, provincial fisheries research officer.

"Not too long ago, a stream would have to cause an epidemic before anybody did anything about it. But companies now realize that if they take reasonable precautions, it's a good investment.

"It's better and cheaper to install control facilities when a plant is built than to have to do it later."

• **1966** Feature Writing •

The salesman: Image and ethics

Betty Lee

Globe and Mail

Aperson never buys life insurance. It is *sold* to him mostly by that persistent, high-pressure creation of the insurance business, the life insurance underwriter.

Technically, the underwriter isn't really an underwriter (a true underwriter is a company employee who sits in judgment on incoming applications for insurance), though he preselects prospects for company consideration. More correctly, he is a salesman; an agent of a life insurance company that probably has been the first to train him, bond him and recommend to the provincial Department of Insurance that he be issued a license.

He works on commission (unless he is a debit man, who works for a graded salary and commission) and he can earn anything from a subsistence income to $100,000 a year.

At the moment, he is part of a Dominion-wide sales force of about 17,000 men and women that has one of the largest occupational turnovers in Canada.

Insurance men at all company levels never seem to tire of discussing the controversial aspects of the field underwriter's job: The importance of the work in the complex structure of the insurance business, the impact of the Hard Soft Sell on the sensitivity of prospective policyholders, the philosophical and psychological pressures on the salesman himself.

"What about the image of the life underwriter?" Roger Martel, agency manager of the Alliance Mutual Life Insurance Co., asked at a meeting of the Canadian Life Insurance Association last year. "In my many years of experience, I have never noticed so much camouflage, so many disguises. More and more agents now call themselves estate consultants, investment counsellors, savings analysts, pension specialists. There are less and less life insurance company representatives!

"Some agents live outside their branch offices and are subsidized by home offices. Some branches are now known not as life insurance agencies but as professional centres, economic bureaus, estate planners, etc. Is it that some fieldmen think their public image is not good enough? Do they feel they are at a disadvantage, for instance, with their colleagues who deal in general insurance lines and call themselves, rotundously, brokers?"

"I don't know how other agents feel about it," says one Torontonian who quit the life insurance business after 18 months in the field, "but I would say an insurance salesman has to be ruthless, somewhat hypocritical and with a skin like a rhino. I couldn't stand knowing I was barging into places where I really wasn't wanted."

"The life insurance business?" counters a prominent Toronto branch manager who rose through the ranks. "It's rewarding, lucrative, one of the most satisfying fields a man can get into. The first years can be discouraging for some, but if an underwriter can get over the hump, he'll never want to do anything else."

Department of Insurance figures show early humps and discouragements nudge 20 to 25 per cent of insurance salesmen into cancelling their licenses the first couple of years on the job. This high dropout rate prompts a certain amount of raiding for experienced agents and keeps the life insurance companies busily recruiting newcomers "or just bodies," as one agent complains.

The company pitch looks attractive enough: A modest salary — around $250-$400 a month — during a training period, depending on the company. When a fledgling agent is finally out of the nest, commissions for whole life policies range between 30 and 80 per cent on a first-year premium plus a continuing two per cent through fewer years. Commissions on term used to be less but the life of a policy or a fatter percentage spread over companies selling it have raised the percentage. Docking of commissions for policy lapses or early surrenders, of course, can cut down income.

To start a man selling, new agents are expected to submit prospect lists of friends and relatives and, just to show how a selling job is done, the branch supervisor invariably talks the tyro into buying a policy, even before he hits the road. "Then come the morning pep talks, the sales contests, the endless charts which compare how underwriters are doing in the field," says the disillusioned ex-salesman.

"Sure there's competition at branch level," counters the Toronto manager. "But isn't there competition in every business? The main thing is, we try to teach our agents they are independent businessmen and that the only capital they possess is discipline and knowledge. The more we can encourage them and the more knowledge we can urge them to acquire, the better job they can do for us, the public and themselves."

Even the life insurance companies will admit the initial training they give new sales recruits can only be a grounding for the really ambitious underwriter.

More than 70 per cent of this country's 17,000 life insurance agents are members of the 60-year-old Life Underwriters Association of Canada, which offers two courses in insurance sales methods and technical principles: The Life Underwriters Association Training Course and the Chartered Life Underwriter degree. At the moment, 2,300 agents are registered in the two-year LUATC program and 1,000 are taking the tough, three-year CLU. Only 2,700 current LUAC members hold the CLU certificate.

But LUAC membership alone can give the insurance salesman a certain amount of status, mainly because of the association's publicized emphasis on business ethics and internal discipline. LUAC dues-payers know, for example, their licenses can be suspended or cancelled if the association chooses to bring a case of wrongdoing to the attention of the Department of Insurance. A handbook of Ethical Practices details some cardinal sins:

A member, for example, may not "make any statements of a misleading or derogatory nature which might cause members or the public to lose confidence in any life insurance company, its policy contracts or its agents." He is warned that rebating is prohibited; in other words, attempting to make any agreement with a policyholder about payments of a premium "other than as plainly set forth in the contract." The LUAC requires members to "respect the confidence of clients and prospects at all times."

Replacement, or twisting, is high on the list of misdemeanors: Talking a policyholder into letting lapse or surrendering one contract "with permanent insurance values" — namely a whole life policy — for one that does not, namely term insurance. Twisting is not only an LUAC sin, it also is illegal and can land an agent in jail. Before an applicant can sign up for a term contract with another company, he must answer a form question: "Are you dropping another policy to get this new one?" If the answer is yes, the application will be refused.

Oddly enough, twisting the other way seems to be condoned by the life insurance companies. They call it conversion, and no agent seems to have been rapped over the knuckles for it.

The LUAC frowns on misrepresentation or "dishonesty or fraud in connection with any business transaction." The association's code states: "While the life underwriter's vocation is basically that of a salesman, he should at all times strive to carry out his activities in a professional manner."

Yet for all of the LUAC's influence, insiders like Mr. Martel still are complaining: "Among the many challenges, the main one, as I see it, is probably the problem of finding ways to raise the stature and the public image of the agent. How can it be done? I suppose by doing more of what many of you have done, like developing not merely salesmen, but knowledgeable and ethical salesmen and women who can do justice to the character of the product we have to offer."

Insurance crusaders offer some tips on how to deal with foot-in-the-door colleagues who might not stick to the rules:

• Never talk to a life insurance agent who has not made an appointment. Even the hard-sell underwriters admit that doormat introductions are an invasion of privacy.

• Always ask a salesman if he is a member of the LUAC. A "yes" to your query can give you confidence the underwriter is at least aware of a code of ethics and you can always complain to the association if you can prove a case of misrepresentation. You might also like to ask the agent if he is studying for his CLU. If you get a nod, you can be sure you are dealing with a first-class insurance man.

- Try to resist signing an application at the first interview. After you have heard the agent's arguments, call up two other companies and ask them for rates on the type of policy you are interested in buying.

- If you are talked into signing, make sure you tell the agent you will inquire from other companies. You can always cancel — and lose your deposit — if you find you can get a better deal, though the second company will be obliged to inform the first of your decision and you can expect some heated talk from the agent who sold you the insurance in the first place. If he succeeds in winning you back within two weeks, the second company will tear up your application.

• 1972 Enterprise Reporting •

A way of life faces upheaval in the Arctic

David Crane

Toronto Star

OTTAWA — The huge northern gas pipeline, which will carry the rich reserves of Arctic natural gas to energy-short United States utilities, is certain to damage the precarious Arctic environment and disrupt the lives and culture of northern Indians and Eskimos.

Although the environmental and social consequences of the planned pipeline are widely viewed as less critical than its economic impact, these questions will have to have a thorough public airing if the pipeline project is to go ahead.

The pipeline itself will run 1,500 miles through one of the last remaining great wilderness areas in the world. It will stretch hundreds of miles over permafrost, cross several hundred rivers and streams, run through treacherous muskeg, and progress south along the banks of Canada's greatest waterway, the Mackenzie River.

In the process, it could cause serious disruption to plant and animal life, create problems with landslides and erosion, and upset the North's fragile ecological balance.

The presence of thousands of construction workers with giant earth-moving machines digging a vast trench through the unbroken country, bulldozing air strips and shipping in thousands of tons of steel pipe, fuel oil and other supplies, is bound to create severe problems.

Unprecedented caution will have to be exercised in carrying out one of the biggest construction projects in history.

For the northern native peoples — about 10,000 Indians, 14,000 Eskimos and several thousand Métis — the northern pipeline project could bring some benefits. But it also would bring social and cultural problems.

Northern natives are gradually moving away from their historic hunting and fishing based on a nomadic way of life.

They are increasingly settling in small communities across the North, moving into a wage economy while their children are being educated in new schools.

This change in lifestyle coincides with a new awareness and militancy. More than ever before, northern natives are concerned about protecting their traditions, languages, culture, and their hunting and fishing grounds.

Led by a new generation of young leaders, they want to determine their own future — and they want their own wealth, instead of continuing to depend on federal government handouts.

The northern natives see the pipeline as the key to their future wealth and independence.

They are determined that the pipeline will not be built — and there have even been threats of dynamite — until their historic land claims are settled.

Treaties dating back to 1899 and 1921 guarantee certain amounts of land to Indians. The Eskimos and Métis have no treaties to back their claims.

The natives, working through militant new organizations, will push their demands for a share of northern wealth through the courts and in direct negotiation with the government. They will count on both legal claims and public opinion.

With one eye on the huge Alaska settlement which gave U.S. natives more than $1 billion and 40 million acres of land, Canadian natives will be seeking cash, land and royalties from resources in northern Canada. They are being advised both by Canadian lawyers and by the U.S. native who engineered the Alaska settlement.

Almost as soon as a pipeline application is filed, some time next year, an injunction to block the pipeline project will likely be brought through the courts.

Just how the environmental and social questions will be handled in the pipeline application itself is still far from clear.

A task force on northern oil development was set up within the federal government in December, 1968, with the deputy minister of the Department of Mines, Energy and Natural Resources as chairman. Its other members include the deputy ministers of the Departments of the Environment, Indian Affairs and Northern Development, and Transport, along with the chairman of the National Energy Board.

During 1970, it made several reports to the cabinet, which resulted in the 1970 northern pipeline guidelines.

These guidelines called for a "comprehensive report" by the pipeline company on the full environmental impact of the project, as part of its application.

Any permit for the project, the guidelines said, "will be strictly conditioned in respect of preservation of the ecology and environment, prevention of pollution, prevention of thermal and other erosion, freedom of navigation, and the protection of the rights of northern residents."

The guidelines also stressed that the pipeline company must provide training programs for northern residents so they could obtain jobs on the pipeline project.

Since then, more detailed guidelines on the environment and native peoples have been issued.

In the meantime, both industry and government have been carrying out extensive environmental research, with industry spending about $20 million and the government about $15 million. Special pipeline test facilities have been built in the North by the pipeline participants, one at Norman Wells and the other at Long Sault.

This is the first time that industry has had to spend millions of dollars on advance ecological planning of a major project.

But the Alaska fiasco, in which pipeline companies moved hundreds of millions of dollars worth of pipe and other supplies to Prudhoe Bay before environmental questions had been dealt with, is engraved on the industry's mind. The pipe stands today as a rusting monument to poor corporate planning and insensitivity to public concerns about ecology while environmentalists still block the proposed Trans-Alaska pipeline.

In the Canadian project, both pipeline groups established special environment research teams as soon as they began to consider a pipeline project. Since the merger of the two consortium groups into Canadian Gas Arctic Study Ltd., the environmental research work has been combined.

So far, only limited environmental findings have been published; and those that have are not totally reassuring.

The environment protection board, established by the Gas Arctic Systems Study Group, one of the two early consortiums, published a report this year. The board, which was funded by the pipeline participants but given freedom to publish and autonomy in its research, included such well-known Canadian scientists as Ian McTaggart-Cowan of the University of British Columbia.

Scientists fear the pipeline project may block migration paths of animals, destroy critical nesting areas of birds, prevent fish spawning through stream-crossing construction or removal of gravel, lead to loss of vegetation, and perhaps produce major forest fires in an area highly susceptible to such disasters.

"The Arctic is environmentally harsh and ecologically fragile," two University of Alberta scientists, I.C. Bliss and R.W. Weit, conclude.

"The North is harsh and demanding," C.H.D. Clarke, another environmental scientist, said in an interview.

"Wildlife in the North is a complex of contrasts — few species and many individuals, feast and famine, short visits and long migrations, large litters and mass death, slow growth and late maturity; the one constant that runs through is the slow growth of plants, on which all animals depend."

According to J.B. Sprague, a zoologist at the University of Guelph, the continent's last big untouched wilderness region must struggle with long periods of low temperatures and a low supply of basic nutrients to support life.

"The eco-systems present in such adverse conditions are literally at the limits of existence in a state of delicate balance," he says. "Even small changes in the environment are likely to produce rather dramatic changes in populations of the larger animals at the top of the food pyramid."

But, says Robert Howland, chairman of the National Energy Board, "there is a danger of the pipeline being priced out of the market if industry is compelled to meet standards which entail unrealistically high-cost components."

According to Howland, "the board is convinced that pipelines can be built and can operate with minimum undesirable impact upon the environment and the society of the North." The National Energy Board will conduct the hearings on the pipeline application.

But before the application is approved, many legal hurdles could arise. The requirements of the Territorial Lands Act, through its land use regulations, must be satisfied. The Northern Inland Waters Act will apply to all stream-crossings, with a license required for the 300 or so streams and rivers that must be crossed. The Fisheries Act applies to the protection of fish. The Canada Water Act may be used by environmentalists to challenge the project. And the Migratory Birds Convention can be used to protect birds in the North.

While the native peoples have less legislation to back their claims, they will be politically organized. The Committee for Original Peoples Settlement has been organized to co-ordinate the strategy of the native peoples and it is led by militant spokesmen such as Nellie Cournoyer of Inuvik.

It is the settlement of outstanding land and aboriginal claims that looms largest in native peoples' minds.

To Chief Elijah Smith of the Yukon Native Brotherhood, a settlement is the beginning of independence for the northern natives, just as the Alaskan settlement was to U.S. natives.

"Those resources will be used to bring new opportunities, and additional education and social advancement."

In 1959, a royal commission proposed a $25-million settlement of outstanding native claims. This was rejected by the government as too expensive. But today the price will be much higher. Eric Goudreau of the Arctic Institute of North America suggests it could run to $20 million a year for the next 10 years, along with an equal amount in payment from the resource companies in royalties. That could run to $400 million.

With a pipeline application now six to 10 months away, and with the pipeline company anxious to get approval as quickly as possible, there may not be that much time for protesters concerned about the environment or native rights to prepare their cases.

• **1973** Enterprise Reporting •

But, by gosh! The price is right!

Henry Aubin

Montreal Gazette

To the casual shopper, the layout of a supermarket may seem like an equally casual arrangement of shelves and aisles — with a little Muzak and colour thrown in.

Marketing experts, however, don't see it that simply.

Supermarket layout, they say, is connected with the fact that about 50 per cent of all purchases in supermarkets are not planned by shoppers before they enter the stores.

That figure may sound high, but it is documented in a study by E.I. du Pont de Nemours & Co., the synthetic goods manufacturer which depends on supermarkets for much of its sales. The figure has been corroborated by a field study of 596 shoppers by David T. Kollat. His study, published by the American Marketing Association, nudges the figure up to 50.5 per cent.

The manufacturing and retailing industries attribute much of their success to this "impulse shopping" phenomenon.

For example, Edward A. Brand in his textbook on supermarket management, *Modern Supermarket Operations*, notes that studies have shown the height of a product on a shelf is important to sales — the closer to eye level the better.

The textbook suggests this technique:

"Shelving is adjusted so that high profit impulse merchandise is stocked over staple items. The customers' eyes automatically come into contact with the high profit impulse merchandise when they reach down to pick up the staple item …"

The 259-page book, complete with diagrams on where to most advantageously place products, continues:

"Eye-level impulse stocking has increased grocery markup and volume and strengthened operations for the companies experimenting with it …

"Stock arrangements that have been successful include:

"1. Cereal on the bottom shelf with candy on the upper shelves.

"2. Cereal on the bottom shelf with jellies, peanut butter and condiments on the upper shelves.

"3. Sanitary napkins on the bottom shelf with drugs on the upper shelves …"

The list goes on and on.

Products sell even better when moved from along aisles to the end of aisles — where displays can be larger and more conspicuous. Manufacturers compete among themselves for "end-aisle" positions for their products.

Again, the statistic may sound high, but New York's Point of Advertising Institute found in a study of 19 products that when they were changed from locations along aisles to the ends of aisles their sales increased by an average 673 per cent.

High or not, Dominion Stores Ltd. can command up to $10,000 per week from manufacturers to promote a product at the end of its aisles in Ontario and to feature that product in its advertisements, according to a well-placed marketing source.

The same study which came up with the 673 per cent figure sought to explain the advantage of end-aisle location by noting: "Most shoppers feel that every (end) displayed item is also on sale … This misunderstanding on the part of the consumer is also one of the chief reasons for the success of end displays in increasing unit sales."

(Inspectors for the food prices review board, incidentally, found this practice flourishing in Canada. Says a board study: "Often, end-aisle displays of products confuse and deceive customers. Instances were reported where the price of a product on the end-aisle display was actually higher than the same product displayed elsewhere in the store.")

Shelf and aisle position are not the only considerations in locating products. Marketing experts say the floorplan of stores is often designed to increase traffic flow through parts of the stores some shoppers — not wanting to buy more than a few items — might otherwise not visit.

As Glenn Walters and Gordon W. Paul, two PhDs in marketing, note in their book *Consumer Behaviour*: "Meat is placed in the rear, so that customers must pass through other areas first, increasing the chance of impulse purchases."

Other high-demand staples besides meat are also often placed at different sides of stores. These include milk, produce, flour and sugar.

As Brand notes, "By strategically placing fast-moving items, complete store shopping is almost assured."

Brand also advises his retailer readers: "Merchandise … it is desirable to group related items together near the faster food items. Items such as dried foods, party foods, beverages and household supplies sell successfully when displayed together.

"High markup, impulse items tend to sell best when located near checkout lines."

Which is why shoppers see so much candy and gum there.

"Try getting a child past this point without having to cope with a request for a tidbit," write Walters and Paul.

A product's location within a store is also changed at intervals, forcing shoppers to hunt for it — prowling the aisles it seldom had for sales.

Another technique for giving shoppers an opportunity to tour the store is to split up similar items — this could help explain why one Montreal chain, for example, puts its salted nuts in one aisle and its unsalted varieties in another.

But the "strategic placement" of goods — as Brand calls it — is not the only stimulus to sales. The emotional state of a harried shopper is another.

Kollat, in an Ama-published article called A Decision-Process Approach to Impulse Purchasing, describes with clinical objectivity the effect that large-scale supermarket shopping may have on a consumer's presence of mind:

"As the number of products to be purchased increases, it becomes more difficult and time consuming for the shopper to give a complete roster of purchase intentions.

"Therefore, as transaction size increases, the divergence between actual and measured purchase intentions also increases, resulting in an increase in the percentage of unplanned purchases.'

In short, the more you buy … the more you buy.

Proliferation of package sizes helps breed confusion. That this has the effect of increasing sales is generally well known, but the extent of this effect may not be.

Monroe P. Friedman, writing in the *Journal of Applied Psychology*, made tests on this effect at Eastern Michigan University. He asked 36 young married women, with at least one year of college education, to select the "best deals" in the purchase of 20 different widely used items (ranging from catchup to toothpaste to detergent). He also gave them three minutes to make each selection — three times as much time as studies show it takes the average shopper to make a purchase.

In other words, the women had more education and more time than average shoppers.

Nonetheless, the women made uneconomical choices 43 per cent of the time.

Based on the needless expenses run up by these shoppers, the study estimated that the average housewife may spend at least nine per cent more than she should on such items. The study ascribed this to such factors as small print on labels, the abundance of sizes and curious labels.

Poliferation of sizes remains high in Canada despite criticism. A governments study this fall found there were, for example, 17 different sizes of cereals, six sizes of instant coffee, 11 of crackers and seven of frozen vegetables. Besides confusing shoppers, this also takes up valuable supermarket shelf space.

(It should be noted that some supermarkets are all for reducing the number of sizes. Steinberg's stated: "In our private-label program we are attempting to reduce the number of package sizes available … We are prepared to support any program of standardization.")

The interest of supermarket managemnt in new floor space and display techniques is reflected in the trade magazines. The journal *Progressive Grocer*, for example, features in each issue a "store of the month" — complete with colour photos of displays which boosted the store's profits.

In a typical issue, the magazine's store of the month was an ultra modern Wisconsin supermarket whose profits were soaring.

"At the front end of the first aisle, just inside the door," the magazine noted approvingly, "customers are attracted to the aroma of the bakery and the snack bar." The bakery's star product was a plain, additive-free fresh bread.

But it was not the bread's nutritional qualities which interested the magazine.

The supermarket owner was quoted: "We don't use preservatives so that people will have to come in every day for fresh loaves. And when they do, they make other purchases."

Many consumers assume that supermarkets charge about the same markup on all their thousands of products. However, as some of the textbook remarks quoted earlier suggested, some goods have much higher markups than others — and it is these high markup items which the grocers have, of course, the most interest in selling.

The markup — or, in retail technology, the "margin" — is the hush-hush difference between what a grocer buys a product for and what he sells it for to the consumer.

In general, staple foods — like milk, bread, sugar, butter and flour — carry low margins. Processed foods and especially the luxury ones have the highest.

Supermarkets don't like to discuss their markups on individual items. But the records of one of the largest Canadian chains show that its margin on butter is about 1.4 per cent and on sugar six per cent. On processed foods the margins are higher.

The chain shows a margin of seven per cent on Heinz baby food, nine per cent on Alymer canned peaches, nine per cent on Campbell's tomato soap, 14 cent on Kellogg's corn flakes, 14.3 per cent on Alymer canned peas and 27 per cent on buns and rolls.

Dry goods — like hardware and toys — are among the highest margins. Thus in promotional material to grocers, A-OK toys suggests margins of 33 per cent and General Electric suggests margins of over 40 per cent for its home electrical supplies. Drugs and vitamin pills are also high.

This helps explain why more than 20 per cent of supermarket sales today come from non-food items, and why the percentage is rising, according to Canadian Grocer figures.

The location of these high markup items — processed or non-food — of course gets priority. As James Cooke, president of Allied Supermarkets in the U.S. has put it, "Obviously more sales result when the average person takes his four-pound consumption of food in products such as cake mix rather than flour."

Indeed, a chain like Steinburg's tends to make bigger overall store-wide margins in its west end stores than in the east end. "The reason is that our high markup stuff — frozen foods, gourmet items and all that — tend to do better in the west end," an official acknowledged.

The markups listed above are actually higher than given. They were listed according to the retailers' method of calculating markup. This method is different from almost anyone else's — and its easy for consumers to be confused.

If a supermarket buys a product from a manufacturer or wholesaler for $1 and sells it to the consumer for $2, the markup is 100 per cent, right? Wrong.

According to the retailers' way of figuring it, it would be 50 per cent.

Supermarkets are not trying to minimize their cut by employing this style of arithmetic. It's a traditional system of calculation which, according to the stores, facilitates book-keeping.

But next time a store says it is marking up an item, say, 25 per cent, keep in mind that according to conventional arithmetic it may be really 33 per cent.

Here's how it works. If a retailer says he marks an item up 25 per cent, he may be saying, for instance, that on a 52 cent sale he made 18 cents. That is, he bought the item for 29 cents and 13 cents is 25 per cent of 52 cents.

Everyone else would say that since the retailer bought the product for 29 cents and sold it for 52 cents he made 33 per cent on the deal, since 13 is one-third of 39.

There has been consumer confusion not only on the statistical but the linguistic usages of supermarkets. Price structures which chains describe as 'miracle discount' or 'deep discount' in nature have left some shoppers puzzled.

A study of profits at Steinberg's, Quebec's largest food chain and the first to begin 'discount' pricing in response to consumer concern over high prices in the late 1960's, shows that the company's profits are higher now than when "miracle" prices were introduced.

A word of caution, however. Margins are not the same thing as profits. The average supermarket chain generally makes a gross margin of about 20 per cent of sales (or according to conventional math, 25 per cent.)

After overhead — notably labour, rent, taxes, etc. — chains are typically left with only one or two cents net profit per sales dollar.

This may not sound like much money, as the chains are frequently pointing out to critics who say their earnings are high.

But in the supermarket industry, good profits come by combining thin margins with high volume. This is why Steinburg's, with only a billion dollars in sales this past year, was able to translate 1.6 cents profit per dollar of sales into net profit of $16.7 million.

When Steinburg's introduced "miracle" pricing in 1969, it dropped stamps and contests and reduced advertising, among other steps. It lowered its gross margins from 21 per cent to 19 per cent.

Profits were lower too during a shake-down period lasting several years. But now they're higher than ever.

The company explains: "Reduced margins and prices were accompanied by increased volume and greater efficiency."

After tax-net profits which had stood at $6.8 million in 1967 and were down to $5.9 million in 1969, soared to almost $15 million in 1972 and $15.7 million last year.

Looking at the profit picture from a percentage standpoint, the 1.67 cents profit per sales dollar the company made last year compares favourably with the 1.00 cents average it maintained for the four years before miracle pricing.

It is perhaps easier to understand, then, why the food price review board and consumer groups have criticized Steinberg's for the term "miracle pricing" and the company says it is an apt description.

• **1974** Enterprise Reporting •

It's easy to get a job IF you want one

Robert Nielsen

Toronto Star

In the face of half a million Canadians officially counted as unemployed and seeking work, I say it's easy to get a job in Canada. Even in the depth of winter, even in the chronically high-employment areas of the country.

The only requirement is a willingness to take any job, however humble or poorly paid, wherever it's available.

This was proved, to my satisfaction at least, by a January job-hunt through 10 cities in five provinces, during which I dressed in labourer's clothes, stayed in cheap hotels and represented myself as an unskilled middle-aged man ready to take any work I could get.

I was hired for six different jobs — fish-plant worker, night cleaner, warehouse labourer, clothing-factory hand, beverage-room bouncer and gold miner.

I was promised four more if I showed up at hiring halls at 6:30 a.m., and a fifth if I would present myself in Forestville, Que., with a chain saw. A papermaking company told me I could qual-ify as a paid trainee (at $4.69 an hour) for woodcutting jobs that pay piece-rate workers $60 to $70 a day.

I learned in the most convincing way — by doing three of those jobs for a day each — why certain kinds of work are shunned by Canadians even when they can't get anything better.

The quest began in St. John's, Nfld., on Jan. 2 and ended at Thunder Bay, Ont., on Jan. 29. I ended it there because it was evident that I would simply be repeating my experiences, with local variations, if I continued through the prairie provinces and British Columbia. Canada Manpower lists hundreds of unskilled job openings in each of the western cities.

The project almost foundered the first day out. In the bar of the Welcome Hotel in St. John's, Bill Cashin, a janitor, talked to me volubly about people who were "riding the welfare" instead of taking well-paid woods jobs, and about his own dream of getting a provincial land grant for a farm.

I realized my imposture as a poor working fellow from Plaster Rock (my New Brunswick home-town) wasn't going over when Bill kept interjecting such remarks as, "I'll be honest wit' ya bye, though ya might be from the government for all I knows …" Asked why he hadn't taken me at face value, Bill replied: "I knowed ya was a gentleman the minute ya asked me to sit down wit' ya. And you're dressed more like an American hunter than a workin' chap."

Damn. If my worn mackinaw jacket, lumberjack's shirt, shapeless work pants and heavy boots hadn't fooled the first Newfie I met in a darkened bar (and one who already had consumed his quota of beer, at that), how could the masquerade possibly succeed with Manpower counsellors and company personnel managers? If I blew my cover in St. John's, Manpower offices across the country might be alerted to watch out for me.

So I stayed away from Manpower and tried major Newfoundland companies in fish processing, lumbering and iron mining by telephone, talking in as backwoodsy a style as I could manage. No unskilled workers needed at the moment, thanks.

Yet I learned later, by phoning back as a *Star* reporter, that the St. John's Manpower office had 793 job openings listed at the turn of the year, some of them labour and service jobs requiring no previous experience. And I could have got hired instantly by Ches's Snacks, a fish-and-chip shop desperate for a short-order cook, by claiming experience in that line.

Thus Bill Cashin's acuteness and my own timidity undid me in Newfoundland. Following a rule I'd made in advance, to keep the assignment from lasting forever — if no definite job within 24 hours, move on — I left for Nova Scotia.

Fortunately, mainland Canadians proved more gullible than Newfoundlanders. Not once in the Maritimes, Quebec and Ontario did anyone show a flicker of doubt about my stated purpose or about the stick-in-the-mud occupational record — 23 years as a sawmill worker and road construction labourer in and around Plaster Rock — which I recited to Manpower officials, employment agencies and employers.

Sunday in Halifax is like Toronto's Sunday used to be, but there's no law against job-hunting on that day, so I answered two newspaper ads.

The first was for a dishwasher at the Flamingo Restaurant, where the woman manager had me fill out a long, detailed application form and then asked me to come back Tuesday; her "regular girl" could manage until then. Two days' wait for a part-time dishwashing job? Forget it.

The second ad I answered out of idle curiosity: "Beef herdsman wanted immediately for North Shore farm. Applicants please call 453-4964 collect." Was it possible that in Nova Scotia, a province whose airwaves ceaselessly keen and moan with country and western music, nobody actually wanted to be a Pictou County cowboy?

A woman answered the phone. "How many head?" I asked.

"About 100."

"That's a lot for one hand to look after."

"Well, the man we had managed it until he took to drinking too much."

"Are the cattle in a barn?"

"No, outdoors in corrals. The job is to feed them corn silage and hay."

"Wouldn't I have to clean up after them too?" (Vivid recollections of my boyhood on a dairy farm.)

"Not much, outdoors in winter."

She said her husband would call me back to set up an interview. He did next day, but I was already on a job.

The lucky employer, found through Manpower, was the National Sea Products Co. on the Halifax waterfront. Within 40 minutes of reporting there, I had passed inspection by the wharf foreman, been togged out in rubber overalls, high rubber boots and rubberized gloves, and set to work at a sorting table at the bottom end of one of the chutes from which the trawler Cape Scotia was disgorging its catch.

Pay $2.17 an hour, rising to $2.27 after 30 days — and more to come in a new union contract, the employment manager said.

The job is to sort gray sole from flounder and throw them into separate bins, after first separating them from the crushed ice in which they were packed aboard ship.

The only way I can tell them apart is that the flounder has a white belly, and since only 50 per cent of them come down the chute belly-up, I have to turn the others over to see which is which. This makes me slower than my partner across the table.

It soon occurs to me, too, that fish are not only slippery, but have an inconvenient lack of handles on them.

As it is, I miss the bins occasionally, and my workmate is sorting and flinging at least 50 per cent more fish than I can manage, going my hardest without stopping.

Every time the table is almost clear, a guy on the boat tips another barrelful of fish down. A sadist.

This isn't a really hard job, but it's wet, dirty, as cold as the weather, tedious and mean. I got used to the powerful smell after an hour or two, but the smell stayed with me, on my clothes, for days afterward. And the inside jobs — beheading, cleaning and filleting fish — are warmer but no easier. This must be despised work, the kind that makes children the target of unkind taunts because their dad smells fishy all the time.

Certainly the pay is insufficient compensation for the job's miseries, in Halifax and many other places. I was told by Manpower and by a plant worker that the job I was on had a very high turnover, and it was notable that there were no young men at the sorting tables — despite the high official rate of unemployment among youth. Only tough old geezers, men brought up to work hard, stick with that job.

A remedy had been suggested in Newfoundland when I checked out a story that fish plants were importing seasonal Portuguese workers because they couldn't recruit Newfoundlanders.

Not so, said Gus Etchegary, vice-president of Fishery Products Ltd. The company hadn't been able to get enough fish-plant workers last year, when it was paying about $110 a week. But since then, a new contract had been negotiated with the Canadian Seafood Workers' Union, and the workers are now getting about $190 a week, counting bonuses. "Now we've got enough hands at all six plants, and on our trawlers," Etchegary said.

A costly remedy, and one that will probably raise the price of seafood. But I for one will gladly pay more for fish if it results from higher wages for the workers in that Halifax plant, and elsewhere. Hordes of people in comfortable city offices, including me, are doing less-probably useful work for better pay.

• **1987** Business Reporting •

Lumber deal may involve
complicated rate setting

Christopher Waddell

Globe and Mail

OTTAWA — Ottawa may face the unprecedented situation of setting separate export tax rates for lumber from each province as a result of a deal signed last week with Washington to end the bitter trade dispute with the United States.

Treasury Board President Robert de Cotret appeared to concede that such a scenario is possible when he said at a press conference on Friday that individual provinces "may wish to act in different fashions" in responding to the agreement.

Under the Dec. 30 deal between the two countries, Canada will impose a 15 per cent export tax on all softwood lumber shipped to the United States, effective Jan. 8.

In return, the U.S. lumber industry dropped its demand that countervailing duties be imposed on softwood imports from Canada, to offset low provincial stumpage fees for cutting timber on Crown land, which the U.S. industry regards as an unfair trade subsidy. In a preliminary ruling in mid-October, the U.S. Commerce Department set those duties at 15 per cent. It would have made a final ruling at midnight on Dec. 30 had a deal not been struck hours before the deadline.

Though the pact allows the export tax to remain in place indefinitely, it is Ottawa's intention to quickly replace it in full or part with what is described in the agreement as "increased stumpage or other charges by provinces on softwood lumber production."

But, after several weeks spent wracking their brains, federal officials admitted at an off-the-record briefing last week that they have been unable to come up with any ideas other than stumpage fee increases for additional taxes to raise the needed revenues.

Because the provinces have total control over stumpage fees, in effect the Dec. 30 agreement merely replaces one bitter set of negotiations involving the federal government with two that will, in coming months, likely prove just as contentious as the initial phase of the softwood dispute with the United States.

First, Ottawa must negotiate stumpage increases with the provinces in a bargaining process that will begin with a meeting of federal and provincial trade and forestry ministers on Jan. 14. Ottawa has accepted Washington's demand that it collect at least $500-million a year through whatever combination of export tax and other duties are levied, setting the stage for the difficult negotiations with provincial governments.

In those sessions each province will have to take care that changes in its stumpage system do not put its industry at a competitive disadvantage with other provinces in the domestic market. The provinces also will have to consider the export situation.

Other problems could arise if, for example, the export tax/ stumpage increases price a significant percentage of British Columbia's production out of the U.S. market. West Coast producers might then ship lumber to eastern Canada, to areas served by Ontario and Quebec mills, forcing them to shut down.

At the First Ministers Conference in Vancouver in late November, Ontario indicated its opposition to Ottawa's decision to negotiate with the United States rather than fight the countervailing duty claim put forward by U.S. lumber producers through various U.S. and international trade tribunals.

What if Ontario, say, with stumpage fees at about $3.75 per 1,000 board feet, now refuses to increase its stumpage levels, which are already high compared with the approximately $1.07 charged by British Columbia?

B.C. Premier William Vander Zalm has given his hearty endorsement to the deal, and presumably his province — which contributes between 65 per cent and 70 per cent of softwood exports to the United States — will increase stumpage fees. But they probably will go up only enough to provide British Columbia's pro rata share of the minimum of the $500- million total to be raised by the various measures.

Would Ottawa then be forced to levy an export tax on Ontario production to make sure that it does not gain a competitive advantage against B.C. output in the American market?

If other provinces also balk at stumpage increases or merely introduce changes to partially off-set their share of the revenue to be raised by the export tax, the federal government would have to charge different rates of tax on each province's exports.

If Ottawa can reach a deal with all the provinces, then a second round of talks must be held with Washington to indicate to the Administration that all stumpage fee alterations are equal to the value of the 15 per cent export tax replaced by the higher fees.

It is that issue that has produced the debate over how much, if any, sovereignty over natural resource pricing and other forest management policies Canada has sacrificed to Washington in the deal.

Brandishing a clarification from the U.S. Embassy, Mr. de Cotret said on Friday that Canadian sovereignty is not diminished by the agreement. Canada retains full rights to determine what changes it wishes to make to forest management practices, he said.

But Washington has an effective veto over such changes, according to any of three documents:
• The agreement's wording that "calculation of the value of any replacement measures in relation to the export charge will be subject to further consultations and agreement between the two Governments;"
• The wording of a Dec. 30 letter from U.S. Commerce Secretary Malcolm Baldrige to U.S. lumber producers that "the U.S. Government would have to approve any changes in the export charge or calculation of the value of any replacement measures";
• The clarification from the U.S. Embassy in Ottawa which said that "the U.S. is concerned with the valuation of those measures and their impact on the export charge." If the Administra-tion, after consultation with U.S. lumber producers, does not agree that any changes introduced by Ottawa have the equivalent impact on exports of the 15 per cent tax, then there is no deal.

Canada must then either alter the value or form of the measures it has introduced, which will almost certainly be stumpage fee increases, or the Americans will simply abrogate the agree-ment on 30 days' notice and impose import duties on Canadian lumber.

Such duties are precisely what would have been introduced had there been no last-minute agreement last week.

• **1990** Business Reporting •

The Edper puzzle: Crisis of confidence

Kimberley Noble

Globe and Mail

B efore the stock market turned treacherous and investors' moods soured, a broker close to the Hees-Edper-Bronfman empire offered an analogy that still stands as the best two-minute guide to how the group works — as well as the reason for a lot of its problems.

He compared investing in Bronfman companies with watching a basketball game in the dark. Shareholder-spectators know there's a game going on because they can hear the ball bouncing and feet scuffling on the floor; they just can't see what's happening.

But there is a big electronic board overhead that periodically flashes the score so spectators can see how their team is doing.

Chief strategist Jack Cockwell and his team of crackerjack lawyers, accountants and bankers tell their shareholders ahead of time what the score will be. They believe the audience should be satisfied as long as the numbers match up to what the managers promised.

Yet investors aren't so easily satisfied, the broker said. They've paid their money, and they want to watch the game itself.

Today, they want more than that. Times are tough, stocks are falling and investors are afraid of things they cannot see or understand.

They are much less willing to bet on the brains and connections of a deal-driven organization that won't tell outsiders how much money it has, where this is held, how it is moved among affiliates, to whom it is lent and how exactly it grows in value.

Canada's largest conglomerate is facing a significant crisis. Confidentiality has given the powerful and innovative Bronfman companies an important competitive edge over the years. It has enabled them to offer their clients — troubled borrowers and blue-chip financiers alike — privacy, speed, flexibility and a hidden network of partners.

But their passion for privacy has backfired in a bad market. Share prices of group companies have plunged faster than the Toronto Stock Exchange's main index, priced-to-sell rights offerings have been left virtually untouched by outside shareholders, and debt traders have found themselves working harder than usual to find buyers for short-term corporate paper.

Bronfman holding companies are finding it difficult to borrow from the banks, sources with inside information said, and some of the operating companies are discovering that investors, lenders and customers are thinking twice or demanding higher returns before entering into deals.

"We feel the taint," an executive in one Bronfman affiliate said. "People are wary of doing business with us. It may not be justified, but it's there."

Yet, as the recession deepens and investor confidence shrivels, it becomes increasingly evident that the managers who run this empire simply do not explain their business in a way that would provide the public with the reassurance it wants.

The Bronfman empire — created by Mr. Cockwell out of Edward and Peter Bronfman's share of the Seagram distilleries fortune — contains many of the oldest and best-known names in Canadian business: Noranda Inc., MacMillan Bloedel Ltd., Falconbridge Ltd., John Labatt Ltd., London Life Ltd., Royal Trust Ltd. and Bramalea Ltd.

Operating companies are controlled through layers of holding companies that culminate in key financing-investing-merchant banking vehicles at the top of the pyramid. These include Brascan Ltd., Hees International Bancorp Inc., Carena Developments Ltd., Trilon Financial Corp., Pagurian Corp. Ltd. and Edper Enterprises Ltd.

The group controls companies that make up 12 per cent of market capitalization of the Toronto Stock Exchange's main index of 300 stocks; both Hees and Brascan are often described as proxies for investing in Corporate Canada.

This organization has grown huge and wealthy by sniffing out and putting to profitable use every nuance and loophole of tax and securities law. In the same way as the avant-garde artist challenges the limits of a medium, the Bronfmans' legal and financial wizards have the creative ability and an obsessive need to push the envelope of federal and provincial regulations if it will add anything to the bottom line.

A senior manager in the group complained once that every time they're frank about these special financial talents, Bronfman companies end up becoming the target of public outrage. This was the case in 1985, when Edper officials were forced to appear before a parliamentary committee on the deregulation of financial institutions to defend their practice of using companies they controlled to underwrite securities of others in the group, a practice known as self-dealing.

It happened again in 1988, when the federal government responded to public pressure over the group's use of the tax savings that flowed from preferred share financing by eliminating many of those benefits.

The group official said that every time this happens, it shows the managers that it's just not worth letting the public know about many of the things they do.

Yet group managers keep trying to change their image and be seen as more open in their public dealings, primarily because they recognize that, otherwise, they will never see their common shares traded for what insiders think they are worth.

Early this year, senior officials stated publicly that they would become more accessible to outside shareholders, provide better explanations of their financial results and eliminate extraneous parts of their byzantine organizational structure — steps that financial analysts say are essential to improve market perception of values within the group.

But so far, the managers have been unable to keep these promises: Low share prices have made reorganizations unattractive and refinancings almost impossible, and both Canadian and U.S. regulators have held up proposals to transfer or redistribute assets.

Moreover, Bronfman companies have been under siege since late spring as a result of some high-profile battles with minority shareholders, as well as from the impact of falling real estate and natural resource values on share prices, balance sheets and dividend flows throughout the empire.

Outside supporters, including some investment analysts, accuse short sellers and brokers of spreading unfounded rumours about cash shortages and other pressures in order to drive stock prices lower and to generate commissions when frightened shareholders bail out of what, they say, are essentially sound but badly misunderstood companies.

One investment analyst argues that the group should be able to withstand any recession short of one that cripples the entire country: "A lot of people are talking about things they don't know anything about."

But he added that this, in itself, "is really key, this tells you something right there.

"The fact that they don't know much about what's going on is a problem. In a bear market, people are looking for bad news, they're looking for a reason to sell. And the unknown generates fear and concern, and then everybody tends to discount."

In September, group managers reacted by making the rounds of investment dealers and institutional shareholders to reassure them that the organization has more than enough cash tucked away to keep the dividends flowing up the pyramid.

But one skeptic who attended these sessions said that while the managers "talked a lot, they didn't say anything. They wouldn't answer the tough questions." Another said they keep insisting that outside observers should view the group they way they do — as a series of otherwise independent companies that can be teamed up if one of them runs into financial trouble.

This view of the group — which combines liquid Hees with cash-strapped Brascan, for example — is a favourite of its managers, but bothers a number of outside observers. "They can't do that," one former director complained. "Those companies are separate legal entities." They cannot ask shareholders to look at group companies as if they can transfer liquidity back and forth, he said.

All the pressures are prompting the Bronfman group to revert to old habits. For one thing, member companies have turned inward and are doing increasing amounts of business with one another — something that a key official in the organization said is a way of exercising better control during uncertain times.

And, following their brief flirtation with openness, Bronfman officials are avoiding contact with anyone outside the investment communities in which they wield financial influence. Senior managers have recently refused all interviews that would address the issues that confront them.

• **1993** Business Reporting •

Northern Telecom: The morning after

Lawrence Surtees

Globe and Mail

In the spring of 1992, Northern Telecom Ltd., Canada's foremost high-technology company, was having a banner year. Revenues were headed for an all-time high and quarterly profits, with one small exception, were marching steadily upward. The company had recently concluded deals that gave it a big foothold in Britain and France.

Northern was walking tall in the world and so was Dr. Paul Stern, the president, chairman and CEO, the man who had been hand-picked to shape the company's global destiny. (The Dr., a title he insisted on, was justified by his PhD in physics.) *Business Week* took note, and was busy preparing a cover story featuring Mr. Stern's square-jawed, steely-eyed and resolute face under the coverline "High-tech star."

Inside the company, however, unease was growing from top to bottom. Many top executives were heading for the exits, some driven out by their boss's relentless focus on short-term profits, his abrasive and often abusive personal behaviour and what they described as a fundamental absence of long-term vision. Key customers of long standing cancelled big orders. Crucial research and development projects languished. Among the rank and file, discontent over Mr. Stern's constant cost-cutting and imperial style had turned into near-rebellion.

The poor morale was evident in the frosty reception Mr. Stern received from employees during a visit to the Ottawa headquarters of Bell-Northern Research Ltd.

"Good morning!" the chairman shouted to a large crowd in the cavernous cafeteria.

No one answered. He repeated the greeting, which again was met with silence. It was not until the third try that a lone voice echoed back.

Mr. Stern, who resigned as CEO last September and as chairman on June 25, has left a lot of mopping up to do. Among his legacies will be a second-quarter loss, the first in almost five years for the company.

News of the loss knocked the share price down almost 30 per cent and shaved $3.3-billion in value off the stock last week. The reasons and the amount haven't been disclosed, but analysts believe the company will take hefty charges, including provisions to pay for overhauls to vital software technology that were delayed too long.

Mr. Stern, who is 54, declined a request to be interviewed for this story and to respond to questions raised by his record and his background. A spokesman says those matters have "been touched on in the press and he's given his best side of it."

But off-the-record interviews with more than 40 current and former senior executives, consultants and customers reveal a legacy of bad blood between Mr. Stern and every group the company has been dependent upon for its success: Its phone company customers; its employees — from the most senior and loyal officers to shopfloor workers — and investors, including its corporate parent, BCE Inc. of Montreal.

Northern Telecom is a strong company with an abundance of assets, both technological and human. But Mr. Stern's tenure is a textbook example of the way that managing for short-term profits can undermine a company's long-term competitive position. There is no doubt that Northern had to cut its costs in order to protect its margins in an ever more competitive world. But in doing so, Mr. Stern sacrificed sales and weakened the company's position in some of its core markets.

"Stern was an opportunist, instead of being a leader, who ... came dangerously close to wrecking what his predecessors had worked so diligently to build," a former officer says.

Northern Telecom is the top telecommunications manufacturer in Canada and owns the country's largest private R&D complex. It employs almost 60,000 people around the world.

But it is more than Canada's high-tech crown jewel. Its prowess in electronics and software tie it to Canada's economic future. With sales of $8.4-billion (U.S.) last year, it ranked as the fifth-largest telephone equipment maker in the world, competing in a global market worth over $120-billion annually.

Northern is a world leader in two market segments: Business telephone systems and the telephone company market for large computer switches used to route calls. Its flagship family of DMS switches gave it access to the huge U.S. market in 1979.

But it wasn't technology that got the company on supplier lists. "What made it for Northern Telecom was personal relationships with key customers," says Rick Oliver, a former vice-president. He left the company last fall and is now a business professor at Vanderbilt University in Nashville.

By the late '80s, the company was poised for a renewed global assault. Northern Telecom's chairman at the time was Edmund Fitzgerald, a respected, independently wealthy businessman from Milwaukee who had been with the company for a decade. He was ready to retire and needed to find a successor.

Mr. Fitzgerald first met Mr. Stern in the late '80s at a gathering of the Electrical Manufacturers' Club, whose purpose was to bring together executives for drinking, fishing and networking. Mr. Stern was then president of Unisys Corp., a large U.S. computer maker, where he had slashed costs after orchestrating a big merger. Mr. Fitzgerald believed Mr. Stern possessed the two ingredients his successor needed most — toughness and a global outlook.

In 1987, Mr. Stern left Unisys when its chairman, W. Michael Blumenthal, decided to expand the executive office and dilute his power. Rather than share his job, Mr. Stern quit — and collected a $6.7-million severance deal. He took up teaching and tennis at Duke University in North Carolina and was hired as a consultant to Northern Telecom by Mr. Fitzgerald. He won a seat on the board in April, 1988.

The board liked what they saw. Mr. Stern, who was born in Czechoslovakia, had a quick and decisive manner, and impressed them with his insights gained from living and working in the United States, Britain, Mexico and Germany. His strengths outweighed the fact that he knew little about the telecommunications business. The board anointed him as Mr. Fitzgerald's successor, and he became chairman in April 1990.

It was Mr. Stern's first job as Number One. On top of that, Northern made it a hat trick. He was president, CEO and chairman. Although he had held big titles at big companies like Braun AG of Germany and Unisys, he had never before been the executive chairman of the board. He had always had someone else to whom he was accountable. But the history of business is littered with effective number two's whose style became a liability when they got to be number one.

Columbia University business professor Donald Hambrick coined the term Idi Amin complex, after Uganda's former dictator, to describe a boss who has all three top titles and wields power unchecked. Some people thought he must have had Mr. Stern in mind. A former officer of the company, who left during Mr. Stern's reign, says, "The image was a veneer that coated an immature, vain and irresponsible individual ill-suited to the discipline of power."

The warning signs were there early on. Even before he became chairman. Mr. Stern exhibited a crudeness in private that clashed with his carefully-crafted image. Mr. Oliver, who was then Mr. Fitzgerald's aide, attended a senior management conference at Naples, Fla., in February, 1990, and recalls Mr. Fitzgerald wanted Mr. Stern to join his table to discuss strategy. When Mr. Oliver invited Mr. Stern to the discussion, he got a shocking reply.

"Tell Fitz to go fuck himself," the incoming chairman said.

"We must become the preferred company for customers," Mr. Stern repeatedly told employees. Yet problems with customers started soon after he took over. One of his first decisions was to relocate the chairman's office to a Washington suburb, predictably inflaming Canadian nationalists. But it also upset some company executives who had to relocate because, they say, they lost close touch with sales groups in the United States and Canada.

In early 1991, Mr. Stern recruited Edward Lucente, 53, from International Business Machines

Corp. to be Northern's global marketing boss. He also reorganized the company, putting all the subsidiary heads under Mr. Lucente and creating separate global product bosses. The shuffle was aimed at ending geographic turf battles over product development and marketing.

"It got rid of the warring tribes, but replaced them with warring towers," a former officer said.

Like Mr. Stern, Mr. Lucente was perceived as arrogant and abrasive. At one point, Mr. Lucente decreed, to widespread disbelief, that all employees who dealt with customers would have to start wearing uniforms. When one widely respected vice-president made the mistake of ridiculing the edict, he was dismissed. The uniform idea was eventually scrapped.

Neither Mr. Stern nor Mr. Lucente were customer men. Insiders say their cost-cutting policies damaged Northern Telecom's critical relationships with its biggest customers — North America's largest telephone companies, a conservative bunch that are used to close-knit connections with their suppliers. The phone companies expect their suppliers to mount plenty of customer seminars and junkets, like golf tournaments. These events are more than perks. They help educate influential buyers about the strategic value of Northern's products, which, after all, run a phone company's network.

Those relationships were damaged when several programs to craft ties with phone companies and Fortune 500 businesses were killed in Mr. Stern's bid to reduce costs, Mr. Oliver says. Mr. Stern and Mr. Lucente also set out to replace Northern's specialized account executives, who could handle a customer's every need, with commodity-type sales forces for different product lines. This scheme also harmed relationships with the U.S. phone companies, says a former U.S. marketing executive.

That change "reinforced the perception these guys didn't know the business," Mr. Oliver says.

The organizational changes distanced customers from knowledgeable executives. Customers were also dismayed by recurrent technical problems and dissatisfaction mounted.

• In the United States, some "Baby Bells" complained of system crashes, late deliveries and pressure to advance orders.

• In Great Britain, Northern Telecom was held back from making additional inroads with BT PLC (formerly British Telecom) — now Northern Telecom's second-largest customer — because Mr. Stern and Mr. Lucente did not listen to BT's concerns about quality, a senior BT officer told a source.

• In Australia, Optus Communications Pty — the alternate long-distance carrier — recently gave a $28-million (U.S.) piece of a major contract with Northern Telecom to a Texas company because Northern could not deliver until the end of 1994.

• In Japan, Nippon Telegraph and Telephone Co. was upset by software problems and bothered by Northern Telecom's unwillingness to put an Asian in charge of its Tokyo-based subsidiary.

Mr. Stern's bottom-line focus caused him to put off launching a much-needed, but expensive, research project to revamp the vast and unwieldy software of Northern Telecom's flagship switches, former officers and consultants say.

The software works very well most of the time. The problem, however, is that there's too much of it. Phone companies began suffering paralyzing problems in the mid-'80s as they installed more software for new services. Northern Telecom solved that problem briefly by developing a more powerful brain for the computer switches. But it was apparent to engineers in the early 1990s that a sweeping redesign was needed to avoid future crashes and to keep customers happy. The project was finally launched last fall, insiders say, after Mr. Stern had stepped aside as president. The cost will be reflected in this year's second-quarter loss.

The majority of former officers and executives interviewed for this story decried Mr. Stern's lack of strategic vision and long-term outlook.

"He is a quarter-to-quarter manager whose sole focus is cutting costs and finding ways to boost the next period's profit," says one.

"We were into very intensive biweekly forecasts," says another.

To beef up revenue, raise profit and boost the company's share price, which flagged in mid-1992, Mr. Stern pressured customers to book more orders in advance.

Some phone companies, like Pacific Bell of San Francisco, resisted.

Pac Bell's president reportedly told Mr. Lucente, "I wish you guys were as concerned about my earnings as you are about your sales."

But Northern Telecom's sister company, Bell Canada, obliged by accelerating its purchases of digital switches. Bell officials admitted the utility did the $390-million (Canadian) deal as a favour. It boosted Northern Telecom's 1992 share profit by 20 cents (U.S.), according to one analyst's estimate.

In 1991, Mr. Stern launched a covert restructuring program involving the layoff of more than 1,000 people. The layoffs were spread out over many months and portrayed as isolated, "local" events. According to a confidential memo written by John Strimas, vice-president of corporate relations, the idea was to keep the extent of the restructuring hidden from "media, politicians and governments, customers, investors (and) employees." Former officers say there was a perception at high levels inside the company that Mr. Stern wanted the layoffs separated to avoid depressing the company's share price.

"Stern was obsessed with the stock price because he used it to measure his own performance," says a former officer, adding that Mr. Stern constantly checked the company's share price throughout the day.

For a strategy, Mr. Stern borrowed something called Vision 2000. Vision 2000 was a slogan that dated from 1987 and referred to the company's goal to attain industry leadership by the year 2000. (To put this goal in perspective, Northern's sales are one-third those of industry leader Alcatel NV of Belgium.)

To promote the Vision, renamed A Journey to Leadership, Mr. Stern took to the hustings on a multimillion-dollar, political-style campaign. The tour was orchestrated by Mr. Strimas, who called himself "Mr. Stern's campaign manager." It took them to every plant in the world. Each stop was filmed for a quarterly employee video.

The hype backfired, says Francis McInerny, a leading U.S. consultant and head of North River Ventures Inc. of New York. "The sales goal of the Vision is unattainable, which has heightened the demoralization and cynicism widely felt through the company," he says.

Another morale-boosting idea was to create an annual chairman's award for employee excellence. It too backfired — when Mr. Stern gave the first award to Mr. Strimas for the Vision campaign. Last fall, Mr. Stern issued a Scrooge-like memo threatening employees with dismissal if any Christmas party involved company money or company time. But his calls for austerity flew in the face of his own opulent lifestyle, which employees perceived as inappropriate. In one widely cited example, he lavished attention on a temporary secretary whom he promoted to "specialist" in charge of special events. She accompanied the chairman on his new corporate jet wherever he travelled and executives bristled at her presence at his side during the senior management conference for the company's top 150 executives at Aventura, Fla., in 1991.

Mr. Stern's wife did not always get the same treatment. Former officers remember how Mr. Stern stranded his spouse on the tarmac at Toronto's Pearson International Airport one Friday afternoon because she forgot her passport. The chairman was taking a group of executives and their spouses to a weekend meeting with some phone company bosses in Bermuda ostensibly to drum up sales. Wives, he declared in his book *Straight to the Top*, are assets to be picked for success.

Mr. Stern repeatedly declared "our people are our strength." In private councils, however, he said employees performed better if they lived in fear of their job.

"He has a very binary mind. Things are either done his way or the wrong way," a former officer says.

The employee in charge of Northern Telecom's corporate jets found that out when he was dismissed after the boss was kept waiting in Chicago because a blizzard grounded his jet in Toronto.

"The old, Neanderthal methods don't produce industry leaders," says Anna VerSteeg, a former deputy manager at Northern's repair facility in Morrisville, N.C., and now president of Competitive Solutions Inc. of Cary, N.C.

Some employees agreed. Half of the more than 20 former executives tracked down for this story say they quit because of Mr. Stern.

"Two years ago, headhunters couldn't pry executives out of Northern Telecom," a former human resources executive says.

But Mr. Stern last year angrily denied a suggestion he was to blame for driving away talent. "I never lost an executive I wanted to keep. Never."

It all began to unravel about 15 months ago.

In April, 1992, Northern Telecom's largest U.S. customer, BellSouth Corp. of Atlanta, suspended further orders for transmission products. Although BellSouth refuses to comment on any of its vendor relationships, several sources, including a former Northern Telecom director, confirm the troubles.

The problems began with delays related to orders for fibre-optic products. Summoned to a meeting by BellSouth chairman John Clendenin in late 1991 to explain how Northern Telecom was going to solve those problems, Mr. Stern instead boasted about the benefits of his big, British acquisition. "Clendenin hit the roof," a consultant says, then cancelled BellSouth's orders. Although the value of that business is undisclosed, BellSouth's purchases totalled $260-million in 1990.

Worse news came in an alarming letter from BellSouth to Northern Telecom's U.S. unit last September. "The letter stated BellSouth was suspending, until further notice, all subsequent switch purchases," says a respected U.S. consultant, who was shown the original copy of the letter. The letter's existence was confirmed by several former Northern Telecom officers.

At the same time, Mr. Stern's relations with the board soured, too. In April, 1992, Mr. Stern took a proposal to Northern Telecom's board of directors to make Mr. Lucente president, give him a seat on the board and make him Mr. Stern's successor. It was a serious misstep. The board vetoed him.

The succession scheme "woke BCE up," a former officer says, adding that J.V. Raymond Cyr, then BCE chairman, is believed to have led the board's veto.

Ian Barclay, a director who retired from Northern Telecom's board last April — and the only board member approached who offered comments on the record — refuses to confirm or deny whether the board vetoed that proposal. But he did say that hypothetically, such a defeat, "if you know your guy, would be more than a vote of non-confidence in his leadership."

Five months later, on Sept. 24, 1992, Mr. Stern suddenly resigned as president and was replaced by Bell Canada president Jean Monty, 45.

Mr. Barclay, who was also a member of the powerful management resources and compensation committee, categorically denies that Mr. Stern was ousted by BCE's outside directors. "At no time did the BCE directors demand, or ask for, his resignation," Mr. Barclay says. "That was entirely his move."

Yet Mr. Barclay and top BCE officers acknowledge the parent was concerned with the deterioration of the company's customer relationships. Bell Canada executives say Mr. Monty was in fact offered the Northern Telecom job in April, 1992, but had to stay put at the telephone company to see it through the crucial regulatory decision on long-distance competition, which was issued last June. At Northern Telecom, Mr. Monty immediately took charge of operations, particularly marketing. Mr. Stern was said to be concentrating on strategy and made it widely known that he was available for the top job at IBM or, failing that, Westinghouse Electric Corp. Mr. Lucente left this March.

In January of this year Mr. Stern gave up the CEO title to become "non-executive" chairman. The way out was eased by a lucrative settlement package. He will get two years' salary (last year his pay was more than $2.1-million, including a $975,000 bonus) and his pension will be credited with an added 10 years of service. His annual payout at retirement will be over $600,000. And the company bought his sprawling house in Potomac, Md.

Earlier this spring Mr. Stern exercised his stock options. He sold 65,000 shares near their 52-week high and netted a profit of $1.8-million.

Mr. Stern has not yet landed another job. Westinghouse turned him down because his "abrasive style" alienated the board, *Business Week* reported.

And had Northern Telecom's board dug deeper into Mr. Stern's past, they would have found that his track record at other companies may not be as good as it first appears and that his resumé contains exaggerations.

Mr. Stern has given at least three different accounts of his 1966 PhD, obtained from the University of Manchester Institute of Science and Technology (UMIST) in Great Britain. His thesis was on a method to interpret X-ray photos.

Yet he told journalists his PhD was in solid-state physics. This conflicts with the claim he made to two Northern Telecom executives, both of whom are physicists, that he earned it in plasma physics. At the time, UMIST had no facilities to study the then-new area of very hot ionized gases. And he told another former officer that he did his research with the co-discoverers of DNA — the biological molecule of heredity.

Records at Wilmington-based chemical giant E. I. du Pont de Nemours & Co. Inc. state he began his career not as a senior physicist, as his official biography claims, but as a junior "research physicist" at du Pont's Spruance plant in Richmond, Va.

He then went to IBM of Armonk, N.Y., and after seven years there, was hired in 1975 by Braun, the German electric shaver and toiletry maker, as a technical director. He was promoted to chairman, which, despite the title, was a job akin to CEO. One month later, he was awarded his sole patent, along with G. Mahlich. It was for a curling tong or hair dryer helmet with a flash-tube discharge lamp to heat hair, according to the World Patents Index data-base.

At Braun, his quest to downsize and shave costs produced mixed results. After the company posted a whopping 25-per-cent decline in profit and a six-per-cent drop in sales for the fiscal year ended March 1979, he left.

Mr. Stern returned to the United States and joined Rockwell International Corp. of Pittsburgh as a vice-president of strategic management, but spent little more than a year at the aerospace and defence conglomerate. He left in January, 1981, only two months after he was promoted to president of the newly created commercial electronics unit.

Next, he was hired for a job at Burroughs Corp. by chairman W. Michael Blumenthal. He was promoted to president and chief operating officer of the computer maker in 1982, then made headlines as the mastermind of Burroughs' 1986 acquisition of rival Sperry Corp. — and enemies by eliminating 9,600 jobs when he created Unisys Corp.

His decision to close Sperry's factory in Bristol, Tenn., has made him a political liability today. A powerful U.S. Senator named Al Gore fought to keep the plant open. Mr. Gore is now U.S. Vice-President. And even if he has forgotten the plant, he won't soon forget Mr. Stern's role as a leading financial bagman for the rival Republican Party and former U.S. president George Bush.

It's a fair question to ask, "What the hell did the fellow do for the corporation?" says Walter Light. Mr. Light, who is a former chairman and CEO of Northern Telecom, applauds Mr. Stern's twin focus of building international markets and curbing costs. Other current officers also give the departed chairman credit for his accomplishments in these areas. And the most recent proxy statement makes much of the company's record 1992 revenue and share price. It also points to growth in international sales during his tenure, the STC PLC acquisition in Britain, the joint venture with Matra SA in France and with Motorola Inc. to justify Mr. Stern's 1992 bonus.

But Mr. Light also says, "I think we have to see if the changes (Mr. Stern made) have kept us competitive and profitable."

On the face of it, the international sales record is good. Sales outside North America rose to 25 per cent of revenue last year, compared with eight per cent in 1988 when Mr. Stern joined the company. But the bulk of the increase is due to the acquisition of STC, the British fibre optics maker.

Mr. Stern cannot take credit, as he is fond of doing, for the STC or Matra deals. Both were initiated by his predecessor. Mr. Fitzgerald spearheaded the STC deal by acquiring 27 per cent of the company in 1987 and contemplated but did not act on a proposal to do the Matra deal around the same time, former officers say. Mr. Stern points to new contracts in Japan and Mexico as a sign of his success and global savvy. Yet Mr. Fitzgerald cracked Japan and Robert Ferchat, the former president of Northern Telecom Canada, did the spadework in Mexico.

Lynton "Red" Wilson, the chairman of Northern's parent, BCE, defends Mr. Stern's emphasis on short-term costs. But in a recent interview he was critical that the focus came "at the expense of the long-term." Northern Telecom's two greatest strengths are its people and its large customer base, he says. "But it must attend to that base."

Although some Northern-watchers say the need to restructure may be more extensive than people think, all believe the company has a bright future. Offsetting the slower growth in its core business of selling switches in North America are opportunities in promising new offshore markets, like China, and in new technologies.

Jean Monty, who has made his mark as a finance whiz, has moved quickly to reorganize Northern's marketing to its largest U.S. phone company customers. Last week, he elevated some of the company's most respected career officers to top positions as he pursues a strategy aimed at improving customer and employee satisfaction.

Mr. Monty did not want to be interviewed for this story. But the course he has set is becoming apparent. When he launched the latest reorganization he said his executives must groom a new generation of leaders. That would compensate for the exodus of some of the top talent during Mr. Stern's tenure. His decision to launch the software improvement program is critical to maintaining technological leadership and keeping customers happy. But as competition increases for fewer contracts in the core switching business, he will have to keep reducing costs to enable the company to bid at ever-lower prices. While work remains to be done, some U.S. customers, like Pacific Bell, have shown signs of renewed confidence in Northern Telecom through major contract awards.

The consensus among analysts and former executives alike is that Northern Telecom is too strong to be wrecked by one bad CEO. Despite everything, says one, "it's still a great company."

• **1997** Business Reporting •
Bre-X: The untold story
John Stackhouse, Paul Waldie, Janet McFarland

Globe and Mail

John Felderhof walked into the Sari Hotel in downtown Jakarta hoping the man he was about to meet for dinner might be his saviour. It was March, 1993, and Mr. Felderhof, once a star geologist, was flat broke and trying to recover from a stock market scandal that had cost him his job.

With him that night were three geologists: Michael de Guzman, a Filipino who had been fired from a job because he'd bought presents for a girlfriend using company money; Jonathan Nassey, an Indonesian who liked to be called doctor even though everyone in Jakarta knew his PhD had come from a mail order company in the United States; and Mike Bird, an Australian who married into a family well connected to Indonesia's military.

The rag-tag group of friends, who had been slashing through the jungles of Indonesia for more than a decade, turned out that night to meet Canadian businessman David Walsh.

None of the men knew Mr. Walsh very well. And they had no idea he needed saviours just as badly as they did.

"I assumed anyone who could afford to fly out from Canada had a fair bit of money," said one of the geologists at the meal that night.

This could hardly have been further from the truth.

Mr. Walsh, who would soon become the celebrated chief executive officer of Bre-X Minerals Ltd., was a bankrupt business owner with a checkered past who had spent his last $10,000 on the trip to Jakarta. He needed Mr. Felderhof as much as Mr. Felderhof needed him. And that night in 1993, they found each other.

The story of Bre-X's rise and fall on North American stock exchanges has been well documented. But few people in Canada know the real story of how a group of geologists came to control the infamous Busang gold site, and how much the promotion of Bre-X echoed their earlier work in Australia.

A new picture has emerged, with a cast of key characters whose names are largely unfamiliar in this country. And it tells a tale of how a small group of men embarked on a decade-long, all-consuming quest for gold in Borneo. Interviews with dozens of key people on several continents have produced some important revelations:

• Mr. Walsh, who has been at the centre of the Bre-X story in Canada, is regarded in Indonesia essentially as a source of cash, a man who had little, if any, control over what happened at Busang. The geologists clearly regarded him solely as a foreign banker.

• Most of Bre-X's team of geologists are well-remembered in Australia, where they left a trail of corporate wreckage and poorer investors in the 1980s and early 1990s. Their activities created a short-lived gold rush in Indonesia and a stock market furor in Australia. The market scandal resulted in a sweeping reform of mining regulations in Australia and gave investors there a healthy dose of skepticism when the same players came along with Bre-X a decade later.

• Mr. Felderhof, Bre-X's chief geologist, is seen as a geological star in Canadian circles. But he is known very differently in Indonesia. His first big break came in 1968 at age 28, when he co-discovered one of the world's biggest gold deposits. Ever since, he has struggled to match his early success. Before joining Bre-X, he was down-and-out and living with his family in a borrowed house in Jakarta. His mining prospects were so dim, he was trying to raise funds to start a shrimp farm in remote Irian Jaya.

• As in Australia in the 1980s, huge amounts of public money have funded virtually the same cast of geologists in their efforts to dig gold out of the ground in the province of East Kalimantan.

It seems remarkable that the group that met at the Sari Hotel that fateful night in 1993 would quickly build one of the most famous mining companies in Canadian history, a company that is today under a cloud. And indeed, the saga started to rival a John Grisham novel as Mr. de Guzman plunged to his death from a helicopter just days before Bre-X partner Freeport-McMoRan Copper & Gold Inc. revealed its preliminary testing had found "insignificant" amounts of gold.

By Monday, new test results from Busang should give the world a better idea whether the site is indeed the world's largest gold find ever — as Bre-X has consistently claimed. But just who are the men behind this tale of intrigue, and riches?

The story of Busang begins long before Bre-X shares began to soar on Canadian stock exchanges in 1995. And it begins long before 1993, when Mr. Walsh entered the picture to handle the finances and shake hands with investors. It goes back more than 20 years, to when the geologists — the people who really run Bre-X — began their work in Borneo.

It begins in the mid-1970s, when Mr. Felderhof walked into Peter Howe's Toronto office looking for work. The young geologist was still basking in the glow of his work in Papua New Guinea, which resulted in the big mine known as Ok Tedi.

Born in the Netherlands early in the Second World War, Mr. Felderhof was the son of a doctor who moved in 1954 from Rotterdam to New Glasgow, N.S., to work in the town's new hospital.

Mr. Felderhof, one of 12 children, graduated from Dalhousie University in 1962 with a geology degree. He went to work for Iron Ore Co. of Canada in Schefferville, Que., but soon left for more exotic places. By the late 1960s, he had worked in Zambia for Britain's Rio Tinto-Zinc Corp., married a South African woman, Denise, and joined an exploration team in Papua New Guinea for a U.S. company, Kennecott Copper Corp. In the rugged Star Mountains, he and another young geologist, Doug Fishburn, made their names by finding Ok Tedi, a copper and gold mine now owned by Broken Hill Pty. Co. Ltd. The find was remarkable, in part because the team used an innovative new theory.

"To find something based on what had been an abstruse [mining] theory, it was really exciting times in mining geology," said Richard Jackson, a professor at James Cook University in North

Queensland, Australia, who has written a book on Ok Tedi. "It definitely … established Mr. Felderhof in the field."

After his big success, Mr. Felderhof moved to Australia and took up new interests. "I'm not sure what he was doing there, mining-wise. I know he was growing macadamia nuts," said Mr. Howe, an old friend. "It was around '74 or '75. He thought he'd better get back to work."

In the Bre-X story, Mr. Howe plays the role of matchmaker, bringing together most of the geologists who run the company today.

Mr. Howe's interest in Indonesia was ignited in the 1970s after the bloody rise of General (now President) Suharto led to a pro-Western, pro-business regime. His company, ACA Howe International Ltd., hired Mr. Felderhof to open its South Africa office, then moved him to Australia in 1979 to launch an assault on Indonesia.

Mr. Howe's first venture was a small mining operation in the far eastern province of Irian Jaya. His man on the ground was Mr. Nassey, the Bre-X geologist who flaunts his PhD from the Beverly Hills School of Engineering — an institution about which no information can be found.

Mr. Nassey was an Irianese national who was educated at a Catholic mission school and held big political aspirations. He was known to his friends as Moses and had a critical role: Only Indonesian nationals could stake mining claims at that time.

What then developed is eerily reminiscent of the Bre-X story: A flood of junior mining companies, backed by investors smelling a possible gold rush, pour into Indonesia.

In this case, they came from Australia, led by Mr. Howe and a geologist named Michael Novotny. His interest in Indonesia dated from the 1960s, when he was one of the first Australians active in the country. He returned in 1977 and started scouting potential gold sites as a freelance prospector. In 1979, Mr. Novotny took his portfolio of properties to a flamboyant Perth businessman named Kevin Parry. A former cabinet maker, Mr. Parry had created a vast business empire that included interests in shopping malls, retail and broadcasting. He had also once planned to make an action film with himself as the star.

Mr. Parry's holdings included an oil company called Pelsart Resources NL, but before long Mr. Novotny convinced him to move Pelsart away from oil and into Indonesia's gold fields. Enamoured by the lure of gold and convinced of Mr. Novotny's connections, Mr. Parry agreed. Mr. Novotny began hiring Mr. Howe's geologists, including Mr. Felderhof, to work over dozens of properties he'd found during his hiatus in Indonesia. The arrangement was ideal for the geologists. Like Mr. Walsh later, Mr. Parry left the geologists to the exploration and provided them with the promise of virtually limitless cash, largely by tenaciously promoting Pelsart's shares on the stock market. He once boasted that Indonesia would soon become the world's second-largest gold producer, behind South Africa.

Investors loved it. Pelsart's shares were hot on the Australian Stock Exchange and Mr. Parry soon raised more than $30-million (U.S.) for his band of geologists. Meanwhile, Mr. Howe persuaded several friends, including Jakarta-based geologist Mr. Bird, to join him in forming Jason Mining Ltd. (named after Jason and the Argonauts, searching for the golden fleece). Mr. Howe and Mr. Felderhof were directors, and Mr. Bird was general manager. Jason went public on the Australian Stock Exchange, which was hot for almost anything connected to Indonesia.

"We started the gold rush," Mr. Howe claimed. "The fact we were active on six properties finding gold attracted the attention of other Australian companies."

Mr. Felderhof and Mr. Bird rented motorcycles and raced around the logging roads of central Kalimantan, where most of the existing development involved timber and coal. Mr. Bird, who speaks the national language fluently, asked Dayak villagers to show them spots where they panned gold from stream beds.

Jason soon had a portfolio of about a dozen properties. Nearly all were joint ventures with Pelsart, which was also still employing many of the same ACA Howe geologists. Thanks to Mr. Parry's chequebook and salesmanship, Mr. Novotny and a friend, Laurie Whitehouse, built a big exploration house for Pelsart that contained 20 properties and 30 expatriate geologists, including Mr. de Guzman. Several of the geologists received thousands of shares and stock options in the companies they were now helping to promote. According to the 1986 Jason annual report, Mr.

Felderhof and Mr. Howe bought nearly two million shares for 20 cents Australian a piece, and also received options allowing each to buy 300,000 company shares at the same price. Promoting the companies to the investment community helped generate glowing reports from analysts. Rosy forecasts were routine, boosted by presentations made by Mr. Felderhof, recalled Australian analyst Warren Staude, who sat through several of them.

"They were fairly upbeat," he says, adding that the Howe group had created such a rush that nearly every mining presentation by any company was buoyant.

"There was just so much hype and things going on at the same time. What obviously does come to mind was that, at the end of the day, there simply wasn't any gold."

More accurately, there weren't any gold mines — at least not until much later, when new owners arrived. In the meantime, things quickly turned sour for the Pelsart and Jason geologists. The ever-ambitious Mr. Parry was diverting money he raised to a new passion, yacht racing. Parry Corp., his holding company, raised $32-million for Pelsart, but almost none of it reached Jakarta. Although colleagues say Mr. Parry hates boats, he was determined to win the America's Cup. In 1987 he spent the money on his yacht Kookaburra III. The final blow came in October, when the stock market crash wiped out any enthusiasm for mining ventures in far-off lands.

The geologists found themselves back operating on a shoestring, with only one prospect even close to producing gold. It was a small, awkward alluvial site where they could dredge up gold-bearing river mud. They knew little about alluvial mining, but they would gamble their companies on it. The property, known as Ampalit, was deep in the Borneo jungle. The dredging equipment they bought sank in the swampy terrain. When they got it working, it moved too slowly, letting gold sink back into the mud, and it often broke down. The venture was expected to produce 18,000 ounces of gold a year. In its first six months, it produced only 1,500. It all came to a messy end by 1988. The market crash dried up their source of funds. The failing Ampalit site had to be shut down.

The America's Cup bid nearly bankrupted Pelsart, which hadn't produced a cent of profit for shareholders throughout the 1980s. In 1988, Mr. Parry, his business empire ruined, was voted off the board of his own company. Mr. Novotny arranged to sell Parry Corp., including Pelsart, to a group of Hong Kong businessmen for around $12-million. That group soon sold it to an Indonesian group for around $7-million. Jason also nearly went bankrupt and eventually changed its name to Imperial Mining NL and hired new management.

Mr. Novotny was furious at the loss. After working for years through the 1980s, none of the geologist gang ended up owning the gold sites they had developed. All of their stock options were unexercised and worthless, and the men made almost no money off the venture — an error they wouldn't repeat with Bre-X.

The Jason and Pelsart gold properties passed into other hands, including Mt. Muro, the only property that later yielded a gold mine. It is a two-million ounce site, and bears one of just two operating gold mines in Borneo.

"I was so pissed off when we had to actually disgorge ourselves from Mt. Muro," Mr. Novotny said. "I had made a deal to buy that a long time before, and I was the first one to step there."

Indeed, Mr. Novotny was the first one to set foot on most of the land explored by Jason and Pelsart — Mt. Muro, Ampalit, Mirah and others. By all accounts, it was his geological work that identified the most promising sites in Indonesia. Mr. Felderhof often gets the credit, but many in the industry say his participation came later when he teamed with Mr. Novotny to decide which sites would be developed.

One of the properties they were offered, but decided not to pick up, was Busang, then a patchwork of staking claims about 500 kilometres north of their main base. Mr. Felderhof decided it was too remote and would cost too much to explore. After Pelsart, Mr. Novotny said he retired. As for Mr. Whitehouse, he said he moved on after being given a less-attractive job with Pelsart. That is disputed, however, by Michael Everett, a former director and executive at Pelsart. He said the two men were dismissed when the new management "brought in consultants from the United States to audit everybody including myself ...

"Basically it was a personality thing. Those that the new manager got on with stayed and those he didn't, didn't. There was a great big clean-out of those who made the grade and those who didn't. You'd be surprised how many who didn't turn out ended up with Canadian companies." Mr. de Guzman, who was a senior geologist at Pelsart, was fired after he was caught spending company money on gifts for a girlfriend. Mr. Everett said the offence wasn't serious, but a senior manager didn't like Mr. de Guzman and fired him.

From there, the future Bre-X gang scattered to try to find work and resurrect their battered reputations.

Mr. de Guzman went to work for another Indonesian mining company and at one point tried to interest Mr. Everett in a property. However, Mr. Everett said his old colleague's work had slipped greatly.

"It was very poor piece of work," he said. "The information available had been written by Mike, and basically the information was a load of baloney. There weren't too many facts in it, let's put it that way." Mr. Novotny and Mr. Whitehouse moved on, right into the arms of a salting scandal.

Mr. Novotny said he was approached in 1990 by two brothers, Len and Dean Ireland, and their buddy Clark Easterday about a fabulous gold find they had discovered near Perth, Australia, in an area called Karpa Springs. Mr. Novotny agreed to buy the property for $6-million.

A second round of drilling soon suggested massive gold reserves, the biggest in Australia. Mr. Novotny attracted new investors to the project including Perilya Mines NL and Noranda Inc., which put up $16.2-million (Canadian) for a stake.

But when the partners asked for core samples — supposedly stored in a shed in Dean Ireland's backyard — he refused until paid the $6-million (Australian) from Mr. Novotny. Then he told the partners the samples, all six million tonnes of dirt, had been stolen. Perilya immediately began its own drilling on the site and turned up virtually no gold. The Irelands and Mr. Easterday were arrested for fraud and sentenced to $3^{1}/_{2}$ years in prison. Of the $6-million paid by Mr. Novotny, only $4-million was ever recovered.

Life for Mr. Felderhof didn't turn out much better.

He drifted to Perth and then to Canada, dabbling in consulting. His second wife, Ingrid, was also dabbling, but in politics. In 1989, she helped start the Australian Conservative Party in Perth and ran for a seat in the Senate on a right-wing platform advocating law-and-order and religious values. The party didn't elect a single member and slowly faded away.

Mr. Felderhof ended up back in Jakarta in 1991 for one more shot, this time teamed up with Armand Beaudoin, a controversial Canadian deal maker well known in Jakarta. Mr. Beaudoin set up Mr. Felderhof and Mr. de Guzman with a new exploration outfit called PT Minindo Perkasasemesta. "It was John's saving grace," one colleague said. "He didn't have a penny in his pocket." Minindo had a few properties and was soon planning a float on the Jakarta Stock Exchange — making it the first junior mining company ever to get listed in Indonesia.

The government saw Minindo as a chance to attract exploration funds and show the world it was serious about helping junior mining companies, not just the big names who could afford a golf game with the president. To bolster the company's image, Minindo's board was stacked with high profile figures including President Suharto's brother-in-law, the former head of the Indonesian intelligence agency, and the brother of the mines minister.

The company got approval to list on the exchange, but problems quickly emerged. The issue was undersubscribed, then the capital market supervisory agency discovered the company had filed false reports. In November, Minindo fired its president, Suharto's brother-in-law, and tried to reorganize. Mr. Felderhof and Mr. de Guzman flogged the shares across town, including to a consultant working for Lac Minerals Ltd. But there were no takers. In March, 1993, the securities agency delisted the company and sanctioned the underwriter. Mr. Felderhof and Mr. de Guzman hadn't been paid for months and quit.

For Mr. Felderhof, 1993 could not look worse. His mining prospects were so dim, he and his friend Mr. Nassey planned a shrimp farm and resort hotel in Irian Jaya — a new dream they could sell to investors. Mr. Nassey was even considering quitting business and entering politics.

"John was pretty desperate. He was pretty broke," said Theo van Leeuwan, who heads Rio Tinto's Indonesian operation. Mr. Felderhof was supported and looked after by various friends in

Indonesia through the difficult period, said Colin Hebbard, an old friend in Perth. "At that stage it was a pretty tough time for him," Mr. Hebbard said.

Fortuitously, Mr. Walsh arrived on the scene, offering hope that a new backer would emerge to replace the unreliable Mr. Parry. Mr. Walsh had first met Mr. Felderhof in 1983 at Mr. Howe's house in Sydney, and the conversation soon turned to gold. Mr. Felderhof "was going up to Indonesia with a client and invited me along," Mr. Walsh recalled last year. They spent a couple of weeks in Borneo, he said.

Ten years later when he was broke, Mr. Walsh turned to Mr. Felderhof on the other side of the world. He remembered asking Mr. Felderhof: "What would the opportunities be in Indonesia?" and being told: "Excellent, because there's no one there."

He went to Jakarta, dined at the Sari and came away with two deals. The one history will remember was Busang, which happened to have drifted back into Mr. Felderhof's grasp. The property had been held by the Syakeranis, a modest family from Kalimantan, the Indonesian part of Borneo. They had several properties staked, including Busang, but lacked cash and clout to get going. They struck a joint venture with Mr. Nassey, an Australian company and Jusuf Merukh, a controversial Indonesian businessman and politician. They drilled 19 holes in 1988-89, but there wasn't enough data to judge how much gold might be there.

Four years later, an out-of-work Mr. Felderhof lucked into an interesting assignment for a company called Montague Gold NL — assisted, no doubt, by his old friend, Mr. Howe, who sat on the board of Montague's parent company.

Mr. Felderhof was hired to review the earlier exploration work, and he called on Mr. de Guzman to help. Both men liked what they saw. According to Warren Beckwith, a former partner in the joint venture, Mr. Felderhof estimated the site contained two million ounces of gold. Mr. Beckwith, however, argues that none of the geological data was sufficient to come up with any estimate. What happened next is the source of one of the many lawsuits that now litter the Busang landscape. According to allegations in this lawsuit, Mr. Felderhof took the information about the drilling to Bre-X and encouraged the Calgary company to take control of the project. According to the lawsuit, Mr. Felderhof was an employee of both companies at the time.

Mr. Walsh soon raised enough money on the Alberta Stock Exchange to start a drilling program. And indeed, Canada seemed like a perfect fit. Australia's regulators had cracked down on junior mining companies after markets were shaken by scandals in the 1980s. All reports to the market had to be okayed by a member of the Australian Institute of Mining and Metallurgy. Reserve figures had to be signed off by an accredited expert. And pension funds were not allowed to invest in exploration firms. Canada seemed like a free-market haven, by contrast.

In May of 1993, Mr. Walsh was issuing the first of many press releases about the site. Three "prime prospects" had been identified on it, the release said. One of them (drilled previously by the Australians) was estimated to contain one million ounces of recoverable gold, it said. Not an earth-shaking number, but a start. Besides issuing press releases, his main job was to round up cash. As far as the folks on the ground in Indonesia were concerned, that was all Mr. Walsh needed to know. Operations weren't part of his mandate.

In sworn affidavits entered into Alberta court as evidence for a continuing lawsuit involving Bre-X, managers of the Indonesian operations explain the Calgary office was told little about what was going on. Mr. Nassey, a senior geologist and project manager for Bre-X in Indonesia, said all developments relating to Busang since Bre-X's involvement began in 1993 occurred under the authority of Mr. Felderhof and other members of the Indonesian management team. "To my knowledge, the Canadian Bre-X office has had no involvement with the activities of the Bre-X office in Jakarta," Mr. Nassey said. "Walsh is not involved in operational decisions in Indonesia. The Indonesian management team has always operated virtually independently of Bre-X's Canadian management."

Mr. Nassey told the *Globe and Mail* that he had met Mr. Walsh only three or four times and only on social occasions. He said he had never talked geology with Mr. Walsh. Similarly, Gregory MacDonald, commercial manager of Bre-X's Jakarta office since 1995, said in his affidavit that there was "no one" in the Calgary office who could provide any assistance regarding any operations in Indonesia.

"From my review, it appeared that the Jakarta office of Bre-X had operated independently of the Calgary office before my arrival, save for requests from Jakarta to Calgary for cash calls," he said. The only contact occurred when Jakarta officials would provide accounting information and "limited" technical information to Calgary, primarily to assist with investor relations.

Mr. Felderhof had been to Alberta only twice, he said, while other project managers such as Mr. Nassey and Mr. de Guzman had never been to Calgary.

"From my perspective as the commercial manager of Bre-X in the Jakarta office, there is very little connection between Alberta and the evolution of the Busang gold project, aside from the continued injection of capital," he said.

It was all reminiscent of the Parry days. By 1995, the money was pouring in as Bre-X shares approached $100 (Canadian) on the ASE. Once again the geologists took stock options, but this time they wouldn't wait to cash out. Mr. Felderhof earned $42-million on options. He also bought a house on the Cayman Islands listed at $3-million (U.S.). Mr. Walsh bought a mansion in the Bahamas called Ocean Place.

And just like in the 1980s, analysts became enchanted with Bre-X. Many kept upping the company's own gold estimates. Soon Bre-X was touted as discovering 30 million ounces, then 50 million, then 70 million with the potential of 100 million. Mr. Felderhof finally topped them all earlier this year by announcing that he felt comfortable at 200 million ounces. Back at the site, work was kept at a feverish pace to match the great expectations. By 1995, Busang had four drilling rigs working around the clock, and the local staff were told that bankers and brokers wanted as many assay results as possible before they could fund a bigger exploration program.

"We were completely, royally understaffed," said one geologist who quit. "I was getting four hours of sleep a night. One reason I left was I would have died of exhaustion." Mr. de Guzman was also busy running three other Bre-X exploration camps in Indonesia.

Much of the work at Busang was managed by his Filipino friend Cesar Puspos, whose rise was sharp and sudden. In 1993, he was turned down for a basic field job with another company. Two years later, he was in charge of the most famous exploration camp in the world. "Cesar is a good geologist, but could he run Busang? I don't think so," said one of his former employers.

The emerging estimates raised eyebrows among long-time geologists in Jakarta and contempt among investors in Australia. "I've been a bit frightened and fascinated by some of the comments I hear back from your company promoters in Canada talking about the potential of ounces," said Mr. Staude, who is a portfolio manager for a large Australian insurance company. "You are not allowed to say that in Australia because we have put a stamp on that. You have to have a degree of credibility before you can make, as a company representative, any statement like that."

The old gang from the Sari Hotel won't be together this weekend, but their futures are once again on the line. Mr. Felderhof is believed to be in Calgary along with Mr. Walsh. Mr. de Guzman's body is buried in the Philippines. Mr. Nassey is at home in Indonesia. Mr. Bird, a consultant in Indonesia, is also in Jakarta along with Mr. Whitehouse. Mr. Novotny lives in Perth, but flew into Jakarta this week.

The world is waiting to find out whether the geologists of Bre-X have, as they claim, discovered the biggest gold find ever — or not. Either way, their names will go down in mining history.

SORRY I ASKED...

Bruce MacKinnon

Halifax Chronicle-Herald

What else could Brian Mulroney say on the day after a national referendum turned thumbs down on his Charlottetown Accord? Bruce MacKinnon gave the former PM a direct hit on the chin with this cartoon for the *Halifax Chronicle-Herald*, his first of two straight NNAs.

Que pouvait dire de plus Brian Mulroney le lendemain du référendum national qui disait non à son accord de Charlottetown? Bruce MacKinnon donnait à l'ancien premier ministre canadien une droite au menton dans cette caricature publiée dans le *Chronicle-Herald* (Halifax), pour remporter le premier de ses deux prix du CCJ en autant d'années.

CHAPTER 7

Voix

*Une sélection de lauréats du CCJ dans les catégories
Éditorial et Chronique. D'autres participations francophones
se retrouvent dans les chapitres « Littérature et journalisme, »
« Comment le Canada voyait le monde » et « Les joutes de nos vies ».*

par Alain Dubuc

Ce qui étonne le plus, lorsqu'on relit les articles publiés par des lauréats québécois du Concours canadien de journalisme des décennies passées, c'est de découvrir que les textes les plus anciens, ceux des années cinquante et soixante, n'ont pas le caractère vieillot et empoussiéré qu'on associe d'habitude aux découpures d'archives jaunies.

Les textes les plus anciens, ceux de journalistes qui sont maintenant passés à l'histoire, Gérard Filion (1951), André Laurendeau (1962) et de Claude Ryan (1964), proposent une langue simple, claire et aussi moderne que celle de leurs successeurs, Gilles Boyer (1973), Lysiane Gagnon (1981) et Pierre Foglia (1994). Même les sujets sont les mêmes! On parlait, il y a presque cinquante ans, de la place des Québécois au Canada, des visions irréconciliables du Canada qu'ont les francophones et les anglophones. Plus ça change, plus c'est pareil.

Non. La différence est moins dans les écrits eux-mêmes que dans la vie de leurs auteurs, dans le rôle public qu'ont joué ces grands journalistes de la génération précédente, pour qui l'action politique et sociale fut un prolongement normal de leur pratique journalistique.

Gérard Filion, André Laurendeau et Claude Ryan, trois artisans du Québec moderne, sont probablement plus connus par leur vie publique que par leurs écrits. Ils se retrouvent par exemple tous trois dans la liste des cent personnes qui ont façonné le siècle que proposait récemment le bimensuel québécois *L'actualité*.

Ce n'est pas dévaloriser mes collègues plus contemporains que de constater qu'aucun journaliste ne pourra plus, peu importe son talent, prétendre à un rôle aussi central dans le façonnement du Québec de cette fin de siècle. Parce que la société a changé, mais aussi parce que le métier s'est également transformé. Les journalistes les plus pénétrants ont cessé d'être des acteurs, pour devenir des observateurs.

Le plus ancien des lauréats, Gérard Filion, qui a remporté le concours trois fois, peut être décrit sans exagération, comme l'un des pères de la « Révolution tranquille », ce mouvement de modernisation de la société québécoise du début des années soixante. Gérard Filion, fut le troisième directeur du *Devoir*, qu'il dirigea pendant 16 ans, de 1947 à 1963. Fils d'agriculteur, seul enfant d'une famille nombreuse à faire des études, il fut d'abord secrétaire général de l'Union catholique des cultivateurs, l'ancêtre du syndicalisme agricole et directeur de son organe d'information, *La terre de chez nous*.

Surnommé le « bagarreur », il a transformé *Le Devoir* en véritable journal de combat, qui a pris fait et cause pour les travailleurs opprimés lors de la grève d'Asbestos, dénoncé la corruption à l'hôtel de ville de Montréal, et surtout, lutté contre l'obscurantisme du duplessisme. Filion était la bête noire de Maurice Duplessis, qu'il n'a jamais rencontré.

Dans son premier éditorial, il écrivait : « C'est mon ambition que *Le Devoir* devienne pour les Canadiens français un guide d'action pratique, un étendard, de conquête. Évidemment, il ne manquera pas de fustiger la bêtise des hommes, mais en indiquant en même temps la route qu'on aurait dû suivre, les actes qu'on aurait dû poser. »

Si la question nationale a occupé une place importante dans sa démarche, Gérard Filion, qui détenait un diplôme de l'École des hautes études commerciales, se préoccupait aussi d'économie, comme on le voit avec le texte primé en 1951 sur l'inflation. Et c'est d'ailleurs vers l'économie qu'il se retournera quand il quittera le journalisme en 1963 pour devenir président de la *Société générale de financement,* un des fleurons de la Révolution tranquille qu'il avait contribué à mettre sur les rails.

Le chemin d'André Laurendeau a souvent croisé celui de Gérard Filion. Pendant la guerre, ils ont participé ensemble à la lutte contre la conscription. Écrivain, penseur, André Laurendeau fit aussi un détour par la politique, comme leader et député du Bloc Populaire en 1944. Il était directeur de l'Action nationale quand il se joint au *Devoir.* Il y resta vingt ans, de 1948 à sa mort, en 1968, comme rédacteur en chef adjoint et ensuite comme rédacteur en chef. Il a été deux fois lauréat du Concours canadien de journalisme.

S'il a participé aux grandes batailles du *Devoir,* à rechercher, comme il le disait, « la vérité toute crue », on se souviendra surtout de la contribution de ce grand nationaliste à la définition de l'identité québécoise.

En 1959, il dénonce la discrimination dont sont l'objet les Canadiens français dans l'administration publique fédérale. C'est d'ailleurs ce thème qu'il aborde dans le texte primé qui figure dans le présent recueil, datant de 1962, et qui vise les pratiques d'embauche du C.N.

C'est lui qui suggérera l'idée d'une commission royale au premier ministre John Diefenbaker. Ce projet sera repris par le gouvernement libéral, et André Laurendeau deviendra l'un des coprésidents de la Commission sur le bilinguisme et le biculturalisme, plus connue sous le nom de *Commission Laurendeau-Dunton,* qui mènera à l'instauration du bilinguisme « coast-to-coast ».

Claude Ryan, directeur du *Devoir* de 1963 à 1978, a poursuivi cette même réflexion sur la place du Québec dans la Confédération, comme le rappelle l'article qui lui a valu un prix en 1964, sur les conceptions différentes que se font du fédéralisme les Québécois francophones et les autres Canadiens. Cette réflexion l'a amené à s'opposer à la formule Fulton-Favreau de rapatriement de la Constitution en 1964, à la charte de Victoria de Pierre Trudeau, en 1970, ou à la loi des mesures de guerre. « S'il a toujours rejeté la solution indépendantiste, il n'a pas cessé au *Devoir* de rechercher une formule — les « deux nations », un statut particulier — qui procurerait au Québec une marge d'autonomie politique propre à garantir aux Québécois la sécurité individuelle et collective qui leur fait défaut dans le cadre constitutionnel actuel », disait de lui le politicologue Léon Dion, père de l'actuel ministre, Stéphane.

Claude Ryan, qui venait de la revue *l'Action catholique,* a fait du *Devoir* un journal d'information moderne. Et ce dont on se souviendra longtemps, c'est son esprit critique acéré, son esprit d'analyse rigoureux et impitoyable, redoutable dans les débats publics. Comme dans le cas de ses prédécesseurs, *Le Devoir* lui servira de tremplin pour d'autres combats. Claude Ryan quittera *Le Devoir* en 1978 pour devenir le chef du Parti libéral du Québec, chef du camp du « Non » en 1980, et par la suite ministre dans les gouvernements Bourassa. Il joue toujours un rôle d'« elder statesman ».

Ces liens intimes entre le journalisme et l'activité politique ont manifestement été un trait de la culture québécoise. Ils sont sans doute amplifiés par le fait que ces trois lauréats proviennent du *Devoir,* un quotidien qui s'est longtemps défini comme un journal de combat, ce qui le rendait atypique par rapport aux quotidiens tant québécois que canadiens.

N'oublions pas que René Lévesque fut journaliste et que Pierre Elliott Trudeau fut l'un des fondateurs de la revue *Cité libre.* Cette symbiose s'expliquait en partie par la nature de la société québécoise de l'après-guerre, une petite société à la recherche de son identité, dont les élites étaient restreintes, où le débat était dominé par une question unique.

Personne ne peut plus prétendre jouer maintenant un rôle de guide dans une société plus complexe, plus éclatée, moins homogène, plus cynique. Aussi respecté soit-il, un journaliste n'est qu'une voix parmi d'autres. Et sa pratique s'inscrit davantage dans un cadre nord-américain, qui valorise une séparation soigneuse des pouvoirs.

C'est à cette école journalistique nord-américaine plus classique qu'appartient *Le Soleil*, le quotidien de la ville de Québec, et Gilles Boyer qui y a œuvré pendant vingt ans, de 1956 à 1976, comme éditorialiste et rédacteur en chef adjoint.

Gilles Boyer, perçu comme un défenseur convaincu du fédéralisme, impressionnait par sa polyvalence, capable de se prononcer sur une multitude de sujets, politique, international, débats locaux, et éducation, comme on le voit dans le texte qui lui a permis de remporter le concours, en 1973, après avoir été en nomination en 1964, 1965 et 1966, porte sur un problème récurrent au Québec, la crise de l'éducation, un problème si chronique qu'on a du mal à se souvenir d'un moment où le système n'était pas en crise.

C'est également dans le domaine de l'éducation que Lysiane Gagnon a d'abord fait sa marque. Chroniqueure à *La Presse* depuis 1979, elle signe également une chronique hebdomadaire dans le *Globe and Mail*, est passée au journalisme d'opinion après une longue présence, remarquée, dans le reportage, notamment comme chroniqueure à l'éducation et correspondante parlementaire à Québec.

Son premier prix du Concours canadien de journalisme (National de journalisme), elle l'a d'ailleurs obtenu en 1975, pour une série d'articles sur l'enseignement du français dans les écoles où, en quelque sorte, elle disséquait les effets de la Révolution tranquille que ses prédécesseurs avaient déclenchée.

Dans la chronique qu'elle signe depuis 1979, en principe politique, mais qui déborde largement sur le social et le culturel, Lysiane Gagnon s'est affirmée comme une grande voix du Québec, lucide et courageuse, dotée d'un instinct remarquable.

La colonne qui lui a permis de remporter en 1981, quelques mois après le référendum, sur l'impasse de la souveraineté, est d'ailleurs tristement prophétique, et aurait presque pu être signée hier.

Lysiane Gagnon peut être décrite comme une enfant de *La Presse*, où elle écrit depuis 1962. C'est donc dire qu'elle y a été pour la quasi-totalité de sa carrière et que c'est à *La Presse* qu'elle a façonné son style et sa démarche.

Pierre Foglia, le gagnant pour 1994, est un autre enfant de *La Presse*, qu'il a joint en 1972, où il a longtemps été journaliste sportif, avant de signer une chronique personnelle, qu'on décrit formellement comme une chronique d'humeurs, mais qui est beaucoup plus que cela.

Dans ses textes, Foglia propose sa vision du monde, aborde des questions culturelles, parle parfois de politique, dénonce des scandales et, souvent, ne fait que décrire des tranches de la vie de tous les jours. Le tout dans un style qui se rapproche plus de celui de l'écrivain que celui du journaliste, et qui lui permet, comme dans la chronique avec laquelle il a remporté le concours en 1994, d'aborder des thèmes aussi difficiles que celui de la mort.

Mais avec un instinct et une lucidité qui font de lui un sociologue du quotidien à l'influence considérable. Très populaire, sa chronique a suscité de nombreuses imitations, le plus souvent pâles. Car derrière son approche en apparence impressionniste, se cache une démarche journalistique, une curiosité et une rigueur qu'il n'a jamais perdues.

• **1951** Éditorial •
La course folle de l'inflation

Gérard Filion

Le Devoir

Le coût de la vie continue de grimper. Au 1er février dernier, l'indice avait atteint 175,2 soit une augmentation de 2,7 pour le seul mois de janvier. C'est la plus forte augmentation enregistrée depuis plusieurs mois.

Chacun a sa théorie sur les causes de la hausse constante de la vie. Les ouvriers disent : Ce sont les patrons qui grossissent indûment leurs bénéfices. Les patrons rétorquent : Les augmentations de salaires que les syndicats nous extorquent rendent nécessaire la hausse des prix.

Les deux ont partiellement raison. Il est exact que les profits ont sensiblement augmenté depuis la fin de la guerre. Certaines corporations ont profité de l'absence de concurrence sérieuse pour gonfler leurs prix de vente et accroître leurs bénéfices. D'autre part, les chiffres d'affaires ont considérablement augmenté : il n'est donc pas surprenant qu'une entreprise double ses bénéfices si elle a doublé son chiffre d'affaires.

Les salaires et les gages ont enregistré des augmentations sensibles depuis cinq ans. Dans certaines industries ils ont plus que doublé. Cette hausse n'est pas l'unique cause de la vie chère, mais elle en est sûrement une importante. La réaction spontanée de l'industriel ou du commerçant qui donne à son personnel une augmentation de salaires, c'est d'en faire porter le coût, si possible, par le consommateur.

■■■

Les ouvriers et les patrons ont donc raison quand ils s'accusent mutuellement de provoquer la cherté de la vie. Mais, il existe un troisième facteur qui a joué à plein depuis le début des hostilités en Corée : le facteur psychologique.

Chacun redoute, pour des raisons obscures, l'éclatement d'une guerre générale. Les préparatifs de défense et peut-être d'attaque qui se font présentement en Amérique du Nord laissent présager un retour plus ou moins proche à une économie contrôlée.

Tout le monde sait qu'il ne peut y avoir de contrôle des prix sans contrôle des salaires et vice versa. Alors patrons et ouvriers se hâtent d'occuper des positions avantageuses. Les industriels majorent leurs prix pour que les régies à venir leur laissent une marge confortable de bénéfices : les ouvriers réclament des hausses de salaires qui protègent contre la trop grande rigidité des régies.

Nous assistons depuis quelques mois à une folle chevauchée. La spirale de l'inflation s'étire à perte de vue. On ne voit pas comment tout cela finira, à moins qu'une détente générale en politique internationale ne renverse la vapeur.

■■■

Chacun propose son remède pour mettre un cran d'arrêt au mouvement inflationnaire. Les uns disent : Il faut une augmentation de la production.

C'est vrai qu'une augmentation de la production mettrait plus de marchandises sur le marché et contribuerait à la stabilisation des prix. Mais le mouvement général est pour la diminution des heures de travail dans la plupart des industries et des commerces ; d'autre part, le rendement des travailleurs n'est sûrement pas à la hausse. Alors comment augmenter la production quand tout le monde veut travailler moins et être mieux payé ?

Sous un régime de dictature, on peut forcer les gens à prolonger leur semaine de travail. Dans un régime de liberté, c'est possible, à moins qu'ils n'y consentent. Nous ne croyons pas que les salariés soient actuellement prêts à travailler plus fort et plus longtemps, afin d'enrayer la montée des prix.

D'autres disent : il faut réduire le pouvoir d'achat de la population. Pour y arriver, il faut accroître les impôts. C'est une théorie qui manque de réalisme psychologique. Quand les taxes augmentent, les salariés réclament des salaires plus élevés pour compenser ce que l'État leur enlève de leur enveloppe de paye. Ce qui est censé être une mise échec de l'inflation devient souvent une cause d'inflation.

■ ■ ■

Le gouverneur de la Banque du Canada, M. Towers, avait raison d'affirmer l'autre jour que les moyens purement fiscaux et financiers d'enrayer l'inflation deviennent de moins en moins efficaces ; il faudra en venir avant longtemps aux méthodes directes, c'est à dire au contrôle des prix, des bénéfices, des salaires, aux coupons de rationnement et à tout l'attirail que nous avons connu durant la dernière guerre.

D'ailleurs, la mise en œuvre de tous ces moyens ne fera que retarder l'inflation, qui se produira fatalement plus tard. Durant la dernière guerre on a essayé de nous faire croire qu'il était possible de faire un effort de guerre total sans provoquer une hausse des prix. C'était tromper la population.

L'inflation est un effet et non une cause. Elle est l'indice d'un appauvrissement général d'un pays. Quand la nation consacre une part importante de ses revenus à des œuvres de destruction, elle s'appauvrit. Il est possible de le cacher pour un certain temps, mais l'évidence vient à apparaître au grand jour.

Les prix et les salaires font présentement une course folle parce que les préparatifs de guerre nous appauvrissent. Voilà la cause du mal, il ne sert à rien de la chercher ailleurs.

● **1962** Éditorial ●

Donnons une direction à notre colère

André Laurendeau

Le Devoir

M. Gordon a-t-il tenu les propos que la plupart des journaux lui ont prêtés, et qu'il répudiait hier ? Il est difficile de croire que tous les chroniqueurs parlementaires se soient trompés en même temps, et qu'ils se soient trompés à deux reprises (les 21 et 24 novembre). Le compte rendu des séances, du comité parlementaire des Chemins de fer tirera l'affaire au clair. D'ici là nous tiendrons pour acquis que selon M. Gordon, il est aujourd'hui impossible de trouver un Canadien français qui puisse occuper avec compétence l'un des plus hauts postes du C.N.

Comment expliquer cela, demandait M. Lionel Chevrier, quand l'an dernier le gouvernement a désigné trois Canadiens français au Conseil d'administration des chemins de fer ? La réponse de M. Gordon est rapportée entre guillemets dans plusieurs journaux :

• Le gouvernement pouvait choisir dans tout le Canada tandis que moi, je dois choisir parmi les employés de la société.

Ce qui revient à affirmer :

• qu'aucun employé actuel du C.N. n'a assez de compétence pour accéder aux plus hauts postes ;

• que M. Gordon est forcé d'effectuer son recrutement au sein du C.N.

Or l'étude de M. Patrick Allen établissait ici même, jeudi, que 12 des 17 dirigeants actuels sur lesquels nous possédons des renseignements (il y en a 28 en tout) ne sont pas «sortis du rang ». Ou bien on les a nommés directement au poste qu'ils occupent (3), ou bien ils n'ont eu que de cinq à dix ans de probation dans des postes déjà importants, avant d'atteindre les sommets (9).

Il ressort de ces faits que M. Gordon n'accorde à peu près aucune attention au problème. Que les Canadiens français ne participent pas à la haute direction du C.N., cela paraît lui être parfaitement indifférent. C'est là qu'est son erreur — erreur qu'il partage avec beaucoup d'autres dirigeants — erreur qui nous blesse et nous irrite.

■ ■ ■

Nous avons brûlé M. Gordon en effigie à Montréal la semaine dernière. Nous l'avons pendu et brûlé à Québec. Chaque journal, chaque groupement à tour de rôle vient donner à son image un bon coup de couteaux. Tous en chœur nous dansons autour de lui, mais de fort loin, une espèce de danse de la mort.

Mais M. Gordon se porte bien. M. Gordon demeure président du C.N. M. Gordon, un peu agacé par tout ce bruit, prend la peine d'émettre une dénégation, mais revient paisiblement à son travail sérieux qui consiste à faire rouler les trains.

Comme d'autres subissent un accès de fièvre, nous faisons un accès de fierté. C'est dans les traditions. Ça se défend, car il est vrai que notre fierté est blessée. Mais c'est insuffisant. La crise passera. M. Gordon va demeurer, il semble qu'on ne puisse se passer de lui et il le sait.

Nous avons raison d'être furieux. Mais il est vain de s'installer dans la colère, de dépenser sur M. Gordon la rancune que tant d'autres frustrations, tant d'autres camouflets, une si longue indifférence outaouaise, sans compter la conscience de nos propres déficiences, ont fait naître en nous.

Nous avons raison d'être furieux. Cette exclusion absolue de la direction de C.N. a quelque chose d'odieux. Mais la colère collective dont nous nous enivrons, il faudrait qu'elle serve d'abord à alimenter des actions et des projets positifs.

N'oublions pas que le cas Gordon n'est pas unique. Je dirais même que M. Gordon a une qualité : il est brutal. Il dit très fort ce que d'autres font aussi bien que lui, mais sans le dire. L'étude de M. Réal Pelletier établissait bien que 23 organismes fédéraux sur 78 pratiquent la même exclusion totale. M. Gordon est le bruyant porte-parole d'une politique d'habitude silencieuse.

■ ■ ■

Première conclusion pratique : le nouvel incident Gordon doit nous convaincre – davantage de chercher pour l'instant à Québec, plutôt qu'à Ottawa, la réalisation de nos ambitions les plus importantes. A Ottawa, nous sommes mal, peu ou pas acceptés ? Nous disons zut à Ottawa. Zut est là pour un autre mot, qui se dit mieux qu'il ne s'écrit. Certes, nous ne cesserons pas de réclamer et d'attaquer et de frapper à la porte : car nous n'acceptons pas d'être exclus des centres où se prennent les principales décisions administratives du gouvernement central. Mais enfin, nous savons que la percée se fera d'abord par Québec. Nous savons que l'œuvre de restauration commence par Québec. Québec est notre appui et sera notre tremplin. Il est capital de le comprendre, afin de stimuler sans cesse le gouvernement qui est à Québec, de le presser d'entreprendre les œuvres que nous jugeons essentielles. Ceci, jusqu'à ce que la porte se débloque à Ottawa.

Deuxième conclusion : notre compétence est publiquement mise en doute. Et il est vrai que dans quelques domaines elle est douteuse. L'important pour un professeur d'université, pour une faculté universitaire, et du reste pour chacun d'entre nous dans toutes les activités professionnelles, c'est donc de ruiner cette mauvaise réputation dans les faits, par les faits. Que la colère, au lieu de tourner à l'aigre ou à la déclamation, devienne rage d'apprendre et volonté personnelle d'acquérir une supériorité. C'est une façon autrement réelle de pendre et brûler Gordon — car c'est substituer à l'opération magique, à la destruction purement symbolique de l'adversaire, l'affirmation de soi par des actes irrécusables.

Enfin les politiciens qui s'efforcent à Ottawa d'utiliser à fond l'affaire Gordon, et qui clament notre compétence, feraient bien d'examiner la leur. La faiblesse de nos équipes politiques au Parlement ne témoigne pas en faveur du renouveau québécois. Elles sont minables, elles sont pauvres, elles nous représentent mal.

Je sais bien qu'il n'est pas toujours facile de faire élire un député compétent. Mais quand un parti se croit fort — comme le parti libéral actuel — s'il ne voit pas à présenter des candidats de valeur dans les comtés qu'il estime sûrs, c'est qu'il démissionne d'avance et se voue à la médiocrité. Samedi dernier, on nous faisait savoir que le parti libéral tentera l'impossible pour apporter du sang neuf à un groupe singulièrement vieilli. C'est ainsi, nous disait-on dans la

Presse, que le parti libéral serait heureux de compter dans sa députation des compétences comme MM. Maurice Lamontagne, Jean-Baptiste Lemoyne, Jean Marchand, Jean-Louis Gagnon et Guy Favreau.

Il ne suffit pas d'être « heureux » pour obtenir de semblables adhésions : un parti sérieux qui veut sérieusement se renouveler parvient à embrigader des compétences et à assurer — moralement — leur élection. Il sabre dans son régiment de nouilles ; et sans violenter la démocratie, il parvient à intégrer ceux qui sauront le servir et servir le pays.

Quand M. Gordon, en comité parlementaire, affronte MM. X et Y, qui feraient à peine de bons échevins dans une petite municipalité, comment voulez-vous que la certitude de notre compétence l'illumine ? Et si rien ne change, quelle sorte de ministres fournirons-nous à un hypothétique gouvernement Pearson ?

Brûlons Gordon en effigie si ça nous chante. Mais appliquons un fer rouge sur tout ce qui donne à Gordon un semblant de raison.

• **1964** Éditorial •

Le Canada anglais : autre point de vue, autre conception

Claude Ryan

Le Devoir

Dans une société civilisée, il est normal de s'intéresser au point de vue de l'autre. Cet « autre », que chacun se représente à travers le prisme de ses propres opinions, est souvent différent de ce qu'on imagine.

Dans cet esprit, j'ai regardé l'autre soir, à la télévision, la première émission d' « O Canada ». Inutile de résumer cette émission. Tout le monde l'a sans doute vue. Mais une question se pose : les réactions qu'on a entendues sont-elles l'écho fidèle de ce que pense le Canada anglais ?

Voici, pour aider le lecteur à se former une opinion, quelques impressions additionnelles recueillies lors d'un récent voyage que je fis dans l'Ouest en compagnie de deux autres Canadiens français.

■ ■ ■

Chaque jour, dans des villes différentes, nous avons rencontré en séance publique des auditoires d'environ deux cents personnes.

À chaque endroit, nous avons dû affronter des questions cinglantes comme celles que posèrent à Halifax et Calgary des personnes présentes aux rencontres convoquées par Radio-Canada.

Il serait facile de monter ces réactions en épingle et d'y répondre de manière non moins cinglante. Mais ces interrogations représentaient, au sein des auditoires que nous avons rencontrés, des points de vue nettement minoritaires. Les auteurs de telles questions faisaient figure, dans leur propre milieu, d'être insolites et dépassés. Il serait injuste de les présenter comme typiques du Canada anglais actuel.

■ ■ ■

Ce que j'ai constaté se résume en deux traits fondamentaux.

D'une part, les éléments éclairés du Canada anglais font montre d'une cordialité accrue envers nous. Ils s'inquiètent, bien sûr, de certaines nouvelles, de certaines déclarations en provenance du Québec ; ils ne sont guère aidés à cet égard par la manière dont leur presse leur présente l'information québécoise. Mais ils veulent en savoir davantage. Ils sont prêts à écouter notre point de vue.

Ils manifestent aussi, comme M. Laurendeau vient de le constater à Vancouver, un intérêt accru pour l'étude de la langue française ; on serait prêt à accueillir du jour au lendemain, en Colombie-Britannique et en Saskatchewan, des douzaines de professeurs de français compétents. On rencontre enfin, dans ces milieux mêmes, des hommes influents qui défendent à longueur d'année auprès de leurs confrères plusieurs de nos propres points de vue.

■ ■ ■

Il existe cependant, entre le Québec et le Canada anglais, de très sérieuses divergences intellectuelles sur lesquelles il serait inutile de se fermer les yeux.

La plus grave opposition porte sur la nature même du pacte confédératif. Pour nous, la Confédération fut le fruit d'une entente entre deux peuples. Pour le Canadien anglais moyen, la Confédération fut plutôt le résultat d'une entente entre quatre provinces qui décidèrent de s'unir d'abord pour des fins économiques.

Pour le Canadien anglais, le Canada s'identifie avec le gouvernement central. Un régionalisme plus accentué lui fait mieux voir maintenant l'importance des provinces. Il reste foncièrement convaincu que le Canada — lisez le gouvernement central — vient en premier lieu et qu'il faut à tout prix maintenir cette ligne de force. D'où sa difficulté à saisir le sens des revendications du Québec et sa crainte que nos demandes n'en viennent à ébranler la Confédération.

Le biculturalisme est, pour le Canadien anglais, une seconde pierre d'achoppement. Cet idéal signifie, pour lui, que le Québec pourrait être bilingue et que le Canada pourrait … demeurer ce qu'il est. Les objections sont surtout d'ordre pratique. Il ne voit pas très bien pourquoi le français jouirait d'une position spéciale dans des provinces où les Ukrainiens sont plus nombreux que les Canadiens français. Il redoute les difficultés concrètes qu'engendrerait un bilinguisme généralisé. Il craint que la thèse du biculturalisme ne soit une camisole un peu étroite pour une population d'origines aussi variées que celle de notre pays.

■ ■ ■

Si nous voulons faire comprendre notre point de vue au Canada anglais, nous devons d'abord lui expliquer ce qui s'est passé au Québec depuis quelques années. Il doit apprendre, pour commencer, que le Québec a accédé, ces dernières années, à une maturité, à une vitalité insoupçonnées. La vie, quand elle s'exprime, provoque toujours l'admiration et le respect.

Nous devons ensuite attirer l'attention de nos amis sur la conception différente que nous nous faisons du fédéralisme. Pour eux, le fédéralisme est surtout administratif, de l'ordre des moyens. Pour nous, il est d'abord culturel, de l'ordre de la vie. Cette conception les étonne.

Mais tout vrai dialogue commence à partir d'un certain étonnement. Cela vaut aussi pour nous …

● **1973** Éditorial ●

Les faiblesses dans les CEGEP

Gilles Boyer

Le Soleil

Les critiques sévères et quasi unanimes exprimées à l'endroit des CEGEP devant le Conseil de l'Université Laval, par des professeurs universitaires de longue expérience, devraient porter à réfléchir. On va jusqu'à affirmer que l'enseignement dans les CEGEP est un «fiasco ». Les scientifiques se plaignent que les programmes y sont essentiellement philosophicolittéraires. Par ailleurs, on déplore une formation philosophique, historique et un enseignement du français déficients.

Du point de vue universitaire, l'opinion du doyen de la faculté des sciences sociales, M. Yves

Dubé, paraît résumer celle de ses collègues : « Les CEGEP sont des institutions, malades, qui affectent la vie de l'université. » Les raisons de semblable situation ne tiennent pas seulement au CEGEP lui-même, mais remontent aux niveaux inférieurs de l'enseignement et filtrent de la société tout entière.

Au stade du CEGEP, la grande faille paraît provenir du défaut de programmes et d'enseignement véritablement structurés. Ces grandes institutions nouvelles, où devaient fleurir la liberté et la spontanéité, se sont lancées dans l'aventure de l'enseignement — mi-secondaire, mi-universitaire — avec la naïveté du néophyte. Sans tradition, on tombait d'autant plus facilement dans les pièges des derniers gadgets pédagogiques à la mode, du genre «tout enseignant est enseigné et tout enseigné est enseignant. »

En raison même de leurs faiblesses structurelles, les CEGEP cristallisent en quelque sorte les carences qui ont cours à d'autres niveaux de l'enseignement et en d'autres milieux que le nôtre et qui témoignent d'un malaise de civilisation : la facilité généralisée, la subjectivité intellectuelle poussée, le refus de l'éducation aux frustrations, qui cantonnent les adolescents dans une sorte d'immaturité perpétuelle. Le CEGEP n'a rien inventé de tout cela, mais il en est peut-être à l'heure actuelle le reflet le plus significatif.

Puisque l'enseignement doit être sans douleur et que tout apprentissage est long et pénible, il faut substituer le faire à l'apprendre. Dès lors, l'enseignement deviendra une sorte de jeu idyllique. Dans les langues, on négligera la grammaire et la syntaxe (exercices abstraits et frustrants), au nom des jeux de l'expression écrite et surtout verbale. Résultats, à l'université, on se plaint presqu'unanimement de la faible qualité de la langue maternelle et seconde. En philosophie, loin de cette logique, de cette métaphysique et de cette morale d'un autre âge (le moyen, très certainement), le professeur enseigne que la vérité est au fond de chacun et qu'il lui appartient de l'exprimer, sans autre barrière. On tombe ainsi dans une subjectivité délirante, dans d'éternels « bla-bla » qui tournent en rond, faute de rigueur et d'un minimum de discipline intellectuelle interne.

Un autre phénomène frappant au niveau du CEGEP est que, parallèlement à cette formation intellectuelle imprécise, on se lance dans la spécialisation hâtive. On demandera à des élèves, qui ne connaissent ni A ni B de l'économie politique, ni les lois élémentaires de l'offre et de la demande, ni les aspects les plus simples de la production, de la circulation et de la répartition des biens, de faire une critique comparée de Samuelson et de Milton Friedman, ce qui relève de la spécialisation universitaire.

Dans à peu près tous les domaines de la connaissance, à des élèves qui ne savent même pas leurs « gammes », on demande de composer des « sonates ». Est-il dès lors étonnant que, faute de préparation théorique, on tombe dans tous les pièges des généralisations hâtives, on gobe les slogans les plus spectaculaires. À un âge où l'on a besoin de certitudes absolues, cela apparaît comme autant de fuites en avant. D'autant plus que les professeurs, dans plusieurs cas, participent eux-mêmes à cet état d'esprit et qu'un nombre s'adonnent sans vergogne à l'endoctrinement politique.

Le débraillé physique qu'on peut observer dans nos écoles, n'est que le signe extérieur d'un débraillé plus profond, psychologique et intellectuel. Psychologiquement, à tous les niveaux de l'enseignement, en maintenant l'élève au niveau du faire au détriment de celui de l'apprendre, ou le limité au niveau infantile et il ne peut que difficilement accéder à celui de l'adulte. La connaissance se transmet par l'apprentissage de l'un à l'autre. Sans compter que cette « société sans père » pour reprendre l'expression de Mitscherlich est également reproduite dans l'école «permissive » d'aujourd'hui.

Intellectuellement, ces facilités psychologiques débouchent sur la subjectivité parfois effrénée. Pourtant, l'une des leçons les plus profitables du travail, intellectuel ou manuel, n'est-elle pas un certain oubli de soi, une objectivité devant la vérité, qui est la plus souvent complexe, difficile à atteindre. C'est dans ce sens que Hegel affirmait que le travail relève de « l'esprit de sacrifice ». Affirmation qui, il est vrai, aurait de quoi faire tomber dans l'hilarité générale tous les CEGEP de la province.

Mais, si à l'université on se plaint des CEGEP, c'est que ceux-ci sont au stade immédiatement inférieur qui leur envoie les élèves. Les CEGEP pourraient également se plaindre de la formation du secondaire, du fouillis des polyvalentes, par exemple, et celles-ci à leur tour de la formation acquise à l'école primaire, particulièrement dans l'enseignement de la langue maternelle.

De plus, tant au ministère de l'Éducation qu'au niveau de la direction générale du CEGEP, il devrait y avoir une autorité responsable et efficace en mesure de contrôler la qualité de l'enseignement, si on veut que celui-ci débouche sur un minimum de rigueur intellectuelle.

● **1981** Chronique ●
Le référendum: la fin d'une époque

Lysiane Gagnon

La Presse

Avec l'année du référendum, s'achève toute une époque : 20 années qui furent marquées par l'émergence, le développement puis le déclin de l'idéologie indépendantiste.

Telle est en effet la conséquence la plus sérieuse du référendum de mai : la démarche vers l'indépendance, amorcée au tournant des années 60 par des mouvements d'avant-garde puis reprise par le PQ de René Lévesque, qui allait lui donner de la respectabilité et des chances de réussite concrète tout en l'édulcorant toutefois considérablement, cette démarche donc a fait long feu le printemps dernier, et l'on peut presque dire que le référendum a marqué la fin du mouvement indépendantiste contemporain.

Rien ne prouve que ce mouvement ne renaîtra pas sous d'autres formes à partir d'aspiration renouvelées, mais rien non plus ne permet d'affirmer que les 40 p.c. de « oui » récoltés au référendum ne représenteraient qu'une étape dans une « marche irréversible » vers l'indépendance.

De ces « oui » en effet, à peine plus de la moitié visaient effectivement la souveraineté, si l'on en croit tous les sondages, les autres s'inspirant surtout d'un calcul d'ordre tactique dans les négociations avec Ottawa et les autres provinces. (Sans compter ceux qui ont voté « oui » parce que ce premier référendum n'engageait à rien.)

D'autre part, s'il est vrai que le nombre de souverainistes ne peut aller qu'en augmentant, comment expliquer que la jeunesse paraisse si peu encline à se mobiliser autour des thèmes nationalistes ? Que ces mêmes thèmes n'inspirent plus du tout les créateurs ? Comment expliquer en outre cette démobilisation si rapide, si soudaine, si irrémédiable apparemment, qui a touché, même les indépendantistes les plus militants ? … On voit bien en effet que l'opération de résistance contre le « le coup de force » du premier ministre Trudeau s'est organisée sans trop d'enthousiasme, et qu'elle ne rejoint guère les milieux naturellement portés à l'action politique.

Impossible de tout expliquer par l'amertume d'une défaite qui date maintenant de sept mois, par l'habileté machiavélique d'un Trudeau ou par la position d'extrême faiblesse du PQ. On dirait plutôt que quelque chose — une volonté, une fibre, un ressort — s'est cassé. Cela se voit et se sent. Un mouvement vraiment fort se laisserait-il abattre par une défaite aux urnes ? Les minorités actives savent pourtant, en général, se ressaisir. (En 1971, la crise d'octobre n'avait pas démoli le mouvement indépendantiste, et les péquistes ont su se relever des deux échecs électoraux de 1970 et de 1973.)

Faudrait-il croire que l'idéologie indépendantiste était déjà, bien avant le référendum, en perte de vitesse ? Et que cette défaite n'a fait qu'accélérer une désaffection déjà installée chez les jeunes et dans les milieux plus progressistes — lesquels se trouvent aujourd'hui sollicités par d'autres idéaux, l'action communautaire, l'écologie, le mouvement féministe, les nouvelles sous-cultures, le tiersmondisme, etc., et qui, tout en étant en général plutôt d'accord avec le principe de l'indépendance du Québec, ne sont pas prêts à s'y consacrer de façon exclusive ni même prioritaire ?

À quoi attribuer cette désaffection ? Sans doute à plusieurs facteurs, dont la stratégie confuse du PQ, qui à toutes fins utiles avait cessé de parler d'indépendance depuis 1974, et dont le discours était plus bureaucratique que mobilisateur. (La nouvelle définition péquiste de l'indépendance, c'était que rien ne changerait sauf qu'un seul gouvernement aurait le pouvoir exclusif de lever les impôts et de faire les lois … voilà une perspective qui n'a d'intérêt que pour les sous-ministres qu'ennuient les dédoublement et les chevauchements, de juridictions !)

Mais il faut admettre par ailleurs que le discours indépendantiste classique, fondé sur l'idéologie de la décolonisation, a aujourd'hui quelque chose de désuet et ne colle plus aux réalités et aux aspirations contemporaines.

Ce discours avait pris forme dans les années 60, à une période d'expansion économique où l'on ne parlait ni d'inflation ni du problème de l'énergie, et où à travers le monde, les mouvements de libération nationale paraissaient porter tous les espoirs.

Ironiquement, le simple fait, pour le PQ, d'être au pouvoir et d'avoir légiféré fortement en faveur des francophones a probablement nui à la cause qu'il défendait : qui, vraiment, se sentait opprimé et menacé d'extinction culturelle, en 1980, sous le régime de la loi 101, sous un gouvernement nationaliste ?

Si Trudeau et son French Power ne s'étaient pas trouvés à Ottawa, peut-être les choses en auraient-elles été autrement … mais le fait est que la majorité a refusé de choisir entre deux gouvernements qu'elle perçoit comme défendant, chacun sur son terrain, les intérêts des Québécois francophones.

Force est de conclure que cette année 1980 fut celle de Pierre Elliott Trudeau, qui a gagné sur toute la ligne sans avoir une seule fois dérogé de la ligne de pensée qui est sienne depuis toujours.

Faut-il pour autant en conclure que la génération qui, depuis 20 ans, a consacré l'essentiel de ses énergies à cette démarche vers l'indépendance, a travaillé en vain ? Sûrement pas. On a vu constamment, durant ces deux décennies, que les aspirations nationales ont constitué un puissant levier d'action, un ferment de progrès social et d'épanouissement culturel. Cette démarche dont nous parlions s'arrête avant la conclusion qui aurait été logique et naturelle, mais les sentiments qui l'animaient continuent d'exister et qui sait si cette bifurcation ne saura pas générer d'autres projets, d'autres espoirs ?

• **1994** Chronique •

Virus

Pierre Foglia

La Presse

C'était un de ces matins de décembre volé à l'hiver, un matin si ensoleillé, si triomphant : qu'on pouvait croire que l'Homme et sa fiancée venaient de remporter une grande victoire sur la mort.

C'était tout le contraire.

C'était un de ces matins où rien n'est vrai. Où l'horreur rôde. Un de ces matins où l'on ne peut s'empêcher de penser que Dieu lui-même est peut-être malade.

J'ai cherché dans ma pile de Time celui qui parlait de la « La revanche des microbes qui tuent » (12 sept.). Je ne l'avais pas lu, tant ces histoires de bactéries dévoreuses de chair me semblaient exotiques. Chasse aux fauves micro-organiques. Montres mythiques agités par des savants en attente de budgets de recherche, croyais-je.

Mais voilà que par ce beau matin d'hiver, le monstre était là, à quatre coins de rue de La Presse, dans une chambre de l'hôpital Saint-Luc.

Et d'autres monstres pas loin. Plus communs. Que l'on croyait vaincus, mais qui resurgissent. Comme la pneumonie qui fait 4 millions de victimes par année (alors que le sida en fait 500 000). La tuberculose 3 millions de victimes. L'hépatite B, 2 millions. La malaria, un million …

Sans parler des nouveaux virus. Celui-là dans l'actualité de ce matin-là, le streptocoque de type A. Mais d'autres pires encore. Le Junin, le Machupo, le Sabia, le Marburg, l'Ebola et le « X », ces deux derniers trop foudroyants, dit-on, pour être dangereux. Comprenez qu'ils tuent si rapidement, que leurs victimes n'ont pas le temps d'infecter leurs proches.

Comme c'est rassurant.

La résurgence des vieux microbes s'explique par leur aptitude nouvelle à se défendre contre les antibiotiques. Le commun dont je suis s'en étonne, oubliant que ces petites choses ont, comme les humains, un grand instinct de survie, et la capacité de s'adapter à leur environnement. Les micro-organismes pathogènes ne nous infectent que par accident, ce n'est pas pour mal faire, ils essaient seulement de vivre et de se reproduire, tout comme nous.

Les nouveaux virus ne seraient pas si nouveaux. Y compris celui du sida. Paraît qu'ils vivaient heureux depuis longtemps, sur la peau des singes, au fin fond des forêts du Soudan.

On semble presque certain aujourd'hui que les virus descendent du singe.

À noter que l'homme aussi.

On oublie ces choses-là.

Et par un de ces matins qui semble avoir été volé à l'hiver, un matin si triomphant qu'on pouvait croire que l'Homme et sa fiancée venaient justement de remporter une grande victoire sur la mort, on apprend que c'est tout le contraire.

L'horreur rôde. Et on ne peut s'empêcher de penser que Dieu lui-même a peut-être été bouffé par une bactérie bouffeuse de dieu.

■ ■ ■

Questions diverses

• Chaque fois que l'on invente un antibiotique plus fort, ne crée-t-on pas une souche de virus plus résistante ? C'est comme la guerre alors ? Où cela va-t-il s'arrêter ?

• Se défendrait-on mieux des virus avec un corps moins aseptisé ?

• La prévention obsessive — je pense par exemple au vaccin contre la grippe, pas à celui contre l'hépatite B — la prévention ne nous a-t-elle pas fragilisés au point d'être ravagés à la moindre attaque ?

• L'ennemi du dehors est-il rendu dedans ?

• Au-delà de ces questions, c'est le progrès qui est en cause. Dans nos vies, le progrès ne prend-il pas plus de place que la vie ?

• J'ai une toune dans la tête depuis que cette histoire est arrivée, je n'arrive pas à mettre un titre dessus, ça dit « It's nature's way of telling you something's wrong », c'est quoi donc ?

■ ■ ■

C'est donc un de ces matins où rien n'est vrai [1]. Où l'horreur rôde. Où l'on ne peut s'empêcher de penser à la mort …

L'autre jour, chez des amis, j'ai entendu un jeune homme raconter comment il avait appris la mort de son père, à deux heures du matin, le 31 octobre dernier. « Venez vite, votre père vient de mourir d'une crise cardiaque »…

« Cela m'a pris dix minutes pour me rendre, a raconté le jeune homme, d'une voix neutre et précise à la fois, comme s'il avait fait un relevé sténographique de l'événement. Mon père habitait seul au coin de Masson et de la 10e. Il venait de se séparer. Il avait 46 ans. J'ai croisé des ambulanciers dans les escaliers. Mon père gisait, nu, sur le plancher du salon. Je me suis dit qu'il faudrait bien mettre une couverture dessus. J'allais le faire, mais un médecin d'Urgences Santé m'a appelé de la cuisine : « Viendrais-tu par ici, on a des papiers à te faire remplir. » Quand cela a été fini, il m'a dit : « Où veux-tu le faire embaumer ? » Je lui ai répondu que je ne savais pas, que j'allais en parler avec mes frères. Mon père était toujours sur le plancher du salon »…

L'autre jour, chez des amis, j'ai entendu ce jeune homme raconter comment il avait appris la mort de son père. J'ai réussi à le retracer …

On s'est rencontrés l'autre soir chez X … Voudrais-tu reprendre ton histoire ?

Pourquoi cela ?

Pour chroniquer sur la banalisation de la mort …

Ouais …

Je te dérange ?

Un peu. Je suis en train d'écouter un film …

■ ■ ■

Supposons que la mort soit la grande dame irréductible que l'on dit. Les guerres que les vivants lui livrent doivent bien l'amuser. Nos vaccins, nos antibiotiques, nos reins et nos poumons, bientôt nos cœurs artificiels, nos acharnements thérapeutiques et nos acharnements théologiques (Dieu lui-même), tout cela ne fait que la conforter dans sa toute-puissance.

Finalement, la seule façon d'insulter vraiment la mort, c'est de l'ignorer. De la banaliser. Banalisation médiatique, lointaine et massive, genre : des milliers d'enfants meurent de faim chaque jour. Et banalisation domestique dans la routine des hôpitaux, et la trivialité administrative.

Viens, un peu dans la cuisine, on a des papiers à te faire signer.

Nue dans le salon, la mort a dû se sentir volée.

La mort de mon père ? Une autre fois, je suis en train de regarder un film …

C'est peut-être pour se venger de notre cinéma que la mort invente des bactéries dévoreuses de chairs. L'horreur pour nous piquer au vif.

[1] *Nothing is true, everything is permitted. (Burroughs, Nova Express)*

Serge Chapleau

La Presse

In the year of the paparazzi, even Quebec Premier Daniel Johnson couldn't wait to get in on the act. This classic entry was the Montreal cartoonist's third straight nomination in the category and his first NNA.

Dans l'année des paparazzi, même le premier ministre Daniel Johnson ne pouvait s'empêcher d'être présent. Cette caricature classique marquait la troisième nomination en autant d'années pour Serge Chapleau, et son premier prix du CCJ.

CHAPTER 8

Voices

*A selection of winners primarily in the NNA category
for Critical Writing, which only began in 1972,
with a sprinkling from Columns, also a latecomer (1980).*

By Nick Russell and Kathy English

To speak one's mind in print demands a certain measure of what might be considered journalistic hubris — a firm belief that readers will care a whit about your views of the topic of the day, be that a new politician, a new play or a playful politician. This section brings together the best of the voices of English-Canadian newspaper journalists who have spoken with both grace and authority in criticism and column writing. As one would expect in a chapter championing the personal voice, the writers featured here are a disparate lot. Their writing, which includes commentaries on such topics as books, booze, ballet and the Beatles, is both confident and compelling.

Confidence may well be the first requirement for the newspaper writer who chooses to review the creative output of others. A reviewer, somebody once quipped, is like someone who watches a battle from the top of a hill, and when it's all over, rushes down to finish off the injured. That's unkind, but then some reviewers have themselves been unkind in their time (one New York reviewer said a film star's nose was like a ziggurat — and didn't get sued). But is that what writing reviews is all about — wielding the pen like a weapon, to slash at anyone who dares to make art or to publicly perform? The half-dozen pieces included in this chapter demonstrate the opposite. They show that reviewers can be subtle, supportive, nurturing and highly constructive when they are at their best. They can also be highly entertaining in their own right — without skewering those they write about.

So, while outsiders may assume reviewers get the best seats free for all the best shows, and then just write their opinion, the professional reviewer knows the craft involves long hours, frequent overdoses of art (six movies a day?), sometimes absurdly demanding deadlines (the concert might end at 10:30 p.m. and the deadline for filing to the entertainment section might be 11 p.m.), and constantly upgrading their knowledge of the field. To compensate, well, there are free seats to the best and the worst shows — and the opportunity to write with verve and élan, so that readers will enjoy reading the review as well as attending the show.

What, then, is the role of the newspaper reviewer? Lloyd Dykk, who reviewed theatre for the *Vancouver Sun* for some years, put it in a nutshell: "I said what I thought and tried not to be boring, which are the critic's main duties."

Good reviews do say what they think. They advise readers where the good art is — and the bad. But at the same time they are challenging the audience, educating it to enjoy art better and to demand better art. So entertainment pages will go beyond reviews to news about the arts (hence William French, in his 1978 piece [page 334], describes the content and mood of a public debate about school textbooks, and William Littler [page 337] provides a glossary of terminology for opera fans). And they will explain why things work or don't work. (David Prosser's extended essay for the *Kingston Whig-Standard* magazine on the Stratford Festival [page 349], spends some 300 words on one tiny *Richard III* scene, analyzing gestures and timing, so the reader will likely think, "Oh, y-e-e-s: I didn't realize that was the problem.")

Does the reviewer have to be an expert in the art form he or she reviews? Certainly the fact that we all eat does not make us all expert food reviewers, but nor does the critic have to be able to cook (or perform an entrechat or direct a movie). As one of Canada's most eminent critics, Nathan Cohen, once said, "I believe that the critic should study his theatre art intensively, and that the way to get this knowledge is partly by reading, and partly by seeing shows through trained eyes and ears."

(Cohen isn't represented here because he flourished before the National Newspaper Awards for Critical Writing, which only began in 1972. This suggests both that entertainment writers were not held in very high esteem before that, and that the number of critics could only increase with growth of the arts in Canada.)

Certainly the reviewer must view art holistically. It may not be enough to review the acting in a play: What about the writing, casting, make-up, costumes, etc.? Dave Billington, for instance, reviews a National Ballet production starring Rudolph Nureyev in the context of the ornate sets. Prosser, again, is not reviewing Stratford in a vacuum: He speaks about the rich possibilities of Shakespeare's *Richard III* and *King Lear*, and about previous interpretations of both plays, as well as the current performances.

What criteria can the writer use? The reviewer's best preparation is comparison. If she can compare tonight's opera with others this season, or this book with others by the same author, or this sculptor with others in the genre, she establishes her own expertise while providing the readers with a yardstick ("Oh, it's even better than that one? I'd better read it!")

And what standard should the writer demand? There is little point in the reviewer at the Woodpecker Weekly expecting that the Woodpecker Women's Institute perform Wagner's Ring Cycle to the standards of the Metropolitan Opera in New York. (Though he can advise against their ever trying!) But nor should he be too patronizing or too gushingly positive. John Fraser's 1974 *Globe and Mail* review, page 333, of *Noye's Fludde*, performed by a local church, is rooted firmly within the capabilities of the amateur performers, and David Prosser speaks constantly in terms of what the performers are capable of, and what the audience can reasonably expect.

Finally, the reviewer must be able to write well: Arts and entertainment pages should, in themselves, be entertaining, whether it's an entire review (Wayne Edmonstone, a *Vancouver Sun* drama critic, once wrote an entire review of *The Canterbury Tales* in Chaucerian rhyme), or just the occasional bon mot ("Monstrousness has its own charisma." — Prosser). (One wicked reviewer, long ago, dismissed the film *I Am A Camera* with one line: "Me no Leica.") While William Littler lectures about opera terminology, he makes it highly digestible (See his contrasting definitions of Baritone, Bass, Castrato and Counter-tenor). Jay Scott, while solemnly comparing two books and their movies (page 341), describes Meryl Streep in *The French Lieutenant's Woman* as "an actress with an aura no more mysterious than that of a Pop Tart."

The other component of this chapter also involves highly opinionated writing — newspaper columns. Like reviewers, the best columnists don't hesitate to speak their mind to their readers. As *New York Times* columnist William Safire advised new columnist Abe Rosenthal, "As you cultivate the garden of controversy, burn the bridges of objectivity. Show me an even-handed columnist and I'll show you an odds-on soporific."

The column writing category was added to the National Newspaper Awards in 1980. More often than not, this award has been captured by columnists commenting on the Canadian political scene. While a selection of those columns can be found in *The Opinion Shapers* (and others in *Voix*, our selection of French voices) the pieces here represent those columnists concerned with issues other than politics.

The best columnists quite literally talk to their readers and we come to recognize their voices. The *Globe*'s Jeffrey Simpson speaks with the voice of authority. The *Star*'s Carol Goar is the voice of compassion. And certainly no one can match the ironic voice of Toronto *Star* columnist Joey Slinger. Canadian columnists have spoken to us with both passion and compassion. The rage and fear voiced in Michele Landsberg's 1980 *Toronto Star* column about Barbara Schlifer (page 340), a young lawyer raped and murdered on the day she was called to the Ontario bar, echoes through today in these words: "I felt what it must be like to be a mother whose child has grown safely up, only to have evil, murdering hands laid upon her in an unexpected hour."

Richard Wagamese, the first native Canadian to win a NNA, speaks in a highly-personal voice, taking readers to a place deep inside his memory where lives the young Ojibway boy taken away from his home and culture (page 355). Once heard, his voice is one not easily forgotten:

I didn't know that balance and harmony with all things is the Indian way. I didn't know that the creed of the warrior included compassion, respect, honour and kindness, just as I didn't know that warriors were allowed to cry. Because I had no one to teach me and I did not understand.

Wagamese teaches us and makes us understand. In newspaper journalism, that is the greatest skill of all.

• **1972** Critical Writing •

Sensuous excess as an art form

Dave Billington

Montreal Gazette

This past weekend (perhaps appropriately since it is the Labour Day celebration) has surely belonged to the Russians.

The hockey team, far from showing that they were here to 'learn' from us, reminded a good many people just what the game of hockey is all about — things like balance, stamina and teamwork.

And on Friday night in Ottawa, one of the most singular Russians to skip the country since 1917 reminded the capacity audience in the National Arts Centre just what ballet is all about — balance, stamina and teamwork.

Rudolph Nureyev, surely ballet's most compelling figure since the tragic Nijinsky, opened the National Ballet of Canada's most ambitious season in its 20-year history with an opulent production of *The Sleeping Beauty*.

Nureyev and his manager Sol Hurok (a sort of cultural Alan Eagleson) have decided that Canada's company is the best vehicle for Rudi's latest royal progress through North America — a progress which will wind up with three weeks in the Metropolitan Opera in New York in the spring.

And if Saturday night's opener is any indication of the company's potential, that New York opening may mark the day that the National Ballet of Canada moves into the very top echelon of the world's classical companies.

If this happens there will be few doubts that it was Nureyev's inspirational presence which was largely responsible. The line between excellent craftmanship and fine art is the line between doing something well and doing something better than you ever thought you could.

When the National passed through Montreal last spring on the warm-up for the European tour, they were displaying a lot of beautiful craftsmanship. On Friday night they were flashing hints of art.

Nurveyev's actual appearances in *Sleeping Beauty* are not all that many, considering the length of the ballet. He is not seen until the opening of the second act and he's only on stage in the third act for the closing pas de deux and the finale.

But from the moment the curtain rose until its final fall, the magic of the Nureyev name was all pervasive.

Nureyev, mod figure though he may seem to be with his jetset friends and his stylish 'defector' status, is basically a 19th-century romantic.

His whole approach to *Sleeping Beauty* fairly drips with the ornate and sensuous excess of the European courts in the 1800s.

Rich browns, golds and reds give an almost oil-painting-like background upon which the dancers themselves are displayed like a light, but colourful patina.

The sets, brilliantly conceived and executed by Georg Schlogl and Nicholas Georgiadis, are at times almost too weighty for this essentially light ballet, but what they lack in subtlety they make up in sheer breath-taking spectacle.

Yet, beneath all this spectacle, there was some fine dancing being done.

Nureyev, who has acted as principle dancer, choreographer and director for this tour, seems to have tightened considerably the sometimes lax discipline in the corps.

The lines are cleaner, the movement more assured and the patterns more cohesive than at any time I've seen them in the past. This is really the mark of Nureyev's success with the National.

If he had done no more than inspire a couple of principal dancers to new highs, then the expense of mounting such a lavish production would hardly have been justified. But the fiery dancer has moved the whole company up a few inches in their climb toward greatness.

After the Margot Fonteyne experience, a story that is more romantic than most ballet plot lines, Nureyev's effect on ballerinas has become legendary.

Veronica Tennant is no exception. Though there were times, in the difficult second act, when she looked terrified of her partner, once she got her blood up, she danced better than she has for some time. Again, as the tour goes on, she will add dimension to her character in direct proportion to adding inspiration to her dancing.

As for the man himself there is little to say that has not already been said about him. His dancing is a splendid mixture of sheer physical vigour refined by the gentler arts.

This is particularly evident in the long, brooding pas seul in the second act.

It is in this scene that Nureyev asserts himself as something more than the brilliantly physical dancer of popular imagination.

He is contemplative, subtle and gentle in his gestures, and yet he uses the whole stage area, never once allowing the character to be swallowed by the vastness of the woodland set.

And when called upon for those famous leaps and bursts of animal strength, he summons them the way any mature artist or athlete can, measured out sufficiently to get the job done well, and to save something for next time.

Nureyev is probably now at his peak as a complete dancer and those who can see him on his tour will not soon forget the experience. Youth can always display effortless brilliance. But these flashes and displays are sparks to a fire. But sparks do not linger in memory as does the glow of a warm hearth.

This is the glow of Nureyev today.

• **1974** Critical Writing •

This medieval play has pertinence today

John Fraser

Globe and Mail

The notion of a medieval morality play having any meaning today might strike some people as being hilariously absurd, but fortunately, Benjamin Britten was not among them in 1957 when he wrote *Noyes' Fludde*, based on the fourteenth-century Chester miracle play about Noah and his crowded ark. The world got a miniature masterpiece as a result, and a work that eloquently recalls the purpose of those ancient church dramas: To instruct, to proselytize and to entertain.

Last night at Grace Church on-the-Hill, as part of this Anglican parish's centennial celebration, a new production of *Noye's Fludde* was given its second of three performances. Despite the presence of one of the New York City Opera's leading bassos, Ara Berberian, as Noah, and the Canadian Opera Company's Diane Loeb as his spiteful, doubting wife, as well as a sprinkling of professional talent strewn about in the orchestra, this was largely an amateur effort, with most of it coming from Grace Church itself.

This amateur nature was one of the major reasons for the success of the brief (one hour) but shining church opera. In fact, it was much more than a mere success, for here was an evening that was sincerely conceived to be inspirational and religious, which didn't have a trace of sanctimoniousness. By concentrating on simplicity, Grace Church has captured a measure of spiritual grandeur.

Of course the church had Britten helping it a bit. The opera is predicated on amateur participation. The music is filled with marvelously virile rhythms that are immediately compelling and since the production requires the active assistance of hordes of children and indeed the full audience, Britten has written a cleanly delineated score that virtually forces you to want to take part.

In such an atmosphere, even the occasional false start by the children's chorus seemed appropriate, so amiable and unpretentious is the music and the tale. Brenda Davies directed all the voyagers on this particular ark and heaven only knows how many people were involved. I lost count of the children who sang the animal parts (Britten has given different groups of animals and birds a variety of ways of singing *Kyrie* as they troop down the central aisle onto Murray Laufer's cardboard cutout vessel), but Mrs. Davies managed somehow to make them disappear much as God did dry land — in a flash.

Derek Holman, Grace Church's musical director, led a 50-piece orchestra (Isidor Desser was concertmaster and George Brough was on the organ) which gave a remarkably good account of itself. One didn't come expecting to hear any sublime sounds from the strings — that there was something more than just competence was a welcome surprise. Between the orchestra and the singers, Holman had a small army to control and he emerged at the end still at the head of the ranks, which included a capacity audience that took part in three hymns. No mean feat.

Berberian had the demanding task of holding the opera's disparate parts together because of the size of his role, which accounts for much of the important music. He knows the part of Mr. Noye, as it is styled in the opera, back to front, having performed it many times. That he made it sound newly minted last night was proof of his artistry and professionalism. Miss Loeb, as his bitchy, cantankerous spouse, handles the harridan business well.

As for Arnold Edinborough, the peripatetic former editor of *Saturday Night* and columnist for the *Financial Times* and *Canadian Churchman*, who took on the part of God — or at least his voice, booming out from the back balcony of the church — he proved once and for all, in case there was any doubt, that the Deity is and always was an Anglican, who speaks with a fine, mellifluous, Cambridge-educated tongue and doesn't muck about.

There were no complaints about this evening, for the flaws were as endearing as the assets.

• **1978** Critical Writing •

The Good Book vs. good books

William French

Globe and Mail

CLINTON, Ont. — It would be easy for urban sophisticates to dismiss the meeting that took place in the high school gym here on Tuesday night as just another example of rural Ontario's redneck conservatism, but that would be much too facile and even dangerous. The meeting turned out to be one of those profoundly revealing events that will somehow shape the lives of many of those who participated in it.

It had the stuff of novels — community tensions, family and generational conflict, philosophical underpinnings. There were elements of a Bible Belt revival meeting, and of the Scopes monkey trial in Tennessee in the 1920s, when a teacher was accused of teaching evolution. Yet it was also a New England town meeting, participatory democracy, revealing in stark detail the classic 20th century confrontation between right and left, and the increasing polarization between liberal humanism and evangelical fundamentalism. And it provided clear warning for those who oppose censorship and who value freedom of information that the strength of the suppressors should not be underestimated. There is a strange mood abroad in the land.

The occasion was unique. The Huron County School Board, which operates five high schools in this rich agricultural area near Goderich, has been under great pressure from parents and religious groups to remove three novels from the Grade 13 English course — Margaret Laurence's *The Diviners*, J.D. Salinger's *Catcher in the Rye* and John Steinbeck's *Of Mice and Men*. It's the kind of pressure the Writer's Union was concerned about at its recent annual meeting, when it offered to come to the aid of beleaguered English teachers.

An English teacher at South Huron High School in Exeter decided to take up the union's offer and asked for help. The union decided to send three members — vice-president June Callwood, children's writer Janet Lunn and Alice Munro, who lives in the eye of storm in Clinton — to a public meeting,

No one knew quite what to expect, but well before the 7:30 p.m. starting time it was clear that this was the only show in town. Cars clogged the streets around the school, and the gym was soon packed with about 500 people — one-sixth of the town's population. A young man in the lobby was handing out sheets of paper which most people thought at first was a program, but turned out to contain the most controversial and raunchy excerpts from the three novels (with Margaret Laurence's name misspelled). It was a valuable community service; the protesting parents then knew exactly what they were complaining about without having to read the offending novels.

I asked the young man whom he represented. "The Christian side," he said, leaving the rest of us to the lions.

The chairman, Colin Lowndes, introduced the three women from the Writer's Union and a poet from London, Ont., Steve Osterlund. Alice Munro had the uncomfortable feeling of looking out at the somewhat hostile faces she usually encounters in more genial circumstances in the grocery store and on Clinton's neighbourly streets.

The five people on the platform made some low-key remarks in defense of freedom generally and the three books specifically, trying not to offend or inflame. Then the meeting was thrown open to questions — speeches, really — and an astonishing parade began to the microphone. It soon became clear the community is deeply divided on the issue, that it's far more important to Huron County right now than the possibility of Quebec's separation, nuclear test bans, a federal election, the price of gas, wheat rust or anything else in the world.

As speaker after speaker trooped up to the microphone — at one point 14 were waiting in line — the crowd applauded or groaned in response. One man led the assembly (or part of it, anyway)

in a fervent prayer, another waved his Bible and said everything needed to be taught in English classes was in there. English teachers in the audience found themselves defending their profession, and explaining the role of literature in society. One woman questioned the morals of the teachers with obvious distaste; she had heard of parties where the teachers drank and used foul language. A fervent anti-novel man launched into a diatribe which threatened to become a long sermon. "Hurry up," someone shouted from the bleachers, "my babysitter has to go in five minutes."

The hostility toward common four-letter words was clearly evident. There was much talk about taking the Lord's name in vain, and one of the excerpts from *The Diviners* objected to was, "Now I'm crying, for God sake." The intensity of the religious feeling in the gym was surprising, and Billy Graham would have felt right at home. The Bible-thumpers were clearly in the majority.

Many of the parents couldn't understand why these three particularly offensive novels had to be on the course when so much other, pure, literature was available. Teacher Lowndes tried to explain that writers reflect society, and that teachers ask students to evaluate a variety of responses to life. The novels were not held up as models, any more than a study of Hitler in a history class was an invitation to students to emulate him. But that view of educational philosophy cut little ice with parents, confused by changing values, and clinging to the old verities and trying to impose them on their children.

In the end, it was the students themselves who made the most powerful contribution to the discussion. They were caught in the middle, and for many of those who spoke, it was obviously an intensely emotional experience. Some stood squarely behind their parents in opposing what they described as filth, and thus risked the censure of their more open-minded peers. Others openly opposed their parents — one girl was in tears as she said she respected their opinion, but didn't believe that four-letter words and descriptions of the sex act could corrupt her. In a small community like Clinton, it isn't easy for teenagers to glimpse and reach for the big world beyond their parents' comfortably limited horizons.

They pleaded for tolerance, for rational discussion, and to be treated as young adults, not immature children. "You parents don't trust your kids enough," said a Grade 12 girl.

The school board will decide in mid-August whether to remove the three novels from the curriculum, and given the tensions in the community, it won't be an easy decision. But whatever happens, the students have gained a maturity from the experience that might even be more valuable than reading the novels — which, now, they'll read for certain anyway.

• **1979** Critical Writing •

An author who can change lives

John Hofsess

Calgary Albertan

He lay there, unconscious, looking much older than 48, his dentures stacked with his wallet and keys on the hospital night table, his right arm and leg paralyzed, his breathing labourious, his naked, bloated body skim-milk blue in the fluorescent light.

When the doctor asked me who he was, I had difficulty saying it was my father. "If he lives," the doctor said, putting an arm around my shoulders and walking me back and forth, "he'll be paralyzed permanently. We found blood in the spinal fluid, indicating a brain hemorrhage. We're waiting to see if he has another — it often happens that way. Did he drink much?"

Sitting in his favorite, dingy, womanless beer parlour, my father had passed out. Nothing unusual, his cronies thought, except maybe it was a little early in the evening. Jake (as they called him) had spent, possibly, one-fifth of his lifetime in that hotel taproom or others like it, trying to find joy in southern Ontario, peering at the world through the bottom of a beer glass.

Though his death certificate doesn't say so, my father died of "lifestyle disease." He smoked a pack and a half of Players a day. He gambled compulsively. In the late '30s he was a partner in a taxi business (which later, for other partners, proved quite profitable) but lost his share through card game debts and the indifferent work habits of a drunk. Even his whoring was dumb and irresponsible: The state had to support two of his illegitimate children. When the Second World War was declared he suddenly became a conscientious objector, claiming he was a Seventh Day Adventist.

My father never tired of telling people he was what he was because the rich and the powerful (especially "the Jews") made him that way and kept him that way. He was the kind of man only a mother, or a Marxist, could love; the first because he was a weak, ineffectual manchild; the latter because he could hold my father up (and most of the time he would have had to hold him up) as a classic example of the downtrodden masses.

When a son watches his father die, he should presumably feel some grief, some sense of a breaking connection. All I could feel was a blackening rage. It was as if some part of my body or brain produced a new chemical that night, an acrid secretion that stunned the mind into bitter lucidity. My father's life was a long, long trail of debris, each day more debris, with nothing but death to finally clean it all up. The doctor's voice was full of professionally seductive sympathy, and I heard him out, with tormented politeness, for his sake not mine. It was all I could do to keep from flinging his hand from my shoulder and shouting, "No more excuses — dammit!"

A week later I picked up Margaret Atwood's *Survival.*

■ ■ ■

Prior to reading *Survival* I had resigned myself to thinking that I would never again be as stimulated by new ideas as I had been in my formative years. Life wore one down. Most of one's friends settled down and dust settled down on top of them. *Survival* was a challenge to change. There's no cage, the door is open, Atwood said in effect: Therefore be bold.

I had pictured us meeting (this was the first time) with a certain memorable grace. Instead, each time I lit a cigarette, or filled my glass again, I fancied that her eyes followed my motions (perhaps our meeting, on a rainy day, in a dark, small, stoically underfurnished room at Massey College, where she was writer-in-residence, was so spare in other gestures of visual interest) with close, clinical amusement. Under her scrutiny, I felt embarrassed by my addictions: Unfree, unfit.

In the days ahead I listened to a new inner voice. Do you realize, it asked, that when John Keats was your age he had been dead for nine years? When, how, is your poetry, music, whatever, going to come, living as you do! Taking refuge in Aesop's fable, I replied, well, if I'm not a creative hare perhaps I'm a creative tortoise, gradually, stealthily, creeping up to achievement. I wouldn't bet on it, snapped this ungullible conscience; nobody who smokes a pack of cigarettes a day (that's 9,125 a year), goes through a couple of Sara Lee cakes a week and rarely gets any exercise other than the odd, slow stroll, is planning to live a long life. You're not fit to carry the torch of Canadiana; you'll probably just sprain your back.

■ ■ ■

She laughed when I told her at our second meeting, which took place in a health food restaurant on Bloor Street, that I was now an ex-smoker, and a marathon runner, as a direct result of reading her work.

"*Survival* has nothing to do with exercise," she said, obviously finding the connection ridiculous.

"I read it spiritually," I replied, faintly surprised that she had not foreseen all possible interpretations. Canadians suffer from a colonialized mentality, she had contended in the book; they were abject self-victimizers. Their literature and movies were mostly about "losers" — down-and-out people without spunk; or else resourceless half-heroes ground down by fate or natural forces. Book after book, film after film, the same grim pattern kept repeating itself. As Atwood has said, if a Canadian were to write *Moby Dick* he would have written it from the whale's point of view. All the unhappy endings of Canadian culture suddenly became transparent to me. To say nothing about all the bleak endings in Canadian life. I wanted to break free of such depressing compulsions.

■ ■ ■

At our most recent meeting, at Ambrosia, in Calgary, where she was delighted to find a restaurant that served fresh juices, whole-grain bread, home-made soups and delicious salads, she filled me in on her growing list of achievements. The filming of *Surfacing* (by Quebec director Claude Jutra) is now complete, and will be released next year. Actress Margot Kidder has taken an option on *Lady Oracle* and commissioned a script of it for a Hollywood studio. (Atwood is not directly involved in either project, mainly because she doesn't like to relive a novel two or three years after it has been published.)

She has also finished a stage play based on *The Servant Girl*, and is interested in having it read and appraised by theatre directors. Then, there is the new novel, *Life Before Man* — which is already the number one fiction best-seller in Canada (McClelland and Stewart is projecting sales in hard-cover of 50,000 copies — an all-time record for a novel in this country).

Perhaps because *Life Before Man* had received cool and reserved reviews from critics I respect and because I believed that fiction was what she did least well, I wasn't prepared for the surprise that occurred upon opening its pages.

The first thing I noticed is the economy of the prose style; every word following into place, with the right weight and cadence. Why had no one commented about that, I wondered. For this is clearly the best-written novel that Atwood has done. Then too, there is the growing fascination of the story itself — the intertwining relationships of Nate and Elizabeth, whose marriage has failed, and the liaison that develops between Nate and Lesje (pronounced Lashia), who is a colleague of Elizabeth's at an institution modeled upon the Royal Ontario Museum in Toronto.

She doesn't want the responsibility — but Atwood's work, at its best, has the power to change lives. That's more than one can say about almost any other Canadian writer.

There are thousands of stories like mine — oddly-shared lifelong relationships between reader and author, in which the reader derives spiritual sustenance. The difference here is that Atwood invites us, ultimately, to move beyond admiration and to become creative in our own right. See me as I am, she says; for I see you as you are. Don't worship me, don't call me wise; instead look at your own limitations and transcend yourself.

• **1980** Critical Writing •

A guide to life on the high Cs

William Littler

Toronto Star

L et's be brutally frank. Not everybody likes opera. The learned Samuel Johnson called it an exotic and irrational entertainment. To the brothers Marx it was the biggest slapstick target this side of Margaret Dumont' derriere.

After all, what could be sillier than grown men and women of a corpulent disposition committing suicide and dying of consumption while bellowing at the top of their lungs in a foreign language? By comparison, politics seems positively sane.

And yet, dear reader, there is a case to be made for this "exotic and irrational entertainment, "even if Perry Mason probably wouldn't take it."

First, let me say that the prosecution case mounted by Harpo, Chico and Groucho in *A Night at the Opera* is irrefutable.

There truly was a time when sopranos, in Victor Borge's famous words, came out on stage in a single pile, when the stuffed of tummy sang to the stuffed of shirt.

There was even a time when, in Anna Russell's equally famous words, it didn't matter what you did, as long as you sang it.

Singers in Samuel Johnson's day often did very little beyond opening their throats and letting fly a couple of available octaves. Since the story made no sense (descents by the gods tended to appear at regular intervals) and since the language made less (it was usually Italian), they functioned essentially as the musical equivalent of circus aerialists, tip-toeing along a vocal high wire.

All that, or at any rate the worst of it, has now changed and at its best opera today is what its founders intended it to be — a species of drama in which music heightens the emotional impact of the words.

Oh, yes, the founders. Opera really was born with a silver spoon in its mouth, of Italian manufacture. Its founders, a group of Florentine aristocrats known as the Camerata, thought they were reviving the ancient Greek drama and didn't realize they were bringing into existence, at the turn of the 17th century, a quite new form of musical theatre.

The important thing for the novice, unlettered in the ways of suicidal sopranos and helmeted tenors, is not to be daunted by their theatrical progeny. Anyone who can make sense of Canadian football can make sense of opera.

So why not give opera a try? Down at the O'Keefe Centre, beginning next Wednesday, a Japanese geisha stands ready to break your heart as hers was broken by a "Yankee vagabondo" named Lt. Pinkerton. The opera in question, Puccini's *Madama Butterfly*, has been known to have a stronger effect on the tear ducts than onions.

But before heading down to Front and Yonge, you may like to learn a few of the terms that will enable you to leave your seat during intermission (in opera you can expect to encounter at least one, often two and sometimes even three of these) without being labeled a card-carrying klutz.

Herewith, then, is Littler's limited glossary, the instant expert's guide to the wonderful world of the flat note and the round chest and the high Cs that don't make you seasick:

Aria: A solo song, the big number, the Pavlovian applause generator.

Bis: The Encore cry. Don't use it. Encores are frowned upon nowadays.

Bravo: If the aria was sung by a women, yell, "Brava!" instead. If it was a duet, yell, "Bravi!" If you're musical, shut up and don't interrupt the music until the scene is over.

Bel canto: Literally, beautiful song. The 19th century Italian vocal style emphasizing beauty of tone and florid technique. A Joan Sutherland specialty.

Brindisi: A drinking song, preferably sung sober, as in Act I of Verdi's *La Traviata*.

Baritone: A high, low male voice. Seldom gets the girl.

Bass: A low, low male voice. Usually fathers the girl.

Castrato: Can't father anything and sounds like nothing else. A 17th and 18th century specialty singer, now defunct and much missed in Handel's operas.

Counter-tenor: Highest adult male voice achievable without surgery. Rare but used by Britten for Oberson, king of the fairies, in *A Midsummer Night's Dream*.

Contralto: Lowest female voice. Usually either the mother, the villainess or a man.

Cabaletta: In elaborate arias, the fancy finish. Frequently more icing than cake.

Claque: Organized enthusiasts, sometimes paid by singers at large houses such as The Met and especially in Italy to postpone retirement.

Coloratura: Flowery ornamentation, a high soprano specialty but at one time a requirement of singers in all vocal ranges.

Cadenza: A showy piece of vocal embroidery inserted into an aria, generally just before the end, for purposes of applause and consequent contract renewal.

Chest voice: The lower vocal register as opposed to the higher register known as the head voice.

Duet: It takes two to tango.

Falsetto: Not what you think it means. This is sung, rather than worn, above the normal male vocal range. A once popular technique now in relative disuse.

Finale: The end of a scene, act or opera, when the singers either whoop it up or die very loudly.

Grand Opera: Originally a French term, now loosely applied to any production with at least three changes of scenery, two choruses and one horse. *Aida*, with or without elephants.

Golden Age: When everyone sang better than today. Usually just beyond accurate recall.

Leitmotiv: A musical theme used throughout an opera to identify a character or idea. Or as Anna Russell put it, the signature tune. A Wagner specialty.

Libretto: The opera book. Frequently criticized, unless by Boito Da Ponte or Hoffmansthal.

Maestro: What people call the conductor when they are feeling polite.

Mezza voice: Singing with half one's usual voice. A way to survive rehearsal.

Mezzo soprano: Lower than a soprano, higher than a contralto and the right voice for Carmen.

Monodrama: A work for one character, such as Schoenberg's *Erwartung*.

Opera: In Italian the plural of opus. Literally, the works.

Opera Buffa: Italian comic opera, usually with accompanied recitative.

Opera Comique: Does not mean the same thing in French. Originally, opera with spoken dialogue, whether comic, à la Offenbach, or tragic, à la Bizet's *Carmen*.

Opera Seria: Italian operatic genre of high seriousness and much pomp. Now obsolete.

Operetta: A catch-all term for light opera, with spoken dialogue and set numbers. *The Student Prince* and all that.

Overture: The orchestral music that introduces an opera. Not necessary and if it's short, it's sometimes called a Prelude.

Prima Donna: The first lady, the Diva, the big vocal cheese. In the 18th century there could also be a Primo Uomo — a castrato or tenor.

Prompter: Hides in a tiny box at the front of the stage and cues singers who, in Anna Russell's phrase, "have resonance where their brains ought to be."

Recitative: A species of vocal writing that resembles declamatory speech and allows greater rhythmic latitude to the singer. Recitative usually advances plot, Arias usually elaborate on a given situation.

Scena: A long vocal solo in several movements, mixing recitatives and arias such as Florestan's dungeon scene in Beethoven's *Fidelio*.

Tenor: Famous for high notes, a big ego and an empty head. Usually the hero, for reasons baritones never understand.

Tessiture: The general lie of the notes in a given passage, whether high or low.

Tremolo: Properly a vocal ornament involving the rapid reiteration of the same pitch. More commonly used to identify excessive vibrato, a wobble in the voice

Vibrato: A slight fluctuation of pitch about a single tone, often deliberately cultivated, sometimes sadly abused.

Had enough? If not, here's a list of books, all of them flawed but packed with information, that may not help you survive intermission but contract the addiction for which there remains no cure:

The Encyclopedia of the Opera, edited by Leslie Orrey, published by Pitmamn. Exactly what its title suggests and profusely illustrated.

The Simon and Schuster Book of the Opera, published by Simon and Schuster. A curiously organized, lavishly illustrated guide to hundreds of operas, many now forgotten.

Understanding Opera, by Robin May, published by Coles. A paperback history with the Canadian Opera production of Tchaikovsky's *Joan of Arc* pictured on the cover.

One Hundred Great Operas and their Stories, by Henry W. Simon, published by Doubleday. A handy act by act, murder by murder guide to the standard repertory, now in paperback.

Opera, by Edward Dent, published by Penguin Books. Probably the best single-volume introduction to the whole world of opera.

Bluff Your Way in Opera, by Francis Coleman, published by Wold Publishing Ltd., in paperback. If all else fails.

• **1980** Columns •

Underlining the dread felt by women

Michele Landsberg

Toronto Star

I didn't know Barbra Schlifer, the young lawyer they laid in her grave yesterday. I only know from the newspaper stories that she was a woman we could ill afford to lose; perhaps because of my shock that such a promising life has been wasted, her death has affected my life.

Barbra was called to the bar last Thursday. Friday they discovered her body. Her friends told reporters that she was enthusiastic about using law as a way to be of service to the community; that she was keen on women's rights, supported rape-crisis centres and women's hostels, worried about consumers and the poor, and did volunteer work with the elderly.

No doubt, in years to come, her family will take some comfort in their pride that Barbra was what we call a mensch: A more than ordinarily decent, idealistic and compassionate human being. When other young women were greedily snatching the new freedoms, hard-won by others, to achieve a narrowly materialistic "success," Barbra Schlifer was intent on giving back more to the community than she had received.

In the painful present, though, it must make it all the harder to accept that a woman of vibrant generosity was so horribly robbed of her own life and breath.

Her death touched me closely. Maybe it was because she loved some of the things I love: Books, reading, family, foreign films, the lake, the French language.

Perhaps because we might well have been friends if our paths had crossed, I felt what I haven't felt before: That this random evil could really happen to me or to mine.

U.S. feminists have been writing, for a decade, about the fear of attack which hobbles women with invisible constraints. I could agree with the analysis, but somehow I never felt it as something real in my own life. Oh, sure, I can remember when the boys were allowed out after supper in the magical dusk, to play under the streetlights, and how our mothers always hesitated when we girls begged to go out. And every one of us has felt that quivering vulnerability between our shoulder blades as we hurried down a dark street at night, trying to reason away the footsteps behind us.

But that isn't the same as being circumscribed. Never, never have I avoided a walk or a trip or a late-night excursion because of feminine fears.

Now Barbra Schlifer has been murdered, and all weekend, in dreadful flashes, I felt what it must be to be a mother whose child has grown safely up, only to have evil murdering hands laid upon her in an unexpected hour …

It comes, sickeningly, after a relentless year of well-reported attacks on women. There have been so many. Hardly a day passes without a terse account of a woman raped by a "date," or a teenager taking a ride or meeting someone in a tavern and being lucky to live to tell the tale.

It's easy to write off the latter with a sneer: "What a little fool." We forget the naive trust of a 15-year-old, or the ridiculous fear of making a fool of oneself by taking unnecessary alarm.

Then we snap back to revolted outrage when some low-life kids, groupies of a motorcycle gang, are terrorized, humiliated and savaged for one long night, and the brutish thugs who never denied raping them are acquitted because the girls had consented to sex acts on previous occasions. The trial of the rapist, who never had to testify, was one long assault on the sexual history of the teenage girls. If you're a tramp, you don't have a right to your own body; you don't have a right to say no; the law will not protect you from gruesome attack.

That hasn't changed. And neither has the equal vulnerability of good, decent women, going home at night after celebrating an academic achievement.

340

Hitchhikers, tavern pick-ups, groupies, grandmas, kids and idealistic lawyers, we're all in this leaky boat together. It's not just urban paranoia; it's urban fact. Violence against women is impartially evil. I don't want to be hobbled or to hobble others, but from now on I'll be insisting on taxis and door-to-door vigilance for women I care about.

And, in memory of Barbra Schlifer, and in sad tribute to her humanity, of which our community has now been deprived, I hope others will join me in contributing to the Toronto Rape Crisis Centre, Box 6597, Station A, Toronto, Ontario M5W 1X4. I'm sending $100, today. We have to keep fighting, and the women's movement is the best way I know.

• **1981** Critical Writing •

Two great beginnings disappoint in the end

Jay Scott

Globe and Mail

Cutter's Way, the Ivan Passer film of Newton Thornburg's novel *Cutter and Bone*, opens with a parade in Santa Barbara, Calif. In slow motion and black and white, flamenco dancers approach, gaining speed and colour as they come.

The French Lieutenant's Woman, the Karl Reisz film of John Fowles' novel, opens with a clapper board calling our attention to the fact that a scene from a film is about to be shot. The scene is the novel's most famous: A lone woman in Victorian England stands "motionless, staring, staring out to sea, more like a living memorial to the drowned, a figure from myth, than any proper fragment of the petty provincial day."

The novels that gave birth to these movies are very good novels with an all but identical theme, a theme elucidated by the narrator of *Cutter and Bone*: "One could spend all his life climbing onto crosses to save people from themselves, and nothing would change. For human beings finally were each as alone as dead stars and no amount of toil or love or litany could alter by a centimetre the terrible precision of their journeys."

In *Cutter's Way*, in modern Santa Barbara, Richard Bone (Jeff Bridges), a good-natured but gone slightly to seed blond hustler, and his friend, Alex Cutter (John Heard), a nasty-tempered, one-eyed, one-legged drunk, attempt to save themselves and, metaphorically, modern idealism, when they discover that a rich man has committed a murder. In *The French Lieutenant's Woman*, in Victorian England, Charles Smithson (Jeremy Irons), a gentleman born and bred, and Sara (Meryl Streep), a provocative woman who walks alone, attempt to save themselves and, metaphorically, modern romance, when they discover that Sara's obsessional feelings for a long-absent French lieutenant have been transferred to Charles. These are two movies about friendship, love and the limits of Good Samaritanism.

These are two movies about the limits of cinematic adaptation. 1. Because Fowles' novel was not only set in Victorian England but was about the process of creating a novel about Victorian England — director Reisz and his illustrious screen writer, playwright Harold Pinter, have decided to make *The French Lieutenant's Woman* a movie about making a movie of *The French Lieutenant's Woman*.

American star Meryl Streep plays an American star playing the French lieutenant's woman — the two stories, of her romance in Victorian England and of her romance with the modern actor playing her Victorian lover, are intercut throughout the film and come together at the end, when one story collapses into the other. But there is a problem: Miss Streep plays a fictitious American actress by the name of Anna having an affair with a fictitious British actor by the name of Mike — Miss Streep and Jeremy Irons, as real people, do not figure in this conceit.

When John Fowles spoke to us in the novel as John Fowles, it was the real novelist speaking: the parallel Pinter has invented for Fowles' voice is false and reductive.

The effect is irritating. The film invites us to consider how closely related we are to the Victorians. We get the point. It invites us to revel in the process of artistic creation — *Day for Night* and *The Stunt Man* go on literary location. But each time the Victoria tale becomes interesting, we are wrenched away to the modern drama. (People who count this sort of thing report that this takes place 14 times.) The modern drama never does become interesting; being wrenched away from it is a matter of being returned to the lesser of two evils.

2. *Cutter and Bone* was one of the toughest and grimmest American novels imaginable. *Cutter's Way* is grim, but not grim enough: It's *lyrically* grim. The novel has been Hollywoodized, and has become a black farce with what in these troubled times amounts to a happy (and asinine, and far-fetched) ending, rather than black comedy with the direly pessimistic (and organic and shattering) conclusion it had. Cutter's wife Maureen (Lisa Eichhorn) has been sentimentalized into a romantically doomed Tennessee Williams dipsomaniac; in the novel, she was a junkie who neglected her baby son. John Heard's performance as the terrifyingly witty Viet vet Cutter proffers the cutest stylized gutter bum since Ratso Rizzo: Tom Waits meets Chester. Miss Eichhorn gives every evidence of wanting to become Gloria Grahame. Only Jeff Bridges' Bone is true to the bitter, decaying, sun-smooched culture Thornburg brought to blistered life.

The performances in *Cutter's Way* are devastated by the script; the performances in *The French Lieutenant's Woman* are the result of perverse casting. In her first lead, Miss Streep, an actress with an aura no more mysterious than that of a Pop Tart, has been asked to play a woman whose mysteriousness approximates that of Garbo — or of Vanessa Redgrave (who would have had the role) in *Blow Up*. Not since Barbra Streisand donned a precarious British accent in *On A Clear Day You Can See Forever* has an American actress fallen so short of bridging the Atlantic. Miss Streep is not mediocre: Her failure is of flamboyance that is its own kind of achievement. During her pièce de résistance monologue — "I have set myself beyond the pale, I am nothing, I am hardly human any more, I am the French Lieutenant's woman" — you can easily become distracted by her carroty pre-Raphaelite hair or the grainy cinematography. She reads one of the most extraordinary speeches in the English language as if deciphering the Rosetta Stone.

Fowles used as an epigraph to the final chapter of *The French Lieutenant's Woman* a Matthew Arnold aphorism that is especially applicable: "True piety is acting what one knows." But there is one good thing to be said of the interminable close-ups of Miss Streep: they keep her co-star, Jeremy Irons, out of the frame. As the romantic hero Charles, a man as crazy in his own way as the French lieutenant's woman is in hers, Irons is an asexual epicene nonentity. His accent is, however, impeccable.

Bastardized film versions of great or good novels are said to be helpful — they are said to make people want to read. Do they? Will anyone pick up *Cutter and Bone* or *The French Lieutenant's Woman* after sitting through these visual aids? We are told that the novel as a form is dying. When a work of fiction does show signs of life, it is quickly clubbed into the oblivion of false fame by a filmic "treatment."

Charles Darwin, whom Fowles quotes in *The French Lieutenant's Woman*, could have been talking about novels and movies, and about their relationship each to the other, when he wrote in *Origin of Species*: "I think it inevitably follows, that as new species in the course of time are formed through natural selection, others will become rarer and rarer, and finally extinct. The forms which stand in closest competition with those undergoing modification and improvement will naturally suffer most."

• **1982** Critical Writing •

For one brief, shining summer — Camelot

Peter Goddard

Toronto Star

I t was the summer of *Sgt. Pepper* and we were going to Expo.

Everybody was going to Expo in Montreal that summer 15 years ago; some because it was the country's centennial, some because they were curious about the place Charles de Gaulle had just called "le Quebec libre"; but most because the summer was sweet, warm and welcoming. Hey, listen; there wasn't much else to do and we weren't going to worry about it.

So three of us piled into an ancient Renault and started out along Bloor St. Barely two blocks later, we saw Bonnie, a friend of ours, and she said she'd come along too. Her boyfriend Terry was already there she said and it sounded like it might be fun to surprise him.

But other surprises were in the works. Hours later, as we came into Kingston, we thought it might be even more interesting to head south instead of east. So we ended up in Miami. Then on a plane. Then on a beach in Nassau. We had about $70 all told and one charge card, the Renault died on a Florida highway on our way back and everywhere we went we heard the music from *Sgt. Pepper's Lonely Hearts Club Band.*

> *It was twenty years ago today*
> *Sgt. Pepper taught the band to play*
> *They've been going in and out of style*
> *But they're guaranteed to raise a smile.*

The album was released in June. Throughout July every radio station played it repeatedly. By August everyone had a copy or knew someone who did. Listening became a ritual. It was the first time when the music did seem to embrace the world around it … and the last.

Europe was about to erupt in violent protest, Nixon was on the way to becoming the next American president, French president Charles de Gaulle during a visit here ignited separatist feeling in Quebec and war still raged in Vietnam. But it was to become the psychedelic summer which would give the entire '60s its most rosey memories. It was the first summer a generation lived without nostalgia — and the last.

It was the first time an album of rock 'n' roll would be a social phenomenon as well as a musical one, and the last.

Other albums, before and since, might be considered artistically superior: The Beatles themselves recorded some (*Rubber Soul, Revolver* and *Abbey Road,* for instance). Other albums have cost more and sold more, although the four months and more than $100,000 spent on it seemed outlandish at the time. (Fleetwood Mac spent two years and more than $1 million on *Tusk*). But *Sgt. Pepper*'s place in pop music is similar to Bach's Well Tempered Clavier in Baroque music; it's a summing up and focal point of most of what had come before. It became the standard point of reference. It was inescapable.

And we were expecting it — sort of. Everyone knew the Beatles were up to something during the winter of 1966. They'd given up touring the year before and had tried to drop out of sight, involved in individual projects. George Harrison went to India twice to study with Ravi Shankar and John Lennon was off to Spain to film *How I Won The War*. Rumours and stories about their drug trips were everywhere, but then again, rumours and stories about *everyone's* drug trips were everywhere.

For the first time in memory, nice, middle-class kids knew something their nice, middle-class parents didn't and the secret was sharded via the radio. The year began with nutty-putty pop songs such as Snoopy Vs The Red Baron by the Royal Guardsmen, Winchester Cathedral by The New Vaudeville Band. Nancy Sinatra's Sugar Town and The Monkees singing

Neil Diamond's I'm A Believer.

But that's exactly what we were doing. Scattered in among the silly pop stuff was something else.

There was the Buffalo Springfield's eerie and memorable For What It's Worth. The Rolling Stones sang Ruby Tuesday on radio but could not sing Let's Spend The Night Together without censorship on *The Ed Sullivan Show*. The Spencer Davis Group had I'm A Man. The Jefferson Airpane released Somebody To Love and from out of nowhere and from a band no one had ever heard of called The Doors, came the most startling piece of them all. It wasn't just the sexuality of Light My Fire that made it seem dangerous. It bordered on anarchy and no one — in North America, anyhow —was ready for that. This wasn't the summer to march on Washington, but to crowd into San Francisco's Haight Ashbury district.

In the midst of all this was the strangest song the Beatles had ever recorded. "Let me take you down," was the way Strawberry Fields Forever began.

They'd begun it in November the year before, and, through John Lennon's insistence and with producer George Martin's help, they recorded it over and over until it was textured perfectly. "To this day, they believe it was the greatest single they ever did," says local radio producer David Pritchard, whose past series on the Beatles is still played on the radio networks.

It was also the start of *Sgt. Pepper*. "The idea," Paul McCartney said after it was released, "was to do a complete thing that you could make what you liked of. Just a little magic presentation. Normally, a new Beatles LP would be just a collection of songs or a nice picture on a cover, nothing more. We wanted to make it something more. A complete show."

From John Fowles' novel, *The Magus*, to Federico Fellini's movie, *Juliet Of The Spirits*, the mid-'60s were fascinated with fantasy and with what Fowles' hero, Nicholas Urfe, called, "the God game." To produce the extraordinary melange of sound on *Sgt. Pepper*, the Beatles began to play the recording studio the way they'd once played their instruments. To produce its show-within-their-show, they played the God game.

The title song yanks up the curtain on their real-life circus. A Little Help From My Friends, which follows, is Ringo Starr's song, a bit of throw-away vaudeville that sets up what's to follow. Lucy In The Sky With Diamonds, criticized as being an acronym for LSD but written, according to Lennon at the time, about his son Julian, is evocatively trippy nonetheless, with its "tangerine trees and marmalade skies."

She's Leaving Home, with its rising harp arpeggios, seemed to be a pretty bit of throw-away fluff at the time, a daughter's disappearance confounding the parents. But knowing that the '60s' true legacy is the politics of the women's movement tells me the young girl "meeting a man from the motor trade" is the real hero of *Sgt. Pepper*.

Right from the start, the album ran into stiff criticism. John Gabree, in *Downbeat*, said that the band had "never been in the vanguard of popular music." Richard Goldstein encouraged an enormous deluge of outraged letters to the *New York Times* when, in his review of the album, he said the work "will be (seen as) Beatles baroque — an elaboration without improvement."

But that wasn't the point. Everyone lived *Sgt. Pepper*. For there was the piece which ended it all, A Day In The Life. Even Goldstein admitted to the staggering impact of this two-part song. A precursor to today's lean, pared-down sound, it began, "I read the news today, oh boy," and ended with, "I'd love to turn you on."

A generation lived between those two lines that summer.

• 1982 Columns •

Martial law, torture, 3 a.m. booze and other friendly gestures

Joey Slinger

Toronto Star

As a diplomatic courtesy, Bill Davis, the premier, is permitting our bars to remain open an extra two hours so the delegates to the International Monetary Fund conference won't get the impression that people in Ontario live under some kind of repressive regime.

He is also selling the world bankers tax-free booze so that after a hard day of staving off intergalactic economic collapse they can drink themselves comatose without suffering the personal economic collapse the good citizens of Ontario suffer when they try to do the same.

He explained he was doing this because some of the Moolah Moguls come from countries where the laws governing such things are different and he wants them to feel at home. That is to say, when in Toronto the Romans would still prefer to do as the Romans do.

Some of the natives are upset about this. What the devil, they say. Here is Bill Davis, that paragon of rectitude, or words not even vaguely to that effect, saying there will be two laws in his domain, one for the rich and powerful and one for the rest of us. He must think we are chopped liver.

Pas de tout. Not at all. Bill Davis is just a terrific host and is probably disappointed that there wasn't time to do more to show that our humble province is the equal of the great countries from which the financial wizards have come.

It's too bad he didn't get a chance to legalize prostitution for the week they are here. A lot of these countries have state-run whorehouses and the premier, doubtless, had he thought of it, would have reserved a hotel and filled the rooms with shady ladies who could make sure the delegates don't want for affection.

And think of the chance he missed to waive the laws on pornography. How much more comfortable some of our visitors would have been to find a stack of hard-core publications beside the Gideons in their bureaus. Some of them, perhaps, are accustomed to making their own, so it's a shame they can't phone room service and order up a couple of speed freaks and a Polaroid to ease the burdens of their deliberations. Surely the Humane Society would be eager to go along and not protest when a Doberman pinscher was enlisted in the cause.

But these are mere delights of the flesh, recreational pastimes some delegates have long been accustomed to in their home countries. We want them to feel that Toronto does more than emulate them in the realm of good times.

For instance, in some of their countries it is considered bad form for women to walk around with their faces uncovered: In some places, indeed, it is an offense. A good host, as Bill Davis is certainly striving to be, would go a long mile in this direction and arrange to have women publicly flogged for not wearing veils.

That would have been a nice touch at last night's flashy reception on the lawn at Queen's Park. Between sips of Ontario champagne and mouthfuls of fried shrimp, the premier could have called his wife to the platform, introduced her, condemned her and beaten her within an inch of her life. "We couldn't have done it better ourselves," some delegates would say.

I'm positive some of the delegates are home-sick because none of us natives have been visited at 3 a.m. by masked men and taken outside and summarily machine-gunned or, failing that, at least taken into the basement at police headquarters to have electrodes affixed to our genitals. Polite society isn't polite society in a lot of the countries our visitors hale from unless there are screams in the background.

If he had it to do all over again, Bill Davis would have been able to declare martial law and suspend the democratic process while the great conference was in session. I'm sure many of our guest are nervous to think that the streets are full of voters.

And this that you're reading. Something like this might ruin some delegates' stay in our city. This wouldn't be allowed where they come from. A good host would have taken over the press.

Me, I'm breaking all my fingers. It's my way of saying, "Welcome!"

• **1985** Critical Writing •
Irving Layton biography
a daring piece of work

Ken Adachi

Toronto Star

Writing a biography of Irving Layton takes a large amount of daring. Not for nothing did his mother call him flamplatz (exploding flame), even as a child. Everyone has come to know Layton as a theatrical and often truculent poet whose life has been marked by a flamboyant style that has attracted as many followers as enemies. Those whom he considers fools, he does not suffer gladly; responding to a negative review by Earle Birney in 1951, he would call him an "uncoiled tapeworm of asininity."

"Writing the biography was a challenge," says Elspeth Cameron. "I expect reactions to be extreme, and won't be surprised if I get hate letters from his followers. I don't expect Layton to like it either. Why would he? Unless you write an outright hagiography praising him as a great thinker and God's gift to the world, I doubt that he would like any book about him."

Her 500-page book, *Irving Layton: A Portrait* will be published in October by Stoddart. It promises to be, among other things, one of the publishing sensations of the fall season, no doubt heightened by the fact that it is heading — some might conjecture — on a collision course with the first volume of Layton's own memoir, *Waiting For The Messiah* (McClelland & Stewart), which will be in the bookstores around the same time. It may even unleash a first-class literary row.

Not that Cameron's book is meant merely to be grist for the gossip mills. Nor is it a grocery-list biography full of tedious annotations. No good biographer dares to be less than an artist, neglecting to give full weight to the task of shape and styling. Cameron, in fact, calls it "an experimental" book, in which she uses "fictional techniques of reconstruction in order to convey the emotional milieu in which Layton lived — the short, dramatic chapters reflecting the essence of a fractured and dislocated like."

Cameron's first book, *Hugh MacLennan: A Writer's Life* (1981), was a model for literary biographers, scholarly but accessible, based on deep research, extensive interviews and analysis of the texts of his novels and essays. She brings the same tools — honed through a background of scholarly publishing and more recent and much-praised journalism, particularly her *Saturday Night* magazine profiles of such literary figures as Jack McClelland, Peter Newman and Timothy Findley.

Of course, no two authors like MacLennan and Layton could be more dissimilar, in personality, background and the thrust of their writings. "I tried to get the feel of each of these people," Cameron says. "They are different men. I tried to present and dramatize their lives, rather than letting them present and dramatize their lives for me. Someone said I have contempt for Layton, but that's not true. But just as MacLennan clearly has respect for the writer and himself, Layton played with fire; he indulged in great binges of guilt and remorse."

Two writers: Two solitudes? Whatever. It would be hard to write a dull account of such a personage as Layton. But can we expect the persona of the biographer herself to remain detached, steady and fixed while selecting this detail for emphasis, while ignoring or minimizing that detail? A biographer may be surprised to find, on digging into his subject's life, that he actively dislikes or disapproves of his subject. Something like this happened, for example, in Lawrence Thompson's work on Robert Frost; Joan Givner, writing about Katherine Anne Porter, described her subject's behaviour at a certain period as "a dismal record of cheating, lying, slander and malice."

Cameron, sitting at the dining-room table in her elegant midtown Toronto home, insists this was not so for her. She exudes admiration for Layton's "drive and energy, the way he picked himself up from his working-class roots in Montreal after growing up in a family in which the prime goal was making money and education was thought of as a waste of time. There's an amazing aliveness in him, and his talent is formidable. His poems are a truly remarkable achievement. Of the approximately 1,000 poems he published, roughly 15 are world-class poems that can stand with the best modern poetry in English."

That is high praise. Certainly, Layton's best poems seem to me to stamp him as a poet who is remarkable for virtuosity of expression and understanding of man's fate. His place in Canadian literature and his role in revitalizing poetry are secure. Indeed, Cameron deftly chronicles all of Layton's accomplishments, exploring the Jewish ambience of his Montreal boyhood, his struggle against anti-Semitism and the Philistines in society, the hard-won recognition of his status as a poet, his subsequent lionization and then fallout in the 1970s when he no longer held centre stage.

These details are set against the dense underbrush of Canada's evolving literary life in which Layton cut a large swath, a bull speared by invective, flourishing an emotional apparatus so overactive that it surrounded molehills of circumstance with mountains of drama. By contrast, a quiet authority — based on an analysis of the text of Layton's poems — also permeates the book.

Good biographies present us with an intelligible whole seen in the multiple mirror images of a life lived and a work achieved and the sources of that life and work. The reader, however, will learn more than he might possibly want to know about Layton's marital and other liaisons, the fury over custody of his children and the detritus of broken trusts, self-indulgences and infidelities.

Cameron's interviewees have been astonishingly frank, even indiscreet, in talking about their life with a man who, after all, is still very much alive and vulnerable, even as he is closing on his 74th birthday.

Here, for flavour, is what Aviva Layton, says about her first encounters with Layton while he was married to his second wife, Betty Sutherland: "He was inhibited sexually, puritanical, not at home in his own body. For weeks he would only touch me, fumbling foreplay stuff. He was more comfortable doing that." Why would she now want to demolish the vibrant macho myth and expose what might be a somewhat different reality? And surely, the details of Layton's first marriage with Faye Lynch ("I never loved her. She was obese — probably 350 pounds") are as depressing as they are embarrassing.

We may be hungry for intense personalities, but it doesn't necessarily follow that enjoying a writer's work predisposes a reader to learn about the nitty-gritty of his life. But perhaps it seems only fair that poets (or novelists) who write about the lives of their times and friends should be prepared to undergo a similar scrutiny.

Cameron ponders the question of propriety. "It was a problem. Some of the raw material is the kind which I've been brought up as a woman — I come from a rather puritanical background — not to talk about. But the anecdotal material is not out of line with the subject of many novels; it doesn't offend community standards. Layton's sexual and emotional turmoil gave rise to much of his poetry.

"I had all this information about his nasty falling-out with friends and lovers; it was given to me freely by people who pride themselves in their honesty. None of them said to me: 'Don't use this.' If I had omitted it, my book wouldn't have elucidated the nature of his poetry, with his experiences. If I didn't convey the hatreds and rejections of his highly emotional life, the book would have been simply an academic exercise."

Cameron, though, wears her scholarship lightly. Born in Toronto and raised in Barrie, where her father was general administrator of the Royal Victoria Hospital, she went to the University of Toronto in 1962 and then quit in disgust. "I got mad. I took a course that was called American and Canadian Literature, only to find out that it did not include Canadian authors. We were simply given a list of Canadian books to read for an optional question on the year-end exam."

She became a cultural nationalist even before the term became fashionable. "I didn't see why we had to study American and British writers exclusively; I hated the condescension toward Canadian literature."

She went on to get a B.A. in English at the University of British Columbia; an M.A. in Canadian literature at the University of New Brunswick, producing a thesis on Robertson Davies; and then a PhD at McGill, writing her doctoral thesis on Victorian fiction.

Why the Victorians? "People told me it would be a waste of time to specialize in CanLit and that I wouldn't be able to get a teaching job if I did so. The irony is that I've virtually never taught Victorian literature. Since 1970, it's been all CanLit."

Now 42 and the mother of three children, aged 15, 13 and 7, Cameron is co-ordinator of the University of Toronto's Canadian literature program based at New College. She teaches the kind of courses which I wish were taught when I was a student. One of them is on postwar Canadian women writers, another is called Intellect and Imagination in Canadian Cultural History, a kind of 'great books' course which takes in Northrop Frye, Marshall McLuhan, Donald Creighton, *The Vertical Mosaic* and Charles Taylor's *Six Journeys*.

She admits to an irrepressible curiosity about people's lives, even the man behind the costume of B.J. Birdy, the Toronto Blue Jays' baseball mascot, about whom she wrote a *Toronto Life* article last year. "My curiosity is both a good and bad thing," she says with a smile.

Together with a desire to fill a gap in CanLit studies — which abounds in books of literary criticism but is lacking in full-length biographies of important writers — curiosity is what partly impelled her to write her MacLennan biography.

"That book was a scholarly exercise, published by the University of Toronto Press. I couldn't have been more astonished at its popular success. I don't have tenure, so I felt the need to excel in academic publishing; it was part of the publish-or-perish syndrome. It was only when I got feedback, from reviews and readers, that I knew I had the talent to write." MacLennan was also bowled over by the book. He told Cameron, "It astounded me. It's meticulously accurate. I'm lost in admiration."

But the history of biographies, both authorized and unauthorized, is full of stories of panic, pressure and even libel suits. It's said that an objective biography cannot be written in the subject's lifetime. The best biographers, like Cameron herself, will accept the notion that they have not told the incontrovertible truth about their subjects and that the view they offer cannot be final, or absolutely true. That no such final truth exists is probably the fascination of biography for those who attempt it.

No one will fault the liveliness and intimacy of Cameron's portrait; it does make Layton terribly human. Layton fully co-operated with Cameron by openly talking to her in a series of interviews beginning in 1981 and the biographer had free range through his papers. But it's highly unlikely that Layton will have the same reaction as that of MacLennan. He will want the last word. "It won't bother me," Cameron says with engaging frankness.

• **1988** Critical Writing •
Reaching for the stillness
(Excerpts)

David Prosser

Kingston Whig-Standard

Plays are a way of remaking the world. This is true not just of plays with a particular social or political "message" — plays that point out specific flaws in the way we run the world and urge that they be corrected — but of all works of the dramatic imagination.

The act of writing a play springs partly from the desire to create a world that is somehow more focused, more significant — though not necessarily "better" or more pleasant — than our own. The same sort of desire informs the act of watching a play, of entering into a world dreamed up by someone else's imagination and allowing oneself to be persuaded of its reality. We hope, every time we go to the theatre, that we're going to visit a world that is sharper and clearer and more purposeful than the rather muddled and arbitrary one in which we have to live our lives. We hope that, even if the contents of this new world are mundane, we will at least be excited by the precision with which the lines are drawn, the vividness of the colours. An ordinary street scene projected by a camera obscura has a strangely captivating power: Even though we might as easily step outside and see the real thing for ourselves, it is more exciting to see the tiny people walking about silently on the screen or table before us. They are somehow crisper, brighter, more real than real; and when we go out into the sunlight again we look about us with a slightly different eye.

The better the play (and, by extension, the better the production, since a play is a play only when it is produced, otherwise it is literature) the more we want to retain in our minds the perspectives and the flavour and the texture of the world it creates — even if that world is an inhospitable one. We would all happily linger in the world Shakespeare creates in *As You Like It*, a forest where sunlight dapples the backs of deer and gilds the dimples of shepherdesses; where passionate youths pin poems on the trunks of trees; where love is tutored by wisdom and every obstacle is a prelude to understanding and reconciliation. But the world of *Macbeth* is full of blood and darkness; and that of *King Lear* is a place of blindness and insanity where men feel like flies in the hands of wanton boys. And yet good productions of those plays can be just as seductive as the Forest of Arden, not because the environment they create is pleasant but because it is so heightened that the world outside the theatre seems flat by comparison. Even a play as despairing as *Waiting for Godot* — a play that posits terminal boredom and abandonment as the essence of the human condition — must, in a successful production, somehow make its universe one that we want to experience.

There are many ways of trying to achieve the clarity that makes us want to linger, as the productions that opened earlier this month at the 1988 Stratford Festival demonstrate. You can make the physical trappings of the performance as convincing, or at least as attractive, as possible. You can have beautiful ball gowns and chandeliers and jewels and leather armchairs and oak bookcases; and for people in search of a certain kind of experience (the kind of experience offered by the musical *My Fair Lady*, for instance) that will do the trick. At the other end of the scale, you can dispense with physical trappings altogether, on the theory that they merely blur a picture that should be painted with words alone.

The eight shows now playing in repertory at the Stratford Festival reveal, within certain predictable limits, a wide variety of styles and approaches. But one thing does emerge. Whatever vision it attempts to embody, the stuff of theatre is finally a question of people speaking words. The stage may be bare as a plank or laden with all the opulence of Cleopatra's barge; it makes little difference. What you're left with are words.

It is impossible to define exactly what it is that makes the performances of, say, Nicholas Pennell as Thomas Becket or William Hutt as King Lear shine with a hard-edged light, except to say that part of it is that the words are spoken with unusual intelligence and unusual belief. If there is intensity in those performances, it is intensity that arises from inside, without the application of external force in the form of shouting or ranting or sawing the air too much with your hand, thus. Something as small as the emphasis of a single word in a phrase or the rise of an inflection can make all the difference between opacity and thrilling, lens-like transparence.

It is, too, an intensity that arises from the actor's scrutiny not just of the desired emotions of the moment, but of the whole pattern of the play, the whole tragic or comic arc beyond the moment. To commandeer some lines by T.S. Eliot, "Only by the form, the pattern, / Can words or music reach / The stillness." It is when we feel that sense of stillness at the heart of motion, when we feel that somehow an individual performance is in tune with the whole, unmoving pattern of a play, that we are experiencing the art of acting being practised at its height.

■ ■ ■

Shakespeare's *Richard III* is a play with a monster at its heart: A monster so wholly, so theatrically evil that he has worked his way into the tiny repertoire of universally recognizable impressions. Just as no party reveller has to do more than stand on one leg and say, "Arrr, Jim lad," to summon up the shade of Robert Newton as Long John Silver, just as all that is required to produce Jimmy Cagney is to bare the teeth, hold the forearms rigidly out from the body and utter the magic words "You — dirty — rat," so one need only raise one shoulder higher than the other and declaim, with swooping inflections, "Nowoo iss the wintah of owwer discontenttt," to be the very incarnation of Laurence Olivier's Richard.

Olivier's has stood for many years as the definitive Richard; the most recent contender for that honour has been the South African-born actor Antony Sher, who gives, in his book *Year of the King*, a uniquely compelling account of his preparation for the role as a member of Royal Shakespeare Company. Sher, modelling his Richard on a phrase used by Queen Margaret in Act I, scene iii: "that bottled spider / Whose deadly web ensnareth thee about," used specially-designed steel crutches that enabled him in effect to play the role on all fours.

Faced with two such memorable precursors, Colm Feore, star of Brian Rintoul's production of *Richard III* at the Festival Theatre, treads the path of least possible grotesqueness. The dark and angularly good-looking Feore, Stratford's current specialist in villains, did a commendable Romeo early in his career with the company but first captured critical attention for his remarkable interpretation of Iachimo in the 1986 production of *Cymbeline*. An actor of impressive technical skills (he's one of the few members of the company who is always clearly audible, whichever direction he's facing), he commands the vault of the Festival Theatre. The stage is bare of setting: The only physical evidence of regal pomp is a golden emblem in the shape of a blazing sun — the "sun of York" to which Feore alludes with the merest tilt of the head in his opening speech.

The physical deformities he affects are the minimum required by the text: One arm hanging useless by his side, its fingers curled around his sword's scabbard, the merest of humps on the back, one leg permanently bent at the knee. And when he speaks, his voice is lightly ironic, almost cheerful: The tones of a perfectly reasonable man. Feore does not hiss or leer; his Richard simply reasons out his situation and comes to conclusions that seem monstrous to us but only coldly logical to him. In fact, there is a lack of apparent emotional motivation to this Richard that is in many ways more alarming than any amount of deeply buried neurosis. His choice of evil is something like an existential act: I'm not really suited to be a lover, so I might as well be a monster. Yes, why don't I try that?

Even in the scene when one of the young princes, crying, "Uncle, my brother mocks both you and me. / Because that I am little, like an ape, / He thinks that you should bear me on your shoulders," leaps up on Richard's crooked back and clings to his neck, causing the whole court to cringe with alarm, Feore does not let Richard lose control. There is a moment, certainly, when he freezes and we imagine that he might seize the wretched child and dash its brains out on the floor, but it is not a moment when madness shows itself. Rather we see cold calculation: Shall I pitch this brat to the floor now or deal with it later in the Tower? Later, I think. When he does fling the child from his back, it is as casually as one might flatten a blackfly.

This kind of Richard is certainly a more real creation than one who is self-consciously monstrous. But it does pose certain problems for the rest of the production. Monstrousness has its own charisma, the quality that presumably attracted Eva Braun to Adolph Hitler. Feore's interpretation necessarily sacrifices much of that charisma, leaving it up to the rest of the cast to make us see the bottled spider through their eyes only. Not all of them are up to the task. The more Feore tries to normalize his Richard, the more those around him seem compelled to resort to melodrama.

There is, for instance, the notoriously difficult scene near the beginning of the play where Richard encounters Lady Anne, whose husband, Prince Edward, and father-in-law, King Henry, he has murdered. The scene begins with Anne spitting, both figuratively and literally, on Richard — "Never hung poison on a fouler toad" — and ends with her agreeing to become his wife. Clearly the only way this scene can work is if Lady Anne is sexually hypnotized by Richard from the start. If Richard is not thrillingly, compellingly evil — as Feore, for the good reasons cited above, is not — then it is up to the actress playing Lady Anne to somehow let us see that irresistibly monstrous Richard through her eyes.

Lucy Peacock doesn't manage to pull this off. When Richard gives Anne his sword, lays bare his breast and invites her, if she really detests him so much, to put an end to him, here is what happens. "Nay, do not pause," says Feore, "for I did kill King Henry." Peacock gasps, opens her eyes wide and raises the sword above her head with both hands to plunge it in. "But 'twas thy beauty that provoked me," hastily interposes Feore, whereupon Peacock pauses and brings the sword slowly down. "Nay now, dispatch," urges Feore, "'twas I that stabbed young Edward." Again the gasp, again the eyes, and again the lifting of the sword. "But 'twas thy heavenly face that set me on." Again the sword wavers and falls.

All this business of feinting with the sword is simply too literal to ring true. It's attempting to signal to the audience the emotions affecting Lady Anne (yes-I'll-kill-him, no-I-won't) instead of just letting them happen. In the end we believe neither her anger nor her attraction: They are as stagey as the coarse-acting crowd noises emitted by the production's hapless spear-carriers.

Susan Wright, always a powerful performer, is properly horrifying as the slightly crazed old Queen Margaret, who flits in and out of the play, Cassandra-like, to hurl insults at Richard. The curse she lays on him at the beginning is truly hair-raising (Wright is second to none in her vituperative skills), but her strength is undermined by the costume designer's decision to dress her in some sort of sacking that seems to emit clouds of dust when she moves, thus reducing her to a kind of regal bag lady.

Among Richard's antagonists, it is only Goldie Semple as Queen Elizabeth who pulls off the feat of making us see the bottled spider. When she looks at Richard it is with the sort of unhysterical horror that comes with full knowledge of just how deadly, just how loathsome, this particular creature is, and with that knowledge comes the victim's fascination for the predator.

There are other exciting details to the production: For his coronation, Richard wears an immensely long scarlet and ermine cloak. When he mounts the throne and his attendants spread the train around him in a huge swirl, the result is a dramatic transformation. With the shrivelled arm and crooked leg concealed, Richard suddenly becomes a towering giant. It is when the physical manifestations of monstrousness are concealed that the monster is most clearly visible.

And if you're a connoisseur of stage fighting, you can't fail to be impressed by the final slug-it-out-to-the-end conflict between Richard and the Earl of Richmond (Geraint Wyn Davies). For this the actors wear real metal armor rather than the fibreglass imitation kind, enabling them to land some bone shatteringly heavy blows on each other with their genuinely lethal weapons. Their fight can't be much less dangerous than it looks, and we watch it with our hearts in our mouths.

One other performance stands out, that of Scott Wentworth as the murderer Tyrrel. It's a small part, but what Wentworth does with it is illuminating. He manages, in the space of a few short speeches, to suggest a multiplicity of levels that makes the rest of the production seem one-dimensional. *Richard III* runs at the Festival Theatre until Oct. 28; on two occasions, Sept. 25 and 27, Wentworth and Feore will exchange roles. It is worth a trip to Stratford to see Feore's Richard; it will be equally so to see Wentworth's.

■ ■ ■

It is, however, in Robin Phillips's Young Company production of *King Lear* that this year's Stratford Festival touches greatness. Lear is generally regarded as Shakespeare's greatest play, and it can be one of his most treacherous. There are elements of Phillips's production that don't quite convince us, and elements — such as the use of masks, and the Edwardian costumes — that we sometimes feel are there not because they spring from a particular vision of the play but just because Phillips happens to be fond of them. But if there are moments that fail to persuade, there is at the centre of the production an awesomely convincing performance by Stratford veteran William Hutt: A performance that simply overshadows anything else in the festival.

Here is a play in which the central metaphor is a storm, a play in which madmen rant and howl and the world seems about to crack. And yet here is a production where the most telling sounds are the chirp of crickets, the pulse of distant drumbeats, and a faint, barely perceptible sustained note that keens through many of the scenes like a stretched nerve. The storm has a literal, physical reality, as the sodden clothes worn by Lear and the Fool remind us, but by far the more terrible part of its force lies silent within, where we hear it only as a shuddering sigh or a shadow of pain across the eyes. To create such a storm, to make it visible and audible while all the time the crickets drowse in the background, is a feat requiring the highest order of control and precision. It requires an actor who can focus words to white heat as effortlessly and as precisely as a lens can focus sunlight to a flame just by being there. William Hutt can suggest rage so great that it can sear away a man's wits, and he can do this while scarcely raising his voice.

Again we have the bare neutral pine stage, this time with a chair and a couple of pillars. Again the performances are equally uncluttered, clear and free of emotional "pointers." In fact, the most remarkable thing about this production is how consistently it seduces us into seeing the plausibility of the evil characters' points of view. There is, for instance, no trace of hypocrisy in the speeches of Goneril (Marion Adler) and Regan (Susan Coyne) during the division of Lear's kingdom: They are, after all, only doing what is expected of them, uttering the proper politely turned phrases in what all the characters on stage understand is a ritual. Indeed, when it comes to Cordelia's turn to make her professions of love for her father, and we observe the stubborn blankness on Melanie Miller's face as she utters that fatal "Nothing," we feel almost irked that she should be so pedantic as to upset the pleasant ceremony. Doesn't she realize it's only words? And later, when Lear, denied shelter by both daughters, vows revenge, the daughters exchange glances, not of collusion or of alarm or of smirking delight in their own wickedness, but of the sort of pain one feels when a relative becomes senile and starts doing embarrassing things in public. Goneril and Regan are not, in other words, conscious villains: They are simply the much put-upon heroines of their own tragedies.

John Ormerod plays the Fool in the costume of a cleric and brings to his handling of the lines a certain ascetic priggishness. In doing so he has to give up some of the Fool's usual laughs, but something is gained too — a clearer sense of the Fool as moral corrective and spiritual comforter. Peter Donaldson is a solid Kent and Stuart Hughes gives us one of the most thoroughly hateful Edmunds imaginable.

But Albert Schultz's performance as Edgar seems fractured into a number of pieces that don't fit together. When he first appears, he is a bespectacled wimp who plays the cello. This isn't in itself a bad idea — his effeteness makes sense as a contributing factor to the more manly Edmund's hatred of him — but as soon as he flees into the storm and poses as Poor Tom, the cellist disappears to be replaced by another version of Feste. (There is even a hint of a limp.) When he returns to challenge Edmund, he has somehow become a Real Man out there on the heath: He now knows how to handle a weapon. It's a difficult role, but Schultz hasn't really managed to integrate it.

And integration is the key to the sort of triumph that William Hutt achieves here. As Nicholas Pennell does in *Murder In The Cathedral*, Hutt here achieves that powered repose that comes from being in touch with the whole pattern, which is stillness, rather than just the detail, which is motion. Consider his masterly reading of the lines. Consider, for instance, how, in the "reason not the need" speech he handles these lines: "No, you unnatural hags, / I will have such revenges on you both / That all the world shall — I will do such things, / What they are yet I know not, but they shall be the terrors of the earth."

The broken sentences suggest that Lear is so beside himself with rage that he cannot find the words, or that he becomes so physically choked with rage that he can't get the words out. Hutt does neither of these things; instead he delivers the lines in absolutely level tones, scornfully discarding the sentence he has begun because the depth of his anger and grief goes beyond something as feeble as words. Because he can convey to us at every instant of the tragedy its entire arc, its entire pattern, he does not have to waste energy in signalling its details. The storm is always there, the madness does not come from nowhere but lies waiting even at the very beginning of the play. All Hutt has to do is let it come.

What he does do in every moment of the play, with Phillips's help, is to keep the pattern in view. In even the early scenes of the play, Lear's mind runs on madness, as if it were a fear that had haunted him all his life. Phillips reinforces this idea with a brilliantly original bit of staging. Lear, having been rejected by Goneril, announces his intention of travelling to Regan's home. "Be my horses ready?" he calls. This is normally a straightforward enough question. But the scene, as Phillips has staged it, is played in Lear's carriage, which, we can tell from the sound of horses' hooves, is already moving. Lear's question thus draws a long, stricken look from the Fool and a gently humouring change of subject. When Lear goes on to cry, "O! Let me not be mad, not mad, sweet heaven," we see with chilling clarity that it is already too late.

King Lear is a painful play, one of the most painful ever written. To experience it in the theatre is to enter a world of pain beyond endurance, of grief that can stop a heart. And yet when this most wrenching of all worlds is wrought with such consummate artistry as it is here, when the bleak, stony landscape of tragedy is delineated in such perfect line, such exquisitely fine shading as it is here, it becomes a place in which one willingly remains, because it is so full of Wordsworth's "still, sad music of humanity."

● **1989** Critical Writing ●
Differences in CBC and CTV newscasts not always subtle

John Haslett Cuff

Globe and Mail

Whether you watch *The National* on CBC television each night at 10 or go to bed after catching the CTV *National News* at 11 may simply depend on your personal timetable, or your preference in anchors — either Peter Mansbridge (CBC) or Lloyd Robertson. Canadian viewers are perhaps uniquely fortunate in having two national newscasts available at different times. In the United States, viewers have to zap back and forth and watch partial national newscasts at 6:30 each evening or simply choose one of the three equally competent and credible anchors from ABC (Peter Jennings), CBS (Dan Rather) or NBC (Tom Brokaw).

The two Canadian newscasts also differ in length at 22 minutes (CBC) and 29 minutes, including commercials (CTV), respectively, but only the private network newscast is interrupted by commercials — about five minutes worth. But other than telecast times and personalities, what differentiates these two newscasts?

According to CTV News vice-president Tim Kotcheff, "Our newscast is a lot punchier and to the point ... I think we're operating with a lot less ... If it takes 10 CBC reporters to change a lightbulb, we use five. I think there are inefficiencies there."

A CTV spokesman said the network has four foreign bureaus with a total of five reporters and plans for an additional bureau to open in Moscow next fall. CTV also has about 15 reporters in seven different domestic bureaus and has announced the imminent opening of another bureau in St. John's, Nfld., to be run by Leslie Jones, recently hired from Global TV.

CBC's *The National* has about 30 reporters, including at least six foreign correspondents. Like the private network, the CBC maintains bureaus in Washington, London, Beijing and Jerusalem, and it already has Moscow covered. On the home front, it covers the same cities as CTV, but completely outguns them in Ottawa where it has double the contingent of reporters (eight).

David Bazay, executive producer of *The National,* claims "there is a significant difference in the quality of our writing and reporting. I would say the CBC reporting — person for person — is better, more thoughtful ... Our political coverage is clearly superior. Our Ottawa bureau has broken many, many more stories than theirs has."

Most observers agree that CTV's national news has improved steadily over the past few years and its expansion last September, from 17 minutes to its current length of 24 actual news minutes, has helped. "Lloyd Robertson is excellent and the journalists at CTV are competent, skilled professionals, but there isn't much that startles me ... It tends to be a formula newscast, a little flat," said Peter Desbarats, a veteran broadcast journalist who is also head of the journalism program at the University of Western Ontario.

The National consistently gets higher ratings in the earlier time slot, pulling in an average of 1.5 million viewers each weeknight from September, 1988, to May of this year. During the same period, the CTV *National News* drew about 1.2 million, but claimed a larger percentage of viewers — 32 per cent — than the CBC's 19 per cent, according to a CTV spokesman.

In 1985, Desbarats helped compile research for the Caplan-Sauvageau Report of the Task Force on Broadcasting Policy, comparing radio and television news in the public and private sector. The study involved some 70 different interviews with broadcasters throughout the country and included content analysis of both CBC, private network and local news in English and French.

"The results indicated little discernible difference between CBC and CTV network news in English ... At the network level, the differences between CTV and CBC lay mainly in the fact that CTV carried commercials ... CBC carried more stories than CTV of a hard, spot-news character and CBC carried more of both short items and those more than two minutes, while CTV had scheduled more stories in the mid range," according to the report.

As well, Desbarats said, the research indicated that "the more thoughtful, more socially aware journalists tended to gravitate toward the CBC ... News was considered an important part of the CBC mandate ... In the private sector, the journalists always felt a little uncertain about the owners' commitment to news."

The differences in the daily newscasts are not often dramatic, but the CBC's obvious advantage in resources and commitment becomes apparent on exceptional news days such as last Sunday when the regular *Sunday Report* (with Peter Mansbridge) was expanded to a full hour to deal with an astonishing roster of events. These included: The massacre of students in Beijing, a terrible gas explosion in the Soviet Union, the Solidarity upset in the Polish elections, and the death of the Ayatollah Khomaini. The CBC news crews rose to the occasion with great resourcefulness and it was a classic example of how exciting and informative breaking television news can be.

In contrast, a slow news day such as Wednesday, June 7, can be equally revealing of a network's news-gathering abilities. A rough count indicates the CBC gave viewers about 10 minutes of news related to what they called "The Crisis in China" and the newscast included about 11 different reports, plus a promotion for *The Journal.*

CTV gave viewers nearly 11 minutes of "Turmoil in China" and a total of about 15 stories in the course of the show. Both had almost identical stories on the murder of a two-year-old boy in Ottawa — and both had "silly" stories to leaven the line-up: CTV on a man in Edmonton who paid more than $2,000 in taxes with Loonies and CBC with a Winnipeg story about a city councillor objecting to the city's cordial welcome of a Chinese mayor and two pandas.

Most obviously missing from the CBC newscast was a story from the Montreal conference on AIDS, but the CTV lead was a "no news" story about the fact that an AIDS cure is still a long way off. The CBC had a longish story from Saskatchewan about a proposed mining development pitting the usual parties against one another with the natives caught somewhere in the middle. It could have run anywhere, anytime. Both had at least one report from a U.S. network. On CBC, it was a harrowing tale of a young boy who accidentally shot his sister; on CTV, another China story. Neither newscast emerged as clearly superior, but there were some startling differences in their lead-off China stories.

Lloyd Robertson came quickly to the point before introducing correspondent Jim Munson and his report from Beijing: "Good evening. Another day of violence and bloodshed as the crisis continues in China and foreigners are scrambling to get out. In Beijing today, soldiers open fire in the streets as they move to new positions, sometimes firing at random — at other times, shooting into crowds and a foreign housing complex. Jim Munson has the story."

Munson's report begins with a voice-over about troop movements and there are pictures of troops marching out of the city square. "As they headed out chanting slogans — 'the people's army loves the people' — they fired into the air" (here is a shot of what seems to be a truck full of soldiers passing a tank that has the number 103 on its turret). "Suddenly a number of soldiers lowered their guns and shot directly into a group of people," (here the soldiers can be seen lowering their guns and firing, but their targets are not in the picture), "citizens taunting the troops (here we see a shot of a sidewalk on which some people are sprawled, some standing, it's hard to tell what's going on). "Once again, death (here's a shot of a bicycle speeding along, pulling a cart which seems to have bodies on it; there are three young people running along side) in Beijing. Seven were killed."

Meanwhile, on the CBC broadcast, there are some of these same shots, but no mention of seven people being killed. Reporter Tom Kennedy's story begins with a description of the "soldiers fanning out" from the square and "moving cautiously and with full battle gear. People scattered, but some not quickly enough," (here is the same shot of the bicycle cart and runners). Kennedy continues, "There were some very tense moments outside a foreign compound (aerial shots of a boulevard) residence for diplomats and journalists ... suddenly there were gunshots" (we hear firing and see the shot of the truck full of soldiers passing tank #103). "The few foreigners left in the compound dove for cover (shot of Oriental-looking folks flattened on pavement, ducking behind planters). "Later, the army said it had been firing at a sniper."

Both reports concur on the army's attack on the compound for foreigners, but they are quite different in their account of the preceding actions, while using several of the same pictures, with completely different voice-overs. CTV has the soldiers killing people in the street on the way to the compound while the CBC has the soldiers going from the square to shooting up the compound in virtually the same length of time.

• **1990** Columns •

Learning vital lessons from inflating frogs

Richard Wagamese

Calgary Herald

W e inflated frogs.
　　We were boys. Young and reckless and full of the joys of unrestrained energies shared by boys the world over. Indian boys. Our world at that time was the rough and tangle of the northern Ontario bush.

It was ours. Every day in climbing, creeping, running and walking through it we became as familiar with its motions and stillnesses as we were with our own unencumbered spirits. It was our playground, our chapel and to a certain degree our teacher.

But we inflated frogs.

We'd head out in droves every springtime. The rivers would be alive with swarms of pickerel on their spawning runs. Simply catching the largest fish of the season was enough to elevate a boy right up into the very stuff of legend. Competition was fierce.

We'd insert a milkshake straw into an appropriate orifice and inflate the frog. Someone had discovered that an adequately inflated frog would thrash wildly along the surface of the water. The pickerel, of course, would go crazy. We could locate the holes where the big fish lay by the chum and gulp of water as the frog disappeared.

Back then I didn't know.

I didn't know that the frog's life, as with all life, was sacred. I didn't know that because of this it should be respected. I didn't know the vital difference between ingenuity and disregard, just as I didn't know that what I was doing was wrong.

Because I had no one to teach me and I did not understand.

The progression of my life found me on the streets at 17. After a decade and a half within the relative security of the foster-care system, I was woefully unprepared.

Suddenly I was seen as just another lazy, shiftless, dirty Indian. No one had told me that these attitudes existed. No one had told me that in the eyes of many I would be pre-judged, pre-destined and pre-labelled.

I reacted badly. Soon enough I found myself in the company of other young Indians. They were angry. They were filled with resentment and hatred for 400 years of abuse and betrayal.

And so I learned anger along with politics. I learned to glare into the face of white society and overtly demand rights I barely understood.

Back then I didn't know.

I didn't know that history can't be changed. I didn't know that anger is an all-consuming thing. I didn't know that balance and harmony with all things is the Indian way. Most of all, I didn't know that the creed of the warrior included compassion, respect, honour and kindness, just as I didn't know that warriors were allowed to cry.

Because I had no one to teach me and I did not understand.

The years have changed me. When I began to sit with the elders of my people and listen to the ancient teachings and values, I began to learn to see. I began to see that this circle of people of which I was a part were much more than the images I'd had presented to me all my life. I began to see the people. I began to learn.

Many people come to me in the course of my daily travels and ask me certain things. One of the most common concerns are the reasons Canada's native peoples are always making such a fuss.

To the untrained eye it might seem that things are reasonably OK out there in Indian country. To those same untrained eyes it might seem that all this political hullabaloo is bothersome and unnecessary.

Because they had no one to teach them and they do not understand.

The answer quite simply is this: In every Indian community, on every reserve, the elders who possess that old, traditional knowledge are dying.

It's this knowledge that Indian people are fighting to preserve. At the bottom of every political confrontation, litigation and news release lies the overriding concern for the preservation of that cultural way.

Because those cultural values and spiritual ways have been what has enabled the Indians to survive the enormous changes they've endured in so short a time.

And it's what will enable them to survive in the future.

Over the course of the next few weeks this column will focus on some of those old, traditional ways. Because in order for one to really begin to see, someone needs to tell you where to look.

It's important, vitally important, that these old ways and teachings be continued. They are what define and sustain us as Indian people. Because the saddest image I carry in my mind is that of the last surviving Indian being asked why it is that he or she has no knowledge of the people and where they came from. And the response:

Because I had no one to teach me and I did not understand.

• **1998** Critical Writing •

Fruit for thought

Doug Saunders

Globe and Mail

Take a close look at your banana. It has a couple things to tell you about television.

Or, rather, a U.S. network is using your banana to tell you a thing or two — not just about television, but about the ever-changing world of advertising. Across North America, 22 million bananas, 4.4 million of them in Canada, have been affixed with little yellow labels bearing the ABC network logo, sporting such clever slogans as "TV. Zero Calories" and "Another Fine Use of Yellow" (referring to ABC's official corporate colour, in case you didn't know).

These tiny billboards, about one centimetre by two centimetres, may have passed a new threshold for brevity in advertising. Then again, this may be one of those thresholds, like the Canadian dollar's latest low, that will be endlessly surpassed.

We seem to be in the midst of a micro-ad revolution. This summer has seen the debut of the one-second TV commercial, packing an entire promotional message into a tick of the clock. The Milwaukee-based padlock maker Master Lock discovered that it could fit its pitch — specifically, a bullet penetrating one of its locks, which remains firmly closed — into one-thirtieth the space of a conventional ad. For the cost of 10, 30-second ads, Master Lock gives us 300, one-second ads over the same period, our sanity be damned.

Though the mini-commercials have so far only been picked up by obscure cable stations and a handful of local broadcasters in the U.S., they are gaining popularity among advertisers. James Shapiro, a Rochester, N.Y., personal-injury lawyer, has used the medium in a particularly obnoxious way: His phone number flashes on the screen while he yells brief, loud slogans such as "Pain!" He calls these "intrusive rantings," and it is probably a blessing that they last only a second.

Even the one-second threshold is about to be broken. Earlier this month, an Israeli inventor patented a device that allows "informational messages" to be inserted into the tiny flashes of empty air time that occur while you're switching channels. As you flip across the dial, you will be hit with tiny commercials lasting a fraction of a second, thus providing either a barrage of slogans or a great incentive to keep watching that old movie.

But nowhere has the brevity barrier been more alarmingly breached than in the case of the banana, that low-technology device that has heretofore been used mainly as a source of potassium and pratfalls. For the people who discovered how to put ads on the fruit, this is a great boon to humanity.

"It is increasingly more difficult to impact consumers, and the banana labels are a very novel medium to cut through the clutter," Brian Fox, president of the Santa Monica, Calif.,-based Fruit Label Company, told reporters in August. His boss, CEO Irv Weinhaus, was even more enthusiastic: "The response we have received to date from potential users of this fun new medium is amazing," he told the Business Wire news service. "Our phones have not stopped ringing."

There are two things to be gleaned from this. First, these are people who, with a straight face, can describe a banana as a "new medium." But more to the point is the astonishing fact that something calling itself the Fruit Label Company can be a successful advertising firm. They are already pasting video-rental ads on apples, and the lineup is growing for banana-sized pitches. All of a sudden, there are all sorts of things that people want to say on a banana.

Some people might find this alarming. What has happened to the sanctity of the yellow fruit? Does the debasement of breakfast know no bounds? Is nothing sacred?

But contrary to what Fox and Weinhaus seem to think, the banana is not some exciting new vehicle of communication that has just been discovered by the corporate world. Bananas have rarely been silent. For decades, they have carried such important, succinct messages as "Dole" and "Chiquita," and occasionally more useful data such as "Sale 49 cents."

No, the story here is not about the encroachment of advertising on previously virgin terrain. That story has been told — toilet stalls, turnstile arms and church pews are among the latest venues for ads — and it is largely misleading.

If you've ever seen a photo of a downtown street in a major city of the 1870s, with slogans and brand names plastered on everything in sight, it quickly becomes apparent that advertising has always abhorred an empty surface. Compared to the ad-addled Victorians, we may still have some catching up to do.

What is new is not the ability to place an ad on a banana, but the fact that there are now things that can be said on an ad on a banana. To deliver a comprehensible sales pitch on a tiny sticker — or on a one-second slice of air time — requires a very special kind of mutual understanding between consumer and producer, a very high level of literacy. Until recently, that sort of bond didn't exist.

In order to sell a bottle of Coca-Cola in the early years of this century, for example, it was necessary to tell consumers this: "Coca-Cola Revives and Sustains." By 1945, the word-count had begun to drop: "Coke Means Coca-Cola." The brevity barrier was demolished again and again: in 1970 with "It's the Real Thing"; in 1976 with "Coke Adds Life"; and in 1982 with the Zen-like "Coke is It." Nowadays, even that sounds prolix. Today it is necessary only to affix the word Coke, or even just the familiar red-and-white wave, onto some other product, such as a burger wrapper (but not a banana).

In the 1950s, if you wanted to sell a pair of running shoes, it was necessary to buy a full minute of TV air time and fill it with an extended sales pitch, probably culminating in a display of super-human feats performed while shod. By the end of the 1960s, the 30-second ad was the industry norm; in the 1980s, 15-second ads became available. But the shoe industry has long since surpassed that barrier: Nike discovered in the early 1990s that its ads didn't need to contain any verbal or textual information at all, not even the word Nike. The company's "swoosh" logo alone was enough to sell gazillions of expensive shoes. The shoe, it seems, is ready to meet the banana.

The results are sure to be slippery. Does this mean the end of human communication as we know it, as we slide from complete sentences and paragraphs to shorter and shorter phrases and slogans, individual words, shapes and colours, and then eventually to a vocabulary of grunts and squawks? Or does it mean that language is evolving and improving, that we no longer need a torrent of words to get an idea across, that we can communicate through a poetic play of hint and allusion? Sentences in novels and newspapers have become shorter over the years, as have TV sound bites. This may mark the end of literacy, or it may portend a higher, more intelligent and efficient form of literacy.

This is sure to be an important debate in coming years, even if it's conducted in a series of staccato utterances on tiny scraps of paper and videotape. In the meantime, stay tuned to your banana.

About the Authors

Les Auteurs

Kathy English

Kathy English fell in love with newspapers in 1976 when she began working as a copygirl at her hometown newspaper, the *Brantford Expositor*. She has held reporting and writing jobs at the *London Free Press*, the *Hamilton Spectator*, the *Toronto Sun* and the *Toronto Star*, where she was a Sunday feature writer. In 1989, she left the *Star* to teach newspaper journalism at Ryerson School of Journalism. Since then, she has completed an M.A. in History, focussing on Canadian newspaper history. She dedicates her work in this anthology to the many editors along the way who taught her and shared their passion for the miracle of the daily paper.

■ ■ ■

C'est en 1976 que débutait l'histoire d'amour entre Kathy English et le journalisme, lorsqu'elle commença à travailler au *Brantford Expositor* à titre de commis aux textes. Elle a, depuis, occupé des postes de reporter et de journaliste pour le *London Free Press*, le *Spectator* (Hamilton), le *Toronto Sun* et le *Toronto Star* ou elle était journaliste aux grands reportages du dimanche. Elle a quitté le *Star* en 1989 pour enseigner le journalisme écrit à l'institut Ryerson. Elle a, depuis lors, obtenu une maîtrise en histoire centrée sur l'histoire des journaux canadiens. Elle dédie le travail qu'elle a accompli dans le cadre de cette anthologie aux nombreux rédacteurs de qui elle a beaucoup appris et qui ont partagé avec elle leur passion du journalisme au quotidien.

Nick Russell

Nick Russell has spent 40 years as a journalist and journalism teacher, ranging from the *Wimbledon Borough News* and Canadian Press to CFCF-TV and Vancouver Community College-Langara. Along the way, he has earned a British certificate in journalism, a BA in English from McGill, a Master's in Medieval English from the University of London, and a PhD in journalism ethics from the University of Wales. In 1998 he took early retirement from the School of Journalism at the University of Regina, and is now living, writing and teaching in Victoria, B.C. He's also consulting and giving editing and ethics workshops from coast to coast. For fun he restores old furniture and drives a 1970 Triumph 500cc motorbike.

■ ■ ■

Nicholas Russell a passé 40 années comme journaliste et professeur de journalisme. Sa carrière a touché divers secteurs, du Wimbledon *Borough News* à *la Presse* canadienne en passant par CFCF-TV et le collège Langara de Vancouver. Durant ces années, il a accumulé un certificat britannique en journalisme, un baccalauréat en langue anglaise de l'université McGill, une maîtrise en anglais médiéval de l'université de London et un doctorat en éthique journalistique de l'université du Pays de Galles. Il a pris une retraite anticipée de l'école de journalisme de l'université de Regina en 1988, et il vit maintenant à Victoria, en Colombie-Britannique, où il écrit et enseigne. Il agit aussi comme conseiller et présente des ateliers sur l'édition et l'étique journalistique d'un bout à l'autre du pays. Dans ses temps libres, il rénove des meubles antiques et conduit une vieille moto de type Triumph 500cc édition 1970.

Something like this comes around only twice in a lifetime.

Tories wanted. **W**ho?

Roy Peterson

Vancouver Sun

The versatile Roy Peterson is right on the mark with his Joe Clark and the Beetle making big comebacks after years out of the spotlight. A seventh NNA for Peterson, setting a new standard for Canadian cartoonists.

Le talentueux Roy Peterson frappe encore juste avec Joe Clark et la Beetle qui reviennent sous les feux des projecteurs après des années d'obscurité. Cette caricature a permis à Roy Peterson d'aller chercher son septième prix du CCJ en carrière, un nouveau record pour un caricaturiste canadien.

For the Record

Pour la Postérité

National Newspaper Award Winners
Histoire des gagnants et gagnantes

Editorial Writing ● Éditorial

1949 Edgar A. Collard
Montreal Gazette

1950 Edgar A. Collard
Montreal Gazette

1951 Gérard Filion
Le Devoir, Montréal

1952 Bruce Hutchison
Victoria Times

1953 Thomas E. Nichols
Hamilton Spectator

1954 Charles R. Pyper
Toronto Telegram

1955 C. Mort Fellman
North Bay Nugget

1956 André Laurendeau
Le Devoir, Montréal

1957 Bruce Hutchison
Victoria Times

1958 Gérard Filion
Le Devoir, Montréal

1959 Edgar A. Collard
Montreal Gazette

1960 Gérard Filion
Le Devoir, Montréal

1961 Lubor Zink
Brandon Sun

1962 André Laurendeau
Le Devoir, Montréal

1963 Anthony Westell
Globe and Mail

1964 Claude Ryan
Le Devoir
Montréal

1965 Eric Wells
Winnipeg Tribune

1966 Ralph Hancox
Peterborough
Examiner

1967 William Gold
Hamilton Spectator

1968 Edgar A. Collard
Montreal Gazette

1969 Martin Dewey
Toronto Star

1970 Jacke Wolfe
New Westminster
Columbian

1971 Cameron M. Smith
Globe and Mail

1972 Peter Worthington
Toronto Sun

1973 Gilles Boyer
Le Soleil, Québec

1974 Pierce Fenhagen
Montreal Gazette

1975 John W. Grace
Ottawa Journal

1976 Cameron M. Smith
Globe and Mail

1977 David Ablett
Vancouver Sun

1978 John Grace
Ottawa Journal

1979 Oakland Ross
Globe and Mail

1980 George Radwanski
Toronto Star

1981 George Radwanski
Toronto Star

1982 Joan Fraser
Montreal Gazette

1983 Terry Moore
Winnipeg Free Press

1984 John Dafoe
Winnipeg Free Press

1985 John Dafoe
Winnipeg Free Press

1986 William Thorsell
Globe and Mail

1987 Raymond Giroux
Le Soleil, Québec

1988 Norman Webster
Globe and Mail

1989 Harvey Schachter
Kingston
Whig-Standard

1990 David Prosser
Kingston
Whig-Standard

1991	Joan Fraser	1994	Linda Goyette	1997	Carol Goar
	Montreal Gazette		*Edmonton Journal*		*Toronto Star*
1992	Andrew Coyne	1995	Andrew Cohen	1998	Murdoch Davis
	Globe and Mail		*Globe and Mail*		*Edmonton Journal*
1993	Andrew Coyne	1996	Andrew Cohen		
	Globe and Mail		*Globe and Mail*		

Critical Writing ● Critique

1972	David Billington	1982	Peter Goddard	1991	Rick Groen
	Montreal Gazette		*Toronto Star*		*Globe and Mail*
1973	David Billington	1983	John Bentley Mays	1992	Val Ross
	Montreal Gazette		*Globe and Mail*		*Globe and Mail*
1974	John Fraser	1984	Jay Scott	1993	Lloyd Dykk
	Globe and Mail		*Globe and Mail*		*Vancouver Sun*
1975	Scott Beaven	1985	Ken Adachi	1994	Heather Mallick
	Calgary Albertan		*Toronto Star*		*Toronto Sun*
1976	John Fraser	1986	Ray Conlogue	1995	Mark Abley
	Globe and Mail		*Globe and Mail*		*Montreal Gazette*
1977	William French	1987	David Prosser	1996	Antonia Zerbisias
	Globe and Mail		*Kingston*		*Toronto Star*
1978	William French		*Whig-Standard*	1997	David Macfarlane
	Globe and Mail	1988	David Prosser		*Globe and Mail*
1979	John Hofsess		*Kingston*	1998	Doug Saunders
	Calgary Albertan		*Whig-Standard*		*Globe and Mail*
1980	William Littler	1989	John Haslett Cuff		
	Toronto Star		*Globe and Mail*		
1981	Jay Scott	1990	John Haslett Cuff		
	Globe and Mail		*Globe and Mail*		

Spot News Reporting ● Nouvelle d'actualité

1949	Edmond Chassé	1955	Richard Snell	1961	Charles King
	Le Canada		*Calgary Herald*		Southam News
	Montréal	1956	Bruce Larsen		Services
1950	Ken W. MacTaggart		*Vancouver Province*	1962	Thomas Hazlitt
	Globe and Mail	1957	Ted Byfield		*Vancouver Province*
1951	Gwyn Thomas		*Winnipeg Free Press*	1963	Bob Hill
	Toronto Star	1958	Halifax Bureau		*Edmonton Journal*
1952	Don Delaplante		Canadian Press	1964	Robert Reguly
	Globe and Mail	1959	Andrew MacFarlane		*Toronto Star*
1953	Judith Robinson		*Toronto Telegram*	1965	Warren Gerard
	Toronto Telegram	1960	Walter McCall		*Globe and Mail*
1954	Gwyn Thomas		*Windsor Star*		
	Toronto Star				

1966	Robert Reguly Robert MacKenzie *Toronto Star*	**1979**	Toronto Bureau Canadian Press	**1989**	Team *Winnipeg Free Press*
1967	Anthony Westell *Globe and Mail*	**1980**	Jean Pelletier *La Presse*, Montréal	**1990**	Team *Ottawa Citizen*
1968	Claire Dutrisac *La Presse*, Montréal	**1981**	Ottawa Bureau Canadian Press	**1991**	Mike Trickey Southam News
1969	Gwyn Thomas *Toronto Star*	**1982**	Christopher Young Southam News Services	**1992**	David Staples Greg Owens *Edmonton Journal*
1970	Tom Hazlitt *Toronto Star*	**1983**	Bob Hepburn *Toronto Star*	**1993**	Beth Gorham Michael Johansen Canadian Press
1971	Ron Haggart *Toronto Telegram*	**1984**	Peter Calamai Southam News Services	**1994**	Paul Wells Geoff Baker *Montreal Gazette*
1972	John Zaritsky *Globe and Mail*	**1985**	Peter Calamai Southam News Services	**1995**	Stephen Thorne Canadian Press
1973	Frank Jones *Toronto Star*	**1986**	John Picton *Toronto Star*	**1996**	Philip Mascoll Dale Brazao Donovan Vincent *Toronto Star*
1974	Steve Krueger Canadian Press	**1987**	James Ferrabee Southam News Services	**1997**	Team/Équipe *Le Soleil*, Québec
1975	Jack Cahill *Toronto Star*	**1988**	Dale Brazao Kevin Donovan *Toronto Star*	**1998**	Halifax Bureau Canadian Press
1976	Richard Cleroux *Globe and Mail*				
1977	Gerald Utting *Toronto Star*				
1978	John Fraser *Globe and Mail*				

Enterprise Reporting ● Grande enquête

1972	David Crane *Toronto Star*	**1981**	Mary Janigan *Montreal Gazette*	**1989**	Linda McQuaig *Globe and Mail*
1973	Henry Aubin *Montreal Gazette*	**1982**	Reporting Team *Vancouver Sun*	**1990**	Greg Weston Jack Aubry *Ottawa Citizen*
1974	Robert Nielsen *Toronto Star*	**1983**	John R. Walker Southam News Services	**1991**	Mark Kennedy *Ottawa Citizen*
1975	Lysiane Gagnon *La Presse*, Montréal	**1984**	Dan Turner *Ottawa Citizen*	**1992**	Paulette Peirol Michael Den Tandt *Kingston* *Whig-Standard*
1976	Henry Aubin *Montreal Gazette*	**1985**	Roger Clavet *Le Droit*, Ottawa	**1993**	Carolyn Adolph William Marsden Andrew McIntosh *Montreal Gazette*
1977	Gerald Utting *Toronto Star*	**1986**	Paul McKay *Kingston* *Whig-Standard*		
1978	Peter Worthington *Toronto Sun*	**1987**	Claude Arpin *Montreal Gazette*	**1994**	Peter Cheney Paul Watson Darcy Henton *Toronto Star*
1979	Bill Dampier *Toronto Star*	**1988**	Robert Lee *Ottawa Citizen*		
1980	Tim Padmore Chris Gainor *Vancouver Sun*				

1995	Philip Mathias *Financial Post*	**1997**	Moira Welsh Kevin Donovan *Toronto Star*	**1998**	Peter Cheney *Toronto Star/* *Globe and Mail*
1996	Brad Evenson Andrew Duffy Southam News				

Feature Writing ● Reportage

1949	Dorothy Howarth *Toronto Telegram*	**1966**	Betty Lee *Globe and Mail*	**1983**	Bill McGuire *London Free Press*
1950	Laurie M. McKechnie *Toronto Telegram*	**1967**	Ray Guy *St. John's Telegram*	**1984**	Ian Brown *Globe and Mail*
1951	Bill Boss Canadian Press	**1968**	Sheila Arnopoulos *Montreal Star*	**1985**	Adele Freedman *Globe and Mail*
1952	Wilfrid List *Globe and Mail*	**1969**	Brian Stewart *Montreal Gazette*	**1986**	Lucinda Chodan *Montreal Gazette*
1953	Gerald Clark Canada Wide Features	**1970**	Michael Popovich *Toronto Telegram*	**1987**	Marilyn Dunlop *Toronto Star*
		1971	Claire Dutrisac *La Presse*, Montréal	**1988**	Kelly Toughill *Toronto Star*
1954	Mac Reynolds *Vancouver Sun*	**1972**	George Hutchison *London Free Press*	**1989**	Catherine Dunphy *Toronto Star*
1955	Frank Lowe *Montreal Star*	**1973**	Del Bell *London Free Press*	**1990**	John Gray *Globe and Mail*
1956	Ralph Hicklin *Chatham News*	**1974**	Carol Hogg *Calgary Herald*	**1991**	John Gray *Globe and Mail*
1957	William Kinmond *Globe and Mail*	**1975**	Nigel Gibson *Montreal Gazette*	**1992**	Pierre Foglia *La Presse*, Montréal
1958	G. E. Mortimore *Victoria Colonist*	**1976**	Joe Hall *Toronto Star*	**1993**	Michael Valpy *Globe and Mail*
1959	Gene Telpner *Winnipeg Free Press*	**1977**	Brenda Zosky *Toronto Star*	**1994**	John Stackhouse *Globe and Mail*
1960	Pierre Berton *Toronto Star*	**1978**	Josh Freed *Montreal Star*	**1995**	Kirk Makin *Globe and Mail*
1961	Guy Lamarche *Le Devoir*	**1979**	Val Sears *Toronto Star*	**1996**	Heather Mallick *Toronto Sun*
1962	Peter Worthington *Toronto Telegram*	**1980**	Richard Gwyn *Toronto Star*	**1997**	Buzz Currie Kim Guttormson Bill Redekop Gord Sinclair Bruce Owen *Winnipeg Free Press*
1963	Robert Turnbull *Globe and Mail*	**1981** **(tie)**	Peter Calamai Southam News, Michelle Landsberg *Toronto Star*		
1964	Peter Newman *Toronto Star*				
1965	Arnie Myers *Vancouver Sun*	**1982**	Glen Allen *Montreal Gazette*	**1998**	Shelley Page *Ottawa Citizen*

● Staff Corresponding ●

1949 Stuart Underhill
Canadian Press
1950 Peter Inglis
Southam News
Services
1951 John Bird
Southam News
Services
1952 William Stevenson
Toronto Star
1953 Jack Scott
Vancouver Sun
1954 Bill Boss
Canadian Press
1955 I. Norman Smith
Ottawa Journal
1956 Ken W. MacTaggart
Toronto Telegram

1957 Jean-Marc Léger
Le Devoir
1958 Andrew MacFarlane
Toronto Telegram
1959 Bruce Hutchison
Victoria Times
1960 Pierre Berton
Toronto Star
1961 Bruce Phillips
Southam News
Services
1962 Michael Barkway
Southam News
Services
1963 Alexander Ross
Vancouver Sun
1964 Charles Lynch
Southam News
Services

1965 Jean-Pierre
Fournier
Le Devoir, Montréal
1966 David Oancia
Globe and Mail
1967 Timothy Traynor
FP Publications,
London
1968 Robert Reguly
Toronto Star
1969 Peter Worthington
Toronto Telegram
1970 Anthony Westell
Toronto Star
1971 Norman Webster
Globe and Mail

● Foreign Reporting ●
Reportage à l'étranger

1985 Michael Valpy
Globe and Mail
1986 Michael Valpy
Globe and Mail

1987 Thomas Walkom
Globe and Mail
1988 Christopher Young
Southam News
Services

1989 Gilles Blanchard
La Presse

● International Reporting ●
Reportage à caractère international

1990 Bill Schiller
Toronto Star
1991 Peter Cheney
Toronto Star
1992 Jan Wong
Globe and Mail

1993 Paul Watson
Toronto Star
1994 John Gray
Globe and Mail
1995 Olivia Ward
Toronto Star

1996 Paul Watson
Toronto Star
1997 John Stackhouse
Globe and Mail
1998 Christina Spencer
Ottawa Citizen

Sports Writing ● Sport

1957	Robert Hesketh *Toronto Telegram*	**1972**	Tim Burke *Montreal Gazette*	**1987**	Jim Proudfoot *Toronto Star*
1958	Scott Young *Globe and Mail*	**1973**	John Robertson *Montreal Star*	**1988**	Michael Clarkson *St. Catharines*
1959	Dick Beddoes *Vancouver Sun*	**1974**	George Gross *Toronto Sun*		*Standard*
1960	Jacques Revelin *L'Action Catholique,* Québec	**1975**	Trent Frayne *Toronto Sun*	**1989**	Lisa Fitterman *Montreal Gazette*
		1976	Al Strachan	**1990**	Michael Farber *Montreal Gazette*
1961	Ted Reeve *Toronto Telegram*		*Montreal Gazette*	**1991**	Red Fisher
1962	Mike Cramond *Vancouver Province*	**1977**	Brodie Snyder, Dick Bacon *Montreal Gazette*		*Montreal Gazette*
				1992	Michael Clarkson *Calgary Herald*
1963	Gary Lautens *Toronto Star*	**1978**	Doug Gilbert *Edmonton Sun*	**1993**	Randy Starkman *Toronto Star*
1964	Bob Hanley *Hamilton Spectator*	**1979**	Allen Abel *Globe and Mail*	**1994**	Randy Starkman *Toronto Star*
1965	Bob Pennington *Toronto Telegram*	**1980**	Archie McDonald *Vancouver Sun*	**1995**	Roy MacGregor *Ottawa Citizen*
1966	James Kearney *Vancouver Sun*	**1981**	Barbara Huck *Winnipeg Free Press*	**1996**	Erin Anderssen *New Brunswick*
1967	Al Sokol *Toronto Telegram*	**1982**	Michael Farber *Montreal Gazette*		*Telegraph Journal* *& Saint John*
1968	Bob Hanley *Hamilton Spectator*	**1983**	Robert Martin *Globe and Mail*		*Times Globe*
1969	Bob Pennington *Toronto Telegram*	**1984**	Wayne Parrish *Toronto Star*	**1997**	Geoff Baker *Montreal Gazette*
1970	Bob Hanley *Hamilton Spectator*	**1985**	Wayne Parrish *Toronto Star*	**1998**	Damien Cox *Toronto Star*
1971	Red Fisher *Montreal Star*	**1986**	Jean Sonmor *Toronto Sun*		

Spot News Photography ● Photographie d'actualité

1949	Jack DeLorme *Calgary Herald*	**1955**	Roger St-Jean *La Presse,* Montréal	**1961**	Gordon Karam United Press International
1950	Harry Befus *Calgary Herald*	**1956**	Ted Jolly *Amherst News*	**1962**	Daniel Scott *Vancouver Sun*
1951	David Bier *Montreal Herald*	**1957**	Jerry Ormond *Calgary Herald*	**1963**	Kent Stevenson *Calgary Herald*
1952	Russell Cooper *Toronto Telegram*	**1958**	Robertson Cochrane *London Free Press*	**1964**	Peter Geddes *Toronto Telegram*
1953	Orval Brunelle *Lethbridge Herald*	**1959**	George Diack *Vancouver Sun*	**1965**	Clifford Knapp *Kingston*
1954	Ted Dinsmore *Toronto Telegram*	**1960**	Jack Bowman *Brantford Expositor*		*Whig-Standard*

1966	Norman James *Toronto Star*	**1977**	Douglas Ball Canadian Press	**1989**	Allen McInnis *Montreal Gazette*
1967	Sean Browne *Toronto Telegram*	**1978**	John Colville *Calgary Herald*	**1990**	Tim McKenna *Toronto Sun*
1968	Ernie Lee *London Free Press*	**1979**	Bill Sandford *Toronto Sun*	**1991**	Nick Brancaccio *Windsor Star*
1969	Tibor Kolley *Globe and Mail*	**1980**	Dick Wallace *London Free Press*	**1992**	Pat McGrath *Ottawa Citizen*
1970	Franz Maier *Globe and Mail*	**1981**	Larry MacDougal *Ottawa Citizen*	**1993**	Paul Watson *Toronto Star*
1971	Doug Griffin *Toronto Star*	**1982**	Robert Taylor *Edmonton Sun*	**1994**	Jon Murray *Vancouver Province*
1972	Frank Lennon *Toronto Star*	**1983**	Chris Mikula *Ottawa Citizen*	**1995**	Patrick McConnell *Toronto Sun*
1973 **(tie)**	Kerry McIntyre Canadian Press, Don Dutton *Toronto Star*	**1984**	Guy Shulhan *Calgary Herald*	**1996**	Fred Sherwin *Ottawa Sun*
		1985	Ralph Bower *Vancouver Sun*	**1997**	Bruno Schlumberger *Ottawa Citizen*
1974	Don Dutton *Toronto Star*	**1986**	Michael Peake *Toronto Sun*	**1998**	Ryan Remiorz Canadian Press
1975	Stephen Liard *Toronto Star*	**1987**	Les Bazso *Vancouver Province*		
1976	Russell Mant Canadian Press	**1988**	Rick MacWilliam *Edmonton Journal*		

Editorial Cartooning ● Caricature

1949	Jack Boothe *Globe and Mail*	**1960**	Duncan Macpherson *Toronto Star*	**1971**	Yardley Jones *Toronto Sun*
1950	James G. Reidford *Montreal Star*	**1961**	Ed McNally *Montreal Star*	**1972**	Duncan Macpherson *Toronto Star*
1951	Leonard Norris *Vancouver Sun*	**1962**	Duncan Macpherson *Toronto Star*	**1973**	John Collins *Montreal Gazette*
1952	Robert La Palme *Le Devoir*, Montréal	**1963**	Jan Kamienski *Winnipeg Tribune*	**1974**	Blaine *Hamilton Spectator*
1953	Robert W. Chambers *Halifax Chronicle-Herald*	**1964**	Ed McNally *Montreal Star*	**1975**	Roy Peterson *Vancouver Sun*
1954	John Collins *Montreal Gazette*	**1965**	Duncan Macpherson *Toronto Star*	**1976**	Andy Donato *Toronto Sun*
1955	Merle R. Tingley *London Free Press*	**1966**	Robert W. Chambers *Halifax Chronicle-Herald*	**1977**	Terry Mosher (Aislin) *Montreal Gazette*
1956	James G. Reidford *Globe and Mail*	**1967**	Raoul Hunter *Le Soleil*, Québec	**1978**	Terry Mosher (Aislin) *Montreal Gazette*
1957	James G. Reidford *Globe and Mail*	**1968**	Roy Peterson *Vancouver Sun*	**1979**	Edd Uluschak *Edmonton Journal*
1958	Raoul Hunter *Le Soleil*, Québec	**1969**	Edd Uluschak *Edmonton Journal*	**1980**	Victor Roschkov *Toronto Star*
1959	Duncan Macpherson *Toronto Star*	**1970**	Duncan Macpherson *Toronto Star*		

1981	Tom Innes	1987	Raffi Anderian	1993	Bruce MacKinnon
	Calgary Herald		*Ottawa Citizen*		*Halifax Herald*
1982	Blaine	1988	Vance Rodewalt	1994	Roy Peterson
	Hamilton Spectator		*Calgary Herald*		*Vancouver Sun*
1983	Dale Cummings	1989	Cameron Cardow	1995	Brian Gable
	Winnipeg Free Press		*Regina Leader-Post*		*Globe and Mail*
1984	Roy Peterson	1990	Roy Peterson	1996	Roy Peterson
	Vancouver Sun		*Vancouver Sun*		*Vancouver Sun*
1985	Ed Franklin	1991	Guy Badeaux	1997	Serge Chapleau
	Globe and Mail		*Le Droit*, Ottawa		*La Presse*, Montréal
1986	Brian Gable	1992	Bruce MacKinnon	1998	Roy Peterson
	Regina Leader-Post		*Halifax Herald*		*Vancouver Sun*

Feature Photography ● Photographie de reportage

1950	John Maclean	1967	Reg Innell	1983	Veronica Milne
	Toronto Telegram		*Toronto Star*		*Toronto Sun*
1951	Peter Dunlop	1968	Boris Spremo	1984	David Lazarowych
	Toronto Telegram		*Toronto Star*		*Calgary Herald*
1952	Harry Befus	1969	Peter Bregg	1985	Gerry Bookhout
	Calgary Herald		Canadian Press		*Kitchener-Waterloo*
1953	Bill Dennett	1970	Glenn Baglo		*Record*
	Vancouver Sun		*Vancouver Sun*	1986	Keith Beaty
1954	Ray Munro	1971	Glenn Baglo		*Toronto Star*
	Vancouver Province		*Vancouver Sun*	1987	Bruno Schlumberger
1955	Jack Marshall	1972	Jack Burnett		*Ottawa Citizen*
	Toronto Star		*London Free Press*	1988	Rick Eglinton
1956	Gordon Sedawie	1973	Rod C. MacIvor		*Toronto Star*
	Vancouver Province		United Press	1989	Fred Thornhill
1957	Villy Svarre		International		*Toronto Sun*
	Vancouver Province	1974	Douglas Ball	1990	Craig Robertson
1958	Ron Laytner		Canadian Press		*Toronto Sun*
	Toronto Telegram	1975	Tedd Church	1991	John Lucas
1959	Bob Olsen		*Montreal Gazette*		*Edmonton Journal*
	Vancouver Province	1976	Allan Leishman	1992	Andrew Stawicki
1960	Don McLeod		*Montreal Star*		*Toronto Star*
	Vancouver Province	1977	Boris Spremo	1993	Diana Nethercott
1961	Jack Jarvie		*Toronto Star*		*Hamilton Spectator*
	Brantford Expositor	1978	Hugh MacKenzie	1994	Patti Gower
1962	Boris Spremo		*Ottawa Citizen*		*Toronto Star*
	Globe and Mail	1979	Bill Keay	1995	Debra Brash
1963	Boris Spremo		*Vancouver Sun*		*Victoria Times-*
	Globe and Mail	1980	Peter Martin		*Colonist*
1964	Bob Olsen		*United*	1996	Peter Power
	Vancouver Times		*Press Canada*		*Toronto Star*
1965	Ken Oakes	1981	Tedd Church	1997	David Chidley
	Vancouver Sun		*Montreal Gazette*		*Calgary Sun*
1966	David Paterson	1982	Bruno Schlumberger	1998	Julie Oliver
	Vancouver Province		*Ottawa Citizen*		*Ottawa Citizen*

Columns ● Chronique

1980	Michele Landsberg *Toronto Star*	**1986**	Carol Goar *Toronto Star*	**1993**	Rick Salutin *Globe and Mail*
1981	Lysiane Gagnon *La Presse*, Montréal	**1987**	William Johnson *Montreal Gazette*	**1994**	Pierre Foglia *La Presse,* Montréal
1982	John Slinger *Toronto Star*	**1988**	Gordon Sinclair *Winnipeg Free Press*	**1995**	Joe Fiorito *Montreal Gazette*
1983	Allan Fotheringham Southam News Service	**1989**	Jeffrey Simpson *Globe and Mail*	**1996**	Thomas Walkom *Toronto Star*
1984	Richard Gwyn *Toronto Star*	**1990**	Richard Wagamese *Calgary Herald*	**1997**	Josh Freed *Montreal Gazette*
1985	Harvey Schachter *Kingston Whig-Standard*	**1991**	Linda Goyette *Edmonton Journal*	**1998**	Marcus Gee *Globe and Mail*
		1992	Dave Brown *Ottawa Citizen*		

Business Reporting ● Économie

1987	Christopher Waddell *Globe and Mail*	**1992**	Jacquie McNish *Globe and Mail*	**1997**	John Stackhouse Janet McFarland Paul Waldie *Globe and Mail*
1988	Christopher Waddell, Jennifer Lewington *Globe and Mail*	**1993**	Lawrence Surtees *Globe and Mail*		
		1994	Jonathan Ferguson James Daw *Toronto Star*	**1998**	David Baines Adrian duPlessis *Vancouver Sun*
1989	David Baines *Vancouver Sun*				
1990	Kimberley Noble *Globe and Mail*	**1995**	Andrew McIntosh *Montreal Gazette*		
1991	Kimberley Noble *Globe and Mail*	**1996**	Jonathan Ferguson *Toronto Star*		

Sports Photography ● Photographie de sport

1988	Stan Behal *Toronto Sun*	**1992**	Mike Cassese *Toronto Sun*	**1997**	Andrew Vaughan Canadian Press
1989	Larry MacDougal *Calgary Herald*	**1993**	Rick Eglinton *Toronto Star*	**1998**	Jeff McIntosh *Calgary Herald*
1990	Wayne Roper *Brantford Expositor*	**1994**	Frank Gunn Canadian Press		
1991 **(tie)**	Barry Gray *Hamilton Spectator,* Fred Thornhill *Toronto Sun*	**1995**	Larry MacDougal *Calgary Herald*		
		1996	Bernard Weil *Toronto Star*		

Layout and Design ● Conception et mise en page

1989	Jim Emerson *Vancouver Sun*	**1993**	Lucie Lacava *Le Devoir*, Montréal	**1997**	Gayle Grin *Montreal Gazette*
1990	Paul Gilligan *Ottawa Citizen*	**1994**	Lucie Lacava *Le Devoir*, Montréal	**1998**	Richard Hoffman Susan Batsford *London Free Press*
1991	Roger B. White *Victoria Times-Colonist*	*1995*	Catherine Pike *Toronto Star*		
1992	Eric Nelson *Globe and Mail*	*1996*	Evelyn Stoynoff *Toronto Star*		

Special Project ● Projet spécial

1989	*Kingston Whig-Standard*	**1994**	*Toronto Star*	**1996**	*Toronto Star*
1990	*Windsor Star*	**1995**	*Saint John Telegraph Journal & Times Globe*	**1997**	*Windsor Star*
1991	*Southam News*			**1998**	*Vancouver Sun*
1992	*Calgary Herald*				
1993	*Edmonton Journal*				

Local Reporting ● Reportage à caractère local

1997	Tracy Huffman Ian Elliot Katherine Sedgwick *Port Hope Evening Guide*	**1998**	Team *New Brunswick Telegraph Journal*